W9-CPH-248

OPPOSING
VIEWPOINTS IN

American
History

VOLUME I:
FROM COLONIAL TIMES
TO RECONSTRUCTION

OPPOSING VIEWPOINTS IN
American History

VOLUME I:
FROM COLONIAL TIMES
TO RECONSTRUCTION

David L. Bender, *Publisher*

Bruno Leone, *Executive Editor*

William Dudley, *Series Editor*

John C. Chalberg, Ph.D., Professor in American History,
Normandale Community College, Minneapolis,
Consulting Editor

ADVISORY BOARD:

Robert A Divine
George W. Littlefield Professor in American History
University of Texas, Austin

Joan R. Gunderson
Professor of American History and Women's Studies
California State University, San Marcos

Robert J.Kaczorowski
Professor of Law and American Constitutional History
Fordham University School of Law, New York

GREENHAVEN PRESS, INC., SAN DIEGO, CALIFORNIA

Cover Photo Credits:

Front Cover, clockwise from top

1. Marquis de Lafayette and George Washington at Valley Forge (also on p. 73) (Library of Congress); 2. Red Cloud Oglala Sioux delegation (National Archives); 3. Civil War soldiers (also on p. 223) (Library of Congress); 4. U.S. Constitution (Library of Congress); 5. Family in covered wagon in Nebraska, 1886 (National Archives); 6. (center) Nineteenth-century illustration of the Pilgrims on Plymouth Rock, 1620 (also on p. 1) (Library of Congress)

Back Cover, left to right

1. Abraham Lincoln (Library of Congress); 2. The Alamo, San Antonio, Texas (Stock Montage); 3. Slaves picking cotton (also on p. 147) (North Wind Picture Archives)

Library of Congress Cataloging-in-Publication Data

Opposing viewpoints in American history / William Dudley, book editor.
    p.   cm.
    Includes bibliographical references and indexes.
    Contents: v. 1. From colonial times to Reconstruction — v. 2. From Reconstruction to the present.
    ISBN 1-56510-348-3 (v. 1 : lib. bdg. : alk paper). — ISBN 1-56510-347-5 (v. 1 : pbk. : alk. paper). — ISBN 1-56510-350-5 (v. 2 : lib. bdg. : alk. paper). — ISBN 1-56510-349-1 (v. 2 : pbk. : alk. paper)
    1. United States—History—Sources. I. Dudley, William, 1964-   .
E173.07 1996   95-33446
973—dc20   CIP

© 1996 by Greenhaven Press, Inc., PO Box 289009,
San Diego, CA 92198-9009

Printed in the U.S.A.

Every effort has been made to trace the owners of copyrighted material.

FOREWORD

Educators have long sought ways to engage and interest students in American history. They have also endeavored to sharpen their students' critical thinking skills—to teach them how to effectively analyze and evaluate the material that they read. *Opposing Viewpoints in American History*, an offshoot of Greenhaven Press's acclaimed *American History Series*, has been designed with both these objectives in mind.

Opposing Viewpoints in American History is an anthology of primary documents—the speeches, letters, articles, and other writings that are the raw material from which historians seek to understand and reconstruct the past. Assembled in two volumes (*volume 1: From Colonial Times to Reconstruction* and *volume 2: From Reconstruction to the Present*), these viewpoints trace American social, political, and diplomatic history from the time of the earliest European contact through the end of the Cold War. Student interest will be sparked by a wide spectrum of American voices, both the famous and the unfamiliar, expressing in their own words their opinions on the critical issues of their times.

To help sustain student interest and stimulate critical thinking, *Opposing Viewpoints in American History*, unlike other primary readers, pairs these primary documents in a running debate format. The guiding philosophy behind this compilation is that by comparing and contrasting opposing viewpoints on an issue, students will be challenged to think critically about what they read. Thus, for example, readers can evaluate Thomas Paine's stirring call for American independence in *Common Sense* by comparing it to the tightly reasoned arguments of Loyalist Charles Inglis. Within these two volumes a white minister and an escaped slave differ on the evils of slavery; Chief Joseph and Theodore Roosevelt provide contrasting perspectives on the takeover of Indian land by whites; Franklin D. Roosevelt's call for a New Deal is complemented by Herbert Hoover's dire warnings about the harms of government meddling; and a nuclear physicist and a secretary of war differ on the merits of dropping the atomic bomb on Japan. The paired structuring of sources found in *Opposing Viewpoints in American History* also reflects the important reality that American history itself has been a story of conflict and controversy. The birth of the nation was the result of a hotly debated decision to break from Great Britain, and Americans have continued to debate the meaning and direction of their nation ever since.

Along with its primary documents, *Opposing Viewpoints in American History* includes several supplemental features intended to enhance the readers' understanding. Introductions and timelines supply basic historical background for each section of the book. In addition, prior to each viewpoint the editors have provided essential biographical information about the author; a brief overview of the issue being debated; and questions designed to stimulate interest, reinforce comprehension, and encourage critical thinking.

The combination of primary texts and background information make *Opposing Viewpoints in American History*, by itself or in conjunction with other American history textbooks, an effective way to teach and engage students in the study of American history. To further aid instructors, a test bank based on the materials in both volumes of *Opposing Viewpoints in American History* is available.

Thomas Jefferson once said that "difference of opinion leads to inquiry, and inquiry to truth"—a statement as valid today as in Jefferson's time. It is the editors' hope that this volume will challenge students to actively inquire into the "difference of opinion" found on the pages of America's history in order to better understand the nation's past and to see how that past helped largely shape the present.

John C. Chalberg
Consulting Editor

CONTENTS

Part IV: Civil War America, 1850–1877

Reconstruction

PART I:
COLONIAL AMERICA,
1607–1750

Origins of English Settlement

European Colonists
and Native Americans

Puritans and the Question
of Religious Tolerance

Labor and Land
in Colonial America

Before 1600
- 1492 Christopher Columbus begins first of six voyages to the New World
- 1502 Spanish begin importing slaves into the New World from Africa
- 1565 Spaniards establish fort at St. Augustine, Florida
- 1580 Richard Hakluyt begins issuing a series of tracts urging Englishmen to engage in "western planting"
- 1585 First English colony in North America founded, under aegis of Walter Raleigh, at Roanoke, North Carolina
- 1588 The English navy defeats the Spanish Armada, giving England control of the seas
- 1591 Roanoke settlement is found deserted

1609
- Dutch navigator Henry Hudson explores New York harbor

1612
- Tobacco introduced into Virginia

1614
- Pocahontas, daughter of Native American leader Powhatan, marries Jamestown settler John Rolfe

1619
- First meeting of Virginia House of Burgesses
- First blacks arrive in Virginia; their status is probably that of indentured servants

1634
- Colony of Maryland is established under George Calvert (Lord Baltimore)

1636
- Banished Puritan dissenter Roger Williams founds Rhode Island colony
- Harvard College founded in Massachusetts
- First settlement in Connecticut

1637
- Pequot War in New England virtually wipes out the Pequot tribe
- Anne Hutchinson tried for heresy in Massachusetts; is banished

1653
- First Indian reservation established in Virginia

1663
- Carolina colony founded

1664
- England takes over New Amsterdam (renamed New York) from the Dutch

1665
- Colony of New Jersey founded

Before 1600   1600   1610   1620   1630   1640   1650   1660

1603
- James I begins reign of Stuart monarchs in England

1607
- First permanent English colony is established at Jamestown, Virginia

1608
- First permanent French colony in North America established at Quebec
- Pilgrims leave England to seek refuge in Holland

1620
- Pilgrims arrive at Cape Cod, Massachusetts, and draft Mayflower Compact

1622
- Members of Powhatan Confederacy attack English settlements in Virginia

1624
- Charter of the Virginia Company revoked; Virginia becomes royal colony

1629
- Colony of Massachusetts founded

1639
- First printing press set up in Cambridge, Massachusetts

1640
- Charles I calls Parliament back into session; migration of Puritans to America decreases

1630
- John Winthrop and 700 fellow Puritans arrive in Massachusetts

1660
- Charles II crowned king of England in Stuart restoration

1660–1663
- Parliament passes a series of Navigation Acts to regulate trade

1649
- Charles I beheaded; 9-year reign of Puritan Oliver Cromwell in England begins
- Maryland establishes principle of religious toleration with its "Act Concerning Religion"

1644
- Last concerted Indian attack in Virginia occurs

1642
- English Civil War begins

1661
- Maryland defines slavery as lifelong, inheritable racial status; other colonies follow suit

1701
•Yale College founded in Connecticut

1701–1713
•Queen Anne's War fought between England and Spain

1734
•Trial of John Peter Zenger establishes that press criticism of government is not libelous if true

1750
•Passage of Iron Act restricts colonists from engaging in metal processing

1681
•William Penn founds Pennsylvania colony

1721
•John Trenchard and Thomas Gordon's antimonarchical "Cato's Letters" begin publication in England

1744–1748
•King George's War fought between England and France; Fort Louisbourg in Nova Scotia is captured by Massachusetts colonists only to be returned to the French at the end of the war

1676
•Bacon's Rebellion takes place against the royal government of Virginia

1697
•Royal African Company's monopoly on the slave trade broken, allowing American competition

1713
•Treaty of Utrecht gives Nova Scotia and Newfoundland to England

1675
•King Philip's War in New England

1682
•French explorer Sieur de La Salle claims Mississippi River area for Louis IV of France

1739
•Stono slave rebellion in South Carolina quelled

1670	1680	1690	1700	1710	1720	1730	1740	1750

1685
•Duke of York becomes King James II; establishes the Dominion of New England, dissolving existing legislative assemblies

1718
•New Orleans founded by France

1746
•College of New Jersey (Princeton) founded

1692
•Salem witch trials
•William and Mary College founded in Virginia

1729
•Carolina is divided into North and South Carolina

1688
•Glorious Revolution in England overthrows James II; William and Mary assume power as joint sovereign

1730–1745
•The religious revival known as the Great Awakening sweeps across the colonies

1747
•Boston mobs resist British navy's impressment of sailors

1691
•New Massachusetts charter restores legislative body of Massachusetts General Court
•Spain establishes province of Texas

1733
•James Oglethorpe founds Georgia as colony without slavery
•Parliament passes the Molasses Act restricting access to British sugar islands in the West Indies

1749
•French construct new fortresses in the Ohio Valley

1689
•Leisler's rebellion takes place in New York against the architects of the Dominion of New England

1689–1697
•King William's War fought between England and France in northern New England

PART I:
COLONIAL AMERICA, 1607–1750

On May 24, 1607, 105 Englishmen on three small ships completed a three-thousand-mile, five-month voyage by landing on a North American river peninsula about fifteen miles inland from the Atlantic Ocean. Their first act was to construct a fort to protect themselves from the native peoples in the region and the Spanish to the south. By January 1608, when a new ship landed with 120 new arrivals, almost two-thirds of the 105 original settlers had perished from malnutrition and disease. Another "starving time" in the winter of 1609–1610 reduced the population to 60; in the spring all survivors boarded a ship to return to England, only to be met at the mouth of the river by another ship from England with new supplies and colonists.

Such was the shaky founding of Jamestown, the first permanent English settlement in America. Over the next 150 years a steady stream of immigrants from England and other European countries followed the Jamestown colonists across the Atlantic Ocean to settle on what is now the eastern seaboard of the United States. These immigrants and their descendants were one of three groups of people whose destinies converged to be part of American colonial history—the others were the native inhabitants of America (who were largely displaced by the newcomers) and black Africans who came to America involuntarily as slaves.

America Before Jamestown

In 1607 perhaps 9 million people lived in what is now the United States of America. Their ancestors had migrated to North America from Asia perhaps as many as forty thousand years earlier, across a now-submerged land bridge connecting Siberia and Alaska. These people lived in more than two hundred separate groups and societies, ranging from small tribal bands of hunter-gatherers to large and complex agricultural societies. Some were organized into powerful political entities such as the Iroquois Confederacy; others lived in scattered small communities. Because most of these peoples did not use writing, there are almost no written records of their life and culture. Most of what is known about the early history of Native Americans is derived from oral tradition, archaeological evidence, and the reports of European explorers.

The relative isolation of the Western Hemisphere and its people from the rest of the globe ended with the voyage of Christopher Columbus in 1492. His voyage opened the way for other explorers, the establishment of colonies, and the migration of people from Europe and Africa to these lands.

European Conquest and Colonization

Columbus, an Italian-born navigator in the employ of Spain, was sailing westward in 1492 in search of a new trade route to India and the Far East. After thirty-three days at sea he landed on a small island east of the North American continent, which he named San Salvador. He mistakenly named the peoples he encountered there "Indians." In this and subsequent expeditions, Columbus explored much of the Gulf of Mexico and the Caribbean. Initially convinced he had discovered new lands in Asia, he was reluctant to admit he had come across a previously unknown continent. Nonetheless, his voyages sparked the attention of European rulers, who soon sent other explorers into what became known as the New World. One of them, Amerigo Vespucci, charted much of the eastern coastline from Mexico to Brazil beginning in 1497; it was his name that was ultimately given to the new lands of "America."

The early European explorers had two general objectives: to chart a trade route to Asia and to find gold. Toward both ends England sent John Cabot in 1497 and his son Sebastian eleven years later; they explored Newfoundland and the Atlantic coastline to its south. Explorers Giovanni da Verrazano and Jacques Cartier probed the coast of North America for France; Cartier ventured up the St. Lawrence River in search of a passage to Asia.

Spain and Portugal took the lead in establishing empires in the New World in the sixteenth century; by 1600 these two nations controlled most of what is now Central and South America. Spanish conquistadores discovered and quickly conquered the advanced Aztec and Inca civilizations in Mexico and Peru, respectively, in the process finding large sources of silver and some veins of gold. Spain soon established profitable colonies in these conquered territories, as well as in the Caribbean islands discovered by Columbus. Relying on native slave labor and, beginning in 1502, on African slave labor, the colonies sent great quantities of silver, gold, sugar, cocoa, and dyes back to Spain.

Spanish explorers also ventured into areas of North America. Hernando de Soto led an expedition in 1539–1543 that explored what is now the southeastern United States and crossed the Mississippi River. In 1540–1542 Francisco Vásquez de Coronado led an expedition that explored the Grand Canyon and ventured north into what is now Kansas. A third expedition led by Juan Rodríguez Cabrillo sailed along the California coastline in 1542–1543. None of these expeditions found riches comparable to what was found in Mexico and Peru. The only lasting settlement founded by Spain in North America during the sixteenth century was St. Augustine, Florida, a military outpost established in 1565 to protect Spanish shipping in the Caribbean.

European explorers had devastating effects on the Native Americans they encountered, with disease perhaps the single most important contributing factor. The populations of the New World had no immunity to such European diseases as smallpox, tuberculosis, and cholera. The native populations of the Caribbean islands where Columbus first landed were nearly extinct within a few decades. The population of Mexico dropped from about 25 million in 1519 to between 1 and 2 million by the early seventeenth century. Diseases were also spread to North America by de Soto and other explorers. The establishment of British colonies in Virginia and Massachusetts was facilitated by prior epidemics that had drastically reduced the local native populations.

England and the New World

While Spain was building an overseas empire in the 1500s, England was preoccupied with domestic affairs. King Henry VIII broke with the Roman Catholic Church in the 1530s, and for the next several decades Catholics battled Protestants for political control of England. Under the reign of Queen Elizabeth I (1558–1603), the Protestant Church of England was firmly established as the official national church. Protestantism and English nationalism were fused in the minds of many, especially after England's dramatic naval victory over Catholic Spain's "Invincible Armada" in 1588. Spain continued to be viewed as England's chief European rival, and many advisers to Queen Elizabeth argued that England needed its own colonies in the New World. Such colonies, they argued, would serve as bases from which to raid Spanish ships of gold and other riches and to control any potential westward passage to Asia—and they would lay the foundation for England's own empire.

In addition to political, military, and religious concerns, many supporters of English colonization advanced economic arguments. Elizabeth's reign was marked by the emergence of a wealthy and influential merchant class that was constantly searching for new markets for wool and other products. These merchants advocated the establishment of American colonies not only as a potential market for English goods, but as a source of raw materials as well. Such colonies, many argued, could also provide an outlet for England's exploding population, which grew from 3 million in 1550 to more than 4 million in 1600. The economic impact of such growth was aggravated by "enclosure"—the conversion of much of England's open farmland into fenced sheep pastures—which had resulted in the eviction of tenant farmers and an increase of England's landless and (some feared) idle and criminal population.

England's initial attempts to establish colonies in Newfoundland in 1583 and Roanoke Island (the Lost Colony) in 1587 both failed. Finally, in 1607, the Jamestown settlement was founded. In 1620 English religious refugees called Pilgrims established another settlement well north of Virginia in Plymouth, Massachusetts. They were followed a decade later by a much larger group of religious refugees, called Puritans, who had obtained a charter from King Charles I to establish the Massachusetts Bay Company with rights of settlement in what is now New England. The new and more populous settlement soon overshadowed the small Plymouth colony, which was eventually absorbed by Massachusetts in 1691. A quick look at the early history of America's first English colonies—Virginia and Massachusetts—suggests that the English had many different motives for colonizing America and that numerous controversies arose among them after they arrived in the New World.

Goals of the Two Colonies

The Jamestown settlement had two important advantages over previous English efforts at colonization: The 1604 peace treaty between Great Britain and Spain reduced the danger of Spanish interference, and the use of a joint-stock company (a new economic innovation) provided sufficient private financial backing for the colony. The Virginia Company of London obtained a charter from Elizabeth's successor, James I, granting them the right to establish a colony and govern it. The purpose of the Jamestown settlement was simple: to make money for its investors.

The stockholders of the Virginia Company hoped to profit quickly by finding precious metals and somewhat more slowly by cultivating mulberry trees (for silk production) and grapes. Many of the colonists were self-described "gentlemen" who expected to re-create an English society in which they would comprise a new noble class and in which others (including Indians) would do the work. All of these expectations proved illusory. No gold was found, despite a great amount of time and energy spent by the colonists in its pursuit. Efforts to develop land for cash crops were unsuccessful and aroused the suspicions and hostilities of the Native Americans residing in the area.

Virginia's first major economic breakthrough—and lure for large numbers of new settlers—was the successful cultivation and curing of tobacco. The breakthrough came too late for the Virginia Company, which was dissolved when Virginia was made a royal colony under the Crown's direct authority in 1624. By then the colony itself was well established and by 1627 was exporting 500,000 pounds of tobacco a year. The valuable crop proved to be a mixed blessing. Tobacco cultivation quickly exhausted the soil, causing settlers to move farther and farther west. Price fluctuations wreaked economic havoc on the colony. Finally, its cultivation required intensive labor, which was in short supply until the colony turned to black slavery later in the seventeenth century.

The Puritans who settled in New England had profoundly different concerns than the fortune seekers of Jamestown. Puritans were English Protestants who wished to "purify" the Church of England from what they regarded as dangerous vestiges of Roman Catholicism. Those Puritans who migrated to America sought not wealth, but the establishment of a pure and godly church and society in conformity with their beliefs. In part, they wanted to create a compelling example of true reform Christianity for those who remained behind in England.

The Puritans, like the Jamestown settlers, had mixed success in achieving their own goals. They established a system in which political control and social influence were limited to "visible saints"—those who could demonstrate that they had personally experienced God's grace. Only such church members could vote and participate in the colonial government (although church attendance was required of all, not all attenders could qualify as members). But at the same time Puritan leaders were compelled to wage wars against the native population and attack religious dissenters within their ranks.

Controversies in Virginia and Massachusetts

Most of the recorded disputes within Virginia revolved around economics and politics. In its earliest days the settlement was constantly riven by disagreements between its leaders, who sometimes resorted to martial law to compel their fellow Virginians to grow their own food, and settlers who resisted all efforts to take them away from searching for gold. The demands of the colonists for a greater say in their own affairs led to the creation in 1619 of the House of Burgesses, the first representative governmental assembly in America.

The cultivation of tobacco brought profits for only some in Virginia. By the mid-1600s the colony was beset by conflicts between the landless poor and an emerging economic and political elite. There were even fears among some that Virginia was replicating the social problems of England and that idleness and crime were undermining the colony. Economic and political divisions erupted in Bacon's Rebellion in 1676, the first major colonial rebellion against English authority. One solution to this persistent problem was the introduction of black slavery in the 1600s (Africans had been captured and sold as slaves in Spanish and Portuguese New World colonies since the 1500s). Not only did slavery provide a stable labor force, it also bridged class divisions between rich and poor whites who were united on the basis of race.

Unlike the Virginians, the main controversies that divided the Massachusetts Puritans revolved around religious issues. Puritan ministers and leaders sought levels of political and religious conformity that proved unattainable. As a result, religious dissenters, such as Anne Hutchinson, were put on trial and banished, or, in the case of Roger Williams, simply encouraged to depart. During the second half of the seventeenth century another kind of dissent proved to be even more insidious: religious indifference. Puritan ministers preached warning sermons ("jeremiads") pleading with their followers to disregard worldly concerns and return to the faith of their forefathers. Devastating Indian attacks in 1675 (King Philip's War) and a disastrous Boston fire in 1679 were seen as signs of God's displeasure with the Puritans. By the end of the century controversy over witchcraft, especially in Salem in 1692, was also tearing the Puritan world apart.

Colonists and Native Americans

King Philip's War of 1675–1676 was one of many conflicts that beset both the Virginia and Massachusetts colonies. The relationship between the Jamestown settlers and the local Powhatan Confederacy of Indian tribes was tense from the beginning and exploded into a major war in 1622 when Indians in a surprise attack killed 347 settlers. The Virginia authorities responded by declaring a policy of "perpetual enmity" toward the Indians and began periodic military expeditions that destroyed Indian villages and food supplies, reduced the Indian population, and drove survivors farther westward. Another Indian uprising in 1644 resulted in the death of 500 settlers but failed to stop the growth of the colony. Thirty years later in New England, Metacom (a Wampanoag Indian leader known to the English as King Philip) led well-armed tribesmen in an attack on fifty-two of New England's ninety towns in retaliation for the execution of three of his people, destroying twelve towns and killing 600 colonists. But in the end Metacom was killed and the Wampanoags defeated.

A New Life

The colonies of Virginia and Massachusetts were soon joined by others. Some, such as New York and Maryland, were the domains of English proprietors who received land grants from the Crown. Others, such as Connecticut and Rhode Island, were formed by colonists who were dissatisfied with existing colonies and who moved to create their own. The colonists created societies that combined ideas brought over from England with experiences in the new environment of America. Left largely to their own devices by the remote English government, the American colonies evolved in ways divergent from their ruling country—a development that would cause new controversies and ultimately result in independence from England in 1776.

Origins of English Settlement

Viewpoint 1A

National and Economic Reasons to Colonize America (1582 & 1585)

Richard Hakluyt the younger (1552–1616) and Richard Hakluyt the elder (dates unknown)

During the long reign of Queen Elizabeth I (1558–1603) England was on the sidelines of the European rush to colonize the New World Christopher Columbus had encountered in 1492. Spain created an empire of profitable colonies in South America and the Caribbean Sea (among their settlements was a military base in St. Augustine, Florida). Ships from Spain's colonies laden with gold and silver made Spain the envy of other European nations. Portugal established a colony in what is now Brazil. France sent explorers up the St. Croix River in an effort to find a trade route to Asia, established fur trading posts, and laid claims to much of North America. England sponsored several exploring expeditions, but its colonizing efforts were limited to small summer fishing settlements off the coast of North America and failed attempts at colonizing Newfoundland in 1583 and Roanoke Island off what is now North Carolina in 1587.

From *The Original Writing and Correspondence of the Two Richard Hakluyts*, edited by E.G.R. Taylor (London: Hakluyt Society, 1935).

A growing number of Englishmen began to promote the idea that England needed to establish colonies in the New World to enrich the nation and to compete with the colonizing efforts of Spain and other nations. The writings of two such promoters, who share the name of Richard Hakluyt, appear below. The first part of the following two-part viewpoint is by Richard Hakluyt the younger, an Anglican minister and geographer who compiled and wrote several volumes on voyages to the new lands in the Western Hemisphere in an effort to encourage English settlement. His first compilation was *Divers Voyages Touching the Discovery of America*, published in 1582. In the dedication, excerpted here, Hakluyt writes to courtier and poet Philip Sidney, bringing out several reasons why colonizing America would be beneficial for England. One of the reasons Hakluyt mentions is the search for a trade route (the fabled Northwest Passage) to the Pacific Ocean and to Asia.

Additional reasons for colonization are given in the second part, excerpted from a treatise by Richard Hakluyt the elder, a lawyer, author, and cousin to his namesake. In 1585 he wrote "Inducements to the Liking of the Voyage Intended towards Virginia," listing 31 reasons why England should begin colonizing efforts in the New World. Although he, like his cousin, mentions the spread of Protestant Christianity as a reason for English settlement, many of his arguments dwell on practical and economic benefits for England and the need for England to catch up with Spain and other countries in the race to exploit the new lands.

What social conditions found in England do the two Hakluyts wish to alleviate through colonization? What resources in America do they describe? How important are religious concerns to their arguments?

I

To the right worshipful and most virtuous gentleman, Master Philip Sidney, Esquire

I marvel not a little (Right Worshipful) that since the first discovery of America (which is now full fourscore-and-ten years), after so great conquest and plantings of the Spaniards and Portugals there, that we of England could never have the grace to set fast footing in such fertile and temperate places as are left as yet unpossessed by them. But, again, when I consider that there is a time for all men, and see the Portugals' time to be out of date, and that the nakedness of the Spaniards and their long-hidden secrets are now at length espied, whereby they went about to delude the world, I conceive great hope that the time approacheth and now is that we of England may share and part stakes (if we will ourselves) both with the Spaniard and the Portugal in part of America and other regions as yet undiscovered.

Advancing the Honour of England

And surely, if there were in us that desire to advance the honour of our country which ought to be in every good man, we would not all this while have forslown [delayed] the possessing of those lands which of equity and right appertain unto us, as by the discourses that follow shall appear most plainly. Yea, if we would behold with the eye of pity how all our prisons are pestered and filled with able men to serve their country, which for small robberies are daily hanged up in great numbers, some twenty at a clap out of one jail (as was seen at the last assizes at Rochester), we would hasten and further, every man to his power, the deducting of some colonies of our superfluous people into those temperate and fertile parts of America, which, being within six weeks' sailing of England, are yet unpossessed by any Christians and seem to offer themselves unto us, stretching nearer unto Her Majesty's dominions than to any other part of Europe.

We read that the bees, when they grow to be too many in their own hive at home, are wont to be led out by their captains to swarm abroad and seek themselves a new dwelling place. If the examples of the Grecians and Carthaginians of old time and the practice of our age may not move us, yet let us learn wisdom of these small, weak, and unreasonable creatures.

It chanced very lately that upon occasion I had great conference in matters of cosmography with an excellent learned man of Portugal [possibly Don Antonio de Castilio], most privy to all the discoveries of his nation, who wondered that those blessed countries from the point of Florida northward were all this while unplanted by Christians, protesting with great affection and zeal that if he were now as young as I (for at this present he is threescore years of age) he would sell all he had (being a man of no small wealth and honour) to furnish a convenient number of ships to sea for the inhabiting of those countries and reducing those gentile people to Christianity. Moreover, he added that John Barros, their chief cosmographer, being moved with the like desire, was the cause that Brasilia was first inhabited by the Portugals; where they have nine baronies or lordships, and thirty *engenhos* or sugar mills, two or three hundred slaves belonging to each mill, with a judge and other officers and a church; so that every mill is as it were a little commonwealth; and that the country was first planted by such men as for small offences were saved from the rope. This spake he, not only unto me and in my hearing, but also in the presence of a friend of mine, a man of great skill in the mathematics. If this man's desire might be executed, we might not only for the present time take possession of that good land, but also in short space by God's grace find out that short and easy passage by the north-west, which we have hitherto so long desired and whereof we have made many good and more than probable conjectures. . . .

————— • —————

"I marvel not a little . . . that since the first discovery of America . . . we of England could never have the grace to set fast footing in such fertile and temperate places."

————— • —————

And here to conclude and shut up this matter, I have heard myself, of merchants of credit that have lived long in Spain, that King Philip hath made a law of late that none of his subjects shall discover to the northwards of five-and-forty degrees of America; which maybe thought to proceed chiefly of two causes: the one, lest passing to the north they shall discover the open passage from the South Sea to our North Sea; the other because they have not people enough to possess and keep that passage but rather thereby should open a gap for other nations to pass that way. Certes [certainly], if hitherto in our own discoveries we had not been led with a preposterous desire of seeking rather gain than God's glory, I assure myself that our labours had taken far better effect. But we forgot that godliness is great riches, and that if we first seek the kingdom of God, all other things will be given unto us, and that as the light accompanieth the sun and the heat the fire, so lasting riches do wait upon them that are jealous for the advancement of the kingdom of Christ and the enlargement of His glorious Gospel; as it is said, 'I will honour them that honour me.' I trust that now, being taught by their manifold losses, our men will take a more godly course and use some part of their goods to His glory; if not, He will turn even their covetousness to serve Him, as He hath done the pride and avarice of the Spaniards and Portugals, who, pretending in glorious words that they made their discoveries chiefly to convert infidels to our most holy faith (as they say) in deed and truth sought not them but their goods and riches. . . .

Here I cease, craving pardon for my own boldness, trusting also that Your Worship will continue and increase your accustomed favour towards these godly and honourable discoveries.

II

Reasons for Colonization

1. The glory of God by planting of religion among those infidels.

2. The increase of the force of the Christians.

3. The possibility of the enlarging of the dominions of the Queen's Most Excellent Majesty, and consequently of her honour, revenues, and of her power by this enterprise.

4. An ample vent in time to come of the woollen cloths of England, especially those of the coarsest sorts, to the maintenance of our poor, that else starve or become burdensome to the realm; and vent also of sundry our commodities upon the tract of that firm land, and possibly in other regions from the northern side of that main.

5. A great possibility of further discoveries of other regions from the north part of the same land by sea, and of unspeakable honour and benefit that may rise upon the same by the trades to ensue in Japan, China, and Cathay, etc.

6. By return thence, this realm shall receive (by reason of the situation of the climate, and by reason of the excellent soil) woad, oil, wines, hops, salt, and most or all the commodities that we receive from the best parts of Europe, and we shall receive the same better cheap than now we receive them, as we may use the matter.

7. Receiving the same thence, the navy, the human strength of this realm, our merchants and their goods, shall not be subject to arrest of ancient enemies and doubtful friends as of late years they have been.

8. If our nation do not make any conquest there but only use traffic and change of commodities, yet, by means the country is not very mighty but divided into petty kingdoms, they shall not dare to offer us any great annoy but such as we may easily revenge with sufficient chastisement to the unarmed people there.

9. Whatsoever commodities we receive by the Steelyard Merchants, or by our own merchants from Eastland, be it flax, hemp, pitch, tar, masts, clapboard, wainscot, or such-like; the like good[s] may we receive from the north and north-east part of that country near unto Cape Breton, in return for our coarse woollen cloths, flannels, and rugs fit for those colder regions.

10. The passage to and fro is through the main ocean sea, so as we are not in danger of any enemy's coast.

Trade Opportunities

11. In the voyage we are not to cross the burnt zone, nor to pass through frozen seas encumbered with ice and fogs, but in temperate climate at all times of the year; and it requireth not, as the East

Indies voyage doth, the taking in of water in divers places, by reason that it is to be sailed in five or six weeks; and by the shortness the merchant may yearly make two returns (a factory [trade center] once being erected there), a matter in trade of great moment.

12. In this trade by the way, in our pass to and fro, we have in tempests and other haps all the ports of Ireland to our aid and no near coast of any enemy.

13. By this ordinary trade we may annoy the enemies to Ireland and succour the Queen's Majesty's friends there, and in time we may from Virginia yield them whatsoever commodity they now receive from the Spaniard; and so the Spaniards shall want the ordinary victual that heretofore they received yearly from thence, and so they shall not continue trade, nor fall so aptly in practice against this government as now by their trade thither they may.

14. We shall, as it is thought, enjoy in this voyage either some small islands to settle on or some one place or other on the firm land to fortify for the safety of our ships, our men, and our goods, the like whereof we have not in any foreign place of our traffic, in which respect we may be in degree of more safety and more quiet.

15. The great plenty of buff hides and of many other sundry kinds of hides there now presently to be had, the trade of whale and seal fishing and of divers other fishings in the great rivers, great bays, and seas there, shall presently defray the charge in good part or in all of the first enterprise, and so we shall be in better case than our men were in Russia, where many years were spent and great sums of money consumed before gain was found.

16. The great broad rivers of that main that we are to enter into, so many leagues navigable or portable into the mainland, lying so long a tract with so excellent and so fertile a soil on both sides, do seem to promise all things that the life of man doth require and whatsoever men may wish that are to plant upon the same or to traffic in the same.

17. And whatsoever notable commodity the soil within or without doth yield in so long a tract, that is to be carried out from thence to England, the same rivers so great and deep do yield no small benefit for the sure, safe, easy, and cheap carriage of the same to shipboard, be it of great bulk or of great weight.

18. And in like sort whatsoever commodity of England the inland people there shall need, the same rivers do work the like effect in benefit for the incarriage of the same aptly, easily, and cheaply.

19. If we find the country populous and desirous to expel us and injuriously to offend us, that seek but just and lawful traffic, then, by reason that we are lords of navigation and they not so, we are the better able to defend ourselves by reason of those great rivers and to annoy them in many places.

20. Where there be many petty kings or lords planted on the rivers' sides, and [who] by all likelihood maintain the frontiers of their several territories by wars, we may by the aid of this river join with this king here, or with that king there, at our pleasure, and may so with a few men be revenged of any wrong offered by any of them; or may, if we will proceed with extremity, conquer, fortify, and plant in soils most sweet, most pleasant, most strong, and most fertile, and in the end bring them all in subjection and to civility.

21. The known abundance of fresh fish in the rivers, and the known plenty of fish on the sea-coast there, may assure us of sufficient victual in spite of the people, if we will use salt and industry.

22. The known plenty and variety of flesh of divers kinds of beasts at land there may seem to say to us that we may cheaply victual our navies to England for our returns, which benefit everywhere is not found of merchants.

23. The practice of the people of the East Indies, when the Portugals came thither first, was to cut from the Portugals their lading of spice; and hereby they thought to overthrow their purposed trade. If these people shall practise the like, by not suffering us to have any commodity of theirs without conquest (which requireth some time), yet may we maintain our first voyage thither till our purpose come to effect by the sea-fishing on the coasts there and by dragging for pearls, which are said to be on those parts; and by return of those commodities the charges in part shall be defrayed: which is a matter of consideration in enterprises of charge.

Employing England's Poor

24. If this realm shall abound too too much with youth, in the mines there of gold (as that of Chisca and Saguenay), of silver, copper, iron, etc., may be an employment to the benefit of this realm; in tilling of the rich soil there for grain and in planting of vines there for wine or dressing of those vines which grow there naturally in great abundance; olives for oil; orange trees, lemons, figs and almonds for fruit; woad, saffron, and madder for dyers; hops for brewers; hemp, flax; and in many such other things, by employment of the soil, our people void of sufficient trades may be honestly employed, that else may become hurtful at home.

25. The navigating of the seas in the voyage, and of the great rivers there, will breed many mariners for service and maintain much navigation.

26. The number of raw hides there of divers kinds of beasts, if we shall possess some island there or settle on the firm, may presently employ many of our idle people in divers several dressings of the same,

and so we may return them to the people that cannot dress them so well, or into this realm, where the same are good merchandise, or to Flanders, etc., which present gain at the first raiseth great encouragement presently to the enterprise.

27. Since great waste woods be there of oak, cedar, pine, walnuts, and sundry other sorts, many of our waste people may be employed in making of ships, hoys, busses [types of ships], and boats, and in making of rosin, pitch, and tar, the trees natural for the same being certainly known to be near Cape Breton and the Bay of Menan, and in many other places thereabout.

28. If mines of white or grey marble, jet, or other rich stone be found there, our idle people may be employed in the mines of the same and in preparing the same to shape, and, so shaped, they may be carried into this realm as good ballast for our ships and after serve for noble buildings.

29. Sugar-canes may be planted as well as they are now in the South of Spain, and besides the employment of our idle people, we may receive the commodity cheaper and not enrich infidels or our doubtful friends, of whom now we receive that commodity.

30. The daily great increase of wools in Spain, and the like in the West Indies, and the great employment of the same into cloth in both places, may move us to endeavour, for vent of our cloth, new discoveries of peopled regions where hope of sale may arise; otherwise in short time many inconveniences may possibly ensue.

Incredible Things May Follow

31. This land that we purpose to direct our course to, lying in part in the 40th degree of latitude, being in like heat as Lisbon in Portugal doth, and in the more southerly part, as the most southerly coast of Spain doth, may by our diligence yield unto us, besides wines and oils and sugars, oranges, lemons, figs, raisins, almonds, pomegranates, rice, raw silks such as come from Granada, and divers commodities for dyers, as anil and cochineal, and sundry other colours and materials. Moreover, we shall not only receive many precious commodities besides from thence, but also shall in time find ample vent of the labour of our poor people at home, by sale of hats, bonnets, knives, fish-hooks, copper kettles, beads, looking-glasses, bugles, and a thousand kinds of other wrought wares that in short time may be brought in use among the people of that country, to the great relief of the multitude of our poor people and to the wonderful enriching of this realm. And in time, such league and intercourse may arise between our stapling seats there, and other ports of our Northern America, and of the islands of the same, that incredible things, and by few as yet dreamed of,

may speedily follow, tending to the impeachment of our mighty enemies and to the common good of this noble government.

The ends of this voyage are these:
1. To plant Christian religion.
2. To traffic.
3. To conquer. } Or, to do all three.

VIEWPOINT 1B

A Puritan's Reasons for Colonizing America (1629)
John Winthrop (1588–1649)

The first two lasting English settlements in what is now the United States were at Jamestown, Virginia, in 1607, and Plymouth, Massachusetts, in 1620. The Jamestown settlement was sponsored by the Virginia Company of London, a joint-stock corporation whose investors (some of whom settled in Jamestown) hoped to make a quick profit from the colony. The Pilgrims who arrived in Massachusetts in 1620, and the Puritans who followed them in subsequent years, had different motives.

The Puritans and Pilgrims were religious people who were dissatisfied with the pace of Protestant reform in the Church of England, the official established church that all English people were obliged to support. Under Queen Elizabeth I and her successor, King James I, the Church of England was closely linked to the royal government. Many Puritans came to America to avoid being persecuted for their beliefs, and to create a new society that harmonized with their conceptions of true Christianity. A passionate summary of Puritan motivations comes from the following viewpoint, excerpted from a 1629 pamphlet by John Winthrop. Winthrop, one of the wealthiest and most distinguished of the Puritan settlers, served as governor of the Massachusetts Bay Colony for thirteen of his nineteen years in America following his migration in 1630. In his 1629 pamphlet he argues that the true Christian church is hopelessly corrupted in England and that the faith can be preserved only by creating a new society in America. In part he echoes practical reasons given by the two Richard Hakluyts (see viewpoint 1A) and others. The settlers of the Puritan colonies, however, were not to be adventurers seeking their fortune or the desperately poor and unemployed, but rather people inspired by God to practice their faith free

From *Reasons to be Considered for Justifying the Undertakers of the Intended Plantation in New England* by John Winthrop (*Proceedings*, vol. 8, Massachusetts Historical Society, 1864–65). Courtesy of the Massachusetts Historical Society.

from the limits of the Church of England.

How do Winthrop's views of religion and of God expressed here differ from those expressed by the two Richard Hakluyts, authors of the opposing viewpoint? In what respects do the authors of the two viewpoints differ in predicting the difficulties in surviving in the New World? How does Winthrop justify the taking of land from the Indians?

Reasons to be considered for justifying the undertakers of the intended plantation in New England and for encouraging such whose hearts God shall move to join with them in it.

First, it will be a service to the church of great consequence to carry the gospel into those parts of the world, to help on the coming in of fullness of the Gentiles, and to raise a bulwark against the kingdom of anti-Christ which the Jesuits labor to rear up in those parts.

Rescuing the Church

2. All other churches of Europe are brought to desolation, and our sins, for which the Lord begins already to frown upon us, do threaten us fearfully, and who knows but that God hath provided this place to be a refuge for many whom he means to save out of the general calamity. And seeing the church hath no place left to fly into but the wilderness, what better work can there be than to go before and provide tabernacles and food for her, against she cometh thither?

3. This land grows weary of her inhabitants, so as man who is the most precious of all creatures is here more vile and base than the earth we tread upon, and of less price among us than a horse or a sheep; masters are forced by authority to entertain servants, parents to maintain their own children. All towns complain of the burthen of their poor, though we have taken up many unnecessary, yea unlawful, trades to maintain them. And we use the authority of the law to hinder the increase of people, as urging the execution of the state against cottages and inmates, and thus it is come to pass that children, servants, and neighbors (especially if the[y] be poor) are counted the greatest burthen, which if things were right it would be the chiefest earthly blessing.

4. The whole earth is the Lord's garden, and He hath given it to the sons of men with a general condition, Gen. 1:28, "Increase and multiply, replenish the earth and subdue it," which was again renewed to Noah. The end is double moral and natural: that man might enjoy the fruits of the earth, and God might have his due glory from the creature. Why then should we stand here striving for places of habitation (many men spending as much labor and cost to recover or keep sometimes an acre or two of land as would procure them many hundred as good or better in an other country) and in the meantime suffer a whole continent as fruitful and convenient for the use of man to lie waste without any improvement?

5. We are grown to that height of intemperance in all excess of riot, as no man's estate almost will suffice to keep sail with his equals, and he who fails herein must live in scorn and contempt. Hence it comes that all arts and trades are carried in that deceitful and unrighteous course, as it is almost impossible for a good and upright man to maintain his charge and live comfortably in any of them.

6. The fountains of learning and religion are so corrupted (as beside the unsupportable charge of the education) most children (even the best wits and fairest hopes) are perverted, corrupted, and utterly overthrown by the multitude of evil examples and the licentious government of those seminaries, where men strain at gnats and swallow camels, use all severity for maintenance of capes and other complements, but suffer all ruffian-like fashion and disorder in manners to pass uncontrolled.

7. What can be a better work and more honorable and worthy a Christian than to help raise and support a particular church while it is in the infancy, and to join his forces with such a company of faithful people as by a timely assistance may grow strong and prosper, and for want of it may be put to great hazard, if not wholly ruined.

8. If any such who are known to be godly, and live in wealth and prosperity here, shall forsake all this to join themselves to this church, and to run a hazard with them of a hard and mean condition, it will be an example of great use both for removing the scandal of worldly and sinister respects which is cast upon the adventurers, to give more life to the faith of God's people in their prayers for the plantation, and to encourage others to join the more willingly in it.

9. It appears to be a work of God for the good of His church, in that He hath disposed the hearts of so many of His wise and faithful servants (both ministers and others) not only to approve of the enterprise but to interest themselves in it, some in their persons and estates, others by their serious advice and help otherwise. And all by their prayers for the welfare of it, Amos 3. The Lord revealeth His secrets to His servants the prophets; it is likely He hath some great work in hand which He hath revealed to His prophets among us, whom He hath stirred up to encourage His servants to this plantation, for He doth not use to seduce His people by His own prophets but commits that office to the ministry of false prophets and lying spirits.

Divers objections which have been made against this plantation with their answers and resolutions.

Objection 1: We have no warrant to enter upon that land which hath been so long possessed by others.

Answer 1: That which lies common and hath never been replenished or subdued is free to any that will possess and improve it, for God hath given to the sons of men a double right to the earth: there is a natural right and a civil right. The first right was natural when men held the earth in common, every man sowing and feeding where he pleased, and then as men and the cattle increased they appropriated certain parcels of ground by enclosing, and peculiar manurance, and this in time gave them a civil right. Such was the right which Ephron the Hittite had in the field of Machpelah, wherein Abraham could not bury a dead corpse without leave, though for the out parts of the country which lay common he dwelt upon them and took the fruit of them at his pleasure. The like did Jacob, which fed his cattle as bold in Hamor's land (for he is said to be the lord of the country) and other places where he came as the native inhabitants themselves. And that in those times and places men accounted nothing their own but that which they had appropriated by their own industry appears plainly by this: that Abimelech's servants in their own country, when they oft contended with Isaac's servants about wells which they had digged, yet never strove for the land wherein they were. So likewise between Jacob and Laban: he would not take a kid of Laban's without his special contract, but he makes no bargain with him for the land where they feed, and it is very probable if the country had not been as free for Jacob as for Laban, that covetous wretch would have made his advantage of it and have upbraided Jacob with it, as he did with his cattle. And for the natives in New England, they enclose no land, neither have any settled habitation, nor any tame cattle to improve the land by, and so have no other but a natural right to those countries. So as if we leave them sufficient for their use, we may lawfully take the rest, there being more than enough for them and us.

Secondly, we shall come in with the good leave of the Natives, who find benefit already by our neighborhood and learn of us to improve part to more use than before they could do the whole. And by this means we come in by valuable purchase, for they have of us that which will yield them more benefit than all the land which we have from them.

Thirdly, God hath consumed the Natives with a great plague in those parts so as there be few inhabitants left.

Objection 2: It will be a great wrong to our church to take away the good people, and we shall lay it the more open to the judgment feared.

Answer 1: The departing of good people from a country doth not cause a judgment but foreshew it, which may occasion such as remain to turn from their evil ways that they may prevent it, or to take some other course that they may escape it.

Secondly, such as go away are of no observation in respects of those who remain, and they are likely to do more good there than here. And since Christ's time, the church is to be considered as universal without distinction of countries, so as he who doeth good in any one place serves the church in all places in regard of the unity.

Thirdly, it is the revealed will of God that the gospel should be preached to all nations, and though we know not whether those barbarians will receive it at first or not, yet it is a good work to serve God's providence in offering it to them; and this is fittest to be done by God's own servants, for God shall have glory by it though they refuse it, and there is good hope that the posterity *shall by this means be gathered into Christ's sheepfold.*

———— • ————

"It will be a service to the church of great consequence to carry the gospel into those parts of the world . . . and to raise a bulwark against the kingdom of anti-Christ which the Jesuits labor to rear up in those parts."

———— • ————

Objection 3: We have feared a judgment a great while, but yet we are safe. It were better therefore to stay till it come, and either we may fly then, or if we be overtaken in it, we may well content ourselves to suffer with such a church as ours is.

Answer: It is likely this consideration made the churches beyond the seas, as the Palatinate, Rochelle, etc., to sit still at home and not to look out for shelter while they might have found it. But the woeful spectacle of their ruin may teach us more wisdom, to avoid the plague when it is foreseen, and not to tarry as they did till it overtake us. If they were now at their former liberty, we might be sure they would take other courses for their safety, and though half of them had miscarried in their escape, yet had it not been so miserable to themselves nor scandalous to religion as this desperate backsliding, and abjuring the truth, which many of the ancient professors among them, and the whole posterity which remain, are now plagued into.

Objection 4: The ill success of other plantations may tell us what will become of this.

Answer 1: None of the former sustained any great damage but Virginia; which happened through their own sloth and security.

2. The argument is not good, for thus it stands: some plantations have miscarried, therefore we should not make any. It consists in particulars and so concludes nothing. We might as well reason thus: many houses have been burnt by kilns, therefore we should use none; many ships have been cast away, therefore we should content ourselves with our home commodities and not adventure men's lives at sea for those things which we might live without; some men have been undone by being advanced to great places, therefore we should refuse our preferment, etc.

3. The fruit of any public design is not to be discerned by the immediate success; it may appear in time that former plantations were all to good use.

4. There were great and fundamental errors in the former which are like to be avoided in this, for first their main end was carnal and not religious; secondly, they used unfit instruments—a multitude of rude and misgoverned persons, the very scum of the people; thirdly, they did not establish a right form of government.

The Way of God Is Difficult

Objection 5: It is attended with many and great difficulties.

Answer: So is every good action. The heathen could say *ardua virtutis via*. And the way of God's kingdom (the best way in the world) is accompanied with most difficulties. Straight is the gate and narrow is the way that leadeth to life. Again, the difficulties are no other than such as many daily meet with and such as God hath brought others well through them.

Objection 6: It is a work above the power of the undertakers.

Answer 1: The welfare of any body consists not so much in quantity as in due portion and disposition of parts, and we see other plantations have subsisted divers years and prospered from weak means.

2. It is no wonder, for great things may arise from weak, contemptible beginnings; it hath been oft seen in kingdoms and states and may as well hold in towns and plantations. The Waldenses were scattered into the Alps and mountains of Piedmont by small companies, but they became famous churches whereof some remain to this day; and it is certain that the Turks, Venetians, and other states were very weak in their beginnings.

Objection 7: The country affords no natural fortifications.

Answer: No more did Holland and many other places which had greater enemies and nearer at hand, and God doth use to place His people in the midst of perils that they may trust in Him and not in outward means and safety; so when He would choose a place to plant His beloved people in, He seateth them not in an island or other place fortified by nature, but in a plain country beset with potent and bitter enemies round about, yet so long as they served Him and trusted in His help they were safe. So the Apostle Paul saith of himself and his fellow laborers, that they were compassed with dangers on every side and were daily under the sentence of death that they might learn to trust in the living God.

Objection 8: The place affordeth no comfortable means to the first planters, and our breeding here at home have made us unfit for the hardship we are like to endure.

Answer 1: No place of itself hath afforded sufficient to the first inhabitants; such things as we stand in need of are usually supplied by God's blessing upon the wisdom and industry of man, and whatsoever we stand in need of is treasured in the earth by the Creator and is to be fetched thence by the sweat of our brows.

2. We must learn with Paul to want as well as to abound; if we have food and raiment (which are there to be had), we ought to be contented. The difference in quality may a little displease us, but it cannot hurt us.

3. It may be by this means God will bring us to repent of our former intemperance, and so cure us of that disease which sends many amongst us untimely to their graves and others to hell; so He carried the Israelites into the wilderness and made them forget the flesh pots of Egypt, which was sorry pinch to them at first, but he disposed to their good in the end. Deut. 30: 3, 16.

Tempting God

Objection 9: We must look to be preserved by miracle if we subsist, and so we shall tempt God.

Answer 1: They who walk under ordinary means of safety and supply do not tempt God, but such will be our condition in this plantation therefore, etc. The proposition cannot be denied; the assumption we prove thus: that place is as much secured from ordinary dangers as many hundred places in the civil parts of the world, and we shall have as much provision beforehand as such towns do use to provide against a siege or dearth, and sufficient means for raising a succeeding store against that is spent. If it be denied that we shall be as secure as other places, we answer that many of our sea towns, and such as are upon the confines of enemies' countries in the continent, lie more upon and nearest to danger than we shall. And though such towns have sometimes been burnt or spoiled, yet men tempt not God to dwell still in them, and though many houses in the country amongst us lie open to thieves and robbers (as many have found by sad experience), yet no man will say that those which dwell in such places must be preserved by miracle.

2. Though miracles be now ceased, yet men may expect more than ordinary blessing from God upon all lawful means, where the work is the Lord's and He is sought in it according to His will, for it is usual with Him to increase or weaken the strength of the means as He is pleased or displeased with the instruments and the action, else we must conclude that God hath left the government of the world and committed all power to the creature, that the success of all things should wholly depend upon the second causes.

For Further Reading

Stephen Greenblatt, *Marvelous Possessions: The Wonders of the New World.* Chicago: University of Chicago Press, 1991.

Peter C. Mancall, ed., *Envisioning America.* Boston: Bedford Books of St. Martin's Press, 1995.

Edmund S. Morgan, *The Puritan Dilemma: The Story of John Winthrop.* Boston: Little, Brown, 1958.

David B. Quinn, *North America from Earliest Discovery to First Settlements: The Norse Voyages to 1612.* New York: Harper & Row, 1975.

David B. Quinn, ed., *The Hakluyt Handbook.* London: The Hakluyt Society, 1974.

Darrett Bruce Rutman, *John Winthrop's Decision for America.* Philadelphia: Lippincott, 1975.

Viewpoint 2A

Virginia Is an Abundant New Paradise (1613)

Alexander Whitaker (?–1617?)

Jamestown, the first enduring English settlement in the New World, was financed by the Virginia Company of London, a private joint-stock company; much of the historical record of Jamestown comes from company records and publications. The company's efforts to recoup its expenses and make a profit in its venture were jeopardized in Jamestown's early years as reports of hardship and starvation reached England. In order to attract additional investors and settlers, the company published several pamphlets describing the resources of the new land of "Virginia" and the riches to be attained there. The following viewpoint is one example of such writing; it is excerpted from a pamphlet written by Alexander Whitaker, a minister who had arrived in the new colony in 1611, and published by the Virginia Company in 1613. The son of a prominent Puritan, Whitaker was motivated to move to America to preach Christianity to the Indians, according to

From *Good News from Virginia* by Alexander Whitaker (London: Virginia Company of London, 1613).

William Crashaw, a minister who stayed in England and who wrote the preface to Whitaker's pamphlet. Little else is known about Whitaker other than a 1617 letter from Deputy Governor Samuel Argall stating that he had drowned.

What Virginia resources does Whitaker describe? What major questions and problems about the new colony does he address?

The whole continent of Virginia, situate within the degrees of 34 and 47, is a place beautified by God with all the ornaments of nature and enriched with His earthly treasures. That part of it which we already possess, beginning at the Bay of Chesapeake and stretching itself in northerly latitude to the degrees of 39 and 40, is interlined with seven most goodly rivers, the least whereof is equal to our river of Thames; and all these rivers are so nearly joined as that there is not very much distance of dry ground between either of them, and those several mainlands are everywhere watered with many veins or creeks of water, which sundry ways do overthwart the land and make it almost navigable from one river to the other. The commodity [advantage] whereof to those that shall inhabit this land is infinite in respect of the speedy and easy transportance of goods from one river to the other. I cannot better manifest it unto you but in advising you to consider whether the water or land hath been more beneficial to the Low Countries; but here we shall have the commodity both of water and land more ready, with less charge and labour, than hath been bestowed by them in turning land into water.

Describing the Land

The [James] river which we inhabit (commonly called Powhatan's River) ebbeth and floweth 140 miles from the main, at the mouth whereof are the two forts of Henrico and Charles. Forty-two miles upward is the first and mother Christian town seated, called Jamestown, and seventy miles beyond that upward is the new town of Henrico, built and so named in the memory of the noble Prince Henry of lasting and blessed memory. Ten miles beyond this town is a place called the Falls, because the river hath there a great descent, falling down between many mineral rocks which be there; twelve miles farther beyond this place is there a crystal rock wherewith the Indians do head many of their arrows; three days' journey from thence is there a rock or stony hill found, which is in the top covered all over with a perfect and most rich silver ore. Our men that went to discover those parts had but two iron pickaxes with them, and those so ill tempered that the points of them turned again and bowed at every stroke, so that we could not search the entrails of that place; yet some trial was made of that ore with good success and argument of much hope.

Six days' journey beyond this mine a great ridge of high hills do run along the mainland, not far from whom the Indians report a great sea doth run, which we commonly call a South Sea, but in respect of our habitation is a West Sea, for there the sun setteth from us. The higher ground is much like unto the mould of France, clay and sand being proportionably mixed together at the top; but if we dig any depth (as we have done for our bricks) we find it to be red clay, full of glistering spangles. There be many rocky places in all quarters, and more than probable likelihoods of rich mines of all sorts: though I knew all, yet it were not convenient at this time that I should utter all, neither have we had means to search for anything as we ought, through present want of men and former wants of provision for the belly. . . .

Health and Climate

The air of the country (especially about Henrico and upward) is very temperate and agreeth well with our bodies. The extremity of summer is not so hot as Spain nor the cold of winter so sharp as the frosts of England. The spring and harvest are the two longest seasons and most pleasant; the summer and winter are both but short. The winter is for the most part dry and fair but the summer watered often with many great and sudden showers of rain, whereby the cold of winter is warmed and the heat of summer cooled. Many have died with us heretofore through their own filthiness and want of bodily comforts for sick men; but now very few are sick among us: not above three persons amongst all the inhabitants of Henrico. I would to God our souls were no sicker than our bodies and that other of God's blessings were as general and common as the bodily health. I have seen it by experience and dare boldly affirm it that sickness doth more rage in England quarterly than here yearly. I doubt [fear] that hereafter, when our hospital or guest house is built up, you hear of many more cut off by the sword of justice (unless the better people be sent over) than perished by the diseases of the country.

The Native Inhabitants

The natural people of the land are generally such as you heard of before: a people to be feared of those that come upon them without defensive armour, but otherwise faint-hearted (if they see their arrows cannot pierce) and easy to be subdued. Shirts of mail or quilted cotton are the best defence against them. There is but one or two of their petty kings that for fear of us have desired our friendship, and those keep good quarter with us, being very pleasant amongst us and (if occasion be) serviceable unto us. Our eldest friends be Pipsco and Chopoke, who are our overthwart neighbours at Jamestown and have been friendly to us in our great want. The other is the werowance of Chesapeake, who but lately traded with us peaceably. If we were once the masters of their country and they stood in fear of us (which might with few hands employed about nothing else be in short time brought to pass), it were an easy matter to make them willingly to forsake the Devil, to embrace the faith of Jesus Christ, and to be baptized. Besides, you cannot easily judge how much they would be available to us in our discoveries of the country, in our buildings and plantings and quiet provision for ourselves, when we may peaceably pass from place to place without need of arms or guard.

Natural Resources

The means for our people to live and subsist here of themselves are many and most certain, both for beasts, birds, fish, and herbs. The beasts of the country are for the most part wild: as lions, bears, wolves, and deer; foxes, black and red; raccoons; beavers; possums; squirrels; wildcats, whose skins are of great price; and muskrats, which yield musk as the muskcats do. There be two kinds of beasts among these most strange: one of them is the female possum, which will let forth her young out of her belly and take them up into her belly again at her pleasure without hurt to herself; neither think this to be a traveller's tale but the very truth, for Nature hath framed her fit for that service: my eyes have been witness unto it and we have sent of them and their young ones into England. The other strange-conditioned creature is the flying squirrel, which, through the help of certain broad flaps of skin growing on each side of her forelegs, will fly from tree to tree twenty or thirty paces at one flight and more, if she have the benefit of a small breath of wind. Besides these, since our coming hither we have brought both kine, goats, and hogs, which prosper well and would multiply exceedingly if they might be provided for.

———— • ————

"Virginia . . . is a place beautified by God with all the ornaments of nature and enriched with His earthly treasures."

———— • ————

This country besides is replenished with birds of all sorts, which have been the best sustenance of flesh which our men have had since they came; also eagles and hawks of all sorts, amongst whom are osprey, fishing hawk, and the cormorant. The woods be everywhere full of wild turkeys, which abound and will run as swift as a greyhound. In winter our fields be full of cranes, herons, pigeons, partridges, and blackbirds; the rivers and creeks be overspread everywhere with water-fowl of the greatest and least sort, as swans, flocks of geese and brants, duck and mallard, sheldrakes, divers, etc., besides many other kinds of rare and delectable birds whose names and natures I cannot yet recite; but we want the means to take them.

The rivers abound with fish both great and small. The sea-fish come into our rivers in March and continue until the end of September; great schools of herrings come in first; shads, of a great bigness, and rock fish, follow them. Trouts, bass, flounders, and other dainty fish come in before the other be gone; then come multitudes of great sturgeons, whereof we catch many and should do more but that we want good nets answerable to the breadth and depth of our rivers: besides our channels are so foul in the bottom with great logs and trees that we often break our nets upon them. I cannot reckon nor give proper names to the divers kinds of fresh fish in our rivers. I have caught with mine angle [fishhook] pike, carp, eel, perches of six several kinds, crayfish, and the torope or little turtle, besides many smaller kinds.

Do Not Fear Starvation

Wherefore, since God hath filled the elements of earth, air, and waters with His creatures, good for our food and nourishment, let not the fear of starving hereafter, or of any great want, dishearten your valiant minds from coming to a place of so great plenty. If the country were ours and means for the taking of them (which shortly I hope shall be brought to pass), then all of these should be ours; we have them now but we are fain to fight for them; then should we have them without that trouble. Fear not, then, to want food, but only provide means to get it here. We have store of wild-fowl in England, but what are they better for them that cannot come by them, wanting means to catch them? Even such is and hath been our case heretofore.

But even these are not all the commodities which we may find here: for the earth will yield much more fruit to our industrious labours, as hath been proved by the corn and other things which we have planted this last year. I have made proof of it, with the help of three more, being a stranger to that business and having not a body inured to such labour, and set so much corn, *horis succisivus unius septimanae* (in the idle hours of one week), as will suffice me for bread one quarter of a year; and one commodity is besides in this corn, that from the time of setting unto the time of gathering five months will abundantly suffice: for we set corn from the beginning of March until the end of May, and reap or gather in July, August, and September. Our English seeds thrive very well here, as peas, onions, turnips, cabbages, coleflowers, carrots, thyme, parsley, hyssop, marjoram, and many other whereof I have tasted and eaten.

What should I name unto you the divers sorts of trees, sweet woods, and physical [medicinal] plants; the divers kinds of oaks and walnut trees; the pines, pitch-trees, soap-ashes trees, sassafras, cedar, ash, maple, cypress, and many more which I daily see and admire at the beauty and riches which God hath bestowed upon this people that yet know not how to use them.

Be Not Discouraged

Wherefore, you (right wise and noble adventurers of Virginia) whose hearts God hath stirred up to build Him a temple, to make Him an house, to conquer a kingdom for Him here: be not discouraged with those many lamentable assaults that the Devil hath made against us: he now rageth most because he knoweth his kingdom is to have a short end. Go forward boldly and remember that you fight under the banner of Jesus Christ, that you plant His kingdom Who hath already broken the serpent's head. God may defer His temporal reward for a season, but be assured that in the end you shall find riches and honour in this world and blessed immortality in the world to come. And you, my brethren, my fellow labourers, send up your earnest prayers to God for His church in Virginia, that, since His harvest here is great but the labourers few, He would thrust forth labourers into His harvest. And pray also for me that the ministration of His Gospel may be powerful and effectual by me, to the salvation of many and advancement of the kingdom of Jesus Christ, to whom, with the Father and the Holy Spirit, be all honour and glory forevermore.

Amen.

VIEWPOINT 2B

Virginia Is Not a New Paradise (1624)

Richard Ffrethorne (dates unknown)

A stark counterpoint to the glowing reports of life in Virginia published by the Virginia Company of London is found in the following viewpoint, a 1623 letter from a Virginia colonist to his parents in England. Richard Ffrethorne came to Virginia an indentured servant, bound to work for a planter for a fixed period of time (probably four years). The letter

Reprinted from *The Records of the Virginia Company of London*, edited by Susan Kingsbury, vol. 4 (Washington, DC: GPO, 1935).

describes the lack of food and harsh conditions in Virginia, and helps to explain why by 1624 four out of five Jamestown colonists had perished. It also includes accounts of Indian attacks. Historians know little about Richard Ffrethorne other than the information found here.

How do Ffrethorne's descriptions of Virginia's food resources and Indian inhabitants differ from those of Alexander Whitaker, author of the opposing viewpoint? Ffrethorne was an indentured servant who was in debt for his voyage to America; is this a focus of complaint in his letter?

———————————

Loveing and kind father and mother my most humble duty remembred to you hopeing in God of your good health, as I my selfe am at the makeing hereof, this is to let you understand that I your Child am in a most heavie Case by reason of the nature of the Country is such that it Causeth much sicknes, as the scurvie and the bloody flix, and divers other diseases, wch maketh the bodie very poore, and Weake, and when wee are sicke there is nothing to Comfort us; for since I came out of the ship, I never at[e] anie thing but pease, and loblollie (that is water gruell) as for deare or venison I never saw anie since I came into this land, ther is indeed some foule, but Wee are not allowed to goe, and get it, but must Worke hard both earelie, and late for a messe of water gruell, and a mouthfull of bread, and beife, a mouthfull of bread for a pennie loafe must serve for 4 men wch is most pitifull if you did knowe as much as I, when people crie out day, and night, Oh that they were in England without their lymbes and would not care to loose anie lymbe to bee in England againe, yea though they beg from doore to doore, for wee live in feare of the Enimy [Indians] everie hower, yet wee have had a Combate with them on the Sunday before Shrovetyde, and wee tooke two alive, and make slaves of them, but it was by pollicie, for wee are in great danger, for our Planta͞con is very weake, by reason of the dearth, and sicknes, of our Companie, for wee came but Twentie for the marchaunts, and they are halfe dead Just; and wee looke everie hower When two more should goe, yet there came some for other men yet to live with us, of which ther is but one alive, and our Leiftenant is dead, and his ffather, and his brother, and there was some 5 or 6 of the last yeares 20 of wch there is but 3 left, so that wee are faine to get other men to plant with us, and yet wee are but 32 to fight against 3000 if they should Come, and the nighest helpe that Wee have is ten miles of us, and when the rogues ouvercame this place last, they slew 80 Persons how then shall wee doe for wee lye even in their teeth, they may easilie take us but that God is mercifull, and can save with few as well as with many; as he shewed to Gilead and like Gilead's Souldiers if they lapt water, wee drinkee water wch is but Weake.

———————— • ————————

*"I have nothing to Comfort me,
nor ther is nothing to be gotten
here but sicknes, and death."*

———————— • ————————

And I have nothing to Comfort me, nor ther is nothing to be gotten here but sicknes, and death, except that one had money to lay out in some thinges for profit; But I have nothing at all, no not a shirt to my backe, but two Ragges nor no Clothes, but one poore suite, nor but one paire of shooes, but one paire of stockins, but one Capp, but two bands, my Cloke is stollen by one of my owne fellowes, and to his dying hower would not tell mee what he did with it but some of my fellows saw him have butter and beife out of a ship, wch my Cloke I doubt [fear] paid for, so that I have not a penny, nor a a penny Worth to helpe me to either spice, or sugar, or strong Waters, without the wch one cannot live here, for as strong beare in England doth fatten and strengthen them so water here doth wash and weaken theis here, onelie keepe life and soule togeather. but I am not halfe a quarter so strong as I was in England, and all is for want of victualls, for I doe protest unto you, that I have eaten more in day at home then I have allowed me here for a Weeke. you have given more then my dayes allowance to a beggar at the doore; and if Mr. Jackson had not releived me, I should bee in a poore Case, but he like a ffather and shee like a loveing mother doth still helpe me, for when wee goe up to James Towne that is 10 myles of us, there lie all the ships that Come to the land, and there they must deliver their goods, and when wee went up to Towne as it may bee on Moonedaye, at noone, and come there by night, then load the next day by ~~night~~ noone, and goe home in the afternoone, and unload, and then away againe in the night, and bee up about midnight, then if it rayned, or blowed never so hard wee must lye in the boate on the water, and have nothing but alitle bread, for when wee go into the boate wee have a loafe allowed to two men, and it is all if we staid there 2 dayes, wch is hard, and must lye all that while in the boate, but that Goodman Jackson pityed me & made me a Cabbin to lye in alwayes when I come up, and he would give me some poore Jacks home with me wch Comforted mee more then pease, or water gruell. Oh they bee verie godlie folkes, and love me verie well, and will doe anie thing for me, and he much marvailed that you would send me a servaunt to the Companie, he saith I had beene better knockd on the head, and Indeede so I fynd it now to my greate greife and miserie, and saith, that if you love me you will redeeme me suddenlie, for wch I doe Intreate and begg, and if you cannot get the marchaunts to redeeme me for some litle money then for God's sake get a gathering or intreat some good folks to lay out some little Sum of moneye, in meale, and Cheese and butter, and beife, anie eating meate will yeald great profit, oile and vyniger is verie good, but ffather ther is greate losse in leakinge, but for God's sake send beife and Cheese and butter or the more of one sort and none of another, but if you send Cheese it must bee very old Cheese, and at the Chesmongers you may buy good Cheese for two-pence farthing or halfepenny that will be liked verie well, but if you send Cheese you must have a Care how you packe it in barrells, and you must put Coop-ers Chips betweene everie Cheese, or els the heat of the hold will rott them, and looke whatsoever you send me be it never so much looke what I make of it I will deale trulie with you I will send it over, and begg the profit to redeeme me, and if I die before it Come I have intreated Goodman Jackson to send you the worth of it, who hath promised he will; If you send you must direct your letters to Goodman Jack-son, at James Towne a Gunsmith. (you must set downe his frayt) because there bee more of his name there; good ffather doe not forget me, but have mer-cie and pittye my miserable Case. I know if you did but see me you would weepe to see me, for I have but one suite, but it is a strange one, it is very well guarded, wherefore for God's sake pittie me, I pray you to remember my love my love to all my ffreinds, and kindred, I hope all my Brothers and Sisters are in good health, and as for my part I have set downe my resolucon that certainelie Wilbe, that is, that the Answeare of this letter wilbee life or death to me, therefore good ffather send as soone as you can, and if you send me anie thing let this bee the marke.

ROT   Richard Ffrethorne
        Martyns Hundred.

For Further Reading

Karen Ordahl Kupperman, *Captain John Smith: A Selected Edition of His Writings.* Chapel Hill: University of North Carolina Press, 1988.

Edmund S. Morgan, *American Slavery, American Freedom: The Ordeal of Colonial Virginia.* New York: Norton, 1975.

Richard Lee Morton, *Colonial Virginia.* Chapel Hill: University of North Carolina Press, 1960.

Edward D. Neill, *History of the Virginia Company of London.* New York: Burt Franklin, 1968.

Alden T. Vaughan, *American Genesis: Captain John Smith and the Founding of Virginia.* Boston: Little, Brown, 1975.

European Colonists and Native Americans

VIEWPOINT 3A

Indians and Colonists Should Live in Peace (1609)

Powhatan (ca. 1550–1618)

Powhatan (also called Wahunsonacock) was the leader of a confederacy of American Indian tribes that lived in what is now the state of Virginia, and was thus one of the first Indian leaders to have extensive contact with European colonists in North America. The following viewpoint is taken from a 1609 speech Powhatan made to John Smith, the leader of the English settlement of Jamestown. Smith recorded Powhatan's call for peaceful relations between the two peoples, which stresses the importance of Indian food assistance to Jamestown's survival. Despite occasional skirmishes and confrontations, the Indians of the Powhatan Confederacy and the English settlers maintained a general truce until 1622 (a truce aided in part by the marriage of Powhatan's daughter, Pocahontas, to English settler John Rolfe in 1614).

———— • ————

"You see us unarmed, and willing to supply your wants, if you will come in a friendly manner."

———— • ————

What benefits of peaceful relations for both colonists and Indians does Powhatan list? What dangers does he say might threaten the settlers if they fail to deal peacefully with him and his tribe?

————————————

I am now grown old, and must soon die; and the succession must descend, in order, to my broth-ers, *Opitchapan, Opekankanough,* and *Cata-taugh,* and then to my two sisters, and their two daughters. I wish their experience was equal to mine; and that your love to us might not be less than ours to you. Why should you take by force that from us which you can have by love? Why should you destroy us, who have provided you with food? What can you get by war? We can hide our provisions, and fly into the woods; and then you must consequently famish by wronging your friends. What is the cause of your

from *Biography and History of the Indians of North America* by Samuel B. Drake, 8th ed. (Boston: Antiquarian Bookstore, 1841).

jealousy? You see us unarmed, and willing to supply your wants, if you will come in a friendly manner, and not with swords and guns, as to invade an enemy. I am not so simple, as not to know it is better to eat good meat, lie well, and sleep quietly with my women and children; to laugh and be merry with the English; and, being their friend, to have copper, hatchets, and whatever else I want, than to fly from all, to lie cold in the woods, feed upon acorns, roots, and such trash, and to be so hunted, that I cannot rest, eat, or sleep. In such circumstances, my men must watch, and if a twig should but break, all would cry out, *"Here comes Capt. Smith;"* and so, in this miserable manner, to end my miserable life; and, Capt. *Smith*, this *might* be soon your fate too, through your rashness and unadvisedness. I, therefore, exhort you to peaceable councils; and, above all, I insist that the guns and swords, the cause of all our jealousy and uneasiness, be removed and sent away.

VIEWPOINT 3B

Indians Should Be Conquered and Exterminated (1622)

The Virginia Company of London

A few years after the death of American Indian leader Powhatan (see viewpoint 3A), his brother Opekankanough (Opachankano), the new leader of the Powhatan Confederacy, launched a surprise attack on English settlements in and around Jamestown, Virginia. The 1622 assault, one of the first major conflicts between English colonists and American Indians, was in part a response to continuing seizures of Indian land by the colonists. The attackers killed 347 Jamestown residents (including Pocahontas's widower, John Rolfe) and destroyed many houses and farms before they were stopped. The following viewpoint contains an account of the violence and its ramifications for the colonization of Virginia. It was written by officials of the Virginia Company of London, which had sponsored the Jamestown settlement, and was in part meant to explain why the colony had yet to show any profit for its investors.

How do the Virginia Company officials characterize the Indians? How does this account compare with the company's earlier optimistic account of Virginia, as presented in viewpoint 2A?

T hat all men may see the impartial ingenuity of this discourse, we freely confess, that the country is not so good, as the natives are bad,

Reprinted from *The Records of the Virginia Company of London*, edited by Susan Kingsbury, vol. 3 (Washington, DC: GPO, 1933).

whose barbarous selves need more cultivation then the ground itself, being more overspread with incivility and treachery, than that with briars. For the land, being tilled and used well by us, deceive not our expectation but rather exceeded it far, being so thankful as to return a hundred for one. But the savages, though never a nation used so kindly upon so small desert, have instead of that harvest which our pains merited, returned nothing but briars and thorns, pricking even to death many of their benefactors. Yet doubt we not, but that as all wickedness is crafty to undo itself, so these also have more wounded themselves than us, God Almighty making way for severity there, where a fair gentleness would not take place. The occasion whereof thus I relate from thence.

The last May there came a letter from Sir Francis Wiat [Wyatt] Governor in Virginia, which did advertise that when in November last [1621] he arrived in Virginia and entered upon his government, he found the country settled in a peace (as all men there thought), sure and unviolable, not only because it was solemnly ratified and sworn, but as being advantageous to both parts; to the savages as the weaker, under which they were safely sheltered and defended; to us, as being the easiest way then thought to pursue and advance our projects of buildings, plantings, and effecting their conversion by peaceable and fair means. And such was the conceit [conception] of firm peace and amity as that there was seldom or never a sword worn. . . . The plantations of particular adventurers and planters were placed scatteringly and stragglingly as a choice vein of rich ground invited them, and the further from neighbors held the better. The houses generally set open to the savages, who were always friendly entertained at the tables of the English, and commonly lodged in their bedchambers. The old planters (as they thought now come to reap the benefit of their long travels) placed with wonderful content upon their private lands, and their familiarity with the natives, seeming to open a fair gate for their conversion to Christianity.

A Surprise Attack

The country being in this estate, an occasion was ministered of sending to Opachankano, the King of these savages, about the middle of March last [1622], what time the messenger returned back with these words from him, that he held the peace concluded so firm as the sky should sooner fall than it dissolve. Yea, such was the treacherous dissimulation of that people who then had contrived our destruction, that even two days before the massacre, some of our men were guided through the woods by them in safety. . . . Yea, they borrowed our own boats to convey themselves across the river (on the banks of both sides whereof all our plantations were) to consult of the devilish murder that ensued, and of our utter extirpation, which God of His mercy (by the means of themselves converted to Christianity) prevented. And as well on the Friday morning (the fatal day) the twenty-second of March, as also in the evening, as on other days before, they came unarmed into our houses, without bows or arrows, or other weapons, with deer, turkey, fish, fur, and other provisions to sell and trade with us for glass, beads, and other trifles. Yet in some places, they sat down at breakfast with our people at their tables, whom immediately with their own tools and weapons either laid down, or standing in their houses, they basely and barbarously murdered, not sparing either age or sex, man, woman, or child, so sudden in their cruel execution that few or none discerned the weapon or blow that brought them to destruction. In which manner they also slew many of our people then at their several work and husbandries in the fields, and without their houses, some in planting corn and tobacco, some in gardening, some in making brick, building, sawing, and other kinds of husbandry, they well knowing in what places and quarters each of our men were, in regard of their daily familiarity and resort to us for trading and other negotiations, which the more willingly was by us continued and cherished for the desire we had of effecting that great masterpiece of works, their conversion. And by this means that fatal Friday morning, there fell under the bloody and barbarous hands of that perfidious and inhuman people, contrary to all laws of God and men, of nature and nations, three hundred forty seven men, women, and children, most by their own weapons. And not being content with taking away life alone, they fell after again upon the dead, making as well as they could, a fresh murder, defacing, dragging, and mangling the dead carcasses into many pieces, and carrying some parts away in derision, with base and brutish triumph. . . .

———— • ————

"The way of conquering them is much more easy than of civilizing them by fair means, for they are a rude, barbarous, and naked people."

———— • ————

That the slaughter had been universal, if God had not put it into the heart of an Indian belonging to one Perry to disclose it, who living in the house of one Pace, was urged by another Indian his brother (who came the night before and lay with him) to kill Pace. Telling further that by such an hour in the morning a number would come from different places to finish the execution, who failed not at the time, Perry's Indian rose out of his bed and revealed it to Pace, that used him as a son. And thus the rest of the colony that had warning given them by this means was saved. Such was (God be thanked for it) the good fruit of an infidel converted to Christianity. For though three hundred and more of ours died by many of these pagan infidels, yet thousands of ours were saved by the means of one of them alone which was made a Christian. Blessed be God forever, whose mercy endureth forever. . . .

Lessons of the Massacre

Thus have you seen the particulars of this massacre, wherein treachery and cruelty have done their worst to us, or rather to themselves; for whose understanding is so shallow, as not to perceive that this must needs be for the good of the plantation after, and the loss of this blood to make the body more healthful, as by these reasons may be manifest.

First, because betraying innocence never rests unpunished. . . .

Secondly, because our hands, which before were tied with gentleness and fair usage, are now set at liberty by the treacherous violence of the savages, not untying the knot, but cutting it. So that we, who hitherto have had possession of no more ground than their waste, and our purchase at a valuable consideration to their own contentment gained, may now, by right of war and law of nations, invade the country, and destroy them who sought to destroy us. Whereby we shall enjoy their cultivated places, possessing the fruits of others' labors. Now their cleared grounds in all their villages (which are situated in the fruitfulest places of the land) shall be inhabited by us, whereas heretofore the grubbing of woods was the greatest labor.

Thirdly, because those commodities which the Indians enjoyed as much or rather more than we, shall now also be entirely possessed by us. The deer and other beasts will be in safety, and infinitely increase, which heretofore not only in the general huntings of the King, but by each particular Indian were destroyed at all times of the year, without any difference of male, dame, or young.

There will be also a great increase of wild turkeys, and other weighty fowl, for the Indians never put difference of destroying the hen, but kill them whether in season or not, whether in breeding time, or sitting on their eggs, or having new hatched, it is all one to them. . . .

Fourthly, because the way of conquering them is much more easy than of civilizing them by fair means, for they are a rude, barbarous, and naked people, scattered in small companies, which are helps to victory, but hindrance to civility. Besides that, a conquest may be of many, and at once; but civility is in particular and slow, the effect of long time, and great industry. Moreover, victory of them may be gained many ways: by force, by surprise, by famine in burning their corn, by destroying and burning their boats, canoes, and houses, by breaking their fishing wares, by assailing them in their huntings, whereby they get the greatest part of their sustenance in winter, by pursuing and chasing them with our horses and bloodhounds to draw after them, and mastiffs to tear them.

For Further Reading

Wesley Frank Craven, *White, Red and Black: The Seventeenth Century Virginian*. Charlottesville: University Press of Virginia, 1971.

Francis Jennings, *The Invasion of America: Indians, Colonialism, and the Cant of Conquest*. Chapel Hill: University of North Carolina Press, 1975.

Karen Ordahl Kupperman, *Settling with the Indians: The Meeting of English and Indian Cultures in America, 1580–1640*. Totowa, NJ: Rowman and Littlefield, 1980.

Helen C. Rountree, *Pocahontas's People: The Powhatan Indians of Virginia Through Four Centuries*. Norman: University of Oklahoma Press, 1990.

Bernard W. Sheehan, *Savagism & Civility: Indians and Englishmen in Colonial Virginia*. New York: Cambridge University Press, 1980.

VIEWPOINT 4A

A Puritan Missionary's Account of Indians (1646)

John Eliot (1604–1690)

A Puritan minister who migrated to America in 1631, John Eliot shared ministerial duties in Roxbury, Massachusetts, with Thomas Welde (author of viewpoint 5B). In the 1640s he learned the Algonquian language from an Indian servant and began missionary work among the Indians—work he continued until his death. Widely known both in America and in England as the "Apostle to the Indians," Eliot translated the Bible into the Algonquian language and wrote numerous pamphlets and tracts about his missionary work. Eliot's views toward the Indians are reflected in the following viewpoint, excerpted from a pamphlet first published in London in 1646. Part of the pamphlet's purpose was to elicit English support for his missionary efforts.

Does Eliot seem to believe that European culture is superior to that of the Indians he describes?

From *The Day-Braking, If Not the Sun-Rising, of the Gospell with the Indians in New-England* by John Eliot (Massachusetts Historical Society, Collections, vol. 3). Courtesy of the Massachusetts Historical Society.

Explain. What reasons does he give for optimism in his missionary work among the Indians?

Methinks now that it is with the Indians as it was with our New English ground when we first came over—there was scarce any man that could believe that English grain would grow, or that the plow could do any good in this woody and rocky soil. And thus they continued in this supine unbelief for some years, till experience taught them otherwise; and now all see it to be scarce inferior to Old English tillage, but bears very good burdens. So we have thought of our Indian people, and, therefore, have been discouraged to put plow to such dry and rocky ground, but God, having begun thus with some few, it may be they are better soil for the gospel than we can think.

I confess I think no great good will be done till they be more civilized. But why may not God begin with some few to awaken others by degrees? Nor do I expect any great good will be wrought by the English (leaving secrets to God, although the English surely begin and lay the first stones of Christ's kingdom and temple among them), because God is wont ordinarily to convert nations and peoples by some of their own countrymen who are nearest to them and can best speak, and, most of all, pity their brethren and countrymen. But yet, if the least beginnings be made by the conversion of two or three, it is worth all our time and travails, and cause of much thankfulness for such seeds, although no great harvests should immediately appear.

Surely this is evident, first, that they never heard heartbreaking prayer and preaching before now in their own tongue, that we know of. Second, that there were never such hopes of a dawning of mercy toward them as now. Certainly those abundant tears which we saw shed from their eyes argue a mighty and blessed presence of the Spirit of Heaven in their hearts, which when once it comes into such kind of spirits will not easily out again.

Hopeful Beginnings

The chief use that I can make of these hopeful beginnings, besides rejoicing for such shinings, is from Is. 2:5: "Oh, house of Israel, let us walk in the light of the Lord," considering that these blind natives begin to look toward God's mountain now.

The observations I have gathered by conversing with them are such as these:

1. That none of them . . . derided God's messenger: Woe unto those English that are grown bold to do that which Indians will not—heathens dare not.

2. That there is need of learning in ministers who preach to Indians, much more [than] to Englishmen

and gracious Christians, for these had sundry philosophical questions which some knowledge of the arts must help to give answer to; and without which these would not have been satisfied. Worse than Indian ignorance has blinded their eyes that renounce learning as an enemy to gospel ministries.

3. That there is no necessity of extraordinary gifts nor miraculous signs always to convert heathens . . . for we see the Spirit of God working mightily upon the hearts of these natives in an ordinary way, and I hope will, they being but a remnant, the Lord using to show mercy to the remnant. For there be but few that are left alive from the plague and pox, which God sent into those parts; and, if one or two can understand, they usually talk of it as we do of news— it flies suddenly far and near, and truth scattered will rise in time, for ought we know.

4. If Englishmen begin to despise the preaching of faith and repentance and humiliation for sin, yet the poor heathens will be glad of it and it shall do good to them; for so they are and so it begins to do. The Lord grant that the foundation of our English woe be not laid in the ruin and contempt of those fundamental doctrines of faith, repentance, humiliation for sin, etc., but rather relishing the novelties and dreams of such men as are surfeited with the ordinary food of the Gospel of Christ. Indians shall weep to hear faith and repentance preached, when Englishmen shall mourn, too late, that are weary of such truths.

5. That the deepest estrangements of man from God is no hindrance to His grace nor to the spirit of grace; for what nation or people ever so deeply degenerated since Adam's fall as these Indians, and yet the Spirit of God is working upon them?

6. That it is very likely if ever the Lord convert any of these natives that they will mourn for sin exceedingly and, consequently, love Christ dearly; for, if by a little measure of light such heartbreakings have appeared, what may we think will be when more is let in? They are some of them very wicked, some very ingenious. These latter are very apt and quick of understanding and naturally sad and melancholy (a good servant to repentance); and, therefore, there is the greater hope of great heartbreakings if ever God brings them effectually home, for which we should affectionately pray. . . .

Creating a Christian Indian Town

We have cause to be very thankful to God who has moved the hearts of the General Court to purchase so much land for them to make their town in which the Indians are much taken with. And it is somewhat observable that, while the court were considering where to lay out their town, the Indians (not knowing of anything) were about that time consulting about laws for themselves, and their company who

sit down with Waaubon [a local Christian Indian leader]. There were ten of them; two of them are forgotten.

Their laws were these:

1. That if any man be idle a week, at most a fortnight, he shall pay 5s [shillings].

2. If any unmarried man shall lie with a young woman unmarried, he shall pay 20s.

3. If any man shall beat his wife, his hands shall be tied behind him and [he shall be] carried to the place of justice to be severely punished.

4. Every young man, if not another's servant and if unmarried, he shall be compelled to set up a wigwam and plant for himself, and not live shifting up and down to other wigwams.

5. If any woman shall not have her hair tied up but hang loose or be cut as men's hair, she shall pay 5s.

6. If any woman shall go with naked breasts, [she] shall pay 2s. 6d [2 shillings 6 pence].

7. All those men that wear long locks shall pay 5s.

8. If any shall kill their lice between their teeth, they shall pay 5s. This law, though ridiculous to English ears, yet tends to preserve cleanliness among Indians.

•

"The deepest estrangements of man from God is no hindrance to His grace . . . ; for what nation or people ever so deeply degenerated since Adam's fall as these Indians, and yet the Spirit of God is working upon them?"

•

It is wonderful in our eyes to understand by these two honest Indians [helpers of Eliot] what prayers Waaubon and the rest of them use to make, for he that preaches to them professes he never yet used any of their words in his prayers, from whom otherwise it might be thought that they had learned them by rote. One is this:

Amanaomen Jehovah tahassen metagh.

(Take away Lord my stony heart.)

Another:

Chechesom Jehovah kekowhogkew.

(Wash Lord my soul.)

Another:

(Lord lead me, when I die, to heaven.)

These are but a taste. They have many more, and these more enlarged than thus expressed, yet what are these but the sprinklings of the spirit and blood of Christ Jesus in their hearts?

And it is no small matter that such dry, barren, and

long-accursed ground should yield such kind of increase in so small a time. I would not readily commend a fair day before night, nor promise much of such kind of beginnings, in all persons, nor yet in all of these, for we know the profession of very many is but a mere paint, and their best graces nothing but mere flashes and pangs, which are suddenly kindled and as soon go out and are extinct again. Yet God does not usually send His plow and seeds-man to a place but there is at least some little piece of good ground, although three to one be naught. And methinks the Lord Jesus would never have made so fit a key for their locks, unless He had intended to open some of their doors, and so to make way for His coming in. He that God has raised úp and enabled to preach unto them is a man (you know) of a most sweet, humble, loving, gracious, and enlarged spirit, whom God hath blessed, and surely will still delight in and do good by.

Considerations

I did think never to have opened my mouth to any to desire those in England to further any good work here, but now I see so many things inviting to speak in this business that it were well if you did lay before those that are prudent and able these considerations:

1. That it is pretty heavy and chargeable to educate and train up those children which are already offered us, in schooling, clothing, diet, and attendance, which they must have.

2. That in all probability, many Indians in other places, especially under our jurisdiction, will be provoked by this example in these, both to desire preaching and also to send their children to us, when they see that some of their fellows fare so well among the English, and the civil authority here so much favoring and countenancing of these; and if many more come in, it will be more heavy to such as only are fit to keep them, and yet have their hands and knees enfeebled so many ways besides.

3. That if any shall do anything to encourage this work, that it may be given to the college for such an end and use, that so from the college may arise the yearly revenue for their yearly maintenance. I would not have it placed in any particular man's hands for fear of cozenage or misplacing or careless keeping and improving; but at the college it is under many hands and eyes, the chief and best of the country who have been and will be exactly careful of the right and comely disposing of such things. And, therefore, if anything be given, let it be put in such hands as may immediately direct it to the president of the college, who you know will soon acquaint the rest with it; and for this end if any in England have thus given anything for this end, I would have them speak to those who have received it to send it this way, which

if it be withheld I think it is no less than sacrilege. But if God moves no hearts to such a work, I doubt not then but that [weaker] means shall have the honor of it in the Day of Christ.

Instructing the Children

This day being December 9, the children being catechized, and that place of Ezekiel touching the dry bones being opened and applied to their condition, the Indians offered all their children to us to be educated among us and instructed by us, complaining to us that they were not able to give anything to the English for their education. For this reason, there are, therefore, preparations made toward the schooling of them, and setting up a school among them or very near unto them. Sundry questions also were propounded by them to us, and of us to them; one of them being asked, "What is sin?" He answered, "A naughty heart." Another old man complained to us of his fears, viz., that he was fully purposed to keep the Sabbath, but still he was in fear whether he should go to hell or heaven; and thereupon the justification of a sinner by faith in Christ was opened unto him as the remedy against all fears of hell. Another complained of other Indians that did revile them and call them rogues and suchlike speeches for cutting off their locks, and for cutting their hair in a modest manner as the New English generally do; for since the Word has begun to work upon their hearts, they have discerned the vanity and pride which they placed in their hair, and have, therefore, of their own accord (none speaking to them that we know of), cut it modestly. They were therefore encouraged by some there present of chief place and account with us not to fear the reproaches of wicked Indians, nor their witchcraft and powwows and poisonings; but let them know that if they did not dissemble but would seek God unfeignedly, that they would stand by them, and that God also would be with them.

They told us also of diverse Indians who would come and stay with them three or four days and one Sabbath, and then they would go from them. But as for themselves, they told us they were fully purposed to keep the Sabbath, to which we encouraged them; and, night drawing on, [we] were forced to leave them for this time.

VIEWPOINT 4B

A Puritan Captive's Account of Indians (1682)

Mary Rowlandson (ca. 1635–ca. 1678)

Mary Rowlandson was the author of one of the best-selling and most widely read works of the colonial era—an account of her three-month captivity by Indians in 1676. She was captured during King Philip's War, a conflict in which Metacom (whom the English called King Philip) led the last major Indian challenge to white settlement in New England.

Little is known of Rowlandson's life besides what is described in her captivity narrative. She was the wife of Joseph Rowlandson, the minister of Lancaster, a small village on the western frontier of Massachusetts. On February 10, 1676, while her husband was absent, a band of Indians attacked the village and captured her and her three children. Her youngest child soon died of wounds sustained during the fighting, and her other children were separated from her. For almost three months the Indians held her prisoner, until on May 2 she was released for a sizable ransom. She was shortly thereafter reunited with her husband and surviving children.

The Sovereignty & Goodness of God . . . Being a Narrative of the Captivity and Restauration of Mrs. Mary Rowlandson, first published several years after Rowlandson's death, is noteworthy for several reasons, including its gripping story of capture and imprisonment, its ruminations on God's power and role in permitting such suffering, and its descriptions of Indian life. It also provides evidence of changing Puritan attitudes toward the Indians. In the relatively peaceful decades before 1675, many Puritans viewed the Indians as unbelievers who needed to be converted, and they supported the efforts of missionaries such as John Eliot. After the shock of King Philip's War, Indians—including those who professed Christianity and lived in special Christian Indian communities—came to be seen as enemies who should be exterminated.

What does Rowlandson describe of the daily life of her captors? How does Rowlandson describe the actions of the "praying Indians" she encounters? What observations does she make concerning the English army sent to fight the Indians?

On the tenth of February 1675 [1676 in modern reckoning] came the Indians with great numbers upon Lancaster. Their first coming was about sunrising. Hearing the noise of some guns, we looked out; several houses were burning and the smoke ascending to heaven. There were five persons taken in one house; the father and the mother and a sucking child they knocked on the head; the other two they took and carried away alive. There were two others, who being out of their garrison upon some occasion were set upon; one was knocked on the head, the other escaped. Another there was who run-

From *The Sovereignty and Goodness of God . . . Being a Narrative of the Captivity and Restauration of Mrs. Mary Rowlandson* (Cambridge, 1682).

ning along was shot and wounded and fell down; he begged of them his life, promising them money (as they told me), but they would not hearken to him but knocked him in [the] head, stripped him naked, and split open his bowels. . . . Thus these murderous wretches went on, burning and destroying before them. . . .

My eldest sister [Elizabeth] being yet in the house and seeing those woeful sights, the infidels hailing mothers one way and children another and some wallowing in their blood, and her elder son telling her that her son William was dead and myself was wounded, she said, "And, Lord, let me die with them." Which was no sooner said, but she was struck with a bullet and fell down dead over the threshold. I hope she is reaping the fruit of her good labors, being faithful to the service of God in her place. . . . But to return: the Indians laid hold of us, pulling me one way and the children another, and said, "Come go along with us." I told them they would kill me. They answered, if I were willing to go along with them they would not hurt me.

Oh, the doleful sight that now was to behold at this house! "Come, behold the works of the Lord, what desolation He has made in the earth." Of thirty-seven persons who were in this one house none escaped either present death or a bitter captivity save only one, who might say as he, Job 1:15, "And I only am escaped alone to tell the news." There were twelve killed, some shot, some stabbed with their spears, some knocked down with their hatchets. . . .

I had often before this said that if the Indians should come I should choose rather to be killed by them than taken alive, but when it came to the trial, my mind changed; their glittering weapons so daunted my spirit that I chose rather to go along with those (as I may say) ravenous beasts than that moment to end my days. And that I may the better declare what happened to me during that grievous captivity, I shall particularly speak of the several removes we had up and down the wilderness.

The First Remove

Now away we must go with those barbarous creatures with our bodies wounded and bleeding and our hearts no less than our bodies. About a mile we went that night up upon a hill within sight of the town where they intended to lodge. There was hard by a vacant house (deserted by the English before for fear of the Indians). I asked them whether I might not lodge in the house that night, to which they answered, "What, will you love English men still?" This was the dolefullest night that ever my eyes saw. Oh, the roaring and singing and dancing and yelling of those black creatures in the night, which made the place a lively resemblance of hell. And as miserable was the waste that was there made of horses, cattle, sheep, swine, calves, lambs, roasting pigs, and fowl (which they had plundered in the town), some roasting, some lying and burning, and some boiling to feed our merciless enemies who were joyful enough though we were disconsolate. To add to the dolefulness of the former day and the dismalness of the present night, my thoughts ran upon my losses and sad bereaved condition. All was gone: my husband gone (at least separated from me, he being in the Bay, and to add to my grief, the Indians told me they would kill him as he came homeward), my children gone, my relations and friends gone, our house and home and all our comforts within door and without, all was gone except my life, and I knew not but the next moment that might go too. There remained nothing to me but one poor wounded babe, and it seemed at present worse than death that it was in such a pitiful condition bespeaking compassion, and I had no refreshing for it nor suitable things to revive it. Little do many think what is the savageness and brutishness of this barbarous enemy, ay, even those that seem to profess more than others among them when the English have fallen into their hands. . . .

———— • ————

"The enemy came upon our town like . . . so many ravenous wolves, rending us and our lambs to death. But what shall I say? God seemed to leave His people to themselves and order all things for His own holy ends."

———— • ————

The morning being come, they prepared to go on their way. One of the Indians got up upon a horse, and they set me up behind him with my poor sick babe in my lap. A very wearisome and tedious day I had of it what with my own wound and my child's being so exceeding sick in a lamentable condition with her wound. It may be easily judged what a poor feeble condition we were in, there being not the least crumb of refreshing that came within either of our mouths from Wednesday night to Saturday night except only a little cold water. This day in the afternoon about an hour by sun we came to the place where they intended, *viz.* an Indian town called Wenimesset, nor[th]ward of Quabaug. When we were come, oh, the number of pagans (now merciless enemies) that there came about me that I may say as David, Psal. 27:13, "I had fainted, unless I had believed," etc. The next day was the Sabbath. I then remembered how careless I had been of God's holy time, how many Sabbaths I had lost and misspent and how evilly I had walked in God's sight, which lay

so close unto my spirit that it was easy for me to see how righteous it was with God to cut the thread of my life and cast me out of His presence forever. Yet the Lord still showed mercy to me and upheld me, and as He wounded me with one hand, so He healed me with the other. . . .

Death of a Child

Nine days I sat upon my knees with my babe in my lap till my flesh was raw again; my child being even ready to depart this sorrowful world, they bade me carry it out to another wigwam (I suppose because they would not be troubled with such spectacles), whither I went with a heavy heart, and down I sat with the picture of death in my lap. About two hours in the night my sweet babe like a lamb departed this life on Feb. 18, 1675 [1676], it being about six years and five months old. It was nine days from the first wounding in this miserable condition without any refreshing of one nature or other except a little cold water. I cannot but take notice how at another time I could not bear to be in the room where any dead person was, but now the case is changed; I must and could lie down by my dead babe side by side all the night after. I have thought since of the wonderful goodness of God to me in preserving me in the use of my reason and senses in that distressed time that I did not use wicked and violent means to end my own miserable life.

In the morning when they understood that my child was dead, they sent for me home to my master's wigwam. (By my master in this writing must be understood Quanopin who was a sagamore and married [to] King Philip's wife's sister, not that he first took me, but I was sold to him by another Narragansett Indian who took me when first I came out of the garrison.) I went to take up my dead child in my arms to carry it with me, but they bid me let it alone. There was no resisting, but go I must and leave it. When I had been at my master's wigwam, I took the first opportunity I could get to go look after my dead child. When I came, I asked them what they had done with it. Then they told me it was upon the hill. Then they went and showed me where it was, where I saw the ground was newly digged, and there they told me they had buried it. There I left that child in the wilderness and must commit it and myself also in this wilderness condition to Him who is above all. . . .

The next day, *viz.* to this, the Indians returned from Medfield all the company, for those that belonged to the other small company came through the town that now we were at. But before they came to us, oh, the outrageous roaring and whooping that there was! They began their din about a mile before they came to us. By their noise and whooping they signified how many they had destroyed, which was at that time twenty-three. Those that were with us at home were gathered together as soon as they heard the whooping, and every time that the other went over their number, these at home gave [such] a shout that the very earth rung again. And thus they continued till those that had been upon the expedition were come up to the sagamore's wigwam. And then, oh, the hideous insulting and triumphing that there was over some Englishmen's scalps that they had taken (as their manner is) and brought with them! . . .

The Eighth Remove

On the morrow morning we must go over the river, i.e. Connecticot, to meet with King Philip. . . .

We traveled on till night, and in the morning we must go over the river to Philip's crew. When I was in the canoe, I could not but be amazed at the numerous crew of pagans that were on the bank on the other side. When I came ashore, they gathered all about me, I sitting alone in the midst. I observed they asked one another questions and laughed and rejoiced over their gains and victories. Then my heart began to fail and I fell a-weeping, which was the first time to my remembrance that I wept before them. Although I had met with so much affliction and my heart was many times ready to break, yet could I not shed one tear in their sight but rather had been all this while in a maze and like one astonished. But now I may say as Psal. 137:1, "By the rivers of Babylon there we sat down; yea, we wept when we remembered Zion." There one of them asked me why I wept; I could hardly tell what to say, yet I answered they would kill me. "No," said he, "none will hurt you." Then came one of them and gave me two spoonfuls of meal to comfort me, and another gave me half a pint of peas which was more worth than many bushels at another time. Then I went to see King Philip. He bade me come in and sit down and asked me whether I would smoke it (a usual compliment nowadays among saints and sinners), but this no way suited me. For though I had formerly used tobacco, yet I had left it ever since I was first taken. It seems to be a bait the devil lays to make men lose their precious time. I remember with shame how formerly when I had taken two or three pipes I was presently ready for another, such a bewitching thing it is. But I thank God He has now given me power over it; surely there are many who may be better employed than to lie sucking a stinking tobacco pipe.

Now the Indians gather their forces to go against Northampton. Overnight one went about yelling and hooting to give notice of the design, whereupon they fell to boiling of groundnuts and parching of corn (as many as had it) for their provision, and in the morning away they went. During my abode in this place

Philip spoke to me to make a shirt for his boy, which I did, for which he gave me a shilling. I offered the money to my master, but he bade me keep it, and with it I bought a piece of horseflesh. Afterwards he asked me to make a cap for his boy, for which he invited me to dinner. I went, and he gave me a pancake about as big as two fingers; it was made of parched wheat, beaten and fried in bear's grease, but I thought I never tasted pleasanter meat in my life. There was a squaw who spoke to me to make a shirt for her *sannup* [husband], for which she gave me a piece of bear. Another asked me to knit a pair of stockings, for which she gave me a quart of peas. I boiled my peas and bear together and invited my master and mistress to dinner, but the proud gossip [i.e., companion], because I served them both in one dish, would eat nothing except one bit that he gave her upon the point of his knife. . . .

My son being now about a mile from me, I asked liberty to go and see him; they bade me go, and away I went. But quickly [I] lost myself, traveling over hills and through swamps, and could not find the way to him. And I cannot but admire at the wonderful power and goodness of God to me in that though I was gone from home and met with all sorts of Indians, and those I had no knowledge of, and there being no Christian soul near me, yet not one of them offered the least imaginable miscarriage to me. . . .

The Treachery of Praying Indians

Then came Tom and Peter [Christian Indians] with the second letter from the [Massachusetts authorities] about the captives. Though they were Indians, I got them by the hand and burst out into tears; my heart was so full that I could not speak to them, but recovering myself, I asked them how my husband did and all my friends and acquaintances. They said they [were] all very well but melancholy. . . .

When the letter was come, the sagamores met to consult about the captives and called me to them to inquire how much my husband would give to redeem me. When I came, I sat down among them as I was wont to do as their manner is. Then they bade me stand up and said they were the General Court. They bid me speak what I thought he would give. Now knowing that all we had was destroyed by the Indians, I was in a great strait. I thought if I should speak of but a little, it would be slighted and hinder the matter; if of a great sum, I knew not where it would be procured. Yet at a venture, I said twenty pounds yet desired them to take less, but they would not hear of that but sent that message to Boston that for twenty pounds I should be redeemed. It was a praying Indian that wrote their letter for them. . . .

There was another praying Indian who, when he had done all the mischief that he could, betrayed his own father into the English hands thereby to purchase his own life. Another praying Indian was at Sudbury fight, though, as he deserved, he was afterward hanged for it. There was another praying Indian so wicked and cruel as to wear a string about his neck strung with Christians' fingers. Another praying Indian, when they went to Sudbury fight, went with them and his squaw also with him with her papoose at her back. . . .

On Tuesday morning they called their General Court (as they call it) to consult and determine whether I should go home or no. And they all as one man did seemingly consent to it that I should go home except Philip who would not come among them.

Observations

But before I go any further, I would take leave to mention a few remarkable passages of providence which I took special notice of in my afflicted time.

1. Of the fair opportunity lost in the long march a little after the fort fight when our English army was so numerous and in pursuit of the enemy and so near as to take several and destroy them, and the enemy in such distress for food that our men might track them by their rooting in the earth for groundnuts while they were flying for their lives. I say that then our army should want provision and be forced to leave their pursuit and return homeward. And the very next week the enemy came upon our town like bears bereft of their whelps or so many ravenous wolves, rending us and our lambs to death. But what shall I say? God seemed to leave His people to themselves and order all things for His own holy ends. . . .

3. Which also I have hinted before when the English army with new supplies were sent forth to pursue after the enemy, and they, understanding it, fled before them till they came to Baquaug River where they forthwith went over safely, that that river should be impassable to the English. I can but admire to see the wonderful providence of God in preserving the heathen for further affliction to our poor country. They could go in great numbers over, but the English must stop. God had an overruling hand in all those things.

4. It was thought if their corn were cut down they would starve and die with hunger, and all their corn that could be found was destroyed, and they driven from that little they had in store into the woods in the midst of winter. And yet how to admiration did the Lord preserve them for His holy ends and the destruction of many still amongst the English! Strangely did the Lord provide for them that I did not see (all the time I was among them) one man, woman, or child die with hunger. Though many times they would eat that that a hog or dog would

hardly touch, yet by that God strengthened them to be a scourge to His people.

The chief and commonest food was groundnuts. They eat also nuts and acorns, artichokes, lily roots, groundbeans, and several other weeds and roots that I know not.

They would pick up old bones and cut them to pieces at the joints, and if they were full of worms and maggots, they would scald them over the fire to make the vermin come out and then boil them and drink up the liquor and then beat the great ends of them in a mortar and so eat them. They would eat horses' guts and ears, and all sorts of wild birds which they could catch; also bear, venison, beaver, tortoise, frogs, squirrels, dogs, skunks, rattlesnakes, yea, the very bark of trees, besides all sorts of creatures and provision which they plundered from the English. I can but stand in admiration to see the wonderful power of God in providing for such a vast number of our enemies in the wilderness where there was nothing to be seen but from hand to mouth. . . .

5. Another thing that I would observe is the strange providence of God in turning things about when the Indians [were] at the highest and the English at the lowest. I was with the enemy eleven weeks and five days, and not one weeks passed without the fury of the enemy and some desolation by fire and sword upon one place or other. They mourned (with their black faces) for their own losses, yet triumphed and rejoiced in their inhuman and many times devilish cruelty to the English. They would boast much of their victories, saying that in two hours' time they had destroyed such a captain and his company at such a place, and such a captain and his company in such a place, and such a captain and his company in such a place, and boast how many towns they had destroyed; and then scoff and say they had done them a good turn to send them to heaven so soon. Again they would say this summer that they would knock all the rogues in the head, or drive them into the sea, or make them fly the country, thinking surely Agag-like, "The bitterness of death is past." Now the heathen begins to think all is their own, and the poor Christians' hopes to fail (as to man), and now their eyes are more to God, and their hearts sigh heavenward and to say in good earnest, "Help Lord, or we perish." When the Lord had brought His people to this that they saw no help in anything but Himself, then He takes the quarrel into His own hand, and though they [the Indians] had made a pit in their own imaginations as deep as hell for the Christians that summer, yet the Lord hurled themselves into it. And the Lord had not so many ways before to preserve them, but now He hath as many to destroy them.

Return Home

But to return again to my going home where we may see a remarkable change of providence. At first they were all against it except my husband would come for me, but afterwards they assented to it and seemed much to rejoice in it. Some asked me to send them some bread, others some tobacco, others shaking me by the hand, offering me a hood and scarf to ride in, not one moving hand or tongue against it. Thus hath the Lord answered my poor desire and the many earnest requests of others put up unto God for me. In my travels an Indian came to me and told me if I were willing, he and his squaw would run away and go home along with me. I told him no. I was not willing to run away but desired to wait God's time that I might go home quietly and without fear. And now God hath granted me my desire. O, the wonderful power of God that I have seen and the experience that I have had! I have been in the midst of those roaring lions and savage bears that feared neither God nor man nor the devil, by night and day, alone and in company, sleeping all sorts together, and yet not one of them ever offered me the least abuse of unchastity to me in word or action. Though some are ready to say I speak it for my own credit, I speak it in the presence of God and to His glory. God's power is as great now and as sufficient to save as when He preserved Daniel in the lion's den or the three children in the fiery furnace. I may well say as his Psal. 107:12, "Oh, give thanks unto the Lord for He is good, for His mercy endureth forever." Let the redeemed of the Lord say so whom He hath redeemed from the hand of the enemy, especially that I should come away in the midst of so many hundreds of enemies quietly and peaceably and not a dog moving his tongue.

For Further Reading

James Axtell, *The Invasion Within: The Conquest of Cultures in Colonial North America.* New York: Oxford University Press, 1985.

Charles M. Segal and David C. Stinebeck, *Puritans, Indians, and Manifest Destiny.* New York: G.P. Putnam's Sons, 1977.

George E. Tinker, *Missionary Conquest: The Gospel and Native American Cultural Genocide.* Minneapolis: Fortress Press, 1993.

Alden T. Vaughan, *The New England Frontier: Puritans and Indians, 1620–1675.* 3rd. ed. Norman: University of Oklahoma Press, 1995.

Alden T. Vaughan and Edward W. Clark, eds., *Puritans Among the Indians: Accounts of Captivity and Redemption, 1676–1724.* Cambridge, MA: The Belknap Press of Harvard University Press, 1981.

Ola Elizabeth Winslow, *John Eliot, Apostle to the Indians.* Boston: Houghton Mifflin, 1968.

Puritans and the Question of Religious Tolerance

VIEWPOINT 5A

The Antinomians Are Following the Spirit of God (1637)

Anne Hutchinson (1591–1643) et al.

The Puritans who settled New England were motivated by the desire to create a "pure" Christian church and society. The leaders of the Massachusetts Bay Colony built a form of government that, while not a theocracy (ministers did not hold public office), limited political power to recognized church members and made Puritan religious orthodoxy a matter for the state to enforce. Thus it is not surprising that the early disputes within the New England colonies revolved around religious issues. One important example of division within the New England Puritans was the Antinomian crisis of 1636–1638.

The central figure of the Antinomian crisis was Anne Hutchinson. Daughter of a dissenting English clergyman, wife of a relatively prosperous English merchant, and mother of fourteen children, she quickly gained standing as a religious lay leader in the Puritan community of Boston, Massachusetts, after moving there from England in 1634. The biweekly meetings held at her home to discuss the sermons of John Cotton, the minister of her church, drew as many as sixty people. The leaders of the Massachusetts Bay Colony were disturbed by reports of what was said at those meetings. They were especially unsettled by suggestions that only Cotton and John Wheelwright (a minister and Hutchinson's brother-in-law) adhered to the "covenant of grace" (the orthodox Puritan idea that God's grace was a free gift that could only be received by those whom God chose), while other ministers were in error by preaching a "covenant of works" (the idea that God's grace could be attained by good deeds and behavior). The community became divided between factions of Hutchinson's supporters and opponents.

A gathering of ministers questioned and examined Cotton, who was able to moderate his views enough to be cleared of heresy. Hutchinson and Wheelwright were not as accommodating, and both were found guilty of sedition and heresy and were banished from the colony. Testimony from Hutchinson's trial before the General Court of Massachusetts held in November 1637, is reprinted here; in the absence of written tracts or other materials by Hutchinson, it provides

From the court records of the examination of Anne Hutchinson at the court of Newtown, Mass., November 1637.

one of the few records of her words.

At first Hutchinson was largely able to parry the questions about her views and to confound her questioners, who included Governor John Winthrop and Deputy Governor Thomas Dudley, when they attempted to pin down her heretical ideas. During the second day of her trial—whether from fatigue from the constant questioning or some other cause is not clear—she launched into a long explanation of why she came to New England, claiming that she received direct revelation from the Holy Spirit. For her questioners this was enough evidence to find her guilty of heresy and to banish her from the colony. Hutchinson moved to Rhode Island, a colony founded by another banished religious leader, Roger Williams. She later moved to what is now Long Island, New York, where she and her family were killed by Indians in 1643.

What seem to be the main complaints of John Winthrop and the other leaders? What defense does Anne Hutchinson offer? Judging from this viewpoint, are there any indications that Anne Hutchinson's gender played a part in her trial? Explain your answer.

The Examination of Mrs. Ann Hutchinson at the court at Newtown.

Mr. Winthrop, governor. Mrs. Hutchinson, you are called here as one of those that have troubled the peace of the commonwealth and the churches here; you are known to be a woman that hath had a great share in the promoting and divulging of those opinions that are causes of this trouble, and to be nearly joined not only in affinity and affection with some of those the court had taken notice of and passed censure upon, but you have spoken divers things as we have been informed very prejudicial to the honour of the churches and ministers thereof, and you have maintained a meeting and an assembly in your house that hath been condemned by the general assembly as a thing not tolerable nor comely in the sight of God nor fitting for your sex, and notwithstanding that was cried down you have continued the same, therefore we have thought good to send for you to understand how things are, that if you be in an erroneous way we may reduce [reform] you that so you may become a profitable member here among us, otherwise if you be obstinate in your course that then the court may take such course that you may trouble us no further, therefore I would intreat you to express whether you do not hold and assent in practice to those opinions and factions that have been handled in court already, that is to say, whether you do not justify Mr. Wheelwright's sermon and the petition.

Mrs. Hutchinson. I am called here to answer before you but I hear no things laid to my charge.

Gov. I have told you some already and more I can tell you. (*Mrs. H.*) Name one Sir.

Gov. Have I not named some already?

Mrs. H. What have I said or done?

Gov. Why for your doings, this you did harbour and countenance those that are parties in this faction that you have heard of. (*Mrs H.*) That's matter of conscience, Sir.

Gov. Your conscience you must keep or it must be kept for you.

Mrs. H. Must not I then entertain the saints because I must keep my conscience.

Gov. Say that one brother should commit felony or treason and come to his other brother's house, if he knows him guilty and conceals him he is guilty of the same. It is his conscience to entertain him, but if his conscience comes into act in giving countenance and entertainment to him that hath broken the law he is guilty too. So if you do countenance those that are transgressors of the law you are in the same fact.

Mrs. H. What law do they transgress?

Gov. The law of God and of the state.

Mrs. H. In what particular?

Gov. Why in this among the rest, whereas the Lord doth say honour thy father and thy mother.

Mrs. H. Ey Sir in the Lord. (*Gov.*) This honour you have broke in giving countenance to them.

Mrs. H. In entertaining those did I entertain them against any act (for there is the thing) or what God hath appointed?

Gov. You knew that Mr. Wheelwright did preach this sermon and those that countenance him in this do break a law.

Mrs. H. What law have I broken?

Gov. Why the fifth commandment.

Mrs. H. I deny that for he saith in the Lord.

Gov. You have joined with them in the faction.

Mrs. H. In what faction have I joined with them?

Gov. In presenting the petition.

Mrs. H. Suppose I had set my hand to the petition what then? (*Gov.*) You saw that case tried before.

Mrs. H. But I had not my hand to the petition.

Gov. You have councelled them. (*Mrs. H.*) Wherein?

Gov. Why in entertaining them.

Mrs. H. What breach of law is that Sir?

Gov. Why dishonouring of parents.

Mrs. H. But put the case Sir that I do fear the Lord and my parents, may not I entertain them that fear the Lord because my parents will not give me leave?

Gov. If they be the fathers of the commonwealth, and they of another religion, if you entertain them then you dishonour your parents and are justly punishable.

Mrs. H. If I entertain them, as they have dishonoured their parents I do.

Gov. No but you by countenancing them above others put honor upon them.

Mrs. H. I may put honor upon them as the children of God and as they do honor the Lord.

Gov. We do not mean to discourse with those of your sex but only this; you do adhere unto them and do endeavour to set forward this faction and so you do dishonour us.

Mrs. H. I do acknowledge no such thing neither do I think that I ever put any dishonour upon you.

Gov. Why do you keep such a meeting at your house as you do every week upon a set day?

Mrs. H. It is lawful for me so to do, as it is all your practices and can you find a warrant for yourself and condemn me for the same thing? The ground of my taking it up was, when I first came to this land because I did not go to such meetings as those were, it was presently reported that I did not allow of such meetings but held them unlawful and therefore in that regard they said I was proud and did despise all ordinances, upon that a friend came unto me and told me of it and I to prevent such aspersions took it up, but it was in practice before I came therefore I was not the first.

Gov. For this, that you appeal to our practice you need no confutation. If your meeting had answered to the former it had not been offensive, but I will say that there was no meeting of women alone, but your meeting is of another sort for there are sometimes men among you.

Mrs. H. There was never any man with us.

Gov. Well, admit there was no man at your meeting and that you was sorry for it, there is no warrant for your doings, and by what warrant do you continue such a course?

Biblical Justification

Mrs. H. I conceive there Lyes a clear rule in Titus, that the elder women should instruct the younger and then I must have a time wherein I must do it.

Gov. All this I grant you, I grant you a time for it, but what is this to the purpose that you Mrs. Hutchinson must call a company together from their callings to come to be taught of you?

Mrs. H. Will it please you to answer me this and to give me a rule for then I will willingly submit to any truth. If any come to my house to be instructed in the ways of God what rule have I to put them away?

Gov. But suppose that a hundred men come unto you to be instructed will you forbear to instruct them?

Mrs. H. As far as I conceive I cross a rule in it.

Gov. Very well and do you not so here?

Mrs. H. No Sir for my ground is they are men.

Gov. Men and women all is one for that, but sup-

pose that a man should come and say Mrs. Hutchinson I hear that you are a woman that God hath given his grace unto and you have knowledge in the word of God I pray instruct me a little, ought you not to instruct this man?

Mrs. H. I think I may.—Do you think it not lawful for me to teach women and why do you call me to teach the court?

————— • —————

"Now if you do condemn me for speaking what in my conscience I know to be truth I must commit myself unto the Lord."

————— • —————

Gov. We do not call you to teach the court but to lay open yourself.

Mrs. H. I desire you that you would then set me down a rule by which I may put them away that come unto me and so have peace in so doing.

Gov. You must shew your rule to receive them.

Mrs. H. I have done it.

Gov. I deny it because I have brought more arguments than you have.

Mrs. H. I say, to me it is a rule.

[John] Endicot. You say there are some rules unto you. I think there is a contradiction in your own words. What rule for your practice do you bring, only a custom in Boston.

Mrs. H. No Sir that was no rule to me but if you look upon the rule in Titus it is a rule to me. If you convince me that it is no rule I shall yield.

Gov. You know that there is no rule that crosses another, but this rule crosses that in the Corinthians. But you must take it in this sense that elder women must instruct the younger about their business, and to love their husbands and not to make them to clash.

Mrs. H. I do not conceive but that it is meant for some publick times.

Gov. Well, have you no more to say but this?

Mrs. H. I have said sufficient for my practice.

Gov. Your course is not to be suffered for, besides that we find such a course as this to be greatly prejudicial to the state, besides the occasion that it is to seduce many honest persons that are called to those meetings and your opinions being known to be different from the word of God may seduce many simple souls that resort unto you, besides that the occasion which hath come of late hath come from none but such as have frequented your meetings, so that now they are flown off from [no longer respect] magistrates and ministers and this since they have come to you, and besides that it will not well stand with the commonwealth that families should be neglected for so many neighbours and dames and so much time spent, we see no rule of God for this, we see not that any should have authority to set up any other exercises besides what authority hath already set up and so what hurt comes of this you will be guilty of and we for suffering you.

Mrs. H. Sir I do not believe that to be so.

Gov. Well, we see how it is we must therefore put it away from you, or restrain you from maintaining this course.

Mrs. H. If you have a rule for it from God's word you may.

Gov. We are your judges, and not you ours and we must compel you to it.

Mrs. H. If it please you by authority to put it down I will freely let you for I am subject to your authority.

[Simon] Bradstreet. I would ask this question of Mrs. Hutchinson, whether you do think this is lawful? for then this will follow that all other women that do not are in a sin.

Mrs. H. I conceive this is a free will offering.

Bradst. If it be a free will offering you ought to forbear it because it gives offence.

Mrs. H. Sir, in regard of myself I could, but for others I do not yet see light but shall further consider of it.

Bradst. I am not against all women's meetings but do think them to be lawful.

The Meetings

[Thomas] Dudley, dep. gov. Here hath been much spoken concerning Mrs. Hutchinson's meetings and among other answers she saith that men come not there, I would ask you this one question then, whether never any man was at your meeting?

Gov. There are two meetings kept at their house.

Dep. Gov. How; is there two meetings?

Mrs. H. Ey Sir, I shall not equivocate, there is a meeting of men and women and there is a meeting only for women.

Dep. Gov. Are they both constant?

Mrs. H. No, but upon occasions they are deferred.

Mr. Endicot. Who teaches in the men's meetings none but men, do not women sometimes?

Mrs. H. Never as I heard, not one.

Dep. Gov. I would go a little higher with Mrs. Hutchinson. About three years ago we were all in peace. Mrs. Hutchinson from that time she came hath made a disturbance, and some that came over with her in the ship did inform me what she was as soon as she was landed. I being then in place dealt with the pastor and teacher of Boston and desired them to enquire of her, and then I was satisfied that she held nothing different from us, but within half a year after, she had vented divers of her strange opin-

ions and had made parties [factions] in the country, and at length it comes that Mr. Cotton and Mr. [Henry] Vane were of her judgment, but Mr. Cotton hath cleared himself that he was not of that mind, but now it appears by this woman's meeting that Mrs. Hutchinson hath so forestalled the minds of many by their resort to her meeting that now she hath a potent party in the country. Now if all these things have endangered us as from that foundation and if she in particular hath disparaged all our ministers in the land that they have preached a covenant of works, and only Mr. Cotton a covenant of grace, why this is not to be suffered, and therefore being driven to the foundation and it being found that Mrs. Hutchinson is she that hath depraved all the ministers and hath been the cause of what is fallen out, why we must take away the foundation and the building will fall.

Mrs. H. I pray Sir prove it that I said they preached nothing but a covenant of works.

Dep. Gov. Nothing but a covenant of works, why a Jesuit may preach truth sometimes.

Mrs. H. Did I ever say they preached a covenant of works then?

Dep. Gov. If they do not preach a covenant of grace clearly, then they preach a covenant of works.

Mrs. H. No Sir, one may preach a covenant of grace more clearly than another, so I said.

Dep. Gov. We are not upon that now but upon position.

Mrs. H. Prove this then Sir that you say I said.

Accusations and Denials

Dep. Gov. When they do preach a covenant of works do they preach truth?

Mrs. H. Yes Sir, but when they preach a covenant of works for salvation, that is not truth.

Dep. Gov. I do but ask you this, when the ministers do preach a covenant of works do they preach a way of salvation?

Mrs. H. I did not come hither to answer to questions of that sort.

Dep. Gov. Because you will deny the thing.

Mrs. H. Ey, but that is to be proved first.

Dep. Gov. I will make it plain that you did say that the ministers did preach a covenant of works.

Mrs. H. I deny that.

Dep. Gov. And that you said they were not able ministers of the new testament, but Mr. Cotton only.

Mrs. H. If ever I spake that I proved it by God's word.

Court. Very well, very well.

Mrs. H. If one shall come unto me in private, and desire me seriously to tell them what I thought of such an one. I must either speak false or true in my answer.

Dep. Gov. Likewise I will prove this that you said the gospel in the letter and words holds forth nothing but a covenant of works and that all that do not hold as you do are in a covenant of works.

Mrs. H. I deny this for if I should so say I should speak against my own judgment.

Mr. Endicot. I desire to speak seeing Mrs. Hutchinson seems to lay something against them that are to witness against her.

Gov. Only I would add this. It is well discerned to the court that Mrs. Hutchinson can tell when to speak and when to hold her tongue. Upon the answering of a question which we desire her to tell her thoughts of she desires to be pardoned.

Mrs. H. It is one thing for me to come before a public magistracy and there to speak what they would have me to speak and another when a man comes to me in a way of friendship privately there is difference in that. . . .

Gov. Here are six undeniable ministers who say it is true and yet you deny that you did say that they did preach a covenant of works and that they were not able ministers of the gospel, and it appears plainly that you have spoken it, and whereas you say that it was drawn from you in a way of friendship, you did profess then that it was out of conscience that you spake and said The fear of man is a snare wherefore should I be afraid, I will speak plainly and freely.

Mrs. H. That I absolutely deny, for the first question was thus answered by me to them. They thought that I did conceive there was a difference between them and Mr. Cotton. At the first I was somewhat reserved, then said Mr. Peters I pray answer the question directly as fully and as plainly as you desire we should tell you our minds. Mrs. Hutchinson we come for plain dealing and telling you our hearts. Then I said I would deal as plainly as I could, and whereas they say I said they were under a covenant of works and in the state of the apostles why these two speeches cross one another. I might say they might preach a covenant of works as did the apostles, but to preach a covenant of works and to be under a covenant of works is another business.

Dep. Gov. There have been six witnesses to prove this and yet you deny it.

Mrs. H. I deny that these were the first words that were spoken.

Gov. You make the case worse, for you clearly shew that the ground of your opening your mind was not to satisfy them but to satisfy your own conscience. . . .

Mrs. H. I acknowledge using the words of the apostle to the Corinthians unto him, that they that were ministers of the letter and not the spirit did preach a covenant of works. Upon his saying there was no such scripture, then I fetched the Bible and

shewed him this place 2 Cor. iii. 6. He said that was the letter of the law. No said I it is the letter of the gospel.

Gov. You have spoken this more than once then.

Mrs. H. Then upon further discourse about proving a good estate and holding it out by the manifestation of the spirit he did acknowledge that to be the nearest way, but yet said he, will you not acknowledge that which we hold forth to be a way too wherein we may have hope; no truly if that be a way it is a way to hell.

Gov. Mrs. Hutchinson, the court you see hath laboured to bring you to acknowledge the error of your way that so you might be reduced, the time now grows late, we shall therefore give you a little more time to consider of it and therefore desire that you attend the court again in the morning.

The Next Morning

Gov. We proceeded the last night as far as we could in hearing of this cause of Mrs. Hutchinson. There were divers things laid to her charge, her ordinary meetings about religious exercises, her speeches in derogation of the ministers among us, and the weakning of the hands and hearts of the people towards them. Here was sufficient proof made of that which she was accused of in that point concerning the ministers and their ministry, as that they did preach a covenant of works when others did preach a covenant of grace, and that they were not able ministers of the new testament, and that they had not the seal of the spirit, and this was spoken not as was pretended out of private conference, but out of conscience and warrant from scripture alledged the fear of man is a snare and seeing God had given her a calling to it she would freely speak. Some other speeches she used, as that the letter of the scripture held forth a covenant of works, and this is offered to be proved by probable grounds. If there be anything else that the court hath to say they may speak. . . .

The Spirit of God

Mrs. H. If you please to give me leave I shall give you the ground of what I know to be true. Being much troubled to see the falseness of the constitution of the church of England, I had like to have turned separatist; whereupon I kept a day of solemn humiliation and pondering of the thing; this scripture was brought unto me—he that denies Jesus Christ to be come in the flesh is antichrist—This I considered of and in considering found that the papists did not deny him to be come in the flesh, nor we did not deny him—who then was antichrist? Was the Turk antichrist only? The Lord knows that I could not open scripture; he must by his prophetical office open it unto me. So after that being unsatisfied in the thing, the Lord was pleased to bring this scripture out of the Hebrews. He that denies the testament denies the testator, and in this did open unto me and give me to see that those which did not teach the new covenant had the spirit of antichrist, and upon this he did discover the ministry unto me and ever since. I bless the Lord, he hath let me see which was the clear ministry and which the wrong. Since that time I confess I have been more choice and he hath let me to distinguish between the voice of my beloved and the voice of Moses, the voice of John Baptist and the voice of antichrist, for all those voices are spoken of in scripture. Now if you do condemn me for speaking what in my conscience I know to be truth I must commit myself unto the Lord.

Mr. Nowell. How do you know that that was the spirit?

Mrs. H. How did Abraham know that it was God that bid him offer his son, being a breach of the sixth commandment?

Dep. Gov. By an immediate voice.

Mrs. H. So to me by an immediate revelation.

Dep. Gov. How! an immediate revelation.

Mrs. H. By the voice of his own spirit to my soul. I will give you another scripture, Jer. 46: 27, 28—out of which the Lord shewed me what he would do for me and the rest of his servants—But after he was pleased to reveal himself to me I did presently like Abraham run to Hagar. And after that he did let me see the atheism of my own heart, for which I begged of the Lord that it might not remain in my heart, and being thus, he did shew me this (a twelvemonth after) which I told you of before. Ever since that time I have been confident of what he hath revealed unto me.

[*Text obliterated*] another place out of Daniel chap. 7. and he and for us all, wherein he shewed me the sitting of the judgment and the standing of all high and low before the Lord and how thrones and kingdoms were cast down before him. When our teacher came to New-England it was a great trouble unto me, my brother Wheelwright being put by also. I was then much troubled concerning the ministry under which I lived, and then that place in the 30th of Isaiah was brought to my mind. Though the Lord give thee bread of adversity and water of affliction yet shall not thy teachers be removed into corners any more, but thine eyes shall see thy teachers. The Lord giving me this promise and they being gone there was none then left that I was able to hear, and I could not be at rest but I must come hither. Yet that place of Isaiah did much follow me, though the Lord give thee the bread of adversity and water of affliction. This place lying I say upon me then this place in Daniel was brought unto me and did shew me that though I should meet with affliction yet I am the

same God that delivered Daniel out of the lion's den, I will also deliver thee.—Therefore I desire you to look to it, for you see this scripture fulfilled this day and therefore I desire you that as you tender the Lord and the church and commonwealth to consider and look what you do. You have power over my body but the Lord Jesus hath power over my body and soul, and assure yourselves thus much, you do as much as in you lies to put the Lord Jesus Christ from you, and if you go on in this course you begin you will bring a curse upon you and your posterity, and the mouth of the Lord hath spoken it. . . .

The Verdict

Gov. The court hath already declared themselves satisfied concerning the things you hear, and concerning the troublesomeness of her spirit and the danger of her course amongst us, which is not to be suffered. Therefore if it be the mind of the court that Mrs. Hutchinson for these things that appear before us is unfit for our society, and if it be the mind of the court that she shall be banished out of our liberties and imprisoned till she be sent away, let them hold up their hands.

All but three. . . .

Mrs. Hutchinson, the sentence of the court you hear is that you are banished from out of our jurisdiction as being a woman not fit for our society, and are to be imprisoned till the court shall send you away.

Mrs. H. I desire to know wherefore I am banished?

Gov. Say no more, the court knows wherefore and is satisfied.

VIEWPOINT 5B

The Antinomians Were Heretics Destroying the Community (1644)

Thomas Welde (1595–1661)

From 1636 to 1638 the Puritan community in New England was sharply divided in what became known as the Antinomian crisis. This controversy pitted the political and religious authorities of the Massachusetts Bay Colony against those (called Antinomians) who questioned their religious fitness to lead. One of the central figures of the Antinomian crisis was Anne Hutchinson, the wife of an English merchant, who had migrated with her family to Massachusetts in

From Thomas Welde's preface to John Winthrop's *A Short Story of the Rise, Reign, and Ruine of the Antinomians, Familists, and Libertines*, 1644, as reprinted in *Antinomianism in the Colony of Massachusetts Bay, 1636–1638*, edited by Charles F. Adams (Boston, 1894).

1634. She made it a practice following Sunday services to hold meetings at which the Scriptures and the sermons of leading Puritan minister John Cotton were discussed, and at which other ministers were criticized. As these meetings grew in popularity, the discussions led to divisions within the Puritan community over who was truly part of God's elect. Opposition to Hutchinson undoubtedly stemmed in part from the fact that she was a woman making judgments and statements in areas traditionally the realm of the all-male clergy. Hutchinson and her brother-in-law John Wheelwright were ultimately excommunicated from their church and forced to leave the colony because of their beliefs.

The following summary of events surrounding Anne Hutchinson's banishment was written by Thomas Welde, a minister who had taken an active role in the campaign against Hutchinson. Welde had returned to England in 1641 to represent the colony in its dealings with the English government. In 1644 he wrote a preface to a work by Massachusetts Bay Colony governor John Winthrop directed primarily at English readers, giving the authorities' view of the Antinomian crisis. This viewpoint is excerpted from Welde's preface.

What were the harms caused by the activities of Anne Hutchinson and other Antinomians, according to Welde? How did the church and civil authorities respond to the Antinomians, as recounted by the author? What signs from God does he describe as discrediting Hutchinson?

———————

After we had escaped the cruel hands of persecuting prelates, and the dangers at sea, and had prettily well outgrown our wilderness troubles in our first plantings in New England; and when our commonwealth began to be founded, and our churches sweetly settled in peace (God abounding to us in more happy enjoyments than we could have expected), lest we should now grow secure, our wise God (who seldom suffers His own in this their wearisome pilgrimage to be long without trouble) sent a new storm after us, which proved the sorest trial that ever befell us since we left our native soil.

Which was this, that some going thither from hence, full fraught with many unsound and loose opinions, after a time began to open their packs and freely vend their wares to any that would be their customers. Multitudes of men and women, church members and others, having tasted of their commodities were eager after them and were straight infected before they were aware, and some being tainted conveyed the infection to others and thus that plague first began amongst us. . . .

But the last and worst of all, which most suddenly diffused the venom of these opinions into the very veins and vitals of the people in the country, was Mistress Hutchinson's double weekly lecture, which she kept under a pretense of repeating sermons, to which resorted sundry of Boston and other towns about, to the number of fifty, sixty, or eighty at once. Where, after she had repeated the sermon, she would make her comment upon it, vent her mischievous opinions as she pleased, and wreathed the scriptures to her own purpose; where the custom was for her scholars to propound questions and she (gravely sitting in the chair) did make answers thereunto. The great respect she had at first in the hearts of all, and her profitable and sober carriage of matters, for a time made this her practice less suspected by the godly magistrates and elders of the church there, so that it was winked at for a time (though afterward reproved by the Assembly and called into Court), but it held so long, until she had spread her leaven so far that had not providence prevented, it had proved the canker of our peace and ruin of our comforts.

———————•———————

"Oh their boldness, pride, insolency, alienations from their old and dearest friends, the disturbances, divisions, contentions they raised amongst us, both in church and state and in families, setting division betwixt husband and wife!"

———————•———————

By all these means and cunning slights they used, it came about that those errors were so soon conveyed before we were aware, not only into the church of Boston, where most of these seducers lived, but also into all the parts of the country round about.

These opinions being thus spread and grown to their full ripeness and latitude through the nimbleness and activity of their fomenters, began now to lift up their heads full high, to stare us in the face and to confront all that opposed them.

And that which added vigor and boldness to them was this, that now by this time they had some of all sorts and quality in all places to defend and patronize them: some of the magistrates, some gentlemen, some scholars and men of learning, some burgesses of our General Court [legislature] , some of our captains and soldiers, some chief men in towns, and some men eminent for religion, parts, and wit. So that wheresoever the case of the opinions came in agitation, there wanted not patrons to stand up to plead for them; and if any of the opinionists were complained of in the courts for their misdemeanors, or brought before the churches for conviction or censure, still some or other of that party would not only suspend giving their vote against them, but would labor to justify them, side with them, and protest against any sentence that should pass upon them, and so be ready not only to harden the delinquent against all means of conviction, but to raise a mutiny if the major part should carry it against them. So in town meetings, military trainings, and all other societies, yea almost in every family, it was hard if that some or other were not ready to rise up in defense of them, even as of the apple of their own eye.

Now, oh their boldness, pride, insolency, alienations from their old and dearest friends, the disturbances, divisions, contentions they raised amongst us, both in church and state and in families, setting division betwixt husband and wife! Oh the sore censures against all sorts that opposed them, and the contempt they cast upon our godly magistrates, churches, ministers, and all that were set over them when they stood in their way!

Criticizing Ministers

Now the faithful ministers of Christ must have dung cast on their faces, and be no better than legal preachers, Baal's priests, Popish factors, scribes, Pharisees, and opposers of Christ himself. Now they must be pointed at, as it were with the finger, and reproached by name—such a church officer is an ignorant man and knows not Christ; such an one is under a covenant of works; such a pastor is a proud man and would make a good persecutor; such a teacher is grossly Popish—so that through these reproaches occasion was given to men to abhor the offerings of the Lord.

Now, one of them in a solemn convention of ministers dared to say to their faces that they did not preach the covenant of free grace and that they themselves had not the seal of the spirit, etc. Now, after our sermons were ended at our public lectures, you might have seen half a dozen pistols discharged at the face of the preacher, I mean so many objections made by the opinionists in the open assembly against our doctrine delivered, if it suited not their new fancies, to the marvelous weakening of holy truths delivered (what in them lay) in the hearts of all the weaker sort; and this done not once and away but from day to day after our sermons. Yea, they would come when they heard a minister was upon such a point as was like to strike at their opinions, with a purpose to oppose him to his face.

Now, you might have seen many of the opinionists rising up and contemptuously turning their backs upon the faithful pastor of that church and going forth from the assembly when he began to pray or preach. . . .

Now, might you have seen open contempt cast upon the face of the whole General Court in subtle words to this very effect: that the magistrates were Ahabs, Amaziahs, scribes, and Pharisees, enemies to Christ, led by Satan, that old enemy of free grace, and that it were better that a millstone were hung about their necks, and they were drowned in the sea, than they should censure one of their judgment, which they were now about to do.

Another of them you might have seen so audaciously insolent, and high flown in spirit and speech, that she bade the Court of Magistrates (when they were about to censure her for her pernicious carriages) take heed what they did to her, for she knew by an infallible revelation that for this act which they were about to pass against her, God would ruin them, their posterity, and that whole commonwealth.

By a little taste of a few passages instead of multitudes here presented, you may see what an height they were grown unto in a short time, and what a spirit of pride, insolency, contempt of authority, division, sedition they were acted by. It was a wonder of mercy that they had not set our commonwealth and churches on a fire, and consumed us all therein.

They being mounted to this height and carried with such a strong hand (as you have heard) and seeing a spirit of pride, subtlety, malice, and contempt of all men that were not of their minds breathing in them (our hearts sadded and our spirits tired), we sighed and groaned to Heaven, we humbled our souls by prayer and fasting that the Lord would find out and bless some means and ways for the cure of this sore and deliver his truth and ourselves from this heavy bondage. Which (when His own time was come) He hearkened unto and in infinite mercy looked upon our sorrows and did, in a wonderful manner, beyond all expectation, free us by these means following.

1. He stirred up all the ministers' spirits in the country to preach against those errors and practices that so much pestered the country to inform, to confute, to rebuke, etc., thereby to cure those that were diseased already and to give antidotes to the rest to preserve them from infection. And though this ordinance went not without its appointed effect in the latter respect, yet we found it not so effectual for the driving away of this infection as we desired for they (most of them) hardened their faces and bent their wits how to oppose and confirm themselves in their way.

2. We spent much time and strength in conference with them, sometimes in private before the elders only, sometimes in our public congregation for all comers. Many, very many hours and half days together we spent therein to see if any means might prevail. We gave them free leave, with all lenity and

patience, to lay down what they could say for their opinions, and answered them, from point to point, and then brought clear arguments from evident scriptures against them and put them to answer us even until they were oftentimes brought to be either silent, or driven to deny common principles, or shuffle off plain scripture. And yet such was their pride and hardness of heart that they would not yield to the truth, but did tell us they would take time to consider our arguments, and in mean space meeting with some of their abetters, strengthened themselves again in their old way, that when we dealt with them next time we found them further off than before, so that our hopes began to languish of reducing them by private means.

3. Then we had an assembly of all the ministers and learned men in the whole country which held for three weeks together at Cambridge (then called New Town), Mr. Hooker and Mr. Bulkeley (alias Buckley) being chosen moderators, or prolocutors, the magistrates sitting present all that time, as hearers and speakers also when they saw fit. A liberty was also given to any of the country to come in and hear (it being appointed, in great part for the satisfaction of the people), and a place was appointed for all the opinionists to come in and take liberty of speech (only due order observed) as much as any of ourselves had, and as freely.

The first week we spent in confuting the loose opinions that we gathered up in the country. . . . The other fortnight we spent in a plain syllogistical dispute (*ad vulgus* [for the common public] as much as might be), gathering up nine of the chiefest points (on which the rest depended), and disputed of them all in order, pro and con. In the forenoons we framed our arguments and in the afternoons produced them in public, and the next day the adversary gave in their answers and produced also their arguments on the same questions; then we answered them and replied also upon them the next day. . . .

4. Then after this mean was tried, the magistrates saw that neither our preaching, conference, nor yet our assembly meeting did effect the cure, but that still after conference had together the leaders put such life into the rest that they all went on in their former course, not only to disturb the churches but miserably interrupt the civil peace, and that they threw contempt both upon courts and churches, and began now to raise sedition amongst us to the endangering [of] the commonwealth. Hereupon, for these grounds named (and not for their opinions, as themselves falsely reported, and as our godly magistrates have been much traduced here in England), for these reasons (I say) being civil disturbances, the magistrate convents [assembles] them . . . and censures them. Some were disfranchised, others fined,

the incurable amongst them banished.

This was another mean of their subduing, some of the leaders being down and others gone, the rest were weakened, but yet they (for all this) strongly held up their heads many a day after.

God's Displeasure

5. Then God Himself was pleased to step in with His casting voice and bring in His own vote and suffrage from Heaven, by testifying His displeasure against their opinions and practices, as clearly as if He had pointed with His finger, in causing the two fomenting women in the time of the height of the opinions to produce out of their wombs, as before they had out of their brains, such monstrous births as no chronicle (I think) hardly ever recorded the like. Mistress Dyer brought forth her birth of a woman child, a fish, a beast, and a fowl, all woven together in one, and without an head. . . . Mistress Hutchinson being big with child, and growing towards the time of her labor as other women do, she brought forth not one (as Mistress Dyer did) but (which was more strange to amazement) thirty monstrous births or thereabouts at once, some of them bigger, some lesser, some of one shape, some of another, few of any perfect shape, none at all of them (as far as I could ever learn) of human shape. . . .

Now I am upon Mistress Hutchinson's story, I will digress a little to give you a further taste of her spirit. . . . The Church of Boston sent unto her four of their members, (men of a lovely and winning spirit, as most likely to prevail) to see if they could convince and reduce her, according to 2 Thes. 3. 13. When they came first unto her, she asked from whom they came, and what was their business; They answered, We are come in the name of the Lord Jesus, from the Church of Christ at Boston, to labour to convince you of &c.—At that word she (being filled with as much disdain in her countenance, as bitterness in her spirit) replied, what, from the Church at Boston? I know no such Church, neither will I own it, call it the Whore and Strumpet of Boston, no Church of Christ; so they said no more, seeing her so desperate, but returned. Behold the spirit of error, to what a pass it drives a man!

Providence from Heaven

This loud-speaking providence from Heaven in the monsters, did much awaken many of her followers (especially the tenderer sort) to attend God's meaning therein; and made them at such a stand, that they dared not sleight so manifest a sign from Heaven, that from that time we found many of their ears boared (as they had good cause) to attend to counsel, but others yet followed them.

6. The last stroke that slew the opinions, was the

falling away of their leaders.

1. Into more hideous and soul-destroying delusions, which ruin (indeed) all Religion; as, that the souls of men are mortal like the beasts.

That there is no such thing as inherent righteousness.

That these bodies of ours shall not rise again.

That their own revelations of particular events were as infallible as the Scripture, &c.

2. They also grew (many of them) very loose and degenerate in their practices (for these opinions will certainly produce a filthy life by degrees). As no prayer in their families, no Sabbath, insufferable pride, frequent and hideous lying; divers of them being proved guilty, some of five, other of ten gross lies; another falling into a lie, God smote him in the very act, that he sunk down into a deepe swoon, and being by hot waters recovered, and coming to himself, said, Oh God, thou mightst have struck me dead, as Ananias and Saphira, for I have maintained a lie. Mistress Hutchinson and others cast out of the Church for lying, and some guilty of fouler sins than all these, which I here name not.

These things exceedingly amazed their followers, (especially such as were led after them in the simplicity of their hearts, as many were) and now they began to see that they were deluded by them. . . .

Now they would freely discover the sleights the Adversaries had used to undermine them by, and steal away their eyes from the truth and their brethren, which before (whiles their hearts were sealed) they could not see. And the fruit of this was, great praise to the Lord, who had thus wonderfully wrought matters about; gladness in all our hearts and faces, and expressions of our renewed affections by receiving them again into our bosoms, and from that time until now have walked (according to their renewed Covenants) humbly and lovingly amongst us, holding forth Truth and Peace with power.

But for the rest, which (notwithstanding all these means of conviction from heaven and earth, and the example of their seduced brethrens return) yet stood obdurate, yea more hardened (as we had cause to fear) than before; we convented those of them that were members before the Churches, and yet, labored once and again to convince them, not only of their errors, but also of sundry exorbitant practices which they had fallen into; as manifest Pride, contempt of authority, neglecting to fear the Church, and lying, &c. but after no means prevailed, we were driven with sad hearts to give them up to Satan: Yet not simply for their opinions (for which I find we have been slanderously traduced) but the chiefest cause of their censure was their miscarriages (as have been said) persisted in with great obstinacy.

The persons cast out of the churches were about nine or ten, as far as I can remember, who for a space continued very hard and impenitent, but afterward some of them were received into fellowship again, upon their repentance.

These persons cast out, and the rest of the ringleaders that had received sentence of banishment, with many others infected by them, that were neither censured in court nor in churches, went all together out of our jurisdiction and precinct into an island, called Rhode Island (surnamed by some the island of errors), and there they live to this day, most of them, but in great strife and contention in the civil estate and otherwise, hatching and multiplying new opinions, and cannot agree, but are miserably divided into sundry sects and factions.

The Fate of Anne Hutchinson

But Mistress Hutchinson being weary of the island, or rather the island weary of her, departed from thence with all her family, her daughter and her children, to live under the Dutch, near a place called by seamen, and in the map, Hellgate. (And now I am come to the last act of her tragedy, a most heavy stroke upon herself and hers, as I received it very lately from a godly hand in New England.) There the Indians set upon them and slew her and all her family, her daughter, and her daughter's husband, and all their children, save one that escaped (her own husband being dead before), a dreadful blow. Some write that the Indians did burn her to death with fire, her house and all the rest named that belonged to her; but I am not able to affirm by what kind of death they slew her, but slain it seems she is, according to all reports. I never heard that the Indians in those parts did ever before this commit the like outrage upon any one family, or families, and therefore God's hand is the more apparently seen herein, to pick out this woeful woman, to make her and those belonging to her an unheard of heavy example of their cruelty above all others.

For Further Reading

Emery John Battis, *Saints and Sectaries.* Chapel Hill: University of North Carolina Press, 1962.

Jean Cameron, *Anne Hutchinson, Guilty or Not?* New York: P. Lang, 1994.

Andrew Delbanco, *The Puritan Ordeal.* Cambridge, MA: Harvard University Press, 1989.

David D. Hall, ed., *The Antinomian Controversy, 1636–1638: A Documentary History.* Middletown, CT: Wesleyan University Press, 1968.

Amy Lang, *Prophetic Woman: Anne Hutchinson and the Problem of Dissent in the Literature of New England.* Berkeley: University of California Press, 1987.

William K.B. Stoever, *A Faire and Easie Way to Heaven: Covenant Theology and Antinomianism in Early Massachusetts.* Middletown, CT: Wesleyan University Press, 1978.

VIEWPOINT 6A

A Defense of the Salem Witch Trials (1692)

Cotton Mather (1663–1728)

The Salem witchcraft trials were one of the most infamous episodes in American colonial history. In early 1692 some children in Salem, a village in Massachusetts close to Boston, accused three women of bewitching them. Charges and countercharges followed, and in June of that year witchcraft trials were authorized by the colonial governor, William Phips. Over the next few months the special court appointed by Phips tried, convicted, and executed nineteen people of witchcraft in the largest such proceedings in American history (one other person was tortured to death after refusing to enter a plea of guilty or not guilty). Amid growing criticism and doubts over the witch trials, Phips turned to Cotton Mather, Boston's leading minister and the author of several books and sermons on witchcraft, to defend the Salem proceedings. The result was *The Wonders of the Invisible World*, a study written by Mather and published in Boston in October 1692. This viewpoint contains excerpts of Mather's tract defending the Salem witch trials.

Mather states his beliefs in the existence of witches and, utilizing the records of Stephen Sewall, clerk of the court in Salem, examines the trials of five Salem people convicted of witchcraft (three are included in this viewpoint). Some historians have argued that Mather was selective in his choice of trials to examine. Mather had been among a group of ministers arguing against the use of "spectral evidence"—testimony that a spirit resembling the accused had been seen tormenting a victim—as sole grounds for conviction of witchcraft. In *Wonders* Mather chose to focus on the cases least affected by such supernatural proof.

What special position is held by New England and its people, according to Mather? What beliefs concerning witches and their powers is displayed by his writings and by the trial testimonies?

The *New-Englanders* are a People of God settled in those, which were once the *Devil's* Territories; and it may easily be supposed that the Devil was exceedingly disturbed, when he perceived such a People here accomplishing the Promise of old made unto our Blessed Jesus, *That He should have the Utmost parts of the Earth for his Possession.*

From *The Wonders of the Invisible World* by Cotton Mather (Boston, 1692).

There was not a greater Uproar among the *Ephesians*, when the Gospel was first brought among them, than there was among, *The Powers of the Air* (after whom those *Ephesians* walked) when first the *Silver Trumpets* of the Gospel here made the *Joyful Sound*. The Devil thus Irritated, immediately try'd all sorts of Methods to overturn this poor Plantation: and so much of the Church, as was *Fled into this Wilderness*, immediately found, *The Serpent cast out of his Mouth a Flood for the carrying of it away*. I believe, that never were more *Satanical Devices* used for the Unsetling of any People under the Sun, than what have been Employ'd for the Extirpation of the *Vine* which God has here *Planted, Casting out the Heathen, and preparing a Room Before it, and causing it to take deep Root, and fill the Land, so that it sent its Boughs unto the* Atlantic *Sea* Eastward, *and its Branches unto the* Connecticut *River* Westward, *and the Hills were covered with the shadows thereof.* But, All those Attempts of Hell, have hitherto been Abortive, many an *Ebenezer* [place of worship] has been Erected unto the Praise of God, by his Poor People here; and, *Having obtained Help from God, we continue to this Day.* Wherefore the Devil is now making one Attempt more upon us; an Attempt more Difficult, more Surprizing, more snarl'd with unintelligible Circumstances than any that we have hitherto Encountred; an Attempt so *Critical,* that if we get well through, we shall soon enjoy *Halcyon* Days with all the *Vultures* of hell *Trodden under our Feet.* He has wanted his *Incarnate Legions* to Persecute us, as the People of God have in the other Hemisphere been Persecuted: he has therefore drawn forth his more *Spiritual* ones to make an Attacque upon us. We have been advised by some Credible Christians yet alive, that a Malefactor, accused of *Witchcraft* as well as *Murder,* and Executed in this place more than Forty Years ago, did then give Notice of, *An Horrible* PLOT *against the Country by* WITCHCRAFT, *and a Foundation of* WITCHCRAFT *then laid, which if it were not seasonably discovered, would probably Blow up, and pull down all the Churches in the Country.* And we have now with Horror seen the *Discovery* of such a *Witchcraft!* An Army of *Devils* is horribly broke in upon the place which is the *Center,* and after a sort, the *First-born* of our *English* Settlements: and the Houses of the Good People there are fill'd with the doleful Shrieks of their Children and Servants, Tormented by Invisible Hands, with Tortures altogether preternatural. After the Mischiefs there Endeavoured, and since in part Conquered, the terrible Plague, of *Evil Angels,* hath made its Progress into some other places, where other Persons have been in like manner Diabolically handled. These our poor Afflicted Neighbours, quickly after they become

Infected and *Infested* with these *Dæmons*, arrive to a Capacity of Discerning those which they conceive the *Shapes* of their Troublers; and notwithstanding the Great and Just Suspicion, that the *Dæmons* might Impose the *Shapes* of Innocent Persons in their *Spectral Exhibitions* upon the Sufferers, (which may perhaps prove no small part of the *Witch-Plot* in the issue) yet many of the Persons thus Represented, being Examined, several of them have been Convicted of a very Damnable *Witchcraft*: yea, more than one *Twenty* have *Confessed*, that they have Signed unto a *Book*, which the Devil show'd them, and Engaged in his Hellish Design of *Bewitching*, and *Ruining* our Land. *We* know not, at least *I* know not, how far the *Delusions* of Satan may be Interwoven into some Circumstances of the *Confessions*; but one would think, all the Rules of Understanding Humane Affairs are at an end, if after so many most Voluntary Harmonious *Confessions*, made by Intelligent Persons of all Ages, in sundry Towns, at several Times, we must not Believe the *main strokes* wherein those *Confessions* all agree: especially when we have a thousand preternatural Things every day before our eyes, wherein the *Confessors* do acknowledge their Concernment, and give Demonstration of their being so Concerned. If the Devils now can strike the minds of men with any *Poisons* of so fine a Composition and Operation, that Scores of Innocent People shall Unite, in *Confessions* of a Crime, which we see actually committed, it is a thing prodigious, beyond the Wonders of the former Ages, and it threatens no less than a sort of a Dissolution upon the World. Now, by these *Confessions* 'tis Agreed, *That* the Devil has made a dreadful Knot of *Witches* in the Country, and by the help of *Witches* has dreadfully increased that Knot: *That* these *Witches* have driven a Trade of Commissioning their *Confederate Spirits*, to do all sorts of Mischiefs to the Neighbours, whereupon there have ensued such Mischievous consequences upon the Bodies and Estates of the Neighbourhood, as could not otherwise be accounted for: yea, *That* at prodigious *Witch-Meetings*, the Wretches have proceeded so far, as to Concert and Consult the Methods of Rooting out the Christian Religion from this Country, and setting up instead of it, perhaps a more gross *Diabolism*, than ever the World saw before. And yet it will be a thing little short of *Miracle*, if in so *spread* a Business as this, the Devil should not get in some of his Juggles, to confound the Discovery of all the rest. . . .

The Salem Tryals

But I shall no longer detain my Reader, from his expected Entertainment, in a brief account of the Tryals which have passed upon some of the Malefactors lately Executed at *Salem*, for the *Witchcrafts*

whereof they stood Convicted. For my own part, I was not present at any of them; nor ever had I any Personal prejudice at the Persons thus brought upon the Stage; much less at the Surviving Relations of those Persons, with and for whom I would be as hearty a Mourner as any Man living in the World: *The Lord Comfort them!* But having received a Command so to do, I can do no other than shortly relate the chief *Matters of Fact*, which occur'd in the Tryals of some that were Executed, in an Abridgment Collected out of the *Court-Papers* on this occasion put into my hands. You are to take the *Truth*, just as it was; and the Truth will hurt no good Man. There might have been more of these, if my Book would not thereby have swollen too big; and if some other worthy hands did not perhaps intend something further in these *Collections*; for which cause I have only singled out Four or Five, which may serve to illustrate the way of Dealing, wherein *Witchcrafts* use to be concerned; and I report matters not as an *Advocate*, but as an *Historian*.

They were some of the Gracious Words inserted in the Advice, which many of the Neighbouring Ministers, did this Summer humbly lay before our Honorable Judges, *We cannot but with all thankfulness, acknowledge the success which the Merciful God has given unto the Sedulous and Assiduous endeavours of Our Honourable Rulers, to detect the abominable Witchcrafts which have been committed in the Country; Humbly Praying, that the discovery of those mysterious and mischievous wickednesses, may be Perfected.* If in the midst of the many Dissatisfactions among us, the Publication of these Tryals, may promote such a Pious Thankfulness unto God, for Justice being so far executed among us, I shall Rejoice that God is Glorified, and pray, that no wrong steps of ours may ever sully any of his Glorious Works. . . .

The Tryal of Susanna Martin at the
COURT OF OYER AND TERMINER, HELD BY ADJOURNMENT AT SALEM, JUNE 29, 1692

SUSANNA MARTIN, pleading *Not Guilty* to the Indictment of *Witchcraft*, brought in against her, there were produced the Evidences of many Persons very sensibly and grievously Bewitched; who all complained of the Prisoner at the Bar, as the Person whom they believed the cause of their Miseries. And now, as well as in the other Trials, there was an extraordinary Endeavour by *Witchcrafts*, with Cruel and frequent Fits, to hinder the poor Sufferers from giving in their Complaints, which the Court was forced with much Patience to obtain, by much waiting and watching for it.

2. There was now also an account given of what passed at her first Examination before the Magis-

trates. The Cast of her *Eye*, then striking the afflict-ed People to the Ground, whether they saw that Cast or no; there were these among other Passages between the Magistrates and the Examinate.

Magistrate. Pray, what ails these People?

Martin. I don't know.

Magistrate. But what do you think ails them?

Martin. I don't desire to spend my Judgment upon it.

Magistrate. Don't you think they are bewitch'd?

Martin. No, I do not think they are.

Magistrate. Tell us your Thoughts about them then.

Martin. No, my thoughts are my own, when they are in, but when they are out they are anothers. Their Master—

Magistrate. Their Master? who do you think is their Master?

Martin. If they be dealing in the Black Art, you may know as well as I.

Magistrate. Well, what have you done towards this?

Martin. Nothing at all.

Magistrate. Why, 'tis you or your Appearance.

Martin. I cannot help it.

Magistrate. Is it not *your* Master? How comes your Appearance to hurt these?

Martin. How do I know? He that appeared in the Shape of Samuel, a glorified Saint, may appear in any ones Shape.

It was then also noted in her, as in others like her, that if the Afflicted went to approach her, they were flung down to the Ground. And, when she was asked the reason of it, she said, *I cannot tell; it may be, the Devil bears me more Malice than another.*

3. The Court accounted themselves, alarum'd by these Things, to enquire further into the Conversation of the Prisoner; and see what there might occur, to render these Accusations further credible. Whereupon, *John Allen* of *Salisbury*, testify'd, That he refusing, because of the weakness of his Oxen, to Cart some Staves at the request of this *Martin*, she was displeased at it; and said, *It had been as good that he had; for his Oxen should never do him much more Service.* Whereupon, this Deponent said, *Dost thou threaten me, thou old Witch? I'll throw thee into the Brook*: Which to avoid, she flew over the Bridge, and escaped. But, as he was going home, one of his Oxen tired, so that he was forced to Unyoke him, that he might get him home. He then put his Oxen, with many more, upon *Salisbury* Beach, where Cattle did use to get *Flesh*. In a few days, all the Oxen upon the Beach were found by their Tracks, to have run unto the Mouth of *Merrimack-River*, and not returned; but the next day they were found come ashore upon *Plum-Island*. They that sought them, used all imag-

inable gentleness, but they would still run away with a violence, that seemed wholly Diabolical, till they came near the mouth of *Merrimack-River*; when they ran right into the Sea, swimming as far as they could be seen. One of them then swam back again, with a swiftness, amazing to the Beholders, who stood ready to receive him, and help up his tired Carcass: But the Beast ran furiously up into the Island, and from thence, through the Marshes, up into *Newbury* Town, and so up into the Woods; and there after a while found near *Amesbury*. So that, of fourteen good Oxen, there was only this saved: The rest were all cast up, some in one place, and some in another, Drowned.

4. *John Atkinson* testifi'd, That he exchanged a Cow with a Son of *Susanna Martin's*, whereat she muttered, and was unwilling he should have it. Going to receive this Cow, tho he Hamstring'd her, and Halter'd her, she, of a Tame Creature, grew so mad, that they could scarce get her along. She broke all the Ropes that were fastned unto her, and though she were ty'd fast unto a Tree, yet she made her escape, and gave them such further trouble, as they could ascribe to no cause but Witchcraft.

5. *Bernard Peache* testifi'd, That being in Bed, on the Lord's-day Night, he heard a scrabbling at the Window, whereat he then saw *Susanna Martin* come in, and jump down upon the Floor. She took hold of this Deponent's Feet, and drawing his Body up into an Heap, she lay upon him near Two Hours; in all which time he could neither speak nor stir. At length, when he could begin to move, he laid hold on her Hand, and pulling it up to his Mouth, he bit three of her Fingers, as he judged, unto the Bone. Whereupon she went from the Chamber, down the Stairs, out at the Door. This Deponent thereupon called unto the People of the House, to advise them of what passed; and he himself did follow her. The People saw her not; but there being a Bucket at the Left-hand of the Door, there was a drop of Blood found upon it; and several more drops of Blood upon the Snow newly fallen abroad: There was likewise the print of her 2 Feet just without the Threshold; but no more sign of any Footing further off.

At another time this Deponent was desired by the Prisoner, to come unto an Husking of Corn, at her House; and she said, *If he did not come, it were better that he did!* He went not; but the Night following, *Susanna Martin*, as he judged, and another came towards him. One of them said, *Here he is!* but he having a Quarter-staff, made a Blow at them. The Roof of the Barn, broke his Blow; but following them to the Window, he made another Blow at them, and struck them down; yet they got up, and got out, and he saw no more of them. About this time, there was a Rumour about the Town, that *Martin* had a Broken

Head; but the Deponent could say nothing to that.

The said *Peache* also testifi'd the Bewitching the Cattle to Death, upon *Martin's* Discontents.

6. *Robert Downer* testified, That this Prisoner being some Years ago prosecuted at Court for a Witch, he then said unto her, *He believed she was a Witch*. Whereat she being dissatisfied, said, *That some She-Devil would shortly fetch him away!* Which words were heard by others, as well as himself. The Night following, as he lay in his Bed, there came in at the Window, the likeness of a *Cat*, which flew upon him, took fast hold of his Throat, lay on him a considerable while, and almost killed him. At length he remembred what *Susanna Martin* had threatned the Day before; and with much striving he cried out, *Avoid, thou She-Devil! In the Name of God the Father, the Son, and the Holy Ghost, Avoid!* Whereupon it left him, leap'd on the Floor, and flew out at the Window.

And there also came in several Testimonies, that before ever *Downer* spoke a word of this Accident, *Susanna Martin* and her Family had related, *How this* Downer *had been handled!* . . .

•

"We cannot but with all thankfulness, acknowledge the success which the Merciful God has given unto the . . . endeavours of Our Honourable Rulers, to detect the abominable Witchcrafts which have been committed in the Country."

•

---

9. *Sarah Atkinson* testify'd, That *Susanna Martin* came from *Amesbury* to their House at *Newbury*, in an extraordinary Season, when it was not fit for any to Travel. She came (as she said, unto *Atkinson*) all that long way on Foot. She brag'd and shew'd how dry she was; nor could it be perceived that so much as the Soles of her Shoes were wet. *Atkinson* was amazed at it; and professed, that she should her self have been wet up to the knees, if she had then came so far; but *Martin* reply'd, *She scorn'd to be Drabbled!* It was noted, that this Testimony upon her Trial, cast her in a very singular Confusion.

10. *John Pressy* testify'd, That being one Evening very unaccountably Bewildred, near a Field of *Martins*, and several times, as one under an Enchantment, returning to the place he had left, at length he saw a marvellous Light, about the bigness of an Halfbushel, near two Rod, out of the way. He went, and struck at it with a Stick, and laid it on with all his might. He gave it near forty blows; and felt it a pal-pable substance. But going from it, his Heels were struck up, and he was laid with his Back on the Ground, sliding, as he thought, into a Pit; from whence he recover'd by taking hold on the Bush; altho' afterwards he could find no such Pit in the place. Having, after his Recovery, gone five or six Rod, he saw *Susanna Martin* standing on his Lefthand, as the Light had done before; but they changed no words with one another. He could scarce find his House in his Return; but at length he got home extreamly affrighted. The next day, it was upon Enquiry understood, that *Martin* was in a miserable condition by pains and hurts that were upon her.

It was further testify'd by this Deponent, That after he had given in some Evidence against *Susanna Martin*, many years ago, she gave him foul words about it; and said, *He should never prosper more*; particularly, *That he should never have more than two Cows; that tho' he was never so likely to have more, yet he should never have them.* And that from that very day to this, namely for twenty years together, he could never exceed that number; but some strange thing or other still prevented his having any more.

11. *Jervis Ring* testify'd, That about seven years ago, he was oftentimes and grievously oppressed in the Night, but saw not who troubled him; until at last he Lying perfectly Awake, plainly saw *Susanna Martin* approach him. She came to him, and forceably bit him by the Finger; so that the Print of the bite is now, so long after, to be seen upon him.

12. But besides all of these Evidences, there was a most wonderful Account of one *Joseph Ring*, produced on this occasion. This Man has been strangely carried about by *Dæmons*, from one *Witch-meeting* to another, for near two years together; and for one quarter of this time, they have made him, and keep him Dumb, tho' he is now again able to speak. There was one *T.H.* who having, as 'tis judged, a design of engaging this *Joseph Ring* in a snare of Devillism, contrived a while, to bring this *Ring* two Shillings in Debt unto him.

Afterwards, this poor Man would be visited with unknown shapes, and this *T.H.* sometimes among them; which would force him away with them, unto unknown Places, where he saw Meetings, Feastings, Dancings; and after his return, wherein they hurried him along through the Air, he gave Demonstrations to the Neighbours, that he had indeed been so transported. When he was brought until these hellish Meetings, one of the first Things they still did unto him, was to give him a knock on the Back, whereupon he was ever as if bound with Chains, uncapable of stirring out of the place, till they should release him. He related, that there often came to him a Man, who presented him a *Book*, whereto he would have him set his Hand; promising to him, that he should then have even what he would; and presenting him with all the delectable Things, Persons, and Places, that he could imagin. But he refusing to subscribe, the business would end with dreadful Shapes, Noises and Screeches, which almost scared him out of his Wits. Once with the Book, there was a Pen offered him, and an Ink-horn with Liquor in it, that seemed like Blood: But he never toucht it.

This Man did now affirm, That he saw the Prisoner at several of those hellish Randezvouzes. Note, this Woman was one of the most impudent, scurrilous, wicked Creatures in the World; and she did now throughout her whole Tryal, discover her self to be such an one. Yet when she was asked, what she had to say for her self? Her chief Plea was, *That she had lead a most virtuous and holy Life.*

The Tryal of Elizabeth How, at the
COURT OF OYER AND TERMINER, HELD BY
ADJOURNMENT AT SALEM, JUNE 30, 1692

ELIZABETH HOW pleading *Not Guilty* to the Indictment of Witchcrafts, then charged upon her; the Court, according to the usual Proceedings of the Courts in *England*, in such Cases, began with hearing the Depositions of several afflicted People, who were grievously tortured by sensible and evident *Witchcrafts*, and all complained of the Prisoner, as the cause of their Trouble. It was also found that the Sufferers were not able to bear her *Look*, as likewise, that in their greatest Swoons, they distinguished her *Touch* from other Peoples, being thereby raised out of them.

And there was other Testimony of People to whom the shape of this *How*, gave trouble nine or ten years ago.

2. It has been a most usual thing for the bewitched Persons, at the same time that the *Spectres* representing the *Witches*, troubled them, to be visited with Apparitions of *Ghosts*, pretending to have been Murdered by the *Witches* then represented. And sometimes the Confessions of the Witches afterwards acknowledged those very Murders, which these *Apparitions* charged upon them; altho' they had never heard what Informations had been given by the Sufferers.

There were such Apparitions of Ghosts testified by some of the present Sufferers; and the Ghosts affirmed, that this *How* had murdered them: Which things were *fear'd* but not *prov'd.*

3. This *How* had made some Attempts of joyning to the Church at *Ipswich*, several years ago; but she was denied an admission into that Holy Society, partly through a suspicion of Witchcraft, then urged against her. And there now came in Testimony, of preternatural Mischiefs, presently befalling some that had been Instrumental to debar her from the Communion whereupon she was intruding.

4. There was a particular Deposition of *Joseph Stafford*, That his Wife had conceived an extream Aversion to this *How*, on the Reports of her Witchcrafts: But *How* one day, taking her by the Hand, and saying, *I believe you are not ignorant of the great Scandal that I lye under, by an evil Report raised upon me,* She immediately, unreasonably and unperswadeably, even like one Enchanted, began to take this Woman's part. *How* being soon after propounded, as desiring an Admission to the Table of the Lord, some of the pious Brethren were unsatisfy'd about her. The Elders appointed a Meeting to hear Matters objected against her; and no Arguments in the World could hinder this Goodwife *Stafford* from going to the Lecture. She did indeed promise, with much ado, that she would not go to the Church-meeting, yet she could not refrain going thither also. *How's* Affairs there were so canvased, that she came off rather *Guilty* than *Cleared*; nevertheless Goodwife *Stafford* could not forbear taking her by the Hand, and saying, *Tho' you are Condemned before Men, you are Justify'd before God.* She was quickly taken in a very strange manner, Ranting, Raving, Raging, and crying out, *Goody* How *must come into the Church; she is a precious Saint; and tho' she be condemned before Men, she is Justify'd before God.* So she continued for the space of two or three Hours; and then fell into a Trance. But coming to her self, she cry'd out, *Ha! I was mistaken*; and afterwards again repeated, *Ha! I was mistaken!* Being asked by a stander by, *Wherein?* she replyed, *I thought Goody* How *had been a precious Saint of God, but now I see she is a Witch: She has bewitched me, and my Child, and we shall never be well, till there be a testimony for her, that she may be taken into the Church.* And *How* said afterwards, that she was very sorry to see *Stafford* at the Church-meeting mentioned. *Stafford*, after this, declared herself to be afflicted by the Shape of *How*; and from that Shape she endured many Miseries.

5. *John How*, Brother to the Husband of the Prisoner, testified, that he refusing to accompany the Prisoner unto her Examination, as was by her desired, immediately some of his Cattle were Bewitched to Death, leaping three or four foot high, turning about, speaking, falling, and dying at once; and going to cut off an Ear, for an use, that might as well perhaps have been omitted, the Hand wherein he held his Knife was taken very numb, and so it remained, and full of Pain, for several Days, being not well at this very Time. And he suspected the Prisoner for the Author of it.

6. *Nehemiah Abbot* testify'd, that unusual and mischievous Accidents would befal his Cattle, whenever he had any Difference with this Prisoner. Once, par-

ticularly, she wished his Ox choaked; and within a little while that Ox was choaked with a Turnep in his Throat. At another Time, refusing to lend his Horse, at the Request of her Daughter, the Horse was in a preternatural manner abused. And several other odd things of that kind were testified.

7. There came in Testimony, that one Goodwife *Sherwin*, upon some Difference with *How*, was bewitched; and that she dyed, charging this *How* with having an Hand in her Death. And that other People had their Barrels of Drink unaccountably mischieved, spoil'd and spilt, upon their displeasing of her.

The things in themselves were trivial, but there being such a Course of them, it made them the more considered. Among others, *Martha Wood*, gave her Testimony, That a little after her Father had been employed in gathering an account of *How's* Conversation, they once and again lost great quantities of Drink out of their Vessels, in such a manner, as they could ascribe to nothing but Witchcraft. As also, That *How* giving her some Apples, when she had eaten of them she was taken with a very strange kind of Amaze, insomuch that she knew not what she said or did.

8. There was likewise a Cluster of Depositions, That one *Isaac Cummings* refusing to lend his Mare unto the husband of this *How*, the Mare was within a day or two taken in a strange condition: The Beast seemed much abused, being bruised as if she had been running over the Rocks, and marked where the Bridle went, as if burnt with a red hot Bridle. Moreover, one using a Pipe of Tobacco for the Cure of the Beast, a blue Flame issued out of her, took hold of her Hair, and not only spread and burnt on her, but it also flew upwards towards the Roof of the Barn, and had like to have set the Barn on Fire: And the Mare dyed very suddenly.

9. *Timothy Pearley* and his Wife, testify'd, Not only unaccountable Mischiefs befel their Cattle, upon their having of Differences with this Prisoner: but also that they had a Daughter destroyed by Witchcrafts; which Daughter still charged *How* as the Cause of her Affliction. And it was noted, that she would be struck down whenever *How* were spoken of. She was often endeavoured to be thrown into the Fire, and into the Water, in her strange Fits: Tho' her Father had corrected her for charging *How* with bewitching her, yet (as was testified by others also) she said, She was sure of it, and must dye standing to it. Accordingly she charged *How* to the very Death; and said, *Tho' How could afflict and torment her Body, yet she could not hurt her Soul*: And, *That the Truth of this matter would appear, when she would be dead and gone. . . .*

11. Afterwards there came in the Confessions of several other (penitent) Witches, which affirmed this

How to be one of those, who with them had been baptized by the Devil in the River, at *Newbury*-Falls: before which he made them there kneel down by the Brink of the River and worshiped him.

The Trial of Martha Carrier, at the
COURT OF OYER AND TERMINER, HELD BY ADJOURNMENT AT SALEM, AUGUST 2, 1692

MARTHA CARRIER was Indicted for the bewitching certain Persons, according to the Form usual in such Cases, pleading *Not Guilty*, to her Indictment; there were first brought in a considerable number of the bewitched Persons; who not only made the Court sensible of an horrid Witchcraft committed upon them, but also deposed, That it was *Martha Carrier*, or her Shape, that grievously tormented them, by Biting, Pricking, Pinching and Choaking of them. It was further deposed, That while this *Carrier* was on her Examination, before the Magistrates, the Poor People were so tortured that every one expected their Death upon the very spot, but that upon the binding of *Carrier* they were eased. Moreover the Look of *Carrier* then laid the Afflicted People for dead; and her Touch, if her Eye at the same time were off them, raised them again: Which Things were also now seen upon her Tryal. And it was testified, That upon the mention of some having their Necks twisted almost round, by the Shape of this *Carrier*, she replyed, *Its no matter though their Necks had been twisted quite off.*

2. Before the Tryal of this Prisoner, several of her own children had frankly and fully confessed, not only that they were Witches themselves, but that this their Mother had made them so. This Confession they made with great Shews of Repentance, and with much Demonstration of Truth. They related Place, Time, Occasion; they gave an account of Journeys, Meetings and Mischiefs by them performed, and were very credible in what they said. Nevertheless, this Evidence was not produced against the Prisoner at the Bar, inasmuch as there was other Evidence enough to proceed upon.

3. *Benjamin Abbot* gave his Testimony, That last *March* was a twelvemonth, this *Carrier* was very angry with him, upon laying out some Land, near her Husband's: Her Expressions in this Anger, were, *That she would stick as close to Abbot as the Bark stuck to the Tree; and that he should repent of it afore seven years came to an End, so as Doctor* Prescot *should never cure him.* These Words were heard by others besides *Abbot* himself; who also heard her say, *She would hold his Nose as close to the Grindstone as ever it was held since his Name was* Abbot. Presently after this, he was taken with a Swelling in his Foot, and then with a Pain in his Side, and exceedingly tormented. It bred into a Sore, which was launced by

Doctor *Prescot*, and several Gallons of Corruption ran out of it. For six Weeks it continued very bad, and then another Sore bred in the Groin, which was also lanced by Doctor *Prescot*. Another Sore then bred in his Groin, which was likewise cut, and put him to very great Misery: He was brought unto Death's Door, and so remained until *Carrier* was taken, and carried away by the Constable, from which very Day he began to mend, and so grew better every Day, and is well ever since.

Sarah Abbot also, his Wife, testified, That her Husband was not only all this while Afflicted in his Body, but also that strange extraordinary and unaccountable Calamities befel his Cattel; their Death being such as they could guess at no Natural Reason for.

4. *Allin Toothaker* testify'd, That *Richard*, the son of *Martha Carrier*, having some difference with him, pull'd him down by the Hair of the Head. When he Rose again, he was going to strike at *Richard Carrier*; but fell down flat on his Back to the ground, and had not power to stir hand or foot, until he told *Carrier* he yielded; and then he saw the shape of *Martha Carrier*, go off his breast.

This *Toothaker*, had Received a wound in the *Wars*; and he now testify'd, that *Martha Carrier* told him, *He should never be Cured.* Just afore the Apprehending of *Carrier*, he could thrust a knitting Needle into his wound, four inches deep; but presently after her being seized, he was thoroughly healed. He further testify'd, that when *Carrier* and he sometimes were at variance, she would clap her hands at him, and say, *He should get nothing by it*; whereupon he several times lost his Cattle, by strange Deaths, whereof no natural causes could be given.

5. *John Rogger* also testifyed, That upon the threatning words of this malicious *Carrier*, his Cattle would be strangely bewitched; as was more particularly then described.

6. *Samuel Preston* testify'd, that about two years ago, having some difference with *Martha Carrier*, he lost a *Cow* in a strange Preternatural unusual manner; and about a month after this, the said *Carrier*, having again some difference with him, she told him; *He had lately lost a Cow, and it should not be long before he lost another*; which accordingly came to pass; for he had a thriving and well-kept *Cow*, which without any known cause quickly fell down and dy'd.

7. *Phebe Chandler* testify'd, that about a Fortnight before the apprehension of *Martha Carrier*, on a Lords-day while the Psalm was singing in the *Church*, this *Carrier* then took her by the shoulder and shaking her, asked her, *where she lived*: she made her no Answer, although as *Carrier*, who lived next door to her Fathers House, could not in reason but know who she was.

Quickly after this, as she was at several times cross-ing the Fields, she heard a voice, that she took to be *Martha Carriers*, and it seem'd as if it was over her head. The voice told her, *she should within two or three days be poisoned.* Accordingly, within such a little time, one half of her right hand, became greatly swollen, and very painful; as also part of her Face: whereof she can give no account how it came. It continued very bad for some dayes; and several times since, she has had a great pain in her breast; and been so seized on her leggs, that she has hardly been able to go. She added, that lately, going well to the House of God, *Richard*, the son of *Martha Carrier*, look'd very earnestly upon her, and immediately her hand, which had formerly been poisoned, as is above-said, began to pain her greatly, and she had a strange Burning at her stomach; but was then struck deaf, so that she could not hear any of the prayer, or singing, till the two or three last words of the Psalm.

8. One *Foster*, who confessed her own share in the Witchcraft for which the Prisoner stood indicted, affirm'd, that she had seen the prisoner at some of their *Witch-meetings*, and that it was this *Carrier*, who perswaded her to be a Witch. She confessed, that the Devil carry'd them on a pole, to a Witch-meeting; but the pole broke, and she hanging about *Carriers* neck, they both fell down, and she then received an hurt by the Fall, whereof she was not at this very time recovered.

9. One *Lacy*, who likewise confessed her share in this Witchcraft, now testify'd, that she and the prisoner were once Bodily present at a *Witch-meeting* in *Salem Village*; and that she knew the prisoner to be a Witch, and to have been at a Diabolical sacrament, and that the prisoner was the undoing of her, and her Children, by enticing them into the snare of the Devil.

10. Another *Lacy*, who also confessed her share in this Witchcraft, now testify'd, that the prisoner was at the *Witch-meeting*, in *Salem Village*, where they had Bread and Wine Administred unto them.

11. In the time of this prisoners Trial, one *Susanna Sheldon*, in open Court had her hands Unaccountably ty'd together with a wheel-band, so fast that without cutting, it could not be loosed: It was done by a *Spectre*; and the Sufferer affirm'd, it was the *Prisoners*.

Memorandum. This rampant Hag, *Martha Carrier*, was the person, of whom the Confessions of the Witches, and of her own children among the rest, agreed, That the Devil had promised her, she should be *Queen of Heb*. . . .

Deliverance from Evil

If a Drop of *Innocent Blood* should be shed, in the Prosecution of the *Witchcrafts* among us, how unhappy are we! For which cause, I cannot express myself in better terms, than those of a most Worthy Person, who lives near the present Center of these things. *The Mind of God in these matters, is to be carefully lookt into, with due Circumspection, that Satan deceive us not with his Devices, who transforms himself into an Angel of Light, and may pretend justice and yet intend mischief.* But on the other side, if the storm of Justice do now fall only on the Heads of those guilty *Witches* and *Wretches* which have defiled our Land, *How Happy!*

The Execution of some that have lately Dyed, has been immediately attended, with a strange Deliverance of some, that had lain for many years, in a most sad Condition, under, they knew not whose *evil hands*. As I am abundantly satisfy'd, That many of the Self-Murders committed here, have been the effects of a Cruel and Bloody *Witchcraft*, letting fly *Dæmons* upon the miserable *Seneca's*; thus, it has been admirable unto me to see, how a Devilish *Witchcraft*, sending Devils upon them, has driven many poor people to *Despair*, and persecuted their minds, with such Buzzes of *Atheism* and *Blasphemy*, as has made them even run *distracted with Terrors*: And some long *Bow'd* down under such a *spirit of Infirmity*, have been marvelously Recovered upon the death of the Witches.

VIEWPOINT 6B

An Attack on the Salem Witch Trials (1692)

Thomas Brattle (1658–1713)

Although the mass prosecutions and several executions for witchcraft in Salem, Massachusetts, in 1692, had the support of much of the public, many were deeply disturbed by the proceedings. One critic was Thomas Brattle, a prominent Boston merchant. Educated at Harvard College (and future treasurer of the institution), Brattle had interests in science and mathematics as well as commerce. He was liberal in his political and religious beliefs and opposed Puritan orthodoxy. The following viewpoint is taken from a letter Brattle wrote to an unknown English clergyman in which he attacks the procedures used in the Salem witch trials, especially the use of "specter" or supernatural evidence. The letter was not published in Brattle's day, but is believed by historians to have been privately circulated, allowing Brattle to discreetly make his views of the witchcraft proceedings known. Governor William Phips sus-

From Thomas Brattle's letter dated 8 October 1692, to an unknown clergyman in England (Massachusetts Historical Society, *Collections*, vol. 5). Courtesy of the Massachusetts Historical Society.

pended the witchcraft trials in October 1692. In all, several hundred people were accused of witchcraft, fifty-five confessed, and twenty were killed.

What does Brattle find most disturbing about the Salem trials? How do Brattle's views of confessions of witchcraft differ from those of Cotton Mather, author of the opposing viewpoint? Does Brattle express a disbelief in witchcraft itself?

I should be very loath to bring myself into any snare by my freedom with you, and therefore hope that you will put the best construction on what I write, and secure me from such as would interpret my lines otherwise than they are designed. Obedience to lawful authority I evermore accounted a great duty; and willingly I would not practise anything that might thwart and contradict such a principle. Too many are ready to despise dominions, and speak evil of dignities; and I am sure the mischiefs which arise from a factious and rebellious spirit are very sad and notorious; insomuch that I would sooner bite my fingers' ends than willingly cast dirt on authority, or any way offer reproach to it. Far, therefore, be it from me to have anything to do with those men your letter mentions, whom you acknowledge to be men of a factious spirit, and never more in their element than when they are declaiming against men in public place, and contriving methods that tend to the disturbance of the common peace. I never accounted it a credit to my cause to have the good liking of such men. "My son! (says Solomon) fear thou the Lord and the king, and meddle not with them that are given to change" (Prov. 24:21).

However, sir, I never thought judges infallible, but reckoned that they, as well as private men, might err; and that when they were guilty of erring, standers-by, who possibly had not half their judgment, might, notwithstanding, be able to detect and behold their errors. And, furthermore, when errors of that nature are thus detected and observed, I never thought it an interfering with dutifulness and subjection for one man to communicate his thoughts to another thereabout, and with modesty and due reverence to debate the premised failings; at least, when errors are fundamental and palpably pervert the great end of authority and government; for as to circumstantial errors, I must confess my principle is that it is the duty of a good subject to cover with his silence a multitude of them.

But I shall no longer detain you with my preface, but pass to some things you look for, and whether you expect such freedom from me, yea or no, yet shall you find that I am very open to communicate my thoughts unto you, and in plain terms to tell you what my opinion is of the Salem proceedings.

First, as to the method which the Salem justices do take in their examinations, it is truly this: A warrant being issued out to apprehend the persons that are charged and complained of by the afflicted children, as they are called; said persons are brought before the justices, the afflicted being present. The justices ask the apprehended why they afflict those poor children; to which the apprehended answer, they do not afflict them. The justices order the apprehended to look upon the said children, which accordingly they do; and at the time of that look (I dare not say *by* that look, as the Salem gentlemen do), the afflicted are cast into a fit. The apprehended are then blinded, and ordered to touch the afflicted; and at that touch, though not *by* the touch (as above), the afflicted ordinarily do come out of their fits. The afflicted persons then declare and affirm that the apprehended have afflicted them; upon which the apprehended persons, though of never so good repute, are forthwith committed to prison on suspicion for witchcraft.

One of the Salem justices was pleased to tell Mr. Alden (when upon his examination) that truly he had been acquainted with him these many years, and had always accounted him a good man; but, indeed, now he should be obliged to change his opinion. This there are more than one or two did hear, and are ready to swear to, if not in so many words, yet as to its natural and plain meaning. He saw reason to change his opinion of Mr. Alden because that, at the time he touched the poor child, the poor child came out of her fit. I suppose His Honor never made the experiment whether there was not as much virtue in his own hand as there was in Mr. Alden's, to cure by a touch. I know a man that will venture two to one with any Salemite whatever that, let the matter be duly managed, and the afflicted person shall come out of her fit upon the touch of the most religious hand in Salem. It is worthily noted by some that at some times the afflicted will not presently come out of their fits upon the touch of the suspected; and, then, forsooth, they are ordered by the justices to grasp hard, harder yet, etc., insomuch that at length the afflicted come out of their fits; and the reason is very good, because that a touch of any hand, and process of time, will work the cure; infallibly they will do it, as experience teaches.

I cannot but condemn this method of the justices, of making this touch of the hand a rule to discover witchcraft; because I am fully persuaded that it is sorcery, and a superstitious method, and that which we have no rule for, either from reason or religion. . . .

Superstition and Mockery

This Salem philosophy some men may call the new philosophy; but I think it rather deserves the name of Salem superstition and sorcery, and it is not fit to be named in a land of such light as New England is. I think the matter might be better solved another way; but I shall not make any attempt that way further than to say that these afflicted children, as they are called, do hold correspondence with the devil, even in the esteem and account of the Salem gentlemen; for when the black man, *i.e.*, say these gentlemen, the devil, does appear to them, they ask him many questions, and accordingly give information to the inquirer; and if this is not holding correspondence with the devil, and something worse, I know not what is. . . .

Second, with respect to the confessors, as they are improperly called, or such as confess themselves to be witches (the second thing you inquire into in your letter), there are now about fifty of them in prison, many of which I have again and again seen and heard; and I cannot but tell you that my faith is strong concerning them, that they are deluded, imposed upon, and under the influence of some evil spirit, and therefore unfit to be evidences, either against themselves or anyone else. I now speak of one sort of them, and of others afterward.

These confessors, as they are called, do very often contradict themselves, as inconsistently as is usual for any crazed, distempered person to do. This the Salem gentlemen do see and take notice of; and even the judges themselves have, at some times, taken these confessors in flat lies, or contradictions, even in the courts; by reason of which one would have thought that the judges would have frowned upon the said confessors, discarded them, and not minded one tittle of anything that they said. But instead thereof, as sure as we are men, the judges vindicate these confessors and salve their contradictions by proclaiming that the devil takes away their memory and imposes upon their brain. If this reflects anywhere, I am very sorry for it. I can but assure you that, upon the word of an honest man, it is truth, and that I can bring you many credible persons to witness it, who have been eye and ear witnesses to these things.

These confessors, then, at least some of them, even in the judges' own account, are under the influence of the devil; and the brain of these confessors is imposed upon by the devil, even in the judges' account. But now, if, in the judges' account, these confessors are under the influence of the devil, and their brains are affected and imposed upon by the devil so that they are not their own men, why then should these judges, or any other men, make such account of, and set so much by, the words of these confessors, as they do? In short, I argue thus:

If the devil does actually take away the memory of them at some times, certainly the devil, at other times, may very reasonably be thought to affect their fancies, and to represent false ideas to their imagination. But, now, if it be thus granted that the devil is able to represent false ideas (to speak vulgarly) to the imaginations of the confessors, what man of sense will regard the confessions, or any of the words, of these confessors?

The great cry of many of our neighbors now is— What, will you not believe the confessors? Will you not believe men and women who confess that they have signed to the devil's book? that they were baptized by the devil; and that they were at the mock sacrament once and again? What! will you not believe that this is witchcraft, and that such and such men are witches, although the confessors do own and assert it?

Thus, I say, many of our good neighbors do argue; but methinks they might soon be convinced that there is nothing at all in all these their arguings, if they would but duly consider of the premises.

———— • ————

"This Salem philosophy . . . rather deserves the name of Salem superstition and sorcery, and it is not fit to be named in a land of such light as New England is."

———— • ————

In the meantime, I think we must rest satisfied in it, and be thankful to God for it, that all men are not thus bereft of their senses; but that we have here and there considerate and thinking men who will not thus be imposed upon, and abused, by the subtle endeavors of the crafty one.

In the next place, I proceed to the form of their indictments and the trials thereupon.

The indictment runs for sorcery and witchcraft, acted upon the body of such a one (say M. Warren), at such a particular time . . . and at diverse other times before and after, whereby the said M. W. is wasted and consumed, pined, etc.

Now for the proof of the said sorcery and witchcraft, the prisoner at the bar pleading not guilty.

1. The afflicted persons are brought into court, and, after much patience and pains taken with them, do take their oaths that the prisoner at the bar did afflict them. And here I think it very observable that often, when the afflicted do mean and intend only the appearance and shape of such a one (say G. Proctor), yet they positively swear that G. Proctor did afflict them; and they have been allowed so to do, as though there was no real difference between G. Proctor and the shape of G. Proctor. This, methinks, may readily prove a stumbling block to the jury, lead them into a very fundamental error, and occasion innocent blood, yea, the innocentest blood imagin-

able, to be in great danger. Whom it belongs unto, to be eyes unto the blind and to remove such stumbling blocks, I know full well; and yet you, and everyone else, do know as well as I who do not.

2. The confessors do declare what they know of the said prisoner; and some of the confessors are allowed to give their oaths, a thing which I believe was never heard of in this world, that such as confess themselves to be witches, to have renounced God and Christ and all that is sacred, should yet be allowed and ordered to swear by the name of the great God! This indeed seems to me to be a gross taking of God's name in vain. I know the Salem gentlemen do say that there is hope that the said confessors have repented; I shall only say that, if they have repented, it is well for themselves, but if they have not, it is very ill for you know who. But then,

3. Whoever can be an evidence against the prisoner at the bar is ordered to come into court; and here it scarce ever fails but that evidences, of one nature and another, are brought in; though, I think, all of them altogether alien to the matter of indictment, for they none of them do respect witchcraft upon the bodies of the afflicted, which is the alone matter of charge in the indictment.

4. They are searched by a jury; and as to some of them, the jury brought in, that on such or such a place there was a preternatural excrescence. And I wonder what person there is, whether man or woman, of whom it cannot be said but that, in some part of their body or other, there is a preternatural excrescence. The term is a very general and inclusive term.

Ignorance of Human Nature

Some of the Salem gentlemen are very forward to censure and condemn the poor prisoner at the bar because he sheds no tears; but such betray great ignorance in the nature of passion, and as great heedlessness as to common passages of a man's life. Some there are who never shed tears; others there are that ordinarily shed tears upon light occasions, and yet for their lives cannot shed a tear when the deepest sorrow is upon their hearts. And who is there that knows not these things? Who knows not that an ecstasy of joy will sometimes fetch tears, when as the quite contrary passion will shut them close up? Why then should any be so silly and foolish as to take an argument from this appearance? But this is by the by. In short, the prisoner at the bar is indicted for sorcery and witchcraft acted upon the bodies of the afflicted. Now, for the proof of this, I reckon that the only pertinent evidences brought in are the evidences of the said afflicted.

It is true that over and above the evidences of the afflicted persons there are many evidences brought in against the prisoner at the bar; either that he was at a witch meeting; or that he performed things which could not be done by an ordinary natural power; or that she sold butter to a sailor, which, proving bad at sea, and the seamen exclaiming against her, she appeared, and soon after there was a storm, or the like. But what if there were ten thousand evidences of this nature; how do they prove the matter of indictment? And if they do not reach the matter of indictment, then I think it is clear that the prisoner at the bar is brought in guilty and condemned, merely from the evidences of the afflicted persons. . . .

I cannot but admire that the justices, whom I think to be well-meaning men, should so far give ear to the devil, as merely upon his authority to issue out their warrants and apprehend people. Liberty was evermore accounted the great privilege of an Englishman; but certainly, if the devil will be heard against us and his testimony taken, to the seizing and apprehending of us, our liberty vanishes, and we are fools if we boast of our liberty. Now, that the justices have thus far given ear to the devil, I think may be mathematically demonstrated to any man of common sense. And for the demonstration and proof hereof, I desire, only, that these two things may be duly considered, viz.:

1. That several persons have been apprehended purely upon the complaints of these afflicted, to whom the afflicted were perfect strangers, and had not the least knowledge of [them] imaginable, before they were apprehended.

2. That the afflicted do own and assert, and the justices do grant, that the devil does inform and tell the afflicted the names of those persons that are thus unknown unto them. Now these two things being duly considered, I think it will appear evident to anyone that the devil's information is the fundamental testimony that is gone upon in the apprehending of the aforesaid people.

If I believe such or such an assertion as comes immediately from the minister of God in the pulpit, because it is the Word of the everliving God, I build my faith on God's testimony; and if I practise upon it, this my practice is properly built on the Word of God; even so in the case before us.

If I believe the afflicted persons as informed by the devil, and act thereupon, this my act may properly be said to be grounded upon the testimony or information of the devil. And now, if things are thus, I think it ought to be for a lamentation to you and me, and all such as would be accounted good Christians.

If any should see the force of this argument, and upon it say (as I heard a wise and good judge once propose) that they know not but that God Almighty, or a good spirit, does give this information to these afflicted persons, I make answer thereto and say that it is most certain that it is neither Almighty God, nor

yet any good spirit, that gives this information; and my reason is good, because God is a God of truth, and the good spirits will not lie; whereas these informations have several times proved false, when the accused were brought before the afflicted.

For Further Reading

Paul S. Boyer and Stephen Nissenbaum, *Salem Possessed: The Social Origins of Witchcraft.* Cambridge, MA: Harvard University Press, 1974.

John Demos, *Entertaining Satan: Witchcraft and the Culture of Early New England.* New York: Oxford University Press, 1982.

Carol F. Karlsen, *The Devil in the Shape of a Woman.* New York: Norton, 1987.

Kenneth Silverman, *The Life and Times of Cotton Mather.* New York: Harper & Row, 1984.

Roger Thompson, ed., *The Witches of Salem: A Documentary Narrative.* London: The Folio Society, 1982.

VIEWPOINT 7A

The Great Awakening Is a Welcome Religious Revival (1743)

An Assembly of Pastors of Churches in New England

For several decades beginning in the 1720s a religious revival—the Great Awakening—swept the American colonies. Traveling preachers such as George Whitefield and Gilbert Tennent, as well as some Puritan preachers such as Jonathan Edwards, emphasized the importance of an emotional commitment to Christianity and stirred the religious passions of thousands. Flamboyant preaching, speaking in tongues, lively singing, and dramatic conversions were all part of the religious gatherings of the awakeners. The traveling evangelists often left in their wake divisions between new converts and those who looked upon the emotionalism of the phenomenon with suspicion. This was perhaps especially true in the New England colonies as people debated whether the religious movement helped the colonies live up to their Puritan heritage or represented a dangerous diversion. In the following viewpoint, a convention of New England ministers who met in July 1743 voice their support for the Great Awakening and the people affected by the religious revival. The ministers do caution against deviations from Puritan orthodoxy, including Antinomianism (the belief that grace and personal revelations from God supersede all divine and human laws), and Arminianism (the belief that,

From *The Testimony and Advice of an Assembly of Pastors of Churches in New England, at a Meeting in Boston, July 7, 1743, Occasioned by the Late Happy Revival of Religion in Many Parts of the Land.*

contrary to orthodox Calvinist teachings about predestination, humans can accept or reject salvation independent of God's will). In general, however, the ministers conclude that the revival and the somewhat unusual behaviors it has inspired are the work of God.

What positive aspects of the Great Awakening do the ministers describe? Judging from their listing of possible errors of the Great Awakening, how might their concerns over their position in the community as ministers have affected their views?

If it is the duty of every one capable of observation and reflection, to take a constant religious notice of what occurs in the daily course of common providence; how much more is it expected that those events in the divine economy, wherein there is a signal display of the power, grace and mercy of God in behalf of the church, should be observed with sacred wonder, pleasure, and gratitude! Nor should the people of God content themselves with a silent notice, but publish with the voice of thanksgiving, and tell of all his wondrous works.

A Revival of Religion

More particularly, when Christ is pleased to come into his church in a plentiful effusion of his Holy Spirit, by whose powerful influences the ministration of the word is attended with uncommon success, salvation-work carried on in an eminent manner, and his kingdom, which is within men, and consists in righteousness and peace and joy in the Holy Ghost, is notably advanced, this is an event which, above all others, invites the notice and bespeaks the praises of the Lord's people, and should be declared abroad for a memorial of the divine grace; as it tends to confirm the divinity of a despised gospel, and manifests the work of the Holy Spirit in the application of redemption, which too many are ready to reproach; as it may have a happy effect, by the divine blessing, for the revival of religion in other places, and the enlargement of the kingdom of Christ in the world; and as it tends to enliven the prayers, strengthen the faith, and raise the hopes, of such as are waiting for the kingdom of God, and the coming on of the glory of the latter days.

But if it is justly expected of all who profess themselves the disciples of Christ, that they should openly acknowledge and rejoice in a work of this nature, wherein the honor of their divine Master is so much concerned; how much more is it to be looked for from those who are employed in the ministry of the Lord Jesus, and so stand in a special relation to him, as servants of his household, and officers in his kingdom! These stand as watchmen upon the walls of Jerusalem; and it is their business not only to give the

alarm of war when the enemy is approaching, but to sound the trumpet of praise when the King of Zion cometh, in a meek triumph, having salvation.

For these and other reasons, we, whose names are hereunto annexed, pastors of churches in New England, met together in Boston, July 7, 1743, think it our indispensable duty, (without judging or censuring such of our brethren as cannot at present see things in the same light with us,) in this open and conjunct manner to declare, to the glory of sovereign grace, our full persuasion, either from what we have seen ourselves, or received upon credible testimony, that there has been a happy and remarkable revival of religion in many parts of this land, through an uncommon divine influence; after a long time of great decay and deadness, and a sensible and very awful withdraw of the Holy Spirit from his sanctuary among us.

Though the work of grace wrought on the hearts of men by the word and Spirit of God, and which has been more or less carried on in the church from the beginning, is always the same for substance, and agrees, at one time and another, in one place or person and another, as to the main strokes and lineaments of it, yet the present work appears to be remarkable and extraordinary,

Proof of God's Work

On account of the numbers wrought upon. We never before saw so many brought under soul concern, and with distress making the inquiry, What must we do to be saved? And these persons of all characters and ages. *With regard to the suddenness and quick progress of it.* Many persons and places were surprised with the gracious visit together, or near about the same time; and the heavenly influence diffused itself far and wide like the light of the morning. *Also in respect of the degree of operation,* both in a way of terror and in a way of consolation; attended in many with unusual bodily effects.

Not that all who are accounted the subjects of the present work, have had these extraordinary degrees of previous distress and subsequent joy. But many, and we suppose the greater number, have been wrought on in a more gentle and silent way, and without any other appearances than are common and usual at other times, when persons have been awakened to a solemn concern about salvation, and have been thought to have passed out of a state of nature into a state of grace.

As to those whose inward concern has occasioned extraordinary outward distresses, the most of them, when we came to converse with them, were able to give, what appeared to us, a rational account of what so affected their minds; viz., a quick sense of their guilt, misery, and danger; and they would often mention the passages in the sermons they heard, or particular texts of Scripture, which were set home upon them with such a powerful impression. And as to such whose joys have carried them into transports and extasies, they in like manner have accounted for them, from a lively sense of the danger they hoped they were freed from, and the happiness they were now possessed of; such clear views of divine and heavenly things, and particularly of the excellencies and loveliness of Jesus Christ, and such sweet tastes of redeeming love, as they never had before. The instances were very few in which we had reason to think these affections were produced by visionary or sensible representations, or by any other images than such as the Scripture itself presents unto us.

———— • ————

"There has been a happy and remarkable revival of religion in many parts of this land."

———— • ————

And here we think it not amiss to declare, that in dealing with these persons, we have been careful to inform them, that the nature of conversion does not consist in these passionate feelings; and to warn them not to look upon their state safe, because they have passed out of deep distress into high joys, unless they experience a renovation of nature, followed with a change of life, and a course of vital holiness. Nor have we gone into such an opinion of the bodily effects with which this work has been attended in some of its subjects, as to judge them any signs that persons who have been so affected, were then under a saving work of the Spirit of God. No; we never so much as called these bodily seisures, convictions; or spake of them as the immediate work of the Holy Spirit. Yet we do not think them inconsistent with a work of God upon the soul at that very time; but judge that those inward impressions which come from the Spirit of God, those terrors and consolations of which he is the author, may, according to the natural frame and constitution which some persons are of, occasion such bodily effects; and therefore that those extraordinary outward symptoms are not an argument that the work is delusive, or from the influence and agency of the evil spirit.

With respect to numbers of those who have been under the impressions of the present day, we must declare there is good ground to conclude they are become real Christians; the account they give of their conviction and consolation agreeing with the standard of the Holy Scriptures, corresponding with the experiences of the saints, and evidenced by the external fruits of holiness in their lives; so that they

appear to those who have the nearest access to them, as so many epistles of Christ, written, not with ink, but by the Spirit of the living God, attesting to the genuineness of the present operation, and representing the excellency of it.

Indeed, many, who appeared to be under convictions, and were much altered in their external behaviour when this work began, and while it was most flourishing, have lost their impressions, and are relapsed into their former manner of life. Yet of those who were judged hopefully converted, and made a public profession of religion, there have been fewer instances of scandal and apostasy than might be expected. So that, as far as we are able to form a judgment, the face of religion is lately changed much for the better in many of our towns and congregations; and together with a reformation observable in divers instances, there appears to be more experimental godliness and lively Christianity, than the most of us can remember we have ever seen before.

Thus we have freely declared our thoughts as to the work of God, so remarkably revived in many parts of this land. And now, we desire to bow the knee in thanksgiving to the God and Father of our Lord Jesus Christ, that our eyes have seen and our ears heard such things. And while these are our sentiments, we must necessarily be grieved at any accounts sent abroad, representing this work as all enthusiasm, delusion and disorder.

Warnings of Satan's Devices

Indeed, it is not to be denied, that in some places many irregularities and extravagances have been permitted to accompany it, which we would deeply lament and bewail before God, and look upon ourselves obliged, for the honor of the Holy Spirit, and of his blessed operations on the souls of men, to bear a public and faithful testimony against; though at the same time it is to be acknowledged with much thankfulness, that in other places, where the work has greatly flourished, there have been few, if any, of these disorders and excesses. But who can wonder, if at such a time as this, Satan should intermingle himself, to hinder and blemish a work so directly contrary to the interests of his own kingdom? Or if, while so much good seed is sowing, the enemy should be busy to sow tares? We would therefore, in the bowels of Jesus, beseech such as have been partakers of this work, or are zealous to promote it, that they be not ignorant of Satan's devices; that they watch and pray against errors and misconduct of every kind, lest they blemish and hinder that which they desire to honor and advance.
Particularly,
That they do not make secret impulses on their minds, without a due regard to the written word, the

rule of their duty: a very dangerous mistake, which, we apprehend, some in these times have gone into. That to avoid Arminianism, they do not verge to the opposite side of Antinomianism; while we would have others take good heed to themselves, lest they be by some led into, or fixed in, Arminian tenets, under the pretense of opposing Antinomian errors. That laymen do not invade the ministerial office, and, under a pretense of exhorting, set up preaching; which is very contrary to gospel order, and tends to introduce errors and confusion into the church. That ministers do not invade the province of others, and in ordinary cases preach in another's parish without his knowledge, and against his consent; nor encourage raw and indiscreet young candidates, in rushing into particular places, and preaching publicly or privately, as some have done, to the no small disrepute and damage of the work in places where it once promised to flourish. Though at the same time we would have ministers show their regard to the spiritual welfare of their people, by suffering them to partake of the gifts and graces of able, sound and zealous preachers of the word, as God in his providence may give opportunity therefor; being persuaded God has in this day remarkably blessed the labors of some of his servants who have travelled in preaching the gospel of Christ. That people beware of entertaining prejudices against their own pastors, and do not run into unscriptural separations. That they do not indulge a disputatious spirit, which has been attended with mischievous effects; nor discover a spirit of censoriousness, uncharitableness, and rash judging the state of others; than which scarce any thing has more blemished the work of God amongst us. And while we would meekly exhort both ministers and Christians, so far as is consistent with truth and holiness, to follow the things that make for peace; we would most earnestly warn all sorts of persons not to despise these outpourings of the Spirit, lest a holy God be provoked to withhold them, and instead thereof, to pour out upon this people the vials of his wrath, in temporal judgments and spiritual plagues; and would call upon every one to improve this remarkable season of grace, and put in for a share of the heavenly blessings so liberally dispensed.

Finally, we exhort the children of God to continue instant in prayer, that He with whom is the residue of the Spirit, would grant us fresh, more plentiful and extensive effusions, that so this wilderness, in all the parts of it, may become a fruitful field; that the present appearances may be an earnest of the glorious things promised to the church in the latter days; when she shall shine with the glory of the Lord arisen upon her, so as to dazzle the eyes of beholders, confound and put to shame all her enemies, rejoice the hearts of her solicitous and now saddened

friends, and have a strong influence and resplendency throughout the earth. Amen! Even so. Come, Lord Jesus; come quickly!

VIEWPOINT 7B

The Great Awakening Has Led to Harmful Religious Zealotry (1742)

Charles Chauncy (1705–1787)

The Great Awakening—the religious revival movement that swept the American colonies in the middle of the eighteenth century—often caused many divisions within communities and their churches. Congregations split between factions of the newly converted (the New Lights) and those who looked on the emotional displays of the Great Awakening with suspicion (the Old Lights). Revivalist preacher Gilbert Tennent called most practicing clergy "dead formalists" who were not true Christians. Some ministers responded by barring Tennent and other preachers from speaking in their churches, and accusing them of being charlatans, deceivers, or even workers of the devil. A prominent clerical critic of the Great Awakening was Charles Chauncy, a minister of the First Church in Boston. In the following viewpoint, taken from a sermon published in Boston in 1742, Chauncy describes the harms of religious "enthusiasm" engendered by the Great Awakening. Like many other detractors, Chauncy criticized the emotionalism and mysticism of the movement, which he felt displaced reason and learning.

How does Chauncy describe "enthusiasm" and contrast it with "the proper work of the Spirit"? The Great Awakening was noteworthy for increasing the involvement of women, slaves, and the poor in religion; some historians have argued that Chauncy's views reflect his class position as a conservative elite gentleman disturbed by the emotional displays of those lower in the social order. What, if anything, do you find in the viewpoint to support this interpretation?

I COR. XIV. xxxvii.

If any Man among you think himself to be a Prophet, or Spiritual, let him acknowledge that the Things that I write unto you are the Commandments of the Lord.

Many Things were amiss in the Church of Corinth, when Paul wrote this Epistle to them. There were envyings, strife and divi-

From *Enthusiasm Described and Caution'd Against* by Charles Chauncy (Boston, 1742).

sions among them, on account of their ministers. Some cried up one, others another: one said, I am of PAUL, another I am of APPOLLOS. They had form'd themselves into parties, and each party so admired the teacher they followed, as to reflect unjust contempt on the other.

Pride and Disorder

Nor was this their only fault. A spirit of pride prevailed exceedingly among them. They were conceited of their gifts, and too generally dispos'd to make an ostentatious shew of them. From this vain glorious temper proceeded the forwardness of those that had the gift of tongues, to speak in languages which others did not understand, to the disturbance, rather than edification of the church: And from the same principle it arose, that they spake not by turns, but several at once, in the same place of worship, to the introducing such confusion, that they were in danger of being tho't mad.

Nor were they without some pretence to justify these disorders. Their great plea was, that in these things they were guided by the Spirit, acted under his immediate influence and direction. This seems plainly insinuated in the words I have read to you. If any man think himself to be a prophet, or spiritual, let him acknowledge that the things that I write unto you are the commandments of the Lord. As if the apostle had said, you may imagine your selves to be spiritual men, to be under a divine afflatus in what you do; but 'tis all imagination, meer pretence, unless you pay a due regard to the commandments I have here wrote to you; receiving them not as the word of man, but of GOD. Make trial of your spiritual pretences by this rule: If you can submit to it, and will order your conduct by it, well; otherwise you only cheat yourselves, while you think yourselves to be spiritual men, or prophets: You are nothing better than Enthusiasts; your being acted by SPIRIT, immediately guided and influenced by him, is meer pretence; you have no good reason to believe any such thing.

From the words thus explained, I shall take occasion to discourse to you upon the following Particulars.

I. I shall give you some account of Enthusiasm, in its nature and influence.

II. Point you to a rule by which you may judge of persons, whether they are under the influence of Enthusiasm.

III. Say what may be proper to guard you against this unhappy turn of mind.

The whole will then be follow'd with some suitable Application.

I am in the first place, to give you some account of Enthusiasm. And as this a thing much talk'd of at present, more perhaps than at any other time that has pass'd over us, it will not be tho't unseasonable, if I take some pains to let you into a true understanding of it.

The word, from its Etymology, carries in it a good meaning, as signifying inspiration from GOD: in which sense, the prophets under the old testament, and the apostles under the new, might properly be called Enthusiasts. For they were under a divine influence, spake as moved by the HOLY GHOST, and did such things as can be accounted for in no way, but by recurring to an immediate extraordinary power, present with them.

The Bad Side of Enthusiasm

But the word is more commonly used in a bad sense, as intending an imaginary, not a real inspiration: according to which sense, the Enthusiast is one, who has a conceit of himself as a person favoured with the extraordinary presence of the Deity. He mistakes the workings of his own passions for divine communications, and fancies himself immediately inspired by the SPIRIT of GOD, when all the while, he is under no other influence than that of an over-heated imagination.

The cause of this enthusiasm is a bad temperament of the blood and spirits; 'tis properly a disease, a sort of madness: And there are few; perhaps none at all, but are subject to it, tho' none are so much in danger of it as those, in whom melancholy is the prevailing ingredient in their constitution. In these it often reigns; and sometimes to so great a degree, that they are really beside themselves, acting as truly by the blind impetus of a wild fancy, as tho' they had neither reason nor understanding.

And various are the ways in which their enthusiasm discovers itself.

Sometimes, it may be seen in their countenance. A certain wildness is discernable in their general look and air; especially when their imaginations are mov'd and fired.

Sometimes, it strangely loosens their tongues, and gives them such an energy, as well as fluency and volubility in speaking, as they themselves, by their utmost efforts, can't so much as imitate, when they are not under the enthusiastick influence.

Sometimes, it affects their bodies, throws them into convulsions and distortions, into quakings and tremblings. This was formerly common among the people called Quakers. I was myself, when a Lad, an eye witness to such violent agitations and foamings, in a boisterous female speaker, as I could not behold but with surprize and wonder.

Sometimes, it will unaccountably mix itself with their conduct, and give it such a tincture of that which is freakish or furious, as none can have an idea of, but those who have seen the behaviour of a person in a phrenzy.

Sometimes, it appears in their imaginary peculiar intimacy with heaven. They are, in their own opinion, the special favourites of GOD, have more familiar converse with him than other good men, and receive immediate, extraordinary communications from him. The tho'ts, which suddenly rise up in their minds, they take for suggestions of the SPIRIT; their very fancies are divine illuminations; nor are they strongly inclin'd to any thing, but 'tis an impulse from GOD, a plain revelation of his will.

And what extravagances, in this temper of mind, are they not capable of, and under the specious pretext too of paying obedience to the authority of GOD? Many have fancied themselves acting by immediate warrant from heaven, while they have been committing the most undoubted wickedness. There is indeed scarce any thing so wild, either in speculation or practice, but they have given into it: They have, in many instances, been blasphemers of GOD, and open disturbers of the peace of the world.

Against All Reason

But in nothing does the enthusiasm of these persons discover it self more, than in the disregard they express to the Dictates of reason. They are above the force of argument, beyond conviction from a calm and sober address to their understandings. As for them, they are distinguish'd persons; GOD himself speaks inwardly and immediately to their souls. "They see the light infused into their understandings, and cannot be mistaken; 'tis clear and visible there, like the light of bright sunshine; shews it self and needs no other proof but its own evidence. They feel the hand of GOD moving them within, and the impulses of his SPIRIT; and cannot be mistaken in what they feel. Thus they support themselves, and are sure reason hath nothing to do with what they see and feel. What they have a sensible experience of, admits no doubt, needs no probation." And in vain will you endeavour to convince such persons of any mistakes they are fallen into. They are certainly in the right, and know themselves to be so. They have the SPIRIT opening their understandings and revealing the truth to them. They believe only as he has taught them: and to suspect they are in the wrong is to do dishonour to the SPIRIT; 'tis to oppose his dictates, to set up their own wisdom in opposition to his, and shut their eyes against that light with which he has shined into their souls. They are not therefore capable of being argued with; you had as good reason with the wind. . . .

This is the nature of Enthusiasm, and this its operation, in a less or greater degree, in all who are under the influence of it. 'Tis a kind of religious Phrenzy, and evidently discovers it self to be so, whenever it rises to any great height.

And much to be pitied are the persons who are seized with it. Our compassion commonly works towards those, who, while under distraction, fondly imagine themselves to be Kings and Emperors: And the like pity is really due to those, who, under the power of enthusiasm, fancy themselves to be prophets; inspired of GOD, and immediately called and commissioned by him to deliver his messages to the world: And tho' they should run into disorders, and act in a manner that cannot but be condemned, they should notwithstanding be treated with tenderness and lenity; and the rather, because they don't commonly act so much under the influence of a bad mind, as a deluded imagination. And who more worthy of christian pity than those, who, under the notion of serving GOD and the interest of religion, are filled with zeal, and exert themselves to the utmost, while all the time they are hurting and wounding the very cause they take so much pains to advance. 'Tis really a pitiable case: And tho' the honesty of their intentions won't legitimate their bad actions, yet it very much alleviates their guilt: We should think as favourably of them as may be, and be dispos'd to judge with mercy, as we would hope to obtain mercy. . . .

Guarding Against Enthusiasm

But as the most suitable guard against the first tendencies towards enthusiasm, let me recommend to you the following words of counsel.

1. Get a true understanding of the proper work of the SPIRIT; and don't place it in those things wherein the gospel does not make it to consist. The work of the SPIRIT is different now from what it was in the first days of christianity. Men were then favored with the extraordinary presence of the SPIRIT. He came upon them in miraculous gifts and powers; as a spirit of prophecy, of knowledge, of revelation, of tongues, of miracles: But the SPIRIT is not now to be expected in these ways. His grand business lies in preparing men's minds for the grace of GOD, by true humiliation, from an apprehension of sin, and the necessity of a Saviour; then in working in them faith and repentance, and such a change as shall turn them from the power of sin and satan unto God; and in fine, by carrying on the good work he has begun in them; assisting them in duty, strengthening them against temptation, and in a word, preserving them blameless thro' faith unto salvation: And all this he does by the word and prayer, as the great means in the accomplishment of these purposes of mercy.

Herein, in general, consists the work of the SPIRIT. It does not lie in giving men private revelations, but in opening their minds to understand the publick ones contained in the scripture. It does not lie in sudden impulses and impressions, in immediate calls and extraordinary missions. Men mistake the business of the SPIRIT, if they understand by it such things as these. And 'tis, probably, from such unhappy mistakes, that they are at first betrayed into enthusiasm. Having a wrong notion of the work of the SPIRIT, 'tis no wonder if they take the uncommon sallies of their own minds for his influences.

You cannot, my brethren, be too well acquainted with what the bible makes the work of the HOLY GHOST, in the affair of salvation: And if you have upon your minds a clear and distinct understanding of this, it will be a powerful guard to you against all enthusiastical impressions.

———— • ————

"Many have fancied themselves acting by immediate warrant from heaven, while they have been committing the most undoubted wickedness."

———— • ————

2. Keep close to the scripture, and admit of nothing for an impression of the SPIRIT, but what agrees with that unerring rule. Fix it in your minds as a truth you will invariably abide by, that the bible is the grand test, by which every thing in religion is to be tried; and that you can, at no time, nor in any instance, be under the guidance of the SPIRIT of GOD, much less his extraordinary guidance, if what you are led to, is inconsistent with the things there revealed, either in point of faith or practice. And let it be your care to compare the motions of your minds, and the workings of your imaginations and passions, with the rule of GOD's word. And see to it, that you be impartial in this matter: Don't make the rule bend to your pre-conceiv'd notions and inclinations; but repair to the bible, with a mind dispos'd, as much as may be, to know the truth as it lies nakedly and plainly in the scripture it self. And whatever you are moved to, reject the motion, esteem it as nothing more than a vain fancy, if it puts you upon any method of thinking, or acting, that can't be evidently reconcil'd with the revelations of GOD in his word.

This adherence to the bible, my brethren is one of the best preservatives against enthusiasm. If you will but express a due reverence to this book of GOD, making it the great rule of judgment, even in respect of the SPIRIT's influences and operations, you will not be in much danger of being led into delusion. Let that be your inquiry under all suppos'd impulses from the SPIRIT, What saith the scripture? To the law, and to the testimony: If your impressions, and imagined spiritual motions agree not therewith, 'tis because there is no hand of the SPIRIT of GOD in

them: They are only the workings of your own imaginations, or something worse; and must at once, without any more ado, be rejected as such.

Make Use of Reason

3. Make use of the Reason and Understanding GOD has given you. This may be tho't an ill-advis'd direction, but 'tis as necessary as either of the former. Next to the scripture, there is no greater enemy to enthusiasm, than reason. 'Tis indeed impossible a man shou'd be an enthusiast, who is in the just exercise of his understanding; and 'tis because men don't pay a due regard to the sober dictates of a well inform'd mind, that they are led aside by the delusions of a vain imagination. Be advised then to shew yourselves men, to make use of your reasonable powers; and not act as the horse or mule, as tho' you had no understanding.

'Tis true, you must not go about to set up your own reason in opposition to revelation: Nor may you entertain a tho't of making reason your rule instead of scripture. The bible, as I said before, is the great rule of religion, the grand test in matters of salvation: But then you must use your reason in order to understand the bible: Nor is there any other possible way, in which, as a reasonable creature, you shou'd come to an understanding of it. . . .

4. You must not lay too great stress upon the workings of your passions and affections. These will be excited, in a less or greater degree, in the business of religion: And 'tis proper they shou'd. The passions, when suitably mov'd, tend mightily to awaken the reasonable powers, and put them upon a lively and vigorous exercise. And this is their proper use: And when address'd to, and excited to this purpose, they may be of good service: whereas we shall mistake the right use of the passions, if we place our religion only or chiefly, in the heat and fervour of them. The soul is the man: And unless the reasonable nature is suitably wro't upon, the understanding enlightned, the judgment convinc'd, the will perswaded, and the mind intirely chang'd, it will avail but to little purpose; tho' the passions shou'd be set all in a blaze. This therefore you shou'd be most concern'd about. And if while you are sollicitous that you may be in transports of affection, you neglect your more noble part, your reason and judgment, you will be in great danger of being carried away by your imaginations. This indeed leads directly to Enthusiasm: And you will in vain, endeavour to preserve yourselves from the influence of it, if you a'nt duly careful to keep your passions in their proper place, under the government of a well inform'd understanding. While the passions are uppermost, and bear the chief sway over a man, he is in an unsafe state: None knows what he may be bro't to. You can't therefore be too careful to

keep your passions under the regimen of a sober judgment. 'Tis indeed a matter of necessity, as you would not be led aside by delusion and fancy. . . .

Real, Sober Religion

There is such a thing as real religion, let the conduct of men be what it will; and 'tis, in its nature, a sober, calm, reasonable thing: Nor is it an objection of any weight against the sobriety or reasonableness of it, that there have been enthusiasts, who have acted as tho' it was a wild, imaginary business. We should not make our estimate of religion as exhibited in the behaviour of men of a fanciful mind; to be sure, we should not take up an ill opinion of it, because in the example they give of it, it don't appear so amiable as we might expect. This is unfair. We shou'd rather judge of it from the conduct of men of a sound judgment; whose lives have been such a uniform, beautiful transcript of that which is just and good, that we can't but think well of religion, as display'd in their example.

For Further Reading

J.M. Bumstead, ed., *The Great Awakening: The Beginnings of Evangelical Pietism in America*. Waltham, MA: Blaisdell Publishing, 1970.

Edwin Scott Gaustad, *The Great Awakening in New England*. Chicago: Quadrangle, 1968.

Edward M. Griffin, *Old Brick: Charles Chauncy of Boston, 1705–1787*. Minneapolis: University of Minnesota Press, 1980.

Alan Heimert and Perry Miller, eds., *The Great Awakening*. Indianapolis: Bobbs-Merrill, 1967.

Henry F. May, *The Enlightenment in America*. New York: Oxford University Press, 1915.

Labor and Land in Colonial America

VIEWPOINT 8A

Poor Europeans Should Come to America as Indentured Servants (1666)

George Alsop (dates unknown)

A significant problem facing Virginia, Maryland, and other American colonies in the 1600s and 1700s was a shortage of labor. One answer devised by the Virginia Company in the late 1610s was indentured servitude, a system by which impoverished people in England and other countries agreed to bind themselves for a fixed period of labor in exchange for passage to America. The exact contractual agreements and conditions of service varied depending on the master, the colony, and the time period. However, servants were often treated harshly and many died before their term of service was over. The lot of those who survived their terms of service also varied. In the 1600s Maryland law entitled ex-servants the right to claim fifty acres of land (if they could afford to have the land surveyed), and many did become landowners. Virginia law only required ex-servants receive a new suit of clothes and a year's supply of corn; many servants there became destitute laborers.

The following viewpoint is taken from a 1666 pamphlet that was published in England, undoubtedly in part to encourage people to settle in America as indentured servants. The author, George Alsop, who was an indentured servant himself in Maryland for four years, describes the positive benefits of his experiences in America.

How does Alsop justify the idea of servitude? How has indentured servitude improved his own life? The viewpoint is excerpted from a pamphlet dedicated to Lord Baltimore, the founder and proprietor of the colony of Maryland; how might that have affected its message?

From *A Character of the Province of Mary-Land* by George Alsop (London, 1666), as reprinted in *Narratives of Early Maryland*, edited by Clayton Colman Hall (New York: Scribner, 1910).

As there can be no Monarchy without the Supremacy of a King and Crown, nor no King without Subjects, nor any Parents without it be by the fruitful off-spring of Children; neither can there be any Masters, unless it be by the inferior Servitude of those that dwell under them, by a commanding enjoyment: And since it is ordained from the original and superabounding wisdom of all things, That there should be Degrees and Diversities amongst the Sons of men, in acknowledging of a Superiority from Inferiors to Superiors; the Servant with a reverent and befitting Obedience is as liable to this duty in a measurable performance to him whom he serves, as the loyalest of Subjects to his Prince. Then since it is a common and ordained Fate, that there must be Servants as well as Masters, and that good Servitudes are those Colledges of Sobriety that checks in the giddy and wild-headed youth from his profuse and uneven course of life, by a limited constrainment, as well as it otherwise agrees with the moderate and discreet Servant: Why should there be such an exclusive Obstacle in the minds and unreasonable dispositions of many people, against the limited time of convenient and necessary Servitude, when it is a thing so requisite, that the best of Kingdoms would be unhing'd from their quiet and well setled Government without it. . . .

There is no truer Emblem of Confusion either in

Monarchy or Domestick Governments, then when either the Subject, or the Servant, strives for the upper hand of his Prince, or Master, and to be equal with him, from whom he receives his present subsistance: Why then, if Servitude be so necessary that no place can be governed in order, nor people live without it, this may serve to tell those which prick up their ears and bray against it, That they are none but Asses, and deserve the Bridle of a strict commanding power to reine them in: For I'me certainly confident, that there are several Thousands in most Kingdoms of Christendom, that could not at all live and subsist, unless they had served some prefixed time, to learn either some Trade, Art, or Science, and by either of them to extract their present livelihood.

———— • ————

"The Servants of this Province . . . live well in the time of their Service, and by their restrainment in that time, they are made capable of living much better when they come to be free."

———— • ————

Then methinks this may stop the mouths of those that will undiscreetly compassionate them that dwell under necessary Servitudes; for let but Parents of an indifferent capacity in Estates, when their Childrens age by computation speak them seventeen or eighteen years old, turn them loose to the wide world, without a seven years working Apprenticeship (being just brought up to the bare formality of a little reading and writing) and you shall immediately see how weak and shiftless they'le be towards the maintaining and supporting of themselves; and (without either stealing or begging) their bodies like a Sentinel must continually wait to see when their Souls will be frighted away by the pale Ghost of a starving want.

Then let such, where Providence hath ordained to live as Servants, either in England or beyond Sea, endure the prefixed yoak of their limited time with patience, and then in a small computation of years, by an industrious endeavour, they may become Masters and Mistresses of Families themselves. And let this be spoke to the deserved praise of Mary-Land, That the four years I served there were not to me so slavish, as a two years Servitude of a Handicraft Apprenticeship was here in London; *Volenti enim nil difficile* [Nothing is difficult to the willing]: Not that I write this to seduce or delude any, or to draw them from their native soyle, but out of a love to my Countrymen, whom in the general I wish well to. . . .

They whose abilities cannot extend to purchase their own transportation over into Mary-Land, (and

surely he that cannot command so small a sum for so great a matter, his life must needs be mighty low and dejected) I say they may for the debarment of a four years sordid liberty, go over into this Province and there live plentiously well. And what's a four years Servitude to advantage a man all the remainder of his dayes, making his predecessors happy in his sufficient abilities, which he attained to partly by the restrainment of so small a time?

Now those that commit themselves unto the care of the Merchant to carry them over, they need not trouble themselves with any inquisitive search touching their Voyage; for there is such an honest care and provision made for them all the time they remain aboard the Ship, and are sailing over, that they want for nothing that is necessary and convenient.

The Merchant commonly before they go aboard the Ship, or set themselves in any forwardness for their Voyage, has Conditions of Agreements drawn between him and those that by a voluntary consent become his Servants, to serve him, his Heirs or Assigns, according as they in their primitive acquaintance have made their bargain, some two, some three, some four years; and whatever the Master or Servant tyes himself up to here in England by Condition, the Laws of the Province will force a performance of when they come there: Yet here is this Priviledge in it when they arrive, If they dwell not with the Merchant they made their first agreement withall, they may choose whom they will serve their prefixed time with; and after their curiosity has pitcht on one whom they think fit for their turn, and that they may live well withall, the Merchant makes an Assignment of the Indenture over to him whom they of their free will have chosen to be their Master, in the same nature as we here in England (and no otherwise) turn over Covenant Servants or Apprentices from one Master to another. Then let those whose chaps are always breathing forth those filthy dregs of abusive exclamations, which are Lymbeckt from their sottish and preposterous brains, against this Country of Mary-Land, saying, That those which are transported over thither, are sold in open Market for Slaves, and draw in Carts like Horses; which is so damnable an untruth, that if they should search to the very Center of Hell, and enquire for a Lye of the most antient and damned stamp, I confidently believe they could not find one to parallel this: For know, That the Servants here in Mary-Land of all Colonies, distant or remote Plantations, have the least cause to complain, either for strictness of Servitude, want of Provisions, or need of Apparel: Five days and a half in the Summer weeks is the alotted time that they work in; and for two months, when the Sun predominates in the highest pitch of his heat, they claim an antient and customary Priviledge, to repose themselves three hours in the day within the house, and this is undeniably granted to them that work in the Fields.

In the Winter time, which lasteth three months (*viz.*) December, January, and February, they do little or no work or imployment, save cutting of wood to make good fires to sit by, unless their Ingenuity will prompt them to hunt the Deer, or Bear, or recreate themselves in Fowling, to slaughter the Swans, Geese, and Turkeys (which this Country affords in a most plentiful manner:) For every Servant has a Gun, Powder and Shot allowed him, to sport him withall on all Holidayes and leasurable times, if he be capable of using it, or be willing to learn.

Rewards of Mary-Land Servitude

Now those Servants which come over into this Province, being Artificers, they never (during their Servitude) work in the Fields, or do any other imployment save that which their Handicraft and Mechanick endeavours are capable of putting them upon, and are esteem'd as well by their Masters, as those that imploy them, above measure. He that's a Tradesman here in Mary-Land (though a Servant), lives as well as most common Handicrafts do in London, though they may want something of that Liberty which Freemen have, to go and come at their pleasure; yet if it were rightly understood and considered, what most of the Liberties of the several poor Tradesmen are taken up about, and what a care and trouble attends that thing they call Liberty, which according to the common translation is but Idleness, and (if weighed in the Ballance of a just Reason) will be found to be much heavier and cloggy then the four years restrainment of a Mary-Land Servitude. He that lives in the nature of a Servant in this Province, must serve but four years by the Custom of the Country; and when the expiration of his time speaks him a Freeman, there's a Law in the Province, that enjoyns his Master whom he hath served to give him Fifty Acres of Land, Corn to serve him a whole year, three Sutes of Apparel, with things necessary to them, and Tools to work withall; so that they are no sooner free, but they are ready to set up for themselves, and when once entred, they live passingly well.

The Women that go over into this Province as Servants, have the best luck here as in any place of the world besides; for they are no sooner on shoar, but they are courted into a Copulative Matrimony, which some of them (for aught I know) had they not come to such a Market with their Virginity, might have kept it by them untill it had been mouldy, unless they had let it out by a yearly rent to some of the Inhabitants of Lewknors-lane [a disreputable London district], or made a Deed of Gift of it to Mother Coney,

having only a poor stipend out of it, untill the Gallows or Hospital called them away. Men have not altogether so good luck as Women in this kind, or natural preferment, without they be good Rhetoricians, and well vers'd in the Art of perswasion, then (probably) they may ryvet themselves in the time of their Servitude into the private and reserved favour of their Mistress, if Age speak their Master deficient.

In short, touching the Servants of this Province, they live well in the time of their Service, and by their restrainment in that time, they are made capable of living much better when they come to be free; which in several other parts of the world I have observed, That after some servants have brought their indented and limited time to a just and legal period by Servitude, they have been much more incapable of supporting themselves from sinking into the Gulf of a slavish, poor, fettered, and intangled life, then all the fastness of their prefixed time did involve them in before.

VIEWPOINT 8B

Poor Europeans Should Not Come to America as Indentured Servants (1754)

Gottlieb Mittelberger (dates unknown)

Many of the people who migrated to the American colonies were indentured servants—people who paid for their passage by pledging themselves to be servants for a set period of time. The following viewpoint is taken from an account by Gottlieb Mittelberger, a German schoolmaster and organist who lived in America as an indentured servant from 1750 to 1754. His account describes the hardships facing servants like himself, and concludes by discouraging people from traveling to America.

Mittelberger's depiction of the indentured servant's life is much more negative than the portrayal by George Alsop (see viewpoint 8A). The differences between the two viewpoints are in part reflective of differing times and circumstances. Alsop's account was written a century earlier at a time most indentured servants came from England and settled in the Chesapeake colonies of Virginia and Maryland. In the eighteenth century the majority of servants came from non-English ethnic backgrounds, including German, Dutch, and Scotch-Irish, and most landed in the Pennsylvania and other neighboring colonies. Many, called "redemptioners," were at the mercy of the sea captains who paid for their passage to Amer-

From *Journey to Pennsylvania in the Year 1750 and Return to Germany in the Year 1754* by Gottlieb Mittelberger, trans. by Carl Theo. Eben (Philadelphia: John Joseph McVey, 1898).

ica and who sold them as servants to the highest bidder at the port of arrival. Despite the conditions described by Mittelberger, many indentured servants chose to go to America; many eventually established themselves as successful independent farmers.

How do the conditions described by Mittelberger differ from those depicted by George Alsop, author of the opposing viewpoint? What are some aspects of American life that Mittelberger finds objectionable?

———————

Both in Rotterdam and in Amsterdam the people are packed densely, like herrings so to say, in the large sea vessels. One person receives a place of scarcely 2 feet width and 6 feet length in the bedstead, while many a ship carries four to six hundred souls, not to mention the innumerable implements, tools, provisions, water-barrels and other things which likewise occupy much space.

On account of contrary winds it takes the ships sometimes 2, 3 and 4 weeks to make the trip from Holland to Kaupp [Cowes] in England. But when the wind is good, they get there in 8 days or even sooner. Everything is examined there and the custom-duties paid, whence it comes that the ships ride there 8, 10 to 14 days and even longer at anchor, till they have taken in their full cargoes. During that time every one is compelled to spend his last remaining money and to consume his little stock of provisions which had been reserved for the sea; so that most passengers, finding themselves on the ocean where they would be in greater need of them, must greatly suffer from hunger and want. Many suffer want already on the water between Holland and Old England.

The Long Voyage

When the ships have for the last time weighed their anchors near the city of Kaupp in Old England, the real misery begins with the long voyage. For from there the ships, unless they have good wind, must often sail 8, 9, 10 to 12 weeks before they reach Philadelphia. But even with the best wind the voyage lasts 7 weeks.

But during the voyage there is on board these ships terrible misery, stench, fumes, horror, vomiting, many kinds of sea-sickness, fever, dysentery, headache, heat, constipation, boils, scurvy, cancer, mouth-rot, and the like, all of which come from old and sharply salted food and meat, also from very bad and foul water, so that many die miserably.

Add to this want of provisions, hunger, thirst, frost, heat, dampness, anxiety, want, afflictions and lamentations, together with other trouble, as . . . the lice abound so frightfully, especially on sick people, that they can be scraped off the body. The misery reaches the climax when a gale rages for 2 or 3 nights and days, so that every one believes that the ship will go to the bottom with all human beings on board. In such a visitation the people cry and pray most piteously.

When in such a gale the sea rages and surges, so that the waves rise often like high mountains one above the other, and often tumble over the ship, so that one fears to go down with the ship; when the ship is constantly tossed from side to side by the storm and waves, so that no one can either walk, or sit, or lie, and the closely packed people in the berths are thereby tumbled over each other, both the sick and the well—it will be readily understood that many of these people, none of whom had been prepared for hardships, suffer so terribly from them that they do not survive it. . . .

Among the healthy, impatience sometimes grows so great and cruel that one curses the other, or himself and the day of his birth, and sometimes come near killing each other. Misery and malice join each other, so that they cheat and rob one another. One always reproaches the other with having persuaded him to undertake the journey. Frequently children cry out against their parents, husbands against their wives and wives against their husbands, brothers and sisters, friends and acquaintances against each other. But most against the soul-traffickers.

Many sigh and cry: "Oh, that I were at home again, and if I had to lie in my pig-sty!" Or they say: "O God, if I only had a piece of good bread, or a good fresh drop of water." Many people whimper, sigh and cry piteously for their homes; most of them get home-sick. Many hundred people necessarily die and perish in such misery, and must be cast into the sea, which drives their relatives, or those who persuaded them to undertake the journey, to such despair that it is almost impossible to pacify and console them. . . .

No one can have an idea of the sufferings which women in confinement have to bear with their innocent children on board these ships. Few of this class escape with their lives; many a mother is cast into the water with her child as soon as she is dead. One day, just as we had a heavy gale, a woman in our ship, who was to give birth and could not give birth under the circumstances, was pushed through a loop-hole [porthole] in the ship and dropped into the sea, because she was far in the rear of the ship and could not be brought forward.

Children from 1 to 7 years rarely survive the voyage. I witnessed . . . misery in no less than 32 children in our ship, all of whom were thrown into the sea. The parents grieve all the more since their children find no resting-place in the earth, but are devoured by the monsters of the sea. . . .

That most of the people get sick is not surprising, because, in addition to all other trials and hardships, warm food is served only three times a week, the rations being very poor and very little. Such meals can hardly be eaten, on account of being so unclean. The water which is served out on the ships is often very black, thick and full of worms, so that one cannot drink it without loathing, even with the greatest thirst. Toward the end we were compelled to eat the ship's biscuit which had been spoiled long ago; though in a whole biscuit there was scarcely a piece the size of a dollar that had not been full of red worms and spiders' nests. . . .

Arrival in America

At length, when, after a long and tedious voyage, the ships come in sight of land, so that the promontories can be seen, which the people were so eager and anxious to see, all creep from below on deck to see the land from afar, and they weep for joy, and pray and sing, thanking and praising God. The sight of the land makes the people on board the ship, especially the sick and the half dead, alive again, so that their hearts leap within them; they shout and rejoice, and are content to bear their misery in patience, in the hope that they may soon reach the land in safety. But alas!

———— • ————

"Who therefore wishes to earn his bread in a Christian and honest way, . . . let him do so in his own country and not in America; for he will not fare better in America."

———— • ————

When the ships have landed at Philadelphia after their long voyage, no one is permitted to leave them except those who pay for their passage or can give good security; the others, who cannot pay, must remain on board the ships till they are purchased, and are released from the ships by their purchasers. The sick always fare the worst, for the healthy are naturally preferred and purchased first; and so the sick and wretched must often remain on board in front of the city for 2 or 3 weeks, and frequently die, whereas many a one, if he could pay his debt and were permitted to leave the ship immediately, might recover and remain alive. . . .

The sale of human beings in the market on board the ship is carried on thus: Every day Englishmen, Dutchmen, and High-German people come from the city of Philadelphia and other places, in part from a great distance, say 20, 30, or 40 hours away, and go on board the newly arrived ship that has

brought and offers for sale passengers from Europe, and select among the healthy persons such as they deem suitable for their business, and bargain with them how long they will serve for their passage money, which most of them are still in debt for. When they have come to an agreement, it happens that adult persons bind themselves in writing to serve 3, 4, 5, or 6 years for the amount due by them, according to their age and strength. But very young people, from 10 to 15 years, must serve till they are 21 years old.

Many parents must sell and trade away their children like so many head of cattle; for if their children take the debt upon themselves, the parents can leave the ship free and unrestrained; but as the parents often do not know where and to what people their children are going, it often happens that such parents and children, after leaving the ship, do not see each other again for many years, perhaps no more in all their lives. . . .

Separation of Families

It often happens that whole families, husband, wife, and children, are separated by being sold to different purchasers, especially when they have not paid any part of their passage money.

When a husband or wife has died at sea, when the ship has made more than half of her trip, the survivor must pay or serve not only for himself or herself, but also for the deceased.

When both parents have died over half-way at sea, their children, especially when they are young and have nothing to pawn or to pay, must stand for their own and their parents' passage, and serve till they are 21 years old. When one has served his or her term, he or she is entitled to a new suit of clothes at parting; and if it has been so stipulated, a man gets in addition a horse, a woman, a cow.

When a serf has an opportunity to marry in this country, he or she must pay for each year which he or she would have yet to serve, 5 to 6 pounds. But many a one who has thus purchased and paid for his bride, has subsequently repented his bargain, so that he would gladly have returned his exorbitantly dear ware, and lost the money besides.

If some one in this country runs away from his master, who has treated him harshly, he cannot get far. Good provision has been made for such cases, so that a runaway is soon recovered. He who detains or returns a deserter receives a good reward.

If such a runaway has been away from his master one day, he must serve for it as a punishment a week, for a week a month, and for a month half a year. But if the master will not keep the runaway after he has got him back, he may sell him for so many years as he would have to serve him yet.

Hard Work

Work and labor in this new and wild land are very hard and manifold, and many a one who came there in his old age must work very hard to his end for his bread. I will not speak of young people. Work mostly consists in cutting wood, felling oak-trees, rooting out, or as they say there, clearing large tracts of forest. Such forests, being cleared, are then laid out for fields and meadows. From the best hewn wood, fences are made around the new fields; for there all meadows, orchards and fruit-fields are surrounded and fenced in with planks made of thickly-split wood, laid one above the other, as in zigzag lines, and within such enclosures, horses, cattle, and sheep are permitted to graze. Our Europeans, who are purchased, must always work hard, for new fields are constantly laid out; and so they learn that stumps of oak-trees are in America certainly as hard as in Germany. In this hot land they fully experience in their own persons what God has imposed on man for his sin and disobedience: for in Genesis we read the words: In the sweat of thy brow shalt thou eat bread. Who therefore wishes to earn his bread in a Christian and honest way, and cannot earn it in his fatherland otherwise than by the work of his hands, let him do so in his own country and not in America; for he will not fare better in America. However hard he may be compelled to work in his fatherland, he will surely find it quite as hard, if not harder, in the new country. Besides, there is not only the long and arduous journey lasting half a year, during which he has to suffer, more than with the hardest work; he has also spent about 200 florins which no one will refund to him. If he has so much money, it will slip out of his hands; if he has it not, he must work his debt off as a slave and poor serf. Therefore let every one stay in his own country and support himself and his family honestly. Besides I say that those who suffer themselves to be persuaded and enticed away by the man-thieves, are very foolish if they believe that roasted pigeons will fly into their mouths in America or Pennsylvania without their working for them.

For Further Reading

Clifford L. Alderman, *Colonists for Sale: The Story of Indentured Servants in America.* New York: Macmillan, 1975.

Bernard Bailyn, *The Peopling of British North America: An Introduction.* New York: Knopf, 1986.

David Galenson, *White Servitude in Colonial America: An Economic Analysis.* New York: Cambridge University Press, 1981.

Gloria L. Main, *Tobacco Colony: Life in Early Maryland, 1650–1720.* Princeton, NJ: Princeton University Press, 1982.

Sharon V. Salinger, *"To Serve Thee Well and Faithfully": Labor and Indentured Servants in Pennsylvania, 1682–1800.* New York: Cambridge University Press, 1987.

VIEWPOINT 9A

Bacon's Rebellion Is a Justified Revolution (1676)

Nathaniel Bacon (1647–1676)

Nathaniel Bacon was the leader of Bacon's Rebellion. The 1676 Virginia uprising was the earliest major popular rebellion against British colonial rule in America, and the events and issues surrounding it tell much of divisions between Virginia's upper and lower classes, Indian-white relations, and the eventual entrenchment of slavery in Virginia and other American colonies.

The son of a nobleman and graduate of Cambridge University in England, Bacon emigrated to Virginia in 1674, and established a plantation on the western frontier of the colony. He found the colony deeply divided. The colonists in the western region consisted largely of former indentured servants with little land struggling to make a living. The Virginians of the eastern (Tidewater) region were the established tobacco planters and merchants who had evolved into an aristocratic class that dominated the ownership of productive land, the tobacco trade, and the colonial government. Elections were seldom held, and in 1670 the vote was restricted to landowners.

A particular bone of contention between the two regions was Indian policy. In 1675 a combination of western colonists' desire for Indian land and revenge for some Indian attacks led many of them to call for open warfare against Indians in their midst. Colonial governor William Berkeley and his allies in government, who had established friendly relations (and a profitable fur trade) with some of the frontier Indians, opposed war, and suggested instead an expensive system of frontier forts, to be paid for by increased taxation. Defying Berkeley's orders against retaliatory action, several hundred western settlers in 1676 elected Bacon to lead them on a punitive expedition against the Indians. Berkeley responded to the unauthorized campaign by calling for new elections to the House of Burgesses (Virginia's legislative assembly), and by declaring Bacon a rebel. In July, Bacon and his followers turned from attacking Indians to attacking the Virginia capital of Jamestown. Bacon's forces forced Berkeley to flee, plundered the estates of Berkeley and his followers, and burned Jamestown in September. The rebellion collapsed shortly after Bacon's sudden death from natural causes in October.

The following viewpoint is taken from Bacon's "Manifesto concerning the Present Troubles in Vir-

From "Manifesto Concerning the Troubles in Virginia" by Nathaniel Bacon, *Virginia Magazine of History and Biography*, vol. 1 (1894).

ginia," which he proclaimed on July 30, 1676. Bacon lists grievances held against the leadership of Governor Berkeley and defends his own actions. Historians have debated how much Bacon actually represented "the people," and whether he was a leader of a political rebellion that was a true precursor to the American Revolution, or simply a political opportunist whose followers were mainly interested in looting plantations and killing Indians for their land.

What are Bacon's complaints against Governor Berkeley? How important were Berkeley's policies on Indians in causing the rebellion, according to Bacon? Does the Manifesto provide evidence for or against the proposition that Bacon was a democratic revolutionary?

———————

If vertue be a sin, if Piety be giult, all the Principles of morality goodness and Justice be perverted, Wee must confesse That those who are now called Rebells may be in danger of those high imputations, Those loud and severall Bulls would affright Innocents and render the defence of our Brethren and the enquiry into our sad and heavy oppressions, Treason. But if there bee as sure there is, a just God to appeal too, if Religion and Justice be a sanctuary here, If to plead ye cause of the oppressed, If sincerely to aime at his Majesties Honour and the Publick good without any reservation or by Interest, If to stand in the Gap after soe much blood of our dear Brethren bought and sold, If after the losse of a great part of his Majesties Colony deserted and dispeopled, freely with our lives and estates to indeavor to save the remaynders bee Treason God Almighty Judge and lett guilty dye, But since wee cannot in our hearts find one single spott of Rebellion or Treason or that wee have in any manner aimed at the subverting ye setled Government or attempting of the Person of any either magistrate or private man not with standing the severall Reproaches and Threats of some who for sinister ends were disaffected to us and censured our ino[cent] and honest designes, and since all people in all places where wee have yet bin can attest our civill quiet peaseable behaviour farre different from that of Rebellion and tumultuous persons let Trueth be bold and all the world know the real Foundations of pretended giult, Wee appeale to the Country itselfe what and of what nature their Oppressions have bin or by what Caball and mistery the designes of many of those whom wee call great men have bin transacted and caryed on, but let us trace these men in Authority and Favour to whose hands the dispensation of the Countries wealth has been commited; let us observe the sudden Rise of their Estates composed with the Quality in which they first entered this Country Or the Reputation they have held here amongst wise and discerning men, And lett us see wither their extractions and Education have not bin vile, And by what pretence of learning and vertue they could soe soon [come] into Imployments of so great Trust and consequence, let us consider their sudden advancement and let us also consider wither any Publick work for our safety and defence or for the Advancement and propogation of Trade, liberall Arts or sciences is here Extant in any [way] adaquate to our vast chardg, now let us compare these things togit[her] and see what spounges have suckt up the Publique Treasure and wither it hath not bin privately contrived away by unworthy Favourites and juggling Parasites whose tottering Fortunes have bin repaired and supported at the Publique chardg, now if it be so Judg what greater giult can bee then to offer to pry into these and to unriddle the misterious wiles of a powerful Cabal let all people Judge what can be of more dangerous Import then to suspect the soe long Safe proceedings of Some of our Grandees and wither People may with safety open their Eyes in soe nice a Concerne.

Concerns About Indians

Another main article of our Giult is our open and manifest aversion of all, not onely the Foreign but the protected and Darling Indians, this wee are informed is Rebellion of a deep dye For that both the Governour and Councell are by Colonell Coales Assertion bound to defend the [Indian] Queen and the Appamatocks with their blood. Now whereas we doe declare and can prove that they have bin for these Many years enemies to the King and Country, Robbers and Theeves and Invaders of his Majesties Right and our Interest and Estates, but yet have by persons in Authority bin defended and protected even against His Majesties loyall Subjects and that in soe high a Nature that even the Complaints and oaths of his Majesties Most loyall Subjects in a lawfull Manner proffered by them afainst those barborous Outlaws have bin by ye right honourable Governour rejected and ye Delinquents from his presence dismissed not only with pardon and indemnitye but with all incouragement and favour, Their Fire Arms soe destructfull to us and by our lawes prohibited, Commanded to be restored them, and open Declaration before Witness made That they must have Ammunition although directly contrary to our law, Now what greater giult can be then to oppose and indeavour the destruction of these Honest quiet neighbours of ours. . . .

Another Article of our Giult is To Assert all those neighbour Indians as well as others to be outlawed, wholly unqualifyed for the benefitt and Protection of the law, For that the law does reciprocally protect and punish, and that all people offending must either in person or Estate make equivalent satisfaction or Restitution according to the manner and merit of ye Offences Debts or Trespasses; Now since the Indians cannot according to the tenure and forme of any law to us known be prosecuted, Seised or Complained against, Their Persons being difficulty distinguished or known, Their many nations languages, and their subterfuges such as makes them incapeable to make us Restitution or satisfaction would it not be very giulty to say They have bin unjustly defended and protected these many years.

If it should be said that the very foundation of all these disasters the Grant of the Beaver trade to the Right Honourable Governour was illegall and not granteable by any power here present as being a monopoly, were not this to deserve the name of Rebell and Traytor.

Judge therefore all wise and unprejudiced men who may or can faithfully or truely with an honest heart attempt ye country's good, their vindication and libertie without the aspersion of Traitor and Rebell, since as soe doing they must of necessity gall such tender and dear concernes, But to manifest Sincerity and loyalty to the World, and how much wee abhorre those bitter names, may all the world know that we doe unanimously desire to represent our sad and heavy grievances to his most sacred Majestie as our Refuge and Sanctuary, where wee doe well know that all our Causes will be impartially heard and Equall Justice administered to all men.

The Declaration of the People

For having upon specious pretences of Publick works raised unjust Taxes upon the Commonalty for the advancement of private Favours and other sinister ends but noe visible effects in any measure adequate.

For not having dureing the long time of his Government in any measure advanced this hopefull Colony either by Fortification, Townes or Trade.

For having abused and rendered Contemptible the Majesty of Justice, of advancing to places of judicature scandalous and Ignorant favourits.

For having wronged his Majesties Prerogative and Interest by assuming the monopoley of the Beaver Trade.

By having in that unjust gaine Bartered and sould his Majesties Country and the lives of his Loyal Subjects to the Barbarous Heathen.

For haveing protected favoured and Imboldened the Indians against his Majesties most Loyall subjects never contriveing requireing or appointing any due or proper meanes of satisfaction for their many Invasions Murthers and Robberies Committed upon us.

For having, when the Army of the English was Just upon the Track of the Indians, which now in all places Burne Spoyle and Murder, and when wee might with ease have destroyed them who then were in open Hostility for having expresly Countermanded and sent back our Army by passing his word for the peaceable demeanour of the said Indians, who imediately prosecuted their evill Intentions Commiting horrid Murders and Robberies in all places being protected by the said Engagement and word pass'd of him the said S'r William Berkley, having ruined and made desolate a great part of his Majesties Country, have now drawne themselves into such obscure and remote places and are by their successes soe imboldened and confirmed and by their Confederacy soe strengthened that the cryes of Bloud are in all places and the Terrour and consternation of the People soe great, that they are now become not only a difficult, but a very formidable Enemy who might with Ease have been destroyed &c. When upon the Loud Outcries of Blood the Assembly had with all care raised and framed an Army for the prevention of future Mischiefs and safeguard of his Majesties Colony.

> *"All people in all places where wee have yet bin can attest our civill quiet peaseable behaviour farre different from that of Rebellion."*

For having with only the privacy of some few favourits without acquainting the People, only by the Alteration of a Figure forged a Commission by wee know not what hand, not only without but against the Consent of the People, for raising and effecting of Civill Warrs and distractions, which being happily and without Bloodshedd prevented.

For haveing the second tyme attempted the same thereby, calling downe our Forces from the defence of the Frontiers, and most weake Exposed Places, for the prevention of civill Mischief and Ruine amongst ourselves, whilst the barbarous Enemy in all places did Invade murder and spoyle us his Majesties most faithfull subjects.

Of these the aforesaid Articles wee accuse S'r William Berkely, as guilty of each and every one of the same, and as one, who hath Traiterously attempted, violated and Injured his Majesties Interest here, by the losse of a great Part of his Colony, and many of his Faithfull and Loyall subjects by him betrayed, and in a barbarous and shamefull manner exposed to the Incursions and murthers of the Heathen.

And we further declare these the Ensueing Persons in this List, to have been his wicked, and pernitious Councellors, Aiders and Assisters against the Commonalty in these our Cruell Commotions

SIR HENRY CHICHERLY, KNT.,	JOS. BRIDGER,
COL. CHARLES WORMLEY,	WM. CLABOURNE,
PHIL. DALOWELL,	THOS. HAWKINS, JUNI'R,
ROBERT BEVERLY,	WILLIAM SHERWOOD,
ROBERT LEE,	JOS. PAGE, CLERK,
THOS. BALLARD,	JO. CLIFFE, ″
WILLIAM COLE,	HUBBERD FARRELL,
RICHARD WHITACRE,	JOHN WEST,
NICHOLAS SPENCER,	THOS. READE.
MATHEW KEMP,	

And wee doe further demand, That the said S'r William Berkley, with all the Persons in this List, be forthwith delivered upp, or surrender themselves, within foure dayes, after the notice hereof, or otherwise wee declare, as followeth, That in whatsoever house, place, or shipp, any of the said Persons shall reside, be hide, or protected, Wee doe declare, that the Owners, masters, or Inhabitants of the said places, to be Confederates, and Traitors to the People, and the Estates of them, as alsoe of all the aforesaid Persons to be Confiscated, This wee the Commons of Virginia doe declare desiring a prime Union among ourselves, that wee may Joyntly, and with one Accord defend ourselves against the Common Enemye. And Let not the Faults of the guilty, be the Reproach of the Innocent, or the Faults or Crimes of ye Oppressors divide and separate us, who have suffered by theire oppressions.

These are therefore in his Majesties name, to Command you forthwith to seize, the Persons above mentioned, as Traytors to ye King and Countrey, and them to bring to Middle Plantation, and there to secure them, till further Order, and in Case of opposition, if you want any other Assistance, you are forthwith to demand it in the Name of the People of all the Counties of Virginia

[signed]   NATH BACON, Gen'l.
By the Consent of ye People.

VIEWPOINT 9B

Bacon's Rebellion Is a Treasonous Insurrection (1676)

William Berkeley (1606–1677)

William Berkeley was appointed colonial governor of Virginia by King Charles I in 1641, and governed the colony from 1642 to 1652. Reappointed by King

From "Declaration and Remonstrance" by William Berkeley, 26 May 1676 (Massachusetts Historical Society, *Collections*, series 4). Courtesy of the Massachusetts Historical Society.

Charles II in 1660, he served again as governor until 1676. He gained popularity among the colonists in the early years of his governorship by leading them to victory against Indians in the Second Powhatan War of 1644–1646, and by promoting economic development in Virginia's interior. But by the 1670s many people, especially from the poorer western districts of the colony, were accusing Berkeley of corruption and favoritism in granting political favors, offices, and land grants to his friends. Efforts to redress their grievances peacefully were thwarted in part because Berkeley chose not to hold elections to the House of Burgesses, Virginia's representative assembly, between 1661 and 1676.

The rumblings of discontent erupted in 1675 over the issue of Indians in the frontier. Several hundred of Virginia's poorer residents formed an impromptu army and placed Nathaniel Bacon, a young, newly arrived English aristocrat, in command of an unauthorized April 1676 mission to attack Indians. Berkeley responded in May by declaring Bacon and his followers traitors, and also calling on new elections for the House of Burgesses. At the end of May he wrote a "Declaration and Remonstrance," from which this viewpoint is taken, in which he defends his record as governor, including his refusal to grant military commissions to Bacon.

Bacon later drove Berkeley out of Jamestown, Virginia's capital, and seemed to be on the verge of taking political control of the colony when he died suddenly in October 1676. Berkeley was able to regain power and execute 23 of the rebels, but shortly afterwards was recalled to England. Bacon's Rebellion had two major effects on American colonial history. One was that no future colonial governor would ever hold as much power as Berkeley. The other was the swift development of a labor replacement for indentured servants (who had participated heavily in Bacon's Rebellion). The new source of labor was slaves imported from Africa.

What are Berkeley's main points in the defense of his governing record? Why is Nathaniel Bacon a traitor, according to Berkeley? What policy toward Indians does Berkeley propose?

The declaration and Remonstrance of Sir William Berkeley his most sacred Majesties Governor and Captain Generall of Virginia.

Sheweth That about the yeare 1660 Coll. [Samuel] Mathews the then Governor dyed and then in consideration of the service I had don the Country, in defending them from, and destroying great numbers of the Indians, without the loss of three men, in all the time that warr lasted, and in contemplation of the equall and uncorrupt Justice I had distributed to all men, Not onely the Assembly but the unanimous votes of all the Country, concurred to make me Governor in a time, when if the [Puritan] Rebells in England had prevailed, I had certainly dyed for accepting itt, 'twas Gentlemen an unfortunate Love, shewed to me, for to shew myselfe gratefull for this, I was willing to accept of this Governement againe, when by my gracious Kings favour I might have had other places much more proffitable, and lesse toylesome then this hath beene. Since that time that I returned into the Country, I call the great God, Judge of all things in heaven and earth to wittness, that I doe not know of any thing relateive to this Country, wherein I have acted unjustly, corruptly, or negligently, in distributeing equall Justice to all men, and takeing all possible care to preserve their proprietys, and defend them from their barbarous enimies.

But for all this, perhapps I have erred in things I know not of, if I have I am soe conscious of humane frailty, and my owne defects, that I will not onely acknowledge them, but repent of, and amend them, and not like the Rebell Bacon persist in an error, onely because I have comitted itt, and tells me in diverse of his Letters that itt is not for his honnor to confess a fault, but I am of opinion that itt is onely for divells to be incorrigable, and men of principles like the worst of divells, and these he hath, if truth be reported to me, of diverse of his expressions of Atheisme, tending to take away all Religion and Laws.

Nathaniel Bacon's Treason

And now I will state the Question betwixt me as a Governor and Mr. Bacon, and say that if any enimies should invade England, any Councellor Justice of peace, or other inferiour officer, might raise what forces they could to protect his Majesties subjects, But I say againe, if after the Kings knowledge of this invasion, any the greatest peere of England, should raise forces against the kings prohibition this would be now, and ever was in all ages and Nations accompted treason. Nay I will goe further, that though this peere was truly zealous for the preservation of his King, and subjects, and had better and greater abillitys then all the rest of his fellow subjects, to doe his King and Country service, yett if the King (though by false information) should suspect the contrary, itt were treason in this Noble peere to proceed after the King's prohibition, and for the truth of this I appeale to all the laws of England, and the Laws and constitutions of all other Nations in the world, And yett further itt is declared by this Parliament that the takeing up Armes for the King and Parliament is treason, for the event shewed that what ever the pretence was to seduce ignorant and well affected people, yett the end was ruinous both to King and people, as this will be if not prevented, I doe therefore againe declair

that Bacon proceedeing against all Laws of all Nations modern and ancient, is Rebell to his sacred Majesty and this Country, nor will I insist upon the sweareing of men to live and dye togeather, which is treason by the very words of the Law.

———— • ————

"I doe therefore againe declair that Bacon . . . is Rebell to his sacred Majesty and this Country."

———— • ————

Now my friends I have lived 34 yeares amongst you, as uncorrupt and dilligent as ever Governor was, Bacon is a man of two yeares amongst you, his person and qualities unknowne to most of you, and to all men else, by any vertuous action that ever I heard of, And that very action which he boasts of, was sickly and fooleishly, and as I am informed treacherously carried to the dishonnor of the English Nation, yett in itt, he lost more men then I did in three yeares Warr, and by the grace of God will putt myselfe to the same daingers and troubles againe when I have brought Bacon to acknowledge the Laws are above him, and I doubt not but by God's assistance to have better success then Bacon hath had, the reason of my hopes are, that I will take Councell of wiser men then my selfe, but Mr. Bacon hath none about him, but the lowest of the people.

Yett I must further enlarge, that I cannot without your helpe, doe any thinge in this but dye in defence of my King, his laws, and subjects, which I will cheerefully doe, though alone I doe itt, and considering my poore fortunes, I can not leave my poore Wife and friends a better legacy then by dyeing for my King and you: for his sacred Majesty will easeily distinguish betweene Mr. Bacons actions and myne, and Kinges have long Armes, either to reward or punish.

Now after all this, if Mr. Bacon can shew one precedent or example where such actings in any Nation what ever, was approved of, I will mediate with the King and you for a pardon, and excuce for him, but I can shew him an hundred examples where brave and great men have beene putt to death for gaineing Victorys against the Comand of their Superiors.

Berkeley's Indian Policy

Lastly my most assured friends I would have preserved those Indians that I knew were howerly att our mercy, to have beene our spyes and intelligence, to finde out our bloody enimies, but as soone as I had the least intelligence that they alsoe were trecherous enimies, I gave out Commissions to distroy them all as the Commissions themselves will speake itt.

To conclude, I have don what was possible both to friend and enimy, have granted Mr. Bacon three pardons, which he hath scornefully rejected, suppoaseing himselfe stronger to subvert then I and you to maineteyne the Laws, by which onely and Gods assisting grace and mercy, all men must hope for peace and safety. I will add noe more though much more is still remaineing to Justifie me and condemne Mr. Bacon, but to desier that this declaration may be read in every County Court in the Country, and that a Court be presently called to doe itt, before the Assembly meet, That your approbation or dissattisfaction of this declaration may be knowne to all the Country, and the Kings Councell to whose most revered Judgments itt is submitted, Given the xxixth day of May, a happy day in the xxviiith yeare of his most sacred Majesties Reigne, Charles the second, who God grant long and prosperously to Reigne, and lett all his good subjects say Amen.

For Further Reading

Charles McClean Andrews, ed., *Narratives of the Insurrections, 1675–1690*. New York: Barnes & Noble, 1952.

John B. Frantz, ed., *Bacon's Rebellion: Prologue to the Revolution?* Lexington, MA: D.C. Heath, 1969.

Robert Middlekauf, *Bacon's Rebellion*. Chicago: Rand McNally, 1964.

Wilcomb E. Washburn, *The Governor and the Rebel: A History of Bacon's Rebellion in Virginia*. Chapel Hill: University of North Carolina Press, 1957.

Stephen S. Webb, *1676: The End of American Independence*. New York: Knopf, 1984.

VIEWPOINT 10A

Slavery Is Immoral (1700)

Samuel Sewall (1652–1730)

The key to profitability in the early American colonies was the raising and selling of cash crops, especially tobacco in Virginia and Maryland and rice in South Carolina. However, successful cultivation of these crops required intensive labor—something in short supply in the thinly populated colonies. Some colonists enslaved Indians captured in wars, but this solution proved unworkable, in part because many Indians quickly succumbed to diseases brought over by the colonists. Another attempted solution was indentured servitude (see viewpoints 8A and 8B), but this method of importing bound workers formed in its wake an impoverished white underclass of former servants—a development that often caused political

From *The Selling of Joseph: A Memorial* by Samuel Sewall, Boston, 1700 (Massachusetts Historical Society, *Proceedings*, vol. 7, 1864).

instability as seen in such upheavals as Bacon's Rebellion in 1676 (see viewpoints 9A and 9B).

A lasting solution to the colonies' labor shortage problem was finally found by importing black Africans as slaves. Since the early 1500s, Africans had been captured and transported to Spanish, Portuguese, and (later) British colonies in South America and the Caribbean. Although blacks were present in Virginia in 1619, it was not until the 1680s that they were imported in large numbers sufficient to begin to replace the white indentured servants as the main source of labor in Virginia, South Carolina, and other colonies. Unlike indentured servants, slaves were bound for life, lacked all legal and political rights, and their different skin color made escape much more difficult. By 1700 slavery was legal in all the English colonies in America, and Africans (mostly slaves) accounted for 15 percent of the population in southern colonies. Although legal in New England colonies, it was not as established or widespread as in colonies farther south.

Even though slavery did seem to many a lasting and workable solution to the colonies' labor shortage, the morality of slavery did not go unquestioned in colonial times. The following viewpoint is taken from one of the earliest antislavery pamphlets written in America. The author, Samuel Sewall, was a Puritan judge then serving on the Massachusetts Superior Court. He was one of the judges who condemned several people to death in the 1692 Salem witch trials, actions about which he later confessed error and remorse. In 1700 he became involved in a legal dispute with another judge, John Saffin, over the fate of a black slave Saffin refused to set free despite a contract calling for the slave's release. In defense of his position, Sewall wrote and circulated a pamphlet attacking slavery, *The Selling of Joseph a Memorial*, that was published in Boston in 1700.

What objections does Sewall have to slavery? How does he support his arguments? Is Sewall racially prejudiced against blacks, judging from this viewpoint? Explain your answer.

Forasmuch *as Liberty is in real value next unto Life: None ought to part with it themselves, or deprive others of it, but upon most mature consideration.*

The Numerousness of Slaves at this Day in the Province, and the Uneasiness of them under their Slavery, hath put many upon thinking whether the Foundation of it be firmly and well laid; so as to sustain the Vast Weight that is built upon it. It is most certain that all Men, as they are the Sons of *Adam*, are Co-heirs, and have equal Right unto Liberty, and all other outward Comforts of Life. God *hath given the*

Earth [with all its commodities] unto the Sons of Adam, Psal., 115, 16. And hath made of one Blood all Nations of Men, for to dwell on all the face of the Earth, and hath determined the Times before appointed, and the bounds of their Habitation: That they should seek the Lord. Forasmuch then as we are the Offspring of God, &c. *Acts* 17. 26, 27, 29. Now, although the Title given by the last Adam doth infinitely better Men's Estates, respecting God and themselves; and grants them a most beneficial and inviolable Lease under the Broad Seal of Heaven, who were before only Tenants at Will; yet through the Indulgence of God to our First Parents after the Fall, the outward Estate of all and every of their Children, remains the same as to one another. So that Originally, and Naturally, there is no such thing as Slavery. *Joseph* was rightfully no more a Slave to his Brethren, than they were to him; and they had no more Authority to *Sell* him, than they had to *Slay* him. And if *they* had nothing to do to sell him; the *Ishmaelites* bargaining with them, and paying down Twenty pieces of Silver, could not make a Title. Neither could *Potiphar* have any better Interest in him than the *Ishmaelites* had. *Gen.* 37, 20, 27, 28. For he that shall in this case plead *Alteration of Property*, seems to have forfeited a great part of his own claim to Humanity. There is no proportion between Twenty Pieces of Silver and Liberty. The Commodity itself is the Claimer. If *Arabian* Gold be imported in any quantities, most are afraid to meddle with it, though they might have it at easy rates; lest it should have been wrongfully taken from the Owners, it should kindle a fire to the Consumption of their whole Estate. 'Tis pity there should be more Caution used in buying a Horse, or a little lifeless dust, than there is in purchasing Men and Women: Whereas they are the Offspring of God, and their Liberty is,

. . . Auro pretiosior Omni.
[To Each More Precious than Gold]

And seeing God hath said, *He that Stealeth a Man, and Selleth him, or if he be found in his Hand, he shall surely be put to Death. Exod.* 21, 16. This Law being of Everlasting Equity, wherein Man-Stealing is ranked among the most atrocious of Capital Crimes: What louder Cry can there be made of that Celebrated Warning.

Caveat Emptor! [Buyer Beware!]

And all things considered, it would conduce more to the Welfare of the Province, to have White Servants for a Term of Years, than to have Slaves for Life. Few can endure to hear of a Negro's being made free; and indeed they can seldom use their Freedom well; yet their continual aspiring after their forbidden Liberty, renders them Unwilling Servants.

And there is such a disparity in their Conditions, Colour, and Hair, that they can never embody with us, & grow up in orderly Families, to the Peopling of the Land; but still remain in our Body Politick as a kind of extravasat Blood. As many Negro Men as there are among us, so many empty Places are there in our Train Bands [militias], and the places taken up of Men that might make Husbands for our Daughters. And the Sons and Daughters of *New England* would become more like *Jacob* and *Rachel*, if this Slavery were thrust quite out of Doors. Moreover it is too well known what Temptations Masters are under, to connive at the Fornication of their Slaves; lest they should be obliged to find them Wives, or pay their Fines. It seems to be practically pleaded that they might be lawless; 'tis thought much of, that the Law should have satisfaction for their Thefts, and other Immoralities; by which means, *Holiness to the Lord* is more rarely engraven upon this sort of Servitude. It is likewise most lamentable to think, how in taking Negroes out of *Africa*, and selling of them here, That which God has joined together, Men do boldly rend asunder; Men from their Country, Husbands from their Wives, Parents from their Children. How horrible is the Uncleanness, Mortality, if not Murder, that the Ships are guilty of that bring great Crouds of these miserable Men and Women. Methinks when we are bemoaning the barbarous Usage of our Friends and Kinsfolk in *Africa*, it might not be unreasonable to enquire whether we are not culpable in forcing the *Africans* to become Slaves amongst ourselves. And it may be a question whether all the Benefit received by *Negro* Slaves will balance the Accompt of Cash laid out upon them; and for the Redemption of our own enslaves Friends out of *Africa*. Besides all the Persons and Estates that have perished there.

Objections and Answers

Obj. 1. *These Blackamores are of the Posterity of Cham, and therefore are under the Curse of Slavery. Gen.* 9, 25, 26, 27.

Ans. Of all Offices, one would not beg this; viz. Uncall'd for, to be an Executioner of the Vindictive Wrath of God; the extent and duration of which is to us uncertain. If this ever was a Commission; How do we know but that it is long since out of Date? Many have found it to their Cost, that a Prophetical Denunciation of Judgment against a Person or People, would not warrant them to inflict that evil. If it would, *Hazael* might justify himself in all he did against his master, and the *Israelites* from *2 Kings* 8, 10, 12.

But it is possible that by cursory reading, this Text may have been mistaken. For *Canaan* is the Person Cursed three times over, without the mentioning of *Cham*. Good Expositors suppose the Curse entailed on him, and that this Prophesie was accomplished in the Extirpation of the *Canaanites*, and in the Servitude of the *Gibeonites*. . . . *Whereas* the Blackamores are not descended of *Canaan*, but of *Cush. Psal.* 68, 31. *Princes shall come out of Egypt* [Mizraim]. *Ethiopia* [Cush] *shall soon stretch out her hands unto God.* Under which Names, all *Africa* may be comprehended; and their Promised Conversion ought to be prayed for. *Jer.* 13, 23. *Can the Ethiopian change his Skin?* This shows that Black Men are the Posterity of *Cush.* Who time out of mind have been distinguished by their Colour. . . .

———— • ————

"It is . . . most lamentable to think, how in taking Negroes out of Africa*, and selling of them here, That which God has joined together, Men do boldly rend asunder; Men from their Country, Husbands from their Wives, Parents from their Children."*

———— • ————

Obj. 2. *The* Nigers *are brought out of a Pagan Country, into places where the Gospel is preached.*

Ans. Evil must not be done, that good may come of it. The extraordinary and comprehensive Benefit accruing to the Church of God, and to *Joseph* personally, did not rectify his Brethren's Sale of him.

Obj. 3. *The Africans have Wars one with another: Our Ships bring lawful Captives taken in those wars.*

Ans. For aught is known, their Wars are much such as were between *Jacob's* Sons and their Brother *Joseph.* If they be between Town and Town; Provincial or National: Every War is upon one side Unjust. An Unlawful War can't make lawful Captives. And by receiving, we are in danger to promote, and partake in their Barbarous Cruelties. I am sure, if some Gentlemen should go down to the [town of] *Brewsters* to take the Air, and Fish: And a stronger Party from *Hull* should surprise them, and sell them for Slaves to a Ship outward bound; they would think themselves unjustly dealt with; both by Sellers and Buyers. And yet 'tis to be feared, we have no other Kind of Title to our *Nigers. Therefore all things whatsoever ye would that men should do to you, do you even so to them: for this is the Law and the Prophets. Matt.* 7, 12.

Obj. 4. Abraham *had Servants bought with his Money and born in his House.*

Ans. Until the Circumstances of *Abraham's* purchase be recorded, no Argument can be drawn from it. In the mean time, Charity obliges us to conclude, that He knew it was lawful and good.

It is Observable that the *Israelites* were strictly forbidden the buying or selling one another for Slaves. *Levit.* 25. 39. 46. *Jer.* 34. 8–22. And God gaged His Blessing in lieu of any loss they might conceit they suffered thereby, *Deut.* 15. 18. And since the partition Wall is broken down, inordinate Self-love should likewise be demolished. God expects that Christians should be of a more Ingenuous and benign frame of Spirit. Christians should carry it to all the World, as the *Israelites* were to carry it one towards another. And for Men obstinately to persist in holding their Neighbours and Brethren under the Rigor of perpetual Bondage, seems to be no proper way of gaining Assurance that God has given them Spiritual Freedom. Our Blessed Saviour has altered the Measures of the ancient Love Song, and set it to a most Excellent New Tune, which all ought to be ambitious of Learning. *Matt.* 5. 43. 44. *John* 13. 34. These *Ethiopians*, as black as they are, seeing they are the Sons and Daughters of the First *Adam*, the Brethren and Sisters of the Last Adam, and the Offspring of God; They ought to be treated with a Respect agreeable.

VIEWPOINT 10B

Slavery Is Moral (1701)

John Saffin (1632–1710)

John Saffin was a wealthy landowner and Massachusetts judge. In 1700 he became embroiled in a legal dispute when he refused to give a black slave in his possession his freedom. He viewed Samuel Sewall's tract *The Selling of Joseph a Memorial* (see viewpoint 10A) as a personal affront, and in 1701 published a reply defending the institution of slavery (and, indirectly, his own actions as a slaveowner). The tract, reprinted here, is notable in that many of its arguments appear repeatedly in later proslavery literature.

How does Saffin respond to Samuel Sewall's arguments? Why do you think both Saffin and Sewall focus on the Bible in developing their arguments? What beliefs does Saffin express about blacks?

————————————

A Brief and Candid Answer to a late Printed Sheet, Entituled, The Selling of Joseph

That Honourable and Learned Gentleman, the Author of a Sheet, Entituled, *The Selling of Joseph*, A Memorial, seems from thence to draw this conclusion, that because the Sons of *Jacob*

From *A Brief and Candid Answer to a Late Printed Sheet Entituled "The Selling of Joseph"* by John Saffin (Boston, 1701), as reprinted in *Notes on the History of Slavery in Massachusetts* by George H. Moore (New York: D. Appleton, 1866).

did very ill in selling their Brother *Joseph* to the *Ishmaelites*, who were Heathens, therefore it is utterly unlawful to Buy and Sell Negroes, though among Christians; which Conclusion I presume is not well drawn from the Premises, nor is the case parallel; for it was unlawfull for the *Israelites* to sell their Brethren upon any account, or pretence whatsoever during life. But it was not unlawful for the Seed of *Abraham* to have Bond men, and Bond women either born in their House, or bought with their Money, as it is written of *Abraham, Gen.* 14.14 & 21.10 & *Exod.* 21.16 & *Levit.* 25.44, 45, 46 v. After the giving of the Law: And in *Josh.* 9.23. That famous Example of the *Gibeonites* is a sufficient proof where there [is] no other.

Different Orders of Men

To speak a little to the Gentleman's first Assertion: *That none ought to part with their Liberty themselves, or deprive others of it but upon mature consideration*; a prudent exception, in which he grants, that upon some consideration a man may be deprived of his Liberty. And then presently in his next Position or Assertion he denies it, *viz.: It is most certain, that all men as they are the Sons of* Adam *are Coheirs, and have equal right to Liberty, and all other Comforts of Life*, which he would prove out of *Psal.* 115.16. *The Earth hath he given to the Children of Men.* True, but what is all this to the purpose, to prove that all men have equal right to Liberty, and all outward comforts of this life; which Position seems to invert the Order that God hath set in the World, who hath Ordained different degrees and orders of men, some to be High and Honourable, some to be Low and Despicable; some to be Monarchs, Kings, Princes and Governours, Masters and Commanders, others to be Subjects, and to be Commanded; Servants of sundry sorts and degrees, bound to obey; yea, some to be born Slaves, and so to remain during their lives, as hath been proved. Otherwise there would be a meer parity among men, contrary to that of the Apostle, I *Cor. 12 from the 13 to the 26 verse*, where he sets forth (by way of comparison) the different sorts and offices of the Members of the Body, indigitating that they are all of use, but not equal, and of like dignity. So God hath set different Orders and Degrees of Men in the World, both in Church and Common weal. Now, if this Position of parity should be true, it would then follow that the ordinary Course of Divine Providence of God in the World should be wrong, and unjust, (which we must not dare to think, much less to affirm) and all the sacred Rules, Precepts and Commands of the Almighty which he hath given the Son of Men to observe and keep in their respective Places, Orders and Degrees, would be to no purpose; which unaccountably derogate from the Divine Wis-

dom of the most High, who hath made nothing in vain, but hath Holy Ends in all his Dispensations to the Children of men.

In the next place, this worthy Gentleman makes a large Discourse concerning the Utility and Conveniency to keep the one, and inconveniency of the other; respecting white and black Servants, which conduceth most to the welfare and benefit of this Province: which he concludes to be white men, who are in many respects to be preferred before Blacks; who doubts that? doth it therefore follow, that it is altogether unlawful for Christians to buy and keep Negro Servants (for this is the Thesis) but that those that have them ought in Conscience to set them free, and so lose all the money they cost (for we must not live in any known sin) this seems to be his opinion; but it is a Question whether it ever was the Gentleman's practice? But if he could perswade the General Assembly to make an Act, That all that have Negroes, and do set them free, shall be Re imbursed out of the Publick Treasury, and that there shall be no more Negroes brought into the Country; 'tis probable there would be more of his opinion; yet he would find it a hard task to bring the Country to consent thereto; for then the Negroes must be all sent out of the Country, or else the remedy would be worse than the Disease; and it is to be feared that those Negroes that are free, if there be not some strict course taken with them by Authority, they will be a plague to this Country.

---•---

"It is no Evil thing to bring them out of their own Heathenish Country, where they may have the Knowledge of the True God, be Converted and Eternally saved."

---•---

Again, If it should be unlawful to deprive them that are lawful Captives, or Bondmen of their Liberty for Life being Heathens; it seems to be more unlawful to deprive our Brethren, of our own or other Christian Nations of the Liberty, (though but for a time) by binding them to Serve some Seven, Ten, Fifteen, and some Twenty Years, which oft times proves for their whole Life, as many have been; which in effect is the same in Nature, though different in the time, yet this was allow'd among the *Jews* by the Law of God; and is the constant practice of our own and other Christian Nations in the World: the which our Author by his Dogmatical Assertions doth condemn as Irreligious; which is Diametrically contrary to the Rules and Precepts which God hath given the diversity of men to observe in their respective Stations, Callings, and Conditions of Life, as hath been observed.

Slavery and the Bible

And to illustrate his Assertion our Author brings in by way of Comparison the Law of God against man Stealing, on pain of Death: Intimating thereby, that Buying and Selling of Negro's is a breach of that Law, and so deserves Death: A severe Sentence: But herein he begs the Question with a *Caveat Emptor*. For, in that very Chapter there is a Dispensation to the People of *Israel*, to have Bond men, Women and Children, even of their own Nation in some case; and Rules given therein to be observed concerning them; Verse the *4th*. And in the before cited place, *Levit.* 25.44, 45, 46. Though the *Israelites* were forbidden (ordinarily) to make Bond men and Women of their own Nation, but of Strangers they might: the words run thus, verse 44. *Both thy Bond men, and thy Bond maids which thou shalt have shall be of the Heathen, that are round about you: of them shall you Buy Bond men and Bond maids*, &c. See also, I *Cor.* 12.13. Whether we be Bond or Free, which shows that in the times of the New Testament, there were Bond men also, etc.

In fine, The sum of this long Haurange, is no other, than to compare the Buying and Selling of Negro's unto the Stealing of men, and the Selling of *Joseph* by his Brethren, which bears no proportion therewith, nor is there any congrueity therein, as appears by the foregoing Texts.

Our Author doth further proceed to answer some Objections of his own framing, which he supposes some might raise.

Object. 1. *That these Blackamores are of the Posterity of* Cham, *and therefore under the Curse of Slavery. Gen.* 9.25, 26, 27. The which the Gentleman seems to deny, saying, *they were the Seed of Canaan that were Cursed*, etc.

Ans. Whether they were so or not, we shall not dispute: this may suffice, that not only the seed of *Cham* or *Canaan*, but any lawful Captives of other Heathen Nations may be made Bond men as hath been proved.

Obj. 2. *That the Negroes are brought out of Pagan Countreys into places where the Gospel is Preached.* To which he Replies, *that we must not doe Evil that Good may come of it.*

Ans. To which we answer, That it is no Evil thing to bring them out of their own Heathenish Country, where they may have the Knowledge of the True God, be Converted and Eternally saved.

African Wars

Obj. 3. *The* Affricans *have Wars one with another*; our Ships bring lawful Captives taken in those Wars.

To which our Author answer Conjecturally, and Doubtfully, *for aught we know*, that which may or may not be; which is insignificant, and proves nothing. He also compares the Negroes Wars, one Nation with another, with the Wars between *Joseph* and his Brethren. But where doth he read of any such War? We read indeed of a Domestick Quarrel they had with him, they envyed and hated *Joseph*; but by what is Recorded, he was meerly passive and meek as a Lamb. This Gentleman farther adds, *That there is not any War but is unjust on one side*, etc. Be it so, what doth that signify: We read of lawful Captives taken in the Wars, and lawful to be Bought and Sold without contracting the guilt of the *Agressors*; for which we have the example of *Abraham* before quoted; but if we must stay while both parties Warring are in the right, there would be no lawful Captives at all to be Bought; which seems to be rediculous to imagine, and contrary to the tenour of Scripture, and all Humane Histories on that subject.

Obj. 4. *Abraham had Servants bought with his Money, and born in his House. Gen.* 14.14. To which our worthy Author answers, *until the Circumstances of Abraham's purchase be recorded, no Argument can be drawn from it.*

Ans. To which we Reply, this is also Dogmatical, and proves nothing. He farther adds, *In the mean time Charity Obliges us to conclude, that he knew it was lawful and good.* Here the gentleman yields the case; for if we are in Charity bound to believe *Abraham's* practice, in buying and keeping *Slaves* in his house to be lawful and good: then it follows, that our Imitation of him in this his Moral Action, is as warrantable as that of his Faith; *who is the Father of all them that believe. Rom.* 4.16.

In the close of all, Our Author Quotes two more places of Scripture, *viz.*; *Levit.* 25.46, and *Jer.* 34, from the 8. to the 22. *v.* To prove that the people of Israel were strictly forbidden the Buying and Selling one another for *Slaves*: who questions that? and what is that to the case in hand? What a strange piece of Logick is this? Tis unlawful for Christians to Buy and Sell one another for slaves. *Ergo*, It is unlawful to Buy and Sell Negroes that are lawful Captiv'd Heathens.

And after a Serious Exhortation to us all to Love one another according to the Command of Christ. *Math.* 5.43, 44. This worthy Gentleman concludes with this Assertion, *That these Ethiopeans as Black as they are, seeing they are the Sons and Daughters of the first* Adam; *the Brethren and Sisters of the Second Adam, and the Offspring of God; we ought to treat them with a respect agreeable.*

Loving All People Equally Is Impossible

Ans. We grant it for a certain and undeniable verity, That all Mankind are the Sons and Daughters of

Adam, and the Creatures of God: But it doth not therefore follow that we are bound to love and respect all men alike; this under favour we must take leave to deny; we ought in charity, if we see our Neighbour in want, to relieve them in a regular way, but we are not bound to give them so much of our Estates, as to make them equal with our selves, because they are our Brethren, the Sons of *Adam*, no, not our own natural Kinsmen: We are Exhorted *to do good unto all, but especially to them who are of the Houshold of Faith, Gal.* 6.10. And we are to love, honour and respect all men according to the gift of God that is in them: I may love my Servant well, but my Son better; Charity begins at home, it would be a violation of common prudence, and a breach of good manners, to treat a Prince like a Peasant. And this worthy Gentleman would deem himself much neglected, if we should show him no more Defference than to an ordinary Porter: And therefore these florid expressions, the Sons and Daughters of the First *Adam*, the Brethren and Sisters of the Second *Adam*, and the Offspring of God, seem to be misapplied to import and insinuate, that we ought to tender Pagan Negroes with all love, kindness, and equal respect as to the best of men.

By all which it doth evidently appear both by Scripture and Reason, the practice of the People of God in all Ages, both before and after the giving of the Law, and in the times of the Gospel, that there were Bond men, Women and Children commonly kept by holy and good men, and improved in Service; and there-fore by the Command of God, *Lev.* 24:44, and their venerable Example, we may keep Bond men, and use them in our Service still; yet with all candour, moderation and Christian prudence, according to their state and condition consonant to the Word of God.

The Negroes Character.

Cowardly and cruel are those Blacks *Innate,*
Prone to Revenge, Imp of inveterate hate.
He that exasperates them, soon espies
Mischief and Murder in their very eyes.
Libidinous, Deceitful, False and Rude,
The Spume Issue of Ingratitude.
The Premises consider'd, all may tell,
How near good Joseph *they are parallel.*

For Further Reading

Peter Charles Hoffer, ed., *Africans Become Afro-Americans: Selected Articles on Slavery in the American Colonies.* New York: Garland, 1988.

Winthrop Jordan, *White over Black: American Attitudes Toward the Negro, 1550–1812.* New York: Norton, 1977.

T. Benson Strandness, *Samuel Sewall: A Puritan Portrait.* East Lansing: Michigan State University Press, 1967.

Larry Tise, *Proslavery: A History of the Defense of Slavery in America, 1701–1840.* Athens: University of Georgia Press, 1987.

Peter H. Wood, *Black Majority: Negroes in Colonial South Carolina from 1670 Through the Stono Rebellion.* New York: Knopf, 1974.

PART II:
FORGING A NEW NATION,
1750–1803

⤜•⤛

The Decision to Break
from Great Britain

Creating a New
Government

Problems of the
New Nation

1754
- May Governor of Virginia sends militia under George Washington into Ohio Valley to challenge French expansion
- June Albany Congress held by delegates of six colonies to discuss defense; Benjamin Franklin drafts Albany Plan of Union

1754–1763
- French and Indian War

1760
- George III becomes king of Great Britain.

1771
- May 16 North Carolina farmers known as Regulators, rebelling against North Carolina governor William Tryon, defeated at Battle of Alamance Creek

1770
- March 5 Boston Massacre
- April Townsend Duties repealed; colonists lift trade embargo

1769
- First permanent European settlement in California established by Fr. Junipero Serra at San Diego

1768
- August Boston merchants adopt colonies' first nonimportation agreement against British goods
- October British soldiers stationed in Boston

1767
- Quartering Act and Townshend Duties passed

1773
- December 16 Boston Tea Party: colonists objecting to tea tax dump English tea into Boston harbor

1776
- January Thomas Paine's pamphlet *Common Sense* published
- March 17 British troops evacuate Boston
- July 2 First colonial statute granting woman's suffrage passed in New Jersey; remains in effect until reversed in 1807
- July 4 Continental Congress approves Declaration of Independence

1778
- February 6 France and U.S. sign treaty of alliance
- July–November Joseph Brant leads Iroquois attacks against American settlers in New York and Pennsylvania

1755	1760	1765	1770	1775

1763
- February 10 France cedes North American territories to England in Treaty of Paris
- May Chief Pontiac of Ottawa tribe leads Indian attacks in Great Lakes region
- October 7 Great Britain declares territory west of Appalachians off limits to American colonization.

1765
- March 22 Stamp Act becomes law
- May Patrick Henry attacks Stamp Act at meeting of Virginia House of Burgesses
- August Riots against Stamp Act take place in Boston
- October 5 Stamp Act Congress meets to protest Stamp Act

1766
- March 18 Parliament repeals Stamp Act and passes Declaratory Act asserting Parliament's supremacy over colonial affairs

1774
- March Parliament passes Coercive Acts (Intolerable Acts)
- September First Continental Congress convenes in Philadelphia; delegates approve Suffolk Resolves, declaring "murderous" Intolerable Acts unconstitutional

1775
- April 14 First American slavery abolition society organized in Pennsylvania
- April 19 Battles of Lexington and Concord between American militia and British troops; Boston placed under siege by colonists
- May Second Continental Congress convenes

1777
- October 4 Washington defeated in Battle of Germantown; Continental Army spends winter at Valley Forge
- October 17 Gen. Horatio Gates scores a major American victory in Battle of Saratoga
- November 17 Continental Congress approves Articles of Confederation

1781
•March 1 Articles of Confederation become effective following Maryland's ratification
•October 17 British general Charles Cornwallis surrenders to combined American-French force at Yorktown

1783
•*The American Speller* by Noah Webster published
•May 30 First daily American newspaper, *Pennsylvania Evening Post*, begins publication
•September 3 Peace treaty signed by U.S. and Great Britain

1784
•Economic depression begins
•March Virginia surrenders to Congress its territory northwest of Ohio River
•June 26 Spain closes New Orleans to American shipping

1789
•March First Congress under Constitution convenes in New York
•April 30 George Washington inaugurated in New York as first president of United States
•September 25 Bill of Rights approved by both houses of Congress
•November 21 North Carolina ratifies Constitution and enters Union

1790
•January 9 Alexander Hamilton submits Report on the Public Credit to Congress

1791
•March 4 Vermont enters Union as fourteenth state
•December 12 Bank of United States opens
•December 15 Bill of Rights becomes law with Virginia's ratification

1798–1800
•U.S. and France fight Quasi-War

1797
•March 4 John Adams inaugurated president

1796
•June 1 Tennessee enters Union
•December 7 John Adams elected president
•September 19 Washington's Farewell Address published

1780   **1785**   **1790**   **1795**   **1800**

1785
•May Ordinance of 1785 creates system for surveying and selling western lands

1786
•January 1 Virginia enacts statute for religious freedom drafted by Thomas Jefferson
•August Shays's Rebellion erupts in western Massachusetts

1787
•January Shays's Rebellion routed by Massachusetts militia
•May 25 Constitutional Convention opens at Philadelphia.
•July 13 Enactment of Northwest Ordinance determines government of lands north of Ohio River
•September 17 Constitutional Convention completed; delegates sign Constitution and send to states for ratification

1792
•Federalists and Democratic Republicans emerge as opposing political parties
•June 1 Kentucky enters Union
•December 5 Washington reelected president

1793
•Eli Whitney invents cotton gin
•May Washington's administration proclaims U.S. neutral in war between Great Britain and France

1788
•May *The Federalist* by James Madison, Alexander Hamilton, and John Jay published in book form
•June 21 Constitution goes into effect as New Hampshire becomes ninth state to ratify

1795
•June Senate ratifies Jay Treaty with Great Britain
•October Pinckney's Treaty secures Mississippi navigation rights from Spain

1794
•August U.S. victory over Miami Indians at Battle of Fallen Timbers in Ohio Valley; subsequent treaty cedes substantial new lands to U.S.

1798
•June–July Congress passes Alien and Sedition Acts in effort to suppress dissent

PART II:
FORGING A NEW NATION, 1750–1803

Relations between Great Britain and its thirteen American colonies began to break down in the mid-1700s, as British efforts to tighten control were resisted by colonists accustomed to running their own affairs. Disputes over taxation and other issues eventually turned into war in April 1775, with the Americans deciding on July 4, 1776, to declare independence. That bold (and disputed) decision was just the beginning of a significant series of turning points and challenges facing the Americans. In the quest to become a new and independent nation the former colonists defeated the world's mightiest military empire in battle, negotiated alliances with other nations, coped with the economic dislocations of war and independence, replaced the colonial governments with new state constitutions, and created a new national constitution and national government. Throughout this time the American people strongly disagreed about many issues concerning the break with Great Britain and on what kind of new nation should be created once independence was declared.

The Maturing American Colonies

By the middle of the eighteenth century the thirteen British colonies were well on their way to becoming established and mature societies. The population of the colonies tripled from 330,000 in 1714 to one million in 1744, and continued to double every twenty-six years. The major factors in the population growth were America's large families and low mortality rates (relative to Europe). Colonial women averaged eight children and forty-two grandchildren. Another important factor was immigration, which became less English-centered in the eighteenth century. From 1713 to 1753 the colonies absorbed 350,000 immigrant newcomers, including approximately 65,000 Germans, 65,000 "Scotch-Irish" (Scottish Presbyterians who had settled in Northern Ireland), and 33,000 Irish. Immigrants also came from France, the Netherlands, and other countries. The largest single group of newcomers were the 140,000 Africans brought to America as slaves.

Many of the new immigrants settled in the Piedmont region along the eastern slope of the Appalachian Mountains. In contrast to 1713, when most colonists lived within fifty miles of the Atlantic coast, one-third of the colonists in 1753 lived and farmed in the Piedmont. The average standard of living of the colonists equaled that of England and exceeded that found in Scotland and Ireland. Literacy was widespread in America, especially in the northern colonies.

British Rule in the 1700s

To govern this realm, Great Britain (created by the 1707 union of England and Scotland) relied on two London-based institutions: a Privy Council to review and sometimes veto colonial laws and a Board of Trade to regulate and enforce British trading rules designed to enrich Great Britain. These governing bodies, however, often received scant attention from the British government and were thus often ineffectual.

In addition to these institutions, Great Britain was represented in the colonies by colonial governors. Appointed in eleven of the thirteen colonies by the British monarch or colonial proprietors, governors in turn appointed the council, or upper house of the colonial legislature, and had the official power to veto legislation and to call or dismiss legislative sessions. However, the governors depended on the colonial assemblies for their salaries. In most colonies in the 1700s the lower house of the colonial assemblies, the only representative instrument of the colonists, grew increasingly assertive in using their control over governors' salaries. They forced governors to sign laws opposed in England and in general governed as they saw fit. In two colonies, Rhode Island and Connecticut, the assembly actually elected the governor.

By the 1760s the leaders of the colonies came to believe that, as Englishmen, they possessed certain fundamental rights of self-government that could not be rescinded. On the other hand, British authorities held that colonial self-government was a mere privilege that could be rescinded unilaterally by the Crown or Parliament.

The French and Indian War

A pivotal event in the relationship between Great Britain and the colonies was the French and Indian War (known in Europe as the Seven Years' War). Part of a larger conflict fought in Europe, India, and elsewhere, the war from the American colonists' perspective was the culmination of a long struggle between Great Britain and France for control of North America. In 1749 France began construction of a chain of forts in the Ohio Valley in territory claimed by both Great Britain and France. Despite early defeats of Virginia militia (commanded by George Washington) and British troops by the French and their Indian allies, Great Britain eventually prevailed. In the 1763 Treaty of Paris, Great Britain acquired all French territory on the North American continent.

Ironically, Britain's defeat of France planted the seeds for eventual American independence. Free from the need for protection from the French threat, colonists in America were emboldened to pursue an independent course. In addition, the immense debt Great Britain had incurred to pay the costs of the French and Indian War convinced members of the British Parliament to attempt to tighten their control and raise revenues from the colonists—actions which soon sparked protest in the colonies.

Taxes and Protest

Beginning in 1763 the British Parliament, at the urging of King George III, passed a series of laws designed to raise revenues from the thirteen colonies and to strengthen British control over them. Parliament voted to maintain a standing army in America, mandated that colonists provide British soldiers with living quarters and supplies, and proclaimed that colonists may not settle west of the Appalachian Mountains until treaties with the Native Americans there could be made. The 1764 Sugar Act strengthened enforcement of laws against trade between the colonies and non-British Caribbean islands. The 1764 Currency Act restricted the ability of colonial assemblies to create paper money.

The single most objectionable act, in the minds of many colonists, was the 1765 Stamp Act, which imposed a tax on all legal documents, pamphlets, almanacs, business licenses, and other items. Many Americans, noting that they had no representatives in Parliament, adopted the slogan of "no taxation without representation." Colonists organized economic boycotts against British goods. Secret clubs called Sons of Liberty engaged in violence and threats of violence to prevent enforcement of the Stamp Act. The Virginia

Assembly, led by Patrick Henry, passed resolutions against taxation by the British Parliament. Representatives of nine colonies met in October 1765 in the Stamp Act Congress and petitioned Parliament to repeal the measure. Parliament repealed the Stamp Act in 1766 but also passed a resolution affirming parliamentary authority over the colonies "in all cases whatsoever."

Parliament again asserted its tax authority in 1767 by passing the Townshend Acts, which created import duties on several British goods. Again the colonists protested, pamphlets and newspapers decried the measure, and a boycott of British goods was organized. Parliament backed down and repealed the taxes but refused to cede the principle of its authority to tax by retaining a small tax on tea. This tax, coupled with British efforts to give a British trading company a monopoly in the American tea trade, inspired perhaps the most significant single act of colonial tax resistance: the 1773 Boston Tea Party, in which a group of colonists boarded British ships in Boston Harbor and threw the tea overboard.

The disputes over taxes reflected a deeper division over political authority. The British held that all parts of the British empire had to yield to the ultimate authority of Parliament, whether they elected members to it or not (many cities in Great Britain, for instance, did not send members to Parliament). But many colonists held that although the colonies should maintain loyalty to the Crown, political authority in the colonies lay with each colonial assembly. Many Americans cited English political writers, such as John Locke, Thomas Gordon, and Joseph Priestley, to justify their views.

The Intolerable Acts

Parliament responded to the Boston Tea Party by passing a series of measures designed to punish Massachusetts. Known in America as the Intolerable Acts, these included closing the port of Boston, requiring the quartering of additional British troops, and increasing the powers of the governor. In an unrelated action (but quickly linked to these punitive measures by many concerned Americans), Parliament passed the Quebec Act to govern its Canadian territories. This act nullified the western land claims of several American colonies by extending the boundaries of Quebec south to the Ohio River and west to the Mississippi.

Leaders in several colonies had by this time established "committees of correspondence" and other political organizations to communicate with each other and to act collectively. In September 1774 the trend toward political union took a further step with the convention of the First Continental Congress in Philadelphia, a gathering of delegates for the purpose of formulating a united colonial response to the Intolerable Acts. Elected by colonial assemblies, many of which were meeting without authorization from the colonial governor, and at other extralegal meetings, few delegates at this time supported American independence; the goal was to express and gain redress for grievances against Great Britain. They expressed these grievances in a petition to King George III that attacked virtually all of Parliament's actions since 1763. The delegates resolved to boycott imported British goods and adjourned after determining to meet again in May 1775 if their concerns had not been addressed.

The Decision for Independence

When the Second Continental Congress convened as planned on May 10, 1775, the first battles of the Revolutionary War had already been fought.

British troops sent from Boston to capture military supplies had exchanged fire with Massachusetts militia (called minutemen) in Lexington and Concord on April 19. By April 20 an army of twenty thousand New England patriots was besieging the British garrison in Boston.

The Second Continental Congress continued to debate independence. King George III declared the colonies in a state of rebellion in December 1775. In January 1776 Thomas Paine's pamphlet *Common Sense* was published and sold thousands of copies. Paine's arguments convinced many Americans of the need for a total break from Great Britain. On July 2 the Continental Congress adopted the resolution "that these United Colonies are, and, of right, ought to be, free and independent states." On July 4 they passed the Declaration of Independence, penned by Thomas Jefferson, to explain to the world the reasons for their decision for independence and war.

The Revolutionary War

The American Revolution had three interrelated components. First, it was a military confrontation between Great Britain and the colonies. It was also a continuation of the struggles between Great Britain and France, with France allying itself with the Americans to avenge defeat in previous wars with Britain. Lastly, the American Revolution was a civil war, with the American population divided between supporters of Great Britain (loyalists) and supporters of independence.

The military confrontation seemed a mismatch. On one side was the British Empire with the powerful British navy and one of the world's leading professional armies. The population of the British Isles in 1776 was 11.5 million, compared to 2.5 million colonists (of which a third were either loyalists or slaves). The armed forces the colonies were able to muster lacked training, experienced officers, naval support, equipment, and money. The Continental Army led by George Washington was defeated repeatedly by British forces in the early years of the war. However, the Americans did have the advantage of fighting on their home territory. The British were fighting in unfamiliar and often unfriendly circumstances and had to be equipped and supplied from abroad. Washington was able to achieve his underlying objective of keeping his forces together and prolonging the war until the British no longer wished to fight.

Diplomacy played a major role in the American Revolution, as many European nations, envious and fearful of Great Britain's worldwide power, took various steps to ensure British defeat and American victory. The most significant of these nations was France. Eager for British defeat, the French government secretly supplied much of the munitions used by the Americans in the first years of the war. In 1778, following American victory in Saratoga, New York, France openly allied itself with the rebelling colonies. French naval and armed forces were instrumental in the Battle of Yorktown in 1781, the last major battle of the war and one of the few outright victories for the Americans.

The Revolutionary War was in some respects a civil war. Many of the colonists remained loyal to Great Britain or were indifferent. The British had planned to enlist the help of loyalists (or Tories), who totaled about a quarter of the American population. Loyalists were drawn from all social ranks and classes, ranging from prominent landowners to African slaves and members of ethnic and religious minorities. Nevertheless, the effectiveness of loyalists in helping the British was hampered by three factors: the vigilant actions of the local patriot (Whig) militia, the cruelty of many English soldiers toward the

American populace, and the decision of about 100,000 loyalists to flee the country during the Revolutionary War.

The State Constitutions and the Articles of Confederation

While the military battles, the diplomatic maneuverings, and the clashes between Whigs and loyalists proceeded, the new United States of America attempted to create a government. All thirteen former colonies had formulated and passed new state constitutions before the Revolutionary War was over. Most of these constitutions included guarantees of civil liberties, including freedom of speech, religion, and the press; many extended suffrage to most white male taxpayers. Meanwhile the Continental Congress, without formal and defined powers, took on more of the trappings and duties of a national government: It created and supplied the Continental Army (with George Washington as commander in chief), issued paper currency, established a post office, and oversaw diplomatic efforts. In 1777 the national body approved the Articles of Confederation. Ratified by all the states by 1781, the Articles formalized some of the powers Congress was already using and created a central government—but a government sharply limited in its powers to tax American citizens or directly regulate the states. Sovereignty and political authority remained with the states and the colonial assemblies that governed them—a deliberate decision by Americans who did not want independence from Britain only to be ruled by a new, large, remote, and potentially tyrannical government.

The major legislative achievements of the Confederation Congress were the Land Ordinance in 1785 and the Northwest Ordinance in 1787. These laws provided for the orderly surveying, sale, and governing of the western territories. The Northwest Ordinance was notable for establishing the principle that these territories should eventually enter the Union as states fully equal to the original thirteen and for banning slavery in the new territories.

Postwar Problems

Great Britain formally recognized American independence in the Treaty of Paris in 1783, in which the United States also gained western territory bordered by Canada to the north, Florida to the south, and the Mississippi River to the west. However, the new nation of 900,000 square miles and 3 million people faced several significant difficulties. An economic depression hit the new nation in 1784, aggravated by the loss of trading privileges with the British West Indies and of British naval protection against North African pirates. Commerce was also hurt by Spain's closure of the Mississippi River to American goods and by the fact that each state set its own tariff rate (the national government under the Articles of Confederation had no authority to regulate trade). The Confederation Congress, unable to levy taxes, could neither support its issued currency nor meet payments on domestic or foreign debt. Diplomacy faltered because the national government was unable to enforce any obligations it entered into with foreign nations. State laws and taxes pitted debtors against creditors. Shays's Rebellion, in which Massachusetts farmers in 1786 violently resisted tax and debt collection, alarmed many Americans fearful of anarchy. Congress also proved unable to respond to conflicts between Native Americans and the rapidly increasing number of white settlers moving west. Attempts to amend the Articles fell short of the required unanimous consent of the states.

In May 1787 leading American figures gathered in Philadelphia to devise a replacement for the Articles of Confederation. The result of their deliberations was the U.S. Constitution. The Philadelphia meeting had been proposed in 1786 at an earlier convention, called by Virginia to discuss problems of interstate commerce. The delegates of the Philadelphia convention, which included such noted national figures as George Washington, Benjamin Franklin, and James Madison, decided to go beyond merely revising the Articles of Confederation by devising a whole new system of government.

The document they created differed from the Articles of Confederation in several important respects. It created a national government with powers to tax and regulate commerce, whose laws would be held supreme over conflicting state laws. States would be forbidden from conducting foreign policy, coining money, or setting tariff rates. Unlike the Articles of Confederation, which concentrated legislative, judicial, and executive functions in Congress, the Constitution established three separate branches of government. In the Confederation Congress each state had one vote; the Constitution, in a crucial compromise, created a divided legislature in which each state had two votes in the Senate, but votes relative to its population in the House of Representatives.

Ratification of the Constitution

Many Americans had been generally satisfied with the government under the Articles of Confederation and were highly suspicious of this attempt to create a new and more powerful central government. The ratification of the Constitution—a step that required the approval of special ratifying conventions by nine of the thirteen states—was marked by an intense public controversy that featured hundreds of newspaper articles and pamphlets debating the merits and demerits of the Constitution. Opponents of the Constitution—termed anti-federalists—criticized the creation of what they viewed as a potentially tyrannical government with supremacy over the states. Many criticized the lack of a bill of rights. In Massachusetts and other states, passage was secured after supporters of the Constitution (federalists) pledged to immediately amend the Constitution by adding a bill of rights. Due in large part to this promise, the Constitution was successfully ratified in 1788. The new Congress passed ten amendments (drafted largely by James Madison) in 1789; they were ratified in 1791 and are known today as the Bill of Rights.

Early Domestic and Foreign Policy Disputes

The first government under the new Constitution assembled in New York City in 1789. George Washington, the nation's first president, took care to appoint to his administration people who had supported the Constitution. Yet this did not prevent divisions within America's government and Washington's administration over important public policy decisions involving foreign policy and finance. Relations with France, Great Britain, and Spain were difficult, especially after those three nations went to war with each other in 1793. The people Washington appointed, especially Secretary of the Treasury Alexander Hamilton and Secretary of State Thomas Jefferson, differed over which nation to support, as well as such issues as the creation of a national bank and the funding of the national debt.

Two political camps emerged within Washington's administration. One, led by Hamilton, advocated a strong and vigorous national government and generally backed Great Britain in foreign policy. The other, led by Jefferson and James Madison, then a member of the House of Representatives, advocated a weaker central government and favored France in foreign disputes. The differences signaled the emergence of opposing political parties—the Federalists, led by Hamilton, and the Democratic-Republicans, led by Jefferson. This development was something the makers of the Constitution did not anticipate. Political parties were bitterly attacked by George Washington in his Farewell Address in 1796. Their emergence clearly shows that the momentous decision for independence, the victorious war with Great Britain, and the successful creation of the Constitution did not mark the end of political controversy within the United States.

The Decision to Break from Great Britain

VIEWPOINT 11A

Parliament Is Abusing the Rights of Americans (1764)

Stephen Hopkins (1707–1785)

Between 1763 and 1765 the British Parliament passed a series of controversial laws meant to recover costs from the French and Indian War. Among these laws were stiffer regulations on colonial trade, and the Stamp Act, a direct tax colonists had to pay on legal documents, pamphlets, and newspapers. The following viewpoint is excerpted from one of the many pamphlets written at this time protesting these new British policies. The author is Stephen Hopkins, then the colonial governor of Rhode Island. Unlike the governors of most other colonies, who were appointed by the colony's proprietor or by the king or queen of England, Rhode Island's governor was elected by members of its colonial assembly. Hopkins's pamphlet, entitled *The Rights of Colonists Examined*, was widely acclaimed and reprinted several times in the colonies and in Great Britain. In it Hopkins argues that Americans share with the citizens of Great Britain the rights and liberties granted under the British constitution (the fundamental rights and freedoms that had evolved in English common law over the previous centuries). Hopkins asserts that recent British actions such as the Stamp Act are jeopardizing these rights. The writings of Hopkins and others, as well as political protests and economic boycotts organized by the colonists, caused Parliament to repeal the Stamp Act in 1766.

Hopkins did not originally advocate American independence from Great Britain. In 1776, however, he was one of the signers of the Declaration of Independence.

How does Hopkins define liberty? How, in his view, have the American colonists fully demonstrated their loyalty to Great Britain? What contrasts does he draw between colonial history and recent developments?

Liberty is the greatest blessing that men enjoy, and slavery the heaviest curse that human nature is capable of.—This being so, makes it a matter of the utmost importance to men, which of the two shall be their portion. Absolute liberty is, perhaps, incompatible with any kind of government.—The safety resulting from society, and the advantage of just and equal laws, hath caused men to forego some part of their natural liberty, and submit to government. This appears to be the most rational account of its beginning; although, it must be confessed, mankind have by no means been agreed about it. Some have found its origin in the divine appointment; others have thought it took its rise from power; enthusiasts have dreamed that dominion was founded in grace. Leaving these points to be settled [in the future], we will consider the British constitution, as it at present stands, on revolution principles; and from thence endeavor to find the measure of the magistrate's power and the people's obedience.

This glorious constitution, the best that ever existed among men, will be confessed by all, to be founded by compact, and established by consent of the people. By this most beneficent compact, British subjects are governed only agreeable to laws to which themselves have some way consented; and are not to be compelled to part with their property, but as it is called for by the authority of such laws. The former, is truly liberty; the latter is really to be possessed of property, and to have something that may be called one's own.

The Rights of Colonists

On the contrary, those who are governed at the will of another, or of others, and whose property may be

From *The Rights of Colonists Examined* by Stephen Hopkins (Providence, RI, 1764). Reprinted in *Records of the Colony of Rhode Island and the Providence Plantations*, vol. 6, edited by John R. Bartlett (Providence, 1861).

taken from them by taxes, or otherwise, without their own consent, and against their will, are in the miserable condition of slaves. "For liberty solely consists in an independency upon the will of another; and by the name of slave, we understand a man who can neither dispose of his person or goods, but enjoys all at the will of his master," says [Algernon] Sidney, on government. These things premised, whether the British American colonies, on the continent, are justly entitled to like privileges and freedom as their fellow subjects in Great Britain are, shall be the chief point examined. In discussing this question, we shall make the colonies in New England, with whose rights we are best acquainted, the rule of our reasoning; not in the least doubting but all the others are justly entitled to like rights with them.

New England was first planted by adventurers, who left England, their native country, by permission of King Charles the First; and, at their own expense, transported themselves to America, with great risk and difficulty settled among savages, and in a very surprising manner formed new colonies in the wilderness. Before their departure, the terms of their freedom, and the relation they should stand in to the mother country, in their emigrant state, were fully settled; they were to remain subject to the King, and dependent on the kingdom of Great Britain. In return, they were to receive protection, and enjoy all the rights and privileges of free-born Englishmen.

The Colonial Charters

This is abundantly proved by the charter given to the Massachusetts colony, while they were still in England, and which they received and brought over with them, as the authentic evidence of the conditions they removed upon. The colonies of Connecticut and Rhode Island, also, afterwards obtained charters from the crown, granting them the like ample privileges. By all these charters, it is in the most express and solemn manner granted, that these adventurers, and their children after them for ever, should have and enjoy all the freedom and liberty that the subjects in England enjoy; that they might make laws for their own government, suitable to their circumstances not repugnant to, but as near as might be, agreeable to the laws of England; that they might purchase lands, acquire goods, and use trade for their advantage, and have an absolute property in whatever they justly acquired. These, with many other gracious privileges, were granted them by several kings; and they were to pay, as an acknowledgment to the crown, only one-fifth part of the ore of gold and silver, that should at any time be found in the said colonies, in lieu of, and full satisfaction for, all dues and demands of the crown and kingdom of England upon them.

There is not any thing new or extraordinary in these rights granted to the British colonies; the colonies from all countries, at all times, have enjoyed equal freedom with the mother state. Indeed, there would be found very few people in the world, willing to leave their native country, and go through the fatigue and hardship of planting in a new uncultivated one, for the sake of losing their freedom. They who settle new countries, must be poor; and, in course, ought to be free. Advantages, pecuniary or agreeable, are not on the side of emigrants; and surely they must have something in their stead.

Colonies in History

To illustrate this, permit us to examine what hath generally been the condition of colonies with respect to their freedom; we will begin with those who went out from the ancient commonwealths of Greece, which are the first, perhaps, we have any good account of. Thucidides, that grave and judicious historian, says of one of them, "they were not sent out to be slaves, but to be the equals of those who remain behind;" and again, the Corinthians gave public notice, "that a new colony was going to Epidamus, into which, all that would enter, should have equal and like privileges with those who stayed at home." This was uniformly the condition of all the Grecian colonies; they went out and settled new countries; they took such forms of government as themselves chose, though it generally nearly resembled that of the mother state, whether democratical or oligarchical. . . .

When we come down to the latter ages of the world, and consider the colonies planted in the three last centuries, in America, from several kingdoms in Europe, we shall find them, says [Samuel von] Puffendorf, very different from the ancient colonies, and gives us an instance in those of the Spaniards. Although it be confessed, these fall greatly short of enjoying equal freedom with the ancient Greek and Roman ones; yet it will be said truly, they enjoy equal freedom with their countrymen in Spain; but as they are all under the government of an absolute monarch, they have no reason to complain that one enjoys the liberty the other is deprived of. The French colonies will be found nearly in the same condition, and for the same reason, because their fellow subjects in France, have also lost their liberty. And the question here is not whether all colonies, as compared one with another, enjoy equal liberty, but whether all enjoy as much freedom as the inhabitants of the mother state; and this will hardly be denied in the case of the Spanish, French, or other modern foreign colonies.

By this, it fully appears, that colonies, in general, both ancient and modern, have always enjoyed as much freedom as the mother state from which they went out; and will any one suppose the British colonies in America, are an exception to this general rule? Colonies that came out from a kingdom renowned for liberty; from a constitution founded on compact; from a people, of all the sons of men, the most tenacious of freedom; who left the delights of their native country, parted from their homes, and all their conveniences, searched out and subdued a foreign country, with the most amazing travail and fortitude, to the infinite advantage and emolument of the mother state; that removed on a firm reliance of a solemn compact, and royal promise and grant, that they, and their successors for ever, should be free; should be partakers and sharers in all the privileges and advantages of the then English, now British constitution.

Equal Liberty

If it were possible a doubt could yet remain, in the most unbelieving mind, that these British colonies are not every way justly and fully entitled to equal liberty and freedom with their fellow subjects in Europe, we might show, that the parliament of Great Britain, have always understood their rights in the same light.

By an act passed in the thirteenth year of the reign of his late majesty King George the Second, entitled an act for naturalizing foreign protestants, &c.; and by another act passed in the twentieth year of the same reign, for nearly the same purposes, by both which it is enacted and ordained, "that all foreign protestants, who had inhabited, and resided for the space of seven years, or more, in any of his majesty's colonies, in America," might, on the conditions therein mentioned, be naturalized, and thereupon should "be deemed, adjudged and taken to be his majesty's natural born subjects of the kingdom of Great Britain, to all intents, constructions and purposes, as if they, and every one of them, had been, or were born within the same." No reasonable man will here suppose the parliament intended by these acts to put foreigners, who had been in the colonies only seven years, in a better condition than those who had been born in them, or had removed from Britain thither, but only to put these foreigners on an equality with them; and to do this, they are obliged to give them all the rights of natural born subjects of Great Britain.

From what hath been shown, it will appear beyond a doubt, that the British subjects in America, have equal rights with those in Britain; that they do not hold those rights as a privilege granted them, nor enjoy them as a grace and favor bestowed; but possess them as an inherent indefeasible right; as they, and their ancestors, were free-born subjects, justly and naturally entitled to all the rights and advantages of the British constitution.

New Laws

And the British legislative and executive powers have considered the colonies as possessed of these rights, and have always heretofore, in the most tender and parental manner, treated them as their dependent, though free, condition required. The protection promised on the part of the crown, with cheerfulness and great gratitude we acknowledge, hath at all times been given to the colonies. The dependence of the colonies to Great Britain, hath been fully testified by a constant and ready obedience to all the commands of His present Majesty, and his royal predecessors; both men and money having been raised in them at all times when called for, with as much alacrity and in as large proportions as hath been done in Great Britain, the ability of each considered. It must also be confessed with thankfulness, that the first adventurers and their successors, for one hundred and thirty years, have fully enjoyed all the freedoms and immunities promised on their first removal from England. But here the scene seems to be unhappily changing. The British ministry, whether induced by a jealousy of the colonies, by false informations, or by some alteration in the system of political government, we have no information; whatever hath been the motive, this we are sure of, the parliament in their last session, passed an act, limiting, restricting and burdening the trade of these colonies, much more than had ever been done before; as also for greatly enlarging the power and jurisdiction of the courts of admiralty in the colonies; and also came to a resolution, that it might be necessary to establish stamp duties, and other internal taxes, to be collected within them. This act and this resolution, have caused great uneasiness and consternation among the British subjects on the continent of America; how much reason there is for it, we will endeavor, in the most modest and plain manner we can, to lay before our readers.

In the first place, let it be considered, that although each of the colonies hath a legislature within itself, to take care of it's interests, and provide for it's peace and internal government; yet there are many things of a more general nature, quite out of the reach of these particular legislatures, which it is necessary should be regulated, ordered and governed. One of this kind is, the commerce of the whole British empire, taken collectively, and that of each kingdom and colony in it, as it makes a part of that whole. Indeed, every thing that concerns the proper interest and fit government of the whole commonwealth, of keeping the peace, and subordination of all the parts towards the whole, and one among another, must be considered in this light. Amongst these general concerns, perhaps, money and paper credit, those grand instruments of all commerce, will be found also to have a place. These, with all other matters of a general nature, it is absolutely necessary should have a general power to direct them; some supreme and over ruling authority, with power to make laws, and form regulations for the good of all, and to compel their execution and observation. It being necessary some such general power should exist somewhere, every man of the least knowledge of the British constitution, will be naturally led to look for, and find it in the parliament of Great Britain; that grand and august legislative body, must, from the nature of their authority, and the necessity of the thing, be justly vested with this power. Hence, it becomes the indispensable duty of every good and loyal subject, cheerfully to obey and patiently submit to all the acts, laws, orders and regulations that may be made and passed by parliament, for directing and governing all these general matters.

Here it may be urged by many, and indeed, with great appearance of reason, that the equity, justice, and beneficence of the British constitution, will require, that the separate kingdoms and distant colonies, who are to obey and be governed by these general laws and regulations, ought to be represented, some way or other, in parliament; at least whilst these general matters are under consideration. Whether the colonies will ever be admitted to have representatives in parliament,—whether it be consistent with their distant and dependent state,—and whether if it were admitted, it would be to their advantage,—are questions we will pass by; and observe, that these colonies ought in justice, and for the very evident good of the whole commonwealth, to have notice of every new measure about to be pursued, and new act that is about to be passed, by which their rights, liberties, or interests will be affected; they ought to have such notice, that they may appear and be heard by their agents, by council, or written representation, or by some other equitable and effectual way. . . .

Unfair Taxes

The resolution of the house of commons, come into during the same session of parliament, asserting their rights to establish stamp duties, and internal taxes, to be collected in the colonies without their own consent, hath much more, and for much more reason, alarmed the British subjects in America, than any thing that had ever been done before. These resolutions, carried into execution, the colonies cannot help but consider as a manifest violation of their just and long enjoyed rights. For it must be confessed by all men, that they who are taxed at pleasure by others, cannot possibly have any property, can have nothing to be called their own; they who have no property, can have no freedom, but are indeed reduced to the most abject slavery; are in a condition far worse than countries conquered and made tributary; for these have only a fixed sum to pay, which they are left to raise among themselves, in the way that they may think most equal and easy; and having paid the stipulated sum, the debt is discharged, and what is left is their own. This is much more tolerable than to be taxed at the mere will of others, without any bounds, without any stipulation and agreement, contrary to their consent, and against their will. If we are told that those who lay these taxes upon the colonies, are men of the highest character for their wisdom, justice and integrity, and therefore cannot be supposed to deal hardly, unjustly, or unequally by any; admitting, and really believing that all this is true, it will make no alteration in the nature of the case; for one who is bound to obey the will of another, is as really a slave, though he may have a good master, as if he had a bad one; and this is stronger in politic bodies than in natural ones, as the former have perpetual succession, and remain the same; and although they may have a very good master at one time, they may have a very bad one at another. And indeed, if the people in America, are to be taxed by the representatives of the people in Britain, their malady is an increasing evil, that must always grow greater by time. Whatever burdens are laid upon the Americans, will be so much taken off the Britons; and the doing this, will soon be extremely popular; and those who put up to be members of the house of commons, must obtain the votes of the people, by promising to take more and more of the taxes off them, by putting it on the Americans. This must most assuredly be the case, and it will not be in the power even of the parliament to prevent it; the people's private interest will be concerned, and will govern them; they will have such, and only such representatives as will act agreeable to this their interest; and these taxes laid on Americans, will be always a part of the supply bill, in which the other branches of the Legislature can make no alteration; and in truth, the subjects in the colonies will be taxed at the will and pleasure of their fellow subjects in Britain.— How equitable, and how just this may be, must be left to every impartial man to determine.

Needed for Defence?

But it will be said, that the monies drawn from the colonies by duties, and by taxes, will be laid up and set apart to be used for their future defence. This will not at all alleviate the hardship, but serves only more strongly to mark the servile state of the people. Free people have ever thought, and always will think, that the money necessary for their defence, lies safest in their own hands, until it be wanted immediately for that purpose. To take the money of the Americans, which they want continually to use in their trade, and lay it up for their defence, at a thousand leagues distance from them, when the enemies they have to fear, are in their own neighborhood, hath not the greatest probability of friendship or of prudence. . . .

Important Questions

We are not insensible, that when liberty is in danger, the liberty of complaining is dangerous; yet, a man on a wreck was never denied the liberty of roaring as loud as he could, says Dean Swift. And we believe no good reason can be given, why the colonies should not modestly and soberly inquire, what right the parliament of Great Britain have to tax them. We know such inquiries, by a late letter writer, have been branded with the little epithet of *mushroom policy*; and he insinuates, that for the colonies to pretend to claim any privileges, will draw down the resentment of the parliament on them.—Is the defence of liberty become so contemptible, and pleading for just rights so dangerous? Can the guardians of liberty be thus ludicrous? Can the patrons of freedom be so jealous and so severe? If the British house of commons are rightfully possessed of a power to tax the colonies in America, this power must be vested in them by the British constitution, as they are one branch of the great legislative body of the nation; as they are the representatives of all the people in Britain, they have, beyond doubt, all the power such a representation can possibly give; yet, great as this power is, surely it cannot exceed that of their constituents. And can it possibly be shown that the people in Britain have a sovereign authority over their fellow subjects in America? Yet such is the authority that must be exercised in taking peoples' estates from them by taxes, or otherwise, without their consent. In all aids granted to the crown, by the parliament, it is said with the greatest propriety, "We freely give unto Your Majesty;" for they give their own money, and the money of those who have entrusted them with a proper power for that purpose. But can they, with the same propriety, give away the money of the Americans, who have never given any such power? Before a thing can be justly given away, the giver must certainly have acquired a property in it; and have the people in Britain justly acquired such a property in the goods and estates of the people in these colonies, that they may give them away at pleasure?

In an imperial state, which consists of many separate governments, each of which hath peculiar privileges, and of which kind it is evident the empire of Great Britain is; no single part, though greater than another part, is by that superiority entitled to make laws for, or to tax such lesser part; but all laws, and all taxations, which bind the whole, must be made by the whole. This may be fully verified by the empire of Germany, which consists of many states; some powerful, and others weak; yet the powerful never make laws to govern or to tax the little and weak ones; neither is it done by the emperor, but only by the diet, consisting of the representatives of the whole body. Indeed, it must be absurd to suppose, that the common people of Great Britain have a sovereign and absolute authority over their fellow subjects in America, or even any sort of power whatsoever, over them; but it will be still more absurd to suppose they can give a power to their representatives, which they have not themselves. If the house of commons do not receive this authority from their constituents, it will be difficult to tell by what means they obtained it, except it be vested in them by mere superiority and power.

Defending the Colonies

Should it be urged, that the money expended by the mother country, for the defence and protection of America, and especially during the late war, must justly entitle her to some retaliation from the colonies; and that the stamp duties and taxes, intended to be raised in them, are only designed for that equitable purpose; if we are permitted to examine how far this may rightfully vest the parliament with the power of taxing the colonies, we shall find this claim to have no sort of equitable foundation. In many of the colonies, especially those in New England, who were planted, as is before observed, not at the charge of the crown or kingdom of England, but at the expense of the planters themselves; and were not only planted, but also defended against the savages, and other enemies, in long and cruel wars, which continued for an hundred years, almost without intermission, solely at their own charge; and in the year 1746, when the Duke D'Anville came out from France, with the most formidable French fleet that ever was in the American seas, enraged at these colonies for the loss of [Fort] Louisbourg, the year before, and with orders to make an attack on them; even in this greatest exigence, these colonies were left to the protection of Heaven and their own efforts. These colonies having thus planted and defended themselves, and removed all enemies from their borders, were in hopes to enjoy peace, and recruit their state, much exhausted by these long struggles; but they were soon called upon to raise men, and send out to the defence of other colonies, and to make conquests for the crown; they dutifully obeyed the requisition, and with ardor entered into those services, and continued in them, until all encroachments were removed, and all Canada, and even the Havana, conquered. They most cheerfully complied with every call of the crown; they rejoiced, yea, even exulted, in the prosperity and exaltation of the British empire. But these colonies, whose bounds were fixed, and whose borders were before cleared from enemies, by their own fortitude, and at their own expense, reaped no sort of advantage by these conquests; they are not enlarged, have not gained a single acre of land, have no part in the Indian or interior trade; the immense tracts of land subdued, and no less immense and profitable commerce acquired, all belong to Great Britain; and not the least share or portion to these colonies, though thousands of their men have lost their lives, and millions of their money have been expended in the purchase of them for great part of which we are yet in debt, and from which we shall not in many years be able to extricate ourselves. Hard will be the fate, yea, cruel the destiny, of these unhappy colonies, if the reward they are to receive for all this, is the loss of their freedom; better for them Canada still remained French; yea, far more eligible that it ever should remain so, than that the price of its reduction should be their slavery.

"The resolution of the house of commons, . . . asserting their rights to establish . . . taxes, to be collected in the colonies without their own consent, hath . . . alarmed the British subjects in America."

If the colonies are not taxed by parliament, are they therefore exempted from bearing their proper share in the necessary burdens of government? This by no means follows. Do they not support a regular internal government in each colony, as expensive to the people here, as the internal government of Britain is to the people there? Have not the colonies here, at all times when called upon by the crown, raised money for the public service, done it as cheerfully as the parliament have done on like occasions? Is not this the most easy, the most natural, and most constitutional way of raising money in the colonies? What occasion then to distrust the colonies? What necessity to fall on an invidious and unconstitutional method, to compel them to do what they have ever done freely? Are not the people in the colonies as loyal and dutiful subjects as any age or nation ever produced? And are they not as useful to the king-

dom, in this remote quarter of the world, as their fellow subjects are who dwell in Britain? The parliament, it is confessed, have power to regulate the trade of the whole empire; and hath it not full power, by this means, to draw all the money and all the wealth of the colonies into the mother country, at pleasure? What motive, after all this, can remain, to induce the parliament to abridge the privileges, and lessen the rights of the most loyal and dutiful subjects; subjects justly entitled to ample freedom, who have long enjoyed, and not abused or forfeited their liberties; who have used them to their own advantage, in dutiful subserviency to the orders and interests of Great Britain? Why should the gentle current of tranquillity, that has so long run with peace through all the British states, and flowed with joy and with happiness in all her countries, be at last obstructed, be turned out of its true course, into unusual and winding channels, by which many of those states must be ruined; but none of them can possibly be made more rich or more happy? . . .

Faithful Subjects

We finally beg leave to assert, that the first planters of these colonies were pious christians; were faithful subjects; who, with a fortitude and perseverance little known, and less considered, settled these wild countries, by God's goodness, and their own amazing labors; thereby added a most valuable dependence to the crown of Great Britain; were ever dutifully subservient to her interests; so taught their children, that not one has been disaffected to this day; but all have honestly obeyed every royal command, and cheerfully submitted to every constitutional law; have as little inclination as they have ability, to throw off their dependency; have carefully avoided every offensive measure, and every interdicted manufacture; have risked their lives as they have been ordered, and furnished their money when it has been called for; have never been troublesome or expensive to the mother country; have kept due order, and supported a regular government; have maintained peace, and practiced christianity; and in all conditions, and in every relation, have demeaned [conducted] themselves as loyal, as dutiful, and as faithful subjects ought; and that no kingdom or state hath, or ever had, colonies more quiet, more obedient, or more profitable, than these have ever been.

May the same divine goodness, that guided the first planters, protected the settlements, inspired kings to be gracious, parliaments to be tender, ever preserve, ever support our present gracious King; give great wisdom to his ministers, and much understanding to his parliaments; perpetuate the sovereignty of the British constitution, and the filial dependency and happiness of all the colonies.

VIEWPOINT 11B

Parliament Is Not Abusing the Rights of Americans (1765)

Martin Howard (ca. 1720–1781)

In February 1765 a pamphlet was published sharply attacking Rhode Island governor Stephen Hopkins's tract *The Rights of Colonists Examined*, in which Hopkins had asserted that American colonists held the same political rights as Englishmen. The anonymous writer purported to be a gentleman from Halifax, Nova Scotia, but was in fact Martin Howard, a resident of Newport, Rhode Island. Howard was a lawyer and landowner involved in a political faction opposed to Hopkins. In his pamphlet, excerpted here, Howard sharply attacks both Hopkins's writing style and his arguments. Howard asserts that the political rights of colonists are limited by their colonial charters, and he refutes Hopkins's arguments that the colonists share equal rights with the English. His sympathies toward Great Britain known (despite his use of a pseudonym in this instance), Howard was forced to flee Rhode Island after being attacked by mobs during the August 1765 Stamp Act riots.

What distinctions does Howard make between personal and political rights? How does he respond to the argument that colonists cannot be taxed by Parliament without representation in that body? How popular does Howard believe to be his own views in the colonies?

My Dear Sir,

I thank you very kindly for the pamphlets and newspapers you was so obliging as to send me. I will, according to your request, give you a few miscellaneous strictures on that pamphlet, wrote by Mr. *H—p—s,* your governor, entitled *The Rights of Colonies Examined.* . . .

The Rights of Colonies Examined is a labored, ostentatious piece, discovers its author to be totally unacquainted with style or diction, and eagerly fond to pass upon the world for a man of letters. . . .

However disguised, polished, or softened the expression of this pamphlet may seem, yet everyone must see that its professed design is sufficiently prominent throughout, namely, to prove *that the colonies have rights independent of, and not controllable by the authority of Parliament.* It is upon this dangerous and indiscreet position I shall communicate to you my real sentiments.

From *A Letter from a Gentleman at Halifax, to His Friend in Rhode Island, Containing Remarks upon a Pamphlet Entitled "The Rights of Colonists Examined"* by Martin Howard (Newport, RI, 1765).

Parliament and the Colonies

To suppose a design of enslaving the colonies by Parliament is too presumptuous; to propagate it in print is perhaps dangerous. Perplexed between a desire of speaking all he thinks and the fear of saying too much, the honorable author is obliged to entrench himself in obscurity and inconsistency in several parts of his performance: I shall bring one instance.

In page eleven he says, "It is the indispensable duty of every good and loyal subject cheerfully to obey, and patiently submit to, all the laws, orders, etc., that may be passed by Parliament."

I do not much admire either the spirit or composition of this sentence. Is it the duty *only* of good and loyal subjects to obey? Are the wicked and disloyal subjects absolved from this obligation? Else why is this passage so marvelously penned? Philoleutherus Lipsiensis would directly pronounce this a figure in rhetoric called nonsense. Believe me, my friend, I did not quote this passage to show my skill in criticism, but to point out a contradiction between it and another passage in page twenty, which runs thus: "It must be absurd to suppose that the common people of Great Britain have a sovereign and absolute authority over their fellow subjects of America, *or even any sort of power whatsoever over them*; but it will be still more absurd to suppose they can give a power to their representatives which they have not themselves," etc. Here it is observable that the first cited passage expresses a full submission to the authority of Parliament; the last is as explicit a denial of that authority. The sum of His Honor's argument is this: the people of Great Britain have not any sort of power over the Americans; the House of Commons have no greater authority than the people of Great Britain who are their constituents; *ergo*, the House of Commons *have not any sort of power over the Americans*. This is indeed a curious invented syllogism, the sole merit of which is due to the first magistrate of an English colony.

I have endeavored to investigate the true natural relation, if I may so speak, between colonies and their mother state, abstracted from compact or positive institution, but here I can find nothing satisfactory. Till this relation is clearly defined upon a rational and natural principle, our reasoning upon the measure of the colonies' obedience will be desultory and inconclusive. Every connection in life has its reciprocal duties; we know the relation between a parent and child, husband and wife, master and servant, and from thence are able to deduce their respective obligations. But we have no notices of any such precise natural relation between a mother state and its colonies, and therefore cannot reason with so much certainty upon the power of the one or the duty of the others. The ancients have transmitted to us nothing that is applicable to the state of modern colonies because the relation between these is formed by political compact, and the condition of each, variant in their original and from each other. The honorable author has not freed this subject from any of its embarrassments: vague and diffuse talk of rights and privileges, and ringing the changes upon the words liberty and slavery only serve to convince us that words may affect without raising images or affording any repose to a mind philosophically inquisitive. For my own part, I will shun the walk of metaphysics in my inquiry, and be content to consider the colonies' rights upon the footing of their charters, which are the only plain avenues that lead to the truth of this matter.

The several New England charters ascertain, define, and limit the respective rights and privileges of each colony, and I cannot conceive how it has come to pass that the colonies now claim any other or greater rights than are therein expressly granted to them. I fancy when we speak or think of the rights of freeborn Englishmen, we confound those rights which are personal with those which are political: there is a distinction between these which ought always to be kept in view.

Personal and Political Rights

Our personal rights, comprehending those of life, liberty, and estate, are secured to us by the common law, which is every subject's birthright, whether born in Great Britain, on the ocean, or in the colonies; and it is in this sense we are said to enjoy all the rights and privileges of Englishmen. The political rights of the colonies or the powers of government communicated to them are more limited, and their nature, quality, and extent depend altogether upon the patent or charter which first created and instituted them. As individuals, the colonists participate of every blessing the English constitution can give them: as corporations created by the crown, they are confined within the primitive views of their institution. Whether, therefore, their indulgence is scanty or liberal can be no cause of complaint; for when they accepted of their charters they tacitly submitted to the terms and conditions of them.

The colonies have no rights independent of their charters; they can claim no greater than those give them; by those the Parliamentary jurisdiction over them is not taken away, neither could any grant of the King abridge that jurisdiction, because it is founded upon common law, as I shall presently show, and was prior to any charter or grant to the colonies: every Englishman, therefore, is subject to this jurisdiction, and it follows him wherever he goes. It is of the essence of government that there should be a supreme head, and it would be a solecism in politics to talk of members independent of it.

With regard to the jurisdiction of Parliament, I shall endeavor to show that it is attached to every English subject wherever he be, and I am led to do this from a clause in page nine of His Honor's pamphlet, where he says "That the colonies do not hold their rights as a privilege granted them, nor enjoy them as a grace and favor bestowed, but possess them as an inherent, indefeasible right." This postulatum cannot be true with regard to political rights, for I have already shown that these are derived from your charters, and are held by force of the King's grant; therefore these inherent, indefeasible rights, as His Honor calls them, must be personal ones, according to the distinction already made. Permit me to say that inherent and indefeasible as these rights may be, the jurisdiction of Parliament over every English subject is equally as inherent and indefeasible: that both have grown out of the same stock, and that if we avail ourselves of the one we must submit to and acknowledge the other.

It might here be properly enough asked, Are these personal rights self-existent? Have they no original source? I answer, They are derived from the constitution of England, which is the common law; and from the same fountain is also derived the jurisdiction of Parliament over us.

British Common Law

But to bring this argument down to the most vulgar apprehension: The common law has established it as a rule or maxim that the plantations are bound by British acts of Parliament if particularly named; and surely no Englishman in his senses will deny the force of a common law maxim. One cannot but smile at the inconsistency of these inherent, indefeasible men: if one of them has a suit at law, in any part of New England, upon a question of land, property, or merchandise, he appeals to the common law to support his claim or defeat his adversary, and yet is so profoundly stupid as to say that an act of Parliament does not bind him when perhaps the same page in a law book which points him out a remedy for a libel or a slap in the face would inform him that it does. In a word, the force of an act of Parliament over the colonies is predicated upon the common law, the origin and basis of all those inherent rights and privileges which constitute the boast and felicity of a Briton.

Can we claim the common law as an inheritance, and at the same time be at liberty to adopt one part of it and reject the other? Indeed we cannot. The common law, pure and indivisible in its nature and essence, cleaves to us during our lives and follows us from Nova Zembla to Cape Horn; and therefore, as the jurisdiction of Parliament arises out of and is supported by it, we may as well renounce our allegiance or change our nature as to be exempt from the jurisdiction of Parliament. Hence it is plain to me that in denying this jurisdiction we at the same time take leave of the common law, and thereby, with equal temerity and folly, strip ourselves of every blessing we enjoy as Englishmen: a flagrant proof, this, that shallow drafts in politics and legislation confound and distract us, and that an extravagant zeal often defeats its own purposes.

Taxation and Representation

I am aware that the foregoing reasoning will be opposed by the maxim "That no Englishman can be taxed but by his own consent or by representatives."

It is this dry maxim, taken in a literal sense and ill understood, that, like the song of "Lillibullero," has made all the mischief in the colonies; and upon this the partisans of the colonies' rights chiefly rest their cause. I don't despair, however, of convincing you that this maxim affords but little support to their argument when rightly examined and explained.

It is the opinion of the House of Commons, and may be considered as a law of Parliament, that they are the representatives of every British subject, wheresoever he be. In this view of the matter, then, the aforegoing maxim is fully vindicated in practice, and the whole benefit of it, in substance and effect, extended and applied to the *colonies.* Indeed the maxim must be considered in this latitude, for in a literal sense or construction it ever was, and ever will be, impracticable. Let me ask, Is the Isle of Man, Jersey, or Guernsey represented? What is the value or amount of each man's representation in the kingdom of Scotland, which contains near two millions of people, and yet not more than three thousand have votes in the election of members of Parliament? But to show still further that in fact and reality this right of representation is not of that consequence it is generally thought to be, let us take into the argument the moneyed interest of Britain, which, though immensely great, has no share in this representation. A worthless freeholder of forty shillings per annum can vote for a member of Parliament, whereas a merchant, though worth one hundred thousand pounds sterling, if it consist only in personal effects, has no vote at all. But yet let no one suppose that the interest of the latter is not equally the object of Parliamentary attention with the former. Let me add one example more. Copyholders in England of one thousand pounds sterling per annum, whose estates in land are nominally but not intrinsically inferior to a freehold cannot, by law, vote for members of Parliament; yet we never hear that these people *"murmur with submissive fear, and mingled rage."* They don't

set up their private humor against the constitution of their country, but submit with cheerfulness to those forms of government which providence, in its goodness, has placed them under.

Suppose that this Utopian privilege of representation should take place. I question if it would answer any other purpose but to bring an expense upon the colonies, unless you can suppose that a few American members could bias the deliberations of the whole British legislature. In short, this right of representation is but a phantom, and if possessed in its full extent would be of no real advantage to the colonies; they would, like Ixion, embrace a cloud in the shape of Juno.

The Danger of Innovations

In addition to this head, I could further urge the danger of innovations. Every change in a constitution in some degree weakens its original frame, and hence it is that legislators and statesmen are cautious in admitting them. The goodly building of the British constitution will be best secured and perpetuated by adhering to its original principles. Parliaments are not of yesterday; they are as ancient as our Saxon ancestors. Attendance in Parliament was originally a duty arising from a tenure of lands, and grew out of the feudal system, so that the privilege of sitting in it is territorial and confined to Britain only. Why should the beauty and symmetry of this body be destroyed and its purity defiled by the unnatural mixture of representatives from every part of the British dominions? *Parthians, Medes, Elamites, and the dwellers of Mesopotamia, etc.,* would not, in such a case, speak the same language. What a heterogeneous council would this form? What a monster in government would it be? In truth, my friend, the matter lies here: the freedom and happiness of every British subject depends not upon his share in elections but upon the sense and virtue of the British Parliament, and these depend reciprocally upon the sense and virtue of the whole nation. When virtue and honor are no more, the lovely frame of our constitution will be dissolved. Britain may one day be what Athens and Rome now are; but may Heaven long protract the hour!

The jurisdiction of Parliament being established, it will follow that this jurisdiction cannot be apportioned; it is transcendent and entire, and may levy internal taxes as well as regulate trade. There is no essential difference in the rights: a stamp duty is confessedly the most reasonable and equitable that can be devised, yet very far am I from desiring to see it established among us; but I fear the shaft is sped and it is now too late to prevent the blow.

The examples cited by His Honor with regard to ancient colonies may show his reading and erudition, but are of no authority in the present question. I am not enough skilled in the Grecian history to correct the proofs drawn from thence, though they amount to very little. If the Grecian colonies, as His Honor says, "took such forms of government as themselves chose," there is no kind of similitude between them and the English colonies, and therefore to name them is nothing to the purpose. The English colonies take their forms of government from the crown; hold their privileges upon condition that they do not abuse them; and hold their lands by the tenure of common socage, which involves in it fealty and obedience to the King. Hence it is plain His Honor's argument is not strengthened by the example of the Grecian colonies; for what likeness is there between independent colonies, as those must be which "took such forms of government as themselves chose," and colonies like ours, which are in a manner feudatory, and holden of a superior? . . .

———— • ————

"The several New England charters ascertain, define, and limit the respective rights and privileges of each colony, and I cannot conceive how it has come to pass that the colonies now claim any other or greater rights than are therein expressly granted to them."

———— • ————

If the practice of the ancients was of any authority in this case, I could name examples to justify the enslaving of colonies. The Carthaginians were a free people, yet they, to render the Sardinians and Corsicans more dependent, forbade their planting, sowing, or doing anything of the like kind under pain of death, so that they supplied them with necessaries from Africa: this was indeed very hard. But there is something extremely weak and inconclusive in recurring to the Grecian and Roman history for examples to illustrate any particular favorite opinion: if a deference to the ancients should direct the practice of the moderns, we might sell our children to pay our debts and justify it by the practice of the Athenians. We might lend our wives to our friends and justify it from the example of Cato, among the Romans. In a word, my dear sir, the belly of a sow, pickled, was a high dish in ancient Rome; and I imagine as you advance in the refinements of luxury this will become a capital part of a Rhode Island feast, so fond you seem of ancient customs and laws. Instead of wandering in the labyrinth of ancient colonies, I would advise His Honor to read the

debates in Parliament in the year one thousand seven hundred and thirty-three, when Mr. Partridge, your agent, petitioned the Commons against the then sugar bill; he will there find more satisfaction upon the subject of colonies than in Thucydides' *History of the Peloponnesian War*. It was declared in the course of that debate that the colonists were a part of the people of Great Britain, and, as such, fully represented in that House. The petition then presented by Mr. Partridge was of a very different temper from those now sent home by the colonies; it was extremely modest, and only intimated that the sugar bill if passed into a law might be prejudicial to their charter. At the bare mention of this Sir William Yonge took fire and said, *"It looked like aiming at an independency, and disclaiming the jurisdiction of that House, as if,"* says he, *"this House had not a power to tax the colonies."* Mr. Winnington, with equal warmth, added, *"I hope they have no charter which debars this House from taxing them as well as any other subject of the nation."* Here you have the opinion of two of the most eminent members of that time; they spoke the sentiments of the whole House, and these sentiments still continue the same. And from hence you may perceive how little prospect there is of the colonies' gaining any point upon the footing of these new supposititious rights; broaching such opinions will excite the jealousy of the Parliament, and you will be looked upon with an evil eye. The promoters of such doctrines are no friends to the colonies, whatever may be their pretensions. Can His Honor be so vain as to imagine that ten thousand such pamphlets as his will influence the Parliament, or that they will be persuaded, by the force of his elocution, to give up their supremacy and right of taxing the colonies? What purpose then can be served by these pamphlets but to embitter the minds of a simple, credulous, and hitherto loyal people, and to alienate their affections from Great Britain, their best friend, their protector, and alma mater? A different behavior would be much more prudent and politic. If we have anything to ask, we should remember that diffidence and modesty will always obtain more from generous minds than forwardness and impertinence.

Hopkins's Arguments Answered

The act of the thirteenth [year of the reign of] of his late Majesty [King George II], entitled An Act for Naturalizing of Foreign Protestants, had better have been omitted by His Honor; for if that act is to be the measure of the colonists' rights they will be more circumscribed than he would willingly choose. In that act there is a proviso that no person who shall become a natural-born subject by virtue of that act should be of the Privy Council, or a member of either house of Parliament, or capable of enjoying in

Great Britain or Ireland any place of trust, civil or military, etc. This statute confirms the distinction I have set up between personal and political rights. After naturalization, foreign Protestants are here admitted subjects to all intents and purposes, that is, to the full enjoyment of those rights which are connected with the person, liberty, or estate of Englishmen; but by the proviso they are excluded from bearing offices or honors. . . .

Believe me, my friend, it gives me great pain to see so much ingratitude in the colonies to the mother country, whose arms and money so lately rescued them from a French government. I have been told that some have gone so far as to say that they would, as things are, prefer such a government to an English one. Heaven knows I have but little malice in my heart, yet, for a moment, I ardently wish that these spurious, unworthy sons of Britain could feel the iron rod of a Spanish inquisitor or a French farmer of the revenue; it would indeed be a punishment suited to their ingratitude. Here I cannot but call to mind the adder in one of the fables of Pilpay, which was preparing to sting the generous traveler who had just rescued him from the flames.

You'll easily perceive that what I have said is upon the general design of His Honor's pamphlet; if he had divided his argument with any precision, I would have followed him with somewhat more of method. The dispute between Great Britain and the colonies consists of two parts: first, the jurisdiction of Parliament, and, secondly, the exercise of that jurisdiction. His Honor hath blended these together, and nowhere marked the division between them. The first I have principally remarked upon. As to the second, it can only turn upon the expediency or utility of those schemes which may, from time to time, be adopted by Parliament relative to the colonies. Under this head, I readily grant, they are at full liberty to remonstrate, petition, write pamphlets and newspapers without number, to prevent any improper or unreasonable imposition. Nay, I would have them do all this with that spirit of freedom which Englishmen always have, and I hope ever will, exert; but let us not use our liberty for a cloak of maliciousness. Indeed I am very sure the loyalty of the colonies has ever been irreproachable; but from the pride of some and the ignorance of others the cry against mother country has spread from colony to colony; and it is to be feared that prejudices and resentments are kindled among them which it will be difficult ever thoroughly to soothe or extinguish. It may become necessary for the supreme legislature of the nation to frame some code, and therein adjust the rights of the colonies with precision and certainty, otherwise Great Britain will always be teased with new claims about liberty and privileges.

I have no ambition in appearing in print, yet if you think what is here thrown together is fit for the public eye you are at liberty to publish it. I the more cheerfully acquiesce in this because it is with real concern I have observed that, notwithstanding the frequent abuse poured forth in pamphlets and newspapers against the mother country, not one filial pen in America hath as yet been drawn, to my knowledge, in her vindication.

For Further Reading

Bernard Bailyn, *The Ideological Origins of the American Revolution.* Enlarged ed. Cambridge, MA: Belknap Press of Harvard University Press, 1992.

Bernard Bailyn, ed., *Pamphlets of the American Revolution.* Cambridge, MA: Belknap Press of Harvard University Press, 1965.

Jack P. Greene, ed., *Colonies to Nation, 1763–1789.* New York: Norton, 1975.

Pauline Maier, *From Resistance to Revolution.* New York: Knopf, 1972.

Edmund S. Morgan and Helen M. Morgan, *The Stamp Act Crisis: Prologue to Revolution.* Chapel Hill: University of North Carolina Press, 1953.

VIEWPOINT 12A

War Against the British Is Not Justified (1776)

The Ancient Testimony and Principles of the People Called Quakers

The start of the war against Great Britain predated America's Declaration of Independence. Most historians date the beginning of the war with the clashes between British troops and American militia in Lexington and Concord, Massachusetts, on April 19, 1775. By the end of that year the bloodiest battle of the entire war, Breed's Hill (also called Bunker Hill), had been fought; George Washington had taken command of the Continental Army; and Americans under Benedict Arnold and Richard Montgomery had launched an ultimately failed invasion of Canada.

The commencement of war did not stop debate on its utility or justification. On January 20, 1776, an address arising from a meeting of Quakers was published in Philadelphia. The full title of the tract was *The Ancient Testimony and Principles of the People Called Quakers, Renewed with Respect to the King and Government; and Touching the Commotions now prevailing in these and other Parts of America.* The pamphlet, reprinted here, calls on the colonists

From *The Ancient Testimony and Principles of the People Called Quakers, Renewed with Respect to the King and Government, and Touching the Commotions Now Prevailing in These and Other Parts of America* (Philadelphia, 1776).

to maintain what it describes as a happy connection to Great Britain. With its expressions of abhorrence of violent measures, the pamphlet reflects the Quaker tradition of pacifism. John Pemberton (1727–1795), who as clerk to the meeting signed his name to the pamphlet, was imprisoned in Philadelphia in September 1777 because of his suspected Loyalist views. He was pardoned by George Washington in April 1778.

Whom do the Quakers blame for recent violent events? What alternatives to violence do they propose? What comments do they make about slavery?

A religious concern for our friends and fellow subjects of every denomination, and more especially for those of all ranks, who, in the present commotions, are engaged in publick employments and stations, induces us earnestly to beseech every individual in the most solemn manner, to consider the end and tendency of the measures they are promoting; and on the most impartial enquiry into the state of their minds, carefully to examine whether they are acting in the fear of God, and in conformity to the precepts and doctrine of our Lord Jesus Christ, whom we profess to believe in, and that by him alone we expect to be saved from our sins.

The calamities and afflictions which now surround us should, as we apprehend, affect every mind with the most awful considerations of the dispensations of Divine Providence to mankind in general in former ages, and that as the sins and iniquities of the people subjected them to grievous sufferings, the same causes still produce the like effects.

Peace and Plenty

The inhabitants of these provinces were long signally favoured with peace and plenty: Have the returns of true thankfulness been generally manifest? Have integrity and godly simplicity been maintained, and religiously regarded? Hath a religious care to do justly, love mercy, and walk humbly, been evident? Hath the precept of Christ, to do unto others as we would they should do unto us, been the governing rule of our conduct? Hath an upright impartial desire to prevent the slavery and oppression of our fellow-men, and to restore them to their natural right, to true christian liberty, been cherished and encouraged? Or have pride, wantonness, luxury, profaneness, a partial spirit, and forgetfulness of the goodness and mercies of God, become lamentably prevalent? Have we not, therefore, abundant occasion to break off from our sins by righteousness, and our iniquities by shewing mercy to the poor; and with true contrition and abasement of soul, to humble ourselves, and supplicate the Almighty Preserver

of men, to shew favour, and to renew unto us a state of tranquillity and peace?

It is our fervent desire that this may soon appear to be the pious resolution of the people in general, of all ranks and denominations: then may we have a well grounded hope, that wisdom from above, which is pure, peaceable, and full of mercy and good fruits, will preside and govern in the deliberations of those who, in these perilous times, undertake the transaction of the most important public affairs; and that by their steady care and endeavours, constantly to act under the influences of this wisdom, those of inferior stations will be incited diligently to pursue those measures which make for peace, and tend to the reconciliation of contending parties, on principles dictated by the spirit of Christ, who "came not to destroy men's lives, but to save them." Luke ix. 56.

We are so fully assured that these principles are the most certain and effectual means of preventing the extreme misery and desolations of wars and bloodshed, that we are constrained to intreat all who profess faith in Christ, to manifest that they really believe in him, and desire to obtain the blessings he pronounced to the makers of peace, Mat. v. 9.

His spirit ever leads to seek for and improve every opportunity of promoting peace and reconciliation; and constantly to remember, that as we really confide in him, he can, in his own time, change the hearts of all men in such manner, that the way to obtain it hath been often opened, contrary to every human prospect or expectation.

---●---

"We therefore firmly unite in the abhorrence of all such writings and measures, as evidence a desire and design to break off the happy connection we have heretofore enjoyed with the kingdom of Great Britain, and our just and necessary subordination to the king."

---●---

May we, therefore, heartily and sincerely unite in supplications to the Father of Mercies, to grant the plentiful effusions of his Spirit to all, and in an especial manner to those in superior stations, that they may, with sincerity, guard against and reject all such measures and councils, as may increase and perpetuate the discord, animosities, and unhappy contentions which now sorrowfully abound.

We cannot but, with distressed minds, beseech all such, in the most solemn and awful manner, to consider that, if by their acting and persisting in a proud, selfish spirit, and not regarding the dictates of true wisdom, such measures are pursued as tend to the shedding of innocent blood; in the day when they and all men shall appear at the judgment-seat of Christ, to receive a reward according to their works, they will be excluded from his favour, and their portion will be in everlasting misery. See Mat. xxv. 41. 2, Cor. v. 10.

Making Peace

The peculiar evidence of divine regard manifested to our ancestors, in the founding and settlement of these provinces, we have often commemorated, and desire ever to remember with true thankfulness and reverent admiration.

When we consider—That at the time they were persecuted and subjected to severe sufferings, as a people unworthy of the benefits of religious or civil society, the hearts of the king and rulers, under whom they thus suffered, were inclined to grant them these fruitful countries, and entrust them with charters of very extensive powers and privileges.—That on their arrival here, the minds of the natives were inclined to receive them with great hospitality and friendship, and to cede to them the most valuable part of their land on very easy terms.—That while the principles of justice and mercy continued to preside, they were preserved in tranquility and peace, free from the desolating calamities of war; and their endeavours were wonderfully blessed and prospered; so that the saying of the wisest of kings was signally verified to them, "When a man's ways please the Lord, he maketh even his enemies to be at peace with him." Prov. xvi. 7.

The benefits, advantages, and favour, we have experienced by our dependence on, and connection with, the kings and government, under which we have enjoyed this happy state, appear to demand from us the greatest circumspection, care, and constant endeavours, to guard against every attempt to alter, or subvert, that dependence and connection.

The scenes lately presented to our view, and the prospect before us, we are sensible, are very distressing and discouraging. And though we lament that such amicable measures, as have been proposed, both here and in England, for the adjustment of the unhappy contests subsisting, have not yet been effectual; nevertheless, we should rejoice to observe the continuance of mutual peaceable endeavours for effecting a reconciliation; having grounds to hope that the divine favour and blessing will attend them.

It hath ever been our judgment and principle, since we were called to profess the Light of Christ Jesus, manifested in our consciences, unto this day, that the setting up, and putting down kings and governments, is God's peculiar prerogative; for causes best known to himself: and that it is not our business to have any hand or contrivance therein: nor to be busy-bodies above our station, much less to plot and contrive the ruin, or overturn any of them; but to pray for the king, and safety of our nation, and good of all men; that we may live a peaceable and quiet life, in all godliness and honesty, under the government which God is pleased to set over us.

Ancient Testimony, 1696, in Sewell's History.

May we therefore firmly unite in the abhorrence of all such writings and measures, as evidence a desire and design to break off the happy connection we have heretofore enjoyed with the kingdom of Great Britain, and our just and necessary subordination to the king, and those who are lawfully placed in authority under him; that thus the repeated solemn declarations made on this subject, in the addresses sent to the king on behalf of the people of America in general, may be confirmed, and remain to be our firm and sincere intentions to observe and fulfil.

VIEWPOINT 12B

War Against the British Is Justified (1775)

John Carmichael (1728–1785)

John Carmichael, a Presbyterian minister serving in Chester County, Pennsylvania, began preaching and writing against British taxes and other actions in the colonies in the late 1760s. On June 4, 1775—less than two months after the April 1775 battles of Lexington and Concord—he preached a sermon to a company of Chester County militia in Lancaster, Pennsylvania. The sermon was later reprinted in a widely circulated pamphlet titled A Self-Defensive War Lawful, from which the following viewpoint is excerpted. Carmichael argues that wars against oppressors are sometimes justified and that British actions against the colonies make violent resistance necessary. Carmichael's writings and sermons persuaded most members of his congregation to join the American cause. He later addressed the Continental Congress and was a frequent visitor to George Washington's Continental Army during the war.

What moral arguments does Carmichael make concerning violence? What does he say should be done about pacifists? about other opponents of revolution?

At a time when the unjust storm of ministerial wrath is discharging itself, in a cruel and ignominious manner, on the noble, patriotic, brave people of the ancient, loyal, important colony

From *A Self-Defensive War Lawful* by John Carmichael (Philadelphia: John Dean, 1775).

of the Massachusetts-Bay, in New-England;—at a time when all the other colonies in North-America, like the true children of a *free-born family*, are roused to some just resentment of such insults, on their natural and legal rights, taking each other as by the hand, and uniting by the invincible chains of love, friendship, and interest, are determined to support this their elder sister colony, now suffering so gloriously in the common cause, or *sink* together;—at a time when the alarm is sounding from east to west, over this vast continent of North-America, to arms! to arms!—in short, at a time when the minds of *all* are in such a ferment, that they can be scarce composed to hear any subject, but what may have some reference to the present times;—it is but reasonable to suppose, that even the Minister of the *Prince of Peace*, whose business for ordinary is neither *war* or *politicks*, in such a situation, being member of civil society, and interested like other men would improve the times, by adopting their public instructions, to the best service of the people, and not offensive or displeasing to God; whose holy word is a blessed directory in every emergency.

It is also but reasonable to suppose, that every judicious, sober American, being now reduced to the dreadful alternative, either to take up arms, apparently against that very government, which he was wont to revere, and under which he expected protection for both life and property; or submit tamely to the galling yoke of *perpetual slavery*; I say, it is supposable, that every such Christian American soldier will be all ear to wholesome instructions, relative to his present duty. . . .

Discerning the Circumstances That Justify War

Although war is in itself a very great evil, and one of those sore judgments, by which a holy God punishes the world for sin, therefore to be deprecated, and avoided as much as possible; yet is, at times, by reason of certain circumstances, so unavoidable, that it is our duty to enter into it—The method I design to pursue, in opening up the doctrine, for improvement, is the following:—

I. Humbly attempt to shew (with submission to better judgment) when a war is so unavoidable and necessary, that it is our duty to enter into it.

II. Shew how we should enter into, and prosecute even a just war.

III. Improve the subject, by the deduction of a few natural inferences from the whole.

You are sensible, my hearers, that there are some Christian people in the world, and some of them in these parts, who merit the regard of the public, by their general character of industry, inoffensiveness and sobriety; yet do maintain it, as a sacred conscientious tenet, not to be dispensed with, *not to go to war, or take up arms on any occasion whatsoever*; and charity, the leading grace of the Christian system, will lead us to deal tenderly with such, as far as we have grounds to believe they are sincere in their profession: We ought to pity such for their mistake, and, if possible, to convince them; but not by any means to urge them against their avowed sentiments, lest we come under the odious appellations of *persecutors*.

———— • ————

"[I]f God is on our side we need not fear what man can do unto us."

———— • ————

As far as these sober people make use of the Bible, to found their principles on, they rely on such passages as these, Gen. ix, 6. *He that sheddeth man's blood, by man shall his blood be shed*; and Exod. xx, 13. *Thou shalt not kill*; and in the New-Testament, *But I say unto you, love your enemies;—if any smite thee on the one cheek turn to him the other also;—for all they that take the sword shall perish by the sword*: Matth. v. 39, 44 and xxvi, 52. and hence conclude, though I think falsely, that all war is unlawful, except the spiritual, with our own corruptions, by the sword of the spirit, in Christ's spiritual kingdom, which is not of this world, else would his children fight.

But if I mistake not, these people regard only such passages of holy scripture, as seem to favour their favourite opinion, let the language of other passages be what they will;—and hence their own imagination is substituted instead of divine revelation, so that when people are determined to keep by a sentiment, be it right or wrong, there is an end of all disputation.

We readily allow, that it would be happy for us all, if there was no moral or natural evil in the world. But how plausible soever such opinions may appear, to the weal of society, they are rather calculated to the condition of innocent, than depraved nature; which now is, and ever has been such, since the fall of our first parents, that there is need of some remedy to curb its evil tendencies, or mankind would scarce be able to subsist in the world; and this our alwise righteous Creator knows; and has therefore set up civil government to keep men from destroying each other: But civil government has no power, if it has not the sword, to be a terror to evil-doers, and a praise to them that do well.—Hence it will follow, that men are under a necessity to part with some of their natural rights, to secure the rest; they must give part of their earnings to such as are chosen by themselves to rule the whole; and then again, they must help the rulers to execute the good and wholesome laws of government, against their violators. Suppose, for instance, a great banditti rise to rescue murderers; if these are not quelled, government is overthrown, if the people do not assist good government, and here then arises a necessity to go to war.

And suppose again, on the other hand, which is very supposable, that the rulers of the people should give way to the many temptations their high stations will lead them to; to indulge the inclinations of a lust for absolute dominion, independent of the people, so that all the barrier of oaths and covenants are broke through, to effect the plan; and the people have no security, for either life or property, but the mere sovereign pleasure of the absolute rulers;—then the people are under a disagreeable, but pressing necessity, rather than be crushed by an iron rod, to re-ascertain their own just rights; and stand forth all of them to oppose such tyranny:—Here then is another instance of self-defence—in which a war is both unavoidable and necessary, and therefore lawful, if self-preservation is lawful; which is the point I shall next, in order, endeavour to prove indisputably, both from the light of nature, and divine revelation; and first from the light of nature.

Self-Preservation

It is certainly evident, wherever we turn our eyes, on any part of the whole creation of God, that the principle of self-love or self-preservation, or the desire of existence, is deeply engraved on the nature of every creature. . . .

The little industrious bee is furnished by her Creator with a sting, to preserve for her own use her sweet honey, the fruit of her toil and industry.

The ox has his horns; and the horse his teeth and hoofs.—The deer her feet for flight, and the fowls their wings to escape danger and preserve themselves. And shall man, the noblest creature in his lower world, be destitute of this necessary principle! which we see engraved by instinct on the irrational creation: Man is blest with reason to direct his enquiries, in search of happiness. His maker God allows him to seek to be as happy as he possibly can, both in this life and the life to come. But since man is a fallen, sinful creature, he has lost his true road to happiness—and can never find it, until his Maker points it out to him in the Holy Bible. Here we are taught how to conduct both in the civil and religious life: We are certain the scriptures allow us to defend ourselves in the best manner we can against an enemy.

Therefore, such passages, as would seem to speak a different language; such as those already quoted, must be understood, in a consistency with this great law of nature; as well as consistent with other parts of scripture. For Christ came not to make void, or destroy the law, but to fulfil—when therefore we are forbid to shed blood, or to kill; it is innocent blood is meant—but this doth not forbid to execute a murderer. The divine law requires, that a murderer should be executed, and forbids to take a ransom for his life.

Also, when a body of wicked people join together, or a nation unite, to fall upon and destroy without any just cause an innocent people: The insulted, or invaded people, are then to unite together, to oppose, expel and punish the guilty invaders—as in Judges v, 23. *Curse ye Meroz, (said the Angel of the Lord) curse ye bitterly the inhabitants thereof: Because they came not to the help of the Lord, against the mighty:* And Jeremiah xlviii, 10. *Cursed be he that doth the work of the Lord deceitfully; and cursed be he that keepeth back his sword from blood:* And in Luke xxii, 36. Jesus Christ told his Disciples to arm themselves against approaching danger.—*And he that hath no sword let him sell his garment and buy one.* . . .

Also, it must of course follow, that where our blessed Lord enjoins us, when smote on the one cheek, to turn the other also, he does not mean to forbid us to use lawful and proper means of self-preservation. But the meaning must be as the phrase is proverbial, that we should at no time discover a revengeful or unforgiving disposition; but should be ready to put up with a good deal of ill-usage, before we would create disturbance,—yea that we should do any thing consistent with our own safety. Again, where our Lord enjoins us to love our enemies—he can't possibly mean that we should love them better than ourselves—that we should put it in the enemy's power to kill us, when we had it in our power to save our own life, by killing the enemy. I say, this cannot be the meaning; for that exposition will thwart the original first great law of self-preservation. The meaning therefore must be, that we do not cherish a spirit of hatred towards the enemies, and would be willing to be reconciled again—and would be desirous, the enemy would be convinced of his evil sentiment against us, that we might be again on friendly terms,—that we can be sincere in our prayer to God, to bring such a desirable event to pass. Again,

That a self-defensive war is lawful, I will prove from the conduct of Jesus Christ himself. If civil government is necessary to self-preservation, and war is necessary, at times, in government, as has been already proved; then it will follow, that those who support civil government, do support war, and so of consequence approve of war. But Jesus Christ did pay his tribute money, to the Emperor Tiberius, Matthew xvii, 27. And those who are acquainted with the life of Tiberius Caesar know that he had frequent wars. . . .

I think I have now proved, from the light of nature, from the reason of things—from the Old and New-

Testament, as well as from the example of Christ and his Apostles, that a self-defensive war is lawful. . . .

It is also equally unfair, to say, *Let us stand still and see the salvation of God*; for if this proves any thing, it proves too much, it proves that we are to use no means at all, for why to use lawful means in our power one time, and not another; we must therefore neither plow or sow; build, raise stock, or do any thing in the use of means, *but stand still and see the salvation of God:* But our reason is given us to use it in a proper manner, to preserve our own lives and the lives of others, as God's servants, in a state of probation in this world; and God will reward every one finally, according to his works; when we have no means in our power, we honor God to trust him, as Israel at the Red-Sea, and in the wilderness;—but when means are in our power, and we do not use them, we then tempt God, and rebel against his government, which he exercises over the world, in the way of free and moral agency.

Do Not Persecute Pacifists

Therefore for these people, to argue as they do now, when they are among other societies,—who they know will preserve the state from slaughter or slavery, in the use of lawful means, as has been now proved, is vastly disingenuous, and will undoubtedly subject their opinions to this censure, that it is a sanctuary of sloth—for greed—cowardice, &c.—*for it is easy to stay at home and earn money, to what it is to spend money and expose life, to protect and defend the worldling coward;—it is easy to pay money, to what it is to be slain in battle*, &c. But after all that has been said, I am myself so warm an advocate for the sacred rights of conscience, that if these people will not be convinced of their duty; can not get their eyes open; they are to be pitied, but not persecuted. I beg of all, for God and conscience sake, to let them alone, if they will not in these terrible times, draw the sword *for* Liberty and their Country; surely they will not *against* Liberty and their Country; and if we can do with them, we can without them: O then, let there be no disturbance on that head! But should any of these inoffensive guiltless anti-warriors be detected in assisting Gage or his army with provisions, &c. for lucre or any other motive whatever conscience could not apologize for them but ought to be dealt with accordingly. . . .

I am happy, that I can with a good conscience, congratulate you and myself this day, on the certainty we have, for the justice and goodness of our cause: The angry tools of power who mislead government, may call us American "rebels, who would throw off all government,—would be independent and what not."—But we can now, with great confidence, appeal to God that that is false—we desire no such things—we desire to be as we were in the beginning of the present unhappy reign—we have tried every lawful, peaceable mean in our power—but all in vain!—we would love them if they would suffer us—we would be peaceable, obedient, loving subjects if they would let us; but it would seem as if the present ministry were determined to cram disloyalty, and disobedience down our throats—and then call us all rebels—then confiscate our country and sell it, to pay their [£] 140,000,000 of debt, or else we know not what they would be at. We do in America all declare ourselves the subjects of King George the third, but we never swore allegiance to the Parliament of Great-Britain—or else we would have above 500 Kings—they are our fellow-subjects, chosen by the freeholders of that island to legislate for them, as our Assembly doth for Pennsylvania; but if their present claims are admitted, we may give up our Assemblies—and our Charters are cyphers!—

In the close of the last war, the King had not in all his dominions so many more affectionate subjects than the Americans—and in every valuable enterprize which would exhaust both treasure and blood the brave New-Englanders took the lead—and by our industry and trade with England, the nation rose to her present eminence; and now the very power we helped to give her, is retorted on us with redoubled vengeance and unheard of cruelty—but if they beat down our trading Cities and oppress us all they can, we will have our woods and liberty; for as we are the descendants of Britons, *we scorn to be slaves.*—We are now come to our *ne plus ultra*—the sword, the last argument must decide the controversy. Therefore, you can, Gentlemen Soldiers, appeal to G O D, for the justice of your cause, he is the judge of all the earth, and will do right, the final determination of all matters is in his righteous, holy, powerful hand. When England went to war with France and Spain in the time of last reign, they invoked the aids of the God of heaven by fasting and prayer—and then government discovered no leanings to popery—But now, when they are going to murder and butcher their own children in America, that have been so obedient, useful and affectionate—we do not hear that they ask counsel of God—but if they do not let us ask counsel and assistance from the God of heaven—he is on our side, we hope, and if God is on our side we need not fear what man can do unto us.

For Further Reading

Patricia U. Bonomi, *Under the Cope of Heaven: Religion, Society, and Politics in Colonial America.* New York: Oxford University Press, 1986.

Edward Countryman, *The American Revolution.* New York: Hill and Wang, 1985.

Robert Gross, *The Minutemen and Their World.* New York: Hill and Wang, 1976.

Don Higginbotham, *The War of American Independence.* New York: Macmillan, 1971.

Arthur J. Mekeel, *The Relation of the Quakers to the American Revolution.* Washington, DC: University Press of America, 1977.

John Wingate Thornton, *The Pulpit of the American Revolution.* New York: Da Capo Press, 1970.

VIEWPOINT 13A

America Must Be Independent of Great Britain (1776)

Thomas Paine (1737–1809)

By the end of 1775, British and American forces had engaged in violent clashes in New England and in Canada and King George III had declared the colonies to be in a state of rebellion. Yet many colonists, including influential members of the Continental Congress, were not ready to contemplate the final step of full independence from Great Britain. Many people still professed loyalty to the king, maintaining that they were merely seeking their rights as English citizens denied by corrupt British ministers.

Perhaps the single document most influential in persuading the American colonists that independence was necessary was a pamphlet first published in Philadelphia on January 10, 1776. It was quickly reprinted throughout the colonies and sold an estimated 120,000 copies over the next three months. The pamphlet was *Common Sense* and its author was Thomas Paine, an impoverished writer who had moved from Great Britain to America in 1774 after a checkered career as a corset maker, customs inspector, and schoolmaster. Following the battles of Lexington and Concord in April 1775, he began to advocate total independence from Great Britain. In the following excerpts from *Common Sense,* Paine attacks the British monarchy and argues the case for independence in forthright language that many Americans found convincing.

What economic arguments for American independence does Paine make? Why is independence inevitable, in his opinion? Which of Paine's arguments do you find most convincing? Which do you find least convincing? Why?

I n the following pages I offer nothing more than simple facts, plain arguments, and common sense: and have no other preliminaries to settle

From *Common Sense* by Thomas Paine (Philadelphia, 1776).

with the reader, than that he will divest himself of prejudice and prepossession, and suffer his reason and his feelings to determine for themselves: that he will put on, or rather that he will not put off the true character of a man, and generously enlarge his views beyond the present day.

Volumes have been written on the subject of the struggle between England and America. Men of all ranks have embarked in the controversy, from different motives, and with various designs; but all have been ineffectual, and the period of debate is closed. Arms as the last resource decide the contest; the appeal [to arms] was the choice of the King, and the Continent has accepted the challenge. . . .

The Sun never shined on a cause of greater worth. 'Tis not the affair of a City, a County, a Province or a Kingdom; but of a Continent—of at least one eighth part of the habitable Globe. 'Tis not the concern of a day, a year, or an age; posterity are virtually involved in the contest, and will be more or less affected even to the end of time by the proceedings now. Now is the seed time of Continental union, faith, and honour. The least fracture now, will be like a name engraved with the point of a pin on the tender rind of a young oak; the wound will enlarge with the tree, and posterity read it in full grown characters.

By referring the matter from argument to arms, a new era for politics is struck—a new method of thinking hath arisen. All plans, proposals, &c. prior to the 19th of April, i.e. to the commencement of hostilities, are like the almanacks of the last year; which tho' proper then, are superceded and useless now. Whatever was advanced by the advocates on either side of the question then, terminated in one and the same point, viz. a union with Great Britain; the only difference between the parties, was the method of effecting it; the one proposing force, the other friendship; but it hath so far happened that the first hath failed, and the second hath withdrawn her influence.

As much hath been said of the advantages of reconciliation, which like an agreeable dream, hath passed away and left us as we were, it is but right, that we should examine the contrary side of the argument, and enquire into some of the many material injuries which these Colonies sustain, and always will sustain, by being connected with and dependant on Great Britain. To examine that connection and dependance on the principles of nature and common sense, to see what we have to trust to if separated, and what we are to expect if dependant.

I have heard it asserted by some, that as America hath flourished under her former connection with Great Britain, that the same connection is necessary towards her future happiness and will always have the same effect—Nothing can be more fallacious than this kind of argument:—we may as well assert that because a child hath thrived upon milk, that it is never to have meat, or that the first twenty years of our lives is to become a precedent for the next twenty. But even this is admitting more than is true, for I answer, roundly, that America would have flourished as much, and probably much more had no European power taken any notice of her. The commerce by which she hath enriched herself are the necessaries of life, and will always have a market while eating is the custom of Europe.

But she has protected us say some. That she hath engrossed us is true, and defended the Continent at our expence as well as her own is admitted; and she would have defended Turkey from the same motive viz. the sake of trade and dominion.

Ancient Prejudices

Alas! we have been long led away by ancient prejudices and made large sacrifices to superstition. We have boasted the protection of Great Britain, without considering, that her motive was *interest* not *attachment*; that she did not protect us from *our enemies* on *our account*, but from *her enemies* on *her own account*, from those who had no quarrel with us on any *other account*, and who will always be our enemies on the *same account*. Let Britain wave [waive] her pretensions to the Continent, or the Continent throw off the dependance, and we should be at peace with France and Spain were they at war with Britain. The miseries of Hanover last war ought to warn us against connections.

It hath lately been asserted in parliament, that the Colonies have no relation to each other but through the Parent Country, i.e. that Pennsylvania and the Jerseys and so on for the rest, are sister Colonies by the way of England; this is certainly a very round-about way of proving relationship, but it is the nearest and only true way of proving enmity (or enemyship, if I may so call it). France and Spain never were, nor perhaps ever will be our enemies as *Americans* but as our being the *subjects of Great Britain*.

But Britain is the parent country say some. Then the more shame upon her conduct. Even brutes do not devour their young, nor savages make war upon their families; wherefore the assertion if true, turns to her reproach; but it happens not to be true, or only partly so, and the phrase, *parent* or *mother country*, hath been jesuitically adopted by the King and his parasites, with a low papistical design of gaining an unfair bias on the credulous weakness of our minds. Europe and not England is the parent country of America. This new World hath been the asylum for the persecuted lovers of civil and religious liberty from *every part* of Europe. Hither have they

fled, not from the tender embraces of the mother, but from the cruelty of the monster; and it is so far true of England, that the same tyranny which drove the first emigrants from home, pursues their descendants still.

In this extensive quarter of the Globe, we forget the narrow limits of three hundred and sixty miles (the extent of England) and carry our friendship on a larger scale; we claim brotherhood with every European Christian, and triumph in the generosity of the sentiment. . . .

The Strength of Britain

Much hath been said of the united strength of Britain and the Colonies, that in conjunction they might bid defiance to the world: But this is mere presumption, the fate of war is uncertain, neither do the expressions mean any thing, for this Continent would never suffer itself to be drained of inhabitants, to support the British Arms in either Asia, Africa, or Europe.

Besides, what have we to do with setting the world at defiance? Our plan is commerce, and that well attended to, will secure us the peace and friendship of all Europe, because it is the interest of all Europe to have America a free port. Her trade will always be a protection, and her barrenness of gold and silver will secure her from invaders.

I challenge the warmest advocate for reconciliation, to shew, a single advantage that this Continent can reap, by being connected with Great Britain. I repeat the challenge, not a single advantage is derived. Our corn will fetch its price in any market in Europe and our imported goods must be paid for buy them where we will.

But the injuries and disadvantages we sustain by that connection, are without number, and our duty to mankind at large, as well as to ourselves, instruct us to renounce the alliance: because any submission to, or dependance on Great Britain, tends directly to involve this Continent in European wars and quarrels. As Europe is our market for trade, we ought to form no political connection with any part of it. 'Tis the true interest of America, to steer clear of European contentions, which she never can do, while by her dependance on Britain, she is made the makeweight in the scale of British politics.

Europe is too thickly planted with Kingdoms, to be long at peace, and whenever a war breaks out between England and any foreign power, the trade of America goes to ruin, *because of her connection with Britain.* The next war may not turn out like the last, and should it not, the advocates for reconciliation now, will be wishing for separation then, because neutrality in that case, would be a safer convoy than a man of war. Every thing that is right or reasonable pleads for separation. The blood of the slain, the weeping voice of nature cries, 'TIS TIME TO PART. Even the distance at which the Almighty hath placed England and America, is a strong and natural proof, that the authority of the one over the other, was never the design of Heaven. The time likewise at which the Continent was discovered, adds weight to the argument, and the manner in which it was peopled encreases the force of it. The Reformation was preceded by the discovery of America as if the Almighty graciously meant to open a sanctuary to the persecuted in future years, when home should afford neither friendship nor safety.

The authority of Great Britain over this Continent is a form of Government which sooner or later must have an end: And a serious mind can draw no true pleasure by looking forward, under the painful and positive conviction, that what he calls "the present constitution," is merely temporary. As parents, we can have no joy, knowing that this government is not sufficiently lasting to ensure any thing which we may bequeath to posterity: And by a plain method of

THE DECLARATION OF INDEPENDENCE

Originally written by Thomas Jefferson, this statement justifying America's revolution was debated, amended, and approved by the Continental Congress on July 4, 1776, and signed by fifty-six of its members.

When in the Course of human events, it becomes necessary for one people to dissolve the political bands which have connected them with another, and to assume among the powers of the earth, the separate and equal station to which the Laws of Nature and of Nature's God entitle them, a decent respect to the opinions of mankind requires that they should declare the causes which impel them to the separation.

We hold these truths to be self-evident, that all men are created equal, that they are endowed by their Creator with certain unalienable Rights, that among these are Life, Liberty and the pursuit of Happiness.

That to secure these rights, Governments are instituted among Men, deriving their just powers from the consent of the governed.

That whenever any Form of Government becomes destructive of these ends, it is the Right of the People to alter or to abolish it, and to institute new Government, laying its foundation on such principles and organizing its powers in such form, as to them shall seem most likely to effect their Safety and Happiness. Prudence, indeed, will dictate that Governments long established should not be changed for light and transient causes; and accordingly all experience hath shewn, that mankind are more disposed to suffer, while evils are sufferable, than to right themselves by abolishing the forms to which they are accustomed. But when a long train of abuses and usurpations, pursuing invariably the same Object evinces a design to reduce them under absolute Despotism, it is their right, it is their duty, to throw off such Government, and to provide new Guards for their future security.

Such has been the patient sufferance of these Colonies; and such is now the necessity which constrains them to alter their former Systems of Government. The history of the present King of Great Britain is a history of repeated injuries and usurpations, all having in direct object the establishment of an absolute Tyranny over these States. To prove this, let Facts be submitted to a candid world.

He has refused his Assent to Laws, the most wholesome and necessary for the public good.

He has forbidden his Governors to pass Laws of immediate and pressing importance, unless suspended in their operation till his Assent should be obtained; and when so suspended, he has utterly neglected to attend to them.

He has refused to pass other Laws for the accommodation of large districts of people, unless those people would relinquish the right of Representation in the Legislature, a right inestimable to them and formidable to tyrants only.

He has called together legislative bodies at places unusual, uncomfortable, and distant from the depository of their public Records, for the sole purpose of fatiguing them into compliance with his measures.

He has dissolved Representative Houses repeatedly, for opposing with manly firmness his invasions on the rights of the people.

He has refused for a long time, after such dissolutions, to cause others to be elected; whereby the Legislative powers, incapable of Annihilation, have returned to the People at large for their exercise; the State remaining in the mean time exposed to all the dangers of invasion from without, and convulsions within.

He has endeavoured to prevent the population of these States; for that purpose obstructing the Laws for Naturalization of Foreigners; refusing to pass others to encourage their migrations hither, and raising the conditions of new Appropriations of Lands.

He has obstructed the Administration of Justice, by refusing his Assent to Laws for establishing Judiciary powers.

He has made Judges dependent on his Will alone, for the tenure of their offices, and the amount and payment of their salaries.

He has erected a multitude of New Offices, and sent hither swarms of Officers to harrass our people, and eat out their substance.

He has kept among us, in times of peace, Standing Armies without the Consent of our legislatures.

He has affected to render the Military independent of and superior to the Civil power.

argument, as we are running the next generation into debt, we ought to do the work of it, otherwise we use them meanly and pitifully. . . .

Those Who Advocate Reconciliation

Though I would carefully avoid giving unnecessary offence, yet I am inclined to believe, that all those who espouse the doctrine of reconciliation, may be included within the following descriptions. Interested men who are not to be trusted, weak men who cannot see, prejudiced men who will not see, and a certain set of moderate men who think better of the

European world than it deserves; and this last class, by an ill-judged deliberation, will be the cause of more calamities to this Continent, than all the other three.

It is the good fortune of many to live distant from the scene of present sorrow; the evil is not sufficiently brought to their doors to make them feel the precariousness with which all American property is possessed. But let our imaginations transport us for a few moments to Boston [where British forces were then under siege by the Continental Army]; that seat of wretchedness will teach us wisdom, and instruct

He has combined with others to subject us to a jurisdiction foreign to our constitution, and unacknowledged by our laws; giving his Assent to their Acts of pretended Legislation:

For quartering large bodies of armed troops among us:

For protecting them, by a mock Trial, from punishment for any Murders which they should commit on the Inhabitants of these States:

For cutting off our Trade with all parts of the world:

For imposing Taxes on us without our Consent:

For depriving us in many cases, of the benefits of Trial by Jury:

For transporting us beyond Seas to be tried for pretended offences:

For abolishing the free System of English Laws in a neighbouring Province, establishing therein an Arbitrary government, and enlarging its Boundaries so as to render it at once an example and fit instrument for introducing the same absolute rule into these Colonies:

For taking away our Charters, abolishing our most valuable Laws, and altering fundamentally the Forms of our Governments:

For suspending our own Legislatures, and declaring themselves invested with power to legislate for us in all cases whatsoever.

He has abdicated Government here, by declaring us out of his Protection and waging War against us.

He has plundered our seas, ravaged our Coasts, burnt our towns, and destroyed the Lives of our people.

He is at this time transporting large Armies of foreign Mercenaries to compleat the works of death, desolation and tyranny, already begun with circumstances of Cruelty & perfidy scarcely paralleled in the most barbarous ages, and totally unworthy the Head of a civilized nation.

He has constrained our fellow Citizens taken Captive on the high Seas to bear Arms against their Country, to become the executioners of their friends and Brethren, or to fall themselves by their Hands.

He has excited domestic insurrections amongst us, and has endeavoured to bring on the inhabitants of our frontiers, the merciless Indian Savages, whose known rule of warfare, is an undistinguished destruction of all ages, sexes and conditions.

In every stage of these Oppressions We have Petitioned for Redress in the most humble terms: Our repeated Petitions have been answered only by repeated injury. A Prince, whose character is thus marked by every act which may define a Tyrant, is unfit to be the ruler of a free people.

Nor have We been wanting in attentions to our British brethren. We have warned them from time to time of attempts by their legislature to extend an unwarrantable jurisdiction over us. We have reminded them of the circumstances of our emigration and settlement here. We have appealed to their native justice and magnanimity, and we have conjured them by the ties of our common kindred to disavow these usurpations, which, would inevitably interrupt our connections and correspondence. They too have been deaf to the voice of justice and of consanguinity. We must, therefore, acquiesce in the necessity, which denounces our Separation, and hold them, as we hold the rest of mankind, Enemies in War, in Peace Friends.

We, therefore, the Representatives of the united States of America, in General Congress, Assembled, appealing to the Supreme Judge of the world for the rectitude of our intentions, do, in the Name, and by Authority of the good People of these Colonies, solemnly publish and declare, That these United Colonies are, and of Right ought to be Free and Independent States; that they are Absolved from all Allegiance to the British Crown, and that all political connection between them and the State of Great Britain, is and ought to be totally dissolved; and that as Free and Independent States, they have full Power to levy War, conclude Peace, contract Alliances, establish Commerce, and to do all other Acts and Things which Independent States may of right do.

And for the support of this Declaration, with a firm reliance on the protection of divine Providence. we mutually pledge to each other our Lives, our Fortunes and our sacred Honor.

us for ever to renounce a power in whom we can have no trust. The inhabitants of that unfortunate city who but a few months ago were in ease and affluence, have now no other alternative than to stay and starve, or turn out to beg. Endangered by the fire of their friends if they continue within the city, and plundered by government if they leave it. In their present condition they are prisoners without the hope of redemption, and in a general attack for their relief, they would be exposed to the fury of both armies.

Men of passive tempers look somewhat lightly over the offences of Britain, and still hoping for the best, are apt to call out: *Come, come, we shall be friends again for all this.* But examine the passions and feelings of mankind: bring the doctrine of reconciliation to the touchstone of nature, and then tell me, whether you can hereafter love, honour, and faithfully serve the power that hath carried fire and sword into your land? If you cannot do all these, then are you only deceiving yourselves, and by your delay bringing ruin upon posterity. Your future connection with Britain whom you can neither love nor honour, will be forced and unnatural, and being formed only on the plan of present convenience, will in a little time, fall into a relapse more wretched than the first. But if you say, you can still pass the violations over, then I ask, hath your house been burnt? Hath your property been destroyed before your face? Are your wife and children destitute of a bed to lie on, or bread to live on? Have you lost a parent or a child by their hands, and yourself the ruined and wretched survivor? If you have not, then are you not a judge of those who have. But if you have and still can shake hands with the murderers, then are you unworthy the name of husband, father, friend, or lover, and whatever may be your rank or title in life, you have the heart of a coward, and the spirit of a sycophant.

This is not inflaming or exaggerating matters, but trying them by those feelings and affections which nature justifies, and without which, we should be incapable of discharging the social duties of life, or enjoying the felicities of it. I mean not to exhibit horror for the purpose of provoking revenge, but to awaken us from fatal and unmanly slumbers, that we may pursue determinately some fixed object. 'Tis not in the power of England or of Europe to conquer America, if she doth not conquer herself by delay and timidity. The present winter is worth an age if rightly employed, but if lost or neglected, the whole Continent will partake of the misfortune; and there is no punishment which that man doth not deserve, be he who, or what, or where he will, that may be the means of sacrificing a season so precious and useful.

'Tis repugnant to reason, to the universal order of things; to all examples from former ages, to suppose, that this Continent can long remain subject to any external power. The most sanguine in Britain doth not think so. The utmost stretch of human wisdom cannot at this time compass a plan, short of separation, which can promise the Continent even a year's security. Reconciliation is *now* a fallacious dream. Nature hath deserted the connection, and art cannot supply her place. For as Milton wisely expresses "never can true reconcilement grow where wounds of deadly hate have pierced so deep."

Every quiet method for peace hath been ineffectual. Our prayers have been rejected with disdain; and hath tended to convince us that nothing flatters vanity or confirms obstinacy in Kings more than repeated petitioning—and nothing hath contributed more, than that very measure, to make the Kings of Europe absolute. Witness Denmark and Sweden. Wherefore since nothing but blows will do, for God's sake let us come to a final separation, and not leave the next generation to be cutting throats under the violated unmeaning names of parent and child.

To say they will never attempt it again is idle and visionary, we thought so at the repeal of the stamp-act, yet a year or two undeceived us; as well may we suppose that nations which have been once defeated will never renew the quarrel.

———— • ————

"'Tis repugnant to reason, to the universal order of things; to all examples from former ages, to suppose, that this Continent can long remain subject to any external power."

———— • ————

As to government matters 'tis not in the power of Britain to do this Continent justice: the business of it will soon be too weighty and intricate to be managed with any tolerable degree of convenience, by a power so distant from us, and so very ignorant of us; for if they cannot conquer us, they cannot govern us. To be always running three or four thousand miles with a tale or a petition, waiting four or five months for an answer, which when obtained requires five or six more to explain it in, will in a few years be looked upon as folly and childishness—There was a time when it was proper, and there is a proper time for it to cease.

Small islands not capable of protecting themselves are the proper objects for government to take under their care: but there is something very absurd, in supposing a Continent to be perpetually governed by an island. In no instance hath nature made the satellite larger than its primary planet, and as England and America with respect to each other reverse the common order of nature, it is evident they belong to different systems. England to Europe: America to itself.

I am not induced by motives of pride, party or resentment to espouse the doctrine of separation and independance; I am clearly, positively, and conscientiously persuaded that 'tis the true interest of this Continent to be so; that every thing short of that is mere patchwork, that it can afford no lasting felicity,—that it is leaving the sword to our children, and shrinking back at a time, when a little more, a little farther, would have rendered this Continent the glory of the earth.

As Britain hath not manifested the least inclination towards a compromise, we may be assured that no terms can be obtained worthy the acceptance of the Continent, or any ways equal to the expence of blood and treasure we have been already put to.

The object contended for, ought always to bear some just proportion to the expence. The removal of [British prime minister Lord] North, or the whole detestable junto, is a matter unworthy the millions we have expended. A temporary stoppage of trade was an inconvenience, which would have sufficiently ballanced the repeal of all the acts complained of, had such repeals been obtained; but if the whole Continent must take up arms, if every man must be a soldier, 'tis scarcely worth our while to fight against a contemptible ministry only. Dearly, dearly, do we pay for the repeal of the acts, if that is all we fight for; for in a just estimation, 'tis as great a folly to pay a Bunker-hill price for law as for land. As I have always considered the independancy of this Continent, as an event which sooner or later must arrive, so from the late rapid progress of the Continent to maturity, the event could not be far off. Wherefore on the breaking out of hostilities, it was not worth the while to have disputed a matter, which time would have finally redressed, unless we meant to be in earnest; otherwise it is like wasting an estate on a suit at law, to regulate the trespasses of a tenant, whose lease is just expiring. No man was a warmer wisher for reconciliation than myself, before the fatal 19th of April 1775, but the moment the event of that day was made known, I rejected the hardened, sullen tempered Pharoah of England for ever; and disdain the wretch, that with the pretended title of FATHER OF HIS PEOPLE can unfeelingly hear of their slaughter, and composedly sleep with their blood upon his soul.

If Reconciliation Were to Happen

But admitting that matters were now made up, what would be the event? I answer, the ruin of the Continent. And that for several reasons.

First. The powers of governing still remaining in the hands of the King, he will have a negative over the whole legislation of this Continent: and as he

hath shewn himself such an inveterate enemy to liberty, and discovered such a thirst for arbitrary power; is he, or is he not, a proper man to say to these Colonies, *You shall make no laws but what I please.* And is there any inhabitant in America so ignorant, as not to know, that according to what is called the *present constitution*, that this Continent can make no laws but what the King gives leave to; and is there any man so unwise, as not to see, that (considering what has happened) he will suffer no laws to be made here, but such as suit his purpose. We may be as effectually enslaved by the want of laws in America, as by submitting to laws made for us in England. After matters are made up (as it is called) can there be any doubt, but the whole power of the crown will be exerted to keep this Continent as low and humble as possible? instead of going forward, we shall go backward, or be perpetually quarrelling or ridiculously petitioning.—We are already greater than the King wishes us to be, and will he not hereafter endeavour to make us less. To bring the matter to one point, is the power who is jealous of our prosperity, a proper power to govern us? Whoever says *no* to this question is an *Independant,* for independancy means no more than whether we shall make our own laws, or, whether the King, the greatest enemy this Continent hath, or can have, shall tell us, *there shall be no laws but such as I like. . . .*

Secondly—That as even the best terms which we can expect to obtain, can amount to no more than a temporary expedient, or a kind of government by guardianship, which can last no longer than till the Colonies come of age, so the general face and state of things in the interim will be unsettled and unpromising. Emigrants of property will not choose to come to a country whose form of government hangs but by a thread, and who is every day tottering on the brink of commotion and disturbance. And numbers of the present inhabitants would lay hold of the interval to dispose of their effects, and quit the Continent.

But the most powerful of all arguments is, that nothing but independance i.e. a Continental form of government, can keep the peace of the Continent and preserve it inviolate from civil wars. I dread the event of a reconciliation with Britain now, as it is more than probable, that it will be followed by a revolt some where or other, the consequences of which may be far more fatal than all the malice of Britain. . . .

I have heard some men say, many of whom I believe spoke without thinking, that they dreaded an independance, fearing that it would produce civil wars. It is but seldom that our first thoughts are truly correct, and that is the case here; for there are ten times more to dread from a patched up connection, than from independance. I make the sufferers' case my own, and I protest, that were I driven from house and home, my property destroyed, and my circumstances ruined, that as a man sensible of injuries, I could never relish the doctrine of reconciliation, or consider myself bound thereby. . . .

Our Natural Right

A government of our own is our natural right: and when a man seriously reflects on the precariousness of human affairs, he will become convinced, that it is infinitely wiser and safer, to form a constitution of our own, in a cool deliberate manner, while we have it in our power, than to trust such an interesting event to time and chance. . . .

Ye that tell us of harmony and reconciliation, can ye restore to us the time that is past? can ye give to prostitution its former innocence? neither can ye reconcile Britain and America. The last cord now is broken, the people of England are presenting addresses against us. There are injuries which nature cannot forgive; she would cease to be nature if she did. As well can the lover forgive the ravisher of his mistress, as the Continent forgive the murders of Britain. The Almighty hath implanted in us these unextinguishable feelings for good and wise purposes. They are the Guardians of his Image in our hearts. They distinguish us from the herd of common animals. The social compact would dissolve, and justice be extirpated from the earth, or have only a casual existence were we callous to the touches of affection. The robber and the murderer would often escape unpunished, did not the injuries which our tempers sustain, provoke us into justice.

O ye that love mankind! Ye that dare oppose not only the tyranny but the tyrant, stand forth! Every spot of the old world is over-run with oppression. Freedom hath been hunted round the Globe. Asia and Africa have long expelled her. Europe regards her like a stranger, and England hath given her warning to depart. O! receive the fugitive, and prepare in time an asylum for mankind.

VIEWPOINT 13B

America Must Seek Reconciliation with Great Britain (1776)

Charles Inglis (1734–1816)

Thomas Paine's famous 1776 work *Common Sense* advocating independence for America inspired sever-

From *The True Interest of America Impartially Stated, in Certain Strictures on a Pamphlet Intitled Common Sense,* by Charles Inglis (Philadelphia, 1776).

al pamphlets rebutting its arguments. The following viewpoint is taken from one such pamphlet, written by Charles Inglis. Inglis, born in Ireland, first arrived in Pennsylvania in 1755 as a missionary to the Mohawk Indians. Ordained an Anglican clergyman in 1758 and assigned to Trinity Church in New York City in 1764, Inglis was a prolific writer of essays who consistently opposed American independence. Inglis's 1776 pamphlet, *The True Interest of America Impartially Stated, in Certain Strictures on a Pamphlet Intitled Common Sense,* begins by listing the advantages Inglis believes the colonies would derive from reconciling with Great Britain. He goes on to list the disadvantages and calamities he believes would result from declaring independence. Inglis was banished to England in 1783 because of his Loyalist views; he later moved to Nova Scotia, Canada, to become its Anglican bishop.

What are the advantages America would gain by remaining under British colonial rule, according to Inglis? What problems does he predict would befall an independent America? How would you summarize the main differences between the beliefs of Inglis and Thomas Paine, author of the opposing viewpoint?

I think it no difficult matter to point out many advantages which will certainly attend our reconciliation and connection with Great Britain on a firm, constitutional plan. I shall select a few of these; and, that their importance may be more clearly discerned, I shall afterward point out some of the evils which inevitably must attend our separating from Britain and declaring for independency. On each article I shall study brevity.

Preventing War

1. By a reconciliation with Britain, a period would be put to the present calamitous war, by which so many lives have been lost, and so many more must be lost if it continues. This alone is an advantage devoutly to be wished for. This author [Paine] says: "The blood of the slain, the weeping voice of nature cries, 'Tis time to part." I think they cry just the reverse. The blood of the slain, the weeping voice of nature cries: It is time to be reconciled; it is time to lay aside those animosities which have pushed on Britons to shed the blood of Britons; it is high time that those who are connected by the endearing ties of religion, kindred, and country should resume their former friendship and be united in the bond of mutual affection, as their interests are inseparably united.

2. By a reconciliation with Great Britain, peace—that fairest offspring and gift of heaven—will be restored. In one respect peace is like health—we do

not sufficiently know its value but by its absence. What uneasiness and anxiety, what evils has this short interruption of peace with the parent state brought on the whole British Empire! Let every man only consult his feelings—I except my antagonist—and it will require no great force of rhetoric to convince him that a removal of those evils and a restoration of peace would be a singular advantage and blessing.

3. Agriculture, commerce, and industry would resume their wonted vigor. At present, they languish and droop, both here and in Britain; and must continue to do so while this unhappy contest remains unsettled.

America's Trade

4. By a connection with Great Britain, our trade would still have the protection of the greatest naval power in the world. England has the advantage, in this respect, of every other state, whether of ancient or modern times. Her insular situation, her nurseries for seamen, the superiority of those seamen above others—these circumstances, to mention no other, combine to make her the first maritime power in the universe—such exactly is the power whose protection we want for our commerce. To suppose, with our author, that we should have no war were we to revolt from England is too absurd to deserve a confutation. I could just as soon set about refuting the reveries of some brainsick enthusiast. Past experience shows that Britain is able to defend our commerce and our coasts; and we have no reason to doubt of her being able to do so for the future.

5. The protection of our trade, while connected with Britain, will not cost us a *fiftieth* part of what it must cost were we ourselves to raise a naval force sufficient for the purpose.

6. While connected with Great Britain, we have a bounty on almost every article of exportation; and we may be better supplied with goods by her than we could elsewhere. What our author says is true, "that our imported goods must be paid for, buy them where we will"; but we may buy them dearer, and of worse quality, in one place than another. The manufactures of Great Britain confessedly surpass any in the world, particularly those in every kind of metal, which we want most; and no country can afford linens and woolens of equal quality cheaper.

7. When a reconciliation is effected, and things return into the old channel, a few years of peace will restore everything to its pristine state. Emigrants will flow in as usual from the different parts of Europe. Population will advance with the same rapid progress as formerly, and our lands will rise in value.

These advantages are not imaginary but real. They are such as we have already experienced; and such as we may derive from a connection with Great Britain for ages to come. Each of these might easily be enlarged on, and others added to them; but I only mean to suggest a few hints. . . .

Consequences of Independence

Let us now, if you please, take a view of the other side of the question. Suppose we were to revolt from Great Britain, declare ourselves independent, and set up a republic of our own—what would be the consequence? I stand aghast at the prospect; my blood runs chill when I think of the calamities, the complicated evils that must ensue, and may be clearly foreseen—it is impossible for any man to foresee them all.

Our author cautiously avoids saying anything of the inconveniences that would attend a separation. He does not even suppose that any inconvenience would attend it. Let us only declare ourselves independent, break loose from Great Britain, and, according to him, a paradisiacal state will follow! But a prudent man will consider and weigh matters well before he consents to such a measure—when on the brink of such a dreadful precipice, he must necessarily recoil and think of the consequences before he advances a step forward. Supposing then we declared for independency, what would follow? I answer:

1. All our property throughout the continent would be unhinged; the greatest confusion and most violent convulsions would take place. It would not be here as it was in England at the Revolution in 1688. That Revolution was not brought about by a defeasance or disannulling the right of succession. James II, by abdicating the throne, left it vacant for the next in succession; accordingly, his eldest daughter and her husband stepped in. Every other matter went on in the usual, regular way; and the constitution, instead of being dissolved, was strengthened. But in case of our revolt, the old constitution would be totally subverted. The common bond that tied us together, and by which our property was secured, would be snapped asunder. It is not to be doubted but our Congress would endeavor to apply some remedy for those evils; but, with all deference to that respectable body, I do not apprehend that any remedy in their power would be adequate, at least for some time. I do not choose to be more explicit; but I am able to support my opinion.

2. What a horrid situation would thousands be reduced to who have taken the oath of allegiance to the King; yet, contrary to their oath as well as inclination, must be compelled to renounce that allegiance or abandon all their property in America! How many thousands more would be reduced to a similar situation, who, although they took not that oath, yet would think it inconsistent with their duty and a good conscience to renounce their sovereign. I

dare say these will appear trifling difficulties to our author; but, whatever he may think, there are thousands and thousands who would sooner lose all they had in the world, nay, life itself, than thus wound their conscience. A declaration of independency would infallibly disunite and divide the colonists.

War Will Lead to Ruin

3. By a declaration for independency, every avenue to an accommodation with Great Britain would be closed; the sword only could then decide the quarrel; and the sword would not be sheathed till one had conquered the other.

The importance of these colonies to Britain need not be enlarged on—it is a thing so universally known. The greater their importance is to her, so much the more obstinate will her struggle be not to lose them. The independency of America would, in the end, deprive her of the West Indies, shake her empire to the foundation, and reduce her to a state of the most mortifying insignificance. Great Britain, therefore, must, for her own preservation, risk everything, and exert her whole strength to prevent such an event from taking place. This being the case,

4. Devastation and ruin must mark the progress of this war along the seacoast of America. Hitherto, Britain has not exerted her power. Her number of troops and ships of war here at present is very little more than she judged expedient in time of peace—the former does not amount to 12,000 men—nor the latter to 40 ships, including frigates. Both she and the colonies hoped for and expected an accommodation; neither of them has lost sight of that desirable object. The seas have been open to our ships; and, although some skirmishes have unfortunately happened, yet a ray of hope still cheered both sides that peace was not distant. But, as soon as we declare for independency, every prospect of this kind must vanish. Ruthless war, with all its aggravated horrors, will ravage our once happy land; our seacoasts and ports will be ruined, and our ships taken. Torrents of blood will be spilled, and thousands reduced to beggary and wretchedness.

This melancholy contest would last till one side conquered. Supposing Britain to be victorious; however high my opinion is of British generosity, I should be exceedingly sorry to receive terms from her in the haughty tone of a conqueror. Or supposing such a failure of her manufactures, commerce, and strength, that victory should incline to the side of America; yet, who can say, in that case, what extremities her sense of resentment and self-preservation will drive Great Britain to? For my part, I should not in the least be surprised if, on such a prospect as the independency of America, she would parcel out this continent to the different European powers. Canada might be restored to France, Florida to Spain, with additions to each; other states also might come in for a portion. Let no man think this chimerical or improbable. The independency of America would be so fatal to Britain that she would leave nothing in her power undone to prevent it. I believe as firmly as I do my own existence that, if every other method failed, she would try some such expedient as this to disconcert our scheme of independency; and let any man figure to himself the situation of these British colonies, if only Canada were restored to France!

———— • ————

"Suppose we were to revolt from Great Britain, declare ourselves independent, and set up a republic of our own. . . . I stand aghast at the prospect; my blood runs chill when I think of . . . the complicated evils that must ensue."

———— • ————

5. But supposing once more that we were able to cut off every regiment that Britain can spare or hire, and to destroy every ship she can send, that we could beat off any other European power that would presume to intrude upon this continent; yet, a republican form of government would neither suit the genius of the people nor the extent of America.

In nothing is the wisdom of a legislator more conspicuous than in adapting his government to the genius, manners, disposition, and other circumstances of the people with whom he is concerned. If this important point is overlooked, confusion will ensue; his system will sink into neglect and ruin. Whatever check or barriers may be interposed, nature will always surmount them and finally prevail. . . .

We Are Britons

The Americans are properly Britons. They have the manners, habits, and ideas of Britons; and have been accustomed to a similar form of government. But Britons never could bear the extremes, either of monarchy or republicanism. Some of their kings have aimed at despotism, but always failed. Repeated efforts have been made toward democracy, and they equally failed. Once, indeed, republicanism triumphed over the constitution; the despotism of one person ensued; both were finally expelled. The inhabitants of Great Britain were quite anxious for the restoration of royalty in 1660, as they were for its expulsion in 1642, and for some succeeding years. If we may judge of future events by past transactions, in similar circumstances, this would most probably be the case of America were a republican form of government adopted in our present ferment. After much blood was shed, those confusions would terminate in the despotism of some one successful adventurer; and should the Americans be so fortunate as to emancipate themselves from that thralldom, perhaps the whole would end in a limited monarchy, after shedding as much more blood. Limited monarchy is the form of government which is most favorable to liberty, which is best adapted to the genius and temper of Britons; although here and there among us a crack-brained zealot for democracy or absolute monarchy may be sometimes found.

Besides the unsuitableness of the republican form to the genius of the people, America is too extensive for it. That form may do well enough for a single city or small territory, but would be utterly improper for such a continent as this. America is too unwieldy for the feeble, dilatory administration of democracy. . . .

It is well known that wages and the price of labor, in general, are much higher in America than in England. Labor must necessarily be dear in every country where land is cheap and large tracts of it unsettled, as is the case here. Hence an American regiment costs us *double* what a British regiment, of equal number, costs Britain. Were it proper to be explicit and descend to particulars, I could evince this past all possibility of doubt; and I appeal for the truth of it to those gentlemen among us who are acquainted with these matters.

The Costs of Revolution

Where the money is to come from which will defray this enormous annual expense of *three millions* sterling, and all those other debts, I know not; unless the author of *Common Sense*, or some other ingenious projector, can discover the Philosopher's Stone, by which iron and other base metals may be transmuted into gold. Certain I am that our commerce and agriculture, the two principal sources of our wealth, will not support such an expense. The whole of our exports from the Thirteen United Colonies, in the year 1769, amounted only to £2,887,898 sterling; which is not so much, by near half a million, as our annual expense would be were we independent of Great Britain. Those exports, with no inconsiderable part of the profits arising from them, it is well known, centered finally in Britain to pay the merchants and manufacturers there for goods we had imported thence—and yet left us still in debt! What then must our situation be, or what the state of our trade, when oppressed with such a burden of annual expense! When every article of commerce, every necessary of life, together with our lands, must be heavily taxed to defray that expense! . . .

But here it may be said *that all the evils above specified are more tolerable than slavery.* With this sentiment I sincerely agree—any hardships, however great, are preferable to slavery. But then I ask—Is there no other alternative in the present case? Is there no choice left us but slavery, or those evils? I am confident there is; and that both may be equally avoided. Let us only show a disposition to treat or negotiate in earnest—let us fall upon some method to set a treaty or negotiation with Great Britain on foot; and, if once properly begun, there is moral certainty that this unhappy dispute will be settled to the mutual satisfaction and interest of both countries. For my part, I have not the least doubt about it.

It would be improper and needless for me to enlarge on the particulars that should be adjusted at such a treaty. The maturest deliberation will be necessary on the occasion, as well as a generous regard to every part of the Empire. I shall just beg leave to suggest my opinion on a few points—I think America should insist that the claim of parliamentary taxation be either explicitly relinquished, or else such security given as the case will admit, and may be equivalent to a formal relinquishment, that this claim shall not be exerted. When this most important point is gained, America should consider that there is a great difference between having her money wrested from her by others and not giving any of it herself when it is proper to give. While she is protected and shares in the advantages resulting from being a part of the British Empire, she should contribute something for that protection and those advantages; and I never heard a sensible American deny this. Moreover, she should stipulate for such a freedom of trade as is consistent with the general welfare of the State; and that this interesting object be settled in such a manner as to preclude, as much as possible, any impolitic or injurious infringements hereafter. All this may be easily done if both sides are only disposed for peace; and there are many other particulars which would be exceedingly beneficial to America, and might be obtained, as they could not interfere with the interest of Great Britain or any other part of the Empire. We have abundant proof of this, as well as several good hints to proceed on, in the late concessions to Nova Scotia from government. . . .

But a declaration for independency on the part of America would preclude treaty entirely and could answer no good purpose. We actually have already every advantage of independency, without its inconveniences. By a declaration of independency, we should instantly lose all assistance from our friends in England. It would stop their mouths; for, were they to say anything in our favor, they would be deemed rebels and treated accordingly.

Our author is much elated with the prospect of

foreign succor, if we once declare ourselves independent, and from thence promises us mighty matters. This, no doubt, is intended to spirit up the desponding—all who might shrink at the thought of America encountering, singly and unsupported, the whole strength of Great Britain. I believe, in my conscience, that he is as much mistaken in this as in anything else; and that this expectation is delusive, vain, and fallacious. My reasons are these, and I submit them to the reader's judgement:

The only European power from which we can possibly receive assistance is France. But France is now at peace with Great Britain; and is it probable that France would interrupt that peace and hazard a war with the power which lately reduced her so low, from a disinterested motive of aiding and protecting these colonies? . . .

It is well known that some of the French and Spanish colonists, not long since, offered to put themselves under the protection of England and declare themselves independent of France and Spain; but England rejected both offers. The example would be rather dangerous to states that have colonies—to none could it be more so than to France and Spain, who have so many and such extensive colonies. "The practice of courts are as much against us" in this as in the instance our author mentions. Can anyone imagine that, because we declared ourselves independent of England, France would *therefore* consider us as really independent! And before England had acquiesced, or made any effort worth mentioning to reduce us? Or can anyone be so weak as to think that France would run the risk of a war with England, unless she (France) were sure of some extraordinary advantage by it, in having the colonies under her *immediate jurisdiction?* If England will not protect us for our trade, surely France will not. . . .

A Blessed Country

America is far from being yet in a desperate situation. I am confident she may obtain honorable and advantageous terms from Great Britain. A few years of peace will soon retrieve all her losses. She will rapidly advance to a state of maturity whereby she may not only repay the parent state amply for all past benefits but also lay under the greatest obligations.

America, till very lately, has been the happiest country in the universe. Blessed with all that nature could bestow with the profusest bounty, she enjoyed, besides, more liberty, greater privileges than any other land. How painful is it to reflect on these things, and to look forward to the gloomy prospects now before us! But it is not too late to hope that matters may mend. By prudent management her former happiness may again return; and continue to increase

for ages to come, in a union with the parent state.

However distant humanity may wish the period, yet, in the rotation of human affairs, a period may arrive when (both countries being prepared for it) some terrible disaster, some dreadful convulsion in Great Britain may transfer the seat of empire to this Western Hemisphere—where the British constitution, like the Phoenix from its parent's ashes, shall rise with youthful vigor and shine with redoubled splendor.

But if America should now mistake her real interest—if her sons, infatuated with romantic notions of conquest and empire, ere things are ripe, should adopt this republican's scheme—they will infallibly destroy this smiling prospect. They will dismember this happy country, make it a scene of blood and slaughter, and entail wretchedness and misery on millions yet unborn.

For Further Reading

Eric Foner, *Tom Paine and Revolutionary America.* New York: Oxford University Press, 1976.

Robert Middlekauf, *The Glorious Cause: The American Revolution, 1763–1789.* New York: Oxford University Press, 1982.

Mary Beth Norton, *Liberty's Daughters: The Revolutionary Experience of American Women, 1750–1800.* Boston: Little, Brown, 1980.

Benjamin Quarles, *The Negro in the American Revolution.* Chapel Hill: University of North Carolina Press, 1961.

Leslie F.S. Upton, ed., *Revolutionary vs. Loyalist.* Waltham, MA: Blaisdell Publishing, 1968.

Creating a New Government

VIEWPOINT 14A

A Republican Form of Government Is Best (1776)

John Adams (1735–1826)

When the United States declared independence from Great Britain in 1776, the former British colonies faced the task of creating new constitutional governments at the state and national levels. One of the most important figures in this process was John Adams, a lawyer from Massachusetts. Adams, first identified with the revolutionary cause when he wrote a series of resolutions condemning the Stamp Act in 1765, became a forceful advocate for indepen-

From *Thoughts on Government, in a Letter from a Gentleman to His Friend* by John Adams (Boston, 1776). Reprinted in *The Works of John Adams*, vol. 4, edited by Charles Francis Adams (Boston: Little, Brown, 1854).

dence while serving in the First and Second Continental Congresses. Like many other revolutionary leaders, however, he was distrustful of the radical forms of democracy advocated by *Common Sense* author Thomas Paine and others, believing that popular democracy carried its own threat of tyranny by the majority. Adams's views on government are spelled out in the following viewpoint, taken from a pamphlet first published in 1776, entitled *Thoughts on Government, in a Letter from a Gentleman to His Friend*. The pamphlet was written in part to counter the influence of Paine and other democratic writers. Adams advocates a "mixed Republican" government consisting of different branches that check the powers of one another, and through which he feels the rule of law and true liberty could be preserved. Adams put his views into practice in 1780 when he wrote most of the provisions of the Massachusetts state constitution. He later became the first vice president and the second president of the United States.

What should be the end of government, according to Adams? Why does Adams oppose a single-house assembly or legislature? What reasons does he give in favor of rotation of political office (term limits)?

My dear Sir,—If I was equal to the task of forming a plan for the government of a colony, I should be flattered with your request, and very happy to comply with it; because, as the divine science of politics is the science of social happiness, and the blessings of society depend entirely on the constitutions of government, which are generally institutions that last for many generations, there can be no employment more agreeable to a benevolent mind than a research after the best.

[Alexander] Pope flattered tyrants too much when he said,

For forms of government let fools contest,
That which is best administered is best.

Nothing can be more fallacious than this. But poets read history to collect flowers, not fruits; they attend to fanciful images, not the effects of social institutions. Nothing is more certain, from the history of nations and nature of man, than that some forms of government are better fitted for being well administered than others.

The End of Government

We ought to consider what is the end of government, before we determine which is the best form. Upon this point all speculative politicians will agree, that the happiness of society is the end of government, as all divines and moral philosophers will agree that the happiness of the individual is the end of man. From this principle it will follow, that the form of government which communicates ease, comfort, security, or, in one word, happiness, to the greatest number of persons, and in the greatest degree, is the best.

All sober inquirers after truth, ancient and modern, pagan and Christian, have declared that the happiness of man, as well as his dignity, consists in virtue. Confucius, Zoroaster, Socrates, Mahomet, not to mention authorities really sacred, have agreed in this.

If there is a form of government, then, whose principle and foundation is virtue, will not every sober man acknowledge it better calculated to promote the general happiness than any other form?

Fear is the foundation of most governments; but it is so sordid and brutal a passion, and renders men in whose breasts it predominates so stupid and miserable, that Americans will not be likely to approve of any political institution which is founded on it.

Honor is truly sacred, but holds a lower rank in the scale of moral excellence than virtue. Indeed, the former is but a part of the latter, and consequently has not equal pretensions to support a frame of government productive of human happiness.

The foundation of every government is some principle or passion in the minds of people. The noblest principles and most generous affections in our nature, then, have the fairest chance to support the noblest and most generous models of government.

A man must be indifferent to the sneers of modern Englishmen, to mention in their company the names of [Algernon] Sidney, [James] Harrington, [John] Locke, [John] Milton, [John] Nedham, [Henry] Neville, [Gilbert] Burnet, and [Benjamin] Hoadly. No small fortitude is necessary to confess that one has read them. The wretched condition of this country, however, for ten or fifteen years past, has frequently reminded me of their principles and reasonings. They will convince any candid mind, that there is no good government but what is republican. That the only valuable part of the British constitution is so; because the very definition of a republic is "an empire of laws, and not of men." That, as a republic is the best of governments, so that particular arrangement of the powers of society, or, in other words, that form of government which is best contrived to secure an impartial and exact execution of the laws, is the best of republics.

Of republics there is an inexhaustible variety, because the possible combinations of the powers of society are capable of innumerable variations.

As good government is an empire of laws, how shall your laws be made? In a large society, inhabiting an extensive country, it is impossible that the whole should assemble to make laws. The first necessary step, then, is to depute power from the many to a few of the most wise and good. But by what rules shall you choose your representatives? Agree upon the number and qualifications of persons who shall have the benefit of choosing, or annex this privilege to the inhabitants of a certain extent of ground.

———— • ————

*"There is no good government
but what is republican."*

———— • ————

The principal difficulty lies, and the greatest care should be employed, in constituting this representative assembly. It should be in miniature an exact portrait of the people at large. It should think, feel, reason, and act like them. That it may be the interest of this assembly to do strict justice at all times, it should be an equal representation, or, in other words, equal interests among the people should have equal interests in it. Great care should be taken to effect this, and to prevent unfair, partial, and corrupt elections. Such regulations, however, may be better made in times of greater tranquillity than the present; and they will spring up themselves naturally, when all the powers of government come to be in the hands of the people's friends. At present, it will be safest to proceed in all established modes, to which the people have been familiarized by habit.

Disadvantages of One Assembly

A representation of the people in one assembly being obtained, a question arises, whether all the powers of government, legislative, executive, and judicial, shall be left in this body? I think a people cannot be long free, nor ever happy, whose government is in one assembly. My reasons for this opinion are as follow:—

1. A single assembly is liable to all the vices, follies, and frailties of an individual; subject to fits of humor, starts of passion, flights of enthusiasm, partialities, or prejudice, and consequently productive of hasty results and absurd judgments. And all these errors ought to be corrected and defects supplied by some controlling power.

2. A single assembly is apt to be avaricious, and in time will not scruple to exempt itself from burdens, which it will lay, without compunction, on its constituents.

3. A single assembly is apt to grow ambitious, and after a time will not hesitate to vote itself perpetual. This was one fault of the Long Parliament [in England, 1640–1660]; but more remarkably of Holland, whose assembly first voted themselves from annual to septennial, then for life, and after a course of years, that all vacancies happening by death or otherwise, should be filled by themselves, without any application to constituents at all.

4. A representative assembly, although extremely well qualified, and absolutely necessary, as a branch of the legislative, is unfit to exercise the executive power, for want of two essential properties, secrecy and despatch.

5. A representative assembly is still less qualified for the judicial power, because it is too numerous, too slow, and too little skilled in the laws.

6. Because a single assembly, possessed of all the powers of government, would make arbitrary laws for their own interest, execute all laws arbitrarily for their own interest, and adjudge all controversies in their own favor.

But shall the whole power of legislation rest in one assembly? Most of the foregoing reasons apply equally to prove that the legislative power ought to be more complex; to which we may add, that if the legislative power is wholly in one assembly, and the executive in another, or in a single person, these two powers will oppose and encroach upon each other, until the contest shall end in war, and the whole power, legislative and executive, be usurped by the strongest.

The judicial power, in such case, could not mediate, or hold the balance between the two contending powers, because the legislative would undermine it. And this shows the necessity, too, of giving the executive power a negative upon the legislative, otherwise this will be continually encroaching upon that.

To avoid these dangers, let a distinct assembly be constituted, as a mediator between the two extreme branches of the legislature, that which represents the people, and that which is vested with the executive power.

Let the representative assembly then elect by ballot, from among themselves or their constituents, or both, a distinct assembly, which, for the sake of perspicuity, we will call a council. It may consist of any number you please, say twenty or thirty, and should have a free and independent exercise of its judgment, and consequently a negative voice in the legislature.

The Governor

These two bodies, thus constituted, and made integral parts of the legislature, let them unite, and by joint ballot choose a governor, who, after being stripped of most of those badges of domination, called prerogatives, should have a free and independent exercise of his judgment, and be made also an integral part of the legislature. This, I know, is liable to objections; and, if you please, you may make him only president of the council, as in Connecticut. But as the governor is to be invested with the executive power, with consent of council, I think he ought to have a negative upon the legislative. If he is annually elective, as he ought to be, he will always have so much reverence and affection for the people, their representatives and counsellors, that, although you give him an independent exercise of his judgment, he will seldom use it in opposition to the two houses, except in cases the public utility of which would be conspicuous; and some such cases would happen.

In the present exigency of American affairs, when, by an act of Parliament, we are put out of the royal protection, and consequently discharged from our allegiance, and it has become necessary to assume government for our immediate security, the governor, lieutenant-governor, secretary, treasurer, commissary, attorney-general, should be chosen by joint ballot of both houses. And these and all other elections, especially of representatives and counsellors, should be annual, there not being in the whole circle of the sciences a maxim more infallible than this, "where annual elections end, there slavery begins."

These great men, in this respect, should be, once a year,

> Like bubbles on the sea of matter borne,
> They rise, they break, and to that sea return.

This will teach them the great political virtues of humility, patience, and moderation, without which every man in power becomes a ravenous beast of prey.

This mode of constituting the great offices of state will answer very well for the present; but if by experiment it should be found inconvenient, the legislature may, at its leisure, devise other methods of creating them, by elections of the people at large, as in Connecticut, or it may enlarge the term for which they shall be chosen to seven years, or three years, or for life, or make any other alterations which the society shall find productive of its ease, its safety, its freedom, or, in one word, its happiness.

A rotation of all offices, as well as of representatives and counsellors, has many advocates, and is contended for with many plausible arguments. It would be attended, no doubt, with many advantages; and if the society has a sufficient number of suitable characters to supply the great number of vacancies which would be made by such a rotation, I can see no objection to it. These persons may be allowed to serve for three years, and then be excluded three years, or for any longer or shorter term.

Any seven or nine of the legislative council may be made a quorum, for doing business as a privy council, to advise the governor in the exercise of the executive branch of power, and in all acts of state.

The governor should have the command of the militia and of all your armies. The power of pardons should be with the governor and council.

Judges, justices, and all other officers, civil and military, should be nominated and appointed by the governor, with the advice and consent of council, unless you choose to have a government more popular; if you do, all officers, civil and military, may be chosen by joint ballot of both houses; or, in order to preserve the independence and importance of each house, by ballot of one house, concurred in by the other. . . .

The Judicial Branch

The dignity and stability of government in all its branches, the morals of the people, and every blessing of society depend so much upon an upright and skilful administration of justice, that the judicial power ought to be distinct from both the legislative and executive, and independent upon both, that so it may be a check upon both, as both should be checks upon that. The judges, therefore, should be always men of learning and experience in the laws, of exemplary morals, great patience, calmness, coolness, and attention. Their minds should not be distracted with jarring interests; they should not be dependent upon any man, or body of men. To these ends, they should hold estates for life in their offices; or, in other words, their commissions should be during good behavior, and their salaries ascertained and established by law. For misbehavior, the grand inquest of the colony, the house of representatives, should impeach them before the governor and council, where they should have time and opportunity to make their defence; but, if convicted, should be removed from their offices, and subjected to such other punishment as shall be thought proper. . . .

Laws for the liberal education of youth, especially of the lower class of people, are so extremely wise and useful, that, to a humane and generous mind, no expense for this purpose would be thought extravagant. . . .

A constitution founded on these principles introduces knowledge among the people, and inspires them with a conscious dignity becoming freemen; a general emulation takes place, which causes good humor, sociability, good manners, and good morals to be general. That elevation of sentiment inspired by such a government, makes the common people brave and enterprising. That ambition which is inspired by it makes them sober, industrious, and frugal. You will find among them some elegance, perhaps, but more solidity; a little pleasure, but a great deal of business; some politeness, but more civility. If you compare such a country with the regions of domination, whether monarchical or aristocratical, you will fancy yourself in Arcadia or Elysium.

If the colonies should assume governments separately, they should be left entirely to their own choice of the forms; and if a continental constitution should be formed, it should be a congress, containing a fair and adequate representation of the colonies, and its authority should sacredly be confined to these cases, namely, war, trade, disputes between colony and colony, the post-office, and the unappropriated lands of the crown, as they used to be called.

These colonies, under such forms of government, and in such a union, would be unconquerable by all the monarchies of Europe.

You and I, my dear friend, have been sent into life at a time when the greatest lawgivers of antiquity would have wished to live. How few of the human race have ever enjoyed an opportunity of making an election of government, more than of air, soil, or climate, for themselves or their children! When, before the present epocha, had three millions of people full power and a fair opportunity to form and establish the wisest and happiest government that human wisdom can contrive? I hope you will avail yourself and your country of that extensive learning and indefatigable industry which you possess, to assist her in the formation of the happiest governments and the best character of a great people. For myself, I must beg you to keep my name out of sight; for this feeble attempt, if it should be known to be mine, would oblige me to apply to myself those lines of the immortal John Milton, in one of his sonnets:—

> I did but prompt the age to quit their clogs
> By the known rules of ancient liberty,
> When straight a barbarous noise environs me
> Of owls and cuckoos, asses, apes, and dogs.

VIEWPOINT 14B

Popular Democracy Is the Best Form of Government (1776)

Anonymous

By 1777 most of the former British colonies had created and adopted new state constitutions. Most of these constitutions, reflecting the ideas of John Adams and other relatively conservative colonial leaders, included a bicameral legislature, the separation of powers, the election of the governor and state officials by the legislature, and property qualifications for voting. The major exception was the Pennsylvania constitution, adopted in September 1776. Among its novel features was a unicameral legislature, an executive president and council elected directly by the public, and a broad franchise enabling all taxpayers and sons of taxpayers to vote. The Pennsylvania constitution was modeled after proposals set forth in several pamphlets and tracts published in

From *The Interest of America* (anonymous), 1776.

1776. Among these tracts was *The Interest of America*, excerpted here. The anonymous author of the pamphlet writes that America has a chance to create an entirely new and more democratic form of government to best serve the interests of the people.

Why does the author oppose a bicameral legislature? What contrasts does he describe between Great Britain and the United States? What points of agreement does he have with John Adams (author of the opposing viewpoint)? What areas of disagreement exist between the two?

The important day is come, or near at hand, that America is to assume a form of Government for herself. We should be very desirous to know what form is best; and that surely is best which is most natural, easy, cheap, and which best secures the rights of the people. We should always keep in mind that great truth, viz: that the good of the people is the ultimate end of civil Government. As we must (some Provinces at least) in a short time assume some new mode of Government, and the matter cannot be deferred so long as to canvass, deliberately weigh, and fully adjust everything that may hereafter appear necessary, we should leave room to alter for the better in time to come. Every Province should be viewed as having a right, either with or without an application to the Continental Congress, to alter their form of Government in some particulars; and that without being liable to raise a clamour, by some who would be glad to say that it was contrary to the Constitution that they first formed upon; that it was overturning the original plan, and leaving people at uncertainties as to the foundation they are upon, and the like. As the Government is for the people, the people, when properly represented, have a right to alter it for their advantage.

Designing a Government

The affair now in view is the most important that ever was before *America*. In my opinion, it is the most important that has been transacted in any nation for some centuries past. If our civil Government is well constructed and well managed, *America* bids fair to be the most glorious State that has ever been on earth. We should now, at the beginning, lay the foundation right. Most, if not all, other Governments have had a corrupt mixture in their very Constitution; they have generally been formed in haste, or out of necessity, or tyrannically, or in a state of ignorance; and, being badly formed, the management of them has been with difficulty. But we have opportunity to form with some deliberation, with free choice, with good advantages for knowledge; we have opportunity to observe what has been right and what wrong in other States, and to profit by them. The plan of *American* Government should, as much as possible, be formed to suit all the variety of circumstances that people may be in—virtuous or vicious, agreeing or contending, moving regularly or convulsed by the intrigues of aspiring men; for we may expect a variety of circumstances in a course of time, and we should be prepared for every condition. We should assume that mode of Government which is most equitable and adapted to the good of mankind, and trust Providence for the event; for *God*, who determines the fate of Governments, is most like to prosper that which is most equitable; and I think there can be no doubt that a well-regulated Democracy is most equitable. An annual or frequent choice of magistrates, who, in a year, or after a few years, are again left upon a level with their neighbours, is most likely to prevent usurpation and tyranny, and most likely to secure the privileges of the people. If rulers know that they shall, in a short term of time, be again out of power, and, it may be, liable to be called to an account for misconduct, it will guard them against maladministration. A truly popular Government has, I believe, never yet been tried in the world. The most remarkable Government that has ever been, viz: the *Roman* Republick, was something near it, but not fully so; and the want of it being fully so, kept a continual contest between the Senate and Plebeians.

America must consist of a number of confederate Provinces, Cantons, Districts, or whatever they may be called. These must be united in a General Congress; but each Province must have a distinct Legislature, and have as much power within itself as possible. The General Congress should not interfere or meddle with Provincial affairs more than needs must. Every Province should be left to do as much within itself as may be; and every Province should allow each County, yea, and each Town, to do as much within themselves as possible. Small bodies manage affairs much easier and cheaper than large ones. If every County and Town manage as much business as may be within themselves, people will be better satisfied, and the Provincial Congress saved much trouble. Our Counties and Towns have heretofore been left to manage many of their own affairs; and it has been a great privilege, and their business has been managed to great advantage. Each County should now choose their own officers, which were heretofore appointed by the Crown. These matters may now be adjusted with much ease. Every Province should be allowed such full power within itself, and receive such advantages by a general union or confederation, that it would choose to continue in that union. The connection of the Provinces should be made to be for the interest of each, and be agreeable

to each. This will keep them quiet and peaceable; and nothing will tend so much to this, as to let every Province have as much power and liberty within itself as will consist with the good of the whole. Neither the Continental Congress, nor any other number of men, should assume or use any power or office for their own sake, but for the good of the whole. Let *America* increase ever so much, there must never be any power like a Kingly power; no power used for its own sake, or for the advantage or dignity of any number of men, as distinct from the good of the whole; and while things are thus managed, a general union will be agreeable, and people will not complain.

Duties of a National Congress

Notwithstanding every Province should have all possible power within itself, yet some things must be left to the General Congress; as, 1. Making and managing war and making peace. 2. Settling differences between Provinces. 3. Making some maritime laws, or general regulations respecting trade; otherwise one Province might unjustly interfere with another. 4. Ordering a currency for the whole Continent; for it would be best that, as soon as may be, there should be one currency for the whole; the General Congress might order the quota for each Province. 5. The forming of new Provinces. 6. The sale of new lands. 7. Treaties with other nations; consequently some general directions of our *Indian* affairs.

As we are now to assume a new mode of Government, I think it ought properly to be new. Some are for keeping as near the old form of Government in each Province as can well be. But I think it is entirely wrong; it is mistaken policy. It is probable that some who propose it mean well; but I humbly conceive they have not thoroughly considered the thing. Others who propose it may have self-interest at bottom, hoping thereby to retain, or obtain, places of profit or honour. We must come as near a new form of Government as we can, without destroying private property. So far as private property will allow, we must form our Government in each Province just as if we had never any form of Government before. It is much easier to form a new Government than to patch up one partly old and partly new, because it is more simple and natural. I speak chiefly with respect to Legislature. We should by all means avoid several branches of Legislature.

One Branch of Legislature Best

One branch of Legislature is much preferable to more than one, because a plurality causes perpetual contention and waste of time. It was so in *Rome*; it has been so in *Great Britain*; and has been remarkably so in these Provinces in times past. The ever-memorable Congress now in *America* has done business infinitely better than if there had been several orders of Delegates to contest, interrupt, and be a negative one upon another.

---•---

"Rulers should be frequently chose to their office."

---•---

A patched Government, consisting of several parts, has been the difficulty, I may call it the disease, of some of the best civil Governments that have been in the world—I mean the *Roman* Republick and the Government of *Great Britain*. Had the *Romans* been a true Democracy, without a Senate, or body different from the Plebeians, they might have avoided those jars and contentions which continually subsisted between those two bodies. Should we admit different branches of Legislature, it might give occasion in time to degenerate into that form of Government, or something like that, which has been so oppressive in our nation. It might open a door for ill-disposed aspiring men to destroy the State. Our having several branches of Legislature heretofore is an argument against, rather than for it, in time to come, because it is a word that not only has been abused, but in its nature tends to abuse. The simplest mode of legislation is certainly best. The *European* nations have, for some centuries past, derived most of their knowledge from the *Greeks* and *Romans*. The *Romans*, especially, have been, in a sort, an example, being excellent in many things. We have been ready to view them so in all things. We are very apt to take in, or imitate, the imperfections as well as the excellencies of those that are excellent. Hence, I suppose, it is that most, if not all, the Republicks in *Europe* have a body of Senators in their form of Government. I doubt not it will be an argument with many, that we in *America* must have something like a Senate, or Council, or Upper House, because the *Romans* and other Republicks have had. But the argument is the other way; it was their imperfection, it was a source of trouble, it was a step towards arbitrary power, and therefore to be avoided. Free Government can better, must better, subsist without it. Different branches of Legislature cause much needless expense, two ways: First, as there are more persons to maintain; and, second, as they waste time, and prolong a session by their contentions. Besides, it is a great absurdity that one branch of a Legislature, that can negative all the rest, should be the principal Executive power in the State. There can be but little chance for proper freedom, where the making and executing the laws of a State lie in the same hand, and that not of the people in general, but of a single person. The

Legislative and Executive power in every Province ought to be kept as distinct as possible. Wise, experienced, and publick-spirited persons should be in places of power, and if so, they must be sought out, chosen, and introduced. For this reason there ought not to be a number that are hereditary, for wisdom is not a birthright; nor a number put in place for life, for men's abilities and manners may change. Rulers should be frequently chose to their office. A Provincial Congress is the whole Province met by Representatives; and there is no need of a representative of a King, for we have none; nor can there be need of a Council to represent the House of Lords, for we have not, and hope never shall have, a hereditary nobility, different from the general body of the people; but if we admit different branches of the Legislature, there is danger that there may be in time.

For Further Reading

Willi P. Adams, *The First American Constitutions.* Chapel Hill: University of North Carolina Press, 1980.

Edward Handler, *America and Europe in the Political Thought of John Adams.* Cambridge: Harvard University Press, 1964.

John Paul Selsam, *The Pennsylvania Constitution of 1776.* New York: Octagon Books, 1971.

Peter Shaw, *The Character of John Adams.* Chapel Hill: University of North Carolina Press, 1976.

Gordon S. Wood, *The Creation of the American Republic, 1776–1787.* Chapel Hill: University of North Carolina Press, 1969.

VIEWPOINT 15A

Shays's Rebellion Indicates the Need for a New Constitution (1786)

George Washington (1732–1799)

One of the key events that led to the 1787 Constitutional Convention was a series of uprisings by Massachusetts farmers in 1786 and 1787 that became known as Shays's Rebellion. Faced with a combination of bad harvests, a shortage of hard currency, and heavy taxes (instituted in part to pay off Revolutionary War debts), farmers were threatened with the loss of their farms and imprisonment for failure to pay debts and taxes. Many farmers, after failing to convince the state legislature to enact debt relief measures, resorted to mob action to shut down local courts and intimidate local authorities. Daniel Shays, a former Revolutionary War army officer, began training a group of farmers in military drills and

Excerpted from *The Writings of George Washington, from Original Manuscript Sources,* edited by John C. Fitzpatrick (Washington, DC: GPO, 1931–44).

became the symbolic leader of the insurrection. The Massachusetts government raised a strong militia force that crushed the rebellion in battles in January and February of 1787.

News of Shays's Rebellion spread throughout the states and was used by many as evidence that a new constitution creating a stronger national government was needed. One important figure to draw this conclusion was George Washington. Having resigned as general of the Continental Army in 1783, Washington was officially retired from public life. But he was disturbed by events in Massachusetts and elsewhere that suggested that the new nation he had helped to create would founder without a stronger government. Washington expressed these views in several letters to friends and associates, including a November 5, 1786, letter to fellow Virginian James Madison. In his letter to Madison, reprinted below, Washington refers to a letter from Henry Knox, one of Washington's generals during the Revolution, which described the situation in Massachusetts as a serious one.

What concerns does Washington express about the future of the nation? What does he find most disturbing about the disturbances in Massachusetts and the beliefs of the people leading them?

———————

My dear Sir:
I thank you for the communications in your letter of the first instt. The decision of the [Virginia] House on the question respecting a paper emission [issuing of paper money], is portentous I hope, of an auspicious Session. It may certainly be classed among the important questions of the present day; and merited the serious consideration of the Assembly. Fain would I hope, that the great, and most important of all objects, the foederal governmt., may be considered with that calm and deliberate attention which the magnitude of it so loudly calls for at this critical moment. Let prejudices, unreasonable jealousies, and local interest yield to reason and liberality. Let us look to our National character, and to things beyond the present period. No morn ever dawned more favourably than ours did; and no day was ever more clouded than the present! Wisdom, and good examples are necessary at this time to rescue the political machine from the impending storm. Virginia has now an opportunity to set the latter, and has enough of the former, I hope, to take the lead in promoting this great and arduous work. Without some alteration in our political creed, the superstructure we have been seven years raising at the expence of so much blood and treasure, must fall. We are fast verging to anarchy and confusion!

A letter which I have just received from Genl Knox, who had just returned from Massachusetts

(whither he had been sent by Congress consequent of the commotion in that State) is replete with melancholy information of the temper, and designs of a considerable part of that people. Among other things he says,

> there creed is, that the property of the United States, has been protected from confiscation of Britain by the joint exertions of *all*, and therefore ought to be the *common property* of all. And he that attempts opposition to this creed is an enemy to equity and justice, and ought to be swept from off the face of the Earth.

Again:

> They are determined to anihillate all debts public and private, and have Agrarian Laws, which are easily effected by the means of unfunded paper money which shall be a tender in all cases whatever.

He adds:

> The numbers of these people amount in Massachusetts to about one fifth part of several populous Counties, and to them may be collected, people of similar sentiments from the States of Rhode Island, Connecticut, and New Hampshire, so as to constitute a body of twelve or fifteen thousand desperate, and unprincipled men. They are chiefly of the young and active part of the Community.

———— • ————

"What stronger evidence can be given of the want of energy in our governments than these disorders?"

———— • ————

How melancholy is the reflection, that in so short a space, we should have made such large strides towards fulfilling the prediction of our transatlantic foe! "Leave them to themselves, and their government will soon dissolve." Will not the wise and good strive hard to avert this evil? Or will their supineness suffer ignorance, and the arts of self-interested designing disaffected and desperate characters, to involve this rising empire in wretchedness and contempt? What stronger evidence can be given of the want of energy in our governments than these disorders? If there exists not a power to check them, what security has a man for life, liberty, or property? To you, I am sure I need not add aught on this subject, the consequences of a lax, or inefficient government, are too obvious to be dwelt on. Thirteen Sovereignties pulling against each other, and all tugging at the foederal head will soon bring ruin on the whole; whereas a liberal, and energetic Constitution, well guarded and closely watched, to prevent incroachments, might restore us to that degree of respectability and consequence, to which we had a fair claim, and the brightest prospect of attaining. With sentiments of the sincerest esteem etc.

VIEWPOINT 15B

The Threat Posed By Shays's Rebellion Has Been Exaggerated (1787)

Thomas Jefferson (1743–1826)

In the years following the American Revolution, many impoverished farmers in several states resorted to mob violence in an effort to attain debt and tax relief. Shays's Rebellion in Massachusetts in 1786 was one of the most serious of these insurrections. Many political leaders throughout America looked upon such events with alarm, believing them evidence that America was falling apart. Thomas Jefferson presents a different view of Shays's Rebellion in two letters reprinted in part here. Jefferson—the author of the Declaration of Independence and a future president of the United States—was at the time of this writing U.S. minister to France. In the first letter, written to Edward Carrington on January 16, 1787, Jefferson maintains that the respect for America among European governments has not been diminished by events in Massachusetts, and he compares favorably the independent state of people in America with the situation in Europe. In the second letter, written to James Madison on January 30, Jefferson argues that occasional rebellions are necessary to preserve free government.

What is the proper relationship between the people and government, according to Jefferson? How do his views on the meaning and significance of Shays's Rebellion compare with those of George Washington, author of the opposing viewpoint?

I

The tumults in America I expected would have produced in Europe an unfavorable opinion of our political state. But it has not. On the contrary, the small effect of these tumults seems to have given more confidence in the firmness of our governments. The interposition of the people themselves on the side of government has had a great effect on the opinion here. I am persuaded myself that the good sense of the people will always be

From *The Writings of Thomas Jefferson*, edited by Paul L. Ford (New York: Putnam, 1892) and *The Writings of Thomas Jefferson: Being His Autobiography, Correspondence, Reports, Messages, Addresses, and Other Writings, Official and Private*, edited by H. A. Washington (Philadelphia, 1871).

found to be the best army. They may be led astray for a moment, but will soon correct themselves.

Inform the People

The people are the only censors of their governors; and even their errors will tend to keep these to the true principles of their institution. To punish these errors too severely would be to suppress the only safeguard of the public liberty. The way to prevent these irregular interpositions of the people is to give them full information of their affairs through the channel of the public papers, and to contrive that those papers should penetrate the whole mass of the people. The basis of our governments being the opinion of the people, the very first object should be to keep that right; and were it left to me to decide whether we should have a government without newspapers, or newspapers without a government, I should not hesitate a moment to prefer the latter. But I should mean that every man should receive those papers, and be capable of reading them.

I am convinced that those societies (as the Indians) which live without government enjoy in their general mass an infinitely greater degree of happiness than those who live under the European governments. Among the former, public opinion is in the place of law, and restrains morals as powerfully as laws ever did anywhere. Among the latter, under pretense of governing, they have divided their nations into two classes, wolves and sheep. I do not exaggerate.

This is a true picture of Europe. Cherish, therefore, the spirit of our people, and keep alive their intention. Do not be too severe upon their errors, but reclaim them by enlightening them. If once they become inattentive to the public affairs, you and I, and Congress and assemblies, judges and governors shall all become wolves. It seems to be the law of our general nature, in spite of individual exceptions; and experience declares that man is the only animal which devours his own kind; for I can apply no milder term to the governments of Europe, and to the general prey of the rich on the poor.

II

My last to you was of the 16th of December; since which, I have received yours of November 25 and December 4, which afforded me, as your letters always do, a treat on matters public, individual, and economical. I am impatient to learn your sentiments on the late troubles in the Eastern states. So far as I have yet seen, they do not appear to threaten serious consequences. Those states have suffered by the stoppage of the channels of their commerce, which have not yet found other issues. This must render money scarce and make the people uneasy. This uneasiness has produced acts absolutely unjustifiable; but I hope they will provoke no severities from their governments. A consciousness of those in power that their administration of the public affairs has been honest may, perhaps, produce too great a degree of indignation; and those characters, wherein fear predominates over hope, may apprehend too much from these instances of irregularity. They may conclude too hastily that nature has formed man insusceptible of any other government than that of force, a conclusion not founded in truth nor experience.

Three Forms of Society

Societies exist under three forms, sufficiently distinguishable: (1) without government, as among our Indians; (2) under governments, wherein the will of everyone has a just influence, as is the case in England, in a slight degree, and in our states, in a great one; (3) under governments of force, as is the case in all other monarchies, and in most of the other republics.

———— • ————

"I hold it that a little rebellion now and then is a good thing, and as necessary in the political world as storms in the physical."

———— • ————

To have an idea of the curse of existence under these last, they must be seen. It is a government of wolves over sheep. It is a problem, not clear in my mind, that the first condition is not the best. But I believe it to be inconsistent with any great degree of population. The second state has a great deal of good in it. The mass of mankind under that enjoys a precious degree of liberty and happiness. It has its evils, too, the principal of which is the turbulence to which it is subject. But weigh this against the oppressions of monarchy, and it becomes nothing. *Malo periculosam libertatem quam quietam servitutem* [I prefer liberty at risk to peaceful servitude]. Even this evil is productive of good. It prevents the degeneracy of government and nourishes a general attention to the public affairs.

I hold it that a little rebellion now and then is a good thing, and as necessary in the political world as storms in the physical. Unsuccessful rebellions, indeed, generally establish the encroachments on the rights of the people which have produced them. An observation of this truth should render honest republican governors so mild in their punishment of rebellions as not to discourage them too much. It is a medicine necessary for the sound health of government.

For Further Reading

Richard B. Bernstein with Kym S. Rice, *Are We to Be a Nation? The Making of the Constitution.* Cambridge, MA: Harvard University Press, 1987.

James T. Flexner, *Washington: The Indispensable Man.* Boston: Little, Brown, 1974.

Richard B. Morris, *The Forging of the Union, 1781–1789.* New York: Harper & Row, 1987.

Merrill Peterson, *Thomas Jefferson and the New Nation.* New York: Oxford University Press, 1970.

David Szatmary, *Shays' Rebellion: The Making of an Agrarian Insurrection.* Amherst: University of Massachusetts Press, 1980.

VIEWPOINT 16A

A Republic Must Be Small and Uniform to Survive (1787)

"Brutus"

The U.S. Constitution was written by delegates meeting in a special convention in Philadelphia from May to September 1787. The product of the Constitutional Convention, which then had to be ratified by the states, faced widespread debate. Numerous pamphlets and newspaper articles were published in the succeeding months as "federalists" (supporters of the Constitution) sparred with "anti-federalists." The following viewpoint is taken from one of the most notable of the anti-federalist essays. It was the first of sixteen articles by "Brutus" published in the *New York Journal* between October 1787 and April 1788 and widely reprinted elsewhere. Some historians have suggested that the author was Robert Yates (1738–1801) a New York delegate to the Constitutional Convention who refused to sign the Constitution.

"Brutus" criticizes the proposed Constitution for greatly centralizing powers in the national government. He argues that republican government has proved practical only in communities where the population was manageably small and homogeneous, unlike that of America. Many anti-federalist writers like "Brutus" cited the size and diversity of America in asserting that a national regime could not effectively govern without sacrificing the personal freedoms and liberties Americans valued.

How does the Constitution grant the national government "absolute" power, according to "Brutus"? What reasons does he give to support the argument that free republics can only exist in small areas? Which, if any, of his predictions have come true?

From an editorial by "Brutus" that appeared in the October 18, 1787, *New York Journal.*

The first question that presents itself on the subject is, whether a confederated government be the best for the United States or not? Or in other words, whether the thirteen United States should be reduced to one great republic, governed by one legislature, and under the direction of one executive and judicial; or whether they should continue thirteen confederated republics, under the direction and controul of a supreme federal head for certain defined national purposes only?

This enquiry is important, because, although the government reported by the convention does not go to a perfect and entire consolidation, yet it approaches so near to it, that it must, if executed, certainly and infallibly terminate in it.

A National Government with Absolute Power

This government is to possess absolute and uncontroulable power, legislative, executive and judicial, with respect to every object to which it extends, for by the last clause of section 8th, article 1st, it is declared "that the Congress shall have power to make all laws which shall be necessary and proper for carrying into execution the foregoing powers, and all other powers vested by this constitution, in the government of the United States; or in any department or office thereof." And by the 6th article, it is declared "that this constitution, and the laws of the United States, which shall be made in pursuance thereof, and the treaties made, or which shall be made, under the authority of the United States, shall be the supreme law of the land; and the judges in every state shall be bound thereby, any thing in the constitution, or law of any state to the contrary notwithstanding." It appears from these articles that there is no need of any intervention of the state governments, between the Congress and the people, to execute any one power vested in the general government, and that the constitution and laws of every state are nullified and declared void, so far as they are or shall be inconsistent with this constitution, or the laws made in pursuance of it, or with treaties made under the authority of the United States. . . .

The legislature of the United States are vested with the great and uncontroulable powers, of laying and collecting taxes, duties, imposts, and excises; of regulating trade, raising and supporting armies, organizing, arming, and disciplining the militia, instituting courts, and other general powers. And are by this clause invested with the power of making all laws, *proper and necessary*, for carrying all these into execution; and they may so exercise this power as entirely to annihilate all the state governments, and reduce this country to one single government. And if

they may do it, it is pretty certain they will; for it will be found that the power retained by individual states, small as it is, will be a clog upon the wheels of the government of the United States; the latter therefore will be naturally inclined to remove it out of the way. Besides, it is a truth confirmed by the unerring experience of ages, that every man, and every body of men, invested with power, are ever disposed to increase it, and to acquire a superiority over every thing that stands in their way. This disposition, which is implanted in human nature, will operate in the federal legislature to lessen and ultimately to subvert the state authority, and having such advantages, will most certainly succeed, if the federal government succeeds at all. It must be very evident then, that what this constitution wants of being a complete consolidation of the several parts of the union into one complete government, possessed of perfect legislative, judicial, and executive powers, to all intents and purposes, it will necessarily acquire in its exercise and operation.

Can a Nation Be Large and Free?

Let us now proceed to enquire, as I at first proposed, whether it be best the thirteen United States should be reduced to one great republic, or not? It is here taken for granted, that all agree in this, that whatever government we adopt, it ought to be a free one; that it should be so framed as to secure the liberty of the citizens of America, and such an one as to admit of a full, fair, and equal representation of the people. The question then will be, whether a government thus constituted, and founded on such principles, is practicable, and can be exercised over the whole United States, reduced into one state?

If respect is to be paid to the opinion of the greatest and wisest men who have ever thought or wrote on the science of government, we shall be constrained to conclude, that a free republic cannot succeed over a country of such immense extent, containing such a number of inhabitants, and these encreasing in such rapid progression as that of the whole United States. Among the many illustrious authorities which might be produced to this point, I shall content myself with quoting only two. The one is the baron [Charles-Louis] de Montesquieu, spirit of laws, chap. xvi. vol. I [book VIII]. "It is natural to a republic to have only a small territory, otherwise it cannot long subsist. In a large republic there are men of large fortunes, and consequently of less moderation; there are trusts too great to be placed in any single subject; he has interest of his own; he soon begins to think that he may be happy, great and glorious, by oppressing his fellow citizens; and that he may raise himself to grandeur on the ruins of his country. In a large republic, the public good is sacrificed to a thousand views; it is subordinate to exceptions, and depends on accidents. In a small one, the interest of the public is easier perceived, better understood, and more within the reach of every citizen; abuses are of less extent, and of course are less protected." Of the same opinion is the marquis Beccarari [Cesare di Beccaria].

History furnishes no example of a free republic, any thing like the extent of the United States. The Grecian republics were of small extent; so also was that of the Romans. Both of these, it is true, in process of time, extended their conquests over large territories of country; and the consequence was, that their governments were changed from that of free government to those of the most tyrannical that ever existed in the world.

Not only the opinion of the greatest men, and the experience of mankind, are against the idea of an extensive republic, but a variety of reasons may be drawn from the reason and nature of things, against it. In every government, the will of the sovereign is the law. In despotic governments, the supreme authority being lodged in one, his will is law, and can be as easily expressed to a large extensive territory as to a small one. In a pure democracy the people are the sovereign, and their will is declared by themselves; for this purpose they must all come together to deliberate, and decide. This kind of government cannot be exercised, therefore, over a country of any considerable extent; it must be confined to a single city, or at least limited to such bounds as that the people can conveniently assemble, be able to debate, understand the subject submitted to them, and declare their opinion concerning it.

The Consent of the People

In a free republic, although all laws are derived from the consent of the people, yet the people do not declare their consent by themselves in person, but by representatives, chosen by them, who are supposed to know the minds of their constituents, and to be possessed of integrity to declare this mind.

In every free government, the people must give their assent to the laws by which they are governed. This is the true criterion between a free government and an arbitrary one. The former are ruled by the will of the whole, expressed in any manner they may agree upon; the latter by the will of one, or a few. If the people are to give their assent to the laws, by persons chosen and appointed by them, the manner of the choice and the number chosen, must be such, as to possess, be disposed, and consequently qualified to declare the sentiments of the people; for if they do not know, or are not disposed to speak the sentiments of the people, the people do not govern, but the sovereignty is in a few. Now, in a large extended country, it is impossible to have a representation, possessing the sentiments, and of integrity, to declare the minds of the people, without having it so numerous and unwieldy, as to be subject in great measure to the inconveniency of a democratic government.

The territory of the United States is of vast extent; it now contains near three millions of souls, and is capable of containing much more than ten times that number. Is it practicable for a country, so large and so numerous as they will soon become, to elect a representation, that will speak their sentiments, without their becoming so numerous as to be incapable of transacting public business? It certainly is not.

The Diversity of the United States

In a republic, the manners, sentiments, and interests of the people should be similar. If this be not the case, there will be a constant clashing of opinions; and the representatives of one part will be continually striving against those of the other. This will retard the operations of government and prevent such conclusions as will promote the public good. If we apply this remark to the condition of the United States, we shall be convinced that it forbids that we should be one government. The United States includes a variety of climates. The productions of the different parts of the union are very variant, and their interests, of consequence, diverse. Their manners and habits differ as much as their climates and productions; and their sentiments are by no means coincident. The laws and customs of the several states are, in many respects, very diverse, and in some opposite; each would be in favor of its own interests and customs, and, of consequence, a legislature, formed of representatives from the respective parts, would not only be too numerous to act with any care or decision, but would be composed of such heterogenous and discordant principles, as would constantly be contending with each other.

The laws cannot be executed in a republic, of an extent equal to that of the United States, with promptitude.

The magistrates in every government must be supported in the execution of the laws, either by an armed force, maintained at the public expence for that purpose; or by the people turning out to aid the magistrate upon his command, in case of resistance.

In despotic governments, as well as in all the monarchies of Europe, standing armies are kept up to execute the commands of the prince or the magistrate, and are employed for this purpose when occasion requires: But they have always proved the destruction of liberty, and abhorrent to the spirit of a free republic. In England, where they depend upon the parliament for their annual support, they have always been complained of as oppressive and unconstitutional, and are seldom employed in executing of the laws; never except on extraordinary occasions, and then under the direction of a civil magistrate.

•

"A free republic cannot succeed over a country of such immense extent, containing such a number of inhabitants . . . as that of the whole United States."

•

A free republic will never keep a standing army to execute its laws. It must depend upon the support of its citizens. But when a government is to receive its support from the aid of the citizens, it must be so constructed as to have the confidence, respect, and affection of the people. Men who, upon the call of the magistrate, offer themselves to execute the laws, are influenced to do it either by affection to the government, or from fear; where a standing army is at hand to punish offenders, every man is actuated by the latter principle, and therefore, when the magistrate calls, will obey: but, where this is not the case, the government must rest for its support upon the confidence and respect which the people have for their government and laws. The body of the people being attached, the government will always be sufficient to support and execute its laws, and to operate upon the fears of any faction which may be opposed to it, not only to prevent an opposition to the execution of the laws themselves, but also to compel the most of them to aid the magistrate; but the people will not be likely to have such confidence in their rulers, in a republic so extensive as the United States, as necessary for these purposes. The confidence which the people have in their rulers, in a free republic, arises from their knowing them, from their being responsible to them for their conduct, and from the power they have of displacing them when they misbehave: but in a republic of the extent of this continent, the people in general would be acquainted with very few of their rulers: the people at large would know little of their proceedings, and it would be extremely difficult to change them. The people in Georgia and New-Hampshire would not know one another's mind, and therefore could not act in concert to enable them to effect a general change of representatives. The different parts of so extensive a country could not possibly be made acquainted with the conduct of their representatives, nor be informed of the reasons upon which measures were founded. The consequence will be, they will have no confidence in their legislature, suspect them of ambitious views, be jealous of every measure they adopt, and will not support the laws they pass. Hence the government will be nerveless and inefficient, and no way will be left to render it otherwise, but by establishing an armed force to execute the laws at the point of the bayonet—a government of all others the most to be dreaded.

In a republic of such vast extent as the United States, the legislature cannot attend to the various concerns and wants of its different parts. It cannot be sufficiently numerous to be acquainted with the local condition and wants of the different districts, and if it could, it is impossible it should have sufficient time to attend to and provide for all the variety of cases of this nature, that would be continually arising.

The Abuse of Power

In so extensive a republic, the great officers of government would soon become above the controul of the people, and abuse their power to the purpose of aggrandizing themselves, and oppressing them. The trust committed to the executive offices, in a country of the extent of the United States, must be various and of magnitude. The command of all the troops and navy of the republic, the appointment of officers, the power of pardoning offences, the collecting of all the public revenues, and the power of expending them, with a number of other powers, must be lodged and exercised in every state, in the hands of a few. When these are attended with great honor and emolument, as they always will be in large states, so as greatly to interest men to pursue them, and to be proper objects for ambitious and designing men, such men will be ever restless in their pursuit after them. They will use the power, when they have acquired it, to the purposes of gratifying their own interest and ambition, and it is scarcely possible, in a very large republic, to call them to account for their misconduct, or to prevent their abuse of power.

These are some of the reasons by which it appears, that a free republic cannot long subsist over a country of the great extent of these states. If then this new constitution is calculated to consolidate the thirteen states into one, as it evidently is, it ought not to be adopted.

VIEWPOINT 16B

A Viable Republic Can Be Large and Diverse (1787)

James Madison (1751–1836)

Political theorist and future president James Madison played a significant role in both instigating and

From an open letter "To the People of the State of New York" by "Publius" (James Madison) that appeared in the November 22, 1787, *New York Daily Advertiser*.

influencing the 1787 Constitutional Convention. During the ensuing months of debate he wrote numerous articles, letters, and pamphlets urging ratification of the Constitution. His most noteworthy and lasting writings in this debate are the famous *Federalist Papers*, a series of newspaper articles he co-authored with Alexander Hamilton and John Jay under the pseudonym "Publius." The following viewpoint is taken from *The Federalist* No. 10, his first and most famous contribution to the series, which was originally published on November 22, 1787, in the *New York Daily Advertiser*. Madison was responding in part to arguments made by "Brutus" and other anti-federalists who believed that republican governments were viable only in smaller communities where the "interests of the people should be similar." Madison argues here that republican governments in such situations are vulnerable to the problem of "factions"—the ability of local majorities motivated by selfish concerns to dominate the government, create bad law, and tyrannize the minority. Creating a government over a larger territory, Madison contends, can "extend the sphere" and prevent a single faction from gaining control over the government.

How does Madison define and describe "factions"? What effect does he say the proposed Constitution will have on factions? How does he differentiate between a republic and a democracy? Which of the arguments found here can be seen as direct answers to arguments by "Brutus" in viewpoint 16A?

To the People of the State of New-York.

Among the numerous advantages promised by a well-constructed Union, none deserves to be more accurately developed than its tendency to break and control the violence of faction. The friend of popular governments never finds himself so much alarmed for their character and fate, as when he contemplates their propensity to this dangerous vice. He will not fail, therefore, to set a due value on any plan which, without violating the principles to which he is attached, provides a proper cure for it. The instability, injustice, and confusion introduced into the public councils, have, in truth, been the mortal diseases under which popular governments have everywhere perished; as they continue to be the favorite and fruitful topics from which the adversaries to liberty derive their most specious declamations. The valuable improvements made by the American [state] constitutions on the popular models, both ancient and modern, cannot certainly be too much admired; but it would be an unwarrantable partiality, to contend that they have as effectually obviated the danger on this side, as was wished and expected.

Complaints are everywhere heard from our most considerate and virtuous citizens, equally the friends of public and private faith, and of public and personal liberty, that our governments are too unstable, that the public good is disregarded in the conflicts of rival parties, and that measures are too often decided, not according to the rules of justice and the rights of the minor party, but by the superior force of an interested and overbearing majority. However anxiously we may wish that these complaints had no foundation, the evidence of known facts will not permit us to deny that they are in some degree true. It will be found, indeed, on a candid review of our situation, that some of the distresses under which we labor have been erroneously charged on the operation of our governments; but it will be found, at the same time, that other causes will not alone account for many of our heaviest misfortunes; and, particularly, for that prevailing and increasing distrust of public engagements, and alarm for private rights, which are echoed from one end of the continent to the other. These must be chiefly, if not wholly, effects of the unsteadiness and injustice with which a factious spirit has tainted our public administrations.

The Dangers of Factions

By a faction, I understand a number of citizens, whether amounting to a majority or minority of the whole, who are united and actuated by some common impulse of passion, or of interest, adverse to the rights of other citizens, or to the permanent and aggregate interests of the community.

There are two methods of curing the mischiefs of faction: the one, by removing its causes; the other, by controlling its effects.

There are again two methods of removing the causes of faction: the one, by destroying the liberty which is essential to its existence; the other, by giving to every citizen the same opinions, the same passions, and the same interests.

It could never be more truly said than of the first remedy, that it was worse than the disease. Liberty is to faction what air is to fire, an aliment without which it instantly expires. But it could not be less folly to abolish liberty, which is essential to political life, because it nourishes faction, than it would be to wish the annihilation of air, which is essential to animal life, because it imparts to fire its destructive agency.

The second expedient is as impracticable as the first would be unwise. As long as the reason of man continues fallible, and he is at liberty to exercise it, different opinions will be formed. As long as the connection subsists between his reason and his self-love, his opinions and his passions will have a reciprocal influence on each other: and the former will be objects to which the latter will attach themselves.

The diversity in the faculties of men, from which the rights of property originate, is not less an insuperable obstacle to a uniformity of interests. The protection of these faculties is the first object of government. From the protection of different and unequal faculties of acquiring property, the possession of different degrees and kinds of property immediately results; and from the influence of these on the sentiments and views of the respective proprietors, ensues a division of the society into different interests and parties.

The Causes of Faction

The latent causes of faction are thus sown in the nature of man; and we see them everywhere brought into different degrees of activity, according to the different circumstances of civil society. A zeal for different opinions concerning religion, concerning government, and many other points, as well of speculation as of practice; an attachment to different leaders ambitiously contending for pre-eminence and power; or to persons of other descriptions whose fortunes have been interesting to the human passions, have, in turn, divided mankind into parties, inflamed them with mutual animosity, and rendered them much more disposed to vex and oppress each other than to co-operate for their common good. So strong is this propensity of mankind to fall into mutual animosities, that where no substantial occasion presents itself, the most frivolous and fanciful distinctions have been sufficient to kindle their unfriendly passions and excite their most violent conflicts. But the most common and durable source of factions has been the various and unequal distribution of property. Those who hold and those who are without property have ever formed distinct interests in society. Those who are creditors, and those who are debtors, fall under a like discrimination. A landed interest, a manufacturing interest, a mercantile interest, a moneyed interest, with many lesser interests, grow up of necessity in civilized nations, and divide them into different classes, actuated by different sentiments and views. The regulation of these various and interfering interests forms the principal task of modern legislation, and involves the spirit of party and faction in the necessary and ordinary operations of the government.

No man is allowed to be a judge in his own cause, because his interest would certainly bias his judgment, and, not improbably, corrupt his integrity. With equal, nay with greater reason, a body of men are unfit to be both judges and parties at the same time; yet what are many of the most important acts of legislation, but so many judicial determinations, not indeed concerning the rights of single persons, but concerning the rights of large bodies of citizens? And what are the different classes of legislators but advocates and parties to the causes which they determine? Is a law proposed concerning private debts? It is a question to which the creditors are parties on one side and the debtors on the other. Justice ought to hold the balance between them. Yet the parties are, and must be, themselves the judges; and the most numerous party, or, in other words, the most powerful faction must be expected to prevail. Shall domestic manufactures be encouraged, and in what degree, by restrictions on foreign manufactures? are questions which would be differently decided by the landed and the manufacturing classes, and probably by neither with a sole regard to justice and the public good. The apportionment of taxes on the various descriptions of property is an act which seems to require the most exact impartiality; yet there is, perhaps, no legislative act in which greater opportunity and temptation are given to a predominant party to trample on the rules of justice. Every shilling with which they overburden the inferior number, is a shilling saved to their own pockets.

It is in vain to say that enlightened statesmen will be able to adjust these clashing interests, and render them all subservient to the public good. Enlightened statesmen will not always be at the helm. Nor, in many cases, can such an adjustment be made at all without taking into view indirect and remote considerations, which will rarely prevail over the immediate interest which one party may find in disregarding the rights of another or the good of the whole.

The inference to which we are brought is, that the *causes* of faction cannot be removed, and that relief is only to be sought in the means of controlling its *effects*.

If a faction consists of less than a majority, relief is supplied by the republican principle, which enables the majority to defeat its sinister views by regular vote. It may clog the administration, it may convulse the society; but it will be unable to execute and mask its violence under the forms of the Constitution. When a majority is included in a faction, the form of popular government, on the other hand, enables it to sacrifice to its ruling passion or interest both the public good and the rights of other citizens. To secure the public good and private rights against the danger of such a faction, and at the same time to preserve the spirit and the form of popular government, is then the great object to which our inquiries are directed. Let me add that it is the great desideratum by which this form of government can be rescued from the opprobrium under which it has so long labored, and be recommended to the esteem and adoption of mankind.

By what means is this object attainable? Evidently by one of two only. Either the existence of the same passion or interest in a majority at the same time must be prevented, or the majority, having such coexistent passion or interest, must be rendered, by their number and local situation, unable to concert and carry into effect schemes of oppression. If the impulse and the opportunity be suffered to coincide, we well know that neither moral nor religious motives can be relied on as an adequate control. They are not found to be such on the injustice and violence of individuals, and lose their efficacy in proportion to the number combined together, that is, in proportion as their efficacy becomes needful.

Comparing Republics and Democracies

From this view of the subject it may be concluded that a pure democracy, by which I mean a society consisting of a small number of citizens, who assemble and administer the government in person, can admit of no cure for the mischiefs of faction. A common passion or interest will, in almost every case, be felt by a majority of the whole; a communication and concert result from the form of government itself; and there is nothing to check the inducements to sacrifice the weaker party or an obnoxious individual. Hence it is that such democracies have ever been spectacles of turbulence and contention; have ever been found incompatible with personal security or the rights of property; and have in general been as short in their lives as they have been violent in their deaths. Theoretic politicians, who have patronized this species of government, have erroneously supposed that by reducing mankind to a perfect equality in their political rights, they would, at the same time, be perfectly equalized and assimilated in their possessions, their opinions, and their passions.

A republic, by which I mean a government in which the scheme of representation takes place, opens a different prospect, and promises the cure for which we are seeking. Let us examine the points in which it varies from pure democracy, and we shall comprehend both the nature of the cure and the efficacy which it must derive from the Union.

The two great points of difference between a democracy and a republic are: first, the delegation of the government, in the latter, to a small number of citizens elected by the rest; secondly, the greater number of citizens, and greater sphere of country, over which the latter may be extended.

The effect of the first difference is, on the one hand, to refine and enlarge the public views, by passing them through the medium of a chosen body of citizens, whose wisdom may best discern the true interest of their country, and whose patriotism and love of justice will be least likely to sacrifice it to temporary or partial considerations. Under such a regulation, it may well happen that the public voice, pronounced by the representatives of the people, will be more consonant to the public good than if pronounced by the people themselves, convened for the purpose. On the other hand, the effect may be inverted. Men of factious tempers, of local prejudices, or of sinister designs, may, by intrigue, by corruption, or by other means, first obtain the suffrages, and then betray the interests, of the people. The question resulting is, whether small or extensive republics are more favorable to the election of proper guardians of the public weal; and it is clearly decided in favor of the latter by two obvious considerations:

In the first place, it is to be remarked that, however small the republic may be, the representatives must be raised to a certain number, in order to guard against the cabals of a few; and that, however large it may be, they must be limited to a certain number, in order to guard against the confusion of a multitude. Hence, the number of representatives in the two cases not being in proportion to that of the two constituents, and being proportionally greater in the small republic, it follows that, if the proportion of fit characters be not less in the large than in the small republic, the former will present a greater option, and consequently a greater probability of a fit choice.

In the next place, as each representative will be chosen by a greater number of citizens in the large than in the small republic, it will be more difficult for unworthy candidates to practise with success the vicious arts by which elections are too often carried; and the suffrages of the people being more free, will be more likely to centre in men who possess the most attractive merit and the most diffusive and established characters.

It must be confessed that in this, as in most other cases, there is a mean, on both sides of which inconveniences will be found to lie. By enlarging too much the number of electors, you render the representative too little acquainted with all their local circumstances and lesser interests; as by reducing it too much, you render him unduly attached to these, and too little fit to comprehend and pursue great and national objects. The federal Constitution forms a happy combination in this respect; the great and aggregate interests being referred to the national, the local and particular to the State legislatures.

Extending the Sphere

The other point of difference is, the greater number of citizens and extent of territory which may be brought within the compass of republican than of democratic government; and it is this circumstance principally which renders factious combinations less to be dreaded in the former than in the latter. The smaller the society, the fewer probably will be the distinct parties and interests composing it; the fewer the distinct parties and interests, the more frequently will a majority be found of the same party; and the smaller the number of individuals composing a majority, and the smaller the compass within which they are placed, the most easily will they concert and execute their plans of oppression. Extend the sphere, and you take in a greater variety of parties and interests; you make it less probable that a majority of the whole will have a common motive to invade the rights of other citizens; or if such a common motive exists, it will be more difficult for all who feel it to discover their own strength, and to act in unison with each other. Besides other impediments, it may be remarked that, where there is a consciousness of unjust or dishonorable purposes, communication is always checked by distrust in proportion to the number whose concurrence is necessary.

Hence, it clearly appears, that the same advantage which a republic has over a democracy, in controlling the effects of faction, is enjoyed by a large over a small republic,—is enjoyed by the Union over the States composing it. Does the advantage consist in the substitution of representatives whose enlightened views and virtuous sentiments render them superior to local prejudices and to schemes of injustice? It will not be denied that the representation of the Union will be most likely to possess these requisite endowments. Does it consist in the greater security afforded by a greater variety of parties, against the event of any one party being able to outnumber and oppress the rest? In an equal degree does the increased variety of parties comprised within the Union, increase this security. Does it, in fine, consist in the greater obstacles opposed to the concert and accomplishment of the secret wishes of an unjust and interested majority? Here, again, the extent of the Union gives it the most palpable advantage.

———— • ————

"The extent of the Union gives it the most palpable advantage."

———— • ————

The influence of factious leaders may kindle a flame within their particular States, but will be unable to spread a general conflagration through the other States. A religious sect may degenerate into a political faction in a part of the Confederacy; but the variety of sects dispersed over the entire face of it must secure the national councils against any danger from that source. A rage for paper money, for an abolition of debts, for an equal division of property, or for any other improper or wicked project, will be less apt to pervade the whole body of the Union than a particular member of it; in the same proportion as such a malady is more likely to taint a particular county or district, than an entire State.

In the extent and proper structure of the Union, therefore, we behold a republican remedy for the diseases most incident to republican government. And according to the degree of pleasure and pride we feel in being republicans, ought to be our zeal in cherishing the spirit and supporting the character of Federalists.

For Further Reading

Bernard Bailyn, ed., *The Debate on the Constitution.* New York: Library of America, 1993.

John P. Kaminski and Richard Leffler, eds., *Creating the Constitution: A History in Documents.* Madison, WI: The Center for the Study of the American Constitution, 1991.

Charles R. Kesler, *Saving the Revolution: The Federalist Papers and the American Founding.* New York: Free Press, 1987.

Marvin Meyers, *The Mind of the Founder: Sources of the Political Thought of James Madison.* Hanover, NH: University Press of New England, 1981.

Herbert Storing, *What the Antifederalists Were For.* Chicago: University of Chicago Press, 1981.

Viewpoint 17A

The Constitution Needs a Bill of Rights (1788)

Patrick Henry (1736–1799)

A recurring criticism of the Constitution by the anti-federalists during the ratification debates was that it lacked a bill of rights—a list of fundamental freedoms retained by the people that the government could not infringe. Beginning with Virginia in 1776, the majority of the states had included a bill of rights in their state constitutions. However, the 1787 Constitutional Convention, rejecting the wishes of some of its members, did not include such a list. People fearful and critical of creating a new and powerful national government argued that this omission was evidence that such a government could threaten people's liberties. One influential advocate of this view was Patrick Henry, perhaps the most prominent and renowned of the anti-federalists. Henry was a longtime Virginia political leader whose acclaimed oratorical skills had helped to inspire the American Revolution. As a multiple-term governor and leading member of Virginia's House of Delegates, he dominated Virginia state politics in the 1770s and 1780s. The following viewpoint is taken from speeches he made in June 1788 before the Virginia ratifying convention. Henry argues that the new Constitution will supersede Virginia's constitution and its bill of rights, thus endangering the people's freedoms.

From Patrick Henry's speech before the Virginia ratifying convention, June 16, and June 17, 1788.

What parts of Virginia's bill of rights should have been included in the proposed national constitution, according to Henry? He claims that most people want a bill of rights; what argument does he make using that claim? Some historians have argued that Henry and other anti-federalists were more concerned to retain the powers of state governments than individual liberties; do the excerpts presented here support this theory?

---

16 June 1788

Mr. Chairman.—The necessity of a Bill of Rights appear to me to be greater in this Government, than ever it was in any Government before. . . .

All nations have adopted this construction—That all rights not expressly and unequivocally reserved to the people, are impliedly and incidentally relinquished to rulers; as necessarily inseparable from the delegated powers. It is so in Great-Britain: For every possible right which is not reserved to the people by some express provision or compact, is within the King's prerogative. It is so in that country which is said to be in such full possession of freedom. It is so in Spain, Germany, and other parts of the world.

Virginia's Example

Let us consider the sentiments which have been entertained by the people of America on this subject. At the revolution, it must be admitted, that it was their sense to put down those great rights which ought in all countries to be held inviolable and sacred. Virginia did so we all remember. She made a compact to reserve, expressly, certain rights. When fortified with full, adequate, and abundant representation, was she satisfied with that representation? No.—She most cautiously and guardedly reserved and secured those invaluable, inestimable rights and privileges, which no people, inspired with the least glow of the patriotic love of liberty, ever did, or ever can, abandon. She is called upon now to abandon them, and dissolve that compact which secured them to her. She is called upon to accede to another compact which most infallibly supercedes and annihilates her present one. Will she do it?—This is the question. If you intend to reserve your unalienable rights, you must have the most express stipulation. For if implication be allowed, you are ousted of those rights. If the people do not think it necessary to reserve them, they will be supposed to be given up. How were the Congressional rights defined when the people of America united by a confederacy to defend their liberties and rights against the tyrannical attempts of Great-Britain? The States were not then contented with implied reservation. No, Mr.

Chairman. It was expressly declared in our Confederation that every right was retained by the States respectively, which was not given up to the Government of the United States. But there is no such thing here. You therefore by a natural and unavoidable implication, give up your rights to the General Government. Your own example furnishes an argument against it. If you give up these powers, without a Bill of Rights, you will exhibit the most absurd thing to mankind that ever the world saw—A Government that has abandoned all its powers—The powers of direct taxation, the sword, and the purse. You have disposed of them to Congress, without a Bill of Rights—without check, limitation, or controul. And still you have checks and guards—still you keep barriers—pointed where? Pointed against your weakened, prostrated, enervated State Government! You have a Bill of Rights to defend you against the State Government, which is bereaved of all power; and yet you have none against Congress, though in full and exclusive possession of all power! You arm yourselves against the weak and defenceless, and expose yourselves naked to the armed and powerful. Is not this a conduct of unexampled absurdity? What barriers have you to oppose to this most strong energetic Government? To that Government you have nothing to oppose. All your defence is given up. This is a real actual defect.—It must strike the mind of every Gentleman. When our Government was first instituted in Virginia, we declared the common law of England to be in force.—That system of law which has been admired, and has protected us and our ancestors, is excluded by that system.—Added to this, we adopted a Bill of Rights. By this Constitution, some of the best barriers of human rights are thrown away. Is there not an additional reason to have a Bill of Rights? By the ancient common law, the trial of all facts is decided by a jury of impartial men from the immediate vicinage. This paper speaks of different juries from the common law, in criminal cases; and in civil controversies excludes trial by jury altogether. There is therefore more occasion for the supplementary check of a Bill of Rights now, than then. Congress from their general powers may fully go into the business of human legislation. They may legislate in criminal cases from treason to the lowest offence, petty larceny. They may define crimes and prescribe punishments. In the definition of crimes, I trust they will be directed by what wise Representatives ought to be governed by. But when we come to punishments, no latitude ought to be left, nor dependence put on the virtue of Representatives. What says our [state] Bill of Rights? "That excessive bail ought not to be required, nor excessive fines imposed, nor cruel and unusual punishments inflicted." Are you not therefore now calling on those Gentlemen who are to compose Congress, to prescribe trials and define punishments without this controul? Will they find sentiments there similar to this Bill of Rights? You let them loose—you do more—you depart from the genius of your country. That paper tells you, that the trial of crimes shall be by jury, and held in the State where the crime shall have been committed.—

Under this extensive provision, they may proceed in a manner extremely dangerous to liberty.—Persons accused may be carried from one extremity of the State to another, and be tried not by an impartial jury of the vicinage, acquainted with his character, and the circumstances of the fact; but by a jury unacquainted with both, and who may be biassed against

THE BILL OF RIGHTS

The first ten articles amending the Constitution, known as the Bill of Rights, were proposed in Congress on September 25, 1789. After being approved by Congress and ratified by the states, they were declared in force on December 15, 1791.

AMENDMENT I

Congress shall make no law respecting an establishment of religion, or prohibiting the free exercise thereof; or abridging the freedom of speech, or of the press; or the right of the people peaceably to assemble, and to petition the Government for a redress of grievances.

AMENDMENT II

A well regulated Militia, being necessary to the security of a free State, the right of the people to keep and bear Arms, shall not be infringed.

AMENDMENT III

No Soldier shall, in time of peace be quartered in any house, without the consent of the Owner, nor in time of war, but in a manner to be prescribed by law.

AMENDMENT IV

The right of the people to be secure in their persons, houses, papers, and effects, against unreasonable searches and seizures, shall not be violated, and no Warrants shall issue, but upon probable cause, supported by Oath or affirmation, and particularly describing the place to be searched, and the persons or things to be seized.

AMENDMENT V

No person shall be held to answer for a capital, or otherwise infamous crime, unless on a presentment or indictment of a Grand Jury, except in cases arising in the land or naval forces, or in the Militia, when in actual service in time of War or public danger; nor shall any person be subject for the same offence to be twice put in jeopardy of life or limb; nor shall be compelled in any criminal case to be a witness against himself, nor be deprived of life, liberty, or property, without due process of law; nor shall private property be taken for public use, without just compensation.

AMENDMENT VI

In all criminal prosecutions, the accused shall enjoy the right to a speedy and public trial, by an impartial jury of the State and district wherein the crime shall have been committed, which district shall have been previously ascertained by law, and to be informed of the nature and cause of the accusation; to be confronted with the witnesses against him; to have compulsory process for obtaining witnesses in his favor, and to have the Assistance of Counsel for his defence.

AMENDMENT VII

In Suits at common law, where the value in controversy shall exceed twenty dollars, the right of trial by jury shall be preserved, and no fact tried by a jury, shall be otherwise re-examined in any Court of the United States, than according to the rules of the common law.

AMENDMENT VIII

Excessive bail shall not be required, nor excessive fines imposed, nor cruel and unusual punishments inflicted.

AMENDMENT IX

The enumeration in the Constitution, of certain rights, shall not be construed to deny or disparage others retained by the people.

AMENDMENT X

The powers not delegated to the United States by the Constitution, nor prohibited by it to the States, are reserved to the States respectively, or to the people.

him.—Is not this sufficient to alarm men?—How different is this from the immemorial practice of your British ancestors, and your own? I need not tell you, that by the [English] common law a number of hundredors [residents from the same group of one hundred] were required to be on a jury, and that afterwards it was sufficient if the jurors came from the same county. With less than this the people of England have never been satisfied. That paper ought to have declared the common law in force.

The People Want a Bill of Rights

In this business of legislation, your Members of Congress will lose the restriction of not imposing excessive fines, demanding excessive bail, and inflicting cruel and unusual punishments.—These are prohibited by your Declaration of Rights. What has distinguished our ancestors?—That they would not admit of tortures, or cruel and barbarous punishments. But Congress may introduce the practice of the civil law, in preference to that of the common law.—They may introduce the practice of France, Spain, and Germany—Of torturing to extort a confession of the crime. They will say that they might as well draw examples from those countries as from Great-Britain; and they will tell you, that there is such a necessity of strengthening the arm of Government that they must have a criminal equity, and extort confession by torture, in order to punish with still more relentless severity. We are then lost and undone.—And can any man think it troublesome, when we can by a small interference prevent our rights from being lost?—If you will, like the Virginian Government, give them knowledge of the extent of the rights retained by the people, and the powers themselves, they will, if they be honest men, thank you for it.—Will they not wish to go on sure grounds?—But if you leave them otherwise, they will not know how to proceed; and being in a state of uncertainty, they will assume rather than give up powers by implication. A Bill of Rights may be summed up in a few words. What do they tell us?—That our rights are reserved.—Why not say so? Is it because it will consume too much paper? Gentlemen's reasonings against a Bill of Rights, do not satisfy me. Without saying which has the right side, it remains doubtful. A Bill of Rights is a favourite thing with the Virginians, and the people of the other States likewise. It may be their prejudice, but the Government ought to suit their geniuses, otherwise its operation will be unhappy. A Bill of Rights, even if its necessity be doubtful, will exclude the possibility of dispute, and with great submission, I think the best way is to have no dispute. In the present Constitution, they are restrained from issuing general warrants to search suspected places, or seize persons not

named, without evidence of the commission of the fact, &c. There was certainly some celestial influence governing those who deliberated on that Constitution:—For they have with the most cautious and enlightened circumspection, guarded those indefeasible rights, which ought ever to be held sacred. The officers of Congress may come upon you, fortified with all the terrors of paramount federal authority.—Excisemen may come in multitudes:—For the limitation of their numbers no man knows.—They may, unless the General Government be restrained by a Bill of Rights, or some similar restriction, go into your cellars and rooms, and search, ransack and measure, every thing you eat, drink and wear. They ought to be restrained within proper bounds. With respect to the freedom of the press, I need say nothing; for it is hoped that the Gentlemen who shall compose Congress, will take care as little as possible, to infringe the rights of human nature.—This will result from their integrity. They should from prudence, abstain from violating the rights of their constituents. They are not however expressly restrained.—But whether they will intermeddle with that palladium of our liberties or not, I leave you to determine.

17 June 1788

[Editor's note: In the following argument Henry examines the ninth section of Article I of the Constitution, which includes a few civil rights provisions, and argues that it is a meager substitute for a substantive bill of rights.]

Mr. Chairman.—We have now come to the ninth section [of Article I], and I consider myself at liberty to take a short view of the whole. I wish to do it very briefly. Give me leave to remark, that there is a Bill of Rights in that Government [established by the Constitution]. There are express restrictions which are in the shape of a Bill of Rights: But they bear the name of the ninth section. The design of the negative expressions in this section is to prescribe limits, beyond which the powers of Congress shall not go. These are the sole bounds intended by the American Government. Where abouts do we stand with respect to a Bill of Rights? Examine it, and compare it to the idea manifested by the Virginian Bill of Rights, or that of the other States. The restraints in this Congressional Bill of Rights, are so feeble and few, that it would have been infinitely better to have said nothing about it. The fair implication is, that they can do every thing they are not forbidden to do. What will be the result if Congress, in the course of their legislation, should do a thing not restrained by this ninth section? It will fall as an incidental power to Congress, not being prohibited expressly in the Constitution. The first prohibition is, that the privilege of the writ of *habeas corpus* shall not be suspended, but when in cases of rebellion, or invasion, the public safety may require it. It results clearly, that if it had not said so, they could suspend it in all cases whatsoever. It reverses the position of the friends of this Constitution, that every thing is retained which is not given up. For instead of this, every thing is given up, which is not expressly reserved. . . .

Limited Protections

You are told, that your rights are secured in this new Government. They are guarded in no other part but this ninth section. The few restrictions in that section are your only safeguards. They may controul your actions, and your very words, without being repugnant to that paper. The existence of your dearest privileges will depend on the consent of Congress: For these are not within the restrictions of the ninth section.

———— • ————

"My mind will not be quieted till I see something substantial come forth in the shape of a Bill of Rights."

———— • ————

If Gentlemen think that securing the slave trade is a capital object; that the privilege of the *habeas corpus* is sufficiently secured; that the exclusion of *ex post facto* laws will produce no inconvenience; that the publication from time to time [of government expenditures] will secure their property; in one word, that this section alone will sufficiently secure their liberties, I have spoken in vain.—Every word of mine, and of my worthy coadjutor [George Mason], is lost. I trust that Gentlemen, on this occasion, will see the great objects of religion, liberty of the press, trial by jury, interdiction of cruel punishments, and every other sacred right secured, before they agree to that paper. These most important human rights are not protected by that section, which is the only safeguard in the Constitution.—My mind will not be quieted till I see something substantial come forth in the shape of a Bill of Rights.

VIEWPOINT 17B

The Constitution Does Not Need a Bill of Rights (1788)

Alexander Hamilton (1755–1804)

Alexander Hamilton, a past military aide to General George Washington and future secretary of the treasury during Washington's presidency, was one of the main supporters of the new Constitution, and he worked hard for its ratification in New York and other states. Among his efforts in support of the Constitution was a collaboration with James Madison and John Jay in writing a series of eighty-five letters to newspapers under the pseudonym "Publius." These essays, which supported and defended the proposed Constitution against various criticisms and urged ratification, were published in 1788 in book form as *The Federalist*.

Hamilton wrote the bulk of the essays, including No. 84, from which the following viewpoint is taken. He directly takes up the criticism that the Constitution lacks a bill of rights. He summarizes the arguments by which many federalists defended the absence of a bill of rights—that the rights of Americans are protected by state constitutions, and the new federal government is not being given express powers to infringe upon individual rights and liberties. The structure of the new government, he asserts, with its separation of powers and guarantees of the right to elect representatives, among other features, is enough to ensure the people's liberties. Hamilton goes on to conclude that a listing of rights might be dangerous, because it could be construed to mean that any rights and freedoms not listed would lack protection.

What are the true sources of liberty, according to Hamilton? In his view, in what ways is the whole Constitution a bill of rights? Does Hamilton's argument that adding a bill of rights would be unnecessary and dangerous contradict his previous citing of civil liberties clauses in the Constitution? Explain.

————————————

To the People of the State of New-York.
   In the course of the foregoing review of the constitution I have taken notice of, and endeavoured to answer, most of the objections which have appeared against it. There however remain a few which either did not fall naturally under any particular head, or were forgotten in their proper places. These shall now be discussed: but as the subject has been drawn into great length, I shall so far consult brevity as to comprise all my observations on these miscellaneous points in a single paper.

The most considerable of these remaining objections is, that the plan of the convention contains no bill of rights. Among other answers given to this, it has been upon different occasions remarked, that the constitutions of several of the states are in a similar predicament. I add, that New-York is of this number. And yet the opposers of the new system in

From *The Federalist* No. 84, by Alexander Hamilton, under the pseudonym Publius (New York, 1788).

this state, who profess an unlimited admiration for its constitution, are among the most intemperate partizans of a bill of rights. To justify their zeal in this matter, they alledge two things; one is, that though the constitution of New-York has no bill of rights prefixed to it, yet it contains in the body of it various provisions in favour of particular privileges and rights, which in substance amount to the same thing; the other is, that the constitution adopts in their full extent the common and statute law of Great-Britain, by which many other rights not expressed in it are equally secured.

Clauses in the Constitution

To the first I answer, that the constitution proposed by the convention contains, as well as the constitution of this state, a number of such provisions.

Independent of those, which relate to the structure of the government, we find the following: Article I. section 3. clause 7. "Judgment in cases of impeachment shall not extend further than to removal from office, and disqualification to hold and enjoy any office of honour, trust or profit under the United States; but the party convicted shall nevertheless be liable and subject to indictment, trial, judgment and punishment, according to law." Section 9. of the same article, clause 2. "The privilege of the writ of habeas corpus shall not be suspended, unless when in cases of rebellion or invasion the public safety may require it." Clause 3. "No bill of attainder or ex post facto law shall be passed." Clause 7. "No title of nobility shall be granted by the United States: And no person holding any office of profit or trust under them, shall, without the consent of congress, accept of any present, emolument, office or title, of any kind whatever, from any king, prince or foreign state." Article III. section 2. clause 3. "The trial of all crimes, except in cases of impeachment, shall be by jury; and such trial shall be held in the state where the said crimes shall have been committed; but when not committed within any state, the trial shall be at such place or places as the congress may by law have directed." Section 3, of the same article, "Treason against the United States shall consist only in levying war against them, or in adhering to their enemies, giving them aid and comfort. No person shall be convicted of treason unless on the testimony of two witnesses to the same overt act, or on confession in open court." And clause 3, of the same section. "The congress shall have power to declare the punishment of treason, but no attainder of treason shall work corruption of blood, or forfeiture, except during the life of the person attainted."

It may well be a question whether these are not upon the whole, of equal importance with any which

are to be found in the constitution of this state. The establishment of the writ of habeas corpus, the prohibition of ex post facto laws, and of Titles of Nobility, to which we have no corresponding provisions in our constitution, are perhaps greater securities to liberty and republicanism than any it contains. The creation of crimes after the commission of the fact, or in other words, the subjecting of men to punishment for things which, when they were done, were breaches of no law, and the practice of arbitrary imprisonments have been in all ages the favourite and most formidable instruments of tyranny. . . .

To the second, that is, to the pretended establishment of the common and statute law by the constitution, I answer, that they are expressly made subject "to such alterations and provisions as the legislature shall from time to time make concerning the same." They are therefore at any moment liable to repeal by the ordinary legislative power, and of course have no constitutional sanction. The only use of the declaration was to recognize the ancient law, and to remove doubts which might have been occasioned by the revolution. This consequently can be considered as no part of a declaration of rights, which under our constitutions must be intended as limitations of the power of the government itself.

———— • ————

"Bills of rights . . . are not only unnecessary in the proposed constitution, but would even be dangerous."

———— • ————

It has been several times truly remarked, that bills of rights are in their origin, stipulations between kings and their subjects, abridgments of prerogative in favor of privilege, reservations of rights not surrendered to the prince. Such was Magna Charta, obtained by the Barons, sword in hand, from king John. . . . Such also was the declaration of right presented by the lords and commons to the prince of Orange in 1688, and afterwards thrown into the form of an act of parliament, called the bill of rights. It is evident, therefore, that according to their primitive signification, they have no application to constitutions professedly founded upon the power of the people, and executed by their immediate representatives and servants. Here, in strictness, the people surrender nothing, and as they retain every thing, they have no need of particular reservations. "We the people of the United States, to secure the blessings of liberty to ourselves and our posterity, do ordain and establish this constitution for the United States of America." Here is a better recognition of popular rights than volumes of those aphorisms which make the principal figure in several of our state bills of rights, and which would sound much better in a treatise of ethics than in a constitution of government.

But a minute detail of particular rights is certainly far less applicable to a constitution like that under consideration, which is merely intended to regulate the general political interests of the nation, than to a constitution which has the regulation of every species of personal and private concerns. If therefore the loud clamours against the plan of the convention on this score, are well founded, no epithets of reprobation will be too strong for the constitution of this state. But the truth is, that both of them contain all, which in relation to their objects, is reasonably to be desired.

A Bill of Rights Would Be Dangerous

I go further, and affirm that bills of rights, in the sense and in the extent in which they are contended for, are not only unnecessary in the proposed constitution, but would even be dangerous. They would contain various exceptions to powers which are not granted; and on this very account, would afford a colourable pretext to claim more than were granted. For why declare that things shall not be done which there is no power to do? Why for instance, should it be said, that the liberty of the press shall not be restrained, when no power is given by which restrictions may be imposed? I will not contend that such a provision would confer a regulating power; but it is evident that it would furnish, to men disposed to usurp, a plausible pretence for claiming that power. They might urge with a semblance of reason, that the constitution ought not to be charged with the absurdity of providing against the abuse of an authority, which was not given, and that the provision against restraining the liberty of the press afforded a clear implication, that a power to prescribe proper regulations concerning it, was intended to be vested in the national government. This may serve as a specimen of the numerous handles which would be given to the doctrine of constructive powers, by the indulgence of an injudicious zeal for bills of rights.

On the subject of the liberty of the press, as much has been said, I cannot forbear adding a remark or two: In the first place, I observe that there is not a syllable concerning it in the constitution of this state, and in the next, I contend that whatever has been said about it in that of any other state, amounts to nothing. What signifies a declaration that "the liberty of the press shall be inviolably preserved"? What is the liberty of the press? Who can give it any definition which would not leave the utmost latitude for evasion? I hold it to be impracticable; and from this,

I infer, that its security, whatever fine declarations may be inserted in any constitution respecting it, must altogether depend on public opinion, and on the general spirit of the people and of the government. And here, after all, as intimated upon another occasion, must we seek for the only solid basis of all our rights.

The Constitution Is a Bill of Rights

There remains but one other view of this matter to conclude the point. The truth is, after all the declamation we have heard, that the constitution is itself in every rational sense, and to every useful purpose, a Bill of Rights. The several bills of rights, in Great-Britain, form its constitution, and conversely the constitution of each state is its bill of rights. And the proposed constitution, if adopted, will be the bill of rights of the union. Is it one object of a bill of rights to declare and specify the political privileges of the citizens in the structure and administration of the government? This is done in the most ample and precise manner in the plan of the convention, comprehending various precautions for the public security, which are not to be found in any of the state constitutions. Is another object of a bill of rights to define certain immunities and modes of proceeding, which are relative to personal and private concerns? This we have seen has also been attended to, in a variety of cases, in the same plan. Adverting therefore to the substantial meaning of a bill of rights, it is absurd to allege that it is not to be found in the work of the convention. It may be said that it does not go far enough, though it will not be easy to make this appear; but it can with no propriety be contended that there is no such thing. It certainly must be immaterial what mode is observed as to the order of declaring the rights of the citizens, if they are to be found in any part of the instrument which establishes the government. And hence it must be apparent that much of what has been said on this subject rests merely on verbal and nominal distinctions, which are entirely foreign from the substance of the thing.

For Further Reading

Richard Beeman, *Patrick Henry: A Biography.* New York: McGraw-Hill, 1974.

James MacGregor Burns and Stewart Burns, *A People's Charter: The Pursuit of Rights in America.* New York: Knopf, 1991.

Paul Goodman, ed., *The American Constitution.* New York: John Wiley & Sons, 1970.

Bernard Schwartz, *The Bill of Rights: A Documentary History.* New York: Chelsea House, 1971.

Garry Wills, *Explaining America: The Federalist.* New York: Doubleday, 1982.

Problems of the New Nation

VIEWPOINT 18A

A National Bank Would Be Unconstitutional (1791)

Thomas Jefferson (1743–1826)

Thomas Jefferson, appointed by newly elected president George Washington to be the nation's first secretary of state, took office in March 1790. During the next four years Jefferson consistently found himself at odds with the policies of Alexander Hamilton, secretary of the treasury. Hamilton was an advocate of a strong national government; Jefferson was for a limited and frugal one. Hamilton pushed for government policies supporting manufacture and commerce; Jefferson wanted America to remain an agrarian nation. One of their earliest disagreements related to the question of a national bank. In December 1790, Hamilton called on Congress to charter a Bank of the United States. Congress passed such a bill in February 1791; Washington then asked his cabinet officials to submit written opinions on whether Congress had the constitutional authority to take such an action. The following viewpoint is excerpted from Jefferson's written answer to Washington, dated February 15, 1791. Jefferson was dubious of the bank's merits on several grounds, believing it unnecessary for the economy and potentially corrupting for the government. In his paper, Jefferson calls for a strict interpretation of the Constitution, which he concludes does not authorize a national bank.

How does Jefferson argue the Constitution should be interpreted? Why, in his view, does the power to establish a bank not fall within Congress's authority "to regulate commerce"?

I consider the foundation of the Constitution as laid on this ground: that "all powers not delegated to the United States, by the Constitution, nor prohibited by it to the states, are reserved to the states, or to the people." (XIIth amendment.) [actually Amendment X] To take a single step beyond the boundaries thus specially drawn around the powers of Congress, is to take possession of a boundless field of power, no longer susceptible of any definition.

From "Opinion on the Constitutionality of the Bank" by Thomas Jefferson, in *The Writings of Thomas Jefferson*, edited by Albert Bergh (Washington, DC: Thomas Jefferson Memorial Association, 1905).

Enumerated Powers

The incorporation of a bank, and the powers assumed by this bill, have not, in my opinion, been delegated to the United States by the Constitution.

I. They are not among the powers specially enumerated: For these are:

1st. A power to lay taxes for the purpose of paying the debts of the United States; but no debt is paid by this bill, nor any tax laid. Were it a bill to raise money, its organization in the Senate would condemn it by the Constitution.

2d. To "borrow money." But this bill neither borrows money nor insures the borrowing of it. The proprietors of the bank will be just as free as any other money holders, to lend or not to lend their money to the public. The operation proposed in the bill, first to lend them two millions, and then borrow them back again, cannot change the nature of the latter act, which will still be a payment, and not a loan, call it by what name you please.

3d. To "regulate commerce with foreign nations, and among the States, and with the Indian tribes." To erect a bank, and to regulate commerce, are very different acts. He who erects a bank creates a subject of commerce in its bills; so does he who makes a bushel of wheat, or digs a dollar out of the mines; yet neither of these persons regulates commerce thereby. To make a thing which may be bought and sold, is not to prescribe regulations for buying and selling. Besides, if this were an exercise of the power of regulating commerce, it would be void, as extending as much to the internal commerce of every State, as to its external. For the power given to Congress by the Constitution does not extend to the internal regulation of the commerce of a State . . . which remain[s] exclusively with its own legislature; but to its external commerce only, that is to say, its commerce with another State, or with foreign nations, or with the Indian tribes. Accordingly, the bill does not propose the measure as a regulation of trade, but as "productive of considerable advantage to trade." Still less are these powers covered by any other of the special enumerations.

Phrases of the Constitution

II. Nor are they within either of the general phrases, which are the two following:—

1. To lay taxes to provide for the general welfare of the United States, that is to say, "to lay taxes for *the purpose* of providing for the general welfare." For the laying of taxes is the *power*, and the general welfare the *purpose* for which the power is to be exercised. They are not to lay taxes *ad libitum, for any purpose they please*; but only to *pay the debts, or provide for the welfare, of the Union*. In like manner,

they are not *to do anything they please*, to provide for the general welfare, but only *to lay taxes* for that purpose. To consider the latter phrase, not as describing the purpose of the first, but as giving a distinct and independent power to do any act they please which might be for the good of the Union, would render all the preceding and subsequent enumerations of power completely useless.

It would reduce the whole instrument to a single phrase, that of instituting a Congress with power to do whatever would be for the good of the United States; and, as they would be the sole judges of the good or evil, it would be also a power to do whatever evil they pleased.

•

"The incorporation of a bank, and the powers assumed by this bill, have not, in my opinion, been delegated to the United States by the Constitution."

•

It is an established rule of construction, where a phrase will bear either of two meanings, to give it that which will allow some meaning to the other parts of the instrument, and not that which will render all the others useless. Certainly no such universal power was meant to be given them. It was intended to lace them up straitly within the enumerated powers, and those without which, as means, these powers could not be carried into effect. It is known that the very power now proposed *as a means* was rejected *as an end* by the Convention which formed the Constitution. A proposition was made to them, to authorize Congress to open canals, and an amendatory one to empower them to incorporate. But the whole was rejected, and one of the reasons of objection urged in debate was, that they then would have a power to erect a bank, which would render great cities, where there were prejudices and jealousies on that subject, adverse to the reception of the Constitution.

2. The second general phrase is, "to make all laws *necessary* and proper for carrying into execution the enumerated powers." But they can all be carried into execution without a bank. A bank, therefore, is not *necessary*, and consequently not authorized by this phrase.

Conveniences vs. Necessity

It has been much urged that a bank will give great facility or convenience in the collection of taxes. Suppose this were true: yet the Constitution allows only the means which are "necessary," not those which are merely "convenient," for effecting the enumerated powers. If such a latitude of construction be allowed to this phrase as to give any nonenumerated power, it will go to every one, for there is no one which ingenuity may not torture into a *convenience*, in some instance *or other*, to *some one* of so long a list of enumerated powers. It would swallow up all the delegated powers, and reduce the whole to one phrase, as before observed. Therefore it was that the Constitution restrained them to the *necessary* means, that is to say, to those means without which the grant of the power would be nugatory. . . .

Perhaps, indeed bank bills may be a more *convenient* vehicle than treasury orders. But a little *difference* in the degree of *convenience*, cannot constitute the necessity which the Constitution makes the ground for assuming any non-enumerated power. . . .

Can it be thought that the Constitution intended that, for a shade or two of *convenience*, more or less, Congress should be authorized to break down the most ancient and fundamental laws of the several states such as those against Mortmain, the laws of Alienage, the rules of descent, the acts of distribution, the laws of escheat and forfeiture, the laws of monopoly? Nothing but a necessity invincible by other means, can justify such a prostitution of laws, which constitute the pillars of our whole system of jurisprudence. Will Congress be too straitlaced to carry the Constitution into honest effect, unless they may pass over the foundation-laws of the state governments, for the slightest convenience of theirs?

The President's Veto Responsibility

The negative of the President is the shield provided by the Constitution to protect against the invasions of the legislature: 1. The right of the Executive. 2. Of the Judiciary. 3. Of the States and State Legislatures. The present is the case of a right remaining exclusively with the States, and consequently one of those intended by the Constitution to be placed under his protection.

VIEWPOINT 18B

A National Bank Would Not Be Unconstitutional (1791)
Alexander Hamilton (1755–1804)

Alexander Hamilton was appointed by President George Washington to be the nation's first secretary of the treasury. Hamilton energetically used his position to shape American commercial policy, to stabilize public credit, and to promote his vision of a strong national government supported by the wealthy and

From *The Works of Alexander Hamilton*, vol. 4, edited by John C. Hamilton (New York: Charles S. Francis, 1850).

merchant classes. Among the elements of his vision was a national bank that would serve as a depository for federal funds, provide banknotes for commerce, and make short-term loans for the government.

Congress passed a law chartering such a bank in February 1791. Washington then asked members of his cabinet—Hamilton, Secretary of State Thomas Jefferson, and Attorney General Edmund Randolph—for opinions on whether to sign or veto the bank bill. Jefferson and Randolph wrote opinions in opposition, arguing that the Constitution did not authorize such activities by the federal government. The following viewpoint is taken from Hamilton's response to Washington's request. He argues against a strict and limited reading of the Constitution and asserts that Congress has implied powers not explicitly stated to govern the nation, including the power of chartering a bank. Washington agreed with Hamilton and signed the bill creating the first Bank of the United States. (Although it was largely successful in achieving Hamilton's goals of stimulating commerce and centralizing the government, its twenty-year charter was ultimately not renewed, and it ended operations in 1811.) Hamilton's views on the Constitution and the implied powers of the federal government became established constitutional law during the long tenure of Supreme Court chief justice John Marshall.

What general principles does Hamilton stress in interpreting the Constitution? What distinction does he make between *implied* and *express* powers? Hamilton had an advantage in that Washington let him read the papers of Jefferson (see viewpoint 18A) and Randolph before composing his own; what direct responses does Hamilton make to Jefferson's arguments?

In entering upon the argument, it ought to be premised that the objections of the Secretary of State and Attorney-General are founded on a general denial of the authority of the United States to erect corporations. The latter, indeed, expressly admits, that if there be anything in the bill which is not warranted by the Constitution, it is the clause of incorporation.

Now it appears to the Secretary of the Treasury that this *general principle* is *inherent* in the very *definition* of government and *essential* to every step of the progress to be made by that of the United States, namely: That every power vested in a government is in its nature *sovereign* and includes, by *force* of the *term*, a right to employ all the *means* requisite and fairly applicable to the attainment of the *ends* of such power, and which are not precluded by restrictions and exceptions specified in the Constitution, or not

immoral, or not contrary to the *essential ends* of political society. . . .

If it would be necessary to bring proof to a proposition so clear, as that which affirms that the powers of the federal government, as to *its objects*, were sovereign, there is a clause of its Constitution which would be decisive. It is that which declares that the Constitution, and the laws of the United States made in pursuance of it, and all treaties made, or which shall be made, under their authority, shall be the *supreme law of the land*. The power which can create the *supreme law of the land* in *any case* is doubtless *sovereign* as to such case.

This general and indisputable principle puts at once an end to the *abstract* question whether the United States have power to erect a *corporation*; that is to say, to give a *legal* or *artificial capacity* to one or more persons, distinct from the *natural*. For it is unquestionably incident to *sovereign power* to erect corporations, and consequently to *that* of the United States, in *relation* to the *objects* intrusted to the management of the government. The difference is this: where the authority of the government is general, it can create corporations in *all cases*; where it is confined to certain branches of legislation, it can create corporations *only* in those cases. . . .

Implied Powers

It is not denied that there are *implied* as well as *express powers* and that the *former* are as effectually delegated as the *latter*. And for the sake of accuracy it shall be mentioned that there is another class of powers which may be properly denominated *resulting powers*. It will not be doubted that, if the United States should make a conquest of any of the territories of its neighbors, they would possess sovereign jurisdiction over the conquered territory. This would be rather a result, from the whole mass of the powers of the government, and from the nature of political society, than a consequence of either of the powers specially enumerated. . . .

It is conceded that *implied powers* are to be considered as delegated equally with *express ones*. Then it follows that, as a power of erecting a corporation may as well be *implied* as any other thing, it may as well be employed as an *instrument* or *mean* of carrying into execution any of the specified powers, as any other *instrument* or *mean* whatever. The only question must be, in this, as in every other case, whether the mean to be employed or, in this instance, the corporation to be erected, has a natural relation to any of the acknowledged objects or lawful ends of the government. Thus a corporation may not be erected by Congress for superintending the police of the city of Philadelphia, because they are not authorized to *regulate* the *police* of that city. But one may be erected in relation to the collection of taxes, or to the trade with foreign countries, or to the trade between the states, or with the Indian tribes; because it is the province of the federal government to *regulate* those objects, and because it is incident to a general *sovereign* or *legislative* power to *regulate* a thing, to employ all the means which relate to its regulation to the best and greatest advantage. . . .

───── • ─────

"The incorporation of a bank is a constitutional measure; . . . the objections taken to the bill, in this respect, are ill founded."

───── • ─────

Through this mode of reasoning respecting the right of employing all the means requisite to the execution of the specified powers of the government, it is objected that none but necessary and proper means are to be employed; and the Secretary of State maintains that no means are to be considered as *necessary* but those without which the grant of the power would be *nugatory.* Nay, so far does he go in his restrictive interpretation of the *word,* as even to make the case of the *necessity* which shall warrant the constitutional exercise of the power to depend on *casual* and *temporary* circumstances; an idea which alone refutes the construction. The *expediency* of exercising a particular power, at a particular time, must, indeed, depend on circumstances; but the constitutional right of exercising it must be uniform and invariable, the same today as tomorrow.

All the arguments, therefore, against the constitutionality of the bill derived from the accidental existence of certain state banks—institutions which happen to exist today and, for aught that concerns the government of the United States, may disappear tomorrow—must not only be rejected as fallacious but must be viewed as demonstrative that there is a *radical* source of error in the reasoning.

The Meaning of *Necessary*

It is essential to the being of the national government that so erroneous a conception of the meaning of the word *necessary* should be exploded.

It is certain that neither the grammatical nor popular sense of the term requires that construction. According to both, *necessary* often means no more than *needful, requisite, incidental, useful,* or *conducive to.* It is a common mode of expression to say that it is *necessary* for a government or a person to do this or that thing, when nothing more is intended or understood than that the interests of the govern-

ment or person require, or will be promoted by, the doing of this or that thing. The imagination can be at no loss for exemplifications of the use of the word in this sense. And it is the true one in which it is to be understood as used in the Constitution. The whole turn of the clause containing it indicates that it was the intent of the Convention, by that clause, to give a liberal latitude to the exercise of the specified powers. The expressions have peculiar comprehensiveness. They are, "to make all *laws* necessary and proper for *carrying into execution the foregoing powers,* and *all other powers* vested by the Constitution in the *government* of the United States, or in any *department* or *officer* thereof."

To understand the word as the Secretary of State does would be to depart from its obvious and popular sense and to give it a restrictive operation, an idea never before entertained. It would be to give it the same force as if the word *absolutely* or *indispensably* had been prefixed to it.

Such a construction would beget endless uncertainty and embarrassment. The cases must be palpable and extreme, in which it could be pronounced, with certainty, that a measure was absolutely necessary, or one, without which, the exercise of a given power would be nugatory. There are few measures of any government which would stand so severe a test. To insist upon it would be to make the criterion of the exercise of any implied power a *case of extreme necessity*; which is rather a rule to justify the overleaping of the bounds of constitutional authority than to govern the ordinary exercise of it. . . .

The *degree* in which a measure is necessary can never be a *test* of the legal right to adopt it; that must be a matter of opinion and can only be a *test* of expediency. The *relation* between the *measure* and the *end*; between the *nature* of the *mean* employed toward the execution of a power and the object of that power, must be the criterion of constitutionality, not the more or less of *necessity* or *utility*. . . .

This restrictive interpretation of the word *necessary* is also contrary to this sound maxim of construction; namely that the powers contained in a constitution of government, especially those which concern the general administration of the affairs of a country, its finances, trade, defense, etc., ought to be construed liberally in advancement of the public good. This rule does not depend on the particular form of a government, or on the particular demarcation of the boundaries of its powers, but on the nature and objects of government itself. The means by which national exigencies are to be provided for, national inconveniences obviated, national prosperity promoted, are of such infinite variety, extent, and complexity, that there must of necessity be great latitude of discretion in the selection and application of those means. Hence, consequently, the necessity and propriety of exercising the authorities intrusted to a government on principles of liberal construction. . . .

But the doctrine which is contended for is not chargeable with the consequences imputed to it. It does not affirm that the national government is sovereign in all respects but that it is sovereign to a certain extent; that is, to the extent of the objects of its specified powers.

It leaves, therefore, a criterion of what is constitutional and of what is not so. This criterion is the *end*, to which the measure relates as a *mean*. If the *end* be clearly comprehended within any of the specified powers, and if the measures have an obvious relation to that *end*, and is not forbidden by a particular provision of the Constitution, it may safely be deemed to come within the compass of the national authority. There is also this further criterion, which may materially assist the decision: Does the proposed measure abridge a pre-existing right of any state or of any individual? If it does not, there is a strong presumption in favor of its constitutionality, and slighter relations to any declared object of the Constitution may be permitted to turn the scale. . . .

The Case for a National Bank

It shall now be endeavored to be shown that there is a power to erect one [bank] of the kind proposed by the bill. This will be done by tracing a natural and obvious relation between the institution of a bank and the objects of several of the enumerated powers of the government; and by showing that, *politically* speaking, it is necessary to the effectual execution of one or more of those powers. . . .

To establish such a right, it remains to show the relation of such an institution to one or more of the specified powers of the government. Accordingly it is affirmed that it has a relation, more or less direct, to the power of collecting taxes, to that of borrowing money, to that of regulating trade between the states, and to those of raising and maintaining fleets and armies. To the two former the relation may be said to be immediate; and in the last place it will be argued that it is clearly within the provision which authorizes the making of all *needful rules and regulations* concerning the *property* of the United States, as the same has been practiced upon by the government.

A bank relates to the collection of taxes in two ways—*indirectly*, by increasing the quantity of circulating medium and quickening circulation, which facilitates the means of paying directly, by creating a *convenient species* of medium in which they are to be paid. . . .

A bank has a direct relation to the power of borrowing money, because it is a usual, and in sudden emergencies an essential, instrument in the obtaining of loans to government.

A nation is threatened with war; large sums are wanted on a sudden to make the necessary preparation. Taxes are laid for the purpose, but it requires time to obtain the benefit of them. Anticipation is indispensable. If there be a bank, the supply can at once be had. If there be none, loans from individuals must be sought. The progress of these is often too slow for the exigency; in some situations they are not practicable at all. Frequently, when they are, it is of great consequence to be able to anticipate the product of them by advance from a bank. . . .

Let it then be supposed that the necessity existed (as but for a casualty would be the case), that proposals were made for obtaining a loan; that a number of individuals came forward and said, "We are willing to accommodate the government with the money"; with what we have in hand, and the credit we can raise upon it, we doubt not of being able to furnish the sum required, but in order to do this it is indispensable that we should be incorporated as a bank. This is essential toward putting it in our power to do what is desired, and we are obliged on that account to make it the *consideration* or *condition* of the loan.

Can it be believed that a compliance with this proposition would be unconstitutional? . . .

The institution of a bank has also a natural relation to the regulation of trade between the states, in so far as it is conducive to the creation of a convenient medium of *exchange* between them, and to the keeping up a full circulation, by preventing the frequent displacement of the metals in reciprocal remittances. Money is the very hinge on which commerce turns. And this does not merely mean gold and silver; many other things have served the purpose, with different degrees of utility. Paper has been extensively employed. . . .

Regulating Commerce

The Secretary of State further argues that if this was a regulation of commerce, it would be void, as *extending as much to the internal commerce of every state as to its external.* But what regulation of commerce does not extend to the internal commerce of every state? What are all the duties upon imported articles, amounting to prohibitions, but so many bounties upon domestic manufactures, affecting the interests of different classes of citizens, in different ways? What are all the provisions in the Coasting Act which relate to the trade between district and district of the same state? In short, what regulation of trade between the states but must affect the internal trade of each state? What can operate upon the whole but must extend to every part?

The relation of a bank to the execution of the powers that concern the common defense has been anticipated. It has been noted that, at this very moment, the aid of such an institution is essential to the measures to be pursued for the protection of our frontiers.

It now remains to show that the incorporation of a bank is within the operation of the provision which authorizes Congress to make all needful rules and regulations concerning the property of the United States. But it is previously necessary to advert to a distinction which has been taken by the Attorney-General.

He admits that the word *property* may signify personal property, however acquired, and yet asserts that it cannot signify money arising from the sources of revenue pointed out in the Constitution, "because," says he, "the disposal and regulation of money is the final cause for raising it by taxes."

But it would be more accurate to say that the *object* to which money is intended to be applied is the *final cause* for raising it than that the disposal and regulation of it is *such*.

The support of government—the support of troops for the common defense—the payment of the public debt, are the true *final causes* for raising money. The disposition and regulation if it, when raised, are the steps by which it is applied to the *ends* for which it was raised, not the *ends* themselves. Hence, therefore, the money to be raised by taxes, as well as any other personal property, must be supposed to come within the meaning, as they certainly do within the letter, of authority to make all needful rules and regulations concerning the property of the United States. . . .

Objections to a National Bank Are Baseless

A hope is entertained that it has, by this time, been made to appear, to the satisfaction of the President, that a bank has a natural relation to the power of collecting taxes—to that of regulating trade—to that of providing for the common defense—and that, as the bill under consideration contemplates the government in the light of a joint proprietor of the stock of the bank, it brings the case within the provision of the clause of the Constitution which immediately respects the property of the United States.

Under a conviction that such a relation subsists, the Secretary of the Treasury, with all deference, conceives, that it will result as a necessary consequence from the position, that all the specified powers of government are sovereign, as to the proper objects; that the incorporation of a bank is a constitutional measure; and that the objections taken to the bill, in this respect, are ill founded.

For Further Reading

Joyce Appleby, *Capitalism and the New Social Order: The Republican Vision of the 1790s.* New York: New York University Press, 1984.

Margaret C.S. Christman, *"The Spirit of Party": Hamilton & Jefferson at Odds.* Washington, DC: National Portrait Gallery, 1992.

Paul Goodman, *The Federalists vs. the Jeffersonian Republicans.* New York: Holt, Rinehart and Winston, 1967.

David N. Mayer, *The Constitutional Thought of Thomas Jefferson.* Charlottesville: University Press of Virginia, 1994.

Gerald Stourzh, *Alexander Hamilton and the Idea of Republican Government.* Stanford, CA: Stanford University Press, 1970.

VIEWPOINT 19A

Jay's Treaty Should Be Rejected (1795)

Robert R. Livingston (1746–1813)

The United States faced significant diplomatic challenges in the earliest years of its existence, especially in its relations with the leading world powers of the time—Great Britain and France. Disagreements over U.S. foreign policy also reflected the growing political divisions within the United States. A major step in both U.S. foreign relations and the development of opposing political parties in America was Jay's Treaty and the national controversy surrounding it.

President George Washington sent lawyer and diplomat John Jay to Great Britain in 1794 to negotiate a treaty at a time the two nations appeared to be heading toward a military showdown. Great Britain was upset with American trade with France (Great Britain and France were then at war) and with losing British sailors who were deserting to serve on American ships. The United States was upset with British naval actions against U.S. trade, which included the seizure and confiscation of American trade goods and the "impressment" of American sailors suspected of being British deserters. Great Britain also had yet to relinquish its military forts in America's western territories (as promised in the 1783 Treaty of Paris). In addition, many Americans believed it was sponsoring Indian attacks on American settlers.

The treaty Jay negotiated with the British caused a nationwide uproar when it was revealed to the public in 1795. Many Americans criticized the agreement as being too favorable to Great Britain. Great Britain did agree to withdraw its forces from its forts in American territory, but elsewhere made few concessions, and it reserved the rights to impress American sailors and to seize (and pay for) American cargo destined for France. The following viewpoint is taken from a pamphlet by "Cato," a pseudonym for

From *Examination of the Treaty of Amity, Commerce, and Navigation, Between the United States and Great-Britain, in Several Numbers* by Cato (Robert R. Livingston), 1795.

Robert R. Livingston, one of the leaders of the opposition to Jay's Treaty. Livingston, a New York lawyer who in 1776 had been on the Continental Congress committee that drafted the Declaration of Independence, later was appointed minister to France.

How does Livingston describe the balance of power in Europe? Why should the United States be especially concerned with Great Britain's presence in the western territories, according to Livingston?

Britain, on the day of the signature of the treaty, was involved in a war with the bravest people in Europe [France]: in the whole course of this war, she had experienced continued defeats and disgraces; her treasures were wasted upon allies that either deserted or were too feeble to afford her effectual aid; her debt had grown to the enormous sum of three hundred millions; her navy could only be manned by the most destructive burthens upon her commerce; her manufactures were languishing; her fleets were unable to protect her trade, which had suffered unexampled losses. And while she was sinking under her burdens, her antagonist was consolidating her government, and growing so rapidly in strength, reputation, and vigour, as to threaten her existence as a nation. The United States were, on the other hand, in the highest prosperity; their numbers had doubled since they had successfully measured swords with Britain; they possessed men, arms, military stores, and an ally, who was alone too powerful for her enemies. Sweden and Denmark who had received insults from Britain, were ready to make a common cause with her; as the marine of England and France were nearly balanced, the weight of America, had she been forced into the war, would have turned the scale, and compleated the ruin of the British commerce, without any other effort than that of granting letters of marque. Independent of which, without a violation of their neutrality by those acts of sovereignty which no one would dispute their right to exercise, they could involve the British trade in the utmost distress, by an additional duty on British tonnage, by granting advantages to rival manufactures, by retaining debts due to her merchants, until the injuries ours had sustained were compensated. By following her example, both in the present and in the late American war, and suffering no part of the public debt to be paid to her citizens until justice was done us, we could have forced her into any measure that it was just or proper for us to ask. And, indeed, so fully satisfied were the Americans, of every party, of the superiority of our situation, that no doubt was entertained of a favorable issue to Mr. Jay's negociation, and all that his friends lamented, and his enemies rejoiced in, was, that the principal credit of

them would be ascribed rather to the victories of France, than to the address of our minister. Under these happy auspices the negociation began. . . .

The Western Territories

By the 2d article of the treaty, the British promise to evacuate the western posts by the 1st of June, 1796. By the treaty of Paris, in 1783, they promised to evacuate with all convenient speed; which, if we may judge by the speed with which they have found it convenient to evacuate all their posts in France, Flanders, Germany, Holland, and Brabant, one would have supposed must have meant a much shorter time than eighteen months, so that all that the treaty acquires with respect to the posts, is less than we were entitled to by the treaty of Paris. Surely we might expect better security than a mere promise, from a nation which has already shewn, in their violation of the past, the little reliance that can be placed on their future engagements. By June, 1796, it is not improbable that our situation, or that of Britain, may be changed; what security shall we then have for the performance of the treaty? It is said (by those shameless apologists who are determined to find every ministerial measure right) that every treaty is a promise, and that if we are not to rely upon a promise, there can be no treaties, I answer, that it is the practice of negociators, where the character of the nation, or other circumstances, give reason to suspect a violation of their engagements, *not to rely* upon a naked promise, but to expect some guarantee or surety for the performance; that in the present case, as the promise was evidently extorted by the pressure of existing circumstances, we should see to the performance while those circumstances continue to exist. It is evident, before Mr. Jay left this country, that the British were so far from intending to evacuate the posts, that they had determined to extend their limits; this may not only be inferred from the encouragement they gave to the depredations of the Indians, but undeniably proved by [governor-general of Canada] Lord Dorchester's speech, which, though disavowed by [British secretary of war Henry] Dundas, is now admitted to have been made in consequence of express instructions. The promise, then to evacuate, has been extorted by French victories, by the humiliation of the British nation, and by their apprehension that we might at last be provoked to do ourselves justice while they were embarrassed with France. Surely then the evacuation should have been insisted upon, while these circumstances operated with full force. . . . Are we not at this moment at war with the savages? Is not this war attended with much expence to the nation, and much private distress? Is not the blood of our citizens daily shed? These evils must continue as long as the posts are in the hands of the British, or a peace, if practicable, must be purchased by the United States at very considerable expence. Were we to estimate the difference on this point of view, between an immediate evacuation, and one that is to take place in June 1796, it would certainly not fall short of one million of dollars, independent of the price. If to this we add the annual profits of the Indian trade, amounting to 800,000, it will appear, that the United States lose above a million of dollars by retention of the posts, supposing (which is at least problematical) that they will be surrendered at the period proposed. Those who think with me, that decision of the part of our government, and firmness in our minister, could not have failed to effect an immediate restitution of our territory, will know to what account to charge this heavy loss of blood and treasure.

Would to God, my fellow citizens, I could here find some source of consolation, some ray of light, to eradicate the sullen gloom!—But alas! every step we take plunges us into thicker darkness. We might, perhaps, have submitted to past losses; have seen our commerce given away without an equivalent; our navigation ruined; our seamen (I blush with shame and indignation while I say it) our citizen seamen delivered over to the insolence of brutal tyrants, could our national honour have been preserved in future—could alliances, formed by interest and gratitude, have been left unimpaired—could peace have been established upon firm and honorable terms; could the private rights of our citizens, the public ones of our government, have remained unviolated—but, the indiscriminate ruin of all these is too much to be borne in silence. Even the coward advocates for peace, feel their spirits rise on the unexampled indignities which this treaty imposes. And for what? Are we nearer peace (if by peace is meant the security of our persons and property, from foreign depredations) than when Mr. Jay left this country? Is there a single outrage which we suffered before which is not continued to this moment? And yet the advocates for the treaty are continually ringing in our ears, the blessings of peace, the horrors of war; and they have the effrontery to assure us, that we enjoy the first and have escaped the last, merely (to borrow a ministerial term) through the instrumentality of the treaty. Does any body believe, that if we had continued to suffer the British to plunder our trade, to man their ships with our seamen, to possess our frontiers in quiet, that they would have declared war upon us, at least till they had conquered France? . . . In a political view, the treaty is bad, as it detaches us from engagements which our interest and honour equally invite us to maintain; as it sacrifices our friends to our enemies, and holds forth to the world, that those nations who treat us worst, will share the

greatest portion of our attachment, and that, like fawning spaniels, we can be beaten into love and submission. . . .

---•---

"In a political view, the treaty is bad, as it . . . holds forth to the world, that those nations who treat us worst, will share the greatest portion of our attachment."

---•---

I trust, however, that enough has been said to shew, that the treaty has obtained no adequate compensation for the injuries we have suffered; that it has relinquished important claims that we had upon British government, that it has given no protection to our seamen, that it is injurious to our commerce, and ruinous to our navigation, that it takes from us the means we possessed of retaliating injuries without the hazard of a war, that it pledged the country for immense sums of money, which it does not owe, while it curtails our demands upon Britain; that it gives the British subjects a variety of privileges in our country, which are but partially returned to us, that it counteracts the existing laws, and violates the federal constitution, and that it infringes the rights of individual states.

VIEWPOINT 19B

Jay's Treaty Should Be Accepted (1796)

Fisher Ames (1758–1808)

The national debate that erupted over Jay's Treaty between Great Britain and America in 1795 reflected the development of opposing political parties that were then forming in the United States around Alexander Hamilton (the Federalists) and Thomas Jefferson (the Democratic-Republicans). Federalists (not to be confused with the federalists that supported ratification of the Constitution) were generally sympathetic toward Great Britain and favored Jay's Treaty. Jefferson's Democratic-Republicans, on the other hand, were more inclined to favor France over Great Britain in U.S. foreign policy, and were harshly critical of Jay's Treaty as being too favorable to Great Britain.

From *Speech in Support of the Motion: Resolved, That It Is Expedient to Pass the Laws Necessary to Carry into Effect the Treaty Between the United States and Great-Britain* by Fisher Ames (Boston, 1796). Reprinted in *American History Told by Contemporaries*, vol. 3, edited by Albert Bushnell Hart (New York: Macmillan, 1896).

The Senate, controlled by Federalists, narrowly voted to ratify Jay's Treaty in 1795. In 1796, however, the House of Representatives debated whether to withhold funding to implement the agreement. The following viewpoint is taken from a speech by Fisher Ames, one of the supporters of Jay's Treaty. Ames, who served in the House from 1789 to 1797, was one of the leading Federalist members of that body. The House ultimately decided to appropriate funding.

What argument does Ames make about opponents of the treaty? Why would rejecting Jay's Treaty at this time be damaging to American prestige, according to Ames? How do his views on Indian hostilities in the west differ from those of Robert R. Livingston, author of the opposing viewpoint?

The Treaty is bad, fatally bad, is the cry. It sacrifices the interest, the honor, the independence of the United States, and the faith of our engagements to France. . . . The language of passion and exaggeration may silence that of sober reason in other places, it has not done it here. The question here is, whether the treaty be really so very fatal as to oblige the nation to break its faith. . . .

Duty to France

It is in vain to alledge that our faith plighted to France is violated by this new Treaty. Our prior Treaties are expressly saved from the operation of the British Treaty. And what do those mean, who say, that our honor was forfeited by treating at all, and especially by such a Treaty? Justice, the laws and practice of nations, a just regard for peace as a duty to mankind, and the known wish of our citizens, as well as that self-respect which required it of the nation to act with dignity and moderation, all these forbid an appeal to arms before we had tried the effect of negociation. The honor of the United States was saved, not forfeited by treating. The Treaty itself by its stipulations for the posts, for indemnity and for a due observation of our neutral rights, has justly raised the character of the nation. Never did the name of America appear in Europe with more lustre than upon the event of ratifying this instrument. The fact is of a nature to overcome all contradiction.

But *the independence of the country—we are colonists again.* This is the cry of the very men who tell us that France will resent our exercise of the rights of an independent nation to adjust our wrongs with an aggressor, without giving her the opportunity to say those wrongs shall subsist and shall not be adjusted. This is an admirable specimen of independence. The Treaty with Great Britain, it cannot be denied is unfavorable to this strange sort of independence. . . .

Why do they complain that the West-Indies are not laid open? Why do they lament that any restriction is stipulated on the commerce of the East-Indies? Why do they pretend that if they reject this, and insist upon more, more will be accomplished? Let us be explicit—more would not satisfy. If all was granted, would not a Treaty of amity with Britain still be obnoxious? Have we not this instant heard it urged against our Envoy, that he was not ardent enough in his hatred of Great-Britain? A Treaty of Amity is condemned because it was not made by a foe, and in the spirit of one. The same gentleman at the same instant repeats a very prevailing objection, that no Treaty should be made with the enemy of France. No Treaty, exclaim others, should be made with a monarch or a despot. There will be no naval security while those sea robbers domineer on the ocean. Their den must be destroyed. That nation must be extirpated. . . .

The Role of the House of Representatives

Our claim to some agency in giving force and obligation to Treaties, is beyond all kind of controversy NOVEL. The sense of the nation is probably against it. The sense of the Government certainly is. The President denies it on constitutional grounds, and therefore cannot ever accede to our interpretation. The Senate ratified the Treaty and cannot without dishonour adopt it . . .

If they refuse to concur, a Treaty once made remains of full force, although a breach on the part of the foreign nation would confer upon our own a right to forbear the execution. I repeat it, even in that case the act of this house cannot be admitted as the act of the nation, and if the President and Senate should not concur, the Treaty would be obligatory. . . .

On every hypothesis therefore, the conclusion is not to be resisted, we are either to execute this treaty, or break our faith.

To expatiate on the value of public faith may pass with some men for declamation—to such men I have nothing to say. To others I will urge, can any circumstance mark upon a people more turpitude and debasement? . . .

It is painful, I hope it is superfluous, to make even the supposition that America should furnish the occasion of this opprobrium. No, let me not even imagine that a republican government sprung, as our own is, from a people enlightened and uncorrupted, a government whose orig[i]n is right, and whose daily discipline is duty, can, upon solemn debate, make its option to be faithless—can dare to act what despots dare not avow, what our own example evinces the states of Barbary are unsuspected of. No, let me rather make the supposition that Great Britain refuses to execute the treaty, after we have done every thing to carry it into effect. Is there any language of reproach pungent enough to express your commentary on the fact? What would you say, or rather what would you not say? Would you not tell them, wherever an Englishman might travel shame would stick to him—he would disown his country. You would exclaim, England, proud of your wealth, and arrogant in the possession of power—blush for these distinctions, which become the vehicles of your dishonor. Such a nation might truly say, to corruption, Thou art my father, and to the worm, Thou art my mother and my sister. We should say of such a race of men, their name is a heavier burden than their debt.

I can scarcely persuade myself to believe that the consideration I have suggested requires the aid of any auxiliary. But, unfortunately, auxiliary arguments are at hand. Five millions of dollars, and probably more, on the score of spoliations committed on our commerce, depend upon the treaty.—The treaty offers the only prospect of indemnity. Such redress is promised as the merchants place some confidence in. Will you interpose and frustrate that hope? Leaving to many families nothing but beggary and despair. . . .

The Western Forts

The refusal of [Great Britain to withdraw from] the posts (inevitable if we reject the treaty) is a measure too decisive in its nature to be neutral in its consequences. From great causes we are to look for great effects. A plain and obvious one will be, the price of the western lands will fall. Settlers will not chuse to fix their habitation on a field of battle. Those who talk so much of the interest of the United States should calculate how deeply it will be affected by rejecting the treaty—how vast a tract of wild land will almost cease to be property. This loss, let it be observed, will fall upon a fund expressly devoted to sink the national debt. . . .

Will the tendency to Indian hostilities be contested by any one? Experience gives the answer. The frontiers were scourged with war until the negociation with Great-Britain was far advanced, and then the state of hostility ceased. Perhaps the public agents of both nations are innocent of fomenting the Indian war, and perhaps they are not. We ought not however to expect that neighbouring nations, highly irritated against each other, will neglect the friendship of the savages, the traders will gain an influence and will abuse it—and who is ignorant that their passions are easily raised and hardly restrained from violence? Their situation will oblige them to chuse between this country and Great-Britain, in case the Treaty should be rejected. They will not be our friends and at the same time the friends of our enemies. . . .

It is not the part of prudence to be inattentive to the tendencies of measures. Where there is any

ground to fear that these will be pernicious, wisdom and duty forbid that we should underate them.—If we reject the treaty, will our peace be as safe as if we execute it with good faith? . . .

———— • ————

"The honor of the United States was saved, not forfeited by treating."

———— • ————

Are the Posts to remain forever in the possession of Great-Britain? Let those who reject them, when the Treaty offers them to our hands, say, if they chuse, they are of no importance. If they are, will they take them by force? The argument I am urging would then come to a point. To use force is war. To talk of Treaty again is too absurd. Posts and redress must come from voluntary good will, Treaty or war.

The conclusion is plain, if the state of peace shall continue, so will the British possession of the posts.

Look again at this state of things: On the sea coast, vast losses uncompensated; on the frontier, Indian war, actual encroachment on our territory. Every where discontent, resentments tenfold more fierce because they will be impotent and humbled. National discord and abasement.

The disputes of the old treaty of 1783, being left to rankle, will revive the almost extinguished animosities of that period. Wars in all countries, and most of all in such as are free, arise from the impetuosity of the public feelings. . . . War might perhaps be delayed, but could not be prevented. The causes of it would remain, would be aggravated, would be multiplied, and soon become intolerable. More captures, more impressments would swell the list of our wrongs, and the current of our rage. . . .

Will our government be able to temper and restrain the turbulence of such a crisis? The government, alas, will be in no capacity to govern. A divided people, and divided councils! Shall we cherish the spirit of peace, or shew the energies of war? Shall we make our adversary afraid of our strength, or dispose him, by the measures of resentment and broken faith, to respect our rights? Do gentlemen rely on the state of peace because both nations will be worse disposed to keep it? Because injuries, and insults still harder to endure, will be mutually offered.

Such a state of things will exist, if we should long avoid war, as will be worse than war. Peace without security, accumulation of injury without redress, or the hope of it, resentment against the aggressor, contempt for ourselves, intestine discord, and anarchy. . . . Is this the station of American dignity which the high-spirited champions of our national independence and honor could endure—nay, which they are anxious and almost violent to seize for the country? What is there in the treaty that could humble us so low? Are they the men to swallow their resentments, who so lately were choking with them? If in the case contemplated by them, it should be peace, I do not hesitate to declare it ought not to be peace. . . .

Let me cheer the mind, weary no doubt and ready to despond on this prospect, by presenting another which it is yet in our power to realise. Is it possible for a real American to look at the prosperity of this country without some desire for its continuance, without some respect for the measures which, many will say, produced, and all will confess have preserved it? . . . The great interest and the general desire of our people was to enjoy the advantages of neutrality. This instrument, however misrepresented, affords America that inestimable security. The causes of our disputes are either cut up by the roots, or referred to a new negociation, after the end of the European war. This was gaining every thing, because it confirmed our neutrality, by which our citizens are gaining every thing. This alone would justify the engagements of the government. For, when the fiery vapors of the war lowered in the skirts of our horizon, all our wishes were concentered in this one, that we might escape the desolation of the storm. This treaty, like a rainbow on the edge of the cloud, marked to our eyes the space where it was raging, and afforded at the same time the sure prognostic of fair weather. If we reject it, the vivid colours will grow pale, it will be a baleful meteor portending tempest and war.

For Further Reading

Jerald A. Combs, *The Jay Treaty: Political Battleground of the Founding Fathers.* Berkeley: University of California Press, 1970.

Daniel G. Lang, *Foreign Policy in the Early Republic: The Law of Nations and the Balance of Power.* Baton Rouge: University of Louisiana Press, 1985.

Gilbert Lycan, *Alexander Hamilton and American Foreign Policy.* Norman: University of Oklahoma Press, 1970.

J. Leitch Wright, *Britain and the American Frontier, 1783–1815.* Athens: University of Georgia Press, 1975.

VIEWPOINT 20A

The Sedition Act Violates the Bill of Rights (1799)

George Hay (1765–1830)

In 1798 the United States again stood on the brink of war with a major European power, only this time

From *An Essay on the Liberty of the Press* by George Hay (Philadelphia, 1799).

instead of Great Britain the hostile nation was France. America's former Revolutionary War ally, angered by Jay's Treaty between Great Britain and the United States (see viewpoints 19A and 19B), was engaged in naval hostilities against American ships.

In preparation for an anticipated war against France, Congress, then controlled by members of the Federalist Party, passed the Alien and Sedition Acts. The fourth of these laws, the Sedition Act, proscribed "any false, scandalous and malicious" writings and utterances against the government and its officials. It called for fines and jail penalties for anyone speaking, writing, or publishing "with intent to defame . . . or bring into contempt or disrepute" the president or other members of government. The fears of some that the law would be used to stifle political criticism of the Federalist Party appeared to be realized after several prominent Democratic-Republican newspaper editors and leaders were jailed.

Many argued that the Sedition Act violated the First Amendment of the Bill of Rights, which stated that "Congress shall make no law . . . abridging the freedom of speech, or of the press." Those who defended the Sedition Act argued that the Bill of Rights prevented Congress only from making laws that created a "prior restraint" on newspaper publications. Congress, they argued, could still punish publishers for newspaper articles they found seditious or otherwise dangerous to the public *after* publication. Others disagreed, and the Sedition Act is credited by some historians as stimulating new theories and defenses of the freedom of the press. One important pamphlet published at this time was by George Hay, a member of the Virginia House of Delegates and a future federal judge. In 1799 under the pseudonym of "Hortensius" he wrote a pamphlet titled *An Essay on the Liberty of the Press.* In it, he argues that the Sedition Act violates the Bill of Rights by limiting freedoms of speech and of the press, which he argues should be defined broadly.

How does Hay define "freedom"? What did the authors of the First Amendment intend, according to Hay? How does he respond to the argument that the First Amendment prohibits only "prior restraint" of newspapers?

It is the object of the succeeding letters, to demonstrate, that so much of the Sedition Bill, as relates to *printed* libels, is expressly forbidden by the constitution of the United States.

This question, in strictness, ought not to be discussed; because, if Congress have not power, either expressly given or by necessary *implication*, to pass the law under consideration, it is totally immaterial whether they are forbidden to pass it or not. But as the "freedom of the press," has never yet been accurately defined, and as there is no subject in which the welfare of society is more essentially concerned, my original undertaking shall be fully performed.

The words of the constitution, which contain the express prohibition here relied on, are, "Congress shall make no law abridging the freedom of speech or of the press.". . .

The words, "freedom of the press," like most other words, have a meaning, a clear, precise, and definite meaning, which the times require, should be unequivocally ascertained. That this has not been done before, is a wonderful and melancholy evidence of the imbecility of the human mind, and of the slow progress which it makes, in acquiring knowledge even on subjects the most useful and interesting.

It will, I presume, be admitted, that the words in question have a meaning, and that the framers of the amendment containing these words, meant something when they declared, that the freedom of the press should not be abridged.

To ascertain what the "freedom of the press" is, we have only to ascertain what freedom itself is. For, surely, it will be conceded, that freedom applied to one subject, means the same, as freedom applied to another subject.

Two Kinds of Freedom

Now freedom is of two kinds, and of two kinds only: one is, that absolute freedom which belongs to man, previous to any social institution; and the other, that qualified or abridged freedom, which he is content to enjoy, for the sake of government and society. I believe there is no other sort of freedom in which man is concerned.

The absolute freedom then, or what is the same thing, the freedom, belonging to man before any social compact, is the power uncontrouled by law, of doing what he pleases, *provided he does no injury to any other individual*. If this definition of freedom be applied to the press, as surely it ought to be, the press, if I may personify it, may do whatever it pleases to do, uncontrouled by any law, *taking care however to do no injury to any individual*. This injury can only be by slander or defamation, and reparation should be made for it in a state of nature as well as in society.

But freedom in society, or what is called civil liberty, is defined to be, natural liberty, so far, restrained by law as the public good requires, and no farther. This is the definition given by a writer, particularly distinguished for the accuracy of his definitions, and which, perhaps, cannot be mended. Now let freedom, under this definition, be applied to the press, and what will the freedom of the press amount to? It will amount precisely to the privilege of publishing, as far as the legislative power shall say, the public

good requires: that is to say, the freedom of the press will be regulated by law. If the word freedom was used in this sense, by the framers of the amendment, they meant to say, Congress shall make no law abridging the freedom of the press, which freedom, however, is to be regulated by law. Folly itself does not speak such language.

———— • ————

"The freedom of the press . . . means the total exemption of the press from any kind of legislative controul."

———— • ————

It has been admitted by the reader, who has advanced thus far, that the framers of the amendment meant something. They knew, no doubt, that the power granted to Congress, did not authorise any controul over the press, but they knew that its freedom could not be too cautiously guarded from invasion. The amendment in question was therefore introduced. Now if they used the word "freedom" under the first definition, they did mean something, and something of infinite importance in all free countries, the total exemption of the press from any kind of legislative controul. But if they used the word freedom under the second definition they meant nothing; for if they supposed that the freedom of the press, was absolute freedom, so far restrained by law as the public good required, and no farther, the amendment left the legislative power of the government on this subject, precisely where it was before. But it has been already admitted that the amendment had a meaning: the construction therefore which allows it no meaning is absurd and must be rejected.

The Meaning of Freedom

This argument may be summed up in a few words. The word "freedom" has meaning. It is either absolute, that is exempt from all law, or it is qualified, that is, regulated by law. If it be exempt from the controul of law, the Sedition Bill which controuls the "freedom of the press" is unconstitutional. But if it is to be regulated by law, the amendment which declares that Congress shall make no law to abridge the freedom of the press, which freedom however may be regulated by law, is the grossest absurdity that ever was conceived by the human mind.

That by the words "freedom of the press," is meant a total exemption of the press from legislative controul, will further appear from the following cases, in which it is manifest, that the word freedom is used with this signification and no other.

It is obvious in itself and it is admitted by all men,

that freedom of speech means the power uncontrouled by law, of speaking either truth or falsehood at the discretion of each individual, *provided no other individual be injured.* This power is, *as yet*, in its full extent in the United States. A man may say every thing which his passion can suggest; he may employ all his time, and all his talents, if he is wicked enough to do so, in *speaking* against the government matters that are false, scandalous, and malicious; but he is admitted by the majority of Congress to be sheltered by the article in question, which forbids a law abridging the freedom of speech. If then freedom of speech means, in the construction of the Constitution, the privilege of speaking *any thing* without controul, the words freedom of the press, which form a part of the same sentence, mean the privilege of printing *any thing* without controul.

Freedom of Speech and Religion

Happily for mankind, the word "freedom" begins now to be applied to religion also. In the United States it is applied in its fullest force, and religious freedom is completely understood to mean the power uncontrouled by law of professing and publishing any opinion on religious topics, which any individual may choose to profess or publish, and of supporting these opinions by any statements he may think proper to make. The fool may not only say in his heart, there is no God, but he may announce if he pleases his atheism to the world. He may endeavor to corrupt mankind, not only by opinions that are erroneous, but by facts which are false. Still however he will be safe, because he lives in a country where religious freedom is established. If then freedom of religion, will not permit a man to be punished, for publishing any opinions on religious topics and supporting those opinions by false facts, surely freedom of the press, which is the medium of all publications, will not permit a man to be punished, for publishing any opinion on any subject, and supporting it by any statement whatever. . . .

I contend therefore, that if the words freedom of the press, have any meaning at all they mean a total exemption from any law making any publication whatever criminal. Whether the unequivocal avowal of this doctrine in the United States would produce mischief or not, is a question which perhaps I may have leisure to discuss. I must be content here to observe, that the mischief if any, which might arise from this doctrine could not be remedied or prevented, but by means of a power fatal to the liberty of the people.

The Sedition Bill

That the real meaning of the words "freedom of the press," has been ascertained by the foregoing remarks, will appear still more clearly, if possible, from the absurdity of those constructions, which have been given by the advocates of the Sedition Bill.

The construction clearly held out in the bill itself, is, that it does not extend to the privilege of printing facts, that are false. This construction cannot be correct. It plainly supposes that "freedom," extends only as far as the power of doing what is morally right. If, then, the freedom of the press can be restrained to the publication of facts that are true, it follows inevitably, that it may also be restrained to the publication of opinions which are correct. There is truth in opinion, as well as in fact. Error in opinion may do as much harm, as falsity in fact: it may be as morally wrong, and it may be propagated from motives as malicious. It may do more harm, because the refutation of an opinion which is erroneous, is more difficult than the contradiction of a fact which is false. But the power of controuling opinions has never yet been claimed; yet it is manifest that the same construction, which warrants a controul in matters of fact, does the same as to matters of opinion. In addition to this, it ought to be remarked, that the difficulty of distinguishing in many cases between fact and opinion, is extremely great, and that no kind of criterion is furnished by the law under consideration. Of this more, perhaps will be said hereafter.

Again, if the congressional construction be right, if the freedom of the press consists in the full enjoyment of the privilege of printing facts that are true, it will be fair to read the amendment, without the words really used, after substituting those said by Congress to have the same import. The clause will then stand thus: "Congress shall make no law abridging the right of the press, to publish facts that are true!" If this was the real meaning of Congress, and the several States, when they spoke in the state constitutions, and in the amendment of the "freedom of the press," the very great solicitude on this subject displayed throughout the continent, was most irrational and absurd. . . .

This venerable and enlightened assembly had too much wisdom to avow a meaning, so totally incompatible with the real object of their wishes. They knew that there never was a government in the world, however despotic, that dared to avow a design to suppress the truth: they knew that the most corrupt and profligate administrations, that ever brought wretchedness and oppression on a happy and free people, speak in their public acts the language of patriotism and virtue only, and that, although their real object is to stop enquiry, and to terrify truth into silence, the vengeance of the law *appears* to be directed against falsehood and malice only: in fact, they knew, that there are many truths, important to society, which are not susceptible of that full, direct, and positive evidence, which alone can be exhibited before a court and jury:

That men might be, and often would be deterred from speaking truths, which they could prove, unless they were absolutely protected from the trouble, disgrace, losses, and expense of a prosecution.

That in the violence of party spirit which government knows too well how to produce, and to inflame evidence the most conclusive, might be rejected, and that juries might be packed, "who would find Abel guilty of the murder of Cain."

That nothing tends more to irritate the minds of men, and disturb the peace of society, than prosecutions of a political nature, which like prosecutions in religion, increase the evils, they were, perhaps, intended to remove.

They knew that the licentiousness of the press, though an evil, was a less evil than that resulting from any law to restrain it, upon the same principle, that the most enlightened part of the world is at length convinced, that the evils arising from the toleration of heresy and atheism, are less, infinitely less, than the evils of persecution.

That the spirit of inquiry and discussion, was of the utmost importance in every free country, and could be preserved only by giving it absolute protection, even in its excesses.

That truth was always equal to the task of combating falsehood without the aid of government; because in most instances it has defeated falsehood, backed by all the power of government.

That truth cannot be impressed upon the human mind by power, with which therefore, it disdains an alliance, but by reason and evidence only. . . .

Prior Restraint

But, it has been said, that the freedom of the press, consists not in the privilege of printing truth; but in an exemption from previous restraint, and as the Sedition Bill imposes no previous restraint, it does not abridge the freedom of the press. This *profound* remark is borrowed from [William] Blackstone and [Jean Louis] De Lolme, and is gravely repeated, by those who are weak enough to take opinions upon trust.

If these writers meant to state what the law was understood to be in England, they are correct. Even if they meant to state what the law ought to be in England, perhaps they are still correct; because it is extremely probable, that a press absolutely free, would in the short course of one year "humble in the dust and ashes" the "stupendous fabric" of the British government. But this definition does not deserve to be transplanted into America. In Britain, a legislative controul over the press, is, perhaps essential to the preservation of the "present order of

things;" but it does not follow, that such controul is essential here. In Britain, a vast standing army is necessary to keep the people in peace, and the monarch on his throne; but it does not follow that the tranquillity of America, or the personal safety of the President, would be promoted by a similar institution.

A single remark will be sufficient to expose the extreme fallacy of the idea, when applied to the Constitution of the United States. If the freedom of the press consists in an exemption from previous restraint, Congress may, without injury to the freedom of the press, punish with death, any thing *actually* published, which a political inquisition may choose to condemn.

But on what ground is this British doctrine respecting the freedom of the press introduced here? In Britain, the parliament is acknowledged to be omnipotent. . . . In Britain there is no constitution, no limitation of legislative power; but in America, there is a constitution, the power of the legislature is limited, and the object of one limitation is to secure the freedom of the press.

Common Law and the Press

If this doctrine is avowed here, under the idea that the common law of England is in force in the United States, even this idea will be of no avail. The common law knows nothing of printing or the liberty of the press. The art of printing was not discovered, until towards the close of the 14th century. It was at first in England a subject of star-chamber jurisdiction, and afterwards put under a licencer by statute. This statute expired just before the commencement of the present century.

Before this event, the rights of the press, were at the mercy of a single individual. There can be no common law, no immemorial usage or custom concerning a thing of so modern a date.

The freedom of the press, therefore, means the total exemption of the press from any kind of legislative controul, and consequently the Sedition Bill, which is an act of legislative controul, is an abridgment of its liberty, and expressly forbidden by the constitution. Which was to be demonstrated.

VIEWPOINT 20B

The Sedition Act Does Not Violate the Bill of Rights (1799)

5th Congress Majority Report

Congress passed the Sedition Act in 1798, which made it a crime for anyone to "print, utter, or publish . . . any false, scandalous, and malicious writing"

From the Majority and Minority Reports on the Repeal of the Sedition Act, *Annals of Congress*, 5th Cong., 3rd sess. (February 25, 1799).

against the government. The Federalist politicians who made and enforced the law interpreted "malicious writing" to include criticism of the Federalist Party and its programs, including their support of war with France. Under the law several prominent newspaper editors who had questioned the policies and motives of Federalists were jailed, as was Congressman Matthew Lyon, who spent four months in prison for publishing a sharp attack on President John Adams. The law was denounced by many who argued that it violated the Bill of Rights prohibition against laws "abridging freedom of speech or of the press."

In 1799 the House of Representatives, then still under Federalist control, debated the constitutionality of the Sedition Act. Members did not agree, resulting in two reports; the following viewpoint is taken from the Majority Report of the Congress. The report defends the Sedition Acts, arguing that while Congress has no power to engage in prior restraint of newspapers and speeches, it is entitled to pass laws punishing false and seditious writing. The primary author of the majority report was Chauncey Goodrich of Connecticut.

The largely negative public reaction to the Sedition Act was in part responsible for the victory of Thomas Jefferson over John Adams in the 1800 presidential election. Jefferson pardoned the people convicted under the act, and allowed it to expire in 1801. The question of its constitutionality never reached the Supreme Court.

Why was it necessary for Congress to pass the Sedition Act, according to the report? How do the members of Congress respond to arguments that the act violates the Bill of Rights?

The "Act in addition to an act entitled an act for the punishment of certain crimes against the United States," commonly called the sedition act, contains provisions of a twofold nature: first, against seditious acts, and, second, against libellous and seditious writings. The first have never been complained of, nor has any objection been made to its validity. The objection applies solely to the second; and on the ground, in the first place, that Congress have no power by the Constitution to pass any act for punishing libels, no such power being expressly given, and all powers not given to Congress, being reserved to the States respectively, or the people thereof.

To this objection it is answered, that a law to punish false, scandalous, and malicious writings against the Government, with intent to stir up sedition, is a law necessary for carrying into effect the power vested by the Constitution in the Government of the United States, and in the departments and officers

thereof, and, consequently, such a law as Congress may pass; because the direct tendency of such writings is to obstruct the acts of the Government by exciting opposition to them, to endanger its existence by rendering it odious and contemptible in the eyes of the people, and to produce seditious combinations against the laws, the power to punish which has never been questioned; because it would be manifestly absurd to suppose that a Government might punish sedition, and yet be void of power to prevent it by punishing those acts which plainly and necessarily lead to it; and, because, under the general power to make all laws proper and necessary for carrying into effect the powers vested by the Constitution in the Government of the United States, Congress has passed many laws for which no express provision can be found in the Constitution, and the constitutionality of which has never been questioned. . . .

It is objected to this act, in the second place, that it is expressly contrary to that part of the Constitution which declares, that "Congress shall make no law respecting an establishment of religion, or prohibiting the free exercise thereof, or abridging the liberty of the press." The act in question is said to be an "abridgment of the liberty of the press," and therefore unconstitutional.

What True Liberty Consists Of

To this it is answered, in the first place, that the liberty of the press consists not in a license for every man to publish what he pleases without being liable to punishment, if he should abuse this license to the injury of others, but in a permission to publish, without previous restraint, whatever he may think proper, being answerable to the public and individuals, for any abuse of this permission to their prejudice. In like manner, as the liberty of speech does not authorize a man to speak malicious slanders against his neighbor, nor the liberty of action justify him in going, by violence, into another man's house, or in assaulting any person whom he may meet in the streets. In the several States the liberty of the press has always been understood in this manner, and no other; and the Constitution of every State which has been framed and adopted since the Declaration of Independence, asserts "the liberty of the press;" while in several, if not all, their laws provide for the punishment of libellous publications, which would be a manifest absurdity and contradiction, if the liberty of the press meant to publish any and everything, without being amenable to the laws for the abuse of this license. According to this just, legal, and universally admitted definition of "the liberty of the press," a law to restrain its licentiousness, in publishing false, scandalous, and malicious libels against the Government, cannot be considered as "an abridgment" of its "liberty."

It is answered, in the second place, that the liberty of the press did never extend, according to the laws of any State, or of the United States, or of England, from whence our laws are derived, to the publication of false, scandalous, and malicious writings against the Government, written or published with intent to do mischief, such publications being unlawful, and punishable in every State; from whence it follows, undeniably, that a law to punish seditious and malicious publications, is not an abridgment of the liberty of the press, for it would be a manifest absurdity to say, that a man's liberty was abridged by punishing him for doing that which he never had a liberty to do.

———— • ————

"The liberty of the press consists not in a license for every man to publish what he pleases without being liable to punishment, if he should abuse this license to the injury of others."

———— • ————

It is answered, thirdly, that the act in question cannot be unconstitutional, because it makes nothing penal that was not penal before, and gives no new powers to the court, but is merely declaratory of the common law, and useful for rendering that law more generally known, and more easily understood. This cannot be denied, if it be admitted, as it must be, that false, scandalous, and malicious libels against the Government of the country, published with intent to do mischief, are punishable by the common law; for, by the 2d section of the 3d article of the Constitution, the judicial power of the United States is expressly extended to all offences arising under the Constitution. By the Constitution, the Government of the United States is established, for many important objects, as the Government of the country; and libels against that Government, therefore, are offences arising under the Constitution, and, consequently, are punishable at common law by the courts of the United States. The act, indeed, is so far from having extended the law and the power of the court, that it has abridged both, and has enlarged instead of abridging the liberty of the press; for, at common law, libels against the Government might be punished

with fine and imprisonment at the discretion of the court, whereas the act limits the fine to two thousand dollars, and the imprisonment to two years; and it also allows the party accused to give the truth in evidence for his justification, which, by the common law, was expressly forbidden.

And, lastly, it is answered, that had the Constitution intended to prohibit Congress from legislating at all on the subject of the press, which is the construction whereon the objections to this law are founded, it would have used the same expressions as in that part of the clause which relates to religion and religious texts; whereas, the words are wholly different: "Congress," says the Constitution, (amendment 3d.) "shall make no law respecting an establishment of religion, or prohibiting the free exercise thereof, or abridging the freedom of speech of the press." Here it is manifest that the Constitution intended to prohibit Congress from legislating at all on the subject of religious establishments, and the prohibition is made in the most express terms. Had the same intention prevailed respecting the press, the same expressions would have been used, and Congress would have been "prohibited from passing any law respecting the press." They are not, however, "prohibited" from legislating at all on the subject, but merely from abridging the liberty of the press. It is evident they may legislate respecting the press, may pass laws for its regulation, and to punish those who pervert it into an engine of mischief, provided those laws do not abridge its liberty. Its liberty, according to the well known and universally admitted definition, consists in permission to publish, without previous restraint upon the press, but subject to punishment afterwards for improper publications. A law, therefore, to impose previous restraint upon the press, and not one to inflict punishment on wicked and malicious publications, would be a law to abridge the liberty of the press, and, as such, unconstitutional.

For Further Reading

James E. Leahy, *The First Amendment, 1791–1991*. Jefferson, NC: McFarland and Company, 1991.

Leonard Levy, *Legacy of Suppression: Freedom of Speech and Press in Early American History*. Cambridge, MA: Belknap Press of Harvard University Press, 1960.

John C. Miller, *Crisis in Freedom*. Boston: Little, Brown, 1951.

James Morton Smith, *Freedom's Fetters*. Ithaca, NY: Cornell University Press, 1956.

PART III:
ANTEBELLUM AMERICA,
1803–1855

~•~

**The Growth of America
and Its Government**

**Social Issues of
the Antebellum Era**

**Manifest Destiny
and War**

1800

•November　John Adams becomes first president to occupy the White House

1802

•October　Spain suspends right of Americans to deposit goods at New Orleans; two weeks later, transfers control of city and all Louisiana to France

1804

•July　Aaron Burr kills Alexander Hamilton in duel

•December 5 Jefferson reelected president

1808

•December 7 James Madison elected president

1811

•November　Battle of Tippecanoe breaks military strength of Tecumseh-led Indian alliance

1812

•June　Congress votes for war with England

•December 2　Madison reelected president

1817

•April　U.S. and England negotiate Rush-Bagot Agreement calling for mutual naval disarmament on the Great Lakes

•April 30 Louisiana enters Union

•July 4 Construction of Erie Canal begins

1818

•December 3 Illinois enters Union

1819

•February 22　U.S. acquires Florida from Spain

•March 6　Supreme Court upholds constitutionality of a national bank

•December 14　Alabama enters Union

1820

•March 15　Missouri Compromise: Missouri enters Union as slave state, Maine as free state, and line is drawn dividing remaining Louisiana territory into free and slave regions

•December 6　Monroe reelected president

1800	1805	1810	1815	1820

1807

•August 17　Successful debut of Robert Fulton's steamboat

•December　Congress passes Embargo Act, suspending all American trade

1803

•February 24　Supreme Court declares a federal law unconstitutional in *Marbury v. Madison*

•March 1　Ohio enters Union

•April　U.S. buys Louisiana Territory from France for $15 million

•May　War resumes between England and France

•May 14　Lewis and Clark expedition begins

1801

•January 20　Adams appoints John Marshall chief justice of Supreme Court

•March 4　Thomas Jefferson inaugurated as president

1816

•April 10　Second National Bank incorporated by act of Congress

•December 4 James Monroe elected president

•December 11 Indiana enters Union

1815

•January 8　Battle of New Orleans makes hero of Gen. Andrew Jackson

1814

•August 24　British troops occupy Washington, D.C.

•September 13　Francis Scott Key writes "Star-Spangled Banner"

•December　Hartford Convention of New England states meets to discuss opposition to war

•December 24　Treaty of Ghent signed between Great Britain and U.S.

1823

•December 2 Monroe Doctrine: Western Hemisphere declared off-limits to European colonization

1825
- March 4   John Quincy Adams inaugurated president after electoral vote throws decision to House of Representatives; opponents decry "corrupt bargain" with Henry Clay
- October 26   Erie Canal opens

1830
- April 6   Mormon Church organized by Joseph Smith
- May 28   Indian Removal Act signed by President Jackson
- December   *Moral Physiology*, first American book on birth control, published

1832
- April 6   Black Hawk War begins in Illinois
- July 10   President Jackson vetoes bill to recharter Second National Bank
- November   South Carolina convention declares federal tariffs of 1828 and 1832 "null, void, and no law"
- December 5   Jackson reelected president
- December 10   Jackson issues proclamation against state nullification of federal laws

1834
- Formation of Whig Party

1841
- First university degrees granted to women in U.S.
- April 4   Harrison becomes first president to die in office; Vice President John Tyler becomes president

1840
- December 2   William Henry Harrison elected president

1846
- May 13   Congress declares war on Mexico
- August 8   Wilmot Proviso introduced in Congress
- September 10   Elias Howe patents sewing machine
- December 28   Iowa enters Union

1847
- September 14   American forces seize Mexico City

1849
- California seeks admission to Union as free state

1825   1830   1835   1840   1845   1850

1828
- December 3   Andrew Jackson elected president

1831
- January 1   First issue of abolitionist newspaper *The Liberator* published
- August 22   Nat Turner slave rebellion
- December   Choctaw Indians begin forced migration from Mississippi

1836
- March 2   Texas declares itself an independent republic
- June 15   Arkansas enters Union
- December 7   Martin Van Buren elected president

1837
- Financial panic leads to economic depression
- January 26   Michigan enters Union
- November   Abolitionist printer Elijah Lovejoy murdered in Alton, Illinois

1838
- December   Remaining Cherokee Indians in Georgia forcibly removed and herded to Oklahoma by U.S. troops

1844
- May 24   First telegraph message sent
- June 27   Mob kills Mormon leader Joseph Smith in Carthage, Illinois
- December 4   James K. Polk elected president

1845
- March 1   Texas annexed to U.S. by joint resolution of Congress
- March 3   Florida enters Union
- December 29   Texas enters Union

1848
- January 24   Gold found in California
- February 2   Treaty ends Mexican War; U.S. gains California and New Mexico territories from Mexico
- May 29   Wisconsin enters Union
- July 19   First women's rights conference held at Seneca Falls, New York
- August 9   Free-Soil Party born
- November 7   Zachary Taylor elected president

PART III:
ANTEBELLUM AMERICA, 1803–1855

The first half of the nineteenth century was a time of tremendous growth and ferment for the United States of America. Through purchase, diplomacy, annexation, and war, the United States attained most of its present territorial dimensions. Fifteen states entered the Union between 1800 and 1850. During that time the nation's population grew from about 5 million to 23 million. Both agricultural and manufacturing production soared to unprecedented levels. The telegraph, newspaper, and railroad all helped knit the country together. The era was marked by national debates over expansion, democracy, and social reform as Americans reacted to the transformation of their country into a nation far different from the one that existed when the Constitution was written in 1787.

The Jeffersonian Era

Thomas Jefferson, Andrew Jackson, and James K. Polk were arguably the three most influential presidents in the years 1800–1850. All three were committed, with different degrees of emphasis, to democratic values and the expansion of the United States.

The first years of the nineteenth century are commonly known as the Jeffersonian era after the author of the Declaration of Independence, who defeated John Adams in the 1800 presidential election. Never again would the Federalists win the presidency. As if to symbolize the party's declining fortunes, the architect of the Federalist economic program, Alexander Hamilton, was killed in a duel in 1804.

However, the Federalists' loss of power did not necessarily result in the reversal of their policies. In part this was because Jefferson the president and politician proved to be more flexible and open to Federalist policies than Jefferson the political theorist. Jefferson's vision for the future of America was focused on a nation of small independent farmers who would be largely self-sufficient and in little need of government. In that context, Jefferson had attacked Hamilton's call for the federal government to fully fund the national debt and establish a national bank. As president, however, he kept much of the broad outline of Hamilton's economic programs in place. Prior to assuming the presidency Jefferson had advocated the doctrine of states' rights and a "strict" reading of the Constitution in which the federal government had only the powers expressly given to it. However, in 1803, as president, Jefferson approved purchasing the Louisiana Territory from France even though the Constitution did not specifically give the federal government the power to buy territory—a decision that helped expand the powers of the national government at the expense of the doctrine of states' rights. (The Louisiana Purchase, by doubling the nation's size and setting the nation on the course of westward expansion, was momentous in several respects.) Jefferson's successors as president also adopted as their own some key Federalist programs, including tariff protection for beginning industries, federal support for internal improvements such as roads, and the reestablishment of a national bank.

Another important reason for the continuing influence of the Federalist Party, despite its failure to elect presidents and congressional majorities, was its hold on America's judicial branch of government through the lifetime judicial appointments made by Presidents George Washington and John Adams. Of special significance was Adams appointee John Marshall, chief justice of the Supreme Court from 1801 to 1835. The Supreme Court under Marshall's leadership issued several significant opinions that established the right of the Supreme Court to disallow federal or state laws as unconstitutional. In several other opinions, notably in *McCulloch v. Maryland*, the Supreme Court under Marshall supported the supremacy of the federal government over the states as well as other important Federalist Party principles, raising charges of "judicial tyranny" from Jefferson and others who argued, to no avail, that Marshall was changing the Constitution without following the amending process.

The War of 1812

Jefferson's administration, like those that preceded and followed it, was buffeted by European wars. In 1803 war broke out between Great Britain and France. Both nations began seizing American merchant ships destined for their opponents, and Great Britain renewed its practice of impressment—seizing American seamen and forcing them to join the British navy. Presidents Thomas Jefferson and James Madison attempted to assert neutral trading rights without resorting to war by imposing economic embargoes that restricted trade between the United States and the warring nations, but these policies seemed to hurt American traders, shipbuilders, and farmers more than the intended targets of Great Britain and France. U.S.-British relations were also marred by the belief of many Americans that the British in Canada were conspiring with American Indians in the Ohio Valley and elsewhere.

In 1812 Congress declared war on Great Britain. Supporters of the war envisioned an easy invasion and conquest of Canada, but such notions were quickly dispelled as early defeats revealed serious weaknesses in American army and naval forces. The British in turn invaded the American capital of Washington, D.C., and burned much of the city, including the president's mansion. In response, the Americans mustered popular support and gained military victories more in defending their homeland than in invading Canada. The country also found a new hero in General Andrew Jackson, who led American forces to a spectacular victory over a British invading force in New Orleans in 1815.

The Treaty of Ghent agreed to by the two nations late in 1814 (shortly before Jackson's New Orleans triumph) resolved none of the trade and impressment issues that were the ostensible reason for the war. However, the War of 1812 had several important effects on the United States. It brought about the final demise of the Federalist Party, many of whose members, consistent with Federalist pro-British leanings, had opposed the war. It signaled the end of significant Native American resistance to white settlement in lands east of the Mississippi River. It laid foundations for an enduring peaceful relationship with Canada. Finally, it created a new feeling of nationalism among Americans, who emerged from the war more united than when they entered it.

American Society Is Transformed

In the decades following the War of 1812 the United States was the site of numerous important economic developments and social controversies. Agricultural production grew significantly. In the South, Eli Whitney's invention of the cotton gin enabled cotton to replace tobacco and rice as the region's leading cash crop—and further entrench the plantation/slavery system of agriculture. Cotton became America's leading export, accounting for about half of America's exports to Great Britain between 1820 and 1860. In the Midwest, Cyrus McCormick's invention of the mechanical reaper helped establish wheat as an important cash crop, with farmers expanding their holdings to sell surplus wheat both to the eastern United States and abroad.

The change in American farms from self-sufficiency to growing cash crops for export was facilitated by a "transportation revolution"—the improvement of roads, the development of steamboats, and the building of canals and railroads. The steamboat, successfully demonstrated by American inventor Robert Fulton in 1807, made two-way river transportation feasible. The Erie Canal, opened in 1825, connected the Hudson River to Lake Erie. Its successful operation greatly reduced shipping costs and sparked a frenzy of canal construction; by 1840 three thousand miles of canals were built. The canal was then supplemented, and in some cases superseded, by the railroad. From a few experimental developments in the 1820s, railroads spread rapidly; by 1850 more than nine thousand miles of track had been laid. The new transportation infrastructure made the movement of people and freight within the nation's interior relatively efficient and helped bind the frontier to the rest of the nation. Railroads made it possible for westward migration to be an individual or family affair, rather than a community wagon-train endeavor.

Cities and Manufacturing

The transportation revolution not only helped people move west but also contributed to the growth of cities in America. Established cities grew in population: New York City, for instance, grew from 124,000 in 1820 to 800,000 in 1860. The number of incorporated towns with populations between 2,500 and 10,000 grew from 56 in 1820 to more than 350 in 1850. The population of America living in towns of 2,500 or more rose from 6.1 percent in 1820 to nearly 20 percent in 1860.

Many of the city residents were immigrants. In the 1840s 1.5 million Europeans moved to America, and 2.5 million did so the following decade. The majority of immigrants came from Ireland and Germany and settled in the North and West. Some Americans reacted to this new wave of immigrants by organizing a large nativist movement to combat the "alien menace" that they believed created slums, stole jobs, and corrupted politics.

Urbanization was also boosted by the rise of manufacturing, which evolved from the household or "cottage" industries of colonial times to larger factories using unskilled workers and power-driven machinery. Manufacturing, like agriculture, was helped by key technological advances, such as Charles Goodyear's invention of vulcanized rubber and Isaac Singer's improvements on the sewing machine. Manufacturing was concentrated in the Northeast, which had more than half of America's manufacturing establishments and more than two-thirds of America's mill and factory workers. The emergence of industrial workers as a new class was another important social development of the period, as was the fact that many of the workers were women. During the 1830s many workers took steps toward organizing in unions and even striking for better working conditions, but the nascent labor movement was set back by the economic depression of 1837 (despite a favorable 1841 ruling by the Massachusetts supreme court in *Commonwealth v. Hunt* that labor unions were not illegal conspiracies).

Andrew Jackson was the leading political figure for much of the 1820s and

1830s, when much of this economic and social transformation was taking place. Jackson lost a controversial presidential election in 1824, despite receiving the most votes of the four candidates; won the next two presidential elections; and handpicked his successor.

Jackson set several important precedents just by being elected. All previous U.S. presidents were from either Massachusetts or Virginia. Jackson was from Tennessee, a frontier state. Past presidents also had significant records of government service. Jackson's main achievements to this time were from military exploits in the War of 1812 and against American Indians. Previous presidents had been born into and were elected by America's social and economic elite. Jackson, although wealthy when he became president, was born and had grown up in poverty and portrayed himself as a self-made man of the people and opponent of elitism. Jackson attained and cultivated an unprecedented popularity with the "common man" at a time when states were revising or repealing property qualification laws to make universal suffrage for white males (but not blacks, women, or Native Americans) the rule.

President Jackson replaced many government employees with his own political supporters (on the theory that just about anyone could do the government's business). He responded to South Carolina's efforts to nullify federal tariff laws within state borders by proclaiming nullification treason and threatening to use the federal military to enforce federal law. He increased efforts to relocate American Indians across the Mississippi River. Perhaps most famously, he vetoed the charter for and effectively closed the Second Bank of the United States. These actions, coupled with Jackson's contentious personality, helped revive the two-party system that had been dormant since the demise of the Federalists. Jackson's supporters created what became known as the Democratic Party (heirs to Jefferson's Democratic Republicans, but re-created in Jackson's image). The Democrats generally espoused a minimal role for the federal government and were especially against government-granted monopolies, charters, and tariffs that they believed favored the rich at the expense of the poor. Opponents to "King Andrew" created the Whig Party in the 1830s, a diverse organization united mainly by opposition to Jackson. Henry Clay and Daniel Webster, two leading Whigs, maintained that the national government could help the economy through a national banking system, a protective tariff, and expenditures for internal improvements.

Reform Ferment

Many Americans in the 1830s and 1840s devoted their energies to various social reforms, both within and outside party politics. Some reformers were inspired by the wave of evangelical revival that swept much of the nation in the 1820s and 1830s. Among the various goals of those seeking reform were free public schools, temperance with alcohol, better treatment of the mentally ill, the preaching of Christianity in foreign lands, and prison reform. Some idealists withdrew from American society to create utopian communities.

Women were very active in many of the reform efforts and often took a leading role in moral reform societies and other public movements. The position of women in the American republic was itself debated. Early feminists, including Frances Wright and Margaret Fuller, wrote and lectured to public audiences on women's need for marriage and divorce rights, legal equality, and equal education. In 1848 the first women's rights meeting was held in Seneca, New York, passing, among other resolutions, the demand for the right to vote.

Women and men were both involved in perhaps the most controversial social reform issue of the period: the abolition of slavery. By the 1820s most northern states had abolished the institution, and antislavery activists sought its gradual repeal in the remaining states by appealing to the consciences of slaveholders. In the 1830s a new militant abolitionist movement harshly criticized slavery in speeches and articles, calling for its immediate abolition. Leaders of the abolitionist movement were often threatened and attacked by mobs in the North, but the movement still attracted thousands of supporters, including free blacks and escaped slaves. In the South, many whites blamed Nat Turner's 1831 slave rebellion in Virginia on William Garrison's antislavery writings. They successfully persuaded the federal post office to destroy and/or refuse to deliver any abolitionist literature within the South. Slavery remained firmly entrenched. Although Congress had outlawed the importation of slaves in 1808, the slave population in the United States grew from 1.2 million in 1810 to around 4 million in 1860.

Polk and the Expansionists

The issue of slavery was firmly intertwined with another important American development—expansion. Politicians from Thomas Jefferson onward had envisioned the expansion of the United States of America to include most of the North American continent. Expansion became a national controversy after 1835 when American settlers in the Mexican province of Texas successfully fought for independence and later sought admission to the Union. After intensive congressional debate, in which Whig/Democratic divisions were overshadowed by North/South ones, America annexed Texas in 1845, worsening relations with Mexico. James K. Polk, who won the 1844 presidential election over Henry Clay in a contest in which expansion was the leading issue, coveted more Mexican territories. Mindful of trade opportunities in Asia, he especially wanted California, with its harbors on the Pacific Ocean.

Polk's aggressive diplomacy with Mexico in quest of the territories, combined with long-standing tensions between the two nations dating almost from Mexico's independence from Spain in 1821, resulted in war with Mexico in 1846. The United States won spectacular military victories, and in 1848 Mexico agreed to cede the territories Polk had sought. Shortly thereafter news of gold discoveries in California inspired thousands of Americans to journey to that territory—a circumstance that to many Americans confirmed their self-image as a nation of special destiny.

The acquisition of new territories, however, intensified the slavery controversy within the United States. In August 1846 Pennsylvania congressman David Wilmot introduced a provision prohibiting slavery in any newly acquired territory. The Wilmot Proviso was passed in the House but defeated in the Senate and was later unsuccessfully attached to many subsequent bills. It gained the support of many Northerners, including some who did not support the abolitionist movement. The debate over whether the new territories should be slave or free divided the nation in the 1850s and ultimately led to Southern secession and the Civil War.

The Growth of America and Its Government

VIEWPOINT 21A

The Louisiana Purchase Should Be Approved (1803)

Thomas Jefferson (1743–1826)

Perhaps the most significant decision Thomas Jefferson made as U.S. president was the Louisiana Purchase, in which America doubled its size by acquiring from France millions of acres of territory extending from the Mississippi River to the Rocky Mountains. When Jefferson was elected president in 1800, he had pledged to trim government expenses and debt and to adhere strictly to limits of power expressed in the Constitution. The Louisiana Purchase seemed to break these campaign promises: The $15 million price tag wiped out all the progress Jefferson had made in reducing the national debt, and the Constitution did not explicitly give the government authority to purchase new territory or incorporate it into the Union.

Jefferson had originally sent ministers to France with congressional authority and approval to purchase the city of New Orleans or otherwise secure a southern port for the goods of America's western farmers, a long-sought goal of the new nation that had been threatened, Jefferson believed, by France's acquisition of the Louisiana Territory from Spain in 1800. When the ministers arrived in France, however, French ruler Napoléon Bonaparte unexpectedly offered to sell all of the Louisiana Territory to the United States. Afraid that Napoleon might change his mind before a new constitutional amendment allowing such an acquisition could be ratified, Jefferson agreed to the purchase in April 1803.

The following viewpoint consists of two parts. The first is from a letter Jefferson wrote in August 1803 to John Breckinridge, a close friend and political associate. (Jefferson later asked Breckinridge to keep the contents of this letter secret.) Jefferson writes about the purchase and the objections raised by Federalist opponents, as well as his own constitutional concerns. The second part is taken from Jefferson's Third Annual Message to Congress, in which he urges approval and ratification of the Louisiana Purchase.

What differences in opinion over the constitutional legality of the Louisiana Purchase exist, if any,

From *Memoirs, Correspondence, and Private Papers of Thomas Jefferson*, edited by Thomas Jefferson Randolph (Charlottesville, VA, 1829) and *The Writings of Thomas Jefferson*, vol. 3, edited by Albert Bergh (Washington, DC: Thomas Jefferson Memorial Society, 1905).

between the private letter and public message of Jefferson? What arguments against the Louisiana Purchase does Jefferson recite? How does he answer them?

I

The enclosed letter . . . gives me occasion to write a word to you on the subject of Louisiana, which, being a new one, an interchange of sentiments may produce correct ideas before we are to act on them.

Our information as to the country is very incomplete. We have taken measures to obtain it in full as to the settled part, which I hope to receive in time for Congress. The boundaries, which I deem not admitting question, are the highlands on the western side of the Mississippi enclosing all its waters, the Missouri, of course, and terminating in the line drawn from the northwestern point of the Lake of the Woods to the nearest source of the Mississippi, as lately settled between Great Britain and the United States. We have some claims to extend on the seacoast westwardly to the Rio Norte or Bravo [Rio Grande], and, better, to go eastwardly to the Rio Perdido, between Mobile and Pensacola, the ancient boundary of Louisiana. These claims will be a subject of negotiation with Spain and if, as soon as she is at war, we push them strongly with one hand, holding out a price in the other, we shall certainly obtain the Floridas, and all in good time.

In the meanwhile, without waiting for permission, we shall enter into the exercise of the natural right we have always insisted on with Spain, to wit, that of a nation holding the upper part of streams having a right of innocent passage through them to the ocean. We shall prepare her to see us practise on this, and she will not oppose it by force.

Federalist Objections

Objections are raising to the eastward [in New England] against the vast extent of our boundaries, and propositions are made to exchange Louisiana, or a part of it, for the Floridas. But, as I have said, we shall get the Floridas without, and I would not give one inch of the waters of the Mississippi to any nation because I see, in a light very important to our peace, the exclusive right to its navigation, and the admission of no nation into it, but as into the Potomac or Delaware, with our consent and under our police.

These Federalists see in this acquisition the formation of a new confederacy, embracing all the waters of the Mississippi on both sides of it, and a separation of its eastern waters from us. These combinations depend on so many circumstances which we cannot foresee that I place little reliance on them. We have seldom seen neighborhood produce affection among nations. The reverse is almost the universal truth. Besides, if it should become the great interest of those nations to separate from this, if their happiness should depend on it so strongly as to induce them to go through that convulsion, why should the Atlantic states dread it? But, especially, why should we, their present inhabitants, take side in such a question?

———— • ————

"The fertility of the country, its climate and extent, promise in due season important aids to our treasury, an ample provision for our posterity, and a widespread field for the blessings of freedom and equal laws."

———— • ————

When I view the Atlantic states, procuring for those on the eastern waters of the Mississippi friendly instead of hostile neighbors on its western waters, I do not view it as an Englishman would the procuring future blessings for the French nation, with whom he has no relations of blood or affection. The future inhabitants of the Atlantic and Mississippi states will be our sons. We leave them in distinct but bordering establishments. We think we see their happiness in their union, and we wish it. Events may prove it otherwise; and if they see their interest in separation, why should we take side with our Atlantic rather than our Mississippi descendants? It is the elder and the younger son differing. God bless them both and keep them in union if it be for their good, but separate them if it be better.

The inhabited part of Louisiana, from Point Coupée to the sea, will of course be immediately a territorial government and soon a state. But, above that, the best use we can make of the country for some time will be to give establishments in it to the Indians on the east side of the Mississippi in exchange for their present country, and open land offices in the last, and thus make this acquisition the means of filling up the eastern side instead of drawing off its population. When we shall be full on this side, we may lay off a range of states on the western bank from the head to the mouth, and so, range after range, advancing compactly as we multiply.

Congress and the Constitution

This treaty must, of course, be laid before both houses, because both have important functions to exercise respecting it. They, I presume, will see their duty to their country in ratifying and paying for it so

as to secure a good which would otherwise probably be never again in their power. But I suppose they must then appeal to the nation for an additional article to the Constitution, approving and confirming an act which the nation had not previously authorized. The Constitution has made no provision for our holding foreign territory, still less for incorporating foreign nations into our Union. The executive, in seizing the fugitive occurrence which so much advances the good of their country, have done an act beyond the Constitution. The legislature in casting behind them metaphysical subtleties, and risking themselves like faithful servants, must ratify and pay for it and throw themselves on their country for doing for them unauthorized what we know they would have done for themselves had they been in a situation to do it.

It is the case of a guardian investing the money of his ward in purchasing an important adjacent territory, and saying to him when of age, I did this for your good; I pretend to no right to bind you; you may disavow me, and I must get out of the scrape as I can; I thought it my duty to risk myself for you. But we shall not be disavowed by the nation, and their act of indemnity will confirm and not weaken the Constitution by more strongly marking out its lines.

II

To the Senate and House of Representatives of the United States:—

In calling you together, fellow citizens, at an earlier day than was contemplated by the act of the last session of Congress, I have not been insensible to the personal inconveniences necessarily resulting from an unexpected change in your arrangements. But matters of great public concernment have rendered this call necessary, and the interest you feel in these will supersede in your minds all private considerations.

The Importance of New Orleans

Congress witnessed, at their last session, the extraordinary agitation produced in the public mind by the suspension of our right of deposit [of agricultural goods for export] at the port of New Orleans, no assignment of another place having been made according to treaty. They were sensible that the continuance of that privation would be more injurious to our nation than any consequences which could flow from any mode of redress, but reposing just confidence in the good faith of the government whose officer had committed the wrong, friendly and reasonable representations were resorted to, and the right of deposit was restored.

Previous, however, to this period, we had not been unaware of the danger to which our peace would be perpetually exposed while so important a key to the commerce of the western country remained under foreign power. Difficulties, too, were presenting themselves as to the navigation of other streams, which, arising within our territories, pass through those adjacent. Propositions had, therefore, been authorized for obtaining, on fair conditions, the sovereignty of New Orleans, and of other possessions in that quarter interesting to our quiet, to such extent as was deemed practicable; and the provisional appropriation of two millions of dollars, to be applied and accounted for by the president of the United States, intended as part of the price, was considered as conveying the sanction of Congress to the acquisition proposed. The enlightened Government of France saw, with just discernment, the importance to both nations of such liberal arrangements as might best and permanently promote the peace, friendship, and interests of both; and the property and sovereignty of all Louisiana, which had been restored to them, have on certain conditions been transferred to the United States by instruments bearing date the 30th of April last. When these shall have received the constitutional sanction of the senate, they will without delay be communicated to the representatives also, for the exercise of their functions, as to those conditions which are within the powers vested by the constitution in Congress. While the property and sovereignty of the Mississippi and its waters secure an independent outlet for the produce of the western States, and an uncontrolled navigation through their whole course, free from collision with other powers and the dangers to our peace from that source, the fertility of the country, its climate and extent, promise in due season important aids to our treasury, an ample provision for our posterity, and a widespread field for the blessings of freedom and equal laws.

With the wisdom of Congress it will rest to take those ulterior measures which may be necessary for the immediate occupation and temporary government of the country; for its incorporation into our Union; for rendering the change of government a blessing to our newly-adopted brethren; for securing to them the rights of conscience and of property; for confirming to the Indian inhabitants their occupancy and self-government, establishing friendly and commercial relations with them, and for ascertaining the geography of the country acquired. Such materials for your information, relative to its affairs in general, as the short space of time has permitted me to collect, will be laid before you when the subject shall be in a state for your consideration. . . .

Debt and Taxes

Should the acquisition of Louisiana be constitutionally confirmed and carried into effect, a sum of nearly thirteen millions of dollars will then be added to our public debt, most of which is payable after fifteen years; before which term the present existing debts will all be discharged by the established operation of the sinking fund. When we contemplate the ordinary annual augmentation of imposts from increasing population and wealth, the augmentation of the same revenue by its extension to the new acquisition, and the economies which may still be introduced into our public expenditures, I cannot but hope that Congress in reviewing their resources will find means to meet the intermediate interests of this additional debt without recurring to new taxes, and applying to this object only the ordinary progression of our revenue. Its extraordinary increase in times of foreign war will be the proper and sufficient fund for any measures of safety or precaution which that state of things may render necessary in our neutral position.

VIEWPOINT 21B

The Louisiana Purchase Should Be Opposed (1803)

Samuel White (1770–1809)

With the Louisiana Purchase, the United States doubled its territory, acquiring 828,000 square miles from France for a few cents an acre. The treaty with France was ratified in the Senate in October 1803 by an overwhelming margin. Voting against the purchase were a few Federalists, whose opposition was based in part on the worry that such a large territorial expansion and subsequent westward migration would weaken the political influence of the New England states, their political stronghold. Most of their stated arguments focused on the constitutionality of the purchase and whether the nation could, without jeopardizing its unity, readily absorb such a large expansion of territory and people (the French and Spanish-speaking population of New Orleans and the rest of Louisiana were to become American citizens without their asking). A summary of the objections against the Louisiana Purchase can be found in the following viewpoint, excerpted from a Senate speech by Samuel White, a lawyer and senator from Delaware from 1801 to 1809.

How does White believe the addition of territory would harm the United States? Why did France decide to sell its territory at that particular time, according to White? What effect does he say that timing should have had on the negotiations?

From Samuel White's Senate speech of November 2, 1803, in *The Debates and Proceedings in the Congress of the United States, First to Eighteenth Congresses, March 3, 1789, to May 27, 1824, Inclusive* (Washington, DC: Gales & Seaton, 1852).

Admitting then, that His Catholic Majesty [the king of Spain] is hostile to the cession of this territory to the United States, and no honorable gentleman will deny it, what reasons have we to suppose that the French Prefect, provided the Spaniards should interfere, can give to us peaceable possession of the country? He is acknowledged there in no public character, is clothed with no authority, nor has he a single soldier to enforce his orders. I speak now, sir, from mere probabilities. I wish not to be understood as predicting that the French will not cede to us the actual and quiet possession of the territory. I hope to God they may, for possession of it we must have—I mean of New Orleans, and of such other positions on the Mississippi as may be necessary to secure to us forever the complete and uninterrupted navigation of that river. This I have ever been in favor of; I think it essential to the peace of the United States, and to the prosperity of our Western country. But as to Louisiana, this new, immense, unbounded world, if it should ever be incorporated into this Union, which I have no idea can be done but by altering the Constitution, I believe it will be the greatest curse that could at present befall us; it may be productive of innumerable evils, and especially of one that I fear even to look upon. Gentlemen on all sides, with very few exceptions, agree that the settlement of this country will be highly injurious and dangerous to the United States; but as to what has been suggested of removing the Creeks and other nations of Indians from the eastern to the western banks of the Mississippi, and of making the fertile regions of Louisiana a howling wilderness, never to be trodden by the foot of civilized man, it is impracticable. The gentleman from Tennessee (Mr. Cocke) has shown his usual candor on this subject, and I believe with him, to use his strong language, that you had as well pretend to inhibit the fish from swimming in the sea as to prevent the population of that country after its sovereignty shall become ours. To every man acquainted with the adventurous, roving, and enterprising temper of our people, and with the manner in which our Western country has been settled, such an idea must be chimerical. The inducements will be so strong that it will be impossible to restrain our citizens from crossing the river. Louisiana must and will become settled, if we hold it, and with the very population that would otherwise occupy part of our present territory. Thus our citizens will be removed to the immense distance of two or three thousand miles from the capital of the Union, where they will scarcely ever feel the rays of the General Government; their affections will become alienated; they will gradually begin to view us as strangers; they will form other commercial connexions, and our interests will become distinct.

"But as to Louisiana, this new, immense, unbounded world, if it should ever be incorporated into this Union, . . . I believe it will be the greatest curse that could at present befall us."

These, with other causes that human wisdom may not now foresee, will in time effect a separation, and I fear our bounds will be fixed nearer to our houses than the waters of the Mississippi. We have already territory enough, and when I contemplate the evils that may arise to these States, from this intended incorporation of Louisiana into the Union, I would rather see it given to France, to Spain, or to any other nation of the earth, upon the mere condition that no citizen of the United States should ever settle within its limits, than to see the territory sold for an hundred millions of dollars, and we retain the sovereignty. But however dangerous the possession of Louisiana might prove to us, I do not presume to say that the retention of it would not have been very convenient to France, and we know that at the time of the mission of Mr. [James] Monroe, our Administration had never thought of the purchase of Louisiana, and that nothing short of the fullest conviction on the part of the First Consul [Napoléon] that he was on the very eve of a war with England; that this being the most defenceless point of his possessions, if such they could be called, was the one at which the British would first strike, and that it must inevitably fall into their hands, could ever have induced his pride and ambition to make the sale. He judged wisely, that he had better sell it for as much as he could get than lose it entirely. And I do say that under existing circumstances, even supposing that this extent of territory was a desirable acquisition, fifteen millions of dollars was a most enormous sum to give. Our Commissioners were negotiating in Paris—they must have known the relative situation of France and England—they must have known at the moment that a war was unavoidable between the two countries, and they knew the pecuniary necessities of France and the naval power of Great Britain. These imperious circumstances should have been turned to our advantage, and if we were to purchase, should have lessened the consideration. Viewing this subject in any point of light—either as it regards the territory purchased, the high consideration to be given, the contract itself, or any of the circumstances attending it, I see no necessity for precipitating the passage of this bill; and if this motion for postponement should fail, and the question on the final passage of the bill be taken now, I shall certainly vote against it.

For Further Reading

Donald B. Chidsey, *The Louisiana Purchase*. New York: Crown, 1972.

Alexander DeConde, *This Affair of Louisiana*. New York: Scribner, 1976.

Forrest McDonald, *The Presidency of Thomas Jefferson*. Lawrence: University Press of Kansas, 1976.

VIEWPOINT 22A

The Federal Government Is Supreme over the States (1819)

John Marshall (1755–1835)

John Marshall, a Virginia politician and jurist, was appointed by President John Adams to be the nation's fourth chief justice of the Supreme Court in 1801. Over the next thirty-four years he dominated the Supreme Court as no chief justice has done before or since, and shaped it into a branch of the federal government coequal with Congress and the presidency. The Supreme Court under Marshall's tenure laid down broad judicial principles that still guide American constitutional interpretation today. Marshall, a supporter of the Federalist Party (which became extinct during his long term on the Supreme Court), consistently ruled in favor of a strong national government during a period when most presidents and many members of Congress were supportive of states' rights. Among the many landmark Supreme Court opinions penned by Marshall were *Marbury v. Madison* (1803), which ruled a congressional law unconstitutional and established the principle of judicial review; *Fletcher v. Peck* (1810), which stated that the Constitution protects private contracts against state laws and established the Supreme Court's authority to declare state laws unconstitutional; and *McCulloch v. Maryland* (1819), represented in this viewpoint.

The case of *McCulloch v. Maryland* arose when the state of Maryland passed a stiff tax on the operations of the Baltimore branch of the Second Bank of the United States, which had been chartered by Congress in 1816. The bank's cashier in Baltimore, James McCulloch, refused to pay and was sued by the state. In the Supreme Court decision delivered by Marshall on March 7, 1819, and excerpted here, the Court answers two fundamental questions: Did Congress have the constitutional right to charter a bank, and do the states have the right to tax an agency of the national government? Marshall defends the constitutionality of the bank by arguing that the Constitution

McCulloch v. Maryland, 4 Wheaton 316, 1819.

gives Congress broad implied powers—an argument reminiscent of Alexander Hamilton's defense of a national bank in 1791 (see viewpoint 10B). He then rules that the supremacy of federal power over state power established by the Constitution prohibits states to tax or otherwise interfere with the lawful operations of the federal government.

From what source does the Constitution, and the federal government it created, derive its authority, according to Marshall? How does this understanding of federal power affect his ruling? On what basis does Marshall object to Maryland's tax on the bank?

In the case now to be determined, the defendant, a sovereign State, denies the obligation of a law enacted by the legislature of the Union, and the plaintiff, on his part, contests the validity of an act which has been passed by the legislature of that State. The constitution of our country, in its most interesting and vital parts, is to be considered; the conflicting powers of the government of the Union and of its members, as marked in that constitution, are to be discussed; and an opinion given, which may essentially influence the great operations of the government. No tribunal can approach such a question without a deep sense of its importance, and of the awful responsibility involved in its decision. But it must be decided peacefully, or remain a source of hostile legislation, perhaps of hostility of a still more serious nature; and if it is to be so decided, by this tribunal alone can the decision be made. On the Supreme Court of the United States has the constitution of our country devolved this important duty.

The first question made in the cause is, has Congress power to incorporate a bank? . . .

In discussing this question, the counsel for the State of Maryland have deemed it of some importance, in the construction of the constitution, to consider that instrument not as emanating from the people, but as the act of sovereign and independent States. The powers of the general government, it has been said, are delegated by the States, who alone are truly sovereign; and must be exercised in subordination to the States, who alone possess supreme dominion.

It would be difficult to sustain this proposition. The Convention which framed the constitution was indeed elected by the State legislatures. But the instrument, when it came from their hands, was a mere proposal, without obligation, or pretensions to it. It was reported to the then existing Congress of the United States, with a request that it might "be submitted to a Convention of Delegates, chosen in each State by the people thereof, under the recommendation of its Legislature, for their assent and ratification." This mode of proceeding was adopted; and by the Convention, by Congress, and by the State Legislatures, the instrument was submitted to the people. They acted upon it in the only manner in which they can act safely, effectively, and wisely, on such a subject, by assembling in Convention. It is true, they assembled in their several States—and where else should they have assembled? No political dreamer was ever wild enough to think of breaking down the lines which separate the States, and of compounding the American people into one common mass. Of consequence, when they act, they act in their States. But the measures they adopt do not, on that account, cease to be the measures of the people themselves, or become the measures of the State governments.

From these Conventions the constitution derives its whole authority. The government proceeds directly from the people; is "ordained and established" in the name of the people; and is declared to be ordained, "in order to form a more perfect union, establish justice, ensure domestic tranquillity, and secure the blessings of liberty to themselves and to their posterity." The assent of the States, in their sovereign capacity, is implied in calling a Convention, and thus submitting that instrument to the people. But the people were at perfect liberty to accept or reject it; and their act was final. It required not the affirmance, and could not be negatived, by the State governments. The constitution, when thus adopted, was of complete obligation, and bound the State sovereignties.

It has been said, that the people had already surrendered all their powers to the State sovereignties, and had nothing more to give. But, surely, the question whether they may resume and modify the powers granted to government does not remain to be settled in this country. Much more might the legitimacy of the general government be doubted, had it been created by the States. The powers delegated to the State sovereignties were to be exercised by themselves, not by a distinct and independent sovereignty, created by themselves. To the formation of a league, such as was the confederation, the State sovereignties were certainly competent. But when, "in order to form a more perfect union," it was deemed necessary to change this alliance into an effective government, possessing great and sovereign powers, and acting directly on the people, the necessity of referring it to the people, and of deriving its powers directly from them, was felt and acknowledged by all.

The government of the Union, then, (whatever may be the influence of this fact on the case,) is, emphatically, and truly, a government of the people. In form and in substance it emanates from them. Its powers are granted by them, and are to be exercised directly on them, and for their benefit.

This government is acknowledged by all to be one of enumerated powers. The principle, that it can exercise only the powers granted to it, would seem too apparent to have required to be enforced by all those arguments which its enlightened friends, while it was depending before the people, found it necessary to urge. That principle is now universally admitted. But the question respecting the extent of the powers actually granted, is perpetually arising, and will probably continue to arise, as long as our system shall exist.

In discussing these questions, the conflicting powers of the general and State governments must be brought into view, and the supremacy of their respective laws, when they are in opposition, must be settled.

National Government Is Supreme

If any one proposition could command the universal assent of mankind, we might expect it would be this—that the government of the Union, though limited in its powers, is supreme within its sphere of action. This would seem to result necessarily from its nature. It is the government of all; its powers are delegated by all; it represents all, and acts for all. Though any one State may be willing to control its operations, no State is willing to allow others to control them. The nation, on those subjects on which it can act, must necessarily bind its component parts. But this question is not left to mere reason: the people have, in express terms, decided it, by saying, "this constitution, and the laws of the United States, which shall be made in pursuance thereof," "shall be the supreme law of the land," and by requiring that the members of the State legislatures, and the officers of the executive and judicial departments of the States, shall take the oath of fidelity to it.

The government of the United States, then, though limited in its powers, is supreme; and its laws, when made in pursuance of the constitution, form the supreme law of the land, "any thing in the constitution or laws of any State to the contrary notwithstanding."

Among the enumerated powers, we do not find that of establishing a bank or creating a corporation. But there is no phrase in the instrument which, like the articles of confederation, excludes incidental or implied powers; and which requires that every thing granted shall be expressly and minutely described. Even the 10th amendment, which was framed for the purpose of quieting the excessive jealousies which had been excited, omits the word "expressly," and declares only that the powers "not delegated to the United States, nor prohibited to the States, are reserved to the States or to the people;" thus leaving the question, whether the particular power which may become the subject of contest has been delegated to the one government, or prohibited to the other, to depend on a fair construction of the whole instrument. The men who drew and adopted this amendment had experienced the embarrassments resulting from the insertion of this word in the articles of confederation, and probably omitted it to avoid those embarrassments. A constitution, to contain an accurate detail of all the subdivisions of which its great powers will admit, and of all the means by which they may be carried into execution, would partake of the prolixity of a legal code, and could scarcely be embraced by the human mind. It would probably never be understood by the public. Its nature, therefore, requires, that only its great outlines should be marked, its important objects designated, and the minor ingredients which compose those objects be deduced from the nature of the objects themselves. That this idea was entertained by the framers of the American constitution, is not only to be inferred from the nature of the instrument, but from the language. Why else were some of the limitations, found in the ninth section of the 1st article, introduced? It is also, in some degree, warranted by their having omitted to use any restrictive term which might prevent its receiving a fair and just interpretation. In considering this question, then, we must never forget, that it is *a constitution* we are expounding.

Means of Execution

Although, among the enumerated powers of government, we do not find the word "bank" or "incorporation," we find the great powers to lay and collect taxes; to borrow money; to regulate commerce; to declare and conduct a war; and to raise and support armies and navies. The sword and the purse, all the external relations, and no inconsiderable portion of the industry of the nation, are entrusted to its government. It can never be pretended that these vast powers draw after them others of inferior importance, merely because they are inferior. Such an idea can never be advanced. But it may with great reason be contended, that a government, entrusted with such ample powers, on the due execution of which the happiness and prosperity of the nation so vitally depends, must also be entrusted with ample means for their execution. The power being given, it is the interest of the nation to facilitate its execution. It can never be their interest, and cannot be presumed to have been their intention, to clog and embarrass its execution by withholding the most appropriate means. Throughout this vast republic, from the St. Croix to the Gulph of Mexico, from the Atlantic to the Pacific, revenue is to be collected and expended, armies are to be marched and supported. The exi-

gencies of the nation may require that the treasure raised in the north should be transported to the south, *that* raised in the east conveyed to the west, or that this order should be reversed. Is that construction of the constitution to be preferred which would render these operations difficult, hazardous, and expensive? Can we adopt that construction, (unless the words imperiously require it,) which would impute to the framers of that instrument, when granting these powers for the public good, the intention of impeding their exercise by withholding a choice of means? If, indeed, such be the mandate of the constitution, we have only to obey; but that instrument does not profess to enumerate the means by which the powers it confers may be executed; nor does it prohibit the creation of a corporation, if the existence of such a being be essential to the beneficial exercise of those powers. It is, then, the subject of fair inquiry, how far such means may be employed.

It is not denied, that the powers given to the government imply the ordinary means of execution. That, for example, of raising revenue, and applying it to national purposes, is admitted to imply the power of conveying money from place to place, as the exigencies of the nation may require, and of employing the usual means of conveyance. But it is denied that the government has its choice of means; or, that it may employ the most convenient means, if, to employ them, it be necessary to erect a corporation.

On what foundation does this argument rest? On this alone: The power of creating a corporation, is one appertaining to sovereignty, and is not expressly conferred on Congress. This is true. But all legislative powers appertain to sovereignty. The original power of giving the law on any subject whatever, is a sovereign power; and if the government of the Union is restrained from creating a corporation, as a means for performing its functions, on the single reason that the creation of a corporation is an act of sovereignty; if the sufficiency of this reason be acknowledged, there would be some difficulty in sustaining the authority of Congress to pass other laws for the accomplishment of the same objects.

The government which has a right to do an act, and has imposed on it the duty of performing that act, must, according to the dictates of reason, be allowed to select the means; and those who contend that it may not select any appropriate means, that one particular mode of effecting the object is excepted, take upon themselves the burden of establishing that exception. . . .

But the constitution of the United States has not left the right of Congress to employ the necessary means, for the execution of the powers conferred on the government, to general reasoning. To its enumeration of powers is added that of making "all laws which shall be necessary and proper, for carrying into execution the foregoing powers, and all other powers vested by this constitution, in the government of the United States, or in any department thereof.". . .

The result of the most careful and attentive consideration bestowed upon this clause is, that if it does not enlarge, it cannot be construed to restrain the powers of Congress, or to impair the right of the legislature to exercise its best judgment in the selection of measures to carry into execution the constitutional powers of the government. If no other motive for its insertion can be suggested, a sufficient one is found in the desire to remove all doubts respecting the right to legislate on that vast mass of incidental powers which must be involved in the constitution, if that instrument be not a splendid bauble.

We admit, as all must admit, that the powers of the government are limited, and that its limits are not to be transcended. But we think the sound construction of the constitution must allow to the national legislature that discretion, with respect to the means by which the powers it confers are to be carried into execution, which will enable that body to perform the high duties assigned to it, in the manner most beneficial to the people. Let the end be legitimate, let it be within the scope of the constitution, and all means which are appropriate, which are plainly adapted to that end, which are not prohibited, but consist with the letter and spirit of the constitution, are constitutional. . . .

Should Congress; in the execution of its powers, adopt measures which are prohibited by the constitution; or should Congress, under the pretext of executing its powers, pass laws for the accomplishment of objects not entrusted to the government; it would become the painful duty of this tribunal, should a case requiring such a decision come before it, to say that such an act was not the law of the land. But where the law is not prohibited, and is really calculated to effect any of the objects entrusted to the government, to undertake here to inquire into the degree of its necessity, would be to pass the line which circumscribes the judicial department, and to tread on legislative ground. This court disclaims all pretensions to such a power. . . .

Maryland's Tax

It being the opinion of the Court, that the act incorporating the bank is constitutional; and that the power of establishing a branch in the State of Maryland might be properly exercised by the bank itself, we proceed to inquire—

2. Whether the State of Maryland may, without violating the constitution, tax that branch?

That the power of taxation is one of vital importance; that it is retained by the States; that it is not abridged by the grant of a similar power to the government of the Union; that it is to be concurrently exercised by the two governments: are truths which have never been denied. But, such is the paramount character of the constitution, that its capacity to withdraw any subject from the action of even this power, is admitted. The States are expressly forbidden to lay any duties on imports or exports, except what may be absolutely necessary for executing their inspection laws. If the obligation of this prohibition must be conceded—if it may restrain a State from the exercise of its taxing power on imports and exports; the same paramount character would seem to restrain, as it certainly may restrain, a State from such other exercise of this power, as is in its nature incompatible with, and repugnant to, the constitutional laws of the Union. A law, absolutely repugnant to another, as entirely repeals that other as if express terms of repeal were used.

———— • ————

"The States have no power, by taxation or otherwise, to retard, impede, burden, or in any manner control, the operations of the constitutional laws enacted by Congress to carry into execution the powers vested in the general government."

———— • ————

On this ground the counsel for the bank place its claim to be exempted from the power of a State to tax its operations. There is no express provision for the case, but the claim has been sustained on a principle which so entirely pervades the constitution, is so intermixed with the materials which compose it, so interwoven with its web, so blended with its texture, as to be incapable of being separated from it, without rending it into shreds.

This great principle is, that the constitution and the laws made in pursuance thereof are supreme; that they control the constitution and laws of the respective States, and cannot be controlled by them. From this, which may be almost termed an axiom, other propositions are deduced as corollaries, on the truth or error of which, and on their application to this case, the cause has been supposed to depend. These are, 1st. that a power to create implies a power to preserve. 2nd. That a power to destroy, if wielded by a different hand, is hostile to, and incompatible with these powers to create and to preserve. 3d. That where this repugnancy exists, that authority which is supreme must control, not yield to that over which it is supreme. . . .

The power of Congress to create, and of course to continue, the bank, was the subject of the preceding part of this opinion; and is no longer to be considered as questionable.

That the power of taxing it by the States may be exercised so as to destroy it, is too obvious to be denied. But taxation is said to be an absolute power, which acknowledges no other limits than those expressly prescribed in the constitution, and like sovereign power of every other description, is trusted to the discretion of those who use it. But the very terms of this argument admit that the sovereignty of the State, in the article of taxation itself, is subordinate to, and may be controlled by the constitution of the United States. How far it has been controlled by that instrument must be a question of construction. In making this construction, no principle not declared, can be admissable, which would defeat the legitimate operations of a supreme government. It is of the very essence of supremacy to remove all obstacles to its action within its own sphere, and so to modify every power vested in subordinate governments, as to exempt its own operations from their own influence. This effect need not be stated in terms. It is so involved in the declaration of supremacy, so necessarily implied in it, that the expression of it could not make it more certain. We must, therefore, keep it in view while construing the constitution. . . .

The sovereignty of a State extends to every thing which exists by its own authority, or is introduced by its permission; but does it extend to those means which are employed by Congress to carry into execution powers conferred on that body by the people of the United States? We think it demonstrable that it does not. Those powers are not given by the people of a single State. They are given by the people of the United States, to a government whose laws, made in pursuance of the constitution, are declared to be supreme. Consequently, the people of a single State cannot confer a sovereignty which will extend over them.

If we measure the power of taxation residing in a State, by the extent of sovereignty which the people of a single State possess, and can confer on its government, we have an intelligible standard, applicable to every case to which the power may be applied. We have a principle which leaves the power of taxing the people and property of a State unimpaired; which leaves to a State the command of all its resources, and which places beyond its reach, all those powers which are conferred by the people of the United States on the government of the Union, and all those means which are given for the purpose of carrying those powers into execution. We have a principle which is safe for the States, and safe for the Union. We are relieved, as we ought to be, from clashing

sovereignty; from interfering powers; from a repugnancy between a right in one government to pull down what there is an acknowledged right in another to build up; from the incompatibility of a right in one government to destroy what there is a right in another to preserve. We are not driven to the perplexing inquiry, so unfit for the judicial department, what degree of taxation is the legitimate use, and what degree may amount to the abuse of the power. The attempt to use it on the means employed by the government of the Union, in pursuance of the constitution, is itself an abuse, because it is the usurpation of a power which the people of a single State cannot give.

We find, then, on just theory, a total failure of this original right to tax the means employed by the government of the Union, for the execution of its powers. The right never existed, and the question whether it has been surrendered, cannot arise.

But, waiving this theory for the present, let us resume the inquiry, whether this power can be exercised by the respective States, consistently with a fair construction of the constitution?

That the power to tax involves the power to destroy; that the power to destroy may defeat and render useless the power to create; that there is a plain repugnance, in conferring on one government a power to control the constitutional measures of another, which other, with respect to those very measures, is declared to be supreme over that which exerts the control, are propositions not to be denied. But all inconsistencies are to be reconciled by the magic of the word CONFIDENCE. Taxation, it is said, does not necessarily and unavoidably destroy. To carry it to the excess of destruction would be an abuse, to presume which, would banish that confidence which is essential to all government.

But is this a case of confidence? Would the people of any one State trust those of another with a power to control the most insignificant operations of their State government? We know they would not. Why, then, should we suppose that the people of any one State should be willing to trust those of another with a power to control the operations of a government to which they have confided their most important and most valuable interests? In the legislature of the Union alone, are all represented. The legislature of the Union alone, therefore, can be trusted by the people with the power of controlling measures which concern all, in the confidence that it will not be abused. This, then, is not a case of confidence, and we must consider it as it really is.

If we apply the principle for which the State of Maryland contends, to the constitution generally, we shall find it capable of changing totally the character of that instrument. We shall find it capable of arresting all the measures of the government, and of prostrating it at the foot of the States. The American people have declared their constitution, and the laws made in pursuance thereof, to be supreme; but this principle would transfer the supremacy, in fact, to the States.

If the States may tax one instrument, employed by the government in the execution of its powers, they may tax any and every other instrument. They may tax the mail; they may tax the mint; they may tax patent rights; they may tax the papers of the custom house; they may tax judicial process; they may tax all the means employed by the government, to an excess which would defeat all the ends of government. This was not intended by the American people. They did not design to make their government dependent on the States. . . .

It has also been insisted, that, as the power of taxation in the general and State governments is acknowledged to be concurrent, every argument which would sustain the right of the general government to tax banks chartered by the States, will equally sustain the right of the States to tax banks chartered by the general government.

But the two cases are not on the same reason. The people of all the States have created the general government, and have conferred upon it the general power of taxation. The people of all the States, and the States themselves, are represented in Congress, and, by their representatives, exercise this power. When they tax the chartered institutions of the States, they tax their constituents; and these taxes must be uniform. But, when a State taxes the operations of the government of the United States, it acts upon institutions created, not by their own constituents, but by people over whom they claim no control. It acts upon the measures of a government created by others as well as themselves, for the benefit of others in common with themselves. The difference is that which always exists, and always must exist, between the action of the whole on a part, and the action of a part on the whole—between the laws of a government declared to be supreme, and those of a government which, when in opposition to those laws, is not supreme. . . .

The Court has bestowed on this subject its most deliberate consideration. The result is a conviction that the States have no power, by taxation or otherwise, to retard, impede, burden, or in any manner control, the operations of the constitutional laws enacted by Congress to carry into execution the powers vested in the general government. This is, we think, the unavoidable consequence of that supremacy which the constitution has declared.

We are unanimously of opinion, that the law passed by the legislature of Maryland, imposing a tax

on the Bank of the United States, is unconstitutional and void.

This opinion does not deprive the States of any resources which they originally possessed. It does not extend to a tax paid by the real property of the bank, in common with the other real property within the State, nor to a tax imposed on the interest which the citizens of Maryland may hold in this institution, in common with other property of the same description throughout the State. But this is a tax on the operations of the bank, and is, consequently, a tax on the operation of an instrument employed by the government of the Union to carry its powers into execution. Such a tax must be unconstitutional.

VIEWPOINT 22B

The Federal Government Is Not Supreme over the States (1819)

Spencer Roane (1762–1822)

In *McCulloch v. Maryland* the U.S. Supreme Court led by Chief Justice John Marshall unanimously ruled that a Maryland state tax on the Baltimore office of the Second Bank of the United States was unconstitutional. The decision, which broadened national authority at the expense of the states, attracted much criticism from those who argued that Marshall's constitutional decisions were imperiling the sovereignty of the states, and in so doing imperiled the freedoms of the American people. One critic was Spencer Roane, a judge of the Virginia Supreme Court of Appeals from 1794 to 1821. In the following viewpoint, taken from two editorials published in the *Richmond Enquirer*, a journal founded by Roane in 1804, the states' rights advocate attacks the *McCulloch v. Maryland* decision. He questions the Supreme Court's arguments that Congress had constitutional authority to establish a national bank, and that states have no constitutional right to tax such an institution.

What three basic assumptions about the Constitution does Roane postulate? How do they differ from the assumptions of John Marshall found in the opposing viewpoint? What does Roane mean when he argues that "a new mode of amending the Constitution" has been created?

I beg leave to address my fellow citizens . . . on a momentous subject. . . . Although some of them will, doubtless, lend a more willing ear than oth-

From Spencer Roane's editorial in the June 11, 1819, *Richmond Enquirer*, as reprinted in *The John P. Branch Historical Papers of Randolph-Macon College* (1905).

ers to the important truths I shall endeavor to articulate, none can hear them with indifference. None of them can be prepared to give a *carte blanche* to our federal rulers, and to obliterate the state governments, forever, from our political system.

A Confederate Republic

It has been the happiness of the American people to be connected together in a confederate republic; to be united by a system which extends the sphere of popular government and reconciles the advantages of monarchy with those of a republic; a system which combines all the internal advantages of the latter with all the force of the former. It has been our happiness to believe that, in the partition of powers between the general and state governments, the former possessed only such as were expressly granted, or passed therewith as necessary incidents, while all the residuary powers were reserved by the latter. It was deemed by the enlightened founders of the Constitution as essential to the internal happiness and welfare of their constituents to reserve some powers to the state governments; as to their external safety, to grant others to the government of the Union. This, it is believed, was done by the Constitution, in its original shape; but such were the natural fears and jealousies of our citizens, in relation to this all-important subject, that it was deemed necessary to quiet those fears by the Tenth Amendment to the Constitution. It is not easy to devise stronger terms to effect that object than those used in that amendment.

Such, however, is the proneness of all men to extend and abuse their power—to "feel power and forget right"— that even this article has afforded us no security. That legislative power, which is everywhere extending the sphere of its activity and drawing all power into its impetuous vortex, has blinked even the strong words of this amendment. That judicial power, which, according to [French political philosopher Charles-Louis de] Montesquieu is "in some measure, next to nothing"; and whose province this great writer limits to "punishing criminals and determining the disputes which arise between individuals"; that judiciary which, in Rome, according to the same author, was not entrusted to decide questions which concerned "the interests of the state, in the relation which it bears to its citizens"; and which, in England, has only invaded the Constitution in the worst of times, and then, always, on the side of arbitrary power, has also deemed its interference necessary in our country. It will readily be perceived that I allude to the decision of the Supreme Court of the United States, in the case of M'Culloch against the State of Maryland.

The warfare carried on by the legislature of the

Union against the rights of "the states" and of "the people" has been with various success and always by detachment. *They* have not dared to break down the barriers of the Constitution by a *general* act declaratory of their power. That measure was too bold for these ephemeral duties of the people. The people hold them in check by a short rein, and would consign them to merited infamy, at the next election. . . . They have adopted a safer course. *Crescit eundo* [it increases as it goes] is their maxim; and they have succeeded in seeing the Constitution expounded, not by what it actually contains but by the *abuses* committed under it.

A new mode of amending the Constitution has been added to the ample ones provided in that instrument, and the strongest checks established in it have been made to yield to the force of precedents! The time will soon arrive, if it is not already at hand, when the Constitution may be expounded without ever looking into it—by merely reading the acts of a renegade Congress, or adopting the outrageous doctrines of Pickering, Lloyd, or Sheffey!

The warfare waged by the judicial body has been of a bolder tone and character. It was not enough for them to sanction, in former times, the detestable doctrines of Pickering & Co., as aforesaid; it was not enough for them to annihilate the freedom of the press by incarcerating all those who dare, with a manly freedom, to canvass the conduct of their public agents; it was not enough for the predecessors of the present judges to preach political sermons from the bench of justice and bolster up the most unconstitutional measures of the most abandoned of our rulers; it did not suffice to do the business in detail, and ratify, one by one, the legislative infractions of the Constitution. That process would have been too slow, and perhaps too troublesome. . . .

They resolved, therefore, to put down all discussions of the kind, in future, by a judicial *coup de main* [sudden attack]; to give a *general* letter of attorney to the future legislators of the Union; and to tread under foot all those parts and articles of the Constitution which had been, heretofore, deemed to set limits to the power of the federal legislature. That man must be a deplorable idiot who does not see that there is no earthly difference between an *unlimited* grant of power and a grant limited in its terms, but accompanied with *unlimited* means of carrying it into execution.

Limited Powers

The Supreme Court of the United States have not only granted this *general* power of attorney to Congress, but they have gone out of the record to do it, in the case in question. It was only necessary, in that case, to decide whether or not the bank law was "necessary and proper," within the meaning of the Constitution, for carrying into effect some of the granted powers; but the Court have, in effect, expunged those words from the Constitution. . . . The power of the Supreme Court is indeed great, but it does not extend to everything; it is not great enough to *change* the Constitution. . . .

I beg leave to lay down the following propositions as being equally incontestable in themselves, and assented to by the enlightened advocates of the Constitution at the time of its adoption.

1. That that Constitution conveyed only a limited grant of powers to the general government, and reserved the residuary powers to the governments of the states and to the people; and that the Tenth Amendment was merely declaratory of this principle, and inserted only to quiet what the Court is pleased to call "the excessive jealousies of the people."

2. That the limited grant to Congress of certain enumerated powers only carried with it such additional powers as were *fairly incidental* to them, or, in other words, were necessary and proper for their execution.

3. That the insertion of the words "necessary and proper," in the last part of the 8th Section of the 1st Article, did not enlarge the powers previously given, but were inserted only through abundant caution.

On the first point it is to be remarked that the Constitution does not give to Congress *general* legislative powers but the legislative powers "*herein granted.*". . . So it is said in *The Federalist*, that the jurisdiction of the general government extends to certain enumerated objects only and leaves to the states a residuary and inviolable sovereignty over all other objects; that in the *new* as well as the old government, the general powers are limited, and the states, in all the unenumerated cases, are left in the enjoyment of their sovereign and independent jurisdiction; that the powers given to the general government are few and defined; and that all authorities of which the states are not *explicitly* divested, in favor of the Union, remain with them in full force; as is admitted by the affirmative grants to the general government, and the prohibitions of some powers by negative clauses to the state governments.

It was said by Mr. [James] Madison, in the convention of Virginia, that the powers of the general government were enumerated and that its legislative powers are on defined objects, beyond which it cannot extend its jurisdiction; that the general government has no power but what is given and delegated, and that the delegation alone warranted the power; and that the powers of the general government are but *few*, and relate to external objects, whereas those of the states relate to those great objects which immediately concern the prosperity of the people. It

was said by Mr. [John] Marshall that Congress cannot go beyond the delegated powers, and that a law not warranted by any of the enumerated powers would be void; and that the powers not given to Congress were *retained* by the states, and that without the aid of implication. Mr. [John] Randolph said that every power not given by this system is left with the states. And it was said by Mr. Geo. Nicholas that the people retain the powers not conferred on the general government, and that Congress cannot meddle with a power not enumerated.

It was resolved in the legislature of Virginia, in acting upon the celebrated report of 1799 [the Virginia Resolutions] (of which Mr. Madison, the great patron of the Constitution, was the author), that the powers vested in the general government result from the *compact*, to which the *states* are the parties; that they are limited by the plain sense of that instrument (the Constitution), and extend no further than they are authorized by the grant; that the Constitution had been constantly discussed and justified by *its friends* on the ground that the powers not given to the government were withheld from it; and that if any doubts could have existed on the original text of the Constitution, they are removed by the Tenth Amendment; that if the powers granted be valid, it is only because they are *granted*, and that all others are retained; that both from the original Constitution and the Tenth Amendment, it results that it is incumbent on the general government to *prove*, from the Constitution, that it grants the *particular* powers; that it is *immaterial* whether unlimited powers be exercised under the name of unlimited powers, or under that of unlimited means of carrying a limited power into execution; that, in all the discussions and ratifications of the Constitution, it was urged as a characteristic of the government that powers not given were retained, and that none were given but those which were *expressly* granted, or were fairly incident to them; and that in the ratification of the Constitution by Virginia, it was expressly asserted that every power *not granted* by the Constitution remained with them (the people of Virginia), and *at their will*.

Powers Expressly Granted

I am to show in the second place that by the provisions of the Constitution (taken in exclusion of the words "necessary and proper" in the 8th [Section] of the 1st Article) such powers were only conveyed to the general government as were expressly granted or were (to use the language of the report) fairly incident to them. I shall afterward show that the insertion of those words, in that article, made no difference whatever and created no extension of the powers previously granted.

I take it to be a clear principle of universal law—of the law of nature, of nations, of war, of reason, and of the common law—that the general grant of a thing or power carries with it all those means (and those only) which are necessary to the perfection of the grant or the execution of the power. All those entirely concur in this respect, and are bestowed upon a clear principle. That principle is one which, while it completely effects the object of the grant or power, is a safe one as it relates to the reserved rights of the other party.

This is the true principle, and it is a universal one, applying to *all* pacts and conventions, high or low, or of which nature or kind soever. It cannot be stretched or extended even in relation to the American government; although, for purposes which can easily be conjectured, the Supreme Court has used high-sounding words as to it. They have stated it to be a government extending from St. Croix to the Gulf of Mexico, and from the Atlantic to the Pacific Ocean. This principle depends on a basis which applies to all cases whatsoever, and is inflexible and universal. . . .

———— • ————

"[The] Constitution conveyed only a limited grant of powers to the general government, and reserved the residuary powers to the governments of the states and to the people."

———— • ————

We are told in *The Federalist* that all powers *indispensably necessary* are granted by the Constitution, though they be not expressly; and that all the particular powers *requisite* to carry the enumerated ones into effect would have resulted to the government by unavoidable implications *without* the words "necessary and proper"; and that when a power is given, every particular power *necessary* for doing it is included. Again, it is said that a power is nothing but the ability or faculty of doing a thing, and that that ability includes the means *necessary* for its execution.

It is laid down in the report before mentioned that Congress under the terms "necessary and proper" have only all incidental powers necessary and proper, etc., and that the only inquiry is whether the power is properly an *incident* to an express power and *necessary* to its execution, and that, if it is not, Congress cannot exercise it; and that this [understanding of the] Constitution provided [was assumed] during all the discussions and ratifications of the Constitution, and is *absolutely necessary to consist* with the idea of defined or particular powers. Again, it is said, that none but the express powers and those *fairly inci-*

dent to them were granted by the Constitution.

The terms "incident" and "incidental powers" are not only the terms used in the early stages and by the *friends* of the Constitution but they are the terms used by the *Court* itself, in more passages than one, in relation to the power in question. . . . Can it be then said that means which are of an independent or paramount character can be implied as incidental ones? Certainly not, unless, to say the least, they be absolutely necessary.

Can it be said, after this, that we are at liberty to invent terms at our pleasure in relation to this all-important question? Are we not tied down to the terms used by the founders of the Constitution; terms, too, of limited, well-defined, and established signification? On the contrary, I see great danger in using the *general* term now introduced; it may cover the latent designs of ambition and change the nature of the general government. It is entirely unimportant, as is before said, by what means this end is effected.

I come in the third place to show that the words "necessary and proper," in the Constitution, add nothing to the powers before given to the general government. They were only added (says *The Federalist*) for greater caution, and are tautologous and redundant, though harmless. It is also said, in the report aforesaid, that these words do not amount to a grant of *new* power, but for the removal of all uncertainty the declaration was made that the means were included in the grant. I might multiply authorities on this point to infinity; but if these do not suffice, neither would one were he to arise from the dead. If this power existed in the government before these words were used, its repetition or reduplication, in the Constitution, does not increase it. The "expression of that which before existed in the grant, has no operation." So these words, "necessary and proper," have no power or other effect than if they had been annexed to and repeated in every specific grant; and in that case they would have been equally unnecessary and harmless. As a friend, however, to the just powers of the general government, I do not object to them, considered as merely declaratory words, and inserted for greater caution. I only deny to them an extension to which they are not entitled, and which may be fatal to the reserved rights by the states and of the people.

For Further Reading

Charles G. Haines, *The Role of the Supreme Court in American Government and Politics.* New York: Da Capo Press, 1973.

Margaret E. Horsnell, *Spencer Roane: Judicial Advocate of Jeffersonian Principles.* New York: Garland, 1986.

Frances N. Stites, *John Marshall: Defender of the Constitution.* Boston: Little, Brown, 1981.

The Bank of the United States Should Be Abolished (1832)

Andrew Jackson (1767–1845)

The role of the federal government and its relation to the people and the states continued to stir national debate during the presidency of Andrew Jackson (1829–1837). One of the flashpoints of controversy was the fate of the Second Bank of the United States, which had been chartered in 1816 (five years after the charter of the original Bank of the United States had expired). To its supporters, the bank was a valuable national institution that served the country well by safekeeping and transferring government funds, supplying credit to the western states (although not enough, according to some), and providing through its banknotes a dependable medium of exchange. To its opponents, including "the common man's president," Andrew Jackson, the bank was a suspicious and corrupting institution that exploited its monopolistic position to benefit wealthy stockholders at the expense of farmers and workers. Some, including Jackson, were suspicious of all banknotes and paper money not fully backed by *specie* (gold and silver).

Jackson was given an opportunity to act on his beliefs in 1832 when Congress passed a bill to recharter the bank (even though its existing charter was not due to expire until 1836). The following viewpoint is excerpted from Jackson's message to Congress explaining his veto of the measure. Drafted primarily by his advisers Amos Kendall and Roger B. Taney, it was sent to Congress on July 10, 1832. Opponents of Jackson, convinced that the public was on their side, printed and distributed 30,000 copies of the message during the 1832 presidential election. Their ploy failed, however, and Jackson handily won the election over Kentucky senator Henry Clay.

Who benefits most from the Bank of the United States, according to Jackson? What, in his view, should the federal government do to promote equality between Americans?

T he bill "to modify and continue" the act entitled "An act to incorporate the subscribers to the Bank of the United States" was presented to me on the 4th July instant. Having considered it with the solemn regard to the principles of the Constitution which the day was calculated to inspire, and come to the conclusion that it ought not to become a

From Andrew Jackson, "Veto of the Bank Renewal Bill," July 10, 1832, reprinted from *House Miscellaneous Documents*, 53rd Cong., 2nd sess., 1893–94, II, 576–91.

law, I herewith return it to the Senate, in which it originated, with my objections.

A bank of the United States is in many respects convenient for the Government and useful to the people. Entertaining this opinion, and deeply impressed with the belief that some of the powers and privileges possessed by the existing bank are unauthorized by the Constitution, subversive of the rights of the States, and dangerous to the liberties of the people, I felt it my duty at an early period of my Administration to call the attention of Congress to the practicability of organizing an institution combining all its advantages and obviating these objections. I sincerely regret that in the act before me I can perceive none of those modifications of the bank charter which are necessary, in my opinion, to make it compatible with justice, with sound policy, or with the Constitution of our country.

Problems with the Bank

The present corporate body, denominated the president, directors, and company of the Bank of the United States, will have existed at the time this act is intended to take effect twenty years. It enjoys an exclusive privilege of banking under the authority of the General Government, a monopoly of its favor and support, and, as a necessary consequence, almost a monopoly of the foreign and domestic exchange. The powers, privileges, and favors bestowed upon it in the original charter, by increasing the value of the stock far above its par value, operated as a gratuity of many millions to the stockholders.

An apology may be found for the failure to guard against this result in the consideration that the effect of the original act of incorporation could not be certainly foreseen at the time of its passage. The act before me proposes another gratuity to the holders of the same stock, and in many cases to the same men, of at least seven millions more. This donation finds no apology in any uncertainty as to the effect of the act. On all hands it is conceded that its passage will increase at least 20 or 30 per cent more the market price of the stock, subject to the payment of the annuity of $200,000 per year secured by the act, thus adding in a moment one-fourth to its par value. It is not our own citizens only who are to receive the bounty of our Government. More than eight millions of the stock of this bank are held by foreigners. By this act the American Republic proposes virtually to make them a present of some millions of dollars. For these gratuities to foreigners and to some of our own opulent citizens the act secures no equivalent whatever. They are the certain gains of the present stockholders under the operation of this act, after making full allowance for the payment of the bonus.

Every monopoly and all exclusive privileges are granted at the expense of the public, which ought to receive a fair equivalent. The many millions which this act proposes to bestow on the stockholders of the existing bank must come directly or indirectly out of the earnings of the American people. It is due to them, therefore, if their Government sell monopolies and exclusive privileges, that they should at least exact for them as much as they are worth in open market. The value of the monopoly in this case may be correctly ascertained. The twenty-eight millions of stock would probably be at an advance of 50 per cent, and command in market at least $42,000,000 subject to the payment of the present bonus. The present value of the monopoly, therefore, is $17,000,000, and this the act proposes to sell for three millions, payable in fifteen annual installments of $200,000 each.

An Unfair Monopoly

It is not conceivable how the present stockholders can have any claim to the special favor of the Government. The present corporation has enjoyed its monopoly during the period stipulated in the original contract. If we must have such a corporation, why should not the Government sell out the whole stock and thus secure to the people the full market value of the privileges granted? Why should not Congress create and sell twenty-eight millions of stock, incorporating the purchasers with all the powers and privileges secured in this act and putting the premium upon the sales into the Treasury?

But this act does not permit competition in the purchase of this monopoly. It seems to be predicated on the erroneous idea that the present stockholders have a prescriptive right not only to the favor but to the bounty of Government. It appears that more than a fourth part of the stock is held by foreigners and the residue is held by a few hundred of our own citizens, chiefly of the richest class. For their benefit does this act exclude the whole American people from competition in the purchase of this monopoly and dispose of it for many millions less than it is worth. This seems the less excusable because some of our citizens not now stockholders petitioned that the door of competition might be opened, and offered to take a charter on terms much more favorable to the Government and country.

But this proposition, although made by men whose aggregate wealth is believed to be equal to all the private stock in the existing bank, has been set aside, and the bounty of our Government is proposed to be again bestowed on the few who have been fortunate enough to secure the stock and at this moment wield the power of the existing institution. I can not perceive the justice or policy of this course. If our Government must sell monopolies, it would seem to be its duty to take nothing less than their full value, and if gratuities must be made once in fifteen or twenty years let them not be bestowed on the subjects of a foreign government nor upon a designated and favored class of men in our own country. It is but justice and good policy, as far as the nature of the case will admit, to confine our favors to our own fellow-citizens, and let each in his turn enjoy an opportunity to profit by our bounty. In the bearings of the act before me upon these points I find ample reasons why it should not become a law.

It has been urged as an argument in favor of rechartering the present bank that the calling in its loans will produce great embarrassment and distress. The time allowed to close its concerns is ample, and if it has been well managed its pressure will be light, and heavy only in case its management has been bad. If, therefore, it shall produce distress, the fault will be its own, and it would furnish a reason against renewing a power which has been so obviously abused. But will there ever be a time when this reason will be less powerful? To acknowledge its force is to admit that the bank ought to be perpetual, and as a consequence the present stockholders and those inheriting their rights as successors be established a privileged order, clothed both with great political power and enjoying immense pecuniary advantages from their connection with the Government.

The modifications of the existing charter proposed by this act are not such, in my view, as make it consistent with the rights of the States or the liberties of the people. The qualification of the right of the bank to hold real estate, the limitation of its power to establish branches, and the power reserved to Congress to forbid the circulation of small notes are restrictions comparatively of little value or importance. All the objectionable principles of the existing corporation, and most of its odious features, are retained without alleviation. . . .

Taxing Citizens, Not Foreigners

The ninth section of the act recognizes principles of worse tendency than any provision of the present charter.

It enacts that "the cashier of the bank shall annually report to the Secretary of Treasury the names of all stockholders who are not resident citizens of the United States, and on the application of the treasurer of any State shall make out and transmit to such treasurer a list of stockholders residing in or citizens of such State, with the amount of stock owned by each." Although this provision, taken in connection with a decision of the Supreme Court, surrenders, by its silence, the right of the States to tax the banking institutions created by this corporation under the name of branches throughout the Union, it is evidently intended to be construed as a concession of their right to tax that portion of the stock which may be held by their own citizens and residents. In this light, if the act becomes a law, it will be understood by the States, who will probably proceed to levy a tax equal to that paid upon the stock of banks incorporated by themselves. In some States that tax is now 1 per cent, either on the capital or on the shares, and that may be assumed as the amount which all citizen or resident stockholders would be taxed under the operation of this act. As it is only the stock *held* in the States and not that *employed* within them which would be subject to taxation, and as the names of foreign stockholders are not to be reported to the treasurers of the States, it is obvious that the stock held by them will be exempt from this burden. Their annual profits will therefore be 1 per cent more than the citizen stockholders, and as the annual dividends of the bank may be safely estimated at 7 per cent, the stock will be worth 10 or 15 per cent more to foreigners than to citizens of the United States. To appreciate the effects which this state of things will produce, we must take a brief review of the operations and present condition of the Bank of the United States.

By documents submitted to Congress at the present session it appears that on the 1st of January, 1832, of the twenty-eight millions of private stock in the corporation, $8,405,500 were held by foreigners, mostly of Great Britain. The amount of stock held in the nine Western and Southwestern States is $140,200, and in the four Southern States is $5,623,100, and in the Middle and Eastern States is about $13,522,000. The profits of the bank in 1831, as shown in a statement to Congress, were about $3,455,598; of this there accrued in the nine Western States about $1,640,048; in the four Southern States about $352,507, and in the Middle and Eastern States about $1,463,041. As little stock is held in the West, it is obvious that the debt of the people in that section to the bank is principally a debt to the Eastern and foreign stockholders; that the interest they pay upon it is carried into the Eastern States and into Europe, and that it is a burden upon their industry and a drain of their currency, which no country can bear without inconvenience and occasional distress. To meet this burden and equalize the exchange operations of the bank, the amount of specie drawn from those States through its branches within the last two years, as shown by its official reports, was about $6,000,000. More than half a million of this amount does not stop in the Eastern States, but passes on to Europe to pay the dividends of the foreign stockholders. In the principle of taxation recognized by this act the Western States find no adequate compensation for this perpetual burden on their industry and drain of their currency. The branch bank at Mobile made last year $95,140, yet under the provisions of this act the State of Alabama can raise no

revenue from these profitable operations, because not a share of the stock is held by any of her citizens. Mississippi and Missouri are in the same condition in relation to the branches at Natchez and St. Louis, and such, in a greater or less degree, is the condition of every Western State. The tendency of the plan of taxation which this act proposes will be to place the whole United States in the same relation to foreign countries which the Western States now bear to the Eastern. When by a tax on resident stockholders the stock of this bank is made worth 10 or 15 per cent more to foreigners than to residents, most of it will inevitably leave the country.

Thus will this provision in its practical effect deprive the Eastern as well as the Southern and Western States of the means of raising a revenue from the extension of business and great profits of this institution. It will make the American people debtors to aliens in nearly the whole amount due to this bank, and send across the Atlantic from two to five millions of specie every year to pay the bank dividends.

Foreign Control

In another of its bearings this provision is fraught with danger. Of the twenty-five directors of this bank five are chosen by the Government and twenty by the citizen stockholders. From all voice in these elections the foreign stockholders are excluded by the charter. In proportion, therefore, as the stock is transferred to foreign holders the extent of suffrage in the choice of directors is curtailed. Already is almost a third of the stock in foreign hands and not represented in elections. It is constantly passing out of the country, and this act will accelerate its departure. The entire control of the institution would necessarily fall into the hands of a few citizen stockholders, and the ease with which the object would be accomplished would be a temptation to designing men to secure that control in their own hands by monopolizing the remaining stock. There is danger that a president and directors would then be able to elect themselves from year to year, and without responsibility or control manage the whole concerns of the bank during the existence of its charter. It is easy to conceive that great evils to our country and its institutions might flow from such a concentration of power in the hands of a few men irresponsible to the people.

Is there no danger to our liberty and independence in a bank that in its nature has so little to bind it to our country? The president of the bank has told us that most of the State banks exist by its forbearance. Should its influence become concentered, as it may under the operation of such an act as this, in the hands of a self-elected directory whose interests are identified with those of the foreign stockholders, will there not be cause to tremble for the purity of our elections in peace and for the independence of our country in war? Their power would be great whenever they might choose to exert it; but if this monopoly were regularly renewed every fifteen or twenty years on terms proposed by themselves, they might seldom in peace put forth their strength to influence elections or control the affairs of the nation. But if any private citizen or public functionary should interpose to curtail its powers or prevent a renewal of its privileges, it can not be doubted that he would be made to feel its influence.

Should the stock of the bank principally pass into the hands of the subjects of a foreign country, and we should unfortunately become involved in a war with that country, what would be our condition? Of the course which would be pursued by a bank almost wholly owned by the subjects of a foreign power, and managed by those whose interests, if not affections, would run in the same direction there can be no doubt. All its operations within would be in aid of the hostile fleets and armies without. Controlling our currency, receiving our public moneys, and holding thousands of our citizens in dependence, it would be more formidable and dangerous than the naval and military power of the enemy.

---●---

"The modifications of the existing charter proposed by this act are not such, in my view, as make it consistent with the rights of the States or the liberties of the people."

---●---

If we must have a bank with private stockholders, every consideration of sound policy and every impulse of American feeling admonishes that it should be *purely American.* Its stockholders should be composed exclusively of our own citizens, who at least ought to be friendly to our Government and willing to support it in times of difficulty and danger. . . .

The bank is professedly established as an agent of the executive branch of the Government, and its constitutionality is maintained on that ground. Neither upon the propriety of present action nor upon the provisions of this act was the Executive consulted. It has had no opportunity to say that it neither needs nor wants an agent clothed with such powers and favored by such exemptions. There is nothing in its legitimate functions which makes it necessary or proper. Whatever interest or influence, whether public or private, has given birth to this act, it can not be found either in the wishes or necessities of the executive department, by which present action is

deemed premature, and the powers conferred upon its agent not only unnecessary, but dangerous to the Government and country.

The Rich and Powerful

It is to be regretted that the rich and powerful too often bend the acts of government to their selfish purposes. Distinctions in society will always exist under every just government. Equality of talents, of education, or of wealth can not be produced by human institutions. In the full enjoyment of the gifts of Heaven and the fruits of superior industry, economy, and virtue, every man is equally entitled to protection by law; but when the laws undertake to add to these natural and just advantages artificial distinctions, to grant titles, gratuities, and exclusive privileges, to make the rich richer and the potent more powerful, the humble members of society—the farmers, mechanics, and laborers—who have neither the time nor the means of securing like favors to themselves, have a right to complain of the injustice of their Government. There are no necessary evils in government. Its evils exist only in its abuses. If it would confine itself to equal protection, and, as Heaven does its rains, shower its favors alike on the high and the low, the rich and the poor, it would be an unqualified blessing. In the act before me there seems to be a wide and unnecessary departure from these just principles.

Nor is our Government to be maintained or our Union preserved by invasions of the rights and powers of the several States. In thus attempting to make our General Government strong we make it weak. Its true strength consists in leaving individuals and States as much as possible to themselves—in making itself felt, not in its power, but in its beneficence; not in its control, but in its protection; not in binding the States more closely to the center, but leaving each to move unobstructed in its proper orbit.

Experience should teach us wisdom. Most of the difficulties our Government now encounters and most of the dangers which impend over our Union have sprung from an abandonment of the legitimate objects of Government by our national legislation, and the adoption of such principles as are embodied in this act. Many of our rich men have not been content with equal protection and equal benefits, but have besought us to make them richer by act of Congress. By attempting to gratify their desires we have in the results of our legislation arrayed section against section, interest against interest, and man against man, in a fearful commotion which threatens to shake the foundations of our Union. It is time to pause in our career to review our principles, and if possible revive that devoted patriotism and spirit of compromise which distinguished the sages of the

Revolution and the fathers of our Union. If we can not at once, in justice to interests vested under improvident legislation, make our Government what it ought to be, we can at least take a stand against all new grants of monopolies and exclusive privileges, against any prostitution of our Government to the advancement of the few at the expense of the many, and in favor of compromise and gradual reform in our code of laws and system of political economy.

I have now done my duty to my country. If sustained by my fellow-citizens, I shall be grateful and happy; if not, I shall find in the motives which impel me ample grounds for contentment and peace. In the difficulties which surround us and the dangers which threaten our institutions there is cause for neither dismay nor alarm. For relief and deliverance let us firmly rely on that kind Providence which I am sure watches with peculiar care over the destinies of our Republic, and on the intelligence and wisdom of our countrymen. Through *His* abundant goodness and *their* patriotic devotion our liberty and Union will be preserved.

VIEWPOINT 23B

The Bank of the United States Should Not Be Abolished (1832)

Daniel Webster (1782–1852)

Daniel Webster was a noted senator, diplomat, lawyer, and perhaps the most famous orator of his time. During the presidency of Andrew Jackson (1829–1837) he represented Massachusetts in the Senate and became the leader of the emerging Whig Party, which consisted mostly of opponents of Jackson and his policies. Webster and his fellow Whigs supported protective tariffs and federal government support for building roads and other "internal improvements." Jackson and his supporters opposed many of these policies as favoring the rich and privileged.

The fate of the Second Bank of the United States was perhaps the most famous single issue dividing Webster and Jackson. In July 1832 Jackson vetoed a bill that would have renewed the charter of the bank. The following viewpoint is excerpted from Webster's July 1832 speech to the U.S. Senate criticizing Jackson's veto, and urging that Congress override it. He strongly condemns Jackson for abusing his presidential powers, and for the veto message's tendency to "inflame the poor against the rich." This was not Webster's first defense of the bank; in 1819 he had argued on its behalf before the U.S. Supreme Court in the case of *McCulloch v. Maryland* (see view-

From *The Works of Daniel Webster*, vol. 3 (Boston, 1853).

points 22A and 22B).

What will be the effects of closing the Bank of the United States, according to Webster? How does he respond to Andrew Jackson's arguments that the bank benefits wealthy (and foreign) stockholders? Webster's ties to the Bank of the United States were reinforced by his personal friendship with its president, Nicholas Biddle, and by the facts that he received a retainer as attorney for the bank and was the recipient of frequent loans from the institution. How do these considerations affect your assessment of his arguments presented here?

M r. President [of the Senate], no one will deny the high importance of the subject now before us. Congress, after full deliberation and discussion, has passed a bill, by decisive majorities, in both houses, for extending the duration of the Bank of the United States. It has not adopted this measure until its attention had been called to the subject, in three successive annual messages of the President [Andrew Jackson]. The bill having been thus passed by both houses, and having been duly presented to the President, instead of signing and approving it, he has returned it with objections. These objections go against the whole substance of the law originally creating the bank. They deny, in effect, that the bank is constitutional; they deny that it is expedient; they deny that it is necessary for the public service.

It is not to be doubted, that the Constitution gives the President the power which he has now exercised; but while the power is admitted, the grounds upon which it has been exerted become fit subjects of examination. The Constitution makes it the duty of Congress, in cases like this, to reconsider the measure which they have passed, to weigh the force of the President's objections to that measure, and to take a new vote upon the question.

Before the Senate proceeds to this second vote, I propose to make some remarks upon those objections. And, in the first place, it is to be observed, that they are such as to extinguish all hope that the present bank, or any bank at all resembling it, or resembling any known similar institution, can ever receive his approbation. He states no terms, no qualifications, no conditions, no modifications, which can reconcile him to the essential provisions of the existing charter. He is against the bank, and against any bank constituted in a manner known either to this or any other country. One advantage, therefore, is certainly obtained by presenting him the bill. It has caused the President's sentiments to be made known. There is no longer any mystery, no longer a contest between hope and fear, or between those prophets who predicted a *veto* and those who foretold an approval. The bill is negatived; the President has assumed the responsibility of putting an end to the bank; and the country must prepare itself to meet that change in its concerns which the expiration of the charter will produce. Mr. President, I will not conceal my opinion that the affairs of the country are approaching an important and dangerous crisis. At the very moment of almost unparalleled general prosperity, there appears an unaccountable disposition to destroy the most useful and most approved institutions of the government. Indeed, it seems to be in the midst of all this national happiness that some are found openly to question the advantages of the Constitution itself; and many more ready to embarrass the exercise of its just power, weaken its authority, and undermine its foundations. How far these notions may be carried, it is impossible yet to say. We have before us the practical result of one of them. The bank has fallen, or is to fall. . . .

The President is of opinion, that this time [three years and nine months] is long enough to close the concerns of the institution without inconvenience. His language is, "The time allowed the bank to close its concerns is ample, and if it has been well managed, its pressure will be light, and heavy only in case its management has been bad. If, therefore, it shall produce distress, the fault will be its own." Sir, this is all no more than general statement, without fact or argument to support it. We know what the management of the bank has been, and we know the present state of its affairs. We can judge, therefore, whether it be probable that its capital can be all called in, and the circulation of its bills withdrawn, in three years and nine months, by any discretion or prudence in management, without producing distress. The bank has discounted liberally, in compliance with the wants of the community. The amount due to it on loans and discounts, in certain large divisions of the country, is great; so great, that I do not perceive how any man can believe that it can be paid, within the time now limited, without distress. Let us look at known facts. Thirty millions of the capital of the bank are now out, on loans and discounts, in the States on the Mississippi and its waters; ten millions of which are loaned on the discount of bills of exchange, foreign and domestic, and twenty millions on promissory notes. Now, Sir, how is it possible that this vast amount can be collected in so short a period without suffering, by any management whatever? We are to remember, that, when the collection of this debt begins, at that same time, the existing medium of payment, that is, the circulation of the bills of the bank, will begin also to be restrained and withdrawn; and thus the means of payment must be limited just when the necessity of making payment becomes

pressing. The whole debt is to be paid, and within the same time the whole circulation withdrawn. . . .

I hesitate not to say, that, as this *veto* travels to the West, it will depreciate the value of the every man's property from the Atlantic States to the capital of Missouri. Its effects will be felt in the price of lands, the great and leading article of Western property, in the price of crops, in the products of labor, in the repression of enterprise, and in embarrassment to every kind of business and occupation. I state this opinion strongly, because I have no doubt of its truth, and am willing its correctness should be judged by the event. Without personal acquaintance with the Western States, I know enough of their condition to be satisfied that what I have predicted must happen. The people of the West are rich, but their riches consist in their immense quantities of excellent land, in the products of these lands, and in their spirit of enterprise. The actual value of money, or rate of interest, with them is high, because their pecuniary capital bears little proportion to their landed interest. At an average rate, money is not worth less than eight per cent. per annum throughout the whole Western country, notwithstanding that it has now a loan or an advance from the bank of thirty millions, at six per cent. To call in this loan, at the rate of eight millions a year, in addition to the interest on the whole, and to take away, at the same time, that circulation which constitutes so great a portion of the medium of payment throughout that whole region, is an operation, which, however wisely conducted, cannot but inflict a blow on the community of tremendous force and frightful consequences. The thing cannot be done without distress, bankruptcy, and ruin, to many. If the President had seen any practical manner in which this change might be effected without producing these consequences, he would have rendered infinite service to the community by pointing it out. But he has pointed out nothing, he has suggested nothing; he contents himself with saying, without giving any reason, that, if the pressure be heavy, the fault will be the bank's. I hope this is not merely an attempt to forestall opinion, and to throw on the bank the responsibility of those evils which threaten the country, for the sake of removing it from himself.

The responsibility justly lies with him, and there it ought to remain. A great majority of the people are satisfied with the bank as it is, and desirous that it should be continued. They wished no change. The strength of this public sentiment has carried the bill through Congress, against all the influence of the administration, and all the power of organized party. But the President has undertaken, on his own responsibility, to arrest the measure, by refusing his assent to the bill. He is answerable for the consequences, therefore, which necessarily follow the change which the expiration of the bank charter may produce; and if these consequences shall prove disastrous, they can fairly be ascribed to his policy only, and the policy of his administration.

Although, Sir, I have spoken of the effects of this *veto* in the Western country, it has not been because I considered that part of the United States exclusively affected by it. Some of the Atlantic States may feel its consequences, perhaps, as sensibly as those of the West, though not for the same reasons. The concern manifested by Pennsylvania for the renewal of the charter shows her sense of the importance of the bank to her own interest, and that of the nation. That great and enterprising State has entered into an extensive system of internal improvements, which necessarily makes heavy demands on her credit and her resources; and by the sound and acceptable currency which the bank affords, by the stability which it gives to private credit, and by occasional advances, made in anticipation of her revenues, and in aid of her great objects, she has found herself benefited, doubtless, in no inconsiderable degree. Her legislature has instructed her Senators here to advocate the renewal of the charter at this session. They have obeyed her voice, and yet they have the misfortune to find that, in the judgment of the President, *the measure is unconstitutional, unnecessary, dangerous to liberty, and is, moreover, ill-timed.*

———— • ————

"At the very moment of almost unparalleled general prosperity, there appears an unaccountable disposition to destroy the most useful and most approved institutions of the government."

———— • ————

But, Mr. President, it is not the local interest of the West, nor the particular interest of Pennsylvania, or any other State, which has influenced Congress in passing this bill. It has been governed by a wise foresight, and by a desire to avoid embarrassment in the pecuniary concerns of the country, to secure the safe collection and convenient transmission of public moneys, to maintain the circulation of the country, sound and safe as it now happily is, against the possible effects of a wild spirit of speculation. Finding the bank highly useful, Congress has thought fit to provide for its continuance.

As to the *time* of passing this bill, it would seem to be the last thing to be thought of, as a ground of objection, by the President; since, from the date of his first message to the present time, he has never failed to call our attention to the subject with all possible apparent earnestness. . . .

An important election is at hand, and the renewal of the bank charter is a pending object of great interest, and some excitement. Should not the opinions of men high in office, and candidates for reëlection, be known, on this, as on other important public questions? Certainly, it is to be hoped that the people of the United States are not yet mere man-worshippers, that they do not choose their rulers without some regard to their political principles, or political opinions. Were they to do this, it would be to subject themselves voluntarily to the evils which the hereditary transmission of power, independent of all personal qualifications, inflicts on other nations. They will judge their public servants by their acts, and continue or withhold their confidence, as they shall think it merited, or as they shall think it forfeited. In every point of view, therefore, the moment had arrived, when it became the duty of Congress to come to a result, in regard to this highly important measure. . . .

There are some other topics, treated in the message, which ought to be noticed. It commences by an inflamed statement of what it calls the "favor" bestowed upon the original bank by the government, or, indeed, as it is phrased, the "monopoly of its favor and support"; and through the whole message all possible changes are rung on the "gratuity," the "exclusive privileges," and "monopoly," of the bank charter. Now, Sir, the truth is, that the powers conferred on the bank are such, and no others, as are usually conferred on similar institutions. They constitute no monopoly, although some of them are of necessity, and with propriety, exclusive privileges. "The original act," says the message, "operated as a gratuity of many millions to the stockholders." What fair foundation is there for this remark? The stockholders received their charter, not gratuitously, but for a valuable consideration in money, prescribed by Congress, and actually paid. At some times the stock has been above *par*, at other times below *par*, according to prudence in management, or according to commercial occurrences. But if, by a judicious administration of its affairs, it had kept its stock always above *par*, what pretence would there be, nevertheless, for saying that such augmentation of its value was a "gratuity" from government? The message proceeds to declare, that the present act proposes another donation, another gratuity, to the same men, of at least seven millions more. It seems to me that this is an extraordinary statement, and an extraordinary style of argument, for such a subject and on such an occasion. In the first place, the facts are all assumed; they are taken for true without evidence. There are no proofs that any benefit to that amount will accrue to the stockholders, nor any experience to justify the expectation of it. It rests on random estimates, or mere conjecture. But suppose the continuance of the charter should prove beneficial to the stockholders: do they not pay for it? They give twice as much for a charter of fifteen years, as was given before for one of twenty. And if the proposed *bonus*, or premium, be not, in the President's judgment, large enough, would he, nevertheless, on such a mere matter of opinion as that, negative the whole bill? May not Congress be trusted to decide even on such a subject as the amount of the money premium to be received by government for a charter of this kind?

Great Public Interests

But, Sir, there is a larger and a much more just view of this subject. The bill was not passed for the purpose of benefiting the present stockholders. Their benefit, if any, is incidental and collateral. Nor was it passed on any idea that they had a *right* to a renewed charter, although the message argues against such right, as if it had been somewhere set up and asserted. No such right has been asserted by any body. Congress passed the bill, not as a bounty or a favor to the present stockholders, nor to comply with any demand of right on their part; but to promote great public interests, for great public objects. Every bank must have some stockholders, unless it be such a bank as the President has recommended, and in regard to which he seems not likely to find much concurrence of other men's opinions; and if the stockholders, whoever they may be, conduct the affairs of the bank prudently, the expectation is always, of course, that they will make it profitable to themselves, as well as useful to the public. If a bank charter is not to be granted, because, to some extent, it may be profitable to the stockholders, no charter can be granted. The objection lies against all banks.

Sir, the object aimed at by such institutions is to connect the public safety and convenience with private interests. It has been found by experience, that banks are safest under private management, and that government banks are among the most dangerous of all inventions. Now, Sir, the whole drift of the message is to reverse the settled judgment of all the civilized world, and to set up government banks, independent of private interest or private control. For this purpose the message labors, even beyond the measure of all its other labors, to create jealousies and prejudices, on the ground of the alleged benefit which individuals will derive from the renewal of this charter. Much less effort is made to show that government, or the public, will be injured by the bill, than that individuals will profit by it. Following up the impulses of the same spirit, the message goes on

gravely to allege, that the act, as passed by Congress, proposes to make a *present* of some millions of dollars to foreigners, because a portion of the stock is held by foreigners. Sir, how would this sort of argument apply to other cases? The President has shown himself not only willing, but anxious, to pay off the three per cent. stock of the United States at *par*, notwithstanding that it is notorious that foreigners are owners of the greater part of it. Why should he not call that a donation to foreigners of many millions?

I will not dwell particularly on this part of the message. Its tone and its arguments are all in the same strain. It speaks of the certain gain of the present stockholders, of the value of the monopoly; it says that all monopolies are granted at the expense of the public; that the many millions which this bill bestows on the stockholders come out of the earnings of the people; that, if government sells monopolies, it ought to sell them in open market; that it is an erroneous idea, that the present stockholders have a prescriptive right either to the favor or the bounty of government; that the stock is in the hands of a few, and that the whole American people are excluded from competition in the purchase of the monopoly. To all this I say, again, that much of it is assumption without proof; much of it is an argument against that which nobody has maintained or asserted; and the rest of it would be equally strong against any charter, at any time. These objections existed in their full strength, whatever that was, against the first bank. They existed, in like manner, against the present bank at its creation, and will always exist against all banks. Indeed, all the fault found with the bill now before us is, that it proposes to continue the bank substantially as it now exists. "All the objectionable principles of the existing corporation," says the message, "and most of its odious features, are retained without alleviation"; so that the message is aimed against the bank, as it has existed from the first, and against any and all others resembling it in its general features.

Contradictory Arguments

Allow me, now, Sir, to take notice of an argument founded on the practical operation of the bank. That argument is this. Little of the stock of the bank is held in the West, the capital being chiefly owned by citizens of the Southern and Eastern States, and by foreigners. But the Western and Southwestern States owe the bank a heavy debt, so heavy that the interest amounts to a million six hundred thousand a year. This interest is carried to the Eastern States, or to Europe, annually, and its payment is a burden on the people of the West, and a drain of their currency, which no country can bear without inconvenience and distress. The true character and the whole value of this argument are manifest by the mere statement of it. The people of the West are, from their situation, necessarily large borrowers. They need money, capital, and they borrow it, because they can derive a benefit from its use, much beyond the interest which they pay. They borrow at six per cent. of the bank, although the value of money with them is at least as high as eight. Nevertheless, although they borrow at this low rate of interest, and although they use all they borrow thus profitably, yet they cannot pay the interest without "inconvenience and distress"; and then, Sir, follows the logical conclusion, that, although they cannot pay even the interest without inconvenience and distress, yet less than four years is ample time for the bank to call in the whole, both principal and interest, without causing more than a light pressure. This is the argument.

Then follows another, which may be thus stated. It is competent to the States to tax the property of their citizens vested in the stock of this bank; but the power is denied of taxing the stock of foreigners; therefore the stock will be worth ten or fifteen per cent. more to foreigners than to residents, and will of course inevitably leave the country, and make the American people debtors to aliens in nearly the whole amount due the bank, and send across the Atlantic from two to five millions of specie every year, to pay the bank dividends.

Foreign Stockholders

Mr. President, arguments like these might be more readily disposed of, were it not that the high and official source from which they proceed imposes the necessity of treating them with respect. In the first place, it may safely be denied that the stock of the bank is any more valuable to foreigners than to our own citizens, or an object of greater desire to them, except in so far as capital may be more abundant in the foreign country, and therefore its owners more in want of opportunity of investment. The foreign stockholder enjoys no exemption from taxation. He is, of course, taxed by his own government for his incomes, derived from this as well as other property; and this is a full answer to the whole statement. But it may be added, in the second place, that it is not the practice of civilized states to tax the property of foreigners under such circumstances. Do we tax, or did we ever tax, the foreign holders of our public debt? Does Pennsylvania, New York or Ohio tax the foreign holders of stock in the loans contracted by either of these States? Certainly not. Sir, I must confess I had little expected to see, on such an occasion as the present, a labored and repeated attempt to produce an impression on the public opinion unfavorable to the bank, from the circumstance that foreigners are among its stockholders. I have no hesitation in saying, that I deem such a train of remark as the message contains

on this point, coming from the President of the United States, to be injurious to the credit and character of the country abroad; because it manifests a jealousy, a lurking disposition not to respect the property, of foreigners invited hither by our own laws. And, Sir, what is its tendency but to excite this jealousy, and create groundless prejudices?

From the commencement of the government, it has been thought desirable to invite, rather than to repel, the introduction of foreign capital. Our stocks have all been open to foreign subscriptions; and the State banks, in like manner, are free to foreign ownership. Whatever State has created a debt has been willing that foreigners should become purchasers, and desirous of it. How long is it, Sir, since Congress itself passed a law vesting new powers in the President of the United States over the cities in this District, for the very purpose of increasing their credit abroad, the better to enable them to borrow money to pay their subscriptions to the Chesapeake and Ohio Canal? It is easy to say that there is danger to liberty, danger to independence, in a bank open to foreign stockholders, because it is easy to say any thing. But neither reason nor experience proves any such danger. The foreign stockholder cannot be a director. He has no voice even in the choice of directors. His money is placed entirely in the management of the directors appointed by the President and Senate and by the American stockholders. So far as there is dependence or influence either way, it is to the disadvantage of the foreign stockholder. He has parted with the control over his own property, instead of exercising control over the property or over the actions of others. And, Sir, let it now be added, in further answer to this class of objections, that experience has abundantly confuted them all. This government has existed forty-three years, and has maintained, in full being and operation, a bank, such as is now proposed to be renewed, for thirty-six years out of the forty-three. We have never for a moment had a bank not subject to every one of these objections. Always, foreigners might be stockholders; always, foreign stock has been exempt from State taxation, as much as at present; always the same power and privileges; always, all that which is now called a "monopoly," a "gratuity," a "present," has been possessed by the bank. And yet there has been found no danger to liberty, no introduction of foreign influence, and no accumulation of irresponsible power in a few hands. I cannot but hope, therefore, that the people of the United States will not now yield up their judgment to those notions which would reverse all our best experience, and persuade us to discontinue a useful institution from the influence of vague and unfounded declamation against its danger to the public liberties. Our liberties, indeed, must stand upon very frail foundations, if the government cannot, without endangering them, avail itself of those common facilities, in the collection of its revenues and the management of its finances, which all other governments, in commercial countries, find useful and necessary.

In order to justify its alarm for the security of our independence, the message supposes a case. It supposes that the bank should pass principally into the hands of the subjects of a foreign country, and that we should be involved in war with that country, and then it exclaims, "What would be our condition?" Why, Sir, it is plain that all the advantages would be on our side. The bank would still be our institution, subject to our own laws, and all its directors elected by ourselves; and our means would be enhanced, not by the confiscation and plunder, but by the proper use, of the foreign capital in our hands. And, Sir, it is singular enough, that this very state of war, from which this argument against a bank is drawn, is the very thing which, more than all others, convinced the country and the government of the necessity of a national bank. So much was the want of such an institution felt in the late war [War of 1812], that the subject engaged the attention of Congress, constantly, from the declaration of that war down to the time when the existing bank was actually established; so that in this respect, as well as in others, the argument of the message is directly opposed to the whole experience of the government, and to the general and long-settled convictions of the country. . . .

Mr. President, we have arrived at a new epoch. We are entering on experiments, with the government and the Constitution of the country, hitherto untried, and of fearful and appalling aspect. This message calls us to the contemplation of a future which little resembles the past. Its principles are at war with all that public opinion has sustained, and all which the experience of the government has sanctioned. It denies first principles; it contradicts truths, heretofore received as indisputable. It denies to the judiciary the interpretation of law, and claims to divide with Congress the power of originating statutes. It extends the grasp of executive pretension over every power of the government. But this is not all. It presents the chief magistrate of the Union in the attitude of arguing away the powers of that government over which he has been chosen to preside; and adopting for this purpose modes of reasoning which, even under the influence of all proper feeling towards high official station, it is difficult to regard as respectable. It appeals to every prejudice which may betray men into a mistaken view of their own interests, and to every passion which may lead them to disobey the impulses of their understanding. It urges all the specious topics of State rights and national

encroachment against that which a great majority of the States have affirmed to be rightful, and in which all of them have acquiesced. It sows, in an unsparing manner, the seeds of jealousy and ill-will against that government of which its author is the official head. It raises a cry, that liberty is in danger, at the very moment when it puts forth claims to powers heretofore unknown and unheard of. It effects alarm for the public freedom, when nothing endangers that freedom so much as its own unparalleled pretenses. This, even, is not all. It manifestly seeks to inflame the poor against the rich; it wantonly attacks whole classes of the people, for the purpose of turning against them the prejudices and the resentments of other classes. It is a state paper which finds no topic too exciting for its use, no passion too inflammable for its address and its solicitation.

Such is this message. It remains now for the people of the United States to choose between the principles here avowed and their government. These cannot subsist together. The one or the other must be rejected. If the sentiments of the message shall receive general approbation, the Constitution will have perished even earlier than the moment which its enemies originally allowed for the termination of its existence. It will not have survived to its fiftieth year.

For Further Reading

Irving H. Bartlett, *Daniel Webster*. New York: Norton, 1978.

Bray Hammond, *Banks and Politics in America from the Revolution to the Civil War*. Princeton, NJ: Princeton University Press, 1957.

Sydney Nathans, *Daniel Webster and Jacksonian Democracy*. Baltimore, MD: Johns Hopkins University Press, 1973.

Edward Pessen, *Jacksonian America: Society, Personality, and Politics*. Homewood, IL: Dorsey Press, 1969.

Robert V. Remini, *Andrew Jackson and the Bank War*. New York: Norton, 1967.

Social Issues of the Antebellum Era

VIEWPOINT 24A

Suffrage Should Not Be Based on Property (1821)

Nathan Sanford (1777–1838)

The state constitutions of the original thirteen states required property ownership as a qualification for voting. However, beginning in 1815, many of

From *Reports of the Proceedings and Debates of the Convention of 1821, Assembled for the Purpose of Amending the Constitution of the State of New York* (Albany, NY 1821).

these states reformed their constitutions to grant the vote to all (white male) taxpayers—in part because they were losing people to the newer western states that had no such suffrage restrictions. During the 1821 New York convention called to revise the state constitution, Nathan Sanford, a lawyer and public official whose career included service as U.S. district attorney for New York and U.S. senator representing that state, chaired a committee that proposed extending the vote to all white male taxpayers. His speech recommending the committee's resolution to the convention is excerpted in the following viewpoint. Among his arguments is that many local community elections and town meetings already have such democratic voting qualifications with no ill effect.

After 1821 only five states still had property qualifications for voting (these were removed within the next three decades). However, with few exceptions, blacks and women were still denied the vote in all states.

What is the basic principle of the proposed voting reforms, according to Sanford? What importance does he attach to the experiences of other states?

The question before us is the right of suffrage—who shall or who shall not have the right to vote. The committee have presented the scheme they thought best; to abolish all existing distinctions and make the right of voting uniform. Is this not right? Where did these distinctions arise? They arose from British precedents. In England they have their three estates [the nobility, the clergy, and the commons], which must always have their separate interests represented Here there is but one estate—the people. To me the only qualifications seem to be the virtue and morality of the people; and if they may be safely entrusted to vote for one class of our rulers, why not for all?

Those Who Bear the Burdens

In my opinion, these distinctions are fallacious. We have the experience of almost all the other states against them. The principle of the scheme now proposed is that those who bear the burdens of the state should choose those that rule it. There is no privilege given to property as such; but those who contribute to the public support we consider as entitled to a share in the election of rulers. The burdens are annual, and the elections are annual, and this appears proper. To me, and the majority of the committee, it appeared the only reasonable scheme that those who are to be affected by the acts of the government should be annually entitled to vote for those who administer it.

Our taxes are of two sorts, on real and personal property. The payment of a tax on either, we thought, equally entitled a man to a vote, and thus we intended to destroy the odious distinctions of property which now exist. But we have considered personal service, in some cases, equivalent to a tax on personal property, as in work on the high roads. This is a burden and should entitle those subject to it to equivalent privileges. The road duty is equal to a poll tax on every male citizen of twenty-one years, of 62½ cents per annum, which is about the value of each individual's work on the road. This work is a burden imposed by the legislature—a duty required by rulers, and which should entitle those subject to it to a choice of those rulers.

Then, sir, the militia next presents itself; the idea of personal service, as applicable to the road duty, is, in like manner, applicable here; and this criterion has been adopted in other states. In Mississippi mere enrollment gives a vote. In Connecticut, as is proposed here, actual service, and that without the right of commutation, is required. The duty in the militia is obligatory and onerous. The militiaman must find his arms and accouterments and lose his time. But, after admitting all these persons, what restrictions, it will be said, are left on the right of suffrage? (1) The voter must be a citizen. (2) The service required must be performed within the year, on the principle that taxation is annual, and election annual; so that when the person ceases to contribute or serve, he ceases to vote.

A residence is also required. We propose the term of six months, because we find it already in the constitution; but we propose this residence in the state and not in the county or town, so that, wherever a voter may be at the time of election, he may vote there if he has been a resident of the state for six months. The object of this was to enable those who move, as very many do, in the six months preceding an election, out of the town or ward in which they have resided, to retain the right of voting in their new habitations. The term of six months is deemed long enough to qualify those who come into our state from abroad to understand and exercise the privileges of a citizen here.

The Whole Male Population

Now, sir, this scheme will embrace almost the whole male population of the state. There is, perhaps, no subject so purely matter of opinion as the question how far the right of suffrage may be safely carried. We propose to carry it almost as far as the male population of the state. The Convention may perhaps think this too broad. On this subject we have much experience; yet there are respectable citizens who think this extension of suffrage unfavorable to the rights of property. Certainly this would be a fatal objection, if well founded; for any government, however constituted, which does not secure property to its rightful owners is a bad government. But how is the extension of the right of suffrage unfavorable to property? Will not our laws continue the same? Will not the administration of justice continue the same? And, if so, how is private property to suffer? Unless these are changed, and upon them rest the rights and security of property, I am unable to perceive how property is to suffer by the extension of the right of suffrage.

•

"The course of things in this country is for the extension and not the restriction of popular rights."

•

But we have abundant experience on this point in other states. Now, sir, in many of the states the right of suffrage has no restriction; every male inhabitant votes. Yet what harm has been done in those states? What evil has resulted to them from this cause? The course of things in this country is for the extension and not the restriction of popular rights. I do not know that in Ohio or Pennsylvania, where the right of suffrage is universal, there is not the same security for private rights and private happiness as elsewhere. . . . In our town meetings too, throughout the state, we have the same principle. In our town elections we have the highest proof of the virtue and intelligence of our people; they assemble in town meetings as a pure democracy and choose their officers and local legislatures, if I may so call them; and if there is any part of our public business well done, it is that done in town meetings. Is not this a strong practical lesson of the beneficial operation of this principle? This scheme has been proposed by a majority of the committee; they think it safe and beneficial, founded in just and rational principles, and in the experience of this and neighboring states. The committee have no attachment, however, to this particular scheme and are willing to see it amended or altered if it shall be judged for the interest of the people.

VIEWPOINT 24B

Suffrage Should Be Limited to Property Holders (1821)

James Kent (1763–1847)

Many if not most of America's leading political figures during and after the American Revolution—John Adams, James Madison, John Marshall, and

others—opposed universal suffrage. Suffrage, many believed, was the right and responsibility only of established and self-supporting property holders. By the 1820s, however, such views were in the minority as a new generation of Americans called for increased democracy in voting and other areas of society. Many states began to lift voting restrictions. At New York's 1821 state constitutional convention, one of the most contentious issues was the suggestion from a special committee chaired by Nathan Sanford (see viewpoint 24A) that property ownership requirements for voting be removed. The move toward universal (white adult male) suffrage was opposed by several prominent delegates, including James Kent. Chief justice of the New York state supreme court from 1804 to 1814 and chancellor of the New York court of chancery (then the state's highest court) from 1814 to 1823, Kent was one of the leading jurists of his generation. In the following viewpoint, he argues that New York should maintain its present voting rules, including a requirement of property ownership for voting in elections for the New York state senate (one half of the state's bicameral legislature).

What contrasts does Kent draw between farmers and manufacturers? What reasons does he give for his opposition to "universal" suffrage? What does he argue about the possible reversibility of such a step?

I must beg leave to trespass for a few moments upon the patience of the [Sanford] committee while I state the reasons which have induced me to wish that the Senate should continue, as heretofore, the representative of the landed interest and exempted from the control of universal suffrage. I hope what I may have to say will be kindly received, for it will be well intended. But, if I thought otherwise, I should still prefer to hazard the loss of the little popularity which I might have in this house, or out of it, than to hazard the loss of the approbation of my own conscience.

I have reflected upon the report of the select committee with attention and with anxiety. We appear to be disregarding the principles of the constitution, under which we have so long and so happily lived, and to be changing some of its essential institutions. I cannot but think that the considerate men who have studied the history of republics, or are read in lessons of experience, must look with concern upon our apparent disposition to vibrate from a well-balanced government to the extremes of the democratic doctrines. Such a broad proposition as that contained in the report, at the distance of ten years past, would

From *Reports of the Proceedings and Debates of the Convention of 1821, Assembled for the Purpose of Amending the Constitution of the State of New York* (Albany, NY 1821).

have struck the public mind with astonishment and terror, so rapid has been the career of our vibration.

American Prosperity

Let us recall our attention, for a moment, to our past history. This state has existed for forty-four years under our present constitution, which was formed by those illustrious sages and patriots who adorned the Revolution. It has wonderfully fulfilled all the great ends of civil government. During that long period we have enjoyed, in an eminent degree, the blessings of civil and religious liberty. We have had our lives, our privileges, and our property protected. We have had a succession of wise and temperate legislatures. The code of our statute law has been again and again revised and corrected, and it may proudly bear a comparison with that of any other people. We have had, during that period (though I am, perhaps, not the fittest person to say it), a regular, stable, honest, and enlightened administration of justice. All the peaceable pursuits of industry, and all the important interests of education and science, have been fostered and encouraged. We have trebled our numbers within the last twenty-five years, have displayed mighty resources, and have made unexampled progress in the career of prosperity and greatness.

Our financial credit stands at an enviable height; and we are now successfully engaged in connecting the Great Lakes with the ocean by stupendous canals, which excite the admiration of our neighbors and will make a conspicuous figure even upon the map of the United States.

These are some of the fruits of our present government; and yet we seem to be dissatisfied with our condition, and we are engaged in the bold and hazardous experiment of remodeling the constitution. Is it not fit and discreet—I speak as to wise men—is it not fit and proper that we should pause in our career and reflect well on the immensity of the innovation in contemplation? Discontent in the midst of so much prosperity, and with such abundant means of happiness, looks like ingratitude and as if we were disposed to arraign the goodness of Providence. Do we not expose ourselves to the danger of being deprived of the blessings we have enjoyed? When the husbandman has gathered in his harvest, and has filled his barns and his granaries with the fruits of his industry, if he should then become discontented and unthankful, would he not have reason to apprehend that the Lord of the harvest might come in His wrath and with His lightning destroy them?

The Idol of Universal Suffrage

The Senate has hitherto been elected by the farmers of the state, by the free and independent lords of the soil, worth at least $250 in freehold estate, over

and above all debts charged thereon. The governor has been chosen by the same electors, and we have hitherto elected citizens of elevated rank and character. Our assembly has been chosen by freeholders, possessing a freehold of the value of $50, or by persons renting a tenement of the yearly value of $5, and who have been rated [valued for purposes of taxation] and actually paid taxes to the state. By the report before us, we propose to annihilate, at one stroke, all those property distinctions and to bow before the idol of universal suffrage. That extreme democratic principle, when applied to the Legislative and Executive departments of government, has been regarded with terror by the wise men of every age, because in every European republic, ancient and modern, in which it has been tried, it has terminated disastrously and been productive of corruption, injustice, violence, and tyranny. And dare we flatter ourselves that we are a peculiar people who can run the career of history, exempted from the passions which have disturbed and corrupted the rest of mankind? If we are like other races of men, with similar follies and vices, then I greatly fear that our posterity will have reason to deplore, in sackcloth and ashes, the delusion of the day.

The Agricultural Interest

It is not my purpose at present to interfere with the report of the committee, so far as respects the qualifications of electors for governor and members of assembly. I shall feel grateful if we may be permitted to retain the stability and security of a Senate, bottomed upon the freehold property of the state. Such a body, so constituted, may prove a sheet anchor amid the future factions and storms of the republic. The great leading and governing interest of this state is, at present, the agricultural; and what madness would it be to commit that interest to the winds. The great body of the people are now the owners and actual cultivators of the soil. With that wholesome population we always expect to find moderation, frugality, order, honesty, and a due sense of independence, liberty, and justice. It is impossible that any people can lose their liberties by internal fraud or violence so long as the country is parceled out among freeholders of moderate possessions, and those freeholders have a sure and efficient control in the affairs of the government. Their habits, sympathies, and employments necessarily inspire them with a correct spirit of freedom and justice; they are the safest guardians of property and the laws.

We certainly cannot too highly appreciate the value of the agricultural interest. It is the foundation of national wealth and power. According to the opinion of her ablest political economists, it is the surplus produce of the agriculture of England that enables her to support her vast body of manufacturers, her formidable fleets and armies, and the crowds of persons engaged in the liberal professions and the cultivation of the various arts.

Now, sir, I wish to preserve our Senate as the representative of the landed interest. I wish those who have an interest in the soil to retain the exclusive possession of a branch in the legislature as a stronghold in which they may find safety through all the vicissitudes which the state may be destined, in the course of Providence, to experience. I wish them to be always enabled to say that their freeholds cannot be taxed without their consent. The men of no property, together with the crowds of dependents connected with great manufacturing and commercial establishments, and the motley and undefinable population of crowded ports, may, perhaps, at some future day, under skillful management, predominate in the assembly, and yet we should be perfectly safe if no laws could pass without the free consent of the owners of the soil. That security we at present enjoy; and it is that security which I wish to retain.

Dangerous Tendencies

The apprehended danger from the experiment of universal suffrage applied to the whole Legislative Department is no dream of the imagination. It is too mighty an excitement for the moral constitution of men to endure. The tendency of universal suffrage is to jeopardize the rights of property and the principles of liberty. There is a constant tendency in human society, and the history of every age proves it; there is a tendency in the poor to covet and to share the plunder of the rich; in the debtor, to relax or avoid the obligation of contracts; in the majority, to tyrannize over the minority and trample down their rights; in the indolent and the profligate, to cast the whole burdens of society upon the industrious and the virtuous; and *there is a tendency in ambitious and wicked men to inflame these combustible materials.*

It requires a vigilant government and a firm administration of justice to counteract that tendency. "Thou shalt not covet," "Thou shalt not steal" are divine injunctions induced by this miserable depravity of our nature. Who can undertake to calculate with any precision how many millions of people this great state will contain in the course of this and the next century, and who can estimate the future extent and magnitude of our commercial ports? The disproportion between the men of property and the men of no property will be in every society in a ratio to its commerce, wealth, and population.

A Changing Nation

We are no longer to remain plain and simple republics of farmers like the New England colonists

or the Dutch settlements on the Hudson. We are fast becoming a great nation, with great commerce, manufactures, population, wealth, luxuries, and with the vices and miseries that they engender. One-seventh of the population of the city of Paris at this day subsists on charity, and one-third of the inhabitants of that city die in the hospitals; what would become of such a city with universal suffrage? France has upward of 4 million, and England upward of 5 million of manufacturing and commercial laborers without property. Could these kingdoms sustain the weight of universal suffrage? The radicals in England, with the force of that mighty engine, would at once sweep away the property, the laws, and the liberties of that island like a deluge.

The growth of the city of New York is enough to startle and awaken those who are pursuing the *ignis fatuus* [will o' the wisp] of universal suffrage. In 1773 it had 21,000 souls; in 1801 it had 60,000; in 1806 it had 76,000; in 1820 it had 123,000. It is rapidly swelling into the unwieldy population, and with the burdensome pauperism, of a European metropolis. New York is destined to become the future London of America; and in less than a century that city, with the operation of universal suffrage and under skillful direction, will govern this state.

The notion that every man that works a day on the road, or serves an idle hour in the militia, is entitled as of right to an equal participation in the whole power of the government is most unreasonable and has no foundation in justice. We had better at once discard from the report such a nominal test of merit. If such persons have an equal share in one branch of the legislature, it is surely as much as they can in justice or policy demand. Society is an association for the protection of property as well as of life, and the individual who contributes only one cent to the common stock ought not to have the same power and influence in directing the property concerns of the partnership as he who contributes his thousands. He will not have the same inducements to care, and diligence, and fidelity. His inducements and his temptation would be to divide the whole capital upon the principles of an agrarian law.

The Abuse of Liberty

Liberty, rightly understood, is an inestimable blessing, but liberty without wisdom and without justice is no better than wild and savage licentiousness. The danger which we have hereafter to apprehend is not the want but the abuse of liberty. We have to apprehend the oppression of minorities and a disposition to encroach on private right; to disturb chartered privileges; and to weaken, degrade, and overawe the administration of justice; we have to apprehend the establishment of unequal and, consequently, unjust systems of taxation and all the mischiefs of a crude and mutable legislation. A stable Senate, exempted from the influence of universal suffrage, will powerfully check these dangerous propensities. . . .

———————— • ————————

"The tendency of universal suffrage is to jeopardize the rights of property and the principles of liberty."

———————— • ————————

We are destined to become a great manufacturing as well as commercial state. We have already numerous and prosperous factories of one kind or another, and one master-capitalist, with his 100 apprentices, and journeymen, and agents, and dependents, will bear down at the polls an equal number of farmers of small estates in his vicinity who cannot safely unite for their common defense. Large manufacturing and mechanical establishments can act in an instant with the unity and efficacy of disciplined troops. It is against such combinations, among others, that I think we ought to give to the freeholders, or those who have interest in land, one branch of the legislature for their asylum and their comfort. Universal suffrage, once granted, is granted forever and never can be recalled. There is no retrograde step in the rear of democracy. However mischievous the precedent may be in its consequences, or however fatal in its effects, universal suffrage never can be recalled or checked but by the strength of the bayonet. We stand, therefore, this moment, on the brink of fate, on the very edge of the precipice. If we let go our present hold on the Senate, we commit our proudest hopes and our most precious interests to the waves.

The Senate's Importance

It ought further to be observed that the Senate is a court of justice in the last resort. It is the last depository of public and private rights, of civil and criminal justice. This gives the subject an awful consideration and wonderfully increases the importance of securing that house from the inroads of universal suffrage. Our country freeholders are exclusively our jurors in the administration of justice, and there is equal reason that none but those who have an interest in the soil should have any concern in the composition of that court. As long as the Senate is safe, justice is safe, property is safe, and our liberties are safe. But when the wisdom, the integrity, and the independence of that court is lost, we may be certain that the freedom and happiness of this state are fled forever. I hope, sir, we shall not carry desolation through all the departments of the fabric erected by our fathers. I hope we shall not put forward to the world a new constitution as will meet with the scorn of the wise and the tears of the patriot.

For Further Reading

Leon F. Litwack, *North of Slavery: The Negro in the Free States, 1790–1860.* Chicago: University of Chicago Press, 1961.

Merrill D. Peterson, ed., *Democracy, Liberty, and Property: The State Constitutional Conventions of the 1820s.* Indianapolis, IN: Bobbs-Merrill Co., 1966.

Chilton Williamson, *American Suffrage from Property to Democracy, 1760–1860.* Princeton, NJ: Princeton University Press, 1960.

VIEWPOINT 25A

Indians Should Be Removed to the West (1829, 1830)

Andrew Jackson (1767–1845)

Between 1815 and 1860 most of the American Indians residing in the territory between the Appalachian Mountains and the Mississippi River were forced to cede their lands to whites and move from their homes. The United States government actively pursued this end by purchasing or seizing Indian territory and persuading Indians (often with military threats) to relocate west of the Mississippi. Some Indian tribes responded with battle; others tried different methods of resistance. Among the latter group were the Cherokee Indians who lived in Georgia, Alabama, and Tennessee. One of what were called the "Five Civilized Tribes" (which also included the Choctaw, Chickasaw, Creek, and Seminole Indians), the Cherokee had adopted numerous traits of white culture. These included writing, a governing constitution modeled after the U.S. Constitution, schools, and agricultural plantations (with black slaves). In 1827 the Cherokee proclaimed themselves an independent nation, much to the dissatisfaction of whites who coveted their land. The state of Georgia promptly passed laws nullifying the Cherokee declaration and extending state authority over Cherokee lands, actions that violated existing treaties between the Cherokee and the federal government. Both sides looked to Washington for support.

The white settlers were to find an ally in Andrew Jackson, who had been elected president in 1828. Jackson had previously gained national fame and popularity as an Indian fighter who had forced tribes to cede millions of acres of territory in Alabama,

From *A Compilation of the Messages and Papers of the Presidents*, vol. 3, edited by James D. Richardson (New York: Bureau of National Literature, 1897).

Georgia, and Florida. The following two-part viewpoint consists of excerpts from Jackson's first and second annual messages to Congress, given on December 8, 1829, and December 6, 1830, respectively. Jackson asserts that the national government has no authority to interfere with the state of Georgia in its dealings with the Indians (despite past treaties), and argues that the only viable solution is the removal of the Indians to lands west of the Mississippi River. Congress responded by passing the Indian Removal Act in 1830, which authorized funds for the removal of all Indian tribes still east of the Mississippi.

How does Jackson defend on humanitarian grounds the removal of the Indians? What does Jackson predict will happen to Indians who choose to remain? Is Jackson's second message more or less sympathetic to the Indians than his first? Explain.

I

The condition and ulterior destiny of the Indian tribes within the limits of some of our States have become objects of much interest and importance. It has long been the policy of Government to introduce among them the arts of civilization, in the hope of gradually reclaiming them from a wandering life. This policy has, however, been coupled with another wholly incompatible with its success. Professing a desire to civilize and settle them, we have at the same time lost no opportunity to purchase their lands and thrust them farther into the wilderness. By this means they have not only been kept in a wandering state, but been led to look upon us as unjust and indifferent to their fate. Thus, though lavish in its expenditures upon the subject, Government has constantly defeated its own policy, and the Indians in general, receding farther and farther to the west, have retained their savage habits. A portion, however, of the Southern tribes, having mingled much with the whites and made some progress in the arts of civilized life, have lately attempted to erect an independent government within the limits of Georgia and Alabama. These States, claiming to be the only sovereigns within their territories, extended their laws over the Indians, which induced the latter to call upon the United States for protection.

The Rights of States

Under these circumstances the question presented was whether the General Government had a right to sustain those people in their pretensions. The Constitution declares that "no new State shall be formed or erected within the jurisdiction of any other State" without the consent of its legislature. If the General Government is not permitted to tolerate the erection of a confederate State within the territory of one of the members of this Union against her consent, much less could it allow a foreign and independent government to establish itself there. Georgia became a member of the Confederacy which eventuated in our Federal Union as a sovereign State, always asserting her claim to certain limits, which, having been originally defined in her colonial charter and subsequently recognized in the treaty of peace, she has ever since continued to enjoy, except as they have been circumscribed by her own voluntary transfer of a portion of her territory to the United States in the articles of cession of 1802. Alabama was admitted into the Union on the same footing with the original States, with boundaries which were prescribed by Congress. There is no constitutional, conventional, or legal provision which allows them less power over the Indians within their borders than is possessed by Maine or New York. Would the people of Maine permit the Penobscot tribe to erect an independent government within their State? And unless they did would it not be the duty of the General Government to support them in resisting such a measure? Would the people of New York permit each remnant of the Six Nations [Iroquois] within her borders to declare itself an independent people under the protection of the United States? Could the Indians establish a separate republic on each of their reservations in Ohio? And if they were so disposed would it be the duty of this Government to protect them in the attempt? If the principle involved in the obvious answer to these questions be abandoned, it will follow that the objects of this Government are reversed, and that it has become a part of its duty to aid in destroying the States which it was established to protect.

Actuated by this view of the subject, I informed the Indians inhabiting parts of Georgia and Alabama that their attempt to establish an independent government would not be countenanced by the Executive of the United States, and advised them to emigrate beyond the Mississippi or submit to the laws of those States.

Our conduct toward these people is deeply interesting to our national character. Their present condition, contrasted with what they once were, makes a most powerful appeal to our sympathies. Our ancestors found them the uncontrolled possessors of these vast regions. By persuasion and force they have been made to retire from river to river and from mountain to mountain, until some of the tribes have become extinct and others have left but remnants to preserve for a while their once terrible names. Surrounded by the whites with their arts of civilization, which by destroying the resources of the savage doom him to weakness and decay, the fate of the Mohegan, the Narragansett, and the Delaware is fast overtaking the Choctaw, the Cherokee, and the Creek. That this fate surely awaits them if they remain within the limits of the States does not admit of a doubt. Humanity and national honor demand that every effort should be made to avert so great a calamity. It is too late to inquire whether it was just in the United States to include them and their territory within the bounds of new States, whose limits they could control. That step can not be retraced. A State can not be dismembered by Congress or restricted in the exercise of her constitutional power. But the people of those States and of every State, actuated by feelings of justice and a regard for our national honor, submit to you the interesting question whether something can not be done, consistently with the rights of the States, to preserve this much-injured race.

A Proposed Solution

As a means of effecting this end I suggest for your consideration the propriety of setting apart an ample district west of the Mississippi, and without [outside] the limits of any State or Territory now formed, to be guaranteed to the Indian tribes as long as they shall occupy it, each tribe having a distinct control over the portion designated for its use. There they may be secured in the enjoyment of governments of their own choice, subject to no other control from the United States than such as may be necessary to preserve peace on the frontier and between the several tribes. There the benevolent may endeavor to teach them the arts of civilization, and, by promoting union and harmony among them, to raise up an interesting commonwealth, destined to perpetuate the race and to attest the humanity and justice of this Government.

———— • ————

"The consequences of a speedy removal will be important to the United States, to individual States, and to the Indians themselves."

———— • ————

This emigration should be voluntary, for it would be as cruel as unjust to compel the aboriginies to abandon the graves of their fathers and seek a home in a distant land. But they should be distinctly informed that if they remain within the limits of the States they must be subject to their laws. In return for their obedience as individuals they will without doubt be protected in the enjoyment of those possessions which they have improved by their industry. But it seems to me visionary to suppose that in this

state of things claims can be allowed on tracts of country on which they have neither dwelt nor made improvements, merely because they have seen them from the mountain or passed them in the chase. Submitting to the laws of the States, and receiving, like other citizens, protection in their persons and property, they will ere long become merged in the mass of our population.

II

It gives me pleasure to announce to Congress that the benevolent policy of the Government, steadily pursued for nearly thirty years, in relation to the removal of the Indians beyond the white settlements is approaching to a happy consummation. Two important tribes [the Choctaws and the Chickasaws] have accepted the provision made for their removal at the last session of Congress, and it is believed that their example will induce the remaining tribes also to seek the same obvious advantages.

The consequences of a speedy removal will be important to the United States, to individual States, and to the Indians themselves. The pecuniary advantages which it promises to the Government are the least of its recommendations. It puts an end to all possible danger of collision between the authorities of the General and State Governments on account of the Indians. It will place a dense and civilized population in large tracts of country now occupied by a few savage hunters. By opening the whole territory between Tennessee on the north and Louisiana on the south to the settlement of the whites it will incalculably strengthen the southwestern frontier and render the adjacent States strong enough to repel future invasions without remote aid. It will relieve the whole State of Mississippi and the western part of Alabama of Indian occupancy, and enable those States to advance rapidly in population, wealth, and power. It will separate the Indians from immediate contact with settlements of whites; free them from the power of the States; enable them to pursue happiness in their own way and under their own rude institutions; will retard the progress of decay, which is lessening their numbers, and perhaps cause them gradually, under the protection of the Government and through the influence of good counsels, to cast off their savage habits and become an interesting, civilized, and Christian community. These consequences, some of them so certain and the rest so probable, make the complete execution of the plan sanctioned by Congress at their last session [the 1830 Indian Removal Act] an object of much solicitude.

Toward the aborigines of the country no one can indulge a more friendly feeling than myself, or would go further in attempting to reclaim them from their wandering habits and make them a happy, prosperous people. I have endeavored to impress upon them my own solemn convictions of the duties and powers of the General Government in relation to the State authorities. For the justice of the laws passed by the States within the scope of their reserved powers they are not responsible to this Government. As individuals we may entertain and express our opinions of their acts, but as a Government we have as little right to control them as we have to prescribe laws for other nations.

With a full understanding of the subject, the Choctaw and the Chickasaw tribes have with great unanimity determined to avail themselves of the liberal offers presented by the act of Congress, and have agreed to remove beyond the Mississippi River. Treaties have been made with them, which in due season will be submitted for consideration. In negotiating these treaties they were made to understand their true condition, and they have preferred maintaining their independence in the Western forests to submitting to the laws of the States in which they now reside. These treaties, being probably the last which will ever be made with them, are characterized by great liberality on the part of the Government. They give the Indians a liberal sum in consideration of their removal, and comfortable subsistence on their arrival at their new homes. If it be their real interest to maintain a separate existence, they will there be at liberty to do so without the inconveniences and vexations to which they would unavoidably have been subject in Alabama and Mississippi.

True Philanthropy

Humanity has often wept over the fate of the aborigines of this country, and Philanthropy has been long busily employed in devising means to avert it, but its progress has never for a moment been arrested, and one by one have many powerful tribes disappeared from the earth. To follow to the tomb the last of his race and to tread on the graves of extinct nations excite melancholy reflections. But true philanthropy reconciles the mind to these vicissitudes as it does to the extinction of one generation to make room for another. In the monuments and fortresses of an unknown people, spread over the extensive regions of the West, we behold the memorials of a once powerful race, which was exterminated or has disappeared to make room for the existing savage tribes. Nor is there anything in this which, upon a comprehensive view of the general interests of the human race, is to be regretted. Philanthropy could not wish to see this continent restored to the condition in which it was found by our forefathers. What good man would prefer a country covered with forests and ranged by a few thousand savages to our extensive Republic, studded with cities, towns, and

prosperous farms, embellished with all the improvements which art can devise or industry execute, occupied by more than 12,000,000 happy people, and filled with all the blessings of liberty, civilization, and religion?

The present policy of the Government is but a continuation of the same progressive change by a milder process. The tribes which occupied the countries now constituting the Eastern States were annihilated or have melted away to make room for the whites. The waves of population and civilization are rolling to the westward, and we now propose to acquire the countries occupied by the red men of the South and West by a fair exchange, and, at the expense of the United States, to send them to a land where their existence may be prolonged and perhaps made perpetual. Doubtless it will be painful to leave the graves of their fathers; but what do they more than our ancestors did or than our children are now doing? To better their condition in an unknown land our forefathers left all that was dear in earthly objects. Our children by thousands yearly leave the land of their birth to seek new homes in distant regions. Does Humanity weep at these painful separations from everything, animate and inanimate, with which the young heart has become entwined? Far from it. It is rather a source of joy that our country affords scope where our young population may range unconstrained in body or in mind, developing the power and faculties of man in their highest perfection. These remove hundreds and almost thousands of miles at their own expense, purchase the lands they occupy, and support themselves at their new homes from the moment of their arrival. Can it be cruel in this Government when, by events which it can not control, the Indian is made discontented in his ancient home to purchase his lands, to give him a new and extensive territory, to pay the expense of his removal, and support him a year in his new abode? How many thousands of our own people would gladly embrace the opportunity of removing to the West on such conditions! If the offers made to the Indians were extended to them, they would be hailed with gratitude and joy.

A Generous Policy

And is it supposed that the wandering savage has a stronger attachment to his home than the settled, civilized Christian? Is it more afflicting to him to leave the graves of his fathers than it is to our brothers and children? Rightly considered, the policy of the General Government toward the red man is not only liberal, but generous. He is unwilling to submit to the laws of the States and mingle with their population. To save him from this alternative, or perhaps utter annihilation, the General Government kindly offers him a new home, and proposes to pay the whole expense of his removal and settlement.

In the consummation of a policy originating at an early period, and steadily pursued by every Administration within the present century—so just to the States and so generous to the Indians—the Executive feels it has a right to expect the cooperation of Congress and of all good and disinterested men. The States, moreover, have a right to demand it. It was substantially a part of the compact which made them members of our Confederacy. With Georgia there is an express contract; with the new States an implied one of equal obligation. Why, in authorizing Ohio, Indiana, Illinois, Missouri, Mississippi, and Alabama to form constitutions and become separate States, did Congress include within their limits extensive tracts of Indian lands, and, in some instances, powerful Indian tribes? Was it not understood by both parties that the power of the States was to be coextensive with their limits, and that with all convenient dispatch the General Government should extinguish the Indian title and remove every obstruction to the complete jurisdiction of the State governments over the soil? Probably not one of those States would have accepted a separate existence—certainly it would never have been granted by Congress—had it been understood that they were to be confined forever to those small portions of their nominal territory the Indian title to which had at the time been extinguished.

The Duties of This Government

It is, therefore, a duty which this Government owes to the new States to extinguish as soon as possible the Indian title to all lands which Congress themselves have included within their limits. When this is done the duties of the General Government in relation to the States and the Indians within their limits are at an end. The Indians may leave the State or not, as they choose. The purchase of their lands does not alter in the least their personal relations with the State government. No act of the General Government has ever been deemed necessary to give the States jurisdiction over the persons of the Indians. That they possess by virtue of their sovereign power within their own limits in as full a manner before as after the purchase of the Indian lands; nor can this Government add to or diminish it.

May we not hope, therefore, that all good citizens, and none more zealously than those who think the Indians oppressed by subjection to the laws of the States, will unite in attempting to open the eyes of those children of the forest to their true condition, and by a speedy removal to relieve them from all the evils, real or imaginary, present or prospective, with which they may be supposed to be threatened.

VIEWPOINT 25B

Indians Should Be Allowed to Remain in Their Homeland (1830)

Cherokee Nation

The Cherokee Indians in the early 1800s had successfully adopted and combined traits of Indian and white culture to create a prosperous agricultural society with plantations, gristmills, a newspaper, and a governing constitution. In 1828, however, the state government of Georgia passed laws ordering the seizure of Indian lands and declaring all Cherokee laws void. Faced with the growing threat of forced removal from their homes, the Cherokees sent a delegation to Washington in 1830 to plead their case before President Andrew Jackson and to Congress. Finding both the president and Congress unreceptive, they published an appeal to the American people, excerpted below, pleading for the right to stay in their homeland.

The Cherokee nation and their white supporters appealed Georgia's assertion of authority over their territory and had their case heard in the U.S. Supreme Court. In 1832 in *Worcester v. Georgia* Chief Justice John Marshall ruled that the state of Georgia had no authority over the Cherokee nation, but the legal decision was ignored by Georgia and President Jackson and had little practical effect. Jackson and others continued to press for their removal west of the Mississippi River. In 1838 U.S. troops forced the remaining Cherokees to leave for lands in Oklahoma. Around 4,000 Cherokees, or one quarter of the population, perished while on the "trail of tears."

On what legal basis do the Cherokee make their arguments? What reasons do they give for not wishing to move? How, in their view, has the state of Georgia treated them unfairly?

Some months ago a delegation was appointed by the constituted authorities of the Cherokee nation to repair to the city of Washington, and in behalf of this nation, to lay before the government of the United States such representations as should seem most likely to secure to us, as a people, that protection, aid, and good neighborhood, which had been so often promised to us, and of which we stand in great need. Soon after their arrival in the city they presented to congress a petition from our national

From the "Memorial of the Cherokee Nation" (July 17, 1830), as reprinted in *Nile's Weekly Register*, August 21, 1830.

council, asking for the interposition of that body in our behalf, especially with reference to the laws of Georgia; which were suspended in a most terrifying manner over a large part of our population, and protesting in the most decided terms against the operation of these laws. In the course of the winter they presented petitions to congress, signed by more than four thousand of our citizens, including probably more than nineteen-twentieths, and for aught we can tell, ninety-nine hundredths, of the adult males of the nation . . . , pleading with the assembled representatives of the American people, that the solemn engagements between their fathers and our fathers may be preserved, as they have been till recently, in full force and continued operation; asking, in a word, for protection against threatened usurpation and for a faithful execution for a guaranty which is perfectly plain in its meaning, has been repeatedly and rigidly endorsed in our favour, and has received the sanction of the government of the United States for nearly forty years.

President Jackson's Unexpected Policies

More than a year ago we were officially given to understand by the secretary of war, that the president could not protect us against the laws of Georgia. This information was entirely unexpected; as it went upon the principle, that treaties made between the United States and the Cherokee nation have no power to withstand the legislation of separate states; and of course, that they have no efficacy whatever, but leave our people to the mercy of the neighboring whites, whose supposed interests would be promoted by our expulsion, or extermination. It would be impossible to describe the sorrow, which affected our minds on learning that the chief magistrate [president] of the United States had come to this conclusion, that all his illustrious predecessors had held intercourse with us on principles which could not be sustained; that they had made promises of vital importance to us, which could not be fulfilled—promises made hundreds of times in almost every conceivable manner,—often in the form of solemn treaties, sometimes in letters written by the chief magistrate with his own hand, very often in letters written by the secretary of war under his direction, sometimes orally by the president and the secretary to our chiefs, and frequently and always, both orally and in writing by the agent of the United States residing among us, whose most important business it was, to see the guaranty of the United States faithfully executed.

Soon after the war of the revolution, as we have learned from our fathers, the Cherokees looked upon the promises of the whites with great distrust and suspicion; but the frank and magnanimous conduct of General Washington did much to allay these feelings. The perseverance of successive presidents, and especially of Mr. Jefferson, in the same course of policy, and in the constant assurance that our country should remain inviolate, except so far as we voluntarily ceded it, nearly banished anxiety in regard to encroachments from the whites. To this result the aid which we received from the United States in the attempts of our people to become civilized, and the kind efforts of benevolent societies, have greatly contributed. Of late years, however, much solicitude was occasioned among our people by the claims of Georgia. This solicitude arose from the apprehension, that by extreme importunity, threats, and other undue influence, a treaty would be made, which should cede the territory, and thus compel the inhabitants to remove. But it never occurred to us for a moment, that without any new treaty, without any assent of our rulers and people, without even a pretended compact, and against our vehement and unanimous protestations, we should be delivered over to the discretion of those, who had declared by a legislative act, that they wanted the Cherokee lands and would have them.

Appealing to Congress

Finding that relief could not be obtained from the chief magistrate, and not doubting that our claim to protection was just, we made our application to congress. During four long months our delegation waited, at the doors of the national legislature of the United States, and the people at home, in the most painful suspense, to learn in what manner our application would be answered; and, now that congress has adjourned, on the very day before the date fixed by Georgia for the extension of her oppressive laws over the greater part of our country, the distressing intelligence has been received that we have received no answer at all; and no department of the government has assured us, that we are to receive the desired protection. But just at the close of the session, an act was passed, by which an half a million of dollars was appropriated towards effecting a removal of Indians; and we have great reason to fear that the influence of this act will be brought to bear most injuriously upon us. The passage of this act was certainly understood by the representatives of Georgia as abandoning us to the oppressive and cruel measures of the state, and as sanctioning the opinion that treaties with Indians do not restrain state legislation. We are informed by those, who are competent to judge, that the recent act does not admit of such construction; but that the passage of it, under the actual circumstances of the controversy, will be considered as sanctioning the pretensions of Georgia, there is too much reason to fear.

Thus have we realized, with heavy hearts, that our supplication has not been heard; that the protection heretofore experienced is now to be withheld; that the guaranty, in consequence of which our fathers laid aside their arms and ceded the best portions of their country, means nothing; and that we must either emigrate to an unknown region and leave the pleasant land to which we have the strongest attachment, or submit to the legislation of a state, which has already made our people outlaws, and enacted that any Cherokee, who shall endeavor to prevent the selling of his country, shall be imprisoned in the penitentiary of Georgia not less than four years. To our countrymen this has been melancholy intelligence, and with the most bitter disappointment has it been received.

But in the midst of our sorrows, we do not forget our obligations to our friends and benefactors. It was with sensations of inexpressible joy that we have learned that the voice of thousands, in many parts of the United States, has been raised in our behalf, and numerous memorials offered in our favor, in both houses of congress. To those numerous friends, who have thus sympathized with us in our low estate, we tender our grateful acknowledgements. In pleading our cause, they have pleaded the cause of the poor and defenceless throughout the world. Our special thanks are due, however, to those honorable men, who so ably and eloquently asserted our rights, in both branches of the national legislature. Their efforts will be appreciated wherever the merits of this question shall be known; and we cannot but think, that they have secured for themselves a permanent reputation among the disinterested advocates of humanity, equal rights, justice, and good faith. We even cherish the hope, that these efforts, seconded and followed by others of a similar character, will yet be available, so far as to mitigate our sufferings, if not to effect our entire deliverance.

A Brief History

Before we close this address, permit us to state what we conceive to be our relations with the United States. After the peace of 1783, the Cherokees were an independent people; absolutely so, as much as any people on earth. They had been allies to Great Britain, and as a faithful ally took a part in the colonial war on her side. They had placed themselves under her protection, and had they, without cause, declared hostility against their protector, and had the colonies been subdued, what might not have been their fate? But her power on this continent was broken. She acknowledged the independence of the United States, and made peace. The Cherokees therefore stood alone; and, in these circumstances, continued the war. They were then under no obliga-

tions to the United States any more than to Great Britain, France or Spain. The United States never subjugated the Cherokees; on the contrary, our fathers remained in possession of their country, and with arms in their hands.

———— • ————

"We wish to remain on the land of our fathers. We have a perfect and original right to remain without interruption or molestation."

———— • ————

The people of the United States sought a peace; and, in 1785, the treaty of Hopewell was formed, by which the Cherokees came under the protection of the United States, and submitted to such limitations of sovereignty as are mentioned in that instrument. None of these limitations, however, affected, in the slightest degree, their rights of self-government and inviolate territory. The citizens of the United States had no right of passage through the Cherokee country till the year 1791, and then only in one direction, and by an express treaty stipulation. When the federal constitution was adopted, the treaty of Hopewell was confirmed, with all other treaties, as the supreme law of the land. In 1791, the treaty of Holston was made, by which the sovereignty of the Cherokees was qualified as follows: The Cherokees acknowledged themselves to be under the protection of the United States, and of no other sovereign.—They engaged that they would not hold any treaty with a foreign power, with any separate state of the union, or with individuals. They agreed that the United States should have the exclusive right of regulating their trade; that the citizens of the United States should have a right of way in one direction through the Cherokee country; and that if an Indian should do injury to a citizen of the United States he should be delivered up to be tried and punished. A cession of lands was also made to the United States. On the other hand, the United States paid a sum of money; offered protection; engaged to punish citizens of the United States who should do any injury to the Cherokees; abandoned white settlers on Cherokee lands to the discretion of the Cherokees; stipulated that white men should not hunt on these lands, nor even enter the country without a passport; and gave a solemn guaranty of all Cherokee lands not ceded. This treaty is the basis of all subsequent compacts; and in none of them are the relations of the parties at all changed.

The Cherokees have always fulfilled their engagements. They have never reclaimed those portions of sovereignty which they surrendered by the treaties of Hopewell and Holston. These portions were surrendered for the purpose of obtaining the guaranty which was recommended to them as the great equivalent. Had they refused to comply with their engagements, there is no doubt the United States would have enforced a compliance. Is the duty of fulfilling engagements on the other side less binding than it would be, if the Cherokees had the power of enforcing their just claims?

The people of the United States will have the fairness to reflect, that all the treaties between them and the Cherokees were made, at the solicitation, and for the benefit, of the whites; that valuable considerations were given for every stipulation, on the part of the United States; that it is impossible to reinstate the parties in their former situation, that there are now hundreds of thousands of citizens of the United States residing upon lands ceded by the Cherokees in these very treaties; and that our people have trusted their country to the guaranty of the United States. If this guaranty fails them, in what can they trust, and where can they look for protection?

We Wish to Remain

We are aware, that some persons suppose it will be for our advantage to remove beyond the Mississippi. We think otherwise. Our people universally think otherwise. Thinking that it would be fatal to their interests, they have almost to a man sent their memorial to congress, deprecating the necessity of a removal. This question was distinctly before their minds when they signed their memorial. Not an adult person can be found, who has not an opinion on the subject, and if the people were to understand distinctly, that they could be protected against the laws of the neighboring states, there is probably not an adult person in the nation, who would think it best to remove; though possibly a few might emigrate individually. There are doubtless many, who would flee to an unknown country, however beset with dangers, privations and sufferings, rather than be sentenced to spend six years in a Georgia prison for advising one of their neighbors not to betray his country. And there are others who could not think of living as outlaws in their native land, exposed to numberless vexations, and excluded from being parties or witnesses in a court of justice. It is incredible that Georgia should ever have enacted the oppressive laws to which reference is here made, unless she had supposed that something extremely terrific in its character was necessary in order to make the Cherokees willing to remove. We are not willing to remove; and if we could be brought to this extremity, it would be not by argument, not because our judgment was satisfied, not because our condition will be improved; but only because we cannot endure to be deprived of

our national and individual rights and subjected to a process of intolerable oppression.

We wish to remain on the land of our fathers. We have a perfect and original right to remain without interruption or molestation. The treaties with us, and laws of the United States made in pursuance of treaties, guaranty our residence and our privileges, and secure us against intruders. Our only request is, that these treaties may be fulfilled, and these laws executed.

But if we are compelled to leave our country, we see nothing but ruin before us. The country west of the Arkansas territory is unknown to us. From what we can learn of it, we have no prepossessions in its favor. All the inviting parts of it, as we believe, are preoccupied by various Indian nations, to which it has been assigned. They would regard us as intruders, and look upon us with an evil eye. The far greater part of that region is, beyond all controversy, badly supplied with wood and water; and no Indian tribe can live as agriculturists without these articles. All our neighbors, in case of our removal, though crowded into our near vicinity, would speak a language totally different from ours, and practice different customs. The original possessors of that region are now wandering savages lurking for prey in the neighborhood. They have always been at war, and would be easily tempted to turn their arms against peaceful emigrants. Were the country to which we are urged much better than it is represented to be, and were it free from the objections which we have made to it, still it is not the land of our birth, nor of our affections. It contains neither the scenes of our childhood, nor the graves of our fathers.

The Harms of Forced Removal

The removal of families to a new country, even under the most favorable auspices, and when the spirits are sustained by pleasing visions of the future, is attended with much depression of mind and sinking of heart. This is the case, when the removal is a matter of decided preference, and when the persons concerned are in early youth or vigorous manhood. Judge, then, what must be the circumstances of a removal, when a whole community, embracing persons of all classes and every description, from the infant to the man of extreme old age, the sick, the blind, the lame, the improvident, the reckless, the desperate, as well as the prudent, the considerate, the industrious, are compelled to remove by odious and intolerable vexations and persecutions, brought upon them in the forms of law, when all will agree only in this, that they have been cruelly robbed of their country, in violation of the most solemn compacts, which it is possible for communities to form with each other; and that, if they should make themselves comfortable in their new residence, they have nothing to expect hereafter but to be the victims of a future legalized robbery!

Such we deem, and are absolutely certain, will be the feelings of the whole Cherokee people, if they are forcibly compelled, by the laws of Georgia, to remove; and with these feelings, how is it possible that we should pursue our present course of improvement, or avoid sinking into utter despondency? We have been called a poor, ignorant, and degraded people. We certainly are not rich; nor have we ever boasted of our knowledge, or our moral or intellectual elevation. But there is not a man within our limits so ignorant as not to know that he has a right to live on the land of his fathers, in the possession of his immemorial privileges, and that this right has been acknowledged and guaranteed by the United States; nor is there a man so degraded as not to feel a keen sense of injury, on being deprived of this right and driven into exile.

An Appeal to the American People

It is under a sense of the most pungent feelings that we make this, perhaps our last appeal to the good people of the United States. It cannot be that the community we are addressing, remarkable for its intelligence and religious sensibilities, and pre-eminent for its devotion to the rights of man, will lay aside this appeal, without considering that we stand in need of its sympathy and commiseration. We know that to the Christian and to the philanthropist the voice of our multiplied sorrows and fiery trials will not appear as an idle tale. In our own land, on our own soil, and in our own dwellings, which we reared for our wives and for our little ones, when there was peace on our mountains and in our valleys, we are encountering troubles which cannot but try our very souls. But shall we, on account of these troubles, forsake our beloved country? Shall we be compelled by a civilized and Christian people, with whom we have lived in perfect peace for the last forty years, and for whom we have willingly bled in war, to bid a final adieu to our homes, our farms, our streams and our beautiful forests? No. We are still firm. We intend still to cling, with our wonted affection, to the land which gave us birth, and which, every day of our lives, brings to us new and stronger ties of attachment. We appeal to the judge of all the earth, who will finally award us justice, and to the good sense of the American people, whether we are intruders upon the land of others. Our consciences bear us witness that we are the invaders of no man's rights—we have robbed no man of his territory—we have usurped no man's authority, nor have we deprived any one of his unalienable privileges. How

then shall we indirectly confess the right of another people to our land by leaving it forever? On the soil which contains the ashes of our beloved men we wish to live—on this soil we wish to die.

Let Them Remember

We intreat those to whom the foregoing paragraphs are addressed, to remember the great law of love. "Do to others as ye would that others should do to you"—Let them remember that of all nations on the earth, they are under the greatest obligation to obey this law. We pray them to remember that, for the sake of principle, their forefathers were *compelled* to leave, therefore *driven* from the old world, and that the winds of persecution wafted them over the great waters and landed them on the shores of the new world, when the Indian was the sole lord and proprietor of these extensive domains—Let them remember in what way they were received by the savage of America, when power was in his hand, and his ferocity could not be restrained by any human arm. We urge them to bear in mind, that those who would now ask of them a cup of cold water, and a spot of earth, a portion of their own patrimonial possessions, on which to live and die in peace, are the descendants of those, whose origin, as inhabitants of North America, history and tradition are alike insufficient to reveal. Let them bring to remembrance all these facts, and they *cannot*, and we are sure, they *will* not fail to remember, and sympathize with us in these our trials and sufferings.

LEWIS ROSS, pres't committee.

James Daniel,	George Sanders,
Jos. Vann,	Daniel Griffin, jun.
David Vann,	James Hamilton,
Edward Gunter,	Alex. McDaniel,
Richard Taylor,	Thos. Foreman,
John Baldridge,	John Timson.
Samuel Ward,	
W.S. Coodey, clerk.	

GOING SNAKE, speaker of the council.

James Bigbey,	J.R. Daniel,
Deer-in-the-water,	Slim Fellow,
Charles Reese,	Situake,
Sleeping Rabbit,	De-gah-le-lu-ge,
Chu-nu-gee,	Robbin,
Bark,	Tah-lah-doo,
Laugh-at-mush,	Nah-hoo-lah,
Chuleowah,	White Path,
Turtle,	Ne-gah-we,
Walking Stick,	Dah-ye-ske.
Moses Parris,	

John Ridge, clerk of the council.
New Echota, C.N. July 17, 1830.

For Further Reading

Michael D. Green, *The Policies of Indian Removal.* Lincoln: University of Nebraska Press, 1982.

Gloria Jahoda, *Trail of Tears.* New York: Holt, Rinehart & Winston, 1975.

Peter Nabokov, ed., *Native American Testimony.* New York: Viking, 1991.

Michael P. Rogin, *Fathers and Children: Andrew Jackson and the Subjugation of the American Indian.* New York: Knopf, 1975.

Virgil J. Vogel, *This Country Was Ours: A Documentary History of the American Indian.* New York: Harper & Row, 1972.

VIEWPOINT 26A

Immigrants Endanger America (1845)

Native American Party

The decades preceding the Civil War were noteworthy for a large influx of American immigrants. Between 1840 and 1860, 4.2 million European immigrants—primarily from Germany and Ireland—entered the United States. Not all Americans welcomed their arrival. Nativism, a movement devoted to the idea that immigrants threatened the economic and political security of "native" Americans—white, Protestant, established citizens—became entrenched in the American political scene during this time.

The fear and resentment many Americans felt toward immigrants had several causes. Anti-Catholic prejudice fueled much nativist sentiment. Some Americans, noting that most Irish and many Germans were Catholic, feared that the Roman Catholic Church might gain unwanted influence in American life and politics. Some American workers worried about immigrants' driving down wages and competing for jobs. Many nativists, viewing newly arrived immigrants as ignorant and unpatriotic, opposed granting immigrants the right to vote.

In 1844 a new nativist organization, the American Republican Party, managed to elect dozens of officials in the states of New York, Pennsylvania, and Massachusetts. Members of the organization held their first national convention the following year in Philadelphia, where they changed their party's name to the Native American Party and adopted a platform delineating the threats they felt immigrants posed to America. The following viewpoint is excerpted from that platform.

How does the Native American Party compare contemporary immigrants with those of the previous two centuries? What importance does it attach to

From *Address of the Delegates of the Native American National Convention, Assembled at Philadelphia, July 4, 1845, to the Citizens of the United States.*

recent democratic reforms (see viewpoints 24A and 24B) giving more people the vote? What ominous future scenarios does it project for America?

We, the delegates elect to the first National Convention of the Native American body of the United States of America, assembled at Philadelphia, on the 4th of July, A.D. 1845, for the purpose of devising a plan of concerted political action in defence of American institutions against the encroachments of foreign influence, open or concealed, hereby solemnly, and before Almighty God, make known to our fellow citizens, our country, and the world, the following incontrovertible facts, and the course of conduct consequent thereon, to which, in duty to the cause of human rights and the claims of our beloved country, we mutually pledge our lives, our fortunes, and our sacred honour.

The danger of foreign influence, threatening the gradual destruction of our national institutions, failed not to arrest the attention of the Father of his Country [George Washington], in the very dawn of American Liberty. Not only its direct agency in rendering the American system liable to the poisonous influence of European policy—a policy at war with the fundamental principles of the American Constitution—but also its still more fatal operation in aggravating the virulence of partisan warfare—has awakened deep alarm in the mind of every intelligent patriot, from the days of Washington to the present time.

The Dangers of Allowing Immigrants to Vote

The influx of a foreign population, permitted after little more than a nominal residence, to participate in the legislation of the country and the sacred right of suffrage, produced comparatively little evil during the earlier years of the Republic; for that influx was then limited by the considerable expenses of a transatlantic voyage, by the existence of many wholesome restraints upon the acquisition of political prerogatives, by the constant exhaustion of the European population in long and bloody continental wars, and by the slender inducements offered for emigration to a young and sparsely peopled country, contending for existence with a boundless wilderness, inhabited by savage men. Evils which are only prospective rarely attract the notice of the masses, and until peculiar changes in the political condition of Europe, the increased facilities for transportation, and the madness of partisan legislation in removing all effective guards against the open prostitution of the right of citizenship had converted the slender current of naturalization into a torrent threatening to overwhelm the influence of the natives of the land, the far-seeing vision of the statesman, only, [was] being fixed upon the distant, but steadily approaching, cloud.

But, since the barriers against the improper extension of the right of suffrage were bodily broken down, for a partisan purpose, by the Congress of 1825, the rapidly increasing numbers and unblushing insolence of the foreign population of the worst classes have caused the general agitation of the question, "How shall the institutions of the country be preserved from the blight of foreign influence, insanely legalized through the conflicts of domestic parties?" Associations under different names have been formed by our fellow citizens, in many States of this confederation, from Louisiana to Maine, all designed to check this imminent danger before it becomes irremediable, and, at length, a National Convention of the great American people, born upon the soil of Washington, has assembled to digest and announce a plan of operation, by which the grievances of an abused hospitality, and the consequent degradation of political morals, may be redressed, and the tottering columns of the temple of Republican Liberty secured upon the sure foundation of an enlightened nationality.

In calling for support upon every American who loves his country pre-eminently, and every adopted citizen of moral and intellectual worth who would secure, to his compatriots yet to come amongst us, the blessings of political protection, the safety of person and property, it is right that we should make known the grievances which we propose to redress, and the manner in which we shall endeavour to effect our object.

Imminent Peril

It is an incontrovertible truth that the civil institutions of the United States of America have been seriously affected, and that they now stand in imminent peril from the rapid and enormous increase of the body of residents of foreign birth, imbued with foreign feelings, and of an ignorant and immoral character, who receive, under the present lax and unreasonable laws of naturalization, the elective franchise and the right of eligibility to political office.

The whole body of foreign citizens, invited to our shores under a constitutional provision adapted to other times and other political conditions of the world, and of our country especially, has been endowed by American hospitality with gratuitous privileges unnecessary to the enjoyment of those inalienable rights of man—life, liberty, and the pursuit of happiness—privileges wisely reserved to the Natives of the soil by the governments of all other civilized nations. But, familiarized by habit with the exercise of these indulgences, and emboldened by increasing numbers, a vast majority of those who constitute this foreign body, now claim as an original right that which has been so incautiously granted as a favour—thus attempting to render inevitable the prospective action of laws adopted upon a principle of mere expediency, made variable at the will of Congress by the express terms of the Constitution, and heretofore repeatedly revised to meet the exigencies of the times.

In former years, this body was recruited chiefly from the victims of political oppression, or the active and intelligent mercantile adventurers of other lands; and it then constituted a slender representation of the best classes of the foreign population well fitted to add strength to the state, and capable of being readily educated in the peculiarly American science of political self-government. Moreover, while welcoming the stranger of every condition, laws then wisely demanded of every foreign aspirant for political rights a certificate of practical good citizenship. Such a class of aliens were followed by no foreign demagogues—they were courted by no domestic demagogues; they were purchased by no parties—they were debauched by no emissaries of kings. A wall of fire separated them from such a baneful influence, erected by their intelligence, their knowledge, their virtue and love of freedom. But for the last twenty years the road to civil preferment and participation in the legislative and executive government of the land has been laid broadly open, alike to the ignorant, the vicious and the criminal; and a large proportion of the foreign body of citizens and voters now constitutes a representation of the worst and most degraded of the European population—victims of social oppression or personal vices, utterly divested, by ignorance or crime, of the moral and intellectual requisites for political self-government.

A New Class of Immigrants

Thus tempted by the suicidal policy of these United States, and favoured by the facilities resulting from the modern improvements of navigation, numerous societies and corporate bodies in foreign countries have found it economical to transport to our shores, at public and private expense, the feeble, the imbecile, the idle, and intractable, thus relieving themselves of the burdens resulting from the vices of the European social systems by availing themselves of the generous errors of our own.

The almshouses of Europe are emptied upon our coast, and this by our own invitation—not casually, or to a trivial extent, but systematically, and upon a constantly increasing scale. The Bedlams [insane asylums] of the old world have contributed their share to the torrent of immigration, and the lives of our citizens have been attempted in the streets of our capital cities by mad-men, just liberated from European hospitals upon the express condition that they should be transported to America. By the orders of European governments, the punishment of crimes has been commuted for banishment to the land of the free; and criminals in iron have crossed the ocean to be cast loose upon society on their arrival upon our shores. The United States are rapidly becoming the lazar house [hospital for the poor with contagious diseases] and penal colony of Europe; nor can we reasonably censure such proceedings. They are legitimate consequences of our own unlimited benevolence; and it is of such material that we profess to manufacture free and enlightened citizens, by a process occupying five short years at most, but practically oftentimes embraced in a much shorter period of time.

———— • ————

"The civil institutions of the United States . . . now stand in imminent peril from the rapid and enormous increase of the body of residents of foreign birth, imbued with foreign feelings."

———— • ————

The mass of foreign voters, formerly lost among the Natives of the soil, has increased from the ratio of 1 in 40 to that of 1 in 7! A like advance in fifteen years will leave the Native citizens a minority in their own land! Thirty years ago these strangers came by units and tens—now they swarm by thousands. Formerly, most of them sought only for an honest livelihood and a provision for their families, and rarely meddled with the institutions, of which it was impossible they could comprehend the nature; now each newcomer seeks political preferment, and struggles to fasten on the public purse with an avidity, in strict proportion to his ignorance and unworthiness of public trust—having been sent for the purpose of obtaining political ascendancy in the government of the nation; having been sent to exalt their allies to power; having been sent to work a revolution from republican freedom to the divine rights of monarchs.

From these unhappy circumstances has arisen an *Imperium in Imperio* [a state within a state]—a body uninformed and vicious—foreign in feeling, prejudice, and manner, yet armed with a vast and often a controlling influence over the policy of a nation, whose benevolence it abuses, and whose kindness it habitually insults; a body as dangerous to the rights of the intelligent foreigner as to the prospect of its own immediate progeny, as it is threatening to the liberties of the country, and the hopes of rational freedom throughout the world; a body ever ready to complicate our foreign relations by embroiling us with the hereditary hates and feuds of other lands, and to disturb our domestic peace by its crude ideas, mistaking license for liberty, and the overthrow of individual rights for republican political equality; a body ever the ready tool of foreign and domestic demagogues, and steadily endeavouring by misrule to establish popular tyranny under a cloak of false democracy. Americans, false to their country, and led on to moral crime by the desire of dishonest gain, have scattered their agents over Europe, inducing the malcontent and the unthrifty to exchange a life of compulsory labour in foreign lands for relative comfort, to be maintained by the tax-paying industry of our overburdened and deeply indebted community. Not content with the usual and less objectionable licenses of trade, these fraudulent dealers habitually deceive a worthier class of victims, by false promises of employment, and assist in thronging the already crowded avenues of simple labour with a host of competitors, whose first acquaintance with American faith springs from a gross imposture, and whose first feeling on discovering the cheat is reasonable mistrust, if not implacable revenge. The importation of the physical necessities of life is burdened with imposts which many deem extravagant; but the importation of vice and idleness—of seditious citizens and factious rulers—is not only unrestricted by anything beyond a nominal tax, but is actually encouraged by a system which transforms the great patrimony of the nation, purchased by the blood of our fathers, into a source of bounty for the promotion of immigration.

Whenever an attempt is made to restrain this fatal evil, the native and adopted demagogues protest against an effort which threatens to deprive them of their most important tools; and such is the existing organization of our established political parties, that should either of them essay the reform of an abuse which both acknowledge to be fraught with ruin, that party sinks upon the instant into a minority, divested of control, and incapable of result.

From such causes has been derived a body, armed with political power, in a country of whose system it is ignorant, and for whose institutions it feels little interest, except for the purpose of personal advancement. . . .

A Future of Foreign Control

The body of adopted citizens, with foreign interests and prejudices, is annually advancing with rapid strides, in geometrical progression. Already it has acquired a control over our elections which cannot be entirely corrected, even by the wisest legislation, until the present generation shall be numbered with the past. Already it has notoriously swayed the course of national legislation, and invaded the purity of local justice. In a few years its unchecked progress would cause it to outnumber the native defenders of our rights, and would then inevitably dispossess our offspring, and its own, of the inheritance for which our fathers bled, or plunge this land of happiness and peace into the horrors of civil war.

The correction of these evils can never be effected by any combination governed by the tactics of other existing parties. If either of the old parties, as such, were to attempt an extension of the term of naturalization, it would be impossible for it to carry out the measure, because they would immediately be abandoned by the foreign voters. This great measure can be carried out only by an organization like our own, made up of those who have given up their former political preferences.

For these reasons, we recommend the immediate organization of the truly patriotic native citizens throughout the United States, for the purpose of resisting the progress of foreign influence in the conduct of American affairs, and the correction of such political abuses as have resulted from unguarded or partisan legislation on the subject of naturalization, so far as these abuses admit of remedy without encroachment upon the vested rights of foreigners who have been already legally adopted into the bosom of the nation.

VIEWPOINT 26B

Immigrants Do Not Endanger America (1845)

Thomas L. Nichols (1815–1901)

In 1845 in New York, Thomas L. Nichols delivered a lecture, later published, on immigration and naturalization—controversial topics of that time when the number of immigrants arriving annually in the United States was approaching 300,000 (the total U.S. population was then about 20 million). Nichols, a doctor, social historian, and journalist, was a supporter of immigration. In the following viewpoint, taken from his lecture, he criticizes the nativist movement to restrict immigration. He cites contributions immigrants have made to the United States, and responds to the arguments made by nativists.

On what basis do people have a "right" to emigrate, according to Nichols? What benefits does he

say immigrants have bestowed on America? How does he characterize opponents of immigrants?

————————

The questions connected with emigration from Europe to America are interesting to both the old world and the new—are of importance to the present and future generations. They have more consequence than a charter or a state election; they involve the destinies of millions; they are connected with the progress of civilization, the rights of man, and providence of God!

I have examined this subject the more carefully, and speak upon it the more earnestly, because I have been to some extent, in former years, a partaker of the prejudices I have since learned to pity. A native of New England and a descendant of the puritans, I early imbibed, and to some extent promulgated, opinions of which reflection and experience have made me ashamed. . . .

But while I would speak of the motives of men with charity, I claim the right to combat their opinions with earnestness. Believing that the principles and practices of Native Americanism are wrong in themselves, and are doing wrong to those who are the objects of their persecution, justice and humanity require that their fallacy should be exposed, and their iniquity condemned. It may be unfortunate that the cause of the oppressed and persecuted, in opinion if not in action, has not fallen into other hands; yet, let me trust that the truth, even in mine, will prove mighty, prevailing from its own inherent power!

The Right to Emigrate

The right of man to emigrate from one country to another, is one which belongs to him by his own constitution and by every principle of justice. It is one which no law can alter, and no authority destroy. "Life, liberty, and the pursuit of happiness" are set down, in our Declaration of Independence, as among the self-evident, unalienable rights of man. If I have a right to live, I have also a right to what will support existence—food, clothing, and shelter. If then the country in which I reside, from a superabundant population, or any other cause, does not afford me these, my right to go from it to some other is self-evident and unquestionable. The *right to live*, then, supposes the right of emigration. . . .

I proceed, therefore, to show that the emigration of foreigners to this country is not only defensible on grounds of abstract justice—what we have no possible right to prevent, but that it has been in various ways highly beneficial to this country.

Emigration first peopled this hemisphere with civilized men. The first settlers of this continent had the

From *Lecture on Immigration and Right of Naturalization* by Thomas L. Nichols (New York, 1845).

same right to come here that belongs to the emigrant of yesterday—no better and no other. They came to improve their condition, to escape from oppression, to enjoy freedom—for the same, or similar, reasons as now prevail. And so far as they violated no private rights, so long as they obtained their lands by fair purchase, or took possession of those which were unclaimed and uncultivated, the highly respectable natives whom the first settlers found here had no right to make any objections. The peopling of this continent with civilized men, the cultivation of the earth, the various processes of productive labor, for the happiness of man, all tend to "the greatest good of the greatest number," and carry out the evident design of Nature or Providence in the formation of the earth and its inhabitants.

Emigration from various countries in Europe to America, producing a mixture of races, has had, and is still having, the most important influence upon the destinies of the human race. It is a principle, laid down by every physiologist, and proved by abundant observation, that man, like other animals, is improved and brought to its highest perfection by an intermingling of the blood and qualities of various races. That nations and families deteriorate from an opposite course has been observed in all ages. The great physiological reason why Americans are superior to other nations in freedom, intelligence, and enterprize, is because that they are the offspring of the greatest intermingling of races. The mingled blood of England has given her predominance over several nations of Europe in these very qualities, and a newer infusion, with favorable circumstances of climate, position, and institutions, has rendered Americans still superior. The Yankees of New England would never have shown those qualities for which they have been distinguished in war and peace throughout the world had there not been mingled with the puritan English, the calculating Scotch, the warm hearted Irish, the gay and chivalric French, the steady persevering Dutch, and the transcendental Germans, for all these nations contributed to make up the New England character, before the Revolution, and ever since to influence that of the whole American people.

America's Destiny

It is not too much to assert that in the order of Providence this vast and fertile continent was reserved for this great destiny; to be the scene of this mingling of the finest European races, and consequently of the highest condition of human intelligence, freedom, and happiness; for I look upon this mixture of the blood and qualities of various nations, and its continual infusion, as absolutely requisite to the perfection of humanity. . . . Continual emigration, and a constant

mixing of the blood of different races, is highly conducive to physical and mental superiority.

This country has been continually benefited by the immense amount of capital brought hither by emigrants. There are very few who arrive upon our shores without some little store of wealth, the hoard of years of industry. Small as these means may be in each case, they amount to millions in the aggregate, and every dollar is so much added to the wealth of the country, to be reckoned at compound interest from the time of its arrival, nor are these sums like our European loans, which we must pay back, both principal and interest. Within a few years, especially, and more or less at all periods, men of great wealth have been among the emigrants driven from Europe, by religious oppression or political revolutions. Vast sums have also fallen to emigrants and their descendants by inheritance, for every few days we read in the papers of some poor foreigner, or descendant of foreigners, as are we all, becoming the heir of a princely fortune, which in most cases, is added to the wealth of his adopted country. Besides this, capital naturally follows labor, and it flows upon this country in a constant current, by the laws of trade.

But it is not money alone that adds to the wealth of a country, but every day's productive labor is to be added to its accumulating capital. Every house built, every canal dug, every railroad graded, has added so much to the actual wealth of society; and who have built more houses, dug more canals, or graded more railroads, than the hardy Irishmen? I hardly know how our great national works could have been carried on without them—then; while every pair of sturdy arms has added to our national wealth, every hungry mouth has been a home market for our agriculture, and every broad shoulder has been clothed with our manufactures.

Europe's Most Valuable Members

From the very nature of the case, America gets from Europe the most valuable of her population. Generally, those who come here are the very ones whom a sensible man would select. Those who are attached to monarchical and aristocratic institutions stay at home where they can enjoy them. Those who lack energy and enterprize can never make up their minds to leave their native land. It is the strong minded, the brave hearted, the free and self-respecting, the enterprizing and the intelligent, who break away from all the ties of country and of home, and brave the dangers of the ocean, in search of liberty and independence, for themselves and for their children, on a distant continent; and it is from this, among other causes, that the great mass of the people of this country are distinguished for the very qualities we should look for in emigrants. The same spirit which sent our fathers across the ocean impels us over the Alleghanies, to the valley of the Mississippi, and thence over the Rocky mountains into Oregon.

For what are we not indebted to foreign emigration, since we are all Europeans or their descendants? We cannot travel on one of our steamboats without remembering that Robert Fulton was the son of an Irishman. . . . Who of the thousands who every summer pass up and down our great thoroughfare, the North River, fails to catch at least a passing glimpse of the column erected to the memory of [Polish immigrant and American Revolutionary War officer Thaddeus] Kosciusko? I cannot forget that only last night a portion of our citizens celebrated with joyous festivities the birthday of the son of Irish emigrants, I mean the Hero of New Orleans [Andrew Jackson]!

———— • ————

"The emigration of foreigners to this country is not only defensible on grounds of abstract justice . . . but . . . it has been in various ways highly beneficial to this country."

———— • ————

Who speaks contemptuously of Alexander Hamilton as a foreigner, because he was born in one of the West India Islands? Who at this day will question the worth or patriotism of Albert Gallatin, because he first opened his eyes among the Alps of Switzerland—though, in fact, this was brought up and urged against him, when he was appointed special minister to Russia by James Madison. What New Yorker applies the epithet of "degraded foreigner" to the German immigrant, John Jacob Astor, a man who has spread his canvas on every sea, drawn to his adopted land the wealth of every clime, and given us, it may be, our best claim to vast territories!

Who would have banished the Frenchman, Stephen Girard, who, after accumulating vast wealth from foreign commerce, endowed with it magnificent institutions for education in his adopted land? So might I go on for hours, citing individual examples of benefits derived by this country from foreign immigration. . . .

I have enumerated some of the advantages which such emigration has given to America. Let us now very carefully inquire, whether there is danger of any injury arising from these causes, at all proportionable to the palpable good.

"Our country is in danger," is the cry of Nativism. During my brief existence I have seen this country on the very verge of ruin a considerable number of times. It is always in the most imminent peril every four years; but, hitherto, the efforts of one party or the other have proved sufficient to rescue it, just in the latest gasp of its expiring agonies, and we have breathed more freely, when we have been assured that "the country's safe." Let us look steadily in the face of this new danger.

Are foreigners coming here to overturn our government? Those who came before the Revolution appear to have been generally favorable to Republican institutions. Those who have come here since have left friends, home, country, all that man naturally holds dearest, that they might live under a free government—they and their children. Is there common sense in the supposition that men would voluntarily set about destroying the very liberties they came so far to enjoy?

"But they lack intelligence," it is said. Are the immigrants of today less intelligent than those of fifty or a hundred years ago? Has Europe and the human race stood still all this time? . . . The facts of men preferring this country to any other, of their desire to live under its institutions, of their migration hither, indicate to my mind anything but a lack of proper intelligence and enterprize. It has been charged against foreigners, by a portion of the whig press, that they generally vote with the democratic party. Allowing this to be so, I think that those who reflect upon the policy of the two parties, from the time of John Adams down to that of Mayor [James] Harper, will scarcely bring this up as the proof of a lack of intelligence!

The truth is, a foreigner who emigrates to this country comes here saying, "Where Liberty dwells, there is my country." He sees our free institutions in the strong light of contrast. The sun seems brighter, because he has come out of darkness. What we know by hearsay only of the superiority of our institutions, he knows by actual observation and experience. Hence it is that America has had no truer patriots—freedom no more enthusiastic admirers—the cause of Liberty no more heroic defenders, than have been found among our adopted citizens. . . .

But if naturalized citizens of foreign birth had the disposition, they have not the power, to endanger our liberties, on account of their comparatively small and decreasing numbers. There appears to be a most extraordinary misapprehension upon this subject. To read one of our "Native" papers one might suppose that our country was becoming overrun by foreigners, and that there was real danger of their having a majority of votes. . . .

There is a point beyond which immigration cannot be carried. It must be limited by the capacity of the vessels employed in bringing passengers, while our entire population goes on increasing in geometrical progression, so that in one century from now, we shall have a population of one hundred and sixty millions, but a few hundred thousands of whom at the utmost can be citizens of foreign birth. Thus it may be seen that foreign immigration is of very little account, beyond a certain period, in the population of a country, and at all times is an insignificant item. . . .

In the infancy of this country the firstborn native found himself among a whole colony of foreigners. Now, the foreigner finds himself surrounded by as great a disproportion of natives, and the native babe and newly landed foreigner have about the same amount, of either power or disposition, to endanger the country in which they have arrived; one, because he chose to come—the other because he could not help it.

I said the power or the disposition, for I have yet to learn that foreigners, whether German or Irish, English or French, are at all disposed to do an injury to the asylum which wisdom has prepared and valor won for the oppressed of all nations and religions. I appeal to the observation of every man in this community, whether the Germans and the Irish here, and throughout the country, are not as orderly, as industrious, as quiet, and in the habit of performing as well the common duties of citizens as the great mass of natives among us.

The worst thing that can be brought against any portion of our foreign population is that in many cases they are poor, and when they sink under labor and privation, they have no resources but the almshouse. Alas! shall the rich, for whom they have labored, the owners of the houses they have helped to build, refuse to treat them as kindly as they would their horses when incapable of further toil? Can they grudge them shelter from the storm, and a place where they may die in peace?

For Further Reading

Edith Abbott, *Historical Aspects of the Immigration Problem: Select Documents.* New York: Arno Press, 1969.

Ray Allen Billington, *The Protestant Crusade, 1800–1860: A Study of the Origins of American Nativism.* New York: Macmillan, 1938.

Maldwyn A. Jones, *American Immigration.* Chicago: University of Chicago Press, 1992.

VIEWPOINT 27A

Women Hold An Exalted Status in America (1841)

Catharine E. Beecher (1800–1878)

The issues of women's rights and the role of women in American society began to gain national prominence in the decades prior to the Civil War. During this time many people wrote and spoke of the importance of women in managing the household and installing character in children. One of the most noted advocates of this point of view was Catharine E. Beecher, a noted author and education reformer. She was a member of a prominent New England family; her father and brother were both famous preachers, and her sister was Harriet Beecher Stowe, author of *Uncle Tom's Cabin.* She founded several educational institutions for women, and her books and writings were widely influential. Believing that homemaking and teaching were the true professions for women, she sought to improve their status by stressing the importance of women in the "domestic sphere." Although active in the abolitionist and other social reform movements (especially women's education), Beecher opposed women's suffrage and other goals of the early feminist movement.

The following viewpoint is taken from the opening chapter of *A Treatise on Domestic Economy, for the Use of Young Ladies At Home, and at School*, a how-to book on homemaking that was a perennial bestseller in the 1840s and 1850s. Beecher argues that American women have attained respect and true equality with men by remaining in the domestic sphere. She compares the United States favorably with Europe regarding the position and treatment of women, quoting extensively from *Democracy in America*, an influential book published in 1835 by French social philosopher Alexis de Tocqueville.

What basic principles guide American society, according to Beecher? What choices does she say women have regarding marriage? What important responsibilities does Beecher argue American women have?

T here are some reasons why American women should feel an interest in the support of the democratic institutions of their Country, which it is important that they should consider. The great maxim, which is the basis of all our civil and political institutions, is, that "all men are created equal," and that they are equally entitled to "life, liberty, and the pursuit of happiness."

But it can readily be seen, that this is only another mode of expressing the fundamental principle which the Great Ruler of the Universe has established, as the law of His eternal government. "Thou shalt love thy neighbor as thyself;" and "Whatsoever ye would that men should do to you, do ye even so to them." These are the Scripture forms, by which the Supreme Lawgiver requires that each individual of our race

From *A Treatise on Domestic Economy* by Catharine E. Beecher (Boston: March, Capen, Lyon, and Webb, 1841).

shall regard the happiness of others, as of the same value as his own; and which forbids any institution, in private or civil life, which secures advantages to one class, by sacrificing the interests of another.

The principles of democracy, then, are identical with the principles of Christianity.

But, in order that each individual may pursue and secure the highest degree of happiness within his reach, unimpeded by the selfish interests of others, a system of laws must be established, which sustain certain relations and dependencies in social and civil life. What these relations and their attending obligations shall be, are to be determined, not with reference to the wishes and interests of a few, but solely with reference to the general good of all; so that each individual shall have his own interest, as much as the public benefit, secured by them.

The Duties of Subordination

For this purpose, it is needful that certain relations be sustained, that involve the duties of subordination. There must be the magistrate and the subject, one of whom is the superior, and the other the inferior. There must be the relations of husband and wife, parent and child, teacher and pupil, employer and employed, each involving the relative duties of subordination. The superior in certain particulars is to direct, and the inferior is to yield obedience. Society could never go forward, harmoniously, nor could any craft or profession be successfully pursued, unless these superior and subordinate relations be instituted and sustained.

But who shall take the higher, and who the subordinate, stations in social and civil life? This matter, in the case of parents and children, is decided by the Creator. He has given children to the control of parents, as their superiors, and to them they remain subordinate, to a certain age, or so long as they are members of their household. And parents can delegate such a portion of their authority to teachers and employers, as the interests of their children require.

In most other cases, in a truly democratic state, each individual is allowed to choose for himself, who shall take the position of his superior. No woman is forced to obey any husband but the one she chooses for herself; nor is she obliged to take a husband, if she prefers to remain single. So every domestic, and every artisan or laborer, after passing from parental control, can choose the employer to whom he is to accord obedience, or, if he prefers to relinquish certain advantages, he can remain without taking a subordinate place to any employer.

Each subject, also, has equal power with every other, to decide who shall be his superior as a ruler. The weakest, the poorest, the most illiterate, has the same opportunity to determine this question, as the richest, the most learned, and the most exalted.

And the various privileges that wealth secures, are equally open to all classes. Every man may aim at riches, unimpeded by any law or institution that secures peculiar privileges to a favored class at the expense of another. Every law, and every institution, is tested by examining whether it secures equal advantages to all; and if the people become convinced that any regulation sacrifices the good of the majority to the interests of the smaller number, they have power to abolish it.

The institutions of monarchical and aristocratic nations are based on precisely opposite principles. They secure, to certain small and favored classes, advantages which can be maintained, only by sacrificing the interests of the great mass of the people. Thus, the throne and aristocracy of England are supported by laws and customs, that burden the lower classes with taxes, so enormous, as to deprive them of all the luxuries, and of most of the comforts, of life. Poor dwellings, scanty food, unhealthy employments, excessive labor, and entire destitution of the means and time for education, are appointed for the lower classes, that a few may live in palaces, and riot in every indulgence.

The Interests of American Women

The tendencies of democratic institutions, in reference to the rights and interests of the female sex, have been fully developed in the United States; and it is in this aspect, that the subject is one of peculiar interest to American women. In this Country, it is established, both by opinion and by practice, that women have an equal interest in all social and civil concerns; and that no domestic, civil, or political, institution, is right, that sacrifices her interest to promote that of the other sex. But in order to secure her the more firmly in all these privileges, it is decided, that, in the domestic relation, she take a subordinate station, and that, in civil and political concerns, her interests be intrusted to the other sex, without her taking any part in voting, or in making and administering laws. The result of this order of things has been fairly tested, and is thus portrayed by M. [Alexis] De Tocqueville, a writer, who, for intelligence, fidelity, and ability, ranks second to none.

The following extracts [from *Democracy in America*] present his views.

> There are people in Europe, who, confounding together the different characteristics of the sexes, would make of man and woman, beings not only equal, but alike. They would give to both the same functions, impose on both the same duties, and grant to both the same rights. They would mix them in all things,—their business, their occupations, their pleasures. It may readily be conceived, that, by

thus attempting to make one sex equal to the other, both are degraded; and from so preposterous a medley of the works of Nature, nothing could ever result, but weak men and disorderly women.

It is not thus that the Americans understand the species of democratic equality, which may be established between the sexes. They admit, that, as Nature has appointed such wide differences between the physical and moral constitutions of man and woman, her manifest design was, to give a distinct employment to their various faculties; and they hold, that improvement does not consist in making beings so dissimilar do pretty nearly the same things, but in getting each of them to fulfil their respective tasks, in the best possible manner. The Americans have applied to the sexes the great principle of political economy, which governs the manufactories of our age, by carefully dividing the duties of man from those of woman, in order that the great work of society may be the better carried on.

In no country has such constant care been taken, as in America, to trace two clearly distinct lines of action for the two sexes, and to make them keep pace one with the other, but in two pathways which are always different. American women never manage the outward concerns of the family, or conduct a business, or take a part in political life; nor are they, on the other hand, ever compelled to perform the rough labor of the fields, or to make any of those laborious exertions, which demand the exertion of physical strength. No families are so poor, as to form an exception to this rule. . . .

Thus the Americans do not think that man and woman have either the duty, or the right, to perform the same offices, but they show an equal regard for both their respective parts; and, though their lot is different, they consider both of them, as beings of equal value. They do not give to the courage of woman the same form, or the same direction, as to that of man; but they never doubt her courage: and if they hold that man and his partner ought not always to exercise their intellect and understanding in the same manner, they at least believe the understanding of the one to be as sound as that of the other, and her intellect to be as clear. Thus, then, while they have allowed the social inferiority of woman to subsist, they have done all they could to raise her, morally and intellectually, to the level of man; and, in this respect, they appear to me to have excellently understood the true principle of democratic improvement.

As for myself, I do not hesitate to avow, that, although the women of the United States are confined within the narrow circle of domestic life, and their situation is, in some respects, one of extreme dependence, I have nowhere seen women occupying a loftier position; and if I were asked, now I am drawing to the close of this work, in which I have spoken of so many important things done by the

Americans, to what the singular prosperity and growing strength of that people ought mainly to be attributed, I should reply,—*to the superiority of their women.*

Women's Lofty Position

This testimony of a foreigner, who has had abundant opportunities of making a comparison, is sanctioned by the assent of all candid and intelligent men, who have enjoyed similar opportunities.

It appears, then, that it is in America, alone, that women are raised to an equality with the other sex; and that, both in theory and practice, their interests are regarded as of equal value. They are made subordinate in station, only where a regard to their best interests demands it, while, as if in compensation for this, by custom and courtesy, they are always treated as superiors. Universally, in this Country, through every class of society, precedence is given to woman, in all the comforts, conveniences, and courtesies, of life.

In civil and political affairs, American women take no interest or concern, except so far as they sympathize with their family and personal friends; but in all cases, in which they do feel a concern, their opinions and feelings have a consideration, equal, or even superior, to that of the other sex.

In matters pertaining to the education of their children, in the selection and support of a clergyman, in all benevolent enterprises, and in all questions relating to morals or manners, they have a superior influence. In all such concerns, it would be impossible to carry a point contrary to their judgement and feelings; while an enterprise, sustained by them, will seldom fail of success.

———— • ————

"The democratic institutions of this Country . . . have secured to American women a lofty and fortunate position."

———— • ————

If those who are bewailing themselves over the fancied wrongs and injuries of women in this Nation, could only see things as they are, they would know, that, whatever remnants of a barbarous or aristocratic age may remain in our civil institutions, in reference to the interests of women, it is only because they are ignorant of it, or do not use their influence to have them rectified; for it is very certain that there is nothing reasonable which American women would unite in asking, that would not readily be bestowed.

The preceding remarks, then, illustrate the position that the democratic institutions of this Country are in reality no other than the principles of Christianity carried into operation, and that they tend to place woman in her true position in society, as having equal rights with the other sex; and that, in fact, they have secured to American women a lofty and fortunate position, which, as yet, has been attained by the women of no other nation. . . .

The Important Task of Women

The success of democratic institutions, as is conceded by all, depends upon the intellectual and moral character of the mass of the people. If they are intelligent and virtuous, democracy is a blessing; but if they are ignorant and wicked, it is only a curse, and as much more dreadful than any other form of civil government, as a thousand tyrants are more to be dreaded than one. It is equally conceded, that the formation of the moral and intellectual character of the young is committed mainly to the female hand. The mother writes the character of the future man; the sister bends the fibres that hereafter are the forest tree; the wife sways the heart, whose energies may turn for good or for evil the destinies of a nation. Let the women of a country be made virtuous and intelligent, and the men will certainly be the same. The proper education of a man decides the welfare of an individual; but educate a woman, and the interests of a whole family are secured.

If this be so, as none will deny, then to American women, more than to any others on earth, is committed the exalted privilege of extending over the world those blessed influences, that are to renovate degraded man, and " clothe all climes with beauty."

No American woman, then, has any occasion for feeling that hers is an humble or insignificant lot. The value of what an individual accomplishes, is to be estimated by the importance of the enterprise achieved, and not by the particular position of the laborer. The drops of heaven that freshen the earth are each of equal value, whether they fall in the lowland meadow, or the princely parterre. The builders of a temple are of equal importance, whether they labor on the foundations, or toil upon the dome.

Thus, also, with those labors that are to be made effectual in the regeneration of the Earth. The woman who is rearing a family of children; the woman who labors in the schoolroom; the woman who, in her retired chamber, earns, with her needle, the mite to contribute for the intellectual and moral elevation of her country; even the humble domestic, whose example and influence may be moulding and forming young minds, while her faithful services sustain a prosperous domestic state;—each and all may be cheered by the consciousness, that they are agents in accomplishing the greatest work that ever was committed to human responsibility. It is the building of a glorious temple, whose base shall be

coextensive with the bounds of the earth, whose summit shall pierce the skies,whose splendor shall beam on all lands, and those who hew the lowliest stone, as much as those who carve the highest capital, will be equally honored when its top-stone shall be laid, with new rejoicings of the morning stars, and shoutings of the sons of God.

VIEWPOINT 27B

Women Hold a Degraded Status in America (1848)
Elizabeth Cady Stanton (1815–1902) and the Seneca Falls Convention

The Seneca Falls Convention, held on July 18–19, 1848, in Seneca Falls, New York, was the first public political meeting on women's rights in the United States. It was organized by Elizabeth Cady Stanton and Lucretia Mott, two abolitionists who had met in 1840 at the World's Anti-Slavery Convention in London, where they and other female delegates were denied recognition and participation because of their gender. Stanton and Mott resolved to start a women's rights movement in the United States; their efforts resulted in the Seneca Falls Convention eight years later. Stanton, who would go on to devote her life to women's rights, drafted a Declaration of Sentiments (based on America's Declaration of Independence) and a series of resolutions calling for women's rights. Both the declaration and the resolutions were debated, reworded slightly, and adopted by the several hundred women and men assembled at Seneca Falls. All the resolutions save one were passed unanimously; the resolution for women's suffrage passed by only a narrow margin.

What resemblances exist between this document and the Declaration of Independence (reprinted on p. 100)? What examples of oppression does Stanton provide? Judging from the contents of viewpoints 27A and 27B, which points of the Seneca Falls Declaration might Catharine E. Beecher, author of the opposing viewpoint, agree with? Which would she most oppose?

Declaration of Sentiments

When, in the course of human events, it becomes necessary for one portion of the family of man to assume among the people of the earth a position different from that which they have hitherto occupied, but one to which the laws of

From *History of Woman Suffrage*, vol. 1, edited by Elizabeth Cady Stanton, Susan B. Anthony, and Matilda Joslyn Gage (New York: Fowler & Wells, 1881).

nature and of nature's God entitle them, a decent respect to the opinions of mankind requires that they should declare the causes that impel them to such a course.

We hold these truths to be self-evident: that all men and women are created equal; that they are endowed by their Creator with certain inalienable rights; that among these are life, liberty, and the pursuit of happiness; that to secure these rights governments are instituted, deriving their just powers from the consent of the governed. Whenever any form of government becomes destructive of these ends, it is the right of those who suffer from it to refuse allegiance to it, and to insist upon the institution of a new government, laying its foundation on such principles, and organizing its powers in such form, as to them shall seem most likely to effect their safety and happiness. Prudence, indeed, will dictate that governments long established should not be changed for light and transient causes; and accordingly all experience hath shown that mankind are more disposed to suffer, while evils are sufferable, than to right themselves by abolishing the forms to which they are accustomed. But when a long train of abuses and usurpations, pursuing invariably the same object, evinces a design to reduce them under absolute despotism, it is their duty to throw off such government, and to provide new guards for their future security. Such has been the patient sufferance of the women under this government, and such is now the necessity which constrains them to demand the equal station to which they are entitled.

The history of mankind is a history of repeated injuries and usurpations on the part of man toward woman, having in direct object the establishment of an absolute tyranny over her. To prove this, let facts be submitted to a candid world.

He has never permitted her to exercise her inalienable right to the elective franchise.

He has compelled her to submit to laws, in the formation of which she had no voice.

He has withheld from her rights which are given to the most ignorant and degraded men—both natives and foreigners.

Having deprived her of this first right of a citizen, the elective franchise, thereby leaving her without representation in the halls of legislation, he has oppressed her on all sides.

He has made her, if married, in the eye of the law, civilly dead.

He has taken from her all right in property, even to the wages she earns.

He has made her, morally, an irresponsible being, as she can commit many crimes with impunity, provided they be done in the presence of her husband. In the covenant of marriage, she is compelled to promise obedience to her husband, he becoming, to all intents and purposes, her master—the law giving him power to deprive her of her liberty, and to administer chastisement.

He has so framed the laws of divorce, as to what shall be the proper causes, and in case of separation, to whom the guardianship of the children shall be given, as to be wholly regardless of the happiness of women—the law, in all cases, going upon a false supposition of the supremacy of man, and giving all power into his hands.

———— • ————

"Because women do feel themselves aggrieved, oppressed, and fraudulently deprived of their most sacred rights, we insist that they have immediate admission to all the rights and privileges which belong to them as citizens of the United States."

———— • ————

After depriving her of all rights as a married woman, if single, and the owner of property, he has taxed her to support a government which recognizes her only when her property can be made profitable to it.

He has monopolized nearly all the profitable employments, and from those she is permitted to follow, she receives but a scanty remuneration. He closes against her all the avenues to wealth and distinction which he considers most honorable to himself. As a teacher of theology, medicine, or law, she is not known.

He has denied her the facilities for obtaining a thorough education, all colleges being closed against her.

He allows her in Church, as well as State, but a subordinate position, claiming Apostolic authority for her exclusion from the ministry, and, with some exceptions, from any public participation in the affairs of the Church.

He has created a false public sentiment by giving to the world a different code of morals for men and women, by which moral delinquencies which exclude women from society, are not only tolerated, but deemed of little account in man.

He has usurped the prerogative of Jehovah himself, claiming it as his right to assign for her a sphere of action, when that belongs to her conscience and to her God.

He has endeavored, in every way that he could, to destroy her confidence in her own powers, to lessen her self-respect and to make her willing to lead a dependent and abject life.

Now, in view of this entire disfranchisement of one-half the people of this country, their social and religious degradation—in view of the unjust laws above mentioned, and because women do feel themselves aggrieved, oppressed, and fraudulently deprived of their most sacred rights, we insist that they have immediate admission to all the rights and privileges which belong to them as citizens of the United States.

In entering upon the great work before us, we anticipate no small amount of misconception, misrepresentation, and ridicule; but we shall use every instrumentality within our power to effect our object. We shall employ agents, circulate tracts, petition the State and National legislatures, and endeavor to enlist the pulpit and the press in our behalf. We hope this Convention will be followed by a series of Conventions embracing every part of the country.

Resolutions

WHEREAS, The great precept of nature is conceded to be, that "man shall pursue his own true and substantial happiness." [William] Blackstone in his *Commentaries [on the Laws of England]* remarks, that this law of Nature being coeval with mankind, and dictated by God himself, is of course superior in obligation to any other. It is binding over all the globe, in all countries and at all times; no human laws are of any validity if contrary to this, and such of them as are valid, derive all their force, and all their validity, and all their authority, mediately and immediately, from this original; therefore,

Resolved, That such laws as conflict, in any way with the true and substantial happiness of woman, are contrary to the great precept of nature and of no validity, for this is "superior in obligation to any other."

Resolved, That all laws which prevent woman from occupying such a station in society as her conscience shall dictate, or which place her in a position inferior to that of man, are contrary to the great precept of nature, and therefore of no force or authority.

Resolved, That woman is man's equal—was intended to be so by the Creator, and the highest good of the race demands that she should be recognized as such.

Resolved, That the women of this country ought to be enlightened in regard to the laws under which they live, that they may no longer publish their degradation by declaring themselves satisfied with their present position, nor their ignorance, by asserting that they have all the rights they want.

Resolved, That inasmuch as man, while claiming for himself intellectual superiority, does accord to woman moral superiority, it is pre-eminently his duty to encourage her to speak and teach, as she has an opportunity, in all religious assemblies.

Resolved, That the same amount of virtue, delicacy, and refinement of behavior that is required of woman in the social state, should also be required of man, and the same transgressions should be visited with equal severity on both man and woman.

Resolved, That the objection of indelicacy and impropriety, which is so often brought against woman when she addresses a public audience, comes with a very ill-grace from those who encourage, by their attendance, her appearance on the stage, in the concert, or in feats of the circus.

Resolved, That woman has too long rested satisfied in the circumscribed limits which corrupt customs and a perverted application of the Scriptures have marked out for her, and that it is time she should move in the enlarged sphere which her great Creator has assigned her.

Resolved, That it is the duty of the women of this country to secure to themselves their sacred right to the elective franchise.

Resolved, That the equality of human rights results necessarily from the fact of the identity of the race in capabilities and responsibilities.

Resolved, therefore, That, being invested by the Creator with the same capabilities, and the same consciousness of responsibility for their exercise, it is demonstrably the right and duty of woman, equally with man, to promote every righteous cause by every righteous means; and especially in regard to the great subjects of morals and religion, it is self-evidently her right to participate with her brother in teaching them, both in private and in public, by writing and by speaking, by any instrumentalities proper to be used, and in any assemblies proper to be held; and this being a self-evident truth growing out of the divinely implanted principles of human nature, any custom or authority adverse to it, whether modern or wearing the hoary sanction of antiquity, is to be regarded as a self-evident falsehood, and at war with mankind.

Resolved, That the speedy success of our cause depends upon the zealous and untiring efforts of both men and women, for the overthrow of the monopoly of the pulpit, and for the securing to women an equal participation with men in the various trades, professions, and commerce.

For Further Reading

Virginia Bernhard and Elizabeth Fox-Genovese, eds., *The Birth of American Feminism: The Seneca Falls Woman's Convention of 1848*. St. James, NY: Brandywine Press, 1995.

Jeanne Boydston et al., *The Limits of Sisterhood: The Beecher Sisters on Women's Rights and Woman's Sphere*. Chapel Hill: University of North Carolina Press, 1988.

Elizabeth Griffith, *In Her Own Right: The Life of Elizabeth Cady Stanton*. New York: Oxford University Press, 1984.

Miriam Gurko, *The Ladies of Seneca Falls: The Birth of the Women's Rights Movement*. New York: Macmillan, 1974.

Keith E. Melder, *Beginnings of Sisterhood: The American Women's Rights Movement, 1800–1850.* New York: Schocken Books, 1977.

Kathryn K. Sklar, *Catharine Beecher: A Study in American Domesticity.* New York: Norton, 1976.

VIEWPOINT 28A

Slavery Is Not Oppressive (1854)
Nehemiah Adams (1806–1878)

Slavery was perhaps the central issue of the antebellum era. Abolitionists traveled throughout the free states lecturing on the evils of the institution and arguing that it should be purged from the United States. Slavery defenders (mostly from the South) responded with increasing intensity that slavery was, as John C. Calhoun declared, a "positive good," and argued that slaves had better lives than impoverished free people in the North and elsewhere.

The following viewpoint is taken from a book frequently cited by slavery advocates. The author is Nehemiah Adams, a Congregationalist minister in Boston, Massachusetts. In 1853 for health reasons he traveled for three months in the South. What he saw there caused him to question his prior views of slavery as an evil and oppressive institution. Adams's observations were published in 1854 in a book titled *A South-Side View of Slavery.* In the excerpts printed here, Adams describes his observations of black slaves in the South and concludes that many of them live contented lives. He enumerates several advantages of the life of a slave, including freedom from starvation.

What factors shape opinions of slavery in the North, according to Adams? Is there evidence in this viewpoint for or against his observations being affected by racial prejudice? Explain.

T he writer has lately spent three months at the south for the health of an invalid. Few professional men at the north had less connection with the south by ties of any kind than he, when the providence of God made it necessary to become for a while a stranger in a strange land. He was too much absorbed by private circumstances to think of entering at all into a deliberate consideration of any important subject of a public nature; yet for this very reason, perhaps, the mind was better prepared to receive dispassionately the impressions which were to be made upon it. The impressions thus made, and

From *A South-Side View of Slavery* by Nehemiah Adams (Boston: Marvin & Mussey, 1854).

the reflections which spontaneously arose, the writer here submits, not as a partisan, but as a Christian; not as a northerner, but as an American; not as a politician, but as a lover and friend of the colored race. . . .

I will relate the impressions and expectations with which I went to the south; the manner in which things appeared to me in connection with slavery in Georgia, South Carolina, and Virginia; the correction or confirmation of my northern opinions and feelings; the conclusions to which I was led; the way in which our language and whole manner toward the south have impressed me; and the duty which it seems to me, as members of the Union, we at the north owe to the subject of slavery and to the south, and with the south to the colored race. I shall not draw upon fictitious scenes and feelings, but shall give such statements as I would desire to receive from a friend to whom I should put the question, "What am I to believe? How am I to feel and act?". . .

How to say enough of preconceived notions respecting slavery, so as to compare subsequent impressions with them, and yet not enough to give southern friends room to exult and say that we all have false and exaggerated notions about slavery, is somewhat difficult. At the risk of disagreeable imputations, and with a desire to be honest and ingenuous, I will merely add, that there was one thing which I felt sure that I should see on landing, viz., the whole black population cowed down. This best expresses in a word my expectation. "I am a slave," will be indented on the faces, limbs, and actions of the bondmen. Hopeless woe, entreating yet despairing, will frequently greet me. How could it be otherwise, if slavery be such as our books, and sermons, and lectures, and newspaper articles represent? nay, if southern papers themselves, especially their advertisements, are to be relied upon as sources of correct impressions?

Arrival and First Impressions

The steam tug reached the landing, and the slaves were all about us. One thing immediately surprised me; they were all in good humor, and some of them in a broad laugh. The delivery of every trunk from the tug to the wharf was the occasion of some hit, or repartee, and every burden was borne with a jolly word, grimace, or motion. The lifting of one leg in laugh seemed as natural as a Frenchman's shrug. I asked one of them to place a trunk with a lot of baggage; it was done; up went the hand to the hat—"Any thing more, please sir?" What a contrast, I involuntarily said to myself, to that troop at the Albany landing on our Western Railroad! and on those piles of boards, and on the roofs of the sheds, and at the piers, in New York! I began to like these slaves. I began to laugh with them. It was irresistible. Who could have convinced me, an hour before, that slaves could have any other effect upon me than to make me feel sad? One fellow, in all the hurry and bustle of landing us, could not help relating how, in jumping on board, his boot was caught between two planks, and "pulled clean off;" and how "dis ole feller went clean over into de wotter," with a shout, as though it was a merry adventure.

One thing seemed clear; they were not so much cowed down as I expected. Perhaps, however, they were a fortunate set. I rode away, expecting soon to have some of my disagreeable anticipations verified. . . .

The city of Savannah abounds in parks, as they are called—squares, fenced in, with trees. Young children and infants were there, with very respectable colored nurses—young women, with bandanna and plaid cambric turbans, and superior in genteel appearance to any similar class, as a whole, in any of our cities. They could not be slaves. Are they slaves? "Certainly," says the friend at your side; "they each belong to some master or mistress.". . .

Every-Day Life

Our fancies with regard to the condition of the slaves proceed from our northern repugnance to slavery, stimulated by many things that we read. The every-day life, the whole picture of society at the south, is not presented to us so frequently—indeed it cannot be, nor can it strike the mind as strongly—as slave auctions and separations of families, fugitives hiding in dismal swamps, and other things which appeal to our sensibilities. Whatever else may be true of slavery, these things, we say, are indisputable; and they furnish materials for the fancy to build into a world of woe.

Without supposing that I had yet seen slavery, it was nevertheless true that a load was lifted from my mind by the first superficial look at the slaves in the city.

It was as though I had been let down by necessity into a cavern which I had peopled with disagreeable sights, and, on reaching bottom, found daylight streaming in, and the place cheerful.

A better-looking, happier, more courteous set of people I had never seen, than those colored men, women, and children whom I met the first few days of my stay in Savannah. It had a singular effect on my spirits. They all seemed glad to see me. I was tempted with some vain feelings, as though they meant to pay me some special respect. I was all the more grateful, because for months sickness and death had covered almost every thing, even the faces of friends at home, with sadness to my eye, and my spirits had drooped. But to be met and accosted with such extremely civil, benevolent looks, to see so many

faces break into pleasant smiles in going by, made one feel that he was not alone in the world, even in a land of strangers.

Taking a Whole Race by the Hand

How such unaffected politeness could have been learned under the lash I did not understand. It conflicted with my notions of slavery. I could not have dreamed that these people had been "down trodden," "their very manhood crushed out of them," "the galling yoke of slavery breaking every human feeling, and reducing them to the level of brutes." It was one of the pleasures of taking a walk to be greeted by all my colored friends. I felt that I had taken a whole new race of my fellow-men by the hand. I took care to notice each of them, and get his full smile and salutation; many a time I would gladly have stopped and paid a good price for a certain "good morning," courtesy, and bow; it was worth more than gold; its charm consisted in its being unbought, unconstrained, for I was an entire stranger. Timidity, a feeling of necessity, the leer of obliged deference, I nowhere saw; but the artless, free, and easy manner which burdened spirits never wear. It was difficult to pass the colored people in the streets without a smile awakened by the magnetism of their smiles. Let any one at the north, afflicted with depression of spirits, drop down among these negroes, walk these streets, form a passing acquaintance with some of them and unless he is a hopeless case, he will find himself in moods of cheerfulness never awakened surely by the countenances of the whites in any strange place. Involuntary servitude did not present itself to my eye or thoughts during the two weeks which I spent in Savannah, except as I read advertisements in the papers of slaves for sale. . . .

The streets of southern cities and towns immediately struck me as being remarkably quiet in the evening and at night.

"What is the cause of so much quiet?" I said to a friend.

"Our colored people are mostly at home. After eight o'clock they cannot be abroad without a written pass, which they must show on being challenged, or go to the guard house. The master must pay fifty cents for a release. White policemen in cities, and in towns patrols of white citizens, walk the streets at night."

Benefits of Restraint

Here I receive my first impression of interference with the personal liberty of the colored people. The white servants, if there be any, the boys, the apprentices, the few Irish, have liberty; the colored men are under restraint.

But though I saw that this was a feature of slavery, I did not conclude that it would be well to dissolve the Union in order to abolish it. Apart from the question of slavery, it was easy to see that to keep such a part of the population out of the streets after a reasonable hour at night, preventing their unrestrained, promiscuous roving, is a great protection to them, as well as to the public peace. In attending evening worship, in visiting at any hour, a written pass is freely given; so that, after all, the bondage is theoretical, but still it is bondage. Is it an illustration, I asked myself, of other things in slavery, which are theoretically usurpations, but practically benevolent? . . .

The Children of the Slaves

But of all the touching sights of innocence and love appealing to you unconsciously for your best feelings of tenderness and affection, the colored young children have never been surpassed in my experience. Might I choose a class of my fellow-creatures to instruct and love, I should be drawn by my present affection toward them to none more readily than to these children of the slaves; nor should I expect my patience and affection to be more richly rewarded elsewhere. Extremes of disposition and character, of course, exist among them, as among others; but they are naturally as bright, affectionate, and capable as other children, while the ways in which your instructions impress them, the reasonings they excite, the remarks occasioned by them, are certainly peculiar. . . .

Going to meeting one Sabbath morning, a child, about eight years old, tripped along before me, with her hymn book and nicely-folded handkerchief in her hand, the flounces on her white dress very profuse, frilled ankles, light-colored boots, mohair mits, and sunshade, all showing that some fond heart and hand had bestowed great care upon her. Home and children came to mind. I thought of the feelings which that flower of the family perhaps occasioned. Is it the pastor's daughter? Is it the daughter of the lady whose garden I had walked in, but which bears no such plant as this? But my musings were interrupted by the child, who, on hearing footsteps behind, suddenly turned, and showed one of the blackest faces I ever saw. It was one of the thousands of intelligent, happy colored children, who on every Sabbath, in every southern town and city, make a northern visitor feel that some of his theoretical opinions at home, with regard to the actual condition of slavery, are much improved by practical views of it.

Labor and Privileges

Life on the cotton plantations is, in general, as severe with the colored people as agricultural life at the north. I have spent summers upon farms, however, where the owners and their hands excited my sympathy by toils to which the slaves on many plantations are strangers. Every thing depends upon the disposition of the master. It happened that I saw some of the best specimens, and heard descriptions of some of the very bad. In the rice swamps, malaria begets diseases and destroys life; in the sugar districts, at certain seasons, the process of manufacture requires labor, night and day, for a considerable time. There the different dispositions of the master affect the comfort of the laborers variously, as in all other situations.

But in the cotton-growing country, the labor, though extending in one form and another nearly through the year, yet taking each day's labor by itself, is no more toilsome than is performed by a hired field hand at the north; still the continuity of labor from February to the last part of December, with a slight intermission in midsummer, when the crop is "laid by," the stalks being matured, and the crop left to ripen, makes plantation life severe.

Some planters allow their hands a certain portion of the soil for their own culture, and give them stated times to work it; some prefer to allow them out of the whole crop a percentage equal to such a distribution of land; and some do nothing of the kind; but their hearts are made of the northern iron and the steel. It is the common law, however, with all who regard public opinion at the south, to allow their hands certain privileges and exemptions, such as long rest in the middle of the day, early dismission from the field at night, a half day occasionally, in addition to holidays, for which the colored people of all denominations are much indebted to the Episcopal church, whose festivals they celebrate with the largest liberty.

Slave Investments

They raise poultry, swine, melons; keep bees; catch fish; peddle brooms, and small articles of cabinet making; and, if they please, lay up the money, or spend it on their wives and children, or waste it for things hurtful, if there are white traders desperate enough to defy the laws made for such cases, and which are apt to be most rigorously executed. Some slaves are owners of bank and railroad shares. A slave woman, having had three hundred dollars stolen from her by a white man, her master was questioned in court as to the probability of her having had so much money. He said that he not unfrequently had borrowed fifty and a hundred dollars of her, and added, that she was always very strict as to his promised time of payment.

It is but fair, in this and all other cases, to describe the condition of things as commonly approved and prevailing; and when there are painful exceptions, it is but just to consider what is the public sentiment with regard to them. By this rule a visitor is made to feel that good and kind treatment of the slaves is the common law, subject, of course, to caprices and passions.

A strong public sentiment protects the person of the slave against annoyances and injuries. Boys and men cannot abuse another man's servant. Wrongs to his person are avenged. It amounts in many cases to a chivalric feeling, increased by a sense of utter meanness and cowardice in striking or insulting one who can not return insult for insult and blow for blow. Instances of this protective feeling greatly interested me. One was rather singular, indeed ludicrous, and made considerable sport; but it shows how far the feeling can proceed. A slave was brought before a mayor's court for some altercation in the street; the master privately requested the mayor to spare him from being chastised, and the mayor was strongly disposed to do so; but the testimony was too palpably against the servant, and he was whipped; in consequence of which the master sent a challenge to the mayor to fight a duel. . . .

Absence of Pauperism

Pauperism is prevented by slavery. This idea is absurd, no doubt, in the apprehension of many at the north, who think that slaves are, as a matter of course, paupers. Nothing can be more untrue.

Every slave has an inalienable claim in law upon his owner for support for the whole of life. He can not be thrust into an almshouse, he can not become a vagrant, he can not beg his living, he can not be wholly neglected when he is old and decrepit.

I saw a white-headed negro at the door of his cabin on a gentleman's estate, who had done no work for ten years. He enjoys all the privileges of the plantation, garden, and orchard; is clothed and fed as carefully as though he were useful. On asking him his age, he said he thought he "must be nigh a hundred;" that he was a servant to a gentleman in the army "when Washington fit Cornwallis and took him at Little York."

At a place called Harris's Neck, Georgia, there is a servant who has been confined to his bed with rheumatism thirty years, and no invalid has more reason to be grateful for attention and kindness. . . .

Thus the pauper establishments of the free States, the burden and care of immigrants, are almost entirely obviated at the south by the colored population. While we bow in submission to the duty of governing or maintaining certain foreigners, we can not any of us conceal that we have natural preferences and tastes as to the ways of doing good. In laboring for the present and future welfare of immigrants, we are subjected to evils of which we are ashamed to complain, but from which the south is enviably free. To have a neighborhood of a certain description of foreigners about your dwellings; to see a horde of

them get possession of a respectable dwelling in a court, and thus force the residents, as they always do, to flee, it being impossible to live with comfort in close connection with them; to have all the senses assailed from their opened doors; to have your Sabbath utterly destroyed,—is not so agreeable as the presence of a respectable colored population, every individual of which is under the responsible oversight of a master or mistress, who restrains and governs him, and has a reputation to maintain in his respectable appearance and comfort, and keeps him from being a burden on the community. . . .

"Judging of them as you meet them in the streets, see them at work, or at church, . . . one must see that they are a happy people."

The following case, that came to my knowledge, offers a good illustration of the views which many slaves take of their dependent condition. A colored woman with her children lived in a separate cabin belonging to her master, washing clothes for families in that place. She paid her master a percentage of her earnings, and had laid up more than enough to buy her freedom and that of her children. Why, as she might be made free, does she not use it rather?

She says that if she were to buy her freedom, she would have no one to take care of her for the rest of her life. Now her master is responsible for her support. She has no care about the future. Old age, sickness, poverty, do not trouble her. "I can indulge myself and children," she says, "in things which otherwise I could not get. If we want new things faster than mistress gets them for us, I can spare money to get them. If I buy my freedom, I cut myself off from the interests of the white folks in me. Now they feel that I belong to them, and people will look to see if they treat me well." Her only trouble is, that her master may die before her; then she will "have to be free."

Wages of Labor

One error which I had to correct in my own opinions was with regard to wages of labor. . . .

The accusation against slavery of working human beings without wages must be modified, if we give a proper meaning to the term *wages*. A stipulated sum per diem is our common notion of wages. A vast many slaves get wages in a better form than this—in provision for their support for the whole of life, with permission to earn something, and more or less according to the disposition of the masters and the ability of the slaves. A statement of the case, which perhaps is not of much value, was made by a slave-holder in this form: You hire a domestic by the week, or a laborer by the month, for certain wages, with food, lodging, perhaps clothing; I hire him for the term of life, becoming responsible for him in his decrepitude and old age. Leaving out of view the involuntariness on his part of the arrangement, he gets a good equivalent for his services; to his risk of being sold, and passing from hand to hand, there is an offset in the perpetual claim which he will have on some owner for maintenance all his days. . . .

The Features of Slavery

We have thus far looked at the slaves apart from the theory of slavery and from slave laws, and from their liability to suffering by being separated and sold. These features of slavery deserve to be considered by themselves; we can give them and things of that class a more just weight, and view the favorable circumstances of their condition with greater candor. This I have endeavored to do, describing every thing just as it struck me, leaving out of the question the evils of slavery, and abstract doctrines respecting it. . . .

Judging of them as you meet them in the streets, see them at work, or at church, or in their prayer meetings and singing meetings, or walking on the Sabbath or holidays, one must see that they are a happy people, their physical condition superior to that of very many of our operatives, far superior to the common Irish people in our cities, and immeasurably above thousands in Great Britain. . . . It is obvious that if one can have all his present wants supplied, with no care about short crops, the markets, notes payable, bills due, be relieved from the necessity of planning and contriving, all the hard thinking being done for him by another, while useful and honorable employment fills his thoughts and hands, he is so far in a situation favorable to great comfort which will show itself in his whole outer man. Some will say, "This is the lowest kind of happiness." Yet it is all that a large portion of the race seek for; and few, except slaves, obtain it. Thus far I am constrained to say, that the relief which my feelings have experienced in going to the south and seeing the slaves at home is very great. Whatever else may be true of their condition, to whatever perils or sorrows, from causes not yet spoken of, they may be subjected, I feel like one who has visited a friend who is sick and reported to be destitute and extremely miserable, but has found him comfortable and happy. The sickness is there, but the patient is not only comfortable, but happy, if the ordinary proofs of it are to be taken. We may wonder that he should be; we may prove on paper that he can not be; but if the colored people of Savannah, Columbia, and Rich-

mond are not, as a whole, a happy people, I have never seen any.

VIEWPOINT 28B

Slavery Is Oppressive (1855)
Peter Randolph (ca. 1825–1897)

Abolitionist writers and speakers frequently emphasized the cruelties of slave life in the United States to gain public support for their cause. Many were former slaves who told of their personal experiences. An example of such writing can be seen in the following viewpoint by Peter Randolph, who grew up a slave in Virginia. Emancipated with his fellow slaves upon his owner's death, Randolph settled in Boston and became a preacher. In 1847 he published and sold *Sketches of a Slave Life*, based on his own life as a slave; he later wrote *From the Slave Cabin to the Pulpit: The Autobiography of Rev. Peter Randolph.*

The following consists of excerpts from *Sketches* taken from a second and enlarged edition published in 1855. Randolph describes how slaves are mistreated by owners and overseers, and attacks observers such as Nehemiah Adams (see viewpoint 28A) for failing to see the truth about the cruelty of slavery.

What is the main point of Randolph's writing? What criticisms does he make of Nehemiah Adams? What are the greatest differences between Randolph's descriptions of slave life and Adams's observations?

T he good Anti-Slavery men have very much to contend with, in their exertions for the cause of freedom. Many people will not believe their statements; call them unreasonable and fanatical. Some call them ignorant deceivers, who have never been out of their own home, and yet pretend to a knowledge of what is going on a thousand miles from them. Many call them dangerous members of society, sowing discord and distrust where there should be nought but peace and brotherly love. My Readers! give attention to the simple words of one who knows what he utters is truth; who is no stranger to the *beauties* of slavery or the *generosity* of the slaveholder. Spend a few moments in reading his statement in regard to the system of American slavery. Do not scoff or doubt. He writes what he does know, what he has seen and experienced; for he has been, for twenty-seven years of his life, a slave; and he here solemnly pledges himself to TRUTH. Not once has he exaggerated, for he could not; the half of the woes and horrors of slavery, his feeble pen could

From Sketches of a Slave Life, 2nd ed., by Peter Randolph (Boston, 1855).

not portray.

This system is one of robbery and cruel wrong, from beginning to end. It robs men and women of their liberty, lives, property, affections, and virtue, as the following pages will show. It is not only a source of misery to those in bonds, but those who fasten the chains are made wretched by it; for a state of war constantly exists between the master and servant. The one would enforce obedience to his every wish, however wrong and unjust; he would exact all the earnings of the slave, to the uttermost farthing. The latter feels the restraint and writhes under it; he sees the injustice, and at times attempts to assert his rights; but he must submit either to the command or the lash; obey implicitly he must.

The argument so often brought forward, that it would be for the interest of the owner to treat his slaves well, and of course he would not injure his own interests, may do for some, but not for the thinking and considerate. When does the angry tyrant reflect upon what, in the end, will be the best for him? To gratify his passion for the moment, to wreak out his revenge upon a helpless menial, is, at the time of excitement, his interest, and he will serve it well. . . .

Some will say, "The slaveholder cannot live without the negro; the climate will not permit the white man to toil there." Very well; admit it. Then let him grant to men their rights; make them free citizens; pay them justly for their honest toil, and see the consequences. All would be happier and better. Slavery enriches not the mind, heart, or soil where it abides; it curses and blights every thing it comes in contact with. Away, away with, tear up by the roots, these noxious weeds, which choke the growth of all fair plants, and sow in their stead the beauteous flowers of freedom, well watered by the pure waters of religion, and what a rich harvest will be yours!

Personal History

Before going into particulars relative to the horrors of slavery, I will give a little of my own history. I was owned, with eighty-one others, by a man named Edloe, and among them all, only myself could either read or write. . . .

My father did not belong to Edloe, but was owned by a Mr. George Harrison, whose plantation adjoined that of my master. Harrison made my father a slave-driver placing an overseer over him. He was allowed to visit my mother every Wednesday and every Saturday night. This was the time usually given to the slaves to see their wives. My father would often tell my mother how the white overseer had made him cruelly whip his fellows, until the blood ran down to the ground. All his days he had to follow this dreadful employment of flogging men, women and chil-

dren, being placed in this helpless condition by the tyranny of his master. I used to think very hard of my father, and that he was a very cruel man; but when I knew that he could not help himself, I could not but alter my views and feelings in regard to his conduct. I was ten years old when he died.

When my father died, he left my mother with five children. We were all young at the time, and mother had no one to help take care of us. Her lot was very hard indeed. She had to work all the day for her owner, and at night for those who were dearer to her than life; for what was allowed her by Edloe was not sufficient for our wants. She used to get a little corn, without his knowledge, and boil it for us to satisfy our hunger. As for clothing, Edloe would give us a coarse suit once in three years; mother sometimes would beg the cast-off garments from the neighbors, to cover our nakedness; and when they had none to give, she would sit and cry over us, and pray to the God of the widow and fatherless for help and succor. At last, my oldest brother was sold from her, and carried where she never saw him again. She went mourning for him all her days, like a bird robbed of her young,—like Rachel bereft of her children, who would not be comforted, because they were not. She departed this life on the 27th of September, 1847, for that world "where the wicked cease from troubling, and the weary are at rest.". . .

The Hours for Work

The slave goes to his work when he sees the day-break in the morning, and works until dark at night. The slaves have their food carried to them in the field; they have one half hour to eat it in, in the winter, and one hour in the summer. Their time for eating is about eight in the morning, and one in the afternoon. Sometimes, they have not so much time given to them. The overseer stands by them until they have eaten, and then he orders them to work.

The slaves return to their huts at night, make their little fires, and lie down until they are awakened for another day of toil. No beds are given them to sleep on; if they have any, they find themselves. The women and the men all have to work on the farms together; they must fare alike in slavery. Husbands and wives must see all that happens to each other, and witness the sufferings of each. They must see their children polluted, without the power to prevent it. . . .

House Slaves

When the slave-master owns a great many slaves, ten or a dozen are always employed to wait on himself and family. They are not treated so cruelly as the field slaves; they are better fed and wear better clothing, because the master and his family always expect to have strangers visit them, and they want their servants to look well. These slaves eat from their master's table, wear broadcloth and calico; they wear ruffled-bosomed shirts, too,—such as Doctor Nehemiah Adams declares he saw while on his visit to the South, where he became so much in love with the "peculiar institution." These slaves, although dressed and fed better than others, have to suffer alike with those whose outward condition is worse. They are much to be compared to galvanized watches, which shine and resemble gold, but are far from being the true metal; so with these slaves who wait upon their masters at table—their broadcloth and calico look fine, but you may examine their persons, and find many a lash upon their flesh. They are sure of their whippings, and are sold the same as others.

Sometimes their masters change, and put them on the farm, that the overseers may whip them. Among those who wait upon the master, there is always one to watch the others, and report them to him. This slave is treated as well as his master, because it is for the master's interest that he does this. This slave he always carries with him when he visits the North; particularly such slaves as cannot be made to leave their master, because they are their master's watchdog at home. So master can trust them. Before leaving, master always talks very kindly to them, and promises something very great for a present, if they are true to him until his return.

These slaves know what they must say when asked as to their treatment at home, and of the treatment of their fellows. They leave their wives, their mothers, brothers and sisters, and children, toiling and being driven and whipped by the overseer, and tortured and insulted on every occasion.

Deceiving Visitors

All the slaves, as well as their owners, are addicted to drinking; so when the slaveholder wants to make a show of his niggers, (as he calls them,) he gives them rum to drink.

When the master knows a Northern man is to visit him, he gives orders to the overseer, and the overseer orders every slave to dress himself, and appear on the field. If the slaves have any best, they must put it on. Perhaps a man has worked hard, extra times all the year, and got his wife a fourpenny gown,—she must put it on, and go to the field to work. About the time the stranger is expected, a jug of rum is sent to the field, and every slave has just enough given him to make him act as if he was crazy.

When such a stranger as Rev. Dr. Adams appears with the master, he does not see the negroes, but the rum that is in them; and when he hears their hurrah, and sees their Jim-Crow actions, he takes it for granted that they are as happy as need be, and their condition could not be bettered.

The owner gives the visitor liberty to ask his "niggers" questions. He will ask them if they love their master, or wish to leave him. Poor slave will say, he would not leave his master for the world; but O, my reader! just let the poor slave get off, and he would be in Canada very soon, where the slaveholder dare not venture.

The slaves do not speak for themselves. The slaveholding master and his rum are working in their heads, speaking for slavery; and this is the way the slaveholder deceives his friend from the North.

Flogging

For whipping the slaves in Virginia, there are no rules. The slave receives from the slaveholder from fifty to five hundred lashes. The slave-owner would think fifty stripes an insult to the slave. If the slave is let off with fifty lashes, he must show a very good temper. Men, women, and children must be whipped alike on their bare backs, it being considered an honor to whip them over their clothes. The slaves are placed in a certain position when they are flogged, with sufficient management to hold them very still, so they cannot work their hands or feet, while they are "wooding them up," as they call it in Virginia.

Some of the slaves have to lie down on their stomachs, flat on the ground, and stretched out so as to keep their skin tight for the lash and thus lie until they receive as much as they choose to put on; if they move, they must receive so many lashes extra. When the slaveholder expects to give his slave five hundred lashes, he gives him about half at a time; then washes him down with salt and water, and then gives him the remainder of what he is to have. At such times, the slave-owner has his different liquors to drink, while he is engaged in draining the blood of the slave. So he continues to drink his rum and whip his victim. When he does not flog his victims on the ground, they are tied by their hands, and swung up to a great tree, just so the end of their toes may touch the ground. In this way, they receive what number of lashes they are destined to. The master has straw brought, that the blood may not touch his shoes. Ah, reader! this is true, every word of it. The poor slave is whipped till the blood runs down to the earth, and then he must work all day, cold or hot, from week's end to week's end. There are hundreds of slaves who change their skins nearly as often as they have a new suit of clothes. . . .

Slave Overseers

The first overseer I served under was Henry Hallingwork, a cruel and a bad man. He often whipped my mother and the children, and worked the slaves almost day and night, in all weather. The men had no comfort with their wives, for any of the latter who pleased him, he would take from their husbands, and use himself. If any refused his lewd embraces, he treated them with the utmost barbarity. At night, he watched the slaves' huts, to find out if they said anything against him, or had any food except what he had allowed them; and if he discovered anything he disliked, they were severely whipped. He continued this conduct for about three years, when Mr. Edloe discovered it, and discharged him.

The next overseer who lived on the plantation did not treat the people so badly as did Hallingwork, but he drove them very hard, and watched them very closely, to see that they took nothing but their allowance. He only lived there two years, when he was discharged for misconduct.

The next overseer, a man named Harris, only remained about six months; his cruelty was so great, it came to Mr. Edloe's ear, and he was discharged.

The successor of Harris was L. Hobbs. He was very cruel to the people, especially to all women who would not submit to him. He used to bind women hand and foot, and whip them until the blood ran down to the earth, and then wash them down in salt and water, and keep them tied all day, when Edloe was not at home. He used to take my cousin and tie her up and whip her so she could not lie down to rest at night until her back got well. All this was done on Edloe's plantation, the *good slaveholder* who owned me; and the other slaveholders used to say to him that he "spoiled his niggers;"—but this was the way he spoiled them. Hobbs continued this ill-treatment for the space of three years, then he was turned off. Thus ends the history of Hobbs on Edloe's plantation, with the exception of leaving what are termed "mulattoes" in Virginia.

———— • ————

"This system is one of robbery and cruel wrong, from beginning to end."

———— • ————

The fifth overseer was B.F. Bishop. He came to the plantation as a tyrant, and proved himself such to men, women and children. He reigned tyrannically for one year, and did many things which decency will not permit me to speak of. He, and all of the overseers, were in the habit of stealing from their employer, and the colored people knew it, but their informing Edloe would have done no good, for he could not believe a slave. According to the laws of Virginia, the testimony of a slave against an overseer could not be taken. This Benj. Bishop reigned "monarch of all he surveyed" (doing as he chose in every thing—cruel as cruel could be) one year, when he was discharged.

The sixth overseer was R. Lacy, a native of Charles City, Va. He reigned seven years. I cannot describe to my readers the malice and madness with which this being treated Edloe's slaves. You cannot find his parallel in history, except it be in Nero or Caligula. Indeed, he was a very wicked man, and a great hypocrite. I cannot point to one good deed he ever performed. He would enter the houses, and bind men and women, and inflict torture upon them, whether innocent or guilty. The blood of innocent slaves is yet crying to the God of justice to avenge their sufferings, and pour out deserved judgment upon the head of Lacy. . . .

Food and Clothing

I shall now show what the slaves have to eat and wear. They have one pair of shoes for the year; if these are worn out in two months, they get no more that year, but must go barefooted the rest of the year, through cold and heat. The shoes are very poor ones, made by one of the slaves, and do not last more than two or three months. One pair of stockings is allowed them for the year; when these are gone, they have no more, although it is cold in Virginia for five months. They have one suit of clothes for the year. This is very poor indeed, and made by the slaves themselves on the plantation. It will not last more than three months, and then the poor slave gets no more from the slaveholder, if he go naked. This suit consists of one shirt, one pair of pants, one pair of socks, one pair of shoes, and no vest at all. The slave has a hat given him once in two years; when this is worn out, he gets no more from the slaveholder, but must go bareheaded till he can get one somewhere else. Perhaps the slave will get him a skin of some kind, and make him a hat.

The food of the slaves is this: Every Saturday night, they receive two pounds of bacon, and one peck and a half of corn meal, to last the men through the week. The women have one half pound of meat, and one peck of meal, and the children one half peck each. When this is gone, they can have no more till the end of the week. This is very little food for the slaves. They have to beg when they can; when they cannot, they must suffer. They are not allowed to go off the plantation; if they do, and are caught, they are whipped very severely, and what they have begged is taken from them. . . .

City and Town Slaves

The slaves in the cities (Petersburg, Richmond and Norfolk, in Virginia) do not fare so hard as on the plantations, where they have farming work to do. Most of the town and city slaves are hired out, to bring in money to their owners. They often have the privilege of hiring themselves out, by paying their owners so much, at stated times,—say once a week, or once a month. Many of them are employed in factories and work at trades. They do very well, for if they are industrious, they can earn considerably more than is exacted of them by their owners. All can dress well, have comfortable homes, and many can read and write. Many of them lay up money to purchase either their own freedom or that of some dear one. These slaves are not subjected to the lash as the poor creatures upon the plantations are, for their owners would feel (as every man should feel, in the true sense) their dignity fallen, their nobility sullied, by raising the whip over their human property.

Slavery, as seen here by the casual observer, might be supposed not to be so hard as one would imagine, after all the outcry of philanthropists, who "sit in their chimney-corners amid the Northern hills, and conjure up demoniac shapes and fiendish spirits, bearing the name of slaveholders." But Slavery is *Slavery*, wherever it is found. Dress it up as you may, in the city or on the plantation, the human being must feel that which binds him to another's will. Be the fetters of silk, or hemp, or iron, all alike warp the mind and goad the soul.

The city slave may escape the evil eye and cruel lash of the overseer, but if he offend the all-important master, there is retribution for him. "Hand this note to Capt. Heart," (of Norfolk,) or "Capt. Thwing," (of Petersburg,)—and well does the shrinking slave know what is to follow. These last-mentioned gentlemen *give* their time to, and improve their talents by, laying the lash upon the naked backs of men and women!

Slavery's Dark Side

Ah, my readers! take what side you will of slavery,—Dr. Adams's "South side," or the Abolitionist's North side,—there is but one *side*, and that is dark, *dark*. You may think you see bright spots, but look at the surroundings of those spots, and you will see nothing but gloom and darkness. While toiling industriously, and living with a dear family in comparative comfort and happiness, the city slave (whose lot is thought to be so easy) suddenly finds himself upon the auction-block, knocked down to the highest bidder, and carried far and forever from those dearer to him than life; a beloved wife, and tender, helpless children are all bereft, in a moment, of husband, father and protector, by a fate worse than death;—and for what? To gratify some spirit of revenge, or add to the weight of the already well-filled purse of some *Christian white man*, who professes ownership in his fellow-man. Wretch! you may command, for a season, the bones and sinews of that brother, so infinitely your superior; but, remember! that form is animated by a never-dying spirit; it will

not always slumber; a God of infinite love and justice reigns over all, and beholds your unholy, inhuman traffic! Believe you, justice will triumph, the guilty shall not go unpunished on the earth; the righteous are to be recompensed, *much more the wicked and the sinner.*

For Further Reading

John Blassingame, ed., *Slave Testimony: Two Centuries of Letters, Speeches, Interviews, and Autobiographies.* Baton Rouge: Louisiana State University Press, 1977.

B.A. Botkin, ed., *Lay My Burden Down: A Folk History of Slavery.* Athens: University of Georgia Press, 1989.

Eugene Genovese, *Roll, Jordan, Roll.* New York: Random House, 1976.

Robert Q. Mallard, *Plantation Life Before Emancipation.* Richmond, VA: Whittet & Shepperson, 1892.

Eric McKitrick, *Slavery Defended: The Views of the Old South.* Englewood Cliffs, NJ: Prentice-Hall, 1963.

Benjamin Quarles, *Black Abolitionists.* New York: Oxford University Press, 1969.

Kenneth M. Stampp, *The Peculiar Institution.* New York: Vintage Books, 1956.

Manifest Destiny and War

VIEWPOINT 29A

America Should Not Annex Texas (1844)

Henry Clay (1777–1852)

Henry Clay served a long and distinguished career as Speaker of the House of Representatives, secretary of state under President John Quincy Adams, and U.S. senator from Kentucky. He was known as the "Great Compromiser" because of his work in Congress in settling disputes, mostly between northern and southern states over the issues of expansion and slavery. Clay was nominated for president by the Whig Party on three occasions, the last being in 1844 when his opponent was James K. Polk and the central issue of the campaign was Texas.

Texas, a former Mexican province with a large population of settlers from the United States, had declared independence from Mexico in 1836, and had almost immediately inquired about admission into the Union. The United States under Presidents Andrew Jackson and Martin Van Buren, however, decided only to recognize Texas as an independent nation, mindful that annexation of Texas might lead

From Henry Clay's letter to the editor of the *Daily National Intelligencer*, April 27, 1844; reprinted in *Niles National Register*, vol. 66.

to war with Mexico. Slavery was also an issue, as some antislavery leaders came out strongly against adding another potential slave state to the Union. These two basic concerns—war with Mexico and division over slavery—are notable in the following viewpoint, excerpted from Henry Clay's "Raleigh Letter." (He sent it to the editors of the *Daily National Intelligencer* while in Raleigh, North Carolina.) Responding to President John Tyler's 1844 annexation treaty with Texas (just submitted to the Senate for ratification), Clay argues against incorporating Texas into the Union. The letter was published in newspapers in April 1844 when Clay was all but assured of the Whig Party's nomination for president. In the subsequent election Clay, who later hedged on his antiannexation position, was narrowly defeated by James K. Polk, a former Tennessee senator who ran on a strong expansionist platform.

Does Clay come out unconditionally against Texas annexation? What does he say the United States needs at this time? Why might admission of Texas into the Union lead to possible U.S. expansion into Canada, according to Clay?

Gentlemen: Subsequent to my departure from Ashland [Clay's Kentucky home], in December last, I received various communications from popular assemblages and private individuals, requesting an expression of my opinion upon the question of the annexation of Texas to the United States. . . . The rejection of the overture of Texas, some years ago, to become annexed to the United States, had met with general acquiescence. Nothing had since occurred materially to vary the question. I had seen no evidence of a desire being entertained, on the part of any considerable portion of the American people, that Texas should become an integral part of the United States. . . . To the astonishment of the whole nation, we are now informed that a treaty of annexation has been actually concluded, and is to be submitted to the senate for its consideration. . . .

I regret that I have not the advantage of a view of the treaty itself, so as to enable me to adapt an expression of my opinion to the actual conditions and stipulations which it contains. Not possessing that opportunity, I am constrained to treat the question according to what I presume to be the terms of the treaty. If, without the loss of national character, without the hazard of foreign war, with the general concurrence of the nation, without any danger to the integrity of the Union, and without giving an unreasonable price for Texas, the question of annexation were presented, it would appear in quite a different light from that in which, I apprehend, it is now to be regarded. . . .

Desire to Prevent War

Annexation and war with Mexico are identical. Now, for one, I certainly am not willing to involve this country in a foreign war for the object of acquiring Texas. I know there are those who regard such a war with indifference and as a trifling affair, on account of the weakness of Mexico, and her inability to inflict serious injury upon this country. But I do not look upon it thus lightly. I regard all wars as great calamities, to be avoided, if possible, and honorable peace as the wisest and truest policy of this country. What the United States most need are union, peace, and patience. Nor do I think that the weakness of a power should form a motive, in any case, for inducing us to engage in or to depreciate the evils of war.—Honor and good faith and justice are equally due from this country towards the weak as towards the strong. And, if an act of injustice were to be perpetrated towards any power, it would be more compatible with the dignity of the nation, and, in my judgment, less dishonorable, to inflict it upon a powerful instead of a weak foreign nation. But are we perfectly sure that we should be free from injury in a state of war with Mexico? Have we any security that countless numbers of foreign vessels, under the authority and flag of Mexico, would not prey upon our defenceless commerce in the Mexican gulf, on the Pacific ocean, and on every other sea and ocean? What commerce, on the other hand, does Mexico offer, as an indemnity for our losses, to the gallantry and enterprise of our countrymen? This view of the subject supposes that the war would be confined to the United States and Mexico as the only belligerents. But have we any certain guaranty that Mexico would obtain no allies among the great European powers? . . .

Assuming that the annexation of Texas is war with Mexico, is it competent to the treaty-making power to plunge this country into war, not only without the concurrence of, but without deigning to consult congress, to which, by the constitution, belongs exclusively the power of declaring war?

Domestic Considerations

I have hitherto considered the question upon the supposition that the annexation is attempted without the assent of Mexico. If she yields her consent, that would materially affect the foreign aspect of the question, if it did not remove all foreign difficulties. On the assumption of that assent, the question would be confined to the domestic considerations which belong to it, embracing the terms and conditions upon which annexation is proposed. I do not think that Texas ought to be received into the Union, as an integral part of it, in decided opposition to the wishes of a considerable and respectable portion of the confederacy. I think it far more wise and important to compose and harmonize the present confederacy, as it now exists, than to introduce a new element of discord and distraction into it. . . . Mr. [Thomas] Jefferson expressed the opinion, and others believed, that it never was in the contemplation of the framers of the constitution to add foreign territory to the confederacy, out of which new states were to be formed. The acquisitions of Louisiana and Florida may be defended upon the peculiar ground of the relation in which they stood to the states of the Union. After they were admitted, we might well pause a while, people our vast wastes, develop our resources, prepare the means of defending what we possess, and augment our strength, power, and greatness. If hereafter further territory should be wanted for an increased population, we need entertain no apprehensions but that it will be acquired by means, it is to be hoped, fair, honorable, and constitutional.

————— • —————

"I consider the annexation of Texas . . . as a measure compromising the national character, involving us certainly in war with Mexico, . . . [and] dangerous to the integrity of the Union."

————— • —————

It is useless to disguise that there are those who espouse and those who oppose the annexation of Texas upon the ground of the influence which it would exert, in the balance of political power, between two great sections of the Union. I conceive that no motive for the acquisition of foreign territory would be more unfortunate, or pregnant with more fatal consequences, than that of obtaining it for the purpose of strengthening one part against another part of the common confederacy. Such a principle, put into practical operation, would menace the existence, if it did not certainly sow the seeds of a dissolution of the Union. It would be to proclaim to the world an insatiable and unquenchable thirst for foreign conquest or acquisition of territory. For if today Texas be acquired to strengthen one part of the confederacy, tomorrow Canada may be required to add strength to another. And, after that might have been obtained, still other and further acquisitions would become necessary to equalize and adjust the balance of political power. Finally, in the progress of this spirit of universal dominion, the part of the confederacy which is now weakest, would find itself still weaker from the impossibility of securing new theatres for

those peculiar institutions which it is charged with being desirous to extend.

Texas and Future States

But would Texas, ultimately, really add strength to that which is now considered the weakest part of the confederacy? If my information be correct, it would not. According to that, the territory of Texas is susceptible of a division into five states of convenient size and form. Of these, two only would be adapted to those peculiar institutions to which I have referred, and the other three, lying west and north of San Antonio, being only adapted to farming and grazing purposes, from the nature of their soil, climate, and productions, would not admit of those institutions. In the end, therefore, there would be two slave and three free states probably added to the Union. If this view of the soil and geography of Texas be correct, it might serve to diminish the zeal both of those who oppose and those who are urging annexation. . . .

In the future progress of events, it is probable that there will be a voluntary or forcible separation of the British North American possessions from the parent country. I am strongly inclined to think that it will be best for the happiness of all parties that, in that event, they should be erected into a separate and independent republic. With the Canadian republic on one side, that of Texas on the other, and the United States, the friend of both, between them, each could advance its own happiness by such constitutions, laws, and measures, as were best adapted to its peculiar condition. They would be natural allies, ready, by co-operation, to repel any European or foreign attack upon either. Each would afford a secure refuge to the persecuted and oppressed driven into exile by either of the others. They would emulate each other in improvements, in free institutions, and in the science of self-government. Whilst Texas has adopted our constitution as the model of hers, she has, in several important particulars, greatly improved upon it.

Against Annexation

Although I have felt compelled, from the nature of the inquiries addressed to me, to extend this communication to a much greater length than I could have wished, I could not do justice to the subject, and fairly and fully expose my own opinions in a shorter space. In conclusion, they may be stated in a few words to be, that I consider the annexation of Texas, at this time, without the assent of Mexico, as a measure compromising the national character, involving us certainly in war with Mexico, probably with other foreign powers, dangerous to the integrity of the Union, inexpedient in the present financial condition of the country, and not called for by any general expression of public opinion.

VIEWPOINT 29B

America Should Annex Texas (1845)

John L. O'Sullivan (1813–1895)

The Senate rejected the Texas annexation treaty submitted by President John Tyler in 1844. Tyler submitted the issue for congressional vote again in 1845, this time proposing that the two houses of Congress pass a joint resolution that Texas be annexed. Such a resolution required only a majority vote in both houses of Congress, thus avoiding the necessity for the two-thirds Senate majority required for treaty ratification. The stratagem worked; in March 1845 the lame-duck president signed a joint resolution inviting Texas to join the Union. However, the issue of whether to admit Texas remained divisive, with opponents of slavery condemning the admission of Texas as a territorial grab intended to create a new slave state or states. In the following viewpoint, newspaper editor John L. O'Sullivan criticizes the opponents of Texas annexation. He goes beyond the immediate issue of Texas to argue that it is the fate of America to grow to encompass much, if not all, of the North American continent. O'Sullivan, founder and editor of the *United States Magazine and Democratic Review* and editor of the *New York Morning News*, is credited with inventing the term "manifest destiny" to describe his expansionist views for America, which were shared by many.

How does O'Sullivan answer Mexican claims to Texas and California? What future vision of America does O'Sullivan describe? What future does he predict for "the Negro race" in America?

It is time now for opposition to the Annexation of Texas to cease, all further agitation of the waters of bitterness and strife, at least in connection with this question, even though it may perhaps be required of us as a necessary condition of the freedom of our institutions, that we must live on forever in a state of unpausing struggle and excitement upon some subject of party division or other. But, in regard to Texas, enough has now been given to party. It is time for the common duty of patriotism to the country to succeed; or if this claim will not be recognized, it is at least time for common sense to acquiesce with decent grace in the inevitable and the irrevocable.

Texas is now ours. Already, before these words are written, her convention has undoubtedly ratified the

John L. O'Sullivan, "Annexation," *United States Magazine and Democratic Review*, July 1845.

acceptance, by her congress, of our proffered invitation into the Union; and made the requisite changes in her already republican form of constitution to adapt it to its future federal relations. Her star and her stripe may already be said to have taken their place in the glorious blazon of our common nationality; and the sweep of our eagle's wing already includes within its circuit the wide extent of her fair and fertile land. She is no longer to us a mere geographical space—a certain combination of coast, plain, mountain, valley, forest, and stream. She is no longer to us a mere country on the map. She comes within the dear and sacred designation of our country; no longer a *pays* [country], she is a part of *la patrie* [homeland]; and that which is at once a sentiment and a virtue, patriotism, already begins to thrill for her too within the national heart.

It is time then that all should cease to treat her as alien, and even adverse—cease to denounce and vilify all and everything connected with her accession—cease to thwart and oppose the remaining steps for its consummation; or where such efforts are felt to be unavailing, at least to embitter the hour of reception by all the most ungracious frowns of aversion and words of unwelcome. There has been enough of all this. It has had its fitting day during the period when, in common with every other possible question of practical policy that can arise, it unfortunately became one of the leading topics of party division, of presidential electioneering. But that period has passed, and with it let its prejudices and its passions, its discords and its denunciations, pass away too. The next session of Congress will see the representatives of the new young state in their places in both our halls of national legislation, side by side with those of the old Thirteen. Let their reception into "the family" be frank, kindly, and cheerful, as befits such an occasion, as comports not less with our own self-respect than patriotic duty towards them. Ill betide those foul birds that delight to file their own nest, and disgust the ear with perpetual discord of ill-omened croak.

Foreign Interference

Why, were other reasoning wanting, in favor of now elevating this question of the reception of Texas into the Union, out of the lower region of our past party dissensions, up to its proper level of a high and broad nationality, it surely is to be found, found abundantly, in the manner in which other nations have undertaken to intrude themselves into it, between us and the proper parties to the case, in a spirit of hostile interference against us, for the avowed object of thwarting our policy and hampering our power, limiting our greatness and checking the fulfillment of our manifest destiny to overspread the continent allotted by Providence for the free development of our yearly multiplying millions. This we have seen done by England, our old rival and enemy; and by France, strangely coupled with her against us, under the influence of the Anglicism strongly tinging the policy of her present prime minister, [Francois-Pierre-Guillaume] Guizot.

The zealous activity with which this effort to defeat us was pushed by the representatives of those governments, together with the character of intrigue accompanying it, fully constituted that case of foreign interference, which Mr. [Henry] Clay himself declared should, and would unite us all in maintaining the common cause of our country against the foreigner and the foe. We are only astonished that this effect has not been more fully and strongly produced, and that the burst of indignation against this unauthorized, insolent, and hostile interference against us, has not been more general even among the party before opposed to annexation, and has not rallied the national spirit and national pride unanimously upon that policy. We are very sure that if Mr. Clay himself were now to add another letter to his former Texas correspondence, he would express this sentiment, and carry out the idea already strongly stated in one of them, in a manner which would tax all the powers of blushing belonging to some of his party adherents.

It is wholly untrue, and unjust to ourselves, the pretense that the Annexation has been a measure of spoliation, unrightful and unrighteous—of military conquest under forms of peace and law—of territorial aggrandizement at the expense of justice, and justice due by a double sanctity to the weak. This view of the question is wholly unfounded, and has been before so amply refuted in these pages, as well as in a thousand other modes, that we shall not again dwell upon it.

———— • ————

"Texas has been absorbed into the Union in the inevitable fulfilment of the general law which is rolling our population westward."

———— • ————

The independence of Texas was complete and absolute. It was an independence, not only in fact, but of right. No obligation of duty toward Mexico tended in the least degree to restrain our right to effect the desired recovery of the fair province once our own—whatever motives of policy might have prompted a more deferential consideration of her feelings and her pride, as involved in the question. If Texas became peopled with an American population,

it was by no contrivance of our government, but on the express invitation of that of Mexico herself; accompanied with such guaranties of state independence, and the maintenance of a federal system analogous to our own, as constituted a compact fully justifying the strongest measures of redress on the part of those afterward deceived in this guaranty, and sought to be enslaved under the yoke imposed by its violation.

She was released, rightfully and absolutely released, from all Mexican allegiance, or duty of cohesion to the Mexican political body, by the acts and fault of Mexico herself, and Mexico alone. There never was a clearer case. It was not revolution; it was resistance to revolution: and resistance under such circumstances as left independence the necessary resulting state, caused by the abandonment of those with whom her former federal association had existed. What then can be more preposterous than all this clamor by Mexico and the Mexican interest, against Annexation, as a violation of any rights of hers, any duties of ours? . . .

Texas and Slavery

Nor is there any just foundation for the charge that Annexation is a great pro-slavery measure—calculated to increase and perpetuate that institution. Slavery had nothing to do with it. Opinions were and are greatly divided, both at the North and South, as to the influence to be exerted by it on slavery and the slave states. That it will tend to facilitate and hasten the disappearance of slavery from all the northern tier of the present slave states, cannot surely admit of serious question. The greater value in Texas of the slave labor now employed in those states, must soon produce the effect of draining off that labor southwardly, by the same unvarying law that bids water descend the slope that invites it.

Every new slave state in Texas will make at least one free state from among those in which that institution now exists—to say nothing of those portions of Texas on which slavery cannot spring and grow—to say nothing of the far more rapid growth of new states in the free West and Northwest, as these fine regions are overspread by the emigration fast flowing over them from Europe, as well as from the Northern and Eastern states of the Union as it exists. On the other hand, it is undeniably much gained for the cause of the eventual voluntary abolition of slavery, that it should have been thus drained off toward the only outlet which appeared to furnish much probability of the ultimate disappearance of the Negro race from our borders.

The Spanish-Indian-American populations of Mexico, Central America, and South America, afford the only receptacle capable of absorbing that race whenever we shall be prepared to slough it off—to emancipate it from slavery, and (simultaneously necessary) to remove it from the midst of our own. Themselves already of mixed and confused blood, and free from the "prejudices" which among us so insuperably forbid the social amalgamation which can alone elevate the Negro race out of a virtually servile degradation; even though legally free the regions occupied by those populations must strongly attract the black race in that direction; and as soon as the destined hour of emancipation shall arrive, will relieve the question of one of its worst difficulties, if not absolutely the greatest. . . .

The country which was the subject of Annexation in this case, from its geographical position and relations, happens to be—or rather the portion of it now actually settled, happens to be—a slave country. But a similar process might have taken place in proximity to a different section of our Union; and indeed there is a great deal of Annexation yet to take place, within the life of the present generation, along the whole line of our northern border. Texas has been absorbed into the Union in the inevitable fulfilment of the general law which is rolling our population westward; the connexion of which with that ratio of growth in population which is destined within a hundred years to swell our numbers to the enormous population of *two hundred and fifty millions* (if not more), is too evident to leave us in doubt of the manifest design of Providence in regard to the occupation of this continent. It was disintegrated from Mexico in the natural course of events, by a process perfectly legitimate on its own part, blameless on ours; and in which all the censures due to wrong, perfidy and folly, rest on Mexico alone. And possessed as it was by a population which was in truth but a colonial detachment from our own, and which was still bound by myriad ties of the very heartstrings to its old relations, domestic and political, their incorporation into the Union was not only inevitable, but the most natural, right and proper thing in the world—and it is only astonishing that there should be any among ourselves to say it nay. . . .

California Is Next

California will, probably, next fall away from the loose adhesion which, in such a country as Mexico, holds a remote province in a slight equivocal kind of dependence on the metropolis. Imbecile and distracted, Mexico never can exert any real government authority over such a country. The impotence of the one and the distance of the other, must make the relation one of virtual independence; unless, by stunting the province of all natural growth, and forbidding that immigration which can alone develope its capabilities and fulfill the purposes of its creation, tyranny may retain a military dominion, which is no

government in the legitimate sense of the term. In the case of California this is now impossible. The Anglo-Saxon foot is already on its borders. Already the advance guard of the irresistible army of Anglo-Saxon emigration has begun to pour down upon it, armed with the plough and the rifle, and marking its trail with schools and colleges, courts and representative halls, mills and meetinghouses. A population will soon be in actual occupation of California, over which it will be idle for Mexico to dream of dominion. They will necessarily become independent. All this without agency of our government, without responsibility of our people—in the natural flow of events, the spontaneous working of principles, and the adaptation of the tendencies and wants of the human race to the elemental circumstances in the midst of which they find themselves placed.

And they will have a right to independence—to self-government—to the possession of the homes conquered from the wilderness by their own labors and dangers, sufferings and sacrifices—a better and a truer right than the artificial title of sovereignty in Mexico, a thousand miles distant, inheriting from Spain a title good only against those who have none better. Their right to independence will be the natural right of self-government belonging to any community strong enough to maintain it—distinct in position, origin and character, and free from any mutual obligations of membership of a common political body, binding it to others by the duty of loyalty and compact of public faith. This will be their title to independence; and by this title, there can be no doubt that the population now fast streaming down upon California will both assert and maintain that independence.

A Transcontinental Railroad

Whether they will then attach themselves to our Union or not, is not to be predicted with any certainty. Unless the projected railroad across the continent to the Pacific be carried into effect, perhaps they may not; though even in that case, the day is not distant when the empires of the Atlantic and Pacific would again flow together into one, as soon as their inland borders should approach each other. But that great work, colossal as appears the plan on its first suggestion, cannot remain long unbuilt. Its necessity for this very purpose of binding and holding together in its iron clasp our fast-settling Pacific region with that of the Mississippi Valley—the natural facility of the route—the ease with which any amount of labor for the construction can be drawn in from the overcrowded populations of Europe, to be paid in the lands made valuable by the progress of the work itself—and its immense utility to the commerce of the world with the whole eastern coast of Asia, alone almost sufficient for the support of such a road—these considerations give assurance that the day cannot be distant which shall witness the conveyance of the representatives from Oregon and California to Washington within less time than a few years ago was devoted to a similar journey by those from Ohio; while the magnetic telegraph will enable the editors of the *San Francisco Union*, the *Astoria Evening Post*, or the *Nootka Morning News*, to set up in type the first half of the President's inaugural before the echoes of the latter half shall have died away beneath the lofty porch of the Capitol, as spoken from his lips.

A Look to the Future

Away, then, with all idle French talk of balances of power on the American Continent. There is no growth in Spanish America! Whatever progress of population there may be in the British Canadas, is only for their own early severance of their present colonial relation to the little island 3,000 miles across the Atlantic; soon to be followed by annexation, and destined to swell the still accumulating momentum of our progress.

And whosoever may hold the balance, though they should cast into the opposite scale all the bayonets and cannon, not only of France and England, but of Europe entire, how would it kick the beam against the simple, solid weight of the 250, or 300 millions—and American millions—destined to gather beneath the flutter of the stripes and stars, in the fast hastening year of the Lord 1945!

For Further Reading

Reginald Horsman, *Race and Manifest Destiny: The Origins of American Racial Anglo-Saxonism.* Cambridge, MA: Harvard University Press, 1981.

Allan O. Kownslar, *Manifest Destiny and Expansionism in the 1840's.* Boston: Heath, 1967.

Frederick Merk, *Manifest Destiny and Mission in American History.* New York: Knopf, 1966.

Robert V. Remini, *Henry Clay: Statesman for the Union.* New York: W.W. Norton, 1991.

VIEWPOINT 30A

The United States Must Enter War with Mexico to Defend Itself (1846)

James K. Polk (1795–1849)

James K. Polk began his presidency in 1845 determined to add the Oregon and California territories

From James K. Polk's message to Congress on May 11, 1846, as reprinted in *A Compilation of the Messages and Papers of the Presidents, 1798–1897*, edited by James D. Richardson (New York, 1896–1899).

to the Union, to go along with the recently annexed Texas. Negotiations with Great Britain were successful in resolving joint ownership claims of Oregon and attaining Polk's goal of a U.S. boundary at the 49th parallel; negotiations with Mexico proved more difficult. Mexico had broken off relations with the United States immediately after America's annexation of Texas in 1845. An attempt to purchase California from Mexico in 1845 failed when Mexico refused to receive American diplomat John Slidell.

In January 1846 Polk responded to Slidell's failed initiative by stationing American troops in Texas on the north bank of the Rio Grande, in territory south of the Nueces River that was claimed by both Mexico and the United States. Several months later, on April 25, Mexican troops crossed the Rio Grande and attacked two companies of American soldiers. News of the attack reached Washington on May 9, just *after* Polk and his cabinet had discussed and agreed on sending a war message to Congress. The attack was quickly incorporated into the message Polk sent to Congress on May 11. Congress responded to the message, excerpted here, by overwhelmingly voting to go to war with Mexico.

What steps has the United States taken to avoid war, according to Polk? What reasons for war besides the attack on April 25 does he cite? What ultimate goals of war with Mexico does Polk mention?

*T*o the Senate and House of Representatives:

The existing state of the relations between the United States and Mexico renders it proper that I should bring the subject to the consideration of Congress. In my message at the commencement of your present session the state of these relations, the causes which led to the suspension of diplomatic intercourse between the two countries in March, 1845, and the long-continued and unredressed wrongs and injuries committed by the Mexican Government on citizens of the United States in their persons and property were briefly set forth. . . .

A Desire for Peace

The strong desire to establish peace with Mexico on liberal and honorable terms, and the readiness of this Government to regulate and adjust our boundary and other causes of difference with that power on such fair and equitable principles as would lead to permanent relations of the most friendly nature, induced me in September last [1845] to seek the reopening of diplomatic relations between the two countries. Every measure adopted on our part had for its object the furtherance of these desired results. In communicating to Congress a succinct statement of the injuries which we had suffered from Mexico, and which have been accumulating during a period of more than twenty years, every expression that could tend to inflame the people of Mexico or defeat or delay a pacific result was carefully avoided. An envoy of the United States [John Slidell] repaired to Mexico with full powers to adjust every existing difference. But though present on the Mexican soil by agreement between the two Governments, invested with full powers, and bearing evidence of the most friendly dispositions, his mission has been unavailing. The Mexican Government not only refused to receive him or listen to his propositions, but after a long-continued series of menaces have at last invaded our territory and shed the blood of our fellow-citizens on our own soil. . . .

The Government of Mexico, though solemnly pledged by official acts in October last to receive and accredit an American envoy, violated their plighted faith and refused the offer of a peaceful adjustment of our difficulties. Not only was the offer rejected, but the indignity of its rejection was enhanced by the manifest breach of faith in refusing to admit the envoy who came because they had bound themselves to receive him. Nor can it be said that the offer was fruitless from the want of opportunity of discussing it; our envoy was present on their own soil. Nor can it be ascribed to a want of sufficient powers; our envoy had full powers to adjust every question of difference. Nor was there room for complaint that our propositions for settlement were unreasonable; permission was not even given our envoy to make any proposition whatever. Nor can it be objected that we, on our part, would not listen to any reasonable terms of their suggestion; the Mexican Government refused all negotiation, and have made no proposition of any kind.

Defending Texas

In my message at the commencement of the present session l informed you that upon the earnest appeal both of the Congress and convention of Texas I had ordered an efficient military force to take a position "between the Nueces and the Del Norte [Rio Grande]." This had become necessary to meet a threatened invasion of Texas by the Mexican forces, for which extensive military preparations had been made. The invasion was threatened solely because Texas had determined, in accordance with a solemn resolution of the Congress of the United States, to annex herself to our Union, and under these circumstances it was plainly our duty to extend our protection over her citizens and soil.

This force was concentrated at Corpus Christi, and remained there until after I had received such information from Mexico as rendered it probable, if not certain, that the Mexican Government would refuse to receive our envoy.

Meantime Texas, by the final action of our Congress, had become an integral part of our Union. The Congress of Texas, by its act of December 19, 1836, had declared the Rio del Norte to be the boundary of that Republic. Its jurisdiction had been extended and exercised beyond the Nueces. The country between that river and the Del Norte had been represented in the Congress and in the convention of Texas, had thus taken part in the act of annexation itself, and is now included within one of our Congressional districts. Our own Congress had, moreover, with great unanimity, by the act approved December 31, 1845, recognized the country beyond the Nueces as a part of our territory by including it within our own revenue system, and a revenue officer to reside within that district has been appointed by and with the advice and consent of the Senate. It became, therefore, of urgent necessity to provide for the defense of that portion of our country. Accordingly, on the 13th of January last [1846] instructions were issued to the general in command of these troops to occupy the left [northeast] bank of the Del Norte. This river, which is the southwestern boundary of the State of Texas, is an exposed frontier. From this quarter invasion was threatened; upon it and in its immediate vicinity, in the judgment of high military experience, are the proper stations for the protecting forces of the Government. In addition to this important consideration, several others occurred to induce this movement. Among these are the facilities afforded by the ports at Brazos Santiago and the mouth of the Del Norte for the reception of supplies by sea, the stronger and more healthful military positions, the convenience for obtaining a ready and a more abundant supply of provisions, water, fuel, and forage, and the advantages which are afforded by the Del Norte in forwarding supplies to such posts as may be established in the interior and upon the Indian frontier.

The movement of the troops to the Del Norte was made by the commanding general under positive instructions to abstain from all aggressive acts toward Mexico or Mexican citizens and to regard the relations between that Republic and the United States as peaceful unless she should declare war or commit acts of hostility indicative of a state of war. He was specially directed to protect private property and respect personal rights.

Mexican Attack

The Army moved from Corpus Christi on the 11th of March, and on the 28th of that month arrived on the left bank of the Del Norte opposite to Matamoras, where it encamped on a commanding position, which has since been strengthened by the erection of fieldworks. A depot has also been established at Point Isabel, near the Brazos Santiago, 30 miles in rear of the encampment. The selection of his position was necessarily confided to the judgment of the general in command.

The Mexican forces at Matamoras assumed a belligerent attitude, and on the 12th of April General [Pedro de] Ampudia, then in command, notified General [Zachary] Taylor to break up his camp within twenty-four hours and to retire beyond the Nueces River, and in the event of his failure to comply with these demands announced that arms, and arms alone, must decide the question. But no open act of hostility was committed until the 24th of April. On that day General [Mariano] Arista, who had succeeded to the command of the Mexican forces, communicated to General Taylor that "he considered hostilities commenced and should prosecute them." A party of dragoons of 63 men and officers were on the same day dispatched from the American camp up the Rio del Norte, on its left bank, to ascertain whether the Mexican troops had crossed or were preparing to cross the river, "became engaged with a large body of these troops, and after a short affair, in which some 16 were killed and wounded, appear to have been surrounded and compelled to surrender."

"As war . . . exists by the act of Mexico herself, we are called upon by every consideration of duty and patriotism to vindicate with decision the honor, the rights, and the interests of our country."

The grievous wrongs perpetrated by Mexico upon our citizens throughout a long period of years remain unredressed, and solemn treaties pledging her public faith for this redress have been disregarded. A government either unable or unwilling to enforce the execution of such treaties fails to perform one of its plainest duties.

Our commerce with Mexico has been almost annihilated. It was formerly highly beneficial to both nations, but our merchants have been deterred from prosecuting it by the system of outrage and extortion which the Mexican authorities have pursued against them, whilst their appeals through their own Government for indemnity have been made in vain. Our forebearance has gone to such an extreme as to be mistaken in its character. Had we acted with vigor in repelling the insults and redressing the injuries inflicted by Mexico at the commencement, we should doubtless have escaped all the difficulties in which we are now involved.

Instead of this, however, we have been exerting our best efforts to propitiate her good will. Upon the pretext that Texas, a nation as independent as herself, thought proper to unite its destinies with our own she has affected to believe that we have severed her rightful territory, and in official proclamations and manifestoes has repeatedly threatened to make war upon us for the purpose of reconquering Texas. In the meantime we have tried every effort at reconciliation. The cup of forbearance had been exhausted even before the recent information from the frontier of the Del Norte. But now, after reiterated menaces, Mexico has passed the boundary of the United States, has invaded our territory and shed American blood upon the American soil. She has proclaimed that hostilities have commenced, and that the two nations are now at war.

Vindicating Our Rights

As war exists, and, notwithstanding all our efforts to avoid it, exists by the act of Mexico herself, we are called upon by every consideration of duty and patriotism to vindicate with decision the honor, the rights, and the interests of our country. . . .

In further vindication of our rights and defense of our territory, I invoke the prompt action of Congress to recognize the existence of the war, and to place at the disposition of the Executive the means of prosecuting the war with vigor, and thus hastening the restoration of peace. To this end I recommend that authority should be given to call into the public service a large body of volunteers to serve for not less than six or twelve months unless sooner discharged. A volunteer force is beyond question more efficient than any other description of citizen soldiers, and it is not to be doubted that a number far beyond that required would readily rush to the field upon the call of their country. I further recommend that a liberal provision be made for sustaining our entire military force and furnishing it with supplies and munitions of war.

The most energetic and prompt measures and the immediate appearance in arms of a large and overpowering force are recommended to Congress as the most certain and efficient means of bringing the existing collision with Mexico to a speedy and successful termination.

Prepared to Negotiate

In making these recommendations I deem it proper to declare that it is my anxious desire not only to terminate hostilities speedily, but to bring all matters in dispute between this Government and Mexico to an early and amicable adjustment; and in this view I shall be prepared to renew negotiations whenever

Mexico shall be ready to receive propositions or to make propositions of her own.

VIEWPOINT 30B

The United States Fought Mexico to Gain Territory (1850)

Ramon Alcaraz (1823–1886) et al.

The Mexican War began in May 1846 when Congress passed a declaration of war following President James K. Polk's call to defend America from Mexican attack in Texas. It ended in February 1848 with the signing of the Treaty of Guadalupe Hidalgo in which the Rio Grande was established as the Texas boundary, and the United States acquired the Upper California, Utah, and New Mexico territories for a payment of $13 million. Counting Texas (which declared independence from Mexico in 1836 and was annexed by the United States in 1845), Mexico had lost half its territory to the United States since becoming independent from Spain in 1821.

A Mexican perspective on the war is found in the following viewpoint, excerpted from a pamphlet written by a group of Mexican writers and patriots. The work, with its strong accusations of American greed and duplicity, was translated and published in the United States in 1850, where it received a sympathetic audience from many Americans critical of what they termed "Mr. Polk's war."

What main disputes do the writers have with the claims of James K. Polk (see viewpoint 30A) concerning the origins of the Mexican War? Is their opinion of the United States totally negative? Explain.

To explain then in a few words the true origin of the war, it is sufficient to say that the insatiable ambition of the United States, favored by our weakness, caused it. But this assertion, however veracious and well founded, requires the confirmation which we will present, along with some former transactions, to the whole world. This evidence will leave no doubt of the correctness of our impressions.

In throwing off the yoke of the mother country [Great Britain], the United States of the North appeared at once as a powerful nation. This was the result of their excellent elementary principles of government established while in colonial subjection. The Republic announced at its birth, that it was called upon to represent an important part in the

From *The Other Side, or Notes for the History of the War Between Mexico and the United States*, edited by Ramon Alcaraz et al., translated by Albert C. Ramsey (New York, 1850).

world of Columbus. Its rapid advancement, its progressive increase, its wonderful territory, the uninterrupted augmentation of its inhabitants, and the formidable power it had gradually acquired, were many proofs of its becoming a colossus, not only for the feeble nations of Spanish America, but even for the old populations of the ancient continent.

A Policy of Expansion

The United States did not hope for the assistance of time in their schemes of aggrandizement. From the days of their independence they adopted the project of extending their dominions, and since then, that line of policy has not deviated in the slightest degree. This conduct, nevertheless, was not perceptible to the most enlightened: but reflecting men, who examined events, were not slow in recognising it. Conde de Aranda [Pedro de Aranda, a participant in Mexico's revolution against Spain], from whose perception the ends which the United States had resolved upon were not concealed, made use of some celebrated words. These we shall now produce as a prophecy verified by events. "This nation has been born a pigmy: in the time to come, it will be a giant, and even a colossus, very formidable in these vast regions. Its first step will be an appropriation of the Floridas to be master of the Gulf of Mexico."

The Ambition of North Americans

The ambition of the North Americans has not been in conformity with this. They desired from the beginning to extend their dominion in such manner as to become the absolute owners of almost all this continent. In two ways they could accomplish their ruling passion: in one by bringing under their laws and authority all America to the Isthmus of Panama; in another, in opening an overland passage to the Pacific Ocean, and making good harbors to facilitate its navigation. By this plan, establishing in some way an easy communication of a few days between both oceans, no nation could compete with them. England herself might show her strength before yielding the field to her fortunate rival, and the mistress of the commercial world might for a while be delayed in touching the point of greatness to which she aspires.

In the short space of some three quarters of a century events have verified the existence of these schemes and their rapid development. The North American Republic has already absorbed territories pertaining to Great Britain, France, Spain, and Mexico. It has employed every means to accomplish this—purchase as well as usurpation, skill as well as force, and nothing has restrained it when treating of territorial acquisition. Louisiana, the Floridas, Oregon, and Texas, have successively fallen into its power. . . .

While the United States seemed to be animated by a sincere desire not to break the peace, their acts of hostility manifested very evidently what were their true intentions. Their ships infested our coasts; their troops continued advancing upon our territory, situated at places which under no aspect could be disputed. Thus violence and insult were united: thus at the very time they usurped part of our territory, they offered to us the hand of treachery, to have soon the audacity to say that our obstinacy and arrogance were the real causes of the war.

The Texas Border Question

To explain the occupation of the Mexican territory by the troops of General [Zachary] Taylor, the strange idea occurred to the United States that the limits of Texas extended to the Rio Bravo del Norte [Rio Grande]. This opinion was predicated upon two distinct principles: one, that the Congress of Texas had so declared it in December, in 1836; and another, that the river mentioned had been the natural line of Louisiana. To state these reasons is equivalent at once to deciding the matter; for no one could defend such palpable absurdities. The first, which this government prizing its intelligence and civilization, supported with refined malice, would have been ridiculous in the mouth of a child. Whom could it convince that the declaration of the Texas Congress bore a legal title for the acquisition of the lands which it appropriated to itself with so little hesitation? If such a principle were recognised, we ought to be very grateful to these gentlemen senators who had the kindness to be satisfied with so little. Why not declare the limits of the rebel state extended to San Luis, to the capital, to our frontier with Guatemala?

———— • ————

"Is there one impartial man who would not consider the forcible occupation of our territory by the North American arms a shameful usurpation?"

———— • ————

The question is so clear in itself that it would only obscure by delaying to examine it further. We pass then to the other less nonsensical than the former. In the first place to pretend that the limits of Louisiana came to the Rio Bravo, it was essential to confound this province with Texas, which never can be tolerated. We have . . . shown the ancient and peaceable possession of Spain over the lands of the latter. Again, this same province, and afterwards State of Texas, never had extended its territory to the Rio Bravo, being only to the Nueces [River], in which

always had been established the boundary. Lastly, a large part of the territory situated on the other side of the Bravo, belonged, without dispute or doubt, to other states of the [Mexican] Republic—to New Mexico, Tamaulipas, Coahuila, and Chihuahua.

Our Treacherous Neighbors

Then, after so many and such plain proceedings, is there one impartial man who would not consider the forcible occupation of our territory by the North American arms a shameful usurpation? Then further, this power desired to carry to the extreme the sneer and the jest. When the question had resolved itself into one of force which is the *ultima ratio* [final argument] of nations as well as of kings, when it had spread desolation and despair in our populations, when many of our citizens had perished in the contest, the bloody hand of our treacherous neighbors was turned to present the olive of peace. The Secretary of State, Mr. [James] Buchanan, on the 27th of July, 1846, proposed anew, the admission of an Envoy to open negotiations which might lead to the concluding of an honorable peace. The national government answered that it could not decide, and left it to Congress to express its opinion of the subject. Soon to follow up closely the same system of policy, they ordered a commissioner with the army, which invaded us from the east, to cause it to be understood that peace would be made when our opposition ceased. Whom did they hope to deceive with such false appearances? Does not the series of acts which we have mentioned speak louder than this hypocritical language? By that test then, as a question of justice, no one who examines it in good faith can deny our indisputable rights. Among the citizens themselves, of the nation which has made war on us, there have been many who defended the cause of the Mexican Republic. These impartial defenders have not been obscure men, but men of the highest distinction. Mexico has counted on the assistance, ineffectual, unfortunately, but generous and illustrious, of a [Henry] Clay, a [John Quincy] Adams, a [Daniel] Webster, an [Albert] Gallatin; that is to say, on the noblest men, the most appreciated for their virtues, for their talents, and for their services. Their conduct deserves our thanks, and the authors of this work have a true pleasure in paying, in this place, the sincere homage of their gratitude.

The Cause of This War

Such are the events that abandoned us to a calamitous war; and, in the relation of which, we have endeavored not to distort even a line of the private data consulted, to prove, on every occasion, all and each of our assertions.

From the acts referred to, it has been demonstrated to the very senses, that the real and effective cause of this war that afflicted us was the spirit of aggrandizement of the United States of the North, availing itself of its power to conquer us.

For Further Reading

Paul H. Bergeron, *The Presidency of James K. Polk.* Lawrence: University Press of Kansas, 1987.

Gene M. Brack, *Mexico Views Manifest Destiny.* Albuquerque: University of New Mexico Press, 1975.

Seymour V. Connor, and Odie B. Faulk, *North America Divided: The Mexican War, 1846–1848.* New York: Oxford University Press, 1971.

Bernard De Voto, *The Year of Decision, 1846.* Boston: Little, Brown, 1943.

Allan Nevins ed., *Polk; the Diary of a President, 1845–1849.* New York: Longmans, Green, 1952.

David M. Pletcher, *The Diplomacy of Annexation: Texas, Oregon, and the Mexican War.* Columbia: University of Missouri Press, 1973.

PART IV:
CIVIL WAR AMERICA, 1850–1877

❧ ⸰ ❧

The Road to Secession

The Civil War

Reconstruction

1850
•July 9   President Zachary Taylor dies in office; Vice President Millard Fillmore becomes president
•September   Compromise of 1850 passed by Congress

1851
•*Moby Dick* by Herman Melville published
•Irish immigration peaks at 221,000

1852
•*Uncle Tom's Cabin* by Harriet Beecher Stowe published
•November 2   Franklin Pierce elected president

1858
•May 11   Minnesota enters Union
•August 2   Admission of Kansas to Union derailed when residents vote to reject proslavery Lecompton constitution
•August 21–October 15 Lincoln-Douglas debates

1857
•*The Impending Crisis of the South*, an antislavery book written by southern resident Hinton R. Helper, published
•March 6   *Dred Scott* decision: Supreme Court rules blacks are not citizens and that slaves can be taken anywhere in U.S.
•August   Panic of 1857 brings economic downturn to northern states

1861
•January–March   Mississippi, Florida, Alabama, Georgia, Louisiana, and Texas secede from Union; Tennessee, North Carolina, Missouri, and Arkansas reject secession
•January 29   Kansas enters Union as free state
•February 7   The Confederate States of America established
•February 27   The Crittenden Compromise (restoring the Missouri Compromise line) rejected by House of Representatives
•March 4   Lincoln inaugurated
•March 29   Lincoln orders resupply of Fort Sumter, South Carolina
•April 12   Fort Sumter attacked by Confederate troops, beginning Civil War
•April–May   Virginia, Arkansas, North Carolina, and Tennessee secede from Union and join Confederacy
•July 21   First Battle of Bull Run fought at Manassas, Virginia

1850   **1855**   **1860**

1853
•December 30 Gadsden Purchase of territory from Mexico

1854
•Formation of Know-Nothing and Republican Parties
•May 30   Pierce signs Kansas-Nebraska Act, voiding 1820 Missouri Compromise
•October   Ostend Manifesto: American diplomats propose seizing Cuba from Spain

1855
•Violent clashes in "Bleeding Kansas" between proslavery and antislavery settlers

1856
•May 23   Abolitionist John Brown and followers kill five proslavery settlers in Kansas in Pottawatomie massacre
•November 4   James Buchanan elected president

1859
•February 14 Oregon enters Union
•August   First oil well drilled in U.S.
•December 2   John Brown executed after conviction for leading October slave insurrection at Harper's Ferry

1860
•June   Democratic Party splits into northern and southern factions
•November 4   Abraham Lincoln elected president
•December 20   South Carolina secedes from Union

1862
•April 12   First official regiment of black troops organized for Union army
•May 20   Homestead Act signed by Lincoln; grants free public land to settlers
•September 22 Lincoln announces Emancipation Proclamation, to take effect January 1, 1863

1863
•March 3   Congress passes conscription law
•June 20   West Virginia enters Union
•July 1–3   Battle of Gettysburg
•July 11   Draft riots hit New York City
•December 8   Lincoln's Proclamation of Amnesty and Reconstruction

1864

•March 12   Ulysses S. Grant placed in charge of all Union armies

•July 2   Congress passes Wade-Davis Bill giving Congress control over reconstruction; Lincoln pocket-vetoes measure

•October 31   Nevada enters Union

•November 8   Lincoln reelected

1865

•March 3   Freedman's Bureau established

•April 9   Robert E. Lee surrenders to Grant at Appomattox Courthouse

•April 14   Lincoln assassinated by John Wilkes Booth; Vice President Andrew Johnson becomes president

•November 24   Mississippi first state to enact Black Code

•December 18   Thirteenth Amendment, abolishing slavery, ratified

•December 24   Ku Klux Klan founded in Tennessee

1870

•January 26   Virginia readmitted to Union

•February 23   Mississippi readmitted to Union

•February 25   Hiram R. Revels of Mississippi becomes nation's first black senator

•March 30   Fifteenth Amendment, forbidding racial restrictions on suffrage, ratified

1871

•March 3   Congress nullifies past treaties and makes Indians wards of federal government

•March 4   First black members of House of Representatives seated

•April 20   Ku Klux Klan Act passed by Congress

•October 8–11   Great Chicago Fire

1872

•March 1   Yellowstone National Park established by Congress

•June 10   Freedman's Bureau abolished

•November 5   Grant reelected president

1877

•March 2   Rutherford B. Hayes declared winner of close and controversial presidential election

•April   Remaining federal troops withdrawn from South, ending Reconstruction era

1865   **1870**   **1875**

1866

•April 9   Congress passes Civil Rights Act of 1866 over Johnson's veto

•July 24   Congress readmits Tennessee to Union

•July 30   Race riot in New Orleans results in 200 casualties

1867

•March 1   Nebraska enters Union

•March 2   Over Johnson's veto, Congress passes First Reconstruction Act dividing Confederacy into five military districts

•March 30   U.S. purchases Alaska from Russia

1869

•March 15   Woman suffrage amendment to the Constitution proposed in Congress

•May 10   Nation's first transcontinental railroad completed

•November 6   First intercollegiate football game played

•December 10   Wyoming Territory grants women right to vote

1868

•May   President Johnson avoids impeachment by one vote

•June 22–25   Arkansas, Alabama, Florida, Louisiana, South Carolina, and North Carolina are readmitted to Union

•July 21   Fourteenth Amendment, guaranteeing blacks civil rights, ratified by the states

•November 3   Ulysses S. Grant elected president

•December 25   President Johnson grants amnesty to all Confederate leaders

1876

•March   Alexander Graham Bell invents telephone

•August 1   Colorado enters Union

1875

•January 5   Grant dispatches federal troops to Vicksburg, Mississippi, to restore order following the killing of 300 blacks by armed whites

•March 1   Civil Rights Act of 1875 forbids racial segregation in public places

1873

•March 3   Comstock Law bars obscenity (including birth control information) from federal mails

•April 14   Supreme Court rules that Fourteenth Amendment protects only rights derived from federal, not state, citizenship

•September   Major banking failures begin five years of economic depression

PART IV:
CIVIL WAR AMERICA, 1850–1877

The United States of America has survived intact many difficulties: foreign invasions, wars with both neighboring and distant countries, economic depressions, massive influxes of new peoples and new ideas, and sharp disagreements over its economic and political policies. Only once has the Union been broken—the result was the Civil War. The causes and consequences of that war, and the Reconstruction Era that followed, have been the subject of great dispute, both among those who lived through that period of American history, and among later historians who have written about it.

Slavery and the Western Territories

In 1849 California, its population enlarged by gold seekers, applied for statehood as a free state. This request triggered a national debate over whether this territory newly won in the Mexican War should become a free or slave state. Many Southerners in Congress began to speak of secession if slavery was forbidden in California. In fact, Southern leaders called for a convention in June 1850 to discuss the possibility of secession.

The United States had faced a similar quandary in 1819, when Missouri (part of the Louisiana Territory) applied for statehood as a slave state. At issue, both in 1819 and 1849, was sectional balance between free and slave states. Also at issue was whether Congress had the power to prevent slavery in a new state (it had, under the Constitution, no power to ban slavery in states where it already existed). In 1820 Congress, led by Henry Clay and other members, passed what became known as the Missouri Compromise. Congress admitted Missouri as a slave state (and Maine concurrently as a free state) and drew a line roughly parallel with Missouri's southern border through the rest of the Louisiana Territory, dividing it into slave and free regions.

In 1849 some people proposed that the Missouri Compromise line be extended to the Pacific Ocean. This suggestion was opposed by two groups: Northerners who wanted slavery banned altogether in the new territories and slavery partisans of the South who argued that they had a right to bring their "property" into the land they had helped to acquire. The development of a militant abolitionist movement in the North, growing Southern fears of slave rebellions, and the rise of more assertive proslavery defenders in the South after 1820 all helped prevent an extension of the Missouri Compromise.

Slavery was believed by many to be indispensable to the economy and society of the Old South. By 1860 the population of the states that formed the Confederacy consisted of less than six million whites and around four million blacks, most of them slaves. Although only a minority of white families actually owned slaves, and a few white Southerners suggested abolishing the institution, most white Southerners were determined not just to preserve the institution of slavery, but to guarantee its expansion into new territories.

The Compromise of 1850

Congress was able to head off a secession crisis caused by California's statehood application by passing a series of laws known collectively as the Compromise of 1850. This compromise was fashioned by Henry Clay and other members of Congress who had helped pass the Missouri Compromise thirty years before, as well as a new generation of congressional leaders including Illinois Democratic senator Stephen A. Douglas. Concessions made by the South included the admission of California to the Union as a free state and the abolition of the slave trade in Washington, D.C. To satisfy the South, Congress agreed to a strengthened Fugitive Slave Act to assist slaveholders in reclaiming slaves who had escaped to the North. As for the other territories won in the Mexican War, their slave status would be decided on the basis of popular sovereignty (the territorial residents would themselves decide whether to allow or ban slavery). The legislative compromise successfully staved off threats of secession by the South for the time being.

The Kansas-Nebraska Act and Popular Sovereignty

Many Americans were optimistic that the Compromise of 1850 could provide lasting peace on the slavery question. Fundamental disputes remained unresolved, however. In 1852 Harriet Beecher Stowe's best-selling novel *Uncle Tom's Cabin* aroused strong sympathy for slaves among many Northern readers and inspired many communities and local courts in the North to resist enforcing the Fugitive Slave Act. Their defiance of the federal law was bitterly decried by Southern leaders.

Even more damaging to national unity was the passage of the Kansas-Nebraska Act in 1854. The law, supported by Douglas and by Southern members of Congress, explicitly repealed the 1820 Missouri Compromise line and organized the Kansas and Nebraska territories on the basis of popular sovereignty. The act and the widespread Northern dismay at the dismantling of the Missouri Compromise line divided the Democratic Party into Northern and Southern factions, broke apart the Whig Party, and led to the formation of the Republican Party. The new party was a sectional Northern organization dedicated to the principle of free soil, or no slavery in all U.S. territories (it was in some respects the successor to the smaller Free-Soil Party that had fielded presidential candidates in 1848 and 1852). The Kansas-Nebraska Act also led to violence in Kansas, where proslavery and antislavery settlers fought to determine whether that territory would became a slave or free state.

Sectional divisions continued to grow during the remainder of the 1850s. Most major Protestant churches split into Northern and Southern wings. The Supreme Court in 1857 further inflamed sectional tension by handing down the *Dred Scott* decision, which ruled that blacks were not citizens, that laws against slavery were unconstitutional, and that slaveowners had the constitutional right to take their slaves anywhere in the nation. This ruling pleased Southerners but angered Northern abolitionists and free-soil advocates alike.

John Brown and Abraham Lincoln

The actions of two very different people finally led South Carolina and other states to take the fateful step of secession. In 1859 radical abolitionist John Brown attempted to lead a slave insurrection in Virginia. A little more than one year later free-soil partisan and Republican Abraham Lincoln was elected to the presidency.

With secret financial support from prominent Northern abolitionists, Brown and eighteen of his followers (including two of his sons and five black men) raided the federal arsenal at Harpers Ferry in Virginia. Brown and his small army were quickly surrounded and captured by local militia and a detachment of U.S. Army troops commanded by Colonel Robert E. Lee. Tried, convicted, and executed by a Virginia state court on charges of treason, Brown proved to be far more effective as a martyr than as a revolutionary. Northern praise of Brown's goals, along with evidence of abolitionist support for his insurrection, disturbed Southerners even more than the original raid and created an even wider chasm between the two sections.

The sectional divisions magnified by John Brown's rebellion were evident during the second major event leading up to secession—the presidential election of 1860. The Democratic Party, which had controlled the White House for twenty-four of the previous thirty-two years and which was one of the few genuinely national organizations remaining, finally split along sectional lines. Southern delegates, insisting on a platform calling for federal protection of slavery in all western territories and refusing to support the leading candidate, Stephen A. Douglas, left the party and nominated their own candidate, John Breckinridge. The two Democrats were opposed by John Bell of the newly formed Constitutional Union Party, which sought to avoid the slavery issue, and Republican Party candidate Abraham Lincoln.

The nomination of Lincoln, an Illinois lawyer who had gained national fame during his debates with Stephen A. Douglas in an 1858 senatorial election, was a victory for the moderate wing of the Republican Party. Seeking to deflect criticisms that they were "Black Republicans" determined to abolish slavery and promote social equality between blacks and whites, Lincoln and the Republicans ran on a platform that, while advocating the restriction of slavery in the territories, also endorsed the right of each state to maintain slavery and condemned John Brown's raid as "the gravest of crimes." However, Lincoln was resolute in opposing slavery in the territories and won almost no votes in the South. He won the election by capturing most of the Northern states; within a few months the entire Lower South seceded from the Union to form the Confederate States of America.

In his inaugural address on March 4, 1861, Lincoln offered to support a constitutional amendment preventing the federal government from interfering with slavery in the states (but not the territories). He went on to argue that no state could leave the Union of its own volition and that he meant to enforce the Constitution and to "hold, occupy, and possess the property and places belonging to the government." Among these properties was Fort Sumter in South Carolina, where a small garrison of soldiers under Major Robert Anderson was attacked by Confederate troops on April 12, 1861. The assault ushered in four years of brutal war.

The Civil War

The Civil War was the most destructive conflict in American history. At least 620,000 soldiers perished, a sum almost equal to all other U.S. wars combined. Property damage was enormous, especially in the South, where many cities, plantations, factories, and railroads lay in ruins after the war. The North began the war with large material advantages over the South in terms of population and industrial production. Despite many early Confederate victories, the North was ultimately able to exploit these advantages and turn the tide. A key to its success was the use of 180,000 black soldiers, many of them escaped or former slaves. On April 9, 1865, General Robert E. Lee, the commander of the Confederate army, surrendered to Union commander General Ulysses S. Grant.

President Lincoln faced many wartime challenges, not the least of which was dissent within the North. Some elements within his party, known as Radical Republicans, fervently called for the abolition of slavery and the use of black troops (steps initially opposed by Lincoln) and in general pushed for a more aggressive war against the South. Lincoln's critics at the other end of the political spectrum consisted of those people (mostly Democrats) who questioned his decision to go to war, who opposed the abolition of slavery, and who argued that Lincoln was becoming dictatorial in directing the war effort. Although not as powerful in Congress as the Radical Republicans, the Peace Democrats (also called Copperheads) were well represented in state and local governments. Worry over espionage and sabotage by the Copperheads was a constant concern for the Lincoln administration. During the war thousands of suspected Confederate sympathizers were jailed, one of the most prominent being Ohio Democratic leader Clement L. Vallandigham.

Confederate president Jefferson Davis faced comparable challenges, including criticism of his leadership. Ironically, the ideal of states' rights—the stated reason for the Southern states' secession and the subsequent creation of the Confederacy—became itself a source of division as some state governors resisted orders from Davis. Another important source of division within the Confederacy was the defiance and resistance of its slaves.

The Emancipation Proclamation

Abolitionists believed that the Civil War presented an opportunity for the United States to extinguish the institution of slavery. Many argued that emancipating the slaves would deprive the South of its labor force, weaken the rebelling states, and hasten the end of war—an argument that gained increasing support even from people who had not been abolitionists before the war Lincoln at first sought to placate slaveowners from the four slave states that did not secede (as the president put it, he liked having God on his side, but he needed Kentucky). He therefore resisted entreaties by abolitionists to use his presidential powers to free the slaves. But later, stating that "we . . . must change our tactics, or risk losing the game," Lincoln finally decided to issue the Emancipation Proclamation, which took effect on January 1, 1863. The proclamation declared freedom for slaves in all areas of the Confederacy still in rebellion against the Union. Although it did not immediately abolish slavery in all the states, it dramatically changed the nature and aims of the war and helped ensure the death of slavery after the war was over.

Overall, Lincoln was able to bridge serious divisions within the North as he led it to victory, ended slavery, and restored the Union. Whether he would have been as successful in leading the nation following the war will never be known; one week after Lee's surrender, Lincoln was assassinated.

Reconstruction

The Civil War may have settled the questions of secession and slavery, but the aftermath of the war presented many puzzling problems to the new president, Andrew Johnson, and the congressional leadership. Two questions were primary: How should the rebellious states be reintegrated into the Union, and how should the four million ex-slaves be integrated into American society?

Northerners divided into two groups in answering these questions. One sought to restore the states to the Union with a minimum of federal interference, thus giving them a free hand in dealing with former slaves. Those in this group included Lincoln and his successor, Johnson, conservative Republicans and Democrats in Congress, and white Southerners. In the summer of 1865 Johnson oversaw the restoration of state governments in most of the former Confederate states after they met the conditions of abolishing slavery, repudiating secession, and abrogating Confederates debts. Southern whites were given a relatively free hand in establishing their restored state governments. Blacks, who had been offered no role in Johnson's reconstruction plans, found themselves bound under state-passed "Black Codes" that punished blacks for "insulting" whites, kept them bound to year-long labor contracts on plantations, and otherwise severely restricted their economic and political freedoms.

Radical Republicans in Congress proposed a much different approach to reconstruction. They considered the South a conquered territory that was under the jurisdiction of Congress and sought to use their authority to recreate Southern society with equality between blacks and whites. In 1866 and 1867 they were able to turn their ideas into law by passing many bills over Johnson's opposition. They abolished the state governments established in 1865 and, under federal military control, established new governments in which blacks and whites shared political power. Among other achievements of the Radical Republicans in Congress were the Fourteenth and Fifteenth Amendments, which granted citizenship to blacks and suffrage to black men, respectively. However, by the 1870s Radical Republicans were in the minority in Congress. Remaining state governments in which blacks had significant political clout fell after federal troops were withdrawn from the South in 1877. Questions of social, political, and economic equality for blacks remained a controversial issue throughout the nation.

The Road to Secession

Viewpoint 31A

Southern States May Be Forced to Leave the Union (1850)

John C. Calhoun (1782–1850)

In 1850 secession was openly discussed by many leaders in the South in response to President Zachary Taylor's proposed admission of California to the Union as a free state. Granting statehood to the territory newly acquired from Mexico would give free states a 16-15 majority over slave states, a prospect bitterly opposed by many Southerners. On January 29, 1850, Senator Henry Clay of Kentucky introduced a series of legislative resolutions that sought to ease sectional tensions over slavery. Clay's proposals included letting California into the Union as a free state; admitting the territories of New Mex-

ico and Utah on the basis of popular sovereignty (allowing local residents to decide whether to legalize slavery); and, to satisfy Southern demands, establishing a stricter federal law for the return of runaway slaves while removing from Congress any role in regulating the slave trade between Southern states. Clay, long noted as an advocate both of the Union and of compromise, argued before Congress on February 6 that his proposals were necessary to preserve the Union, and warned that "the dissolution of the Union and war are identical and inseparable."

The following viewpoint is taken from a Senate speech written by John C. Calhoun in response to Clay's proposals. Calhoun, who at various times in his long political career was secretary of war, vice president, secretary of state, and U.S. senator, was recognized as the preeminent defender of the South and its institutions, including slavery. Calhoun's speech (read on the Senate floor on March 4, 1850, by Virginia senator James M. Mason because of Calhoun's ill health) begins with the question "How can the Union be preserved?" and goes on to summarize his views on the history and the political situation of the

From John C. Calhoun's speech before the U.S. Senate on March 4, 1850.

United States. He argues that the "equilibrium" between Northern and Southern interests that existed at the time of the nation's birth has been lost, and asserts that nothing less than a permanent halt to antislavery "agitation," the opening of all western territories for slaveholders to bring their slaves without fear of loss, more stringent enforcement of fugitive slave laws, and amending the Constitution to restore the South's previous power in national affairs (in essence, giving the Southern states veto power over any attempt to abolish slavery) will preserve the "cords" that bind the Union.

Calhoun died less than one month later. His last appearance at the Senate was on March 7, to hear Daniel Webster's rebuttal to his arguments and support of Clay's compromise measures. Calhoun's warnings notwithstanding, the Compromise of 1850 was passed after his death; it is credited with preventing war for another few years. Calhoun's analysis, however, proved in many ways prophetic.

What are the causes of Northern dominance over the South, according to Calhoun? Why, in his view, are abolitionists responsible for the national discord? Who, in Calhoun's opinion, is ultimately responsible for preserving the Union? Why?

I have, Senators, believed from the first that the agitation of the subject of slavery would, if not prevented by some timely and effective measure, end in disunion. Entertaining this opinion, I have, on all proper occasions, endeavored to call the attention of both the two great parties which divide the country to adopt some measure to prevent so great a disaster, but without success. The agitation has been permitted to proceed, with almost no attempt to resist it, until it has reached a point when it can no longer be disguised or denied that the Union is in danger. You have thus had forced upon you the greatest and gravest question that can ever come under your consideration—How can the Union be preserved?

To give a satisfactory answer to this mighty question, it is indispensable to have an accurate and thorough knowledge of the nature and the character of the cause by which the Union is endangered. Without such knowledge it is impossible to pronounce, with any certainty, by what measure it can be saved; just as it would be impossible for a physician to pronounce, in the case of some dangerous disease, with any certainty, by what remedy the patient could be saved, without similar knowledge of the nature and character of the cause which produced it. The first question, then, presented for consideration, in the investigation I propose to make, in order to obtain such knowledge, is—What is it that has endangered the Union?

Southern Discontent

To this question there can be but one answer,— that the immediate cause is the almost universal discontent which pervades all the States composing the Southern section of the Union. This widely-extended discontent is not of recent origin. It commenced with the agitation of the slavery question, and has been increasing ever since. The next question, going one step further back, is—What has caused this widely diffused and almost universal discontent?

It is a great mistake to suppose, as is by some, that it originated with demagogues, who excited the discontent with the intention of aiding their personal advancement, or with the disappointed ambition of certain politicians, who resorted to it as the means of retrieving their fortunes. On the contrary, all the great political influences of the section were arrayed against excitement, and exerted to the utmost to keep the people quiet. The great mass of the people of the South were divided, as in the other section, into Whigs and Democrats. The leaders and the presses of both parties in the South were very solicitous to prevent excitement and to preserve quiet; because it was seen that the effects of the former would necessarily tend to weaken, if not destroy, the political ties which united them with their respective parties in the other section. Those who know the strength of party ties will readily appreciate the immense force which this cause exerted against agitation, and in favor of preserving quiet. But, great as it was, it was not sufficient to prevent the widespread discontent which now pervades the section. No; some cause, far deeper and more powerful than the one supposed, must exist, to account for discontent so wide and deep. The question then recurs— What is the cause of this discontent? It will be found in the belief of the people of the Southern States, as prevalent as the discontent itself, that they cannot remain, as things now are, consistently with honor and safety, in the Union. The next question to be considered is—What has caused this belief?

"The South asks for justice, simple justice, and less she ought not to take."

One of the causes is, undoubtedly, to be traced to the long-continued agitation of the slave question on the part of the North, and the many aggressions which they have made on the rights of the South during the time. I will not enumerate them at present, as it will be done hereafter in its proper place.

There is another lying back of it—with which this

is intimately connected—that may be regarded as the great and primary cause. This is to be found in the fact that the equilibrium between the two sections, in the Government as it stood when the constitution was ratified and the Government put in action, has been destroyed. At that time there was nearly a perfect equilibrium between the two, which afforded ample means to each to protect itself against the aggression of the other; but, as it now stands, one section has the exclusive power of controlling the Government, which leaves the other without any adequate means of protecting itself against its encroachment and oppression. To place this subject distinctly before you, I have, Senators, prepared a brief statistical statement, showing the relative weight of the two sections in the Government under the first census of 1790 and the last census of 1840.

Changing Populations

According to the former, the population of the United States, including Vermont, Kentucky, and Tennessee, which then were in their incipient condition of becoming States, but were not actually admitted, amounted to 3,929,827. Of this number the Northern States had 1,997,899, and the Southern 1,952,072, making a difference of only 45,827 in favor of the former States. The number of States, including Vermont, Kentucky, and Tennessee, were sixteen; of which eight, including Vermont, belonged to the Northern section, and eight, including Kentucky and Tennessee, to the Southern—making an equal division of the States between the two sections under the first census. There was a small preponderance in the House of Representatives, and in the electoral college, in favor of the Northern, owing to the fact that, according to the provisions of the constitution, in estimating federal numbers five slaves count but three; but it was too small to affect sensibly the perfect equilibrium which, with that exception, existed at the time. Such was the equality of the two sections when the States composing them agreed to enter into a Federal Union. Since then the equilibrium between them has been greatly disturbed.

According to the last census the aggregate population of the United States amounted to 17,063,357, of which the Northern section contained 9,728,920, and the Southern 7,334,437, making a difference, in round numbers, of 2,400,000. The number of States had increased from sixteen to twenty-six, making an addition of ten States. In the mean time the position of Delaware had become doubtful as to which section she properly belonged. Considering her as neutral, the Northern States will have thirteen and the Southern States twelve, making a difference in the Senate of two Senators in favor of the former.

According to the apportionment under the census of 1840, there were two hundred and twenty-three members of the House of Representatives, of which the Northern States had one hundred and thirty-five, and the Southern States (considering Delaware as neutral) eighty-seven, making a difference in favor of the former in the House of Representatives of forty-eight. The difference in the Senate of two members, added to this, gives to the North, in the electoral college, a majority of fifty. Since the census of 1840, four States have been added to the Union—Iowa, Wisconsin, Florida, and Texas. They leave the difference in the Senate as it stood when the census was taken; but add two to the side of the North in the House, making the present majority in the House in its favor fifty, and in the electoral college fifty-two.

The result of the whole is to give the Northern section a pre-dominance in every department of the Government, and thereby concentrate in it the two elements which constitute the Federal Government,—majority of States, and a majority of their population, estimated in federal numbers. Whatever section concentrates the two in itself possesses the control of the entire Government.

But we are just at the close of the sixth decade, and the commencement of the seventh. The census is to be taken this year, which must add greatly to the decided preponderance of the North in the House of Representatives and in the electoral college. The prospect is, also, that a great increase will be added to its present preponderance in the Senate, during the period of the decade, by the addition of new States. Two territories, Oregon and Minnesota, are already in progress, and strenuous efforts are making to bring in three additional States from the territory recently conquered from Mexico; which, if successful, will add three other States in a short time to the Northern section, making five States; and increasing the present number of its States from fifteen to twenty, and of its Senators from thirty to forty. On the contrary, there is not a single territory in progress in the Southern section, and no certainty that any additional State will be added to it during the decade. The prospect then is, that the two sections in the Senate, should the efforts now made to exclude the South from the newly acquired territories succeed, will stand, before the end of the decade, twenty Northern States to fourteen Southern (considering Delaware as neutral), and forty Northern Senators to twenty-eight Southern. This great increase of Senators, added to the great increase of members of the House of Representatives and the electoral college on the part of the North, which must take place under the next decade, will effectually and irretrievably destroy the equilibrium which existed when the Government commenced.

Had this destruction been the operation of time, without the interference of Government, the South would have had no reason to complain; but such was not the fact. It was caused by the legislation of this Government, which was appointed, as the common agent of all, and charged with the protection of the interests and security of all. The legislation by which it has been effected, may be classed under three heads. The first is, that series of acts [including the 1787 Northwest Ordinance, the 1820 Missouri Compromise, and the 1848 admission of Oregon as a free territory] by which the South has been excluded from the common territory belonging to all the States as members of the Federal Union—which have had the effect of extending vastly the portion allotted to the Northern section, and restricting within narrow limits the portion left the South. The next consists in adopting a system of revenue and disbursements, by which an undue proportion of the burden of taxation has been imposed upon the South, and an undue proportion of its proceeds appropriated to the North; and the last is a system of political measures, by which the original character of the Government has been radically changed. . . .

The Changing Government

That the Government claims, and practically maintains the right to decide in the last resort, as to the extent of its powers, will scarcely be denied by any one conversant with the political history of the country. That it also claims the right to resort to force to maintain whatever power it claims, against all opposition, is equally certain. Indeed it is apparent, from what we daily hear, that this has become the prevailing and fixed opinion of a great majority of the community. Now, I ask, what limitation can possibly be placed upon the powers of a government claiming and exercising such rights? And, if none can be, how can the separate governments of the States maintain and protect the powers reserved to them by the constitution—or the people of the several States maintain those which are reserved to them, and among others, the sovereign powers by which they ordained and established, not only their separate State Constitutions and Governments, but also the Constitution and Government of the United States? But, if they have no constitutional means of maintaining them against the right claimed by this Government, it necessarily follows, that they hold them at its pleasure and discretion, and that all the powers of the system are in reality concentrated in it. It also follows, that the character of the Government has been changed in consequence, from a federal republic, as it originally came from the hands of its framers, into a great national consolidated democracy. It has indeed, at present, all the characteristics of the latter, and not

one of the former, although it still retains its outward form.

The result of the whole of these causes combined is—that the North has acquired a decided ascendancy over every department of this Government, and through it a control over all the powers of the system. A single section governed by the will of the numerical majority, has now, in fact, the control of the Government and the entire powers of the system. What was once a constitutional federal republic, is now converted, in reality, into one as absolute as that of the Autocrat of Russia, and as despotic in its tendency as any absolute government that ever existed.

As, then, the North has the absolute control over the Government, it is manifest, that on all questions between it and the South, where there is a diversity of interests, the interest of the latter will be sacrificed to the former, however oppressive the effects may be; as the South possesses no means by which it can resist, through the action of the Government. But if there was no question of vital importance to the South, in reference to which there was a diversity of views between the two sections, this state of things might be endured, without the hazard of destruction to the South. But such is not the fact. There is a question of vital importance to the Southern section, in reference to which the views and feelings of the two sections are as opposite and hostile as they can possibly be.

The Two Races

I refer to the relation between the two races in the Southern section, which constitutes a vital portion of her social organization. Every portion of the North entertains views and feelings more or less hostile to it. Those most opposed and hostile, regard it as a sin, and consider themselves under the most sacred obligation to use every effort to destroy it. Indeed, to the extent that they conceive they have power, they regard themselves as implicated in the sin, and responsible for not suppressing it by the use of all and every means. Those less opposed and hostile, regard it as a crime—an offence against humanity, as they call it; and, although not so fanatical, feel themselves bound to use all efforts to effect the same object; while those who are least opposed and hostile, regard it as a blot and a stain on the character of what they call the Nation, and feel themselves accordingly bound to give it no countenance or support. On the contrary, the Southern section regards the relation as one which cannot be destroyed without subjecting the two races to the greatest calamity, and the section to poverty, desolation, and wretchedness; and accordingly they feel bound, by every consideration of interest and safety, to defend it.

This hostile feeling on the part of the North

towards the social organization of the South long lay dormant, but it only required some cause to act on those who felt most intensely that they were responsible for its continuance, to call it into action. The increasing power of this Government, and of the control of the Northern section over all its departments, furnished the cause. It was this which made an impression on the minds of many, that there was little or no restraint to prevent the Government from doing whatever it might choose to do. This was sufficient of itself to put the most fanatical portion of the North in action, for the purpose of destroying the existing relation between the two races in the South.

The first organized movement towards it commenced in 1835. Then, for the first time, societies were organized, presses established, lecturers sent forth to excite the people of the North, and incendiary publications scattered over the whole South, through the mail. The South was thoroughly aroused. Meetings were held every where, and resolutions adopted, calling upon the North to apply a remedy to arrest the threatened evil, and pledging themselves to adopt measures for their own protection, if it was not arrested. At the meeting of Congress, petitions poured in from the North, calling upon Congress to abolish slavery in the District of Columbia, and to prohibit, what they called, the internal slave trade between the States—announcing at the same time, that their ultimate object was to abolish slavery, not only in the District, but in the States and throughout the Union. At this period, the number engaged in the agitation was small, and possessed little or no personal influence. . . .

[Yet] the [abolitionist] party succeeded in their first movements, in gaining what they proposed—a position in Congress, from which agitation could be extended over the whole Union. This was the commencement of the agitation, which has ever since continued, and which, as is now acknowledged, has endangered the Union itself.

As for myself, I believed at that early period, if the party who got up the petitions should succeed in getting Congress to take jurisdiction, that agitation would follow, and that it would in the end, if not arrested, destroy the Union. I then so expressed myself in debate, and called upon both parties to take grounds against assuming jurisdiction; but in vain. Had my voice been heeded, and had Congress refused to take jurisdiction, by the united votes of all parties, the agitation which followed would have been prevented, and the fanatical zeal that gives impulse to the agitation, and which has brought us to our present perilous condition, would have become extinguished, from the want of fuel to feed the flame. *That* was the time for the North to have shown her devotion to the Union; but, unfortunately, both of the great parties of that section were so intent on obtaining or retaining party ascendancy, that all other considerations were overlooked or forgotten.

What has since followed are but natural consequences. With the success of their first movement, this small fanatical party began to acquire strength; and with that, to become an object of courtship to both the great parties. The necessary consequence was, a further increase of power, and a gradual tainting of the opinions of both of the other parties with their doctrines, until the infection has extended over both; and the great mass of the population of the North, who, whatever may be their opinion of the original abolition party, which still preserves its distinctive organization, hardly ever fail, when it comes to acting, to co-operate in carrying out their measures. . . .

Such is a brief history of the agitation, as far as it has yet advanced. Now I ask, Senators, what is there to prevent its further progress, until it fulfills the ultimate end proposed, unless some decisive measure should be adopted to prevent it? Has any one of the causes, which has added to its increase from its original small and contemptible beginning until it has attained its present magnitude, diminished in force? Is the original cause of the movement—that slavery is a sin, and ought to be suppressed—weaker now than at the commencement? Or is the abolition party less numerous or influential, or have they less influence with, or control over the two great parties of the North in elections? Or has the South greater means of influencing or controlling the movements of this Government now, than it had when the agitation commenced? To all these questions but one answer can be given: No—no—no. The very reverse is true. Instead of being weaker, all the elements in favor of agitation are stronger now than they were in 1835, when it first commenced, while all the elements of influence on the part of the South are weaker. Unless something decisive is done, I again ask, what is to stop this agitation, before the great and final object at which it aims—the abolition of slavery in the States—is consummated? Is it, then, not certain, that if something is not done to arrest it, the South will be forced to choose between abolition and secession? Indeed, as events are now moving, it will not require the South to secede, in order to dissolve the Union. Agitation will of itself effect it, of which its past history furnishes abundant proof—as I shall next proceed to show.

The Breaking Cords of Union

It is a great mistake to suppose that disunion can be effected by a single blow. The cords which bound these States together in one common Union, are far too numerous and powerful for that. Disunion must be the work of time. It is only through a long process, and successively, that the cords can be snapped, until the whole fabric falls asunder. Already the agitation of the slavery question has snapped some of the most important, and has greatly weakened all the others, as I shall proceed to show.

The cords that bind the States together are not only many, but various in character. Some are spiritual or ecclesiastical; some political; others social. Some appertain to the benefit conferred by the Union, and others to the feeling of duty and obligation.

The strongest of those of a spiritual and ecclesiastical nature, consisted in the unity of the great religious denominations, all of which originally embraced the whole Union. . . . The ties which held each denomination together formed a strong cord to hold the whole Union together; but, powerful as they were, they have not been able to resist the explosive effect of slavery agitation.

The strongest cord, of a political character, consists of the many and powerful ties that have held together the two great parties which have, with some modifications, existed from the beginning of the Government. They both extended to every portion of the Union, and strongly contributed to hold all its parts together. But this powerful cord has fared no better than the spiritual. It resisted, for a long time, the explosive tendency of the agitation, but has finally snapped under its force—if not entirely, in a great measure. Nor is there one of the remaining cords which has not been greatly weakened. To this extent the Union has already been destroyed by agitation, in the only way it can be, by sundering and weakening the cords which bind it together.

If the agitation goes on, the same force, acting with increased intensity, as has been shown, will finally snap every cord, when nothing will be left to hold the States together except force. But, surely, that can, with no propriety of language, be called a Union, when the only means by which the weaker is held connected with the stronger portion is *force*. It may, indeed, keep them connected; but the connection will partake much more of the character of subjugation, on the part of the weaker to the stronger, than the union of free, independent, and sovereign States, in one confederation, as they stood in the early stages of the Government, and which only is worthy of the sacred name of Union.

How Can the Union Be Saved?

Having now, Senators, explained what it is that endangers the Union, and traced it to its cause, and explained its nature and character, the question again recurs—How can the Union be saved? To this I answer, there is but one way by which it can be—and that is—by adopting such measures as will satisfy the States belonging to the Southern section, that they can remain in the Union consistently with their honor and their safety. There is, again, only one way by which this can be effected, and that is—by removing the causes by which this belief has been produced. Do *this*, and discontent will cease—harmony and kind feelings between the sections be restored—and every apprehension of danger to the Union removed. The question, then, is—How can this be done? But, before I undertake to answer this question, I propose to show by what the Union cannot be saved.

It cannot, then, be saved by eulogies on the Union, however splendid or numerous. The cry of "Union, Union—the glorious Union!" can no more prevent disunion than the cry of "Health, health—glorious health!" on the part of the physician, can save a patient lying dangerously ill. So long as the Union, instead of being regarded as a protector, is regarded in the opposite character, by not much less than a majority of the States, it will be in vain to attempt to conciliate them by pronouncing eulogies on it. . . .

Nor can the Union be saved by invoking the name of the illustrious Southerner [George Washington] whose mortal remains repose on the western bank of the Potomac. He was one of us—a slaveholder and a planter. We have studied his history, and find nothing in it to justify submission to wrong. On the contrary, his great fame rests on the solid foundation, that, while he was careful to avoid doing wrong to others, he was prompt and decided in repelling wrong. I trust that, in this respect, we profited by his example.

Nor can we find any thing in his history to deter us from seceding from the Union, should it fail to fulfill the objects for which it was instituted, by being permanently and hopelessly converted into the means of oppressing instead of protecting us. On the contrary, we find much in his example to encourage us, should we be forced to the extremity of deciding between submission and disunion. . . .

Nor can the plan proposed by the distinguished Senator from Kentucky [Henry Clay], nor that of the administration save the Union. . . .

Simple Justice

Having now shown what cannot save the Union, I return to the question with which I commenced, How can the Union be saved? There is but one way by which it can with any certainty; and that is, by a full and final settlement, on the principle of justice, of all the questions at issue between the two sections. The South asks for justice, simple justice, and less she ought not to take. She has no compromise to offer, but the constitution; and no concession or surrender to make. She has already surrendered so much that she has little left to surrender. Such a settlement would go to the root of the evil, and remove all cause of discontent, by satisfying the South, she could remain honorably and safely in the Union, and thereby restore the harmony and fraternal feelings between the sections, which existed anterior to the Missouri agitation. Nothing else can, with any certainty, finally and for ever settle the questions at issue, terminate agitation, and save the Union.

But can this be done? Yes, easily; not by the weaker party, for it can of itself do nothing—not even protect itself—but by the stronger. The North has only to will it to accomplish it—to do justice by conceding to the South an equal right in the acquired territory, and to do her duty by causing the stipulations relative to fugitive slaves to be faithfully fulfilled—to cease the agitation of the slave question, and to provide for the insertion of a provision in the constitution, by an amendment, which will restore to the South, in substance, the power she possessed of protecting herself, before the equilibrium between the sections was destroyed by the action of this Government. There will be no difficulty in devising such a provision—one that will protect the South, and which, at the same time, will improve and strengthen the Government, instead of impairing and weakening it.

But will the North agree to this? It is for her to answer the question. But, I will say, she cannot refuse, if she has half the love of the Union which she professes to have, or without justly exposing herself to the charge that her love of power and aggrandizement is far greater than her love of the Union. At all events, the responsibility of saving the Union rests on the North, and not on the South. The South cannot save it by any act of hers, and the North may save it without any sacrifice whatever, unless to do justice, and to perform her duties under the constitution, should be regarded by her as a sacrifice.

It is time, Senators, that there should be an open and manly avowal on all sides, as to what is intended to be done. If the question is not now settled, it is uncertain whether it ever can hereafter be; and we, as the representatives of the States of this Union, regarded as governments, should come to a distinct understanding as to our respective views, in order to ascertain whether the great questions at issue can be settled or not. If you, who represent the stronger portion, cannot agree to settle them on the broad principle of justice and duty, say so; and let the States we both represent agree to separate and part in peace. If you are unwilling we should part in peace, tell us so, and we shall know what to do, when you reduce the question to submission or resistance. If you remain silent, you will compel us to infer by your acts what you intend. In that case, California will become the

test question. If you admit her, under all the difficulties that oppose her admission, you compel us to infer that you intend to exclude us from the whole of the acquired territories, with the intention of destroying, irretrievably, the equilibrium between the two sections. We would be blind not to perceive in that case, that your real objects are power and aggrandizement, and infatuated not to act accordingly.

I have now, Senators, done my duty in expressing my opinions fully, freely, and candidly, on this solemn occasion. In doing so, I have been governed by the motives which have governed me in all the stages of the agitation of the slavery question since its commencement. I have exerted myself, during the whole period, to arrest it, with the intention of saving the Union, if it could be done; and if it could not, to save the section where it has pleased Providence to cast my lot, and which I sincerely believe has justice and the constitution on its side. Having faithfully done my duty to the best of my ability, both to the Union and my section, throughout this agitation, I shall have the consolation, let what will come, that I am free from all responsibility.

VIEWPOINT 31B

The Union Must Be Preserved (1850)

Daniel Webster (1782–1852)

Daniel Webster of Massachusetts, Henry Clay of Kentucky, and John C. Calhoun of South Carolina, all noted for their oratorical and legislative skills, were the "great triumvirate" of U.S. senators whose achievements and disagreements dominated American political life from 1815 to 1850. Like Clay and Calhoun, Webster capped his long political career by playing a major role in the debate on and passing of the Compromise of 1850, a series of legislative measures aimed at incorporating the territories won in the Mexican War while preventing the nation's rupturing over slavery.

Webster, a strong Unionist, supported the compromise package of legislation proposed by Clay in January 1850. Clay's proposals included admitting California to the Union as a free state (one that banned slavery), organizing New Mexico and Utah as territories without deciding their status on slavery (allowing people who lived there to choose), compensating Texas for relinquishing its claims to New Mexican territory, and strengthening national laws to make it easier for slave owners to recover slaves who had escaped to free states. The proposed compro-

From Daniel Webster's speech before the U.S. Senate on March 7, 1850.

mise was opposed by Northern antislavery leaders who wanted slavery banned from all new U.S. territories, and by Southern proslavery leaders (notably Senator John C. Calhoun of South Carolina) who wanted their property rights to slaves protected in the new territories, and who insisted on measures ensuring slavery's continued existence in the South.

The following viewpoint consists of excerpts from Daniel Webster's famous speech of March 7, 1850, partially in response to Calhoun's speech given three days earlier (see viewpoint 31A) and partially addressed to Northern opponents of slavery. Webster attacks both sides for extremism and refusal to compromise.

How does Webster identify himself at the start of his speech? How do his views on U.S. history (especially the relative strength of the country's Northern and Southern sections) differ from those expressed by John C. Calhoun in the opposing viewpoint? What are Webster's views on slavery?

M r. President [of the Senate],—I wish to speak to-day, not as a Massachusetts man, nor as a Northern man, but as an American, and a member of the Senate of the United States. It is fortunate that there is a Senate of the United States; a body not yet moved from its propriety, not lost to a just sense of its own dignity and its own high responsibilities, and a body to which the country looks, with confidence, for wise, moderate, patriotic, and healing counsels. It is not to be denied that we live in the midst of strong agitations, and are surrounded by very considerable dangers to our institutions and government. The imprisoned winds are let loose. The East, the North, and the stormy South combine to throw the whole sea into commotion, to toss its billows to the skies, and disclose its profoundest depths. I do not affect to regard myself, Mr. President, as holding, or as fit to hold, the helm in this combat with the political elements; but I have a duty to perform, and I mean to perform it with fidelity, not without a sense of existing dangers, but not without hope. I have a part to act, not for my own security or safety, for I am looking out for no fragment upon which to float away from the wreck, if wreck there must be, but for the good of the whole, and the preservation of all; and there is that which will keep me to my duty during this struggle, whether the sun and the stars shall appear, or shall not appear for many days. I speak to-day for the preservation of the Union. "Hear me for my cause." I speak to-day, out of a solicitous and anxious heart, for the restoration to the country of that quiet and that harmony which make the blessings of this Union so rich, and so dear to us all. These are the topics that

I propose to myself to discuss; these are the motives, and the sole motives, that influence me in the wish to communicate my opinions to the Senate and the country; and if I can do any thing, however little, for the promotion of these ends, I shall have accomplished all that I expect. . . .

The Question of Slavery

It is obvious that the question which has so long harassed the country, and at some times very seriously alarmed the minds of wise and good men, has come upon us for a fresh discussion; the question of slavery in these United States. . . .

Now, sir, upon the general nature and influence of slavery there exists a wide difference of opinion between the northern portion of this country and the southern. It is said on the one side, that, although not the subject of any injunction or direct prohibition in the New Testament, slavery is a wrong; that it is founded merely in the right of the strongest; and that it is an oppression, like unjust wars, like all those conflicts by which a powerful nation subjects a weaker to its will; and that, in its nature, whatever may be said of it in the modifications which have taken place, it is not according to the meek spirit of the Gospel. It is not "kindly affectioned"; it does not "seek another's, and not its own"; it does not "let the oppressed go free." These are sentiments that are cherished, and of late with greatly augmented force, among the people of the Northern States. They have taken hold of the religious sentiment of that part of the country, as they have, more or less, taken hold of the religious feelings of a considerable portion of mankind. The South, upon the other side, having been accustomed to this relation between the two races all their lives, from their birth, having been taught, in general, to treat the subjects of this bondage with care and kindness, and I believe, in general, feeling great kindness for them, have not taken the view of the subject which I have mentioned. There are thousands of religious men, with consciences as tender as any of their brethren at the North, who do not see the unlawfulness of slavery; and there are more thousands, perhaps, that, whatsoever they may think of it in its origin, and as a matter depending upon natural right, yet take things as they are, and, finding slavery to be an established relation of the society in which they live, can see no way in which, let their opinions on the abstract question be what they may, it is in the power of the present generation to relieve themselves from this relation. And candor obliges me to say, that I believe they are just as conscientious, many of them, and the religious people, all of them, as they are at the North who hold different opinions. . . .

But we must view things as they are. Slavery does

exist in the United States. It did exist in the States before the adoption of this Constitution, and at that time. Let us, therefore, consider for a moment what was the state of sentiment, North and South, in regard to slavery, at the time this Constitution was adopted. A remarkable change has taken place since; but what did the wise and great men of all parts of the country think of slavery then? In what estimation did they hold it at the time when this Constitution was adopted? It will be found, sir, if we will carry ourselves by historical research back to that day, and ascertain men's opinions by authentic records still existing among us, that there was then no diversity of opinion between the North and South upon the subject of slavery. It will be found that both parts of the country held it equally an evil, a moral and political evil. It will not be found that, either at the North or at the South, there was much, though there was some, invective against slavery as inhuman and cruel. The great ground of objection to it was political; that it weakened the social fabric; that, taking the place of free labor, society became less strong and labor less productive; and therefore we find from all the eminent men of the time the clearest expression of their opinion that slavery is an evil. . . .

The Nation's Founders

Then, sir, when this Constitution was framed, this was the light in which the Federal Convention viewed it. That body reflected the judgment and sentiments of the great men of the South. . . . They thought that slavery could not be continued in the country if the importation of slaves were made to cease, and therefore they provided that, after a certain period, the importation might be prevented by the act of the new government. The period of twenty years was proposed by some gentleman from the North, I think, and many members of the Convention from the South opposed it as being too long. . . .

Now, at the very time when the Convention in Philadelphia was framing this Constitution, the Congress in New York was framing the Ordinance of 1787, for the organization and government of the territory northwest of the Ohio. They passed that Ordinance on the 13th of July, 1787, at New York, the very month, perhaps the very day, on which these questions about the importation of slaves and the character of slavery were debated in the Convention at Philadelphia. So far as we can now learn, there was a perfect concurrence of opinion between these two bodies; and it resulted in this Ordinance of 1787, excluding slavery from all the territory over which the Congress of the United States had jurisdiction, and that was all the territory northwest of the Ohio. . . .

Mr. President, three things are quite clear as historical truths. One is, that there was an expectation that, on the ceasing of the importation of slaves from Africa, slavery would begin to run out here. That was hoped and expected. Another is, that, as far as there was any power in Congress to prevent the spread of slavery in the United States, that power was executed in the most absolute manner, and to the fullest extent. An honorable member [John C. Calhoun], whose health does not allow him to be here to-day—

(A SENATOR. *He is here.*)

I am very happy to hear that he is; may he long be here, and in the enjoyment of health to serve his country! The honorable member said, the other day, that he considered this Ordinance as the first in the series of measures calculated to enfeeble the South, and deprive them of their just participation in the benefits and privileges of this government. He says, very properly, that it was enacted under the old Confederation, and before this Constitution went into effect; but my present purpose is only to say, Mr. President, that it was established with the entire and unanimous concurrence of the whole South. Why, there it stands! The vote of every State in the Union was unanimous in favor of the Ordinance, with the exception of a single individual vote, and that individual vote was given by a Northern man. This Ordinance prohibiting slavery for ever northwest of the Ohio has the hand and seal of every Southern member in Congress. It was therefore no aggression of the North on the South. The other and third clear historical truth is, that the Convention meant to leave slavery in the States as they found it, entirely under the authority and control of the States themselves.

———— • ————

"Secession! Peaceable secession! Sir, your eyes and mine are never destined to see that miracle."

———— • ————

This was the state of things, sir, and this the state of opinion, under which those very important matters were arranged, and those three important things done; that is, the establishment of the Constitution of the United States with a recognition of slavery as it existed in the States; the establishment of the Ordinance for the government of the Northwestern Territory, prohibiting, to the full extent of all territory owned by the United States, the introduction of slavery into that territory, while leaving to the States all power over slavery in their own limits; and creating a power, in the new government, to put an end to the importation of slaves, after a limited period. There was entire coincidence and concurrence of sentiment between the North and the South, upon all these questions, at the period of the adoption of the Constitution. But opinions, sir, have changed, greatly changed; changed North and changed South. Slavery is not regarded in the South now as it was then. . . .

Slavery and Cotton

What, then, have been the causes which have created so new a feeling in favor of slavery in the South, which have changed the whole nomenclature of the South on that subject, so that, from being thought and described in the terms I have mentioned and will not repeat, it has now become an institution, a cherished institution, in that quarter; no evil, no scourge, but a great religious, social, and moral blessing, as I think I have heard it latterly spoken of? I suppose this, sir, is owing to the rapid growth and sudden extension of the *cotton* plantations of the South. So far as any motive consistent with honor, justice, and general judgment could act, it was the *cotton* interest that gave a new desire to promote slavery, to spread it, and to use its labor. I again say that this change was produced by causes which must always produce like effects. The whole interest of the South became connected, more or less, with the extension of slavery. . . .

The age of cotton became the golden age of our Southern brethren. It gratified their desire for improvement and accumulation, at the same time that it excited it. The desire grew by what it fed upon, and there soon came to be an eagerness for other territory, a new area or new areas for the cultivation of the cotton crop; and measures leading to this result were brought about rapidly, one after another, under the lead of Southern men at the head of the government, they having a majority in both branches of Congress to accomplish their ends. The honorable member from South Carolina observed that there has been a majority all along in favor of the North. If that be true, sir, the North has acted either very liberally and kindly, or very weakly; for they never exercised that majority efficiently five times in the history of the government, when a division or trial of strength arose. Never. Whether they were out-generalled, or whether it was owing to other causes, I shall not stop to consider; but no man acquainted with the history of the Union can deny that the general lead in the politics of the country, for three fourths of the period that has elapsed since the adoption of the Constitution, has been a Southern lead.

In 1802, in pursuit of the idea of opening a new cotton region, the United States obtained a cession from Georgia of the whole of her western territory, now embracing the rich and growing States of Alabama and Mississippi. In 1803 Louisiana was purchased from France, out of which the States of Louisiana, Arkansas, and Missouri have been framed, as slave-holding States. In 1819 the cession of Florida was made, bringing in another region adapted to cultivation by slaves. Sir, the honorable member from South Carolina thought he saw in certain operations of the government, such as the manner of collecting the revenue, and the tendency of measures calculated to promote emigration into the country, what accounts for the more rapid growth of the North than the South. He ascribes that more rapid growth, not to the operation of time, but to the system of government and administration established under this Constitution. That is a matter of opinion. To a certain extent it may be true; but it does seem to me that, if any operation of the government can be shown in any degree to have promoted the population, and growth, and wealth of the North, it is much more sure that there are sundry important and distinct operations of the government, about which no man can doubt, tending to promote, and which absolutely have promoted, the increase of the slave interest and the slave territory of the South. It was not time that brought in Louisiana; it was the act of men. It was not time that brought in Florida; it was the act of men. And lastly, sir, to complete those acts of legislation which have contributed so much to enlarge the area of the institution of slavery, Texas, great and vast and illimitable Texas, was added to the Union as a slave State in 1845. . . .

Now, as to California and New Mexico, I hold slavery to be excluded from those territories by a law even superior to that which admits and sanctions it in Texas. I mean the law of nature, of physical geography, the law of the formation of the earth. That law settles for ever, with a strength beyond all terms of human enactment, that slavery cannot exist in California or New Mexico. Understand me, sir; I mean slavery as we regard it; the slavery of the colored race as it exists in the Southern States. . . . It is as impossible that African slavery, as we see it among us, should find its way, or be introduced, into California and New Mexico, as any other natural impossibility. California and New Mexico are Asiatic in their formation and scenery. They are composed of vast ridges of mountains, of great height, with broken ridges and deep valleys. The sides of these mountains are entirely barren; their tops capped by perennial snow. There may be in California, now made free by its constitution, and no doubt there are, some tracts of valuable land. But it is not so in New Mexico. Pray, what is the evidence which every gentleman must have obtained on this subject, from information sought by himself or communicated by others? I have inquired and read all I could find, in order to acquire information on this important subject. What is there in New Mexico that could, by any possibility, induce any body to go there with slaves? There are some narrow strips of tillable land on the borders of the rivers; but the rivers themselves dry up before midsummer is gone. All that the people can do in that region is to raise some little articles, some little wheat for their *tortillas*, and that by irrigation. And who expects to see a hundred black men cultivating tobacco, corn, cotton, rice, or any thing else, on lands in New Mexico, made fertile only by irrigation?

I look upon it, therefore, as a fixed fact, to use the current expression of the day, that both California and New Mexico are destined to be free, so far as they are settled at all, which I believe, in regard to New Mexico, will be but partially for a great length of time; free by the arrangement of things ordained by the Power above us. I have therefore to say, in this respect also, that this country is fixed for freedom, to as many persons as shall ever live in it, by a less repealable law than that which attaches to the right of holding slaves in Texas; and I will say further, that, if a resolution or a bill were now before us, to provide a territorial government for New Mexico, I would not vote to put any prohibition into it whatever. Such a prohibition would be idle, as it respects any effect it would have upon the territory; and I would not take pains uselessly to reaffirm an ordinance of nature, nor to reënact the will of God. I would put in no Wilmot Proviso [banning slavery in New Mexico] for the mere purpose of a taunt or a reproach. I would put into it no evidence of the votes of superior power, exercised for no purpose but to wound the pride, whether a just and a rational pride, or an irrational pride, of the citizens of the Southern States. I have no such object, no such purpose. . . .

I repeat, therefore, sir, and, as I do not propose to address the Senate often on this subject, I repeat it because I wish it to be distinctly understood, that, for the reasons stated, if a proposition were now here to establish a government for New Mexico, and it was moved to insert a provision for a prohibition of slavery, I would not vote for it. . . .

Sir, wherever there is a substantive good to be done, wherever there is a foot of land to be prevented from becoming slave territory, I am ready to assert the principle of the exclusion of slavery. I am pledged to it from the year 1837; I have been pledged to it again and again; and I will perform those pledges; but I will not do a thing unnecessarily that wounds the feelings of others, or that does discredit to my own understanding.

Now, Mr. President, I have established, so far as I proposed to do so, the proposition with which I set out, and upon which I intend to stand or fall; and that is, that the whole territory within the former United States, or in the newly acquired Mexican provinces, has a fixed and settled character, now fixed and settled by law which cannot be repealed; in the case of Texas without a violation of public faith,

and by no human power in regard to California or New Mexico; that, therefore, under one or other of these laws, every foot of land in the States or in the Territories has already received a fixed and decided character.

Fugitive Slaves

Mr. President, in the excited times in which we live, there is found to exist a state of crimination and recrimination between the North and South. There are lists of grievances produced by each; and those grievances, real or supposed, alienate the minds of one portion of the country from the other, exasperate the feelings, and subdue the sense of fraternal affection, patriotic love, and mutual regard. I shall bestow a little attention, sir, upon these various grievances existing on the one side and on the other. I begin with complaints of the South. I will not answer, further than I have, the general statements of the honorable Senator from South Carolina [Calhoun], that the North has prospered at the expense of the South in consequence of the manner of administering this government, in the collecting of its revenues, and so forth. These are disputed topics, and I have no inclination to enter into them. But I will allude to other complaints of the South, and especially to one which has in my opinion just foundation; and that is, that there has been found at the North, among individuals and among legislators, a disinclination to perform fully their constitutional duties in regard to the return of persons bound to service who have escaped into the free States. In that respect, the South, in my judgment, is right, and the North is wrong. Every member of every Northern legislature is bound by oath, like every other officer in the country, to support the Constitution of the United States; and the article of the Constitution which says to these States that they shall deliver up fugitives from service is as binding in honor and conscience as any other article. . . . What right have they, in their legislative capacity or any other capacity, to endeavor to get round this Constitution, or to embarrass the free exercise of the rights secured by the Constitution to the persons whose slaves escape from them? None at all; none at all. Neither in the forum of conscience, nor before the face of the Constitution, are they, in my opinion, justified in such an attempt. . . .

I repeat, therefore, sir, that here is a well-founded ground of complaint against the North, which ought to be removed, which it is now in the power of the different departments of this government to remove; which calls for the enactment of proper laws authorizing the judicature of this government, in the several States, to do all that is necessary for the recapture of fugitive slaves and for their restoration to those who claim them. Wherever I go, and whenever I speak on the subject, and when I speak here I desire to speak to the whole North, I say that the South has been injured in this respect, and has a right to complain; and the North has been too careless of what I think the Constitution peremptorily and emphatically enjoins upon her as a duty. . . .

Then, sir, there are the Abolition societies, of which I am unwilling to speak, but in regard to which I have very clear notions and opinions. I do not think them useful. I think their operations for the last twenty years have produced nothing good or valuable. At the same time, I believe thousands of their members to be honest and good men, perfectly well-meaning men. They have excited feelings; they think they must do something for the cause of liberty; and, in their sphere of action, they do not see what else they can do than to contribute to an Abolition press, or an Abolition society, or to pay an Abolition lecturer. I do not mean to impute gross motives even to the leaders of these societies, but I am not blind to the consequences of their proceedings. I cannot but see what mischiefs their interference with the South has produced. And is it not plain to every man? . . .

It is said, I do not know how true it may be, that they sent incendiary publications into the slave States; at any rate, they attempted to arouse, and did arouse, a very strong feeling; in other words, they created great agitation in the North against Southern slavery. Well, what was the result? The bonds of the slaves were bound more firmly than before, their rivets were more strongly fastened. Public opinion, which in Virginia had begun to be exhibited against slavery, and was opening out for the discussion of the question, drew back and shut itself up in its castle. . . . We all know the fact, and we all know the cause; and every thing that these agitating people have done has been, not to enlarge, but to restrain, not to set free, but to bind faster, the slave population of the South. . . .

Now, sir, so far as any of these grievances have their foundation in matters of law, they can be redressed, and ought to be redressed; and so far as they have their foundation in matters of opinion, in sentiment, in mutual crimination and recrimination, all that we can do is to endeavor to allay the agitation, and cultivate a better feeling and more fraternal sentiments between the South and the North.

Secession Without War Is Impossible

Mr. President, I should much prefer to have heard from every member on this floor declarations of opinion that this Union could never be dissolved, than the declaration of opinion by any body, that, in any case, under the pressure of any circumstances, such a dissolution was possible. I hear with distress and anguish the word "secession," especially when it falls from the lips of those who are patriotic, and known to the country, and known all over the world, for their political services. Secession! Peaceable secession! Sir, your eyes and mine are never destined to see that miracle. The dismemberment of this vast country without convulsion! The breaking up of the fountains of the great deep without ruffling the surface! Who is so foolish, I beg every body's pardon, as to expect to see any such thing? Sir, he who sees these States, now revolving in harmony around a common centre, and expects to see them quit their places and fly off without convulsion, may look the next hour to see the heavenly bodies rush from their spheres, and jostle against each other in the realms of space, without causing the wreck of the universe. There can be no such thing as a peaceable secession. Peaceable secession is an utter impossibility. Is the great Constitution under which we live, covering this whole country, is it to be thawed and melted away by secession, as the snows on the mountain melt under the influence of a vernal sun, disappear almost unobserved, and run off? No, sir! No, sir! I will not state what might produce the disruption of the Union; but, sir, I see as plainly as I see the sun in heaven what that disruption itself must produce; I see that it must produce war, and such a war as I will not describe, *in its twofold character.*

Peaceable secession! Peaceable secession! The concurrent agreement of all the members of this great republic to separate! A voluntary separation, with alimony on one side and on the other. Why, what would be the result? Where is the line to be drawn? What States are to secede? What is to remain American? What am I to be? An American no longer? Am I to become a sectional man, a local man, a separatist, with no country in common with the gentlemen who sit around me here, or who fill the other house of Congress? Heaven forbid! Where is the flag of the republic to remain? Where is the eagle still to tower? or is he to cower, and shrink, and fall to the ground? Why, sir, our ancestors, our fathers and our grandfathers, those of them that are yet living amongst us with prolonged lives, would rebuke and reproach us; and our children and our grandchildren would cry out shame upon us, if we of this generation should dishonor these ensigns of the power of the government and the harmony of that union which is every day felt among us with so much joy and gratitude. What is to become of the army? What is to become of the navy? What is to become of the public lands? How is each of the thirty States to defend itself? I know, although the idea has not been stated distinctly, there is to be, or it is supposed possible that there will be, a Southern Confederacy. I do not mean, when I allude to this statement, that any one seriously contemplates such a state of things. I do not mean to say that it is true, but I have heard it suggested elsewhere, that the idea has been entertained, that, after the dissolution of this Union, a Southern Confederacy might be formed. I am sorry, sir, that it has ever been thought of, talked of, or dreamed of, in the wildest flights of human imagination. But the idea, so far as it exists, must be of a separation, assigning the slave States to one side and the free States to the other. Sir, I may express myself too strongly, perhaps, but there are impossibilities in the natural as well as in the physical world, and I hold the idea of a separation of these States, those that are free to form one government, and those that are slave-holding to form another, as such an impossibility. We could not separate the States by any such line, if we were to draw it. We could not sit down here to-day and draw a line of separation that would satisfy any five men in the country. There are natural causes that would keep and tie us together, and there are social and domestic relations which we could not break if we would, and which we should not if we could. . . .

And now, Mr. President, instead of speaking of the possibility or utility of secession, instead of dwelling in those caverns of darkness, instead of groping with those ideas so full of all that is horrid and horrible, let us come out into the light of day; let us enjoy the fresh air of Liberty and Union; let us cherish those hopes which belong to us; let us devote ourselves to those great objects that are fit for our consideration and our action; let us raise our conceptions to the magnitude and the importance of the duties that devolve upon us; let our comprehension be as broad as the country for which we act, our aspirations as high as its certain destiny; let us not be pigmies in a case that calls for men. Never did there devolve on any generation of men higher trusts than now devolve upon us, for the preservation of this Constitution and the harmony and peace of all who are destined to live under it. Let us make our generation one of the strongest and brightest links in that golden chain which is destined, I fondly believe, to grapple the people of all the States to this Constitution for ages to come.

For Further Reading

Maurice G. Baxter, *One and Inseparable: Daniel Webster and the Union.* Cambridge, MA: Harvard University Press, 1984.

Holman Hamilton, *Prologue to Conflict: The Crisis and Compromise of 1850.* Lexington: University of Kentucky Press, 1964.

Michael F. Holt, *The Political Crisis of the 1850s.* New York: Norton, 1983.

John Niven, *John C. Calhoun and the Price of Union.* Baton Rouge: Louisiana State University Press, 1988.

VIEWPOINT 32A

Constitutional Rights Do Not Extend to Blacks (1857)

Roger Taney (1777–1864)

Roger Taney was the chief justice of the U.S. Supreme Court from 1836 until his death in 1864. He is best remembered for a single case: the Dred Scott decision of 1857, in which Taney attempted to interject the Supreme Court into the national debate over slavery and the power of Congress to regulate it.

Congress and the nation were enmeshed in controversy over the extension of slavery to the western territories, and whether new states, as they were admitted, should allow slavery. In the 1787 Northwest Ordinance and the 1820 Missouri Compromise, Congress had sought to limit slavery by forbidding its introduction into western territories north of certain latitudes, thus dividing the country into slave and free regions. Dred Scott was a slave who had accompanied his master when he moved from Missouri, where slavery was allowed, to the state of Illinois and to the Wisconsin Territory, both of which outlawed slavery. Shortly after they moved back to Missouri, his master died, and Scott, backed and encouraged by abolitionists, sued the widow for his freedom on the grounds that his residence in a free state and a free territory had ended his bondage. The case eventually made it to the federal court system and ultimately to the U.S. Supreme Court, where, by a 7-2 vote, Scott lost his bid for freedom. Each of the nine justices wrote a separate opinion on the case; the following viewpoint is excerpted from the opinion written by Taney.

The Dred Scott case involved three important issues. One was whether Scott's residence in a free state freed him from slavery. A second was the constitutionality of the 1820 Missouri Compromise, and whether Congress had the power to limit or regulate slavery. Taney ruled against Scott on both these matters, and in so doing ruled that Congress had no power to regulate slavery in the territories and that the Missouri Compromise was unconstitutional.

The excerpts reprinted here concentrate on a third issue: whether Scott was a citizen of Missouri and thus able to sue in a federal court. Taney argues that slaves and their descendants were never meant to be part of the political community of citizens envisioned by the writers of the U.S. Constitution, and that Scott had no legal standing as a U.S. citizen.

From Roger Taney's majority opinion in the *Dred Scott* case, as recorded in the *Report of the Decision of the Supreme Court of the United States and the Opinions of the Judges Thereof, in the Case of Dred Scott v. John F. A. Sandford* (Washington, D.C., 1857).

The Dred Scott decision, which Taney hoped would settle the national controversy over slavery, instead intensified it. Taney's reputation was severely tarnished by the case. Dred Scott was freed in 1857 (he had been purchased by abolitionists who had planned to free Scott in any case); he died in the same year. The decision itself was nullified after the Civil War by the Thirteenth and Fourteenth Amendments to the U.S. Constitution.

What reasoning and historical evidence does Taney use in arguing that the language in the Declaration of Independence stating that "all men are created equal" does not refer to blacks? Which clauses in the Constitution does he cite to argue that the document treats blacks as noncitizens?

The question is simply this: Can a negro, whose ancestors were imported into this country, and sold as slaves, become a member of the political community formed and brought into existence by the Constitution of the United States, and as such become entitled to all the rights, and privileges, and immunities, guarantied by that instrument to the citizen? One of which rights is the privilege of suing in a court of the United States in the cases specified in the Constitution.

Can Blacks Be Citizens?

It will be observed, that the plea applies to that class of persons only whose ancestors were negroes of the African race, and imported into this country, and sold and held as slaves. The only matter in issue before the court, therefore, is, whether the descendants of such slaves, when they shall be emancipated, or who are born of parents who had become free before their birth, are citizens of a State, in the sense in which the word citizen is used in the Constitution of the United States. And this being the only matter in dispute on the pleadings, the court must be understood as speaking in this opinion of that class only, that is, of those persons who are the descendants of Africans who were imported into this country, and sold as slaves. . . .

The Constitution has conferred on Congress the right to establish a uniform rule of naturalization, and this right is evidently exclusive, and has always been held by this court to be so. Consequently, no State, since the adoption of the Constitution, can by naturalizing an alien invest him with the rights and privileges secured to a citizen of a State under the Federal Government. . . .

It is very clear, therefore, that no State can, by any act or law of its own, passed since the adoption of the Constitution, introduce a new member into the political community created by the Constitution of the United States. It cannot make him a member of this community by making him a member of its own. And for the same reason it cannot introduce any person, or description of persons, who were not intended to be embraced in this new political family, which the Constitution brought into existence, but were intended to be excluded from it.

The question then arises, whether the provisions of the Constitution, in relation to the personal rights and privileges to which the citizen of a State should be entitled, embraced the negro African race, at that time in this country, or who might afterwards be imported, who had then or should afterwards be made free in any State; and to put it in the power of a single State to make him a citizen of the United States, and endue him with the full rights of citizenship in every other State without their consent? Does the Constitution of the United States act upon him whenever he shall be made free under the laws of a State, and raised there to the rank of a citizen, and immediately clothe him with all the privileges of a citizen in every other State, and in its own courts?

The court thinks the affirmative of these propositions cannot be maintained. And if it cannot, the plaintiff in error [Dred Scott] could not be a citizen of the State of Missouri, within the meaning of the Constitution of the United States, and, consequently, was not entitled to sue in its courts.

Members of the Political Body

It is true, every person, and every class and description of persons, who were at the time of the adoption of the Constitution recognised as citizens in the several States, became also citizens of this new political body; but none other; it was formed by them, and for them and their posterity, but for no one else. And the personal rights and privileges guarantied to citizens of this new sovereignty were intended to embrace those only who were then members of the several State communities, or who should afterwards by birthright or otherwise become members, according to the provisions of the Constitution and the principles on which it was founded. It was the union of those who were at that time members of distinct and separate political communities into one political family, whose power, for certain specified purposes, was to extend over the whole territory of the United States. And it gave to each citizen rights and privileges outside of his State which he did not before possess, and placed him in every other State upon a perfect equality with its own citizens as to rights of person and rights of property; it made him a citizen of the United States.

It becomes necessary, therefore, to determine who were citizens of the several States when the Constitution was adopted. And in order to do this, we must recur to the Governments and institutions of the thirteen colonies, when they separated from Great Britain and formed new sovereignties, and took their places in the family of independent nations. We must inquire who, at that time, were recognised as the people or citizens of a State, whose rights and liberties had been outraged by the English Government; and who declared their independence, and assumed the powers of Government to defend their rights by force of arms.

In the opinion of the court, the legislation and histories of the times, and the language used in the Declaration of Independence, show, that neither the class of persons who had been imported as slaves, nor their descendants, whether they had become free or not, were then acknowledged as a part of the people, nor intended to be included in the general words used in that memorable instrument.

It is difficult at this day to realize the state of public opinion in relation to that unfortunate race, which prevailed in the civilized and enlightened portions of the world at the time of the Declaration of Independence, and when the Constitution of the United States was framed and adopted. But the public history of every European nation displays it in a manner too plain to be mistaken.

An Inferior Race

They had for more than a century before been regarded as beings of an inferior order, and altogether unfit to associate with the white race, either in social or political relations; and so far inferior, that they had no rights which the white man was bound to respect; and that the negro might justly and lawfully be reduced to slavery for his benefit. He was bought and sold, and treated as an ordinary article of merchandise and traffic, whenever a profit could be made by it. This opinion was at that time fixed and universal in the civilized portion of the white race. It was regarded as an axiom in morals as well as in politics, which no one thought of disputing, or supposed to be open to dispute; and men in every grade and position in society daily and habitually acted upon it in their private pursuits, as well as in matters of public concern, without doubting for a moment the correctness of this opinion.

And in no nation was this opinion more firmly fixed or more uniformly acted upon than by the English Government and English people. They not only seized them on the coast of Africa, and sold them or held them in slavery for their own use; but they took them as ordinary articles of merchandise to every country where they could make a profit on them, and were far more extensively engaged in this commerce than any other nation in the world.

The opinion thus entertained and acted upon in England was naturally impressed upon the colonies they founded on this side of the Atlantic. And, accordingly, a negro of the African race was regarded by them as an article of property, and held, and bought and sold as such, in every one of the thirteen colonies which united in the Declaration of Independence, and afterwards formed the Constitution of the United States. The slaves were more or less numerous in the different colonies, as slave labor was found more or less profitable. But no one seems to have doubted the correctness of the prevailing opinion of the time.

The legislation of the different colonies furnishes positive and indisputable proof of this fact. . . .

They show that a perpetual and impassable barrier was intended to be erected between the white race and the one which they had reduced to slavery, and governed as subjects with absolute and despotic power, and which they then looked upon as so far below them in the scale of created beings, that intermarriages between white persons and negroes or mulattoes were regarded as unnatural and immoral, and punished as crimes, not only in the parties, but in the person who joined them in marriage. And no distinction in this respect was made between the free negro or mulatto and the slave, but this stigma, of the deepest degradation, was fixed upon the whole race.

We refer to these historical facts for the purpose of showing the fixed opinions concerning that race, upon which the statesmen of that day spoke and acted. It is necessary to do this, in order to determine whether the general terms used in the Constitution of the United States, as to the rights of man and the rights of the people, was intended to include them, or to give to them or their posterity the benefit of any of its provisions.

The Declaration of Independence

The language of the Declaration of Independence is equally conclusive:

It begins by declaring that, "when in the course of human events it becomes necessary for one people to dissolve the political bands which have connected them with another, and to assume among the powers of the earth the separate and equal station to which the laws of nature and nature's God entitle them, a decent respect for the opinions of mankind requires that they should declare the causes which impel them to the separation."

It then proceeds to say: "We hold these truths to be self-evident: that all men are created equal; that they are endowed by their Creator with certain unalienable rights; that among them is life, liberty, and the pursuit of happiness; that to secure these rights, Governments are instituted, deriving their just powers from the consent of the governed." [The Declaration of Independence appears on pages 100–101.]

The general words above quoted would seem to embrace the whole human family, and if they were used in a similar instrument at this day would be so understood. But it is too clear for dispute, that the enslaved African race were not intended to be included, and formed no part of the people who framed and adopted this declaration; for if the language, as understood in that day, would embrace them, the conduct of the distinguished men who framed the Declaration of Independence would have been utterly and flagrantly inconsistent with the principles they asserted; and instead of the sympathy of mankind, to which they so confidently appealed, they would have deserved and received universal rebuke and reprobation.

Yet the men who framed this declaration were great men—high in literary acquirements—high in their sense of honor, and incapable of asserting principles inconsistent with those on which they were acting. They perfectly understood the meaning of the language they used, and how it would be understood by others; and they knew that it would not in any part of the civilized world be supposed to embrace the negro race, which, by common consent, had been excluded from civilized Governments and the family of nations, and doomed to slavery. They spoke and acted according to the then established doctrines and principles, and in the ordinary language of the day, and no one misunderstood them. The unhappy black race were separated from the white by indelible marks, and laws long before established, and were never thought of or spoken of except as property, and when the claims of the owner or the profit of the trader were supposed to need protection.

This state of public opinion had undergone no change when the Constitution was adopted, as is equally evident from its provisions and language.

The U.S. Constitution

The brief preamble sets forth by whom it was formed, for what purposes, and for whose benefit and protection. It declares that it is formed by the *people* of the United States; that is to say, by those who were members of the different political communities in the several States; and its great object is declared to be to secure the blessings of liberty to themselves and their posterity. It speaks in general terms of the *people* of the United States, and of *citizens* of the several States, when it is providing for the exercise of the powers granted or the privileges secured to the citizen. It does not define what description of persons are intended to be included under these terms, or who shall be regarded as a citizen and one of the people. It uses them as terms so

well understood, that no further description or definition was necessary.

But there are two clauses in the Constitution which point directly and specifically to the negro race as a separate class of persons, and show clearly that they were not regarded as a portion of the people or citizens of the Government they formed.

———— • ————

"There are two clauses in the Constitution which point directly and specifically to the negro race as a separate class of persons, and show clearly that they were not regarded as a portion of the people or citizens of the Government they formed."

———— • ————

One of these clauses reserves to each of the thirteen States the right to import slaves until the year 1808, if it thinks proper. And the importation which it thus sanctions was unquestionably of persons of the race of which we are speaking, as the traffic in slaves in the United States had always been confined to them. And by the other provision the States pledge themselves to each other to maintain the right of property of the master, by delivering up to him any slave who may have escaped from his service, and be found within their respective territories. By the first above-mentioned clause, therefore, the right to purchase and hold this property is directly sanctioned and authorized for twenty years by the people who framed the Constitution. And by the second, they pledge themselves to maintain and uphold the right of the master in the manner specified, as long as the Government they then formed should endure. And these two provisions show, conclusively, that neither the description of persons therein referred to, nor their descendants, were embraced in any of the other provisions of the Constitution; for certainly these two clauses were not intended to confer on them or their posterity the blessings of liberty, or any of the personal rights so carefully provided for the citizen.

No one of that race had ever migrated to the United States voluntarily; all of them had been brought here as articles of merchandise. The number that had been emancipated at that time were but few in comparison with those held in slavery; and they were identified in the public mind with the race to which they belonged, and regarded as a part of the slave population rather than the free. It is obvious that they were not even in the minds of the framers of the Constitution when they were conferring special rights and privileges upon the citizens of a State in every other part of the Union.

Indeed, when we look to the condition of this race in the several States at the time, it is impossible to believe that these rights and privileges were intended to be extended to them.

It is very true, that in that portion of the Union where the labor of the negro race was found to be unsuited to the climate and unprofitable to the master, but few slaves were held at the time of the Declaration of Independence; and when the Constitution was adopted, it had entirely worn out in one of them, and measures had been taken for its gradual abolition in several others. But this change had not been produced by any change of opinion in relation to this race; but because it was discovered, from experience, that slave labor was unsuited to the climate and productions of these States: for some of the States, where it had ceased or nearly ceased to exist, were actively engaged in the slave trade, procuring cargoes on the coast of Africa, and transporting them for sale to those parts of the Union where their labor was found to be profitable, and suited to the climate and productions. And this traffic was openly carried on, and fortunes accumulated by it, without reproach from the people of the States where they resided. And it can hardly be supposed that, in the States where it was then countenanced in its worst form—that is, in the seizure and transportation—the people could have regarded those who were emancipated as entitled to equal rights with themselves.

State Laws

And we may here again refer, in support of this proposition, to the plain and unequivocal language of the laws of the several States, some passed after the Declaration of Independence and before the Constitution was adopted, and some since the Government went into operation. . . .

It would be impossible to enumerate and compress in the space usually allotted to an opinion of a court, the various laws, marking the condition of this race, which were passed from time to time after the Revolution, and before and since the adoption of the Constitution of the United States. In addition to those already referred to, it is sufficient to say, that Chancellor [James] Kent, whose accuracy and research no one will question, states in the sixth edition of his *Commentaries*, (published in 1848, 2 vol., 258, note b,) that in no part of the country except Maine, did the African race, in point of fact, participate equally with the whites in the exercise of civil and political rights.

The legislation of the States therefore shows, in a manner not to be mistaken, the inferior and subject condition of that race at the time the Constitution was adopted. . . . It cannot be believed that the large slaveholding States regarded them as included in the word citizens, or would have consented to a Constitution which might compel them to receive them in that character from another State. . . .

No one, we presume, supposes that any change in public opinion or feeling, in relation to this unfortunate race, in the civilized nations of Europe or in this country, should induce the court to give to the words of the Constitution a more liberal construction in their favor than they were intended to bear when the instrument was framed and adopted. Such an argument would be altogether inadmissable in any tribunal called on to interpret it. If any of its provisions are deemed unjust, there is a mode prescribed in the instrument itself by which it may be amended; but while it remains unaltered, it must be construed now as it was understood at the time of its adoption. It is not only the same in words, but the same in meaning, and delegates the same powers to the Government, and reserves and secures the same rights and privileges to the citizen; and as long as it continues to exist in its present form, it speaks not only in the same words, but with the same meaning and intent with which it spoke when it came from the hands of its framers, and was voted on and adopted by the people of the United States. Any other rule of construction would abrogate the judicial character of this court, and make it the mere reflex of the popular opinion or passion of the day. This court was not created by the Constitution for such purposes. Higher and graver trusts have been confided to it, and it must not falter in the path of duty.

What the construction was at that time, we think can hardly admit of doubt. We have the language of the Declaration of Independence and of the Articles of Confederation, in addition to the plain words of the Constitution itself; we have the legislation of the different States, before, about the time, and since, the Constitution was adopted; we have the legislation of Congress, from the time of its adoption to a recent period; and we have the constant and uniform action of the Executive Department, all concurring together, and leading to the same result. And if anything in relation to the construction of the Constitution can be regarded as settled, it is that which we now give to the word "citizen" and the word "people."

And upon a full and careful consideration of the subject, the court is of opinion, that, upon the facts stated in the plea in abatement, Dred Scott was not a citizen of Missouri within the meaning of the Constitution of the United States, and not entitled as such to sue in its courts; and, consequently, that the Circuit Court had no jurisdiction of the case, and that the judgment on the plea in abatement is erroneous. . . .

The right of property in a slave is distinctly and

expressly affirmed in the Constitution. The right to traffic in it, like an ordinary article of merchandise and property, was guarantied to the citizens of the United States, in every State that might desire it, for twenty years. And the Government in express terms is pledged to protect it in all future time, if the slave escapes from his owner. This is done in plain words—too plain to be misunderstood. And no word can be found in the Constitution which gives Congress a greater power over slave property, or which entitles property of that kind to less protection than property of any other description. The only power conferred is the power coupled with the duty of guarding and protecting the owner in his rights.

Upon these considerations, it is the opinion of the court that the act of Congress which prohibited a citizen from holding and owning property of this kind in the territory of the United States north of the line therein mentioned [the 1820 Missouri Compromise], is not warranted by the Constitution, and is therefore void; and that neither Dred Scott himself, nor any of his family, were made free by being carried into this [Wisconsin] territory; even if they had been carried there by the owner, with the intention of becoming a permanent resident.

We have so far examined the case, as it stands under the Constitution of the United States, and the powers thereby delegated to the Federal Government.

But there is another point in the case which depends on State power and State law. And it is contended, on the part of the plaintiff, that he is made free by being taken to Rock Island, in the State of Illinois, independently of his residence in the territory of the United States; and being so made free, he was not again reduced to a state of slavery by being brought back to Missouri.

Our notice of this part of the case will be very brief; for the principle on which it depends was decided in this court, upon much consideration, in the case of *Strader et al, v. Graham.* . . . In that case, the slaves had been taken from Kentucky to Ohio, with the consent of the owner, and afterwards brought back to Kentucky. And this court held that their *status* or condition, as free or slave, depended upon the laws of Kentucky, when they were brought back into that State, and not of Ohio; and that this court had no jurisdiction to revise the judgment of a State court upon its own laws. This was the point directly before the court, and the decision that this court had not jurisdiction turned upon it, as will be seen by the report of the case.

So in this case. As Scott was a slave when taken into the State of Illinois by his owner, and was there held as such, and brought back in that character, his *status*, as free or slave, depended on the laws of Missouri, and not of Illinois.

VIEWPOINT 32B

Constitutional Rights Do Extend to Blacks (1857)

Benjamin Robbins Curtis (1809–1874)

Massachusetts-born Benjamin Robbins Curtis was a Supreme Court justice from 1851 to 1857. He is most famous for his dissent on the Dred Scott case in 1857, a dissent that ultimately led to his resignation from the court.

Dred Scott was a slave who had sued for his freedom on the grounds that he had resided with his master for a time in a state where slavery was outlawed. The Supreme Court, led by Chief Justice Roger Taney, ruled against him, partly on the basis that slaves and their descendants had no standing as citizens under the U.S. Constitution. In the following excerpts from his dissenting opinion in the case, Curtis challenges this reasoning. He argues that the Constitution contains no provisions excluding blacks from U.S. citizenship. He concludes that the states themselves have the power to determine citizenship, and that all citizens of the states are also citizens of the United States.

What are the major differences between the analysis of Curtis and that of Roger Taney, author of the opposing viewpoint? How does Curtis respond to the argument that the Constitution was meant for whites only?

The question is, whether any person of African descent, whose ancestors were sold as slaves in the United States, can be a citizen of the United States. If any such person can be a citizen, this plaintiff has the right to the judgment of the court that he is so; for no cause is shown by the plea why he is not so, except his descent and the slavery of his ancestors.

The first section of the second article of the Constitution uses the language, "a citizen of the United States at the time of the adoption of the Constitution." One mode of approaching this question is, to inquire who were citizens of the United States at the time of the adoption of the Constitution.

Citizens of the United States at the time of the adoption of the Constitution can have been no other than citizens of the United States under the Confederation. By the Articles of Confederation, a Government was organized, the style whereof was, "The

From Benjamin Robbins Curtis's dissenting opinion in the *Dred Scott* case, as recorded in the *Report of the Decision of the Supreme Court of the United States and the Opinions of the Judges Thereof, in the Case of Dred Scott v. John F.A. Sandford* (Washington, D.C., 1857).

United States of America." This Government was in existence when the Constitution was framed and proposed for adoption, and was to be superseded by the new Government of the United States of America, organized under the Constitution. When, therefore, the Constitution speaks of citizenship of the United States, existing at the time of the adoption of the Constitution, it must necessarily refer to citizenship under the Government which existed prior to and at the time of such adoption.

Without going into any question concerning the powers of the Confederation to govern the territory of the United States out of the limits of the States, and consequently to sustain the relation of Government and citizen in respect to the inhabitants of such territory, it may safely be said that the citizens of the several States were citizens of the United States under the Confederation.

Citizens of the States

That Government was simply a confederacy of the several States, possessing a few defined powers over subjects of general concern, each State retaining every power, jurisdiction, and right, not expressly delegated to the United States in Congress assembled. And no power was thus delegated to the Government of the Confederation, to act on any question of citizenship, or to make any rules in respect thereto. The whole matter was left to stand upon the action of the several States, and to the natural consequence of such action, that the citizens of each State should be citizens of that Confederacy into which that State had entered, the style whereof was, "The United States of America."

To determine whether any free persons, descended from Africans held in slavery, were citizens of the United States under the Confederation, and consequently at the time of the adoption of the Constitution of the United States, it is only necessary to know whether any such persons were citizens of either of the States under the Confederation, at the time of the adoption of the Constitution.

Of this there can be no doubt. At the time of the ratification of the Articles of Confederation, all free native-born inhabitants of the States of New Hampshire, Massachusetts, New York, New Jersey, and North Carolina, though descended from African slaves, were not only citizens of those States, but such of them as had the other necessary qualifications possessed the franchise of electors, on equal terms with other citizens. . . .

An argument from speculative premises, however well chosen, that the then state of opinion in the Commonwealth of Massachusetts was not consistent with the natural rights of people of color who were born on that soil, and that they were not, by the Con-

stitution of 1780 of that State, admitted to the condition of citizens, would be received with surprise by the people of that State, who know their own political history. It is true, beyond all controversy, that persons of color, descended from African slaves, were by that Constitution made citizens of the State; and such of them as have had the necessary qualifications, have held and exercised the elective franchise, as citizens, from that time to the present. . . .

The Constitution of New Hampshire conferred the elective franchise upon "every inhabitant of the State having the necessary qualifications," of which color or descent was not one. . . .

That of New Jersey, to "all inhabitants of this colony, of full age, who are worth £50 proclamation money, clear estate."

———————— • ————————

"That [the Constitution] was made exclusively for the white race is, in my opinion, not only an assumption not warranted by anything in the Constitution, but contradicted by its opening declaration, that it was ordained and established by the people of the United States, for themselves and their posterity."

———————— • ————————

New York, by its Constitution of 1820, required colored persons to have some qualifications as prerequisites for voting, which white persons need not possess. And New Jersey, by its present Constitution, restricts the right to vote to white male citizens. But these changes can have no other effect upon the present inquiry, except to show, that before they were made, no such restrictions existed; and colored in common with white persons, were not only citizens of those States, but entitled to the elective franchise on the same qualifications as white persons, as they now are in New Hampshire and Massachusetts. I shall not enter into an examination of the existing opinions of that period respecting the African race, nor into any discussion concerning the meaning of those who asserted, in the Declaration of Independence, that all men are created equal; that they are endowed by their Creator with certain inalienable rights; that among these are life, liberty, and the pursuit of happiness. My own opinion is, that a calm comparison of these assertions of universal abstract truths, and of their own individual opinions and acts, would not leave these men under any reproach of inconsistency; that the great truths they asserted on that solemn occasion, they were ready and anxious to make effectual, wherever a necessary regard to circumstances, which no statesman can disregard without producing more evil than good, would allow; and that it would not be just to them, nor true in itself, to allege that they intended to say that the Creator of all men had endowed the white race, exclusively, with the great natural rights which the Declaration of Independence asserts. But this is not the place to vindicate their memory. As I conceive, we should deal here, not with such disputes, if there can be a dispute concerning this subject, but with those substantial facts evinced by the written Constitutions of States, and by the notorious practice under them. And they show, in a manner which no argument can obscure, that in some of the original thirteen States, free colored persons, before and at the time of the formation of the Constitution, were citizens of those States. . . .

Did the Constitution of the United States deprive them or their descendants of citizenship?

The Constitution and Black Citizenship

That Constitution was ordained and established by the people of the United States, through the action, in each State, of those persons who were qualified by its laws to act thereon, in behalf of themselves and all other citizens of that State. In some of the States, as we have seen, colored persons were among those qualified by law to act on this subject. These colored persons were not only included in the body of "the people of the United States," by whom the Constitution was ordained and established, but in at least five of the States they had the power to act, and doubtless did act, by their suffrages, upon the question of its adoption. It would be strange, if we were to find in that instrument anything which deprived of their citizenship any part of the people of the United States who were among those by whom it was established.

I can find nothing in the Constitution which, *proprio vigore* [by its own force], deprives of their citizenship any class of persons who were citizens of the United States at the time of its adoption, or who should be native-born citizens of any State after its adoption; nor any power enabling Congress to disfranchise persons born on the soil of any State, and entitled to citizenship of such State by its Constitution and laws. And my opinion is, that, under the Constitution of the United States, every free person born on the soil of a State, who is a citizen of that State by force of its Constitution or laws, is also a citizen of the United States.

I will proceed to state the grounds of that opinion.

The first section of the second article of the Constitution uses the language, "a natural-born citizen." It thus assumes that citizenship may be acquired by birth. . . .

The Constitution having recognised the rule that persons born within the several States are citizens of the United States, one of four things must be true:

First. That the Constitution itself has described what native-born persons shall or shall not be citizens of the United States; or,

Second. That it has empowered Congress to do so; or,

Third. That all free persons, born within the several States, are citizens of the United States; or,

Fourth. That it is left to each State to determine what free persons, born within its limits, shall be citizens of such State, and *thereby* be citizens of the United States.

If there be such a thing as citizenship of the United States acquired by birth within the States, which the Constitution expressly recognises, and no one denies, then these four alternatives embrace the entire subject, and it only remains to select that one which is true.

That the Constitution itself has defined citizenship of the United States by declaring what persons, born within the several States, shall or shall not be citizens of the United States, will not be pretended. It contains no such declaration. We may dismiss the first alternative, as without doubt unfounded.

Has it empowered Congress to enact what free persons, born within the several States, shall or shall not be citizens of the United States?

Before examining the various provisions of the Constitution which may relate to this question, it is important to consider for a moment the substantial nature of this inquiry. It is, in effect, whether the Constitution has empowered Congress to create privileged classes within the States, who alone can be entitled to the franchises and powers of citizenship of the United States. If it be admitted that the Constitution has enabled Congress to declare what free persons, born within the several States, shall be citizens of the United States, it must at the same time be admitted that it is an unlimited power. If this subject is within the control of Congress, it must depend wholly on its discretion. For, certainly, no limits of that discretion can be found in the Constitution, which is wholly silent concerning it; and the necessary consequence is, that the Federal Government may select classes of persons within the several States who alone can be entitled to the political privileges of citizenship of the United States. If this power exists, what persons born within the States may be President or Vice President of the United States, or members of either House of Congress, or hold any office or enjoy any privilege whereof citizenship of the United States is a necessary qualification, must depend solely on the will of Congress. By virtue of it, though Congress can grant no title of nobility, they may create an oligarchy, in whose hands would be concentrated the entire power of the Federal Government.

It is a substantive power, distinct in its nature from all others; capable of affecting not only the relations of the States to the General Government, but of controlling the political condition of the people of the United States. Certainly we ought to find this power granted by the Constitution, at least by some necessary inference, before we can say it does not remain to the States or the people. I proceed therefore to examine all the provisions of the Constitution which may have some bearing on this subject.

Among the powers expressly granted to Congress is "the power to establish a uniform rule of naturalization." It is not doubted that this is a power to prescribe a rule for the removal of the disabilities consequent on foreign birth. To hold that it extends further than this, would do violence to the meaning of the term naturalization. . . .

Whether there be anything in the Constitution from which a broader power may be implied, will best be seen when we come to examine the two other alternatives, which are, whether all free persons, born on the soil of the several States, or only such of them as may be citizens of each State, respectively, are thereby citizens of the United States. The last of these alternatives, in my judgment, contains the truth. . . .

It may be proper here to notice some supposed objections to this view of the subject.

It has been often asserted that the Constitution was made exclusively by and for the white race. It has already been shown that in five of the thirteen original States, colored persons then possessed the elective franchise, and were among those by whom the Constitution was ordained and established. If so, it is not true, in point of fact, that the Constitution was made exclusively by the white race. And that it was made exclusively for the white race is, in my opinion, not only an assumption not warranted by anything in the Constitution, but contradicted by its opening declaration, that it was ordained and established by the people of the United States, for themselves and their posterity. And as free colored persons were then citizens of at least five States, and so in every sense part of the people of the United States, they were among those for whom and whose posterity the Constitution was ordained and established.

Again, it has been objected, that if the Constitution has left to the several States the rightful power to determine who of their inhabitants shall be citizens of the United States, the States may make aliens citizens.

The answer is obvious. The Constitution has left to the States the determination what persons, born within their respective limits, shall acquire by birth citizenship of the United States; it has not left to them any power to prescribe any rule for the removal of the disabilities of alienage. This power is exclusively in Congress.

It has been further objected, that if free colored persons, born within a particular State, and made citizens of that State by its Constitution and laws, are thereby made citizens of the United States, then, under the second section of the fourth article of the Constitution, such persons would be entitled to all the privileges and immunities of citizens in the several States; and if so, then colored persons could vote, and be eligible to not only Federal offices, but offices even in those States whose Constitutions and laws disqualify colored persons from voting or being elected to office.

But this position rests upon an assumption which I deem untenable. Its basis is, that no one can be deemed a citizen of the United States who is not entitled to enjoy all the privileges and franchises which are conferred on any citizen. That this is not true, under the Constitution of the United States, seems to me clear.

Citizens and Their Rights

A naturalized citizen cannot be President of the United States, nor a Senator till after the lapse of nine years, nor a Representative till after the lapse of seven years, from his naturalization. Yet, as soon as naturalized, he is certainly a citizen of the United States. Nor is any inhabitant of the District of Columbia, or of either of the Territories, eligible to the office of Senator or Representative in Congress, though they may be citizens of the United States. So, in all the States, numerous persons, though citizens, cannot vote, or cannot hold office, either on account of their age, or sex, or the want of the necessary legal qualifications. The truth is, that citizenship, under the Constitution of the United States, is not dependent on the possession of any particular political or even of all civil rights; and any attempt so to define it must lead to error. To what citizens the elective franchise shall be confided, is a question to be determined by each State, in accordance with its own views of the necessities or expediencies of its condition. What civil rights shall be enjoyed by its citizens, and whether all shall enjoy the same, or how they may be gained or lost, are to be determined in the same way. . . .

It may be further objected, that if free colored persons may be citizens of the United States, it depends only on the will of a master whether he will emancipate his slave, and thereby make him a citizen. Not so. The master is subject to the will of the State. Whether he shall be allowed to emancipate his slave at all; if so, on what conditions; and what is to be the political *status* of the freed man, depend, not on the will of the master, but on the will of the State, upon which the political *status* of all its native-born inhabitants depends. Under the Constitution of the United States, each State has retained this power of determining the political *status* of its native-born inhabitants, and no exception thereto can be found in the Constitution. And if a master in a slaveholding State should carry his slave into a free State, and there emancipate him, he would not thereby make him a native-born citizen of that State, and consequently no privileges could be claimed by such emancipated slave as a citizen of the United States. For, whatever powers the States may exercise to confer privileges of citizenship on persons not born on their soil, the Constitution of the United States does not recognise such citizens. As has already been said, it recognises the great principle of public law, that allegiance and citizenship spring from the place of birth. It leaves to the States the application of that principle to individual cases. It secured to the citizens of each State the privileges and immunities of citizens in every other State. But it does not allow to the States the power to make aliens citizens, or permit one State to take persons born on the soil of another State, and, contrary to the laws and policy of the State where they were born, make them its citizens, and so citizens of the United States. No such deviation from the great rule of public law was contemplated by the Constitution; and when any such attempt shall be actually made, it is to be met by applying to it those rules of law and those principles of good faith which will be sufficient to decide it, and not, in my judgment, by denying that all the free native-born inhabitants of a State, who are its citizens under its Constitution and laws, are also citizens of the United States.

It has sometimes been urged that colored persons are shown not to be citizens of the United States by the fact that the naturalization laws apply only to white persons. But whether a person born in the United States be or be not a citizen, cannot depend on laws which refer only to aliens, and do not affect the *status* of persons born in the United States. The utmost effect which can be attributed to them is, to show that Congress has not deemed it expedient generally to apply the rule to colored aliens. That they might do so, if thought fit, is clear. The Constitution has not excluded them. And since that has conferred the power on Congress to naturalize colored aliens, it certainly shows color is not a necessary qualification for citizenship under the Constitution of the United States. It may be added, that the power to make colored persons citizens of the United States, under the Constitution, has been actually exercised in repeated and important instances. (See the Treaties with the Choctaws, of September 27, 1830, art. 14; with the Cherokees, of May 23, 1836, art. 12; Treaty of Guadalupe Hidalgo [with Mexico following the Mexican War], February 2, 1848, art. 8.)

I do not deem it necessary to review at length the legislation of Congress having more or less bearing on the citizenship of colored persons. It does not seem to me to have any considerable tendency to prove that it has been considered by the legislative department of the Government, that no such persons are citizens of the United States. Undoubtedly they have been debarred from the exercise of particular rights or privileges extended to white persons, but, I believe, always in terms which, by implication, admit they may be citizens. Thus the act of May 17, 1792, for the organization of the militia, directs the enrollment of "every free, able-bodied, white male citizen." An assumption that none but white persons are citizens, would be as inconsistent with the just import of this language, as that all citizens are able-bodied, or males. . . .

Conclusions

The conclusions at which I have arrived on this part of the case are:

First. That the free native-born citizens of each State are citizens of the United States.

Second. That as free colored persons born within some of the States are citizens of those States, such persons are also citizens of the United States.

Third. That every such citizen, residing in any State, has the right to sue and is liable to be sued in the Federal courts, as a citizen of that State in which he resides.

Fourth. That as the plea to the jurisdiction in this case shows no facts, except that the plaintiff was of African descent, and his ancestors were sold as slaves, and as these facts are not inconsistent with his citizenship of the United States, and his residence in the State of Missouri, the plea to the jurisdiction was bad, and the judgment of the Circuit Court overruling it was correct.

I dissent, therefore, from that part of the opinion of the majority of the court, in which it is held that a person of African descent cannot be a citizen of the United States.

For Further Reading

Walter Ehrlich, *They Have No Rights: Dred Scott's Struggle for Freedom.* Westport, CT: Greenwood Press, 1979.

Don E. Fehrenbacher, *Slavery, Law, and Politics: The Dred Scott Case in Historical Perspective.* New York: Oxford University Press, 1981.

Stanley I. Kutler, *The Dred Scott Decision: Law or Politics?* Boston: Houghton Mifflin, 1967.

VIEWPOINT 33A

Popular Sovereignty Should Settle the Slavery Question (1858)

Stephen A. Douglas (1813–1861)

Stephen A. Douglas, U.S. senator from Illinois, was one of America's leading political figures of the 1850s. Today he is best remembered for his political rivalry with Abraham Lincoln.

Elected to the U.S. Senate in 1846, Douglas played major roles in passing the Compromise of 1850 and the Kansas-Nebraska Act of 1854—both attempts by Congress to resolve the issue of legalizing slavery in America's western territories. Douglas's sponsorship of these laws, especially the Kansas-Nebraska Act, positioned him as the champion of "popular sovereignty"—the idea that territorial settlers should at some point make their own decision whether to legalize slavery.

By 1858 the doctrine of popular sovereignty was under attack from several quarters. For four years the territory of Kansas had been beset by violent confrontations between proslavery and abolitionist settlers who sought to influence the territory's decision on slavery. The Supreme Court had ruled in 1857 in the Dred Scott case that Congress lacked the authority to exclude slavery from the territories—a decision that many people argued made slavery legal in all territories regardless of the desires of their inhabitants. Eventually, the controversy over slavery and popular sovereignty helped give birth to a new political party. The Republican Party was formed to oppose the spread of slavery into the territories; it fielded as its candidate for Douglas's senatorial seat in 1858 a relatively unknown lawyer named Abraham Lincoln.

Lincoln and Douglas held a series of seven celebrated debates on the future of slavery and of America. The following viewpoint is from Douglas's opening speech at the last debate, which was held in Alton, Illinois, on October 15, 1858. In the speech Douglas reviews what he regards as the basic issues of the debate, and makes his case for popular sovereignty as the true democratic and constitutional alternative to civil war. Douglas won the senatorial race, but two years later was defeated by Lincoln in the 1860 election for president.

What does Douglas argue to be Lincoln's three main errors? Why, according to Douglas, are blacks

From *Political Debates Between Hon. Abraham Lincoln and Hon. Stephen A. Douglas, in the Celebrated Campaign of 1858*, published by Follett, Foster & Co., 1860, for the Ohio Republican State Central Committee.

not referred to in the Declaration of Independence's claim that "all men are created equal"? In 1860 Douglas was unable to garner Southern support in his campaign for the presidency; what clues do the excerpts here provide as to why Southerners would not support him?

It is now nearly four months since the canvass between Mr. Lincoln and myself commenced. On the sixteenth of June the Republican Convention assembled at Springfield and nominated Mr. Lincoln as their candidate for the United States Senate, and he, on that occasion, delivered a speech in which he laid down what he understood to be the Republican creed and the platform on which he proposed to stand during the contest.

The principal points in that speech of Mr. Lincoln's were: First, that this government could not endure permanently divided into free and slave states, as our fathers made it; that they must all become free or all become slave; all become one thing or all become the other, otherwise this Union could not continue to exist. I give you his opinions almost in the identical language he used. His second proposition was a crusade against the Supreme Court of the United States because of the Dred Scott decision; urging as an especial reason for his opposition to that decision that it deprived the Negroes of the rights and benefits of that clause in the Constitution of the United States which guarantees to the citizens of each state all the rights, privileges, and immunities of the citizens of the several states.

> *"This Union was established on the right of each state to do as it pleased on the question of slavery and every other question."*

On the tenth of July I returned home and delivered a speech to the people of Chicago. . . . In that speech I joined issue with Mr. Lincoln on the points which he had presented. Thus there was an issue clear and distinct made up between us on these two propositions laid down in the speech of Mr. Lincoln at Springfield and controverted by me in my reply to him at Chicago.

On the next day, the eleventh of July, Mr. Lincoln replied to me at Chicago, explaining at some length, and reaffirming the positions which he had taken in his Springfield speech. In that Chicago speech he even went further than he had before and uttered sentiments in regard to the Negro being on an equality with the white man. . . . He insisted, in that speech, that the Declaration of Independence included the Negro in the clause, asserting that all men were created equal, and went so far as to say that if one man was allowed to take the position that it did not include the Negro, others might take the position that it did not include other men. He said that all these distinctions between this man and that man, this race and the other race, must be discarded, and we must all stand by the Declaration of Independence, declaring that all men were created equal.

Lincoln's Three Errors

The issue thus being made up between Mr. Lincoln and myself on three points, we went before the people of the state. . . . In my speeches I confined myself closely to those three positions which he had taken, controverting his proposition that this Union could not exist as our fathers made it, divided into free and slave states, controverting his proposition of a crusade against the Supreme Court because of the Dred Scott decision, and controverting his proposition that the Declaration of Independence included and meant the Negroes as well as the white men when it declared all men to be created equal. . . . I took up Mr. Lincoln's three propositions in my several speeches, analyzed them, and pointed out what I believed to be the radical errors contained in them. First, in regard to his doctrine that this government was in violation of the law of God, which says that a house divided against itself cannot stand, I repudiated it as a slander upon the immortal framers of our Constitution. I then said, I have often repeated, and now again assert, that in my opinion our government can endure forever, divided into free and slave states as our fathers made it—each state having the right to prohibit, abolish, or sustain slavery, just as it pleases. This government was made upon the great basis of the sovereignty of the states, the right of each state to regulate its own domestic institutions to suit itself, and that right was conferred with the understanding and expectation that, inasmuch as each locality had separate interests, each locality must have different and distinct local and domestic institutions, corresponding to its wants and interests. Our fathers knew when they made the government that the laws and institutions which were well adapted to the Green Mountains of Vermont were unsuited to the rice plantations of South Carolina. They knew then, as well as we know now, that the laws and institutions which would be well adapted to the beautiful prairies of Illinois would not be suited to the mining regions of California. They knew that in a republic as broad as this, having such a variety of soil, climate, and interest, there must necessarily be a corresponding variety of local laws—the policy and institutions of each state adapted to its condition and wants. For this reason this Union was established on the right of each state to do as it pleased on the question of slavery and every other question; and the various states were not allowed to complain of, much less interfere with, the policy of their neighbors. . . .

You see that if this abolition doctrine of Mr. Lincoln had prevailed when the government was made, it would have established slavery as a permanent institution, in all the states, whether they wanted it or not, and the question for us to determine in Illinois now as one of the free states is whether or not we are willing, having become the majority section, to enforce a doctrine on the minority which we would have resisted with our heart's blood had it been attempted on us when we were in a minority. How has the South lost her power as the majority section in this Union, and how have the free states gained it, except under the operation of that principle which declares the right of the people of each state and each territory to form and regulate their domestic institutions in their own way. It was under that principle that slavery was abolished in New Hampshire, Rhode Island, Connecticut, New York, New Jersey, and Pennsylvania; it was under that principle that one-half of the slaveholding states became free; it was under that principle that the number of free states increased until, from being one out of twelve states, we have grown to be the majority of states of the whole Union, with the power to control the House of Representatives and Senate, and the power, consequently, to elect a President by northern votes without the aid of a southern state. Having obtained this power under the operation of that great principle, are you now prepared to abandon the principle and declare that merely because we have the power you will wage a war against the southern states and their institutions until you force them to abolish slavery everywhere . . . ?

A Time for Compromise

My friends, there never was a time when it was as important for the Democratic party, for all national men, to rally and stand together as it is today. We find all sectional men giving up past differences and continuing the one question of slavery, and, when we find sectional men thus uniting, we should unite to resist them and their treasonable designs. Such was the case in 1850, when [Henry] Clay left the quiet and peace of his home and again entered upon public life to quell agitation and restore peace to a distracted Union. Then we Democrats, with [Lewis] Cass at our head, welcomed Henry Clay, whom the whole nation regarded as having been preserved by God for the times. He became our leader in that great fight [to pass the Compromise of 1850], and we rallied around him the same as the Whigs rallied around "Old Hickory" [Democratic president Andrew Jackson] in 1832 to put down nullification [an attempt by South Carolina to declare federal tariff laws "null and void" within its borders]. Thus you see that whilst Whigs and Democrats fought fearlessly in old times about banks, the tariff, distribution, the specie circular, and the sub-treasury, all united as a band of brothers when the peace, harmony, or integrity of the Union was imperiled. It was so in 1850, when abolitionism had even so far divided this country, North and South, as to endanger the peace of the Union; Whigs and Democrats united in establishing the compromise measures of that year and restoring tranquillity and good feeling. These measures passed on the joint action of the two parties. They rested on the great principle that the people of each state and each territory should be left perfectly free to form and regulate their domestic institutions to suit themselves. You Whigs and we Democrats justified them in that principle. In 1854, when it became necessary to organize the territories of Kansas and Nebraska, I brought forward the bill on the same principle. In the Kansas-Nebraska Bill you find it declared to be the true intent and meaning of the act not to legislate slavery into any state or territory, nor to exclude it therefrom, but to leave the people thereof perfectly free to form and regulate their domestic institutions in their own way. I stand on that same platform in 1858 that I did in 1850, 1854, and 1856. . . .

I say to you that there is but one hope, one safety, for this country, and that is to stand immovably by that principle which declares the right of each state and each territory to decide these questions for themselves. This government was founded on that principle and must be administered in the same sense in which it was founded.

Declaration of Independence for Whites

But the Abolition party really think that under the Declaration of Independence the Negro is equal to the white man and that Negro equality is an inalienable right conferred by the Almighty, and hence that all human laws in violation of it are null and void. With such men it is no use for me to argue. I hold that the signers of the Declaration of Independence had no reference to Negroes at all when they declared all men to be created equal. They did not mean Negro, nor the savage Indians, nor the Fiji Islanders, nor any other barbarous race. They were speaking of white men. They alluded to men of European birth and European descent—to white men and to none others—when they declared that doctrine. I hold that this government was established on the white basis. It was established by white men

for the benefit of white men and their posterity forever and should be administered by white men and none others. But it does not follow, by any means, that merely because the Negro is not a citizen, and merely because he is not our equal, that, therefore, he should be a slave. On the contrary, it does follow that we ought to extend to the Negro race, and to all other dependent races all the rights, all the privileges, and all the immunities which they can exercise consistently with the safety of society. Humanity requires that we should give them all these privileges; Christianity commands that we should extend those privileges to them. The question then arises: What are those privileges and what is the nature and extent of them. My answer is that that is a question which each state must answer for itself. We in Illinois have decided it for ourselves. We tried slavery, kept it up for twelve years, and, finding that it was not profitable, we abolished it for that reason, and became a free state. We adopted in its stead the policy that a Negro in this state shall not be a slave and shall not be a citizen. We have a right to adopt that policy. For my part I think it is a wise and sound policy for us. You in Missouri must judge for yourselves whether it is a wise policy for you. If you choose to follow our example, very good; if you reject it, still well, it is your business, not ours. So with Kentucky. Let Kentucky adopt a policy to suit herself. If we do not like it, we will keep away from it, and if she does not like ours let her stay at home, mind her own business and let us alone. If the people of all the states will act on that great principle, and each state mind its own business, attend to its own affairs, take care of its own Negroes, and not meddle with its neighbors, then there will be peace between the North and the South, the East and the West, throughout the whole Union. Why can we not thus have peace? Why should we thus allow a sectional party to agitate this country, to array the North against the South, and convert us into enemies instead of friends, merely that a few ambitious men may ride into power on a sectional hobby?

VIEWPOINT 33B

Slavery Should Not Be Allowed to Spread (1858)
Abraham Lincoln (1809–1865)

Abraham Lincoln's election to the presidency in 1860 was due in part to the national prominence he gained while campaigning unsuccessfully for the

From *Political Debates Between Hon. Abraham Lincoln and Hon. Stephen A. Douglas, in the Celebrated Campaign of 1858*, published by Follett, Foster & Co., 1860, for the Ohio Republican State Central Committee.

U.S. Senate in 1858. During the 1858 senatorial contest, Lincoln and his opponent, incumbent Illinois senator Stephen A. Douglas, held a series of seven public debates in which the main issues discussed were slavery and the future of the American nation.

Lincoln, a self-taught lawyer who had served a term in Congress and had established a successful and busy legal practice, opened his senatorial campaign with a famous speech in Springfield, Illinois. Quoting a passage from the Bible, Lincoln stated:

> "A house divided against itself cannot stand." I believe this government cannot endure, permanently, half slave and half free. . . . It will become all one thing, or all the other.

This statement and others by him were attacked by Douglas, who accused Lincoln of being a radical, a "Black Republican" who wished to abolish slavery in the Southern states and promote racial equality and whose policies would lead the nation into war. In his debates with Douglas, Lincoln denied all of these charges. The following viewpoint is taken from Lincoln's last speech in the debates, given in Alton, Illinois, on October 15, 1858.

On what issues does Lincoln express agreement with his opponent, Stephen A. Douglas? What does he say is their fundamental difference? What position does Lincoln take on the abolition of slavery?

———

It is not true that our fathers, as Judge Douglas assumes, made this government part slave and part free. Understand the sense in which he puts it. He assumes that slavery is a rightful thing within itself—was introduced by the framers of the Constitution. The exact truth is that they found the institution existing among us, and they left it as they found it. But, in making the government, they left this institution with many clear marks of disapprobation upon it. They found slavery among them, and they left it among them because of the difficulty—the absolute impossibility—of its immediate removal. And when Judge Douglas asks me why we cannot let it remain part slave and part free, as the fathers of the government made it, he asks a question based upon an assumption which is itself a falsehood; and I turn upon him and ask him the question, when the policy that the fathers of the government had adopted in relation to this element among us was the best policy in the world—the only wise policy—the only policy that we can ever safely continue upon—that will ever give us peace, unless this dangerous element masters us all and becomes a national institution—*I turn upon him and ask him why he could not leave it alone.* I turn and ask him why he was driven to the necessity of introducing a *new policy* in regard to it. . . . I ask, too, of Judge Douglas and his friends why

we shall not again place this institution upon the basis on which the fathers left it. I ask you, when he infers that I am in favor of setting the free and slave states at war, when the institution was placed in that attitude by those who made the Constitution, *did they make any war?* If we had no war out of it, when thus placed, wherein is the ground of belief that we shall have war out of it if we return to that policy? Have we had any peace upon this matter springing from any other basis? I maintain that we have not. I have proposed nothing more than a return to the policy of the fathers.

I confess, when I propose a certain measure of policy, it is not enough for me that I do not intend anything evil in the result, but it is incumbent on me to show that it has not a *tendency* to that result. I have met Judge Douglas in that point of view. I have not only made the declaration that I do not *mean* to produce a conflict between the states, but I have tried to show by fair reasoning, and I think I have shown to the minds of fair men, that I propose nothing but what has a most peaceful tendency. The quotation that I happened to make in that Springfield speech, that "a house divided against itself cannot stand," and which has proved so offensive to the Judge, was part and parcel of the same thing. He tries to show that variety in the domestic institutions of the different states is necessary and indispensable. I do not dispute it. I have no controversy with Judge Douglas about that. . . .

States and Territories

The Judge alludes very often in the course of his remarks to the exclusive right which the states have to decide the whole thing [slavery] for themselves. I agree with him very readily that the different states have that right. He is but fighting a man of straw when he assumes that I am contending against the right of the states to do as they please about it. Our controversy with him is in regard to the new territories. We agree that when the states come in as states they have the right and the power to do as they please. We have no power as citizens of the free states, or in our federal capacity as members of the federal Union through the general government, to disturb slavery in the states where it exists.

We profess constantly that we have no more inclination than belief in the power of the government to disturb it; yet we are driven constantly to defend ourselves from the assumption that we are warring upon the rights of the *states*. What I insist upon is that the new territories shall be kept free from it while in the territorial condition. Judge Douglas assumes that we have no interest in them, that we have no right whatever to interfere. I think we have some interest. I think that as white men we have.

Do we not wish for an outlet for our surplus population, if I may so express myself? Do we not feel an interest in getting to that outlet with such institutions as we would like to have prevail there? If you go to the territory opposed to slavery, and another man comes upon the same ground with his slaves, upon the assumption that the things are equal, it turns out that he has the equal right all his way, and you have no part of it your way. If he goes in and makes it a slave territory and, by consequence, a slave state, is it not time that those who desire to have it a free state were on equal ground?

———— • ————

"[Slavery] should, as far as may be, be treated *as a wrong, and one of the methods of treating it as a wrong is to* make provision that it shall grow no larger."

———— • ————

Let me suggest it in a different way. How many Democrats are there about here who have left slave states and come into the free state of Illinois to get rid of the institution of slavery? I reckon there are a thousand and one. I will ask you, if the policy you are now advocating had prevailed when this country was in a territorial condition, where would you have gone to get rid of it? Where would you have found your free state or territory to go to? And when, hereafter, for any cause, the people in this place shall desire to find new homes, if they wish to be rid of the institution, where will they find the place to go to? . . .

Now irrespective of the moral aspect of this question as to whether there is a right or wrong in enslaving a Negro, I am still in favor of our new territories being in such a condition that white men may find a home—may find some spot where they can better their condition—where they can settle upon new soil and better their condition in life. I am in favor of this not merely (I must say it here as I have elsewhere) for our own people who are born amongst us, but as an outlet for *free white people everywhere,* the world over—in which Hans and Baptiste and Patrick, and all other men from all the world, may find new homes and better their conditions in life.

The Real Issue

I have stated upon former occasions, and I may as well state again, what I understand to be the real issue in this controversy between Judge Douglas and myself. On the point of my wanting to make war between the free and the slave states, there has been no issue between us. So, too, when he assumes that I am in favor of introducing a perfect social and political equality between the white and black races. These are false issues, upon which Judge Douglas has tried to force the controversy. There is no foundation in truth for the charge that I maintain either of these propositions. The real issue in this controversy—the one pressing upon every mind—is the sentiment on the part of one class that looks upon the institution of slavery *as a wrong* and of another class that *does not* look upon it as a wrong. The sentiment that contemplates the institution of slavery in this country as a wrong is the sentiment of the Republican party. It is the sentiment around which all their actions—all their arguments circle—from which all their propositions radiate. They look upon it as being a moral, social, and political wrong; and, while they contemplate it as such, they nevertheless have due regard for its actual existence among us, and the difficulties of getting rid of it in any satisfactory way and to all the constitutional obligations thrown about it. Yet having a due regard for these, they desire a policy in regard to it that looks to its not creating any more danger. They insist that it should, as far as may be, *be treated* as a wrong, and one of the methods of treating it as a wrong is to *make provision that it shall grow no larger.* They also desire a policy that looks to a peaceful end of slavery at some time as being wrong. These are the views they entertain in regard to it as I understand them; and all their sentiments—all their arguments and propositions—are brought within this range. I have said, and I repeat it here, that if there be a man amongst us who does not think that the institution of slavery is wrong in any one of the aspects of which I have spoken, he is misplaced and ought not to be with us. And if there be a man amongst us who is so impatient of it as a wrong as to disregard its actual presence among us and the difficulty of getting rid of it suddenly in a satisfactory way, and to disregard the constitutional obligations thrown about it, that man is misplaced if he is on our platform. We disclaim sympathy with him in practical action. He is not placed properly with us.

On this subject of treating it as a wrong, and limiting its spread, let me say a word. Has anything ever threatened the existence of this Union save and except this very institution of slavery? What is it that we hold most dear amongst us? Our own liberty and prosperity. What has ever threatened our liberty and prosperity save and except this institution of slavery? If this is true, how do you propose to improve the condition of things by enlarging slavery—by spreading it out and making it bigger? You may have a wen or cancer upon your person and not be able to cut it out lest you bleed to death; but surely it is no way to cure it, to engraft it and spread it over your whole body. That is no proper way of treating what you regard a wrong. You see this peaceful way of dealing with it as a wrong—restricting the spread of it, and not allowing it to go into new countries where it has not already existed. That is the peaceful way, the old-fashioned way, the way in which the fathers themselves set us the example.

Is Slavery Wrong?

On the other hand, I have said there is a sentiment which treats it as *not* being wrong. That is the Democratic sentiment of this day. I do not mean to say that every man who stands within that range positively asserts that it is right. That class will include all who positively assert that it is right, and all who like Judge Douglas treat it as indifferent and do not say it is either right or wrong. These two classes of men fall within the general class of those who do not look upon it as a wrong. . . .

The Democratic policy in regard to that institution will not tolerate the merest breath, the slightest hint, of the least degree of wrong about it. Try it by some of Judge Douglas' arguments. He says he "don't care whether it is voted up or voted down" in the territories. I do not care myself in dealing with that expression, whether it is intended to be expressive of his individual sentiments on the subject or only of the national policy he desires to have established. It is alike valuable for my purpose. Any man can say that who does not see anything wrong in slavery, but no man can logically say it who does see a wrong in it; because no man can logically say he does not care whether a wrong is voted up or voted down. He may say he does not care whether an indifferent thing is voted up or down, but he must logically have a choice between a right thing and a wrong thing. He contends that whatever community wants slaves has a right to have them. So they have if it is not a wrong. But if it is a wrong, he cannot say people have a right to do wrong. He says that, upon the score of equality, slaves should be allowed to go in a new territory, like other property. This is strictly logical if there is no difference between it and other property. If it and other property are equal, his argument is entirely logical. But if you insist that one is wrong and the other right, there is no use to institute a comparison between right and wrong. You may turn over everything in the Democratic policy from beginning to end, whether in the shape it takes on the statute book, in the shape it takes in the Dred Scott decision, in the shape it takes in conversation, or the shape it takes in short maxim-like arguments—it everywhere carefully excludes the idea that there is anything wrong in it.

That is the real issue. That is the issue that will continue in this country when these poor tongues of Judge Douglas and myself shall be silent. It is the

eternal struggle between these two principles—right and wrong—throughout the world. They are the two principles that have stood face to face from the beginning of time and will ever continue to struggle. The one is the common right of humanity and the other the divine right of kings. It is the same principle in whatever shape it develops itself. It is the same spirit that says, "You work and toil and earn bread, and I'll eat it." No matter in what shape it comes, whether from the mouth of a king who seeks to bestride the people of his own nation and live by the fruit of their labor, or from one race of men as an apology for enslaving another race, it is the same tyrannical principle.

For Further Reading

Don E. Fehrenbacher, *Prelude to Greatness: Lincoln in the 1850s.* Stanford, CA: Stanford University Press, 1962.

Eric Foner, *Free Soil, Free Labor, Free Men: The Ideology of the Republican Party Before the Civil War.* New York: Oxford University Press, 1970.

Harold Holzer, ed., *The Lincoln-Douglas Debates.* New York: HarperCollins, 1993.

Harry V. Jaffa, *Crisis of the House Divided.* Chicago: University of Chicago Press, 1982.

Robert W. Johannsen, *Stephen A. Douglas.* New York: Oxford University Press, 1973.

VIEWPOINT 34A

Secession Is Justified (1860)

South Carolina Declaration

Many leaders of the Southern states threatened secession if Abraham Lincoln, the Republican presidential candidate in 1860, was elected president. South Carolina's state legislature was in session when news arrived of Lincoln's election, and legislators immediately called for a special secession convention. On December 20, 1860, by unanimous convention vote, the state became the first to secede from the United States. It presented its reasons for seceding in the form of a declaration, a document parallel in some respects to America's 1776 Declaration of Independence from Great Britain—which this declaration, reprinted here, mentions several times.

What legal arguments does the secession convention make concerning the United States? What grievances against the Northern states does South Carolina cite? What similarities do you find between this viewpoint and the views of John Calhoun as expressed in viewpoint 31A?

From *The Rebellion Record: A Diary of American Events, with Documents, Narratives, Illustrative Incidents, Poetry, etc., etc.*, vol. 1, edited by Frank Moore (New York: Putnam, 1861).

The people of the state of South Carolina, in convention assembled, on the 2nd day of April, A.D. 1852, declared that the frequent violations of the Constitution of the United States by the federal government, and its encroachments upon the reserved rights of the states, fully justified this state in their withdrawal from the federal Union; but in deference to the opinions and wishes of the other slaveholding states, she forbore at that time to exercise this right. Since that time, these encroachments have continued to increase, and further forbearance ceases to be a virtue.

And, now, the state of South Carolina, having resumed her separate and equal place among nations, deems it due to herself, to the remaining United States of America, and to the nations of the world, that she should declare the immediate causes which have led to this act.

The Right of Self-Government

In the year 1765, that portion of the British empire embracing Great Britain undertook to make laws for the government of that portion composed of the thirteen American colonies. A struggle for the right of self-government ensued, which resulted, on the 4th of July, 1776, in a Declaration, by the colonies, "that they are, and of right ought to be, FREE AND INDEPENDENT STATES; and that, as free and independent states, they have full power to levy war, conclude peace, contract alliances, establish commerce, and to do all other acts and things which independent states may of right do."

They further solemnly declared that whenever any "form of government becomes destructive of the ends for which it was established, it is the right of the people to alter or abolish it, and to institute a new government." Deeming the government of Great Britain to have become destructive of these ends, they declared that the colonies "are absolved from all allegiance to the British Crown, and that all political connection between them and the state of Great Britain is, and ought to be, totally dissolved."

In pursuance of this Declaration of Independence, each of the thirteen states proceeded to exercise its separate sovereignty; adopted for itself a constitution, and appointed officers for the administration of government in all its departments—Legislative, Executive, and Judicial. For purposes of defense, they united their arms and their counsels, and, in 1778, they entered into a league known as the Articles of Confederation, whereby they agreed to entrust the administration of their external relations to a common agent, known as the Congress of the United States, expressly declaring, in the 1st Article, "that each state retains its sovereignty, freedom, and independence, and every power, jurisdiction, and right which is not, by this Confederation, expressly delegated to the United States in Congress assembled."

Under this Confederation, the War of the Revolution was carried on; and on the 3rd of September, 1783, the contest ended, and a definite treaty was signed by Great Britain, in which she acknowledged the independence of the colonies in the following terms:

> Article I. His Britannic Majesty acknowledges the said United States, viz.: New Hampshire, Massachusetts Bay, Rhode Island and Providence Plantations, Connecticut, New York, New Jersey, Pennsylvania, Delaware, Maryland, Virginia, North Carolina, South Carolina, and Georgia, to be FREE, SOVEREIGN, AND INDEPENDENT STATES; that he treats with them as such; and, for himself, his heirs, and successors, relinquishes all claims to the government, propriety, and territorial rights of the same and every part thereof.

Thus were established the two great principles asserted by the colonies, namely, the right of a state to govern itself; and the right of a people to abolish a government when it becomes destructive of the ends for which it was instituted. And concurrent with the establishment of these principles was the fact that each colony became and was recognized by the mother country as a FREE, SOVEREIGN, AND INDEPENDENT STATE.

The Constitution

In 1787, deputies were appointed by the states to revise the Articles of Confederation; and on Sept. 17, 1787, these deputies recommended, for the adoption of the states, the Articles of Union, known as the Constitution of the United States.

The parties to whom this Constitution was submitted were the several sovereign states; they were to agree or disagree, and when nine of them agreed, the compact was to take effect among those concurring; and the general government, as the common agent, was then to be invested with their authority.

If only nine of the thirteen states had concurred, the other four would have remained as they then were—separate, sovereign states, independent of any of the provisions of the Constitution. In fact, two of the states did not accede to the Constitution until long after it had gone into operation among the other eleven; and during that interval, they each exercised the functions of an independent nation.

By this Constitution, certain duties were imposed upon the several states, and the exercise of certain of their powers was restrained, which necessarily impelled their continued existence as sovereign states. But, to remove all doubt, an amendment was added which declared that the powers not delegated to the United States by the Constitution, nor prohibited by it to the states, are reserved to the states respectively, or to the people. On the 23rd of May, 1788, South Carolina, by a convention of her people, passed an ordinance assenting to this Constitution, and afterward altered her own constitution to conform herself to the obligations she had undertaken.

Thus was established, by compact between the states, a government with defined objects and powers, limited to the express words of the grant. This limitation left the whole remaining mass of power subject to the clause reserving it to the states or the people, and rendered unnecessary any specification of reserved rights. We hold that the government thus established is subject to the two great principles asserted in the Declaration of Independence; and we hold further that the mode of its formation subjects it to a third fundamental principle, namely, the law of compact. We maintain that in every compact between two or more parties, the obligation is mutual; that the failure of one of the contracting parties to perform a material part of the agreement entirely releases the obligation of the other; and that, where no arbiter is provided, each party is remitted to his own judgment to determine the fact of failure, with all its consequences.

In the present case, the fact is established with certainty. We assert that fourteen of the states have deliberately refused for years past to fulfill their constitutional obligations, and we refer to their own statutes for the proof.

The Fugitive Slave Provision

The Constitution of the United States, in its 4th Article, provides as follows: "No person held to service or labor in one state, under the laws thereof, escaping into another shall, in consequence of any law or regulation therein, be discharged from such service or labor, but shall be delivered up, on claim of the party to whom such service or labor may be due."

This stipulation was so material to the compact that without it that compact would not have been made. The greater number of the contracting parties held slaves, and they had previously evinced their estimate of the value of such a stipulation by making it a condition in the ordinance for the government of the territory ceded by Virginia, which obligations, and the laws of the general government, have ceased to effect the objects of the Constitution. The states of Maine, New Hampshire, Vermont, Massachusetts, Connecticut, Rhode Island, New York, Pennsylvania, Illinois, Indiana, Michigan, Wisconsin, and Iowa have enacted laws which either nullify the acts of Congress or render useless any attempt to execute them. In many of these states the fugitive is discharged from the service of labor claimed, and in none of them has the state government complied with the stipulation made in the Constitution.

The state of New Jersey, at an early day, passed a law in conformity with her constitutional obligation; but the current of antislavery feeling has led her more recently to enact laws which render inoperative the remedies provided by her own laws and by the laws of Congress. In the state of New York even the right of transit for a slave has been denied by her tribunals; and the states of Ohio and Iowa have refused to surrender to justice fugitives charged with murder and with inciting servile insurrection in the state of Virginia. Thus the constitutional compact has been deliberately broken and disregarded by the nonslaveholding states; and the consequence follows that South Carolina is released from her obligation.

The ends for which this Constitution was framed are declared by itself to be "to form a more perfect union, to establish justice, insure domestic tranquility, provide for the common defense, promote the general welfare, and secure the blessings of liberty to ourselves and our posterity." These ends it endeavored to accomplish by a federal government in which each state was recognized as an equal and had separate control over its own institutions. The right of property in slaves was recognized by giving to free persons distinct political rights; by giving them the right to represent, and burdening them with direct taxes for, three-fifths of their slaves; by authorizing the importation of slaves for twenty years; and by stipulating for the rendition of fugitives from labor.

Antislavery Agitation

We affirm that these ends for which this government was instituted have been defeated, and the government itself has been destructive of them by the action of the nonslaveholding states. Those states have assumed the right of deciding upon the propriety of our domestic institutions; and have denied the rights of property established in fifteen of the states and recognized by the Constitution. They have denounced as sinful the institution of slavery; they have permitted the open establishment among them of societies, whose avowed object is to disturb the peace of and eloign [take away] the property of the citizens of other states. They have encouraged and assisted thousands of our slaves to leave their homes; and, those who remain, have been incited by emissaries, books, and pictures to servile insurrection.

For twenty-five years this agitation has been steadily increasing, until it has now secured to its aid the power of the common government. Observing the *forms* of the Constitution, a sectional party has found, within that article establishing the Executive

Department, the means of subverting the Constitution itself. A geographical line has been drawn across the Union, and all the states north of that line have united in the election of a man to the high office of President of the United States whose opinions and purposes are hostile to slavery. He is to be entrusted with the administration of the common government, because he has declared that "Government cannot endure permanently half slave, half free," and that the public mind must rest in the belief that slavery is in the course of ultimate extinction.

———— • ————

"The constitutional compact has been deliberately broken and disregarded by the nonslaveholding states; and . . . South Carolina is released from her obligation."

———— • ————

This sectional combination for the subversion of the Constitution has been aided, in some of the states, by elevating to citizenship persons who, by the supreme law of the land, are incapable of becoming citizens; and their votes have been used to inaugurate a new policy, hostile to the South and destructive of its peace and safety.

On the 4th of March next this party will take possession of the government. It has announced that the South shall be excluded from the common territory, that the judicial tribunal shall be made sectional, and that a war must be waged against slavery until it shall cease throughout the United States.

The guarantees of the Constitution will then no longer exist; the equal rights of the states will be lost. The slaveholding states will no longer have the power of self-government or self-protection, and the federal government will have become their enemy.

Sectional interest and animosity will deepen the irritation; and all hope of remedy is rendered vain by the fact that the public opinion at the North has invested a great political error with the sanctions of a more erroneous religious belief.

We, therefore, the people of South Carolina, by our delegates in convention assembled, appealing to the Supreme Judge of the world for the rectitude of our intentions, have solemnly declared that the Union heretofore existing between this state and the other states of North America is dissolved; and that the state of South Carolina has resumed her position among the nations of the world, as [a] separate and independent state, with full power to levy war, conclude peace, contract alliances, establish commerce, and to do all other acts and things which independent states may of right do.

VIEWPOINT 34B

Secession Is Not Justified (1861)

Abraham Lincoln (1809–1865)

Abraham Lincoln was elected president of the United States on November 6, 1860. In the four months between the election and Lincoln's inauguration, momentous events rocked the nation. South Carolina seceded from the Union on December 20, 1860, and was shortly joined by Mississippi, Florida, Alabama, Georgia, Louisiana, and Texas. On February 4, 1861, representatives from these states (except Texas) met in Montgomery, Alabama, to form a new government—the Confederate States of America. They wrote a new constitution and elected Jefferson Davis as president. Southern politicians resigned from Congress, and Southern states seized federal property. Lame-duck U.S. president James Buchanan hesitated to act, arguing that the Constitution gave the states no legal right to secede, but that Congress and the president had no power under the Constitution to prevent them. States in the upper South—Virginia, North Carolina, and Maryland—as well as states farther west, including Kentucky, Missouri, and Tennessee, were deeply divided over whether to join the Confederacy. Various settlement proposals were discussed in Congress and elsewhere. Most foundered on the issue of federal protection of slavery in the western territories, something both sides refused to compromise on.

It was against this backdrop that Lincoln was inaugurated on March 4, 1861; took the presidential oath "to preserve, protect, and defend the Constitution of the United States"; and gave the address reprinted here before a relatively small crowd of 10,000 in Washington, D.C. In his address the new president seeks to placate the South by pledging not to interfere with slavery in the Southern states, while promising to enforce fugitive slave laws in the Northern states. But he also refutes the legal arguments found in the secession declarations of South Carolina and other states, arguing that "the union of these states is perpetual" and that ordinances of secession by individual states are meaningless. Six weeks later, Confederate guns fired on Fort Sumter marking the advent of the Civil War.

What is the basic difference between Lincoln's views on the founding of the United States and the views expressed by South Carolina in the opposing viewpoint? What does Lincoln take to be the only substantial issue dividing the North and the South?

From Abraham Lincoln's first inaugural address, March 4, 1861, as reprinted in *A Compilation of the Messages and Papers of the Presidents, 1798–1897,* edited by James D. Richardson (New York, 1896–1899).

What passages of Lincoln's speech are conciliatory to the South? Which are not?

———————————————

Fellow Citizens of the United States:
In compliance with a custom as old as the government itself, I appear before you to address you briefly and to take, in your presence, the oath prescribed by the Constitution of the United States to be taken by the President "before he enters on the execution of his office."

I do not consider it necessary, at present, for me to discuss those matters of administration about which there is no special anxiety or excitement. Apprehension seems to exist among the people of the Southern states that, by the accession of a Republican administration, their property and their peace and personal security are to be endangered. There has never been any reasonable cause for such apprehension. Indeed, the most ample evidence to the contrary has all the while existed and been open to their inspection. It is found in nearly all the published speeches of him who now addresses you.

No Intent to Abolish Slavery

I do but quote from one of those speeches when I declare that "I have no purpose, directly or indirectly, to interfere with the institution of slavery in the states where it exists. I believe I have no lawful right to do so, and I have no inclination to do so." Those who nominated and elected me did so with full knowledge that I had made this and many similar declarations, and had never recanted them. And, more than this, they placed in the platform, for my acceptance, and as a law to themselves and to me, the clear and emphatic resolution which I now read:

Resolved, that the maintenance inviolate of the rights of the states, and especially the right of each state, to order and control its own domestic institutions according to its own judgment exclusively is essential to that balance of power on which the perfection and endurance of our political fabric depend; and we denounce the lawless invasion by armed force of the soil of any state or territory, no matter under what pretext, as among the gravest of crimes.

I now reiterate these sentiments; and in doing so, I only press upon the public attention the most conclusive evidence, of which the case is susceptible, that the property, peace, and security of no section are to be in any way endangered by the now incoming administration. I add, too, that all the protection which, consistently with the Constitution and the laws, can be given will be cheerfully given to all the states when lawfully demanded, for whatever cause—as cheerfully to one section as to another.

There is much controversy about the delivering up of fugitives from service or labor. The clause I now read is as plainly written in the Constitution as any other of its provisions:

No person held to service or labor in one state, under the laws thereof, escaping into another, shall, in consequence of any law or regulation therein, be discharged from such service or labor, but shall be delivered up on claim of the party to whom such service or labor may be due.

It is scarcely questioned that this provision was intended by those who made it for the reclaiming of what we call fugitive slaves; and the intention of the lawgiver is the law.

All members of Congress swear their support to the whole Constitution—to this provision as much as to any other. To the proposition, then, that slaves whose cases come within the terms of this clause "shall be delivered up," their oaths are unanimous. Now, if they would make the effort in good temper, could they not, with nearly equal unanimity, frame and pass a law by means of which to keep good that unanimous oath?

There is some difference of opinion whether this clause should be enforced by national or by the state authority; but surely that difference is not a very material one. If the slave is to be surrendered, it can be of but little consequence to him or to others by which authority it is done. And should anyone, in any case, be content that his oath shall go unkept on a merely unsubstantial controversy as to how it shall be kept?

Again, in any law upon this subject, ought not all the safeguards of liberty known in civilized and humane jurisprudence to be introduced, so that a freeman be not, in any case, surrendered as a slave? And might it not be well, at the same time, to provide by law for the enforcement of that clause in the Constitution which guarantees that "the citizens of each state shall be entitled to all privileges and immunities of citizens in the several states"?

———————— • ————————

"No state, upon its own mere motion, can lawfully get out of the Union."

———————— • ————————

I take the official oath today with no mental reservations and with no purpose to construe the Constitution or laws by any hypercritical rules. And while I do not choose now to specify particular acts of Congress as proper to be enforced, I do suggest that it will be much safer for all, both in official and private stations, to conform to and abide by all those acts which stand unrepealed than to violate any of them, trusting to find impunity in having them held to be unconstitutional.

It is seventy-two years since the first inauguration of a President under our national Constitution. During that period fifteen different and greatly distinguished citizens have, in succession, administered the executive branch of the government. They have conducted it through many perils, and generally with great success. Yet, with all this scope of precedent, I now enter upon the same task for the brief constitutional term of four years under great and peculiar difficulties.

A disruption of the federal Union, heretofore only menaced, is now formidably attempted.

The Union Is Perpetual

I hold that, in contemplation of universal law and of the Constitution, the Union of these states is perpetual. Perpetuity is implied, if not expressed, in the fundamental law of all national governments. It is safe to assert that no government proper ever had a provision in its organic law for its own termination. Continue to execute all the express provisions of our national Constitution, and the Union will endure forever—it being impossible to destroy it except by some action not provided for in the instrument itself.

Again, if the United States be not a government proper, but an association of states in the nature of contract merely, can it, as a contract, be peaceably unmade by less than all the parties who made it? One party to a contract may violate it—break it, so to speak—but does it not require all to lawfully rescind it? Descending from these general principles, we find the proposition that in legal contemplation, the Union is perpetual, confirmed by the history of the Union itself.

The Union is much older than the Constitution. It was formed, in fact, by the Articles of Association in 1774. It was matured and continued by the Declaration of Independence in 1776. It was further matured, and the faith of all the then thirteen states expressedly plighted and engaged, that it should be perpetual by the Articles of Confederation of 1778. And finally, in 1787, one of the declared objects for ordaining and establishing the Constitution, was *"to form a more perfect Union."*

But if destruction of the Union by one or by a part only of the states be lawfully possible, the Union is *less* perfect than before the Constitution, having lost the vital element of perpetuity.

It follows from these views that no state, upon its own mere motion, can lawfully get out of the Union—that *resolves* and *ordinances* to that effect are legally void; and that acts of violence within any state or states against the authority of the United States are insurrectionary or revolutionary, according to circumstances.

I therefore consider that, in view of the Constitution and the laws, the Union is unbroken; and to the extent of my ability, I shall take care, as the Constitution itself expressly enjoins upon me, that the laws of the Union be faithfully executed in all the states. Doing this I deem to be only a simple duty on my part; and I shall perform it, so far as practicable, unless my rightful masters, the American people, shall withhold the requisite means or in some authoritative manner direct the contrary.

No Need for Violence

I trust this will not be regarded as a menace but only as the declared purpose of the Union that it *will* constitutionally defend and maintain itself. In doing this, there needs to be no bloodshed or violence; and there shall be none unless it be forced upon the national authority.

The power confided to me will be used to hold, occupy, and possess the property and places belonging to the government, and to collect the duties and imposts; but beyond what may be necessary for these objects, there will be no invasion—no using of force against or among the people anywhere.

Where hostility to the United States, in any interior locality, shall be so great and universal as to prevent competent resident citizens from holding the federal offices, there will be no attempt to force obnoxious strangers among the people for that object. While the strict legal right may exist in the government to enforce the exercise of these offices, the attempt to do so would be so irritating, and so nearly impracticable withal, that I deem it best to forego, for the time, the uses of such offices.

The mails, unless repelled, will continue to be furnished in all parts of the Union.

So far as possible, the people everywhere shall have that sense of perfect security which is most favorable to calm thought and reflection.

The course here indicated will be followed unless current events and experience shall show a modification or change to be proper; and in every case and exigency, my best discretion will be exercised, according to circumstances actually existing, and with a view and a hope of a peaceful solution of the national troubles, and the restoration of fraternal sympathies and affections.

That there are persons in one section or another who seek to destroy the Union at all events and are glad of any pretext to do it, I will neither affirm nor deny; but if there be such, I need address no word to them. To those, however, who really love the Union, may I not speak?

Before entering upon so grave a matter as the destruction of our national fabric, with all its benefits, its memories, and its hopes, would it not be wise to ascertain precisely why we do it? Will you hazard so desperate a step while there is any possibility that any portion of the ills you fly from have no real existence? Will you, while the certain ills you fly to are greater than all the real ones you fly from—will you risk the commission of so fearful a mistake?

All profess to be content in the Union if all constitutional rights can be maintained. Is it true, then, that any right plainly written in the Constitution has been denied? I think not. Happily, the human mind is so constituted that no party can reach to the audacity of doing this. Think, if you can, of a single instance in which a plainly written provision of the Constitution has ever been denied. If, by the mere force of numbers, a majority should deprive a minority of any clearly written constitutional right, it might, in a moral point of view, justify revolution—certainly would, if such right were a vital one. But such is not our case.

All the vital rights of minorities and of individuals are so plainly assured to them by affirmations and negations, guarantees and prohibitions, in the Constitution that controversies never arise concerning them. But no organic law can ever be framed with a provision specifically applicable to every question which may occur in practical administration. No foresight can anticipate nor any document of reasonable length contain express provisions for all possible questions. Shall fugitives from labor be surrendered by national or by state authority? The Constitution does not expressly say. *May* Congress prohibit slavery in the territories? The Constitution does not expressly say. *Must* Congress protect slavery in the territories? The Constitution does not expressly say.

Secession Is Anarchy

From questions of this class spring all our constitutional controversies, and we divide upon them into majorities and minorities. If the minority will not acquiesce, the majority must, or the government must cease. There is no other alternative; for continuing the government is acquiescence on one side or the other. If a minority, in such case, will secede rather than acquiesce, they make a precedent which in turn will divide and ruin them; for a minority of their own will secede from them whenever a majority refuses to be controlled by such minority.

For instance, why may not any portion of a new confederacy, a year or two hence, arbitrarily secede again, precisely as portions of the present Union now claim to secede from it? All who cherish disunion sentiments are now being educated to the exact temper of doing this. Is there such perfect identity of interests among the states to compose a new Union as to produce harmony only and prevent renewed

secession?

Plainly, the central idea of secession is the essence of anarchy. A majority, held in restraint by constitutional checks and limitations, and always changing easily with deliberate changes of popular opinions and sentiments, is the only true sovereign of a free people. Whoever rejects it does of necessity fly to anarchy or to despotism. Unanimity is impossible. The rule of a minority, as a permanent arrangement, is wholly inadmissible; so that, rejecting the majority principle, anarchy or despotism in some form is all that is left.

The Supreme Court

I do not forget the position assumed by some, that constitutional questions are to be decided by the Supreme Court; nor do I deny that such decisions must be binding in any case upon the parties to a suit as to the object of that suit, while they are also entitled to very high respect and consideration, in all parallel cases, by all other departments of the government. And while it is obviously possible that such decision may be erroneous in any given case, still the evil effect following it, being limited to that particular case, with the chance that it may be overruled and never become a precedent for other cases, can better be borne than could the evils of a different practice.

At the same time, the candid citizen must confess that if the policy of the government, upon vital questions affecting the whole people, is to be irrevocably fixed by decisions of the Supreme Court, the instant they are made, in ordinary litigation between parties in personal actions, the people will have ceased to be their own rulers, having, to that extent, practically resigned their government into the hands of that eminent tribunal.

Nor is there, in this view, any assault upon the Court or the judges. It is a duty from which they may not shrink to decide cases properly brought before them; and it is no fault of theirs if others seek to turn their decisions to political purposes.

One section of our country believes slavery is *right* and ought to be extended, while the other believes it is *wrong* and ought not to be extended. This is the only substantial dispute. The fugitive slave clause of the Constitution and the law for the suppression of the foreign slave trade are each as well enforced, perhaps, as any law can ever be in a community where the moral sense of the people imperfectly supports the law itself. The great body of the people abide by the dry legal obligation in both cases, and a few break over in each. This, I think, cannot be perfectly cured; and it would be worse in both cases *after* the separation of the sections than before. The foreign slave trade, now imperfectly suppressed, would be ultimately revived without restriction in one section; while fugitive slaves, now only partially surrendered, would not be surrendered at all by the other.

We Cannot Separate

Physically speaking, we cannot separate. We cannot remove our respective sections from each other, nor build an impassable wall between them. A husband and wife may be divorced, and go out of the presence and beyond the reach of each other, but the different parts of our country cannot do this. They cannot but remain face to face; and intercourse, either amicable or hostile, must continue between them. Is it possible, then, to make that intercourse more advantageous or more satisfactory *after* separation than *before?* Can aliens make treaties easier than friends can make laws? Can treaties be more faithfully enforced between aliens than laws can among friends? Suppose you go to war, you cannot fight always; and when, after much loss on both sides and no gain on either, you cease fighting, the identical old questions as to terms of intercourse are again upon you.

This country, with its institutions, belongs to the people who inhabit it. Whenever they shall grow weary of the existing government, they can exercise their *constitutional* right of amending it or their *revolutionary* right to dismember or overthrow it. I cannot be ignorant of the fact that many worthy and patriotic citizens are desirous of having the national Constitution amended. While I make no recommendation of amendments, I fully recognize the rightful authority of the people over the whole subject, to be exercised in either of the modes prescribed in the instrument itself; and I should, under existing circumstances, favor rather than oppose a fair opportunity being afforded the people to act upon it.

I will venture to add that, to me, the convention mode seems preferable, in that it allows amendments to originate with the people themselves, instead of only permitting them to take or reject propositions originated by others, not especially chosen for the purpose, and which might not be precisely such as they would wish to either accept or refuse. I understand a proposed amendment to the Constitution—which amendment, however, I have not seen—has passed Congress, to the effect that the federal government shall never interfere with the domestic institutions of the states, including that of persons held to service. To avoid misconstruction of what I have said, I depart from my purpose not to speak of particular amendments so far as to say that, holding such a provision to now be implied constitutional law, I have no objection to its being made express and irrevocable.

The chief magistrate derives all his authority from the people, and they have conferred none upon him to fix terms for their separation of the states. The people themselves can do this also if they choose; but the executive, as such, has nothing to do with it. His duty is to administer the present government, as it came to his hands, and to transmit it, unimpaired by him, to his successor. Why should there not be a patient confidence in the ultimate justice of the people? Is there any better or equal hope in the world? In our present differences, is either party without faith of being in the right?

If the Almighty Ruler of nations, with His eternal truth and justice, be on your side of the North, or on yours of the South, that truth and that justice will surely prevail, by the judgment of this great tribunal, the American people. By the frame of the government under which we live, this same people have wisely given their public servants but little power for mischief; and have, with equal wisdom, provided for the return of that little to their own hands at very short intervals. While the people retain their virtue and vigilance, no administration, by any extreme of wickedness or folly, can very seriously injure the government in the short space of four years.

My countrymen, one and all, think calmly and *well* upon this whole subject. Nothing valuable can be lost by taking time. If there be an object to *hurry* any of you, in hot haste, to a step which you would never take *deliberately*, that object will be frustrated by taking time; but no good object can be frustrated by it.

Such of you as are now dissatisfied still have the old Constitution unimpaired, and, on the sensitive point, the laws of your own framing under it; while the new administration will have no immediate power, if it would, to change either.

If it were admitted that you who are dissatisfied hold the right side in the dispute, there still is no single good reason for precipitate action. Intelligence, patriotism, Christianity, and a firm reliance on Him, who has never yet forsaken this favored land, are still competent to adjust, in the best way, all our present difficulty.

In *your* hands, my dissatisfied fellow countrymen, and not in *mine* is the momentous issue of civil war. The government will not assail *you*. You can have no conflict without being yourselves the aggressors. *You* have no oath registered in heaven to destroy the government, while *I* shall have the most solemn one to "preserve, protect, and defend" it.

Friends, Not Enemies

I am loath to close. We are not enemies but friends. We must not be enemies. Though passion may have strained, it must not break our bonds of affection.

The mystic chords of memory, stretching from

every battlefield and patriot grave to every living heart and hearthstone all over this broad land, will yet swell the chorus of the Union, when again touched, as surely they will be, by the better angels of our nature.

For Further Reading

Dwight Dumond, *The Secession Movement*. New York: Octagon Books, 1963.

John Hope Franklin, *The Militant South, 1860–1861*. Boston: Beacon Press, 1968.

David M. Potter, *The Impending Crisis*. New York: Harper & Row, 1976.

Kenneth M. Stampp, *And the War Came: The North and the Secession Crisis, 1860–1861*. Baton Rouge: Louisiana State University Press, 1970.

The Civil War

VIEWPOINT 35A

Freeing the Slaves Should Be the Primary War Aim (1862)

Horace Greeley (1811–1872)

During the first half of the Civil War the issue of slave emancipation was a divisive one in the North. Many people called for President Abraham Lincoln to use his powers as commander in chief to issue a legal edict emancipating the slaves. Lincoln—mindful of the importance of keeping border slave states out of the Confederacy—at first not only resisted such a step, he also rescinded orders Union generals John C. Frémont and David Hunter had made freeing all slaves within their military jurisdiction. Lincoln's actions angered antislavery leaders, including Horace Greeley, a prominent newspaper editor and political leader.

Greeley founded the *New York Tribune* in 1841, and edited the influential newspaper for more than thirty years. On August 19, 1862, the newspaper carried an open letter from Greeley to Lincoln entitled "The Prayer of Twenty Millions." In the essay, excerpted here, Greeley excoriates Lincoln for timidity and inaction on the slavery issue. He urges Lincoln to actively enforce the Confiscation Act, a law passed by Congress in August 1861 and revised in July 1862, which authorized the confiscation of Confederate property, including slaves, and to put them to use in the war effort.

How have some slaves who have escaped to Union armies been treated, according to Greeley? How

From "The Prayer of Twenty Millions" by Horace Greeley, *New York Tribune*, August 19, 1862. Reprinted in *The Rebellion Record*, Supplement, vol. 1, edited by Frank Moore (New York: Putnam, 1866).

might those slaves be helpful to the Union cause, in his view? What connection does he make between emancipation and prospects for Northern victory?

---

*D*ear Sir:

I do not intrude to tell you—for you must know already—that a great proportion of those who triumphed in your election, and of all who desire the unqualified suppression of the rebellion now desolating our country, are sorely disappointed and deeply pained by the policy you seem to be pursuing with regard to the slaves of Rebels. I write only to set succinctly and unmistakably before you what we require, what we think we have a right to expect, and of what we complain.

I. We require of you, as the first servant of the republic, charged especially and pre-eminently with this duty, that you EXECUTE THE LAWS. Most emphatically do we demand that such laws as have been recently enacted, which therefore may fairly be presumed to embody the public will and to be dictated by the *present* needs of the republic, and which, after due consideration, have received your personal sanction, shall by you be carried into full effect and that you publicly and decisively instruct your subordinates that such laws exist, that they are binding on all functionaries and citizens, and that they are to be obeyed to the letter.

II. We think you are strangely and disastrously remiss in the discharge of your official and imperative duty with regard to the emancipating provisions of the new Confiscation Act. Those provisions were designed to fight slavery with liberty. They prescribe that men loyal to the Union, and willing to shed their blood in her behalf, shall no longer be held, with the nation's consent, in bondage to persistent, malignant traitors, who for twenty years have been plotting and for sixteen months have been fighting to divide and destroy our country. Why these traitors should be treated with tenderness by you, to the prejudice of the dearest rights of loyal men, we cannot conceive.

Slavery the Cause of Treason

III. We think you are unduly influenced by the councils, the representations, the menaces, of certain fossil politicians hailing from the border Slave states. Knowing well that the heartily, unconditionally loyal portion of the white citizens of those states do not expect nor desire that slavery shall be upheld to the prejudice of the Union . . . we ask you to consider that slavery is everywhere the inciting cause and sustaining base of treason: the most slaveholding sections of Maryland and Delaware being this day, though under the Union flag, in full sympathy with the rebellion, while the free labor portions of Tennessee and of Texas, though writhing under the bloody heel of treason, are unconquerably loyal to the Union. . . .

———— • ————

"The Union cause has suffered and is now suffering immensely from mistaken deference to Rebel slavery."

———— • ————

It seems to us the most obvious truth that whatever strengthens or fortifies slavery in the border states strengthens also treason and drives home the wedge intended to divide the Union. Had you, from the first, refused to recognize in those states, as here, any other than unconditional loyalty—that which stands for the Union, whatever may become of slavery—those states would have been, and would be, far more helpful and less troublesome to the defenders of the Union than they have been, or now are.

IV. We think timid counsels in such a crisis calculated to prove perilous, and probably disastrous. It is the duty of a government so wantonly, wickedly assailed by rebellion as ours has been to oppose force to force in a defiant, dauntless spirit. It cannot afford to temporize with traitors, nor with semi-traitors. . . .

Deference to Slavery

V. We complain that the Union cause has suffered and is now suffering immensely from mistaken deference to Rebel slavery. Had you, sir, in your inaugural address, unmistakably given notice that in case the rebellion already commenced were persisted in and your efforts to preserve the Union and enforce the laws should be resisted by armed force, *you would recognize no loyal person as rightfully held in slavery by a traitor*, we believe the rebellion would therein have received a staggering if not fatal blow. At that moment, according to the returns of the most recent elections, the Unionists were a large majority of the voters of the Slave states. But they were composed in good part of the aged, the feeble, the wealthy, the timid—the young, the reckless, the aspiring, the adventurous had already been largely lured by the gamblers and Negro traders, the politicians by trade and the conspirators by instinct, into the toils of treason. Had you then proclaimed that rebellion would strike the shackles from the slaves of every traitor, the wealthy and the cautious would have been supplied with a powerful inducement to remain loyal. . . .

VI. We complain that the Confiscation Act which you approved is habitually disregarded by your generals, and that no word of rebuke for them from you

has yet reached the public ear. [John G.] Fremont's Proclamation and [David] Hunter's Order favoring emancipation were promptly annulled by you; while [Henry] Halleck's Number Three, forbidding fugitives from slavery to Rebels to come within his lines—an order as unmilitary as inhuman, and which received the hearty approbation of every traitor in America—with scores of like tendency, have never provoked even your remonstrance.

Refusing to Welcome Slaves

We complain that the officers of your armies have habitually repelled rather than invited the approach of slaves who would have gladly taken the risks of escaping from their Rebel masters to our camps, bringing intelligence often of inestimable value to the Union cause. We complain that those who *have* thus escaped to us, avowing a willingness to do for us whatever might be required, have been brutally and madly repulsed, and often surrendered to be scourged, maimed, and tortured by the ruffian traitors who pretend to own them. We complain that a large proportion of our regular Army officers, with many of the volunteers, evince far more solicitude to uphold slavery than to put down the rebellion.

And, finally, we complain that you, Mr. President, elected as a Republican, knowing well what an abomination slavery is and how emphatically it is the core and essence of this atrocious rebellion, seem never to interfere with these atrocities and never give a direction to your military subordinates, which does not appear to have been conceived in the interest of slavery rather than of freedom. . . .

VIII. On the face of this wide earth, Mr. President, there is not one disinterested, determined, intelligent champion of the Union cause who does not feel that all attempts to put down the rebellion and at the same time uphold its inciting cause are preposterous and futile; that the rebellion, if crushed out tomorrow, would be renewed within a year if slavery were left in full vigor; that Army officers who remain to this day devoted to slavery can at best be but halfway loyal to the Union; and that every hour of deference to slavery is an hour of added and deepened peril to the Union. I appeal to the testimony of your ambassadors in Europe. It is freely at your service, not at mine. Ask them to tell you candidly whether the seeming subserviency of your policy to the slaveholding, slavery-upholding interest is not the perplexity, the despair of statesmen of all parties, and be admonished by the general answer!

Execute the Laws

IX. I close as I began with the statement that what an immense majority of the loyal millions of your countrymen require of you is a frank, declared, unqualified, ungrudging execution of the laws of the land, more especially of the Confiscation Act. That act gives freedom to the slaves of Rebels coming within our lines, or whom those lines may at any time enclose—we ask you to render it due obedience by publicly requiring all your subordinates to recognize and obey it. The Rebels are everywhere using the late anti-Negro riots in the North, as they have long used your officers' treatment of Negroes in the South, to convince the slaves that they have nothing to hope from a Union success, that we mean in that case to sell them into a bitter bondage to defray the cost of the war.

Let them impress this as a truth on the great mass of their ignorant and credulous bondmen, and the Union will never be restored—never. We cannot conquer 10 million people united in solid phalanx against us, powerfully aided by Northern sympathizers and European allies. We must have scouts, guides, spies, cooks, teamsters, diggers, and choppers from the blacks of the South, whether we allow them to fight for us or not, or we shall be baffled and repelled.

As one of the millions who would gladly have avoided this struggle at any sacrifice but that of principle and honor, but who now feel that the triumph of the Union is indispensable, not only to the existence of our country but to the well-being of mankind, I entreat you to render a hearty and unequivocal obedience to the law of the land.

VIEWPOINT 35B

Preserving the Union Should Be the Primary War Aim (1862)

Abraham Lincoln (1809–1865)

Abraham Lincoln, president of the United States from 1861 to 1865, faced the supreme challenge of national division after eleven Southern states seceded from the United States and formed a separate Confederacy, in large part to preserve the institution of slavery. Noted for his single-minded devotion to preserving the Union, Lincoln was continually challenged during his presidency, both by abolitionists who considered him too mild on the subject of slavery and by those who sought to end the Civil War by accepting the division and negotiating with the Confederacy.

Lincoln, although not an active abolitionist during his political career, was personally opposed to slavery, and during the first part of his term he tried to persuade the leaders of the Southern slaveholding

From *The Rebellion Record*, Supplement, vol. 1, edited by Frank Moore (New York: Putnam, 1866).

states that remained in the Union to plan for the gradual and compensated emancipation of their slaves. But he hesitated to issue a general proclamation abolishing slavery, believing that preserving the Union should take highest priority. Lincoln succinctly expresses his views in the following viewpoint, a letter he wrote in response to *New York Tribune* editor Horace Greeley's criticism of his policies (see viewpoint 35A). Lincoln's reply, dated August 22, 1862, was published in the *Tribune* and elsewhere.

How does Lincoln respond to the criticisms of Greeley? Is his message aimed solely at Greeley and the abolitionists? Who else might he be addressing? Lincoln had in July 1862 discussed with his cabinet his intention of issuing an emancipation proclamation, had prepared a draft of such a proclamation, and was waiting for the right moment (after a Northern military victory) to announce his decision; how does this affect your understanding of this letter written and published in August of that year?

*D**ear Sir:*
     I have just read yours of the 19th, addressed to myself through the *New York Tribune*. If there be in it any statements or assumptions of fact which I may know to be erroneous, I do not now and here controvert them. If there be in it any inferences which I may believe to be falsely drawn, I do not now and here argue against them. If there be perceptible in it an impatient and dictatorial tone, I waive it in deference to an old friend, whose heart I have always supposed to be right.

As to the policy I "seem to be pursuing," as you say, I have not meant to leave anyone in doubt.

The Union Must Be Saved

I would save the Union. I would save it the shortest way under the Constitution. The sooner the national authority can be restored, the nearer the Union will be "the Union as it was." If there be those who would not save the Union unless they could at the same time *save* slavery, I do not agree with them. If there be those who would not save the Union unless they could at the same time *destroy* slavery, I do not agree with them. My paramount object in this struggle *is* to save the Union, and is *not* either to save or destroy slavery. If I could save the Union without freeing *any* slave, I would do it; and if I could save it by freeing *all* the slaves, I would do it; and if I could do it by freeing some and leaving others alone, I would also do that.

What I do about slavery and the colored race I do because I believe it helps to save this Union; and what I forbear I forbear because I do *not* believe it would help to save the Union. I shall do *less* whenever I shall believe what I am doing hurts the cause, and I shall do *more* whenever I shall believe doing more will help the cause. I shall try to correct errors when shown to be errors; and I shall adopt new views so fast as they shall appear to be true views.

———— • ————

"My paramount object in this struggle is to save the Union, and is not either to save or destroy slavery."

———— • ————

I have here stated my purpose according to my view of *official* duty, and I intend no modification of my oft-expressed *personal* wish that all men, everywhere, could be free.

For Further Reading

Harlan H. Horner, *Lincoln and Greeley.* Urbana: University of Illinois Press, 1953.

Erik S. Lunde, *Horace Greeley.* Boston: Twayne Publishers, 1981.

James McPherson, *Abraham Lincoln and the Second American Revolution.* New York: Oxford University Press, 1991.

James A. Rawley, *Turning Points of the Civil War.* Lincoln: University of Nebraska Press, 1966.

VIEWPOINT 36A

The Emancipation Proclamation Is a Significant Achievement (1862)

Frederick Douglass (1817–1895)

Abraham Lincoln issued a preliminary Emancipation Proclamation on September 22, 1862, shortly after the partial Northern success in the Battle of Antietam. The proclamation stated that on January 1, 1863, all slaves residing in every part of the South still in rebellion would be declared "then, thenceforward, and forever free." The following viewpoint expresses the elated reaction of Frederick Douglass, an escaped slave who had gained national and international fame as an abolitionist, lecturer, and writer. Douglass viewed the Civil War as a moral crusade against slavery, and was an early advocate of both emancipation of the slaves and enlistment of black soldiers for the Union. In the October 1862 issue of *Douglass' Monthly*, a newspaper Douglass published and edited, he criticizes Lincoln for acting too slowly to free the slaves, but praises the proclamation and

From an editorial of Frederick Douglass, *Douglass' Monthly*, October 1862.

calls for renewed efforts to defeat the Confederacy.

What does Douglass predict will be the effects of the Emancipation Proclamation? What comments does he make on the character of Abraham Lincoln? What reasons does he give for his expressed confidence that the Confederacy will be defeated?

————————

Common sense, the necessities of the war, to say nothing of the dictation of justice and humanity have at last prevailed. We shout for joy that we live to record this righteous decree. *Abraham Lincoln,* President of the United States, Commander-in-Chief of the army and navy, in his own peculiar, cautious, forbearing and hesitating way, slow, but we hope sure, has, while the loyal heart was near breaking with despair, proclaimed and declared: *"That on the First of January, in the Year of Our Lord One Thousand, Eight Hundred and Sixty-three, All Persons Held as Slaves Within Any State or Any Designated Part of a State, The People Whereof Shall Then be in Rebellion Against the United States, Shall be Thenceforward and Forever Free."* "Free forever" oh! long enslaved millions, whose cries have so vexed the air and sky, suffer on a few more days in sorrow, the hour of your deliverance draws nigh! Oh! Ye millions of free and loyal men who have earnestly sought to free your bleeding country from the dreadful ravages of revolution and anarchy, lift up now your voices with joy and thanksgiving for with freedom to the slave will come peace and safety to your country. President Lincoln has embraced in this proclamation the law of Congress passed more than six months ago, prohibiting the employment of any part of the army and naval forces of the United States, to return fugitive slaves to their masters, commanded all officers of the army and navy to respect and obey its provisions. He has still further declared his intention to urge upon the Legislature of all the slave States not in rebellion the immediate or gradual abolishment of slavery. But read the proclamation for it is the most important of any to which the President of the United States has ever signed his name.

Reactions

Opinions will widely differ as to the practical effect of this measure upon the war. All that class at the North who have not lost their affection for slavery will regard the measure as the very worst that could be devised, and as likely to lead to endless mischief. All their plans for the future have been projected with a view to a reconstruction of the American Government upon the basis of compromise between slaveholding and non-slaveholding States. The thought of a country unified in sentiments, objects and ideas, has not entered into their political calculations, and hence this newly declared policy of the Government, which contemplates one glorious homogeneous people, doing away at a blow with the whole class of compromisers and corrupters, will meet their stern opposition. Will that opposition prevail? Will it lead the President to reconsider and retract? Not a word of it. Abraham Lincoln may be slow, Abraham Lincoln may desire peace even at the price of leaving our terrible national sore untouched, to fester on for generations, but Abraham Lincoln is not the man to reconsider, retract and contradict words and purposes solemnly proclaimed over his official signature.

Lincoln Will Take No Step Backward

The careful, and we think, the slothful deliberation which he has observed in reaching this obvious policy, is a guarantee against retraction. But even if the temper and spirit of the President himself were other than what they are, events greater than the President, events which have slowly wrung this proclamation from him may be relied on to carry him forward in the same direction. To look back now would only load him with heavier evils, while diminishing his ability, for overcoming those with which he now has to contend. To recall his proclamation would only increase rebel pride, rebel sense of power and would be hailed as a direct admission of weakness on the part of the Federal Government, while it would cause heaviness of heart and depression of national enthusiasm all over the loyal North and West. No, Abraham Lincoln will take no step backward. His word has gone out over the country and the world, giving joy and gladness to the friends of freedom and progress wherever those words are read, and he will stand by them, and carry them out to the letter. If he has taught us to confide in nothing else, he has taught us to confide in his word. The want of Constitutional power, the want of military power, the tendency of the measure to intensify Southern hate, and to exasperate the rebels, the tendency to drive from him all that class of Democrats at the North, whose loyalty has been conditioned on his restoring the union as it was, slavery and all, have all been considered, and he has taken his ground notwithstanding. The President doubtless saw, as we see, that it is not more absurd to talk about restoring the union, without hurting slavery, than restoring the union without hurting the rebels. As to exasperating the South, there can be no more in the cup than the cup will hold, and that was full already. The whole situation having been carefully scanned, before Mr. Lincoln could be made to budge an inch, he will now stand his ground. Border State influence, and the influence of half-loyal men, have been exerted and have done their worst. The end of these two influences is implied in this proclamation. Hereafter, the inspiration as well as the men and the money for carrying on the war will come from the North, and not from half-loyal border States.

The effect of this paper upon the disposition of Europe will be great and increasing. It changes the character of the war in European eyes and gives it an important principle as an object, instead of national pride and interest. It recognizes and declares the real nature of the contest, and places the North on the side of justice and civilization, and the rebels on the side of robbery and barbarism. It will disarm all purpose on the part of European Government to intervene in favor of the rebels and thus cast off at a blow one source of rebel power. All through the war thus far, the rebel ambassadors in foreign countries have been able to silence all expression of sympathy with the North as to slavery. With much more than a show of truth, they said that the Federal Government, no more than the Confederate Government, contemplated the abolition of slavery.

———— • ————

"Read the proclamation for it is the most important of any to which the President of the United States has ever signed his name."

———— • ————

But will not this measure be frowned upon by our officers and men in the field? We have heard of many thousands who have resolved that they will throw up their commissions and lay down their arms, just so soon as they are required to carry on a war against slavery. Making all allowances for exaggeration there are doubtless far too many of this sort in the loyal army. Putting this kind of loyalty and patriotism to the test, will be one of the best collateral effects of the measure. Any man who leaves the field on such a ground will be an argument in favor of the proclamation, and will prove that his heart has been more with slavery than with his country. Let the army be cleansed from all such pro-slavery vermin, and its health and strength will be greatly improved. But there can be no reason to fear the loss of many officers or men by resignation or desertion. We have no doubt that the measure was brought to the attention of most of our leading Generals, and blind as some of them have seemed to be in the earlier part of the war, most of them have seen enough to convince them that there can be no end to this war that does not end slavery. At any rate, we may hope that for every pro-slavery man that shall start from the ranks of our loyal army, there will be two anti-slavery men to fill up the vacancy, and in this war one truly devoted to the cause of Emancipation is worth two of the opposite sort.

Two Necessary Conditions

Whether slavery will be abolished in the manner now proposed by President Lincoln, depends of course upon two conditions, the first specified and the second implied. The first is that the slave States shall be in rebellion on and after the first day of January 1863 and the second is we must have the ability to put down that rebellion. About the first there can be very little doubt. The South is thoroughly in earnest and confident. It has staked everything upon the rebellion. Its experience thus far in the field has rather increased its hopes of final success than diminished them. Its armies now hold us at bay at all points, and the war is confined to the border States slave and free. If Richmond were in our hands and Virginia at our mercy, the vast regions beyond would still remain to be subdued. But the rebels confront us on the Potomac, the Ohio, and the Mississippi. Kentucky, Maryland, Missouri, and Virginia are in debate on the battlefields and their people are divided by the line which separates treason from loyalty. In short we are yet, after eighteen months of war, confined to the outer margin of the rebellion. We have scarcely more than touched the surface of the

---

THE EMANCIPATION PROCLAMATION

The official Emancipation Proclamation was issued and signed by President Abraham Lincoln on January 1, 1863, one hundred days after he issued a preliminary proclamation stating his intent to free the slaves residing in rebelling states.

Whereas, on the 22nd day of September, in the year of our Lord 1862, a proclamation was issued by the President of the United States, containing, among other things, the following, to wit:

> That on the 1st day of January, in the year of our Lord 1863, all persons held as slaves within any state or designated part of a state, the people whereof shall then be in rebellion against the United States, shall be then, thenceforward, and forever free; and the executive government of the United States, including the military and naval authority thereof, will recognize and maintain the freedom of such persons and will do no act or acts to repress such persons, or any of them, in any efforts they may make for their actual freedom.

> That the executive will, on the 1st day of January aforesaid, by proclamation, designate the states and parts of states, if any, in which the people thereof, respectively, shall then be in rebellion against the United States; and the fact that any state or the people thereof shall on that day be in good faith represented in the Congress of the United States by members chosen thereto at elections wherein a majority of the qualified voters of such states shall have participated shall, in the absence of strong countervailing testimony, be deemed conclusive evidence that such state and the people thereof are not then in rebellion against the United States.

Now, therefore, I, Abraham Lincoln, President of the United States, by virtue of the power in me vested as commander in chief of the Army and Navy of the United States, in time of actual armed rebellion against the authority and government of the United States, and as a fit and necessary war measure for suppressing said rebellion, do, on this 1st day of January, in the year of our Lord 1863, and in accordance with my purpose so to do, publicly proclaimed for the full period of 100 days from the day first above mentioned, order and designate as the states and parts of states wherein the people thereof, respectively, are this day in rebellion against the United States the following, to wit:

Arkansas, Texas, Louisiana (except the parishes of St. Bernard, Plaquemines, Jefferson, St. John, St. Charles, St. James, Ascension, Assumption, Terrebonne, Lafourche, St. Mary, St. Martin, and Orleans, including the city of New Orleans), Mississippi, Alabama, Florida, Georgia, South Carolina, North Carolina, and Virginia (except the forty-eight counties designated as West Virginia, and also the counties of Berkeley, Accomac, Northampton, Elizabeth City, York, Princess Anne, and Norfolk, including the cities of Norfolk and Portsmouth), and which excepted parts are for the present left precisely as if this proclamation were not issued.

And, by virtue of the power and for the purpose aforesaid, I do order and declare that all persons held as slaves within said designated states and parts of states are, and henceforward shall be, free; and that the executive government of the United States, including the military and naval authorities thereof, will recognize and maintain the freedom of said persons.

And I hereby enjoin upon the people so declared to be free to abstain from all violence, unless in necessary self-defense; and I recommend to them that, in all cases when allowed, they labor faithfully for reasonable wages.

And I further declare and make known that such persons of suitable condition will be received into the armed service of the United States to garrison forts, positions, stations, and other places, and to man vessels of all sorts in said service.

And upon this act, sincerely believed to be an act of justice, warranted by the Constitution upon military necessity, I invoke the considerate judgment of mankind and the gracious favor of Almighty God.

terrible evil. It has been raising large quantities of food during the past summer. While the masters have been fighting abroad, the slaves have been busy working at home to supply them with the means of continuing the struggle. They will not [back] down at the bidding of this Proclamation, but may be safely relied upon till January and long after January. A month or two will put an end to general fighting for the winter. When the leaves fall we shall hear again of bad roads, winter quarters and spring campaigns. The South which has thus far withstood our arms will not fall at once before our pens. All fears for the abolition of slavery arising from this apprehension may be dismissed. Whoever, therefore, lives to see the first day of next January, should Abraham Lincoln be then alive and President of the United States, may confidently look in the morning papers for the final proclamation, granting freedom, and freedom forever, to all slaves within the rebel States. On the next point nothing need be said. We have full power to put down the rebellion. Unless one man is more than a match for four, unless the South breeds braver and better men than the North, unless slavery is more precious than liberty, unless a just cause kindles a feebler enthusiasm than a wicked and villainous one, the men of the loyal States will put down this rebellion and slavery, and all the sooner will they put down that rebellion by coupling slavery with that object. Tenderness towards slavery has been the loyal weakness during the war. Fighting the slaveholders with one hand and holding the slaves with the other, has been fairly tried and has failed. We have now inaugurated a wiser and better policy, a policy which is better for the loyal cause than an hundred thousand armed men. The Star Spangled Banner is now the harbinger of Liberty and the millions in bondage, inured to hardships, accustomed to toil, ready to suffer, ready to fight, to dare and to die, will rally under that banner wherever they see it gloriously unfolded to the breeze. Now let the Government go forward in its mission of Liberty as the only condition of peace and union, by weeding out the army and navy of all such officers as the late Col. [Dixon] Miles, whose sympathies are now known to have been with the rebels. Let only the men who assent heartily to the wisdom and the justice of the anti-slavery policy of the Government be lifted into command; let the black man have an arm as well as a heart in this war, and the tide of battle which has thus far only waved backward and forward, will steadily set in our favor. The rebellion suppressed, slavery abolished, and America will, higher than ever, sit as a queen among the nations of the earth.

Now for the work. During the interval between now and next January, let every friend of the long enslaved bondman do his utmost in swelling the tide of anti-slavery sentiment, by writing, speaking, money and example. Let our aim be to make the North a unit in favor of the President's policy, and see to it that our voices and votes, shall forever extinguish that latent and malignant sentiment at the North, which has from the first cheered on the rebels in their atrocious crimes against the union, and has systematically sought to paralyze the national arm in striking down the slaveholding rebellion. We are ready for this service or any other, in this, we trust the last struggle with the monster slavery.

VIEWPOINT 36B

The Emancipation Proclamation Is a Worthless Act (1863)

Clement L. Vallandigham (1820–1871) and Jefferson Davis (1808–1889)

Abraham Lincoln's Emancipation Proclamation on January 1, 1863 (following a preliminary proclamation on September 22, 1862) declared all the slaves in rebelling states to be free. (For the text of the Emancipation Proclamation see p. 270) The proclamation, while highly praised by abolitionists, provoked criticism in both the North and the South. The following two-part viewpoint consists of reactions of a leading Northern dissenter and the president of the Confederacy.

Part I is by Clement L. Vallandigham, a Democratic representative from Ohio and leader of the "Peace Democrats" or "Copperheads," who opposed most of Lincoln's policies and denounced the war as an unjust and unnecessary conflict. In a speech delivered on January 14, 1863, in the House of Representatives, and excerpted here, he argues that the September preliminary proclamation, which announced and warned of the pending emancipation in January for the slaves in any state "in rebellion" had failed to persuade any Confederate state from ceasing its rebellion. The Emancipation Proclamation will not end slavery, he predicts, but it will prevent ending the Civil War by a peaceful compromise with the South—something he had long advocated. Part II is by Jefferson Davis, a former U.S. senator from Mississippi who was the first and only president of the Confederacy. In a special message to the Confederate Congress on January 12, 1863, Davis argues that Lincoln's actions both fully justify the Confederacy's decision to leave the United States and make restora-

From Clement L. Vallandigham's speech before Congress, January 14, 1863, in *Appendix to the Congressional Globe*, 1863, and Jefferson Davis's message to the Confederate Congress, January 12, 1863, in *Jefferson Davis, Constitutionalist*, edited by Dunbar Rowland, 1923; courtesy of the Mississippi Dept. of Archives and History.

tion of the Union impossible.

Why do Vallandigham and Davis consider the Emancipation Proclamation an admission of defeat for the North? What three possible consequences of the Emancipation Proclamation does Davis predict will happen?

I

Now, sir, on the 14th of April [1861], I believed that coercion would bring on war, and war disunion. More than that, I believed, what you all in your hearts believe to-day, that the South could never be conquered—never. And not that only, but I was satisfied—and you of the abolition party have now proved it to the world—that the secret but real purpose of the war was to abolish slavery in the States. In any event, I did not doubt that whatever might be the momentary impulses of those in power, and whatever pledges they might make in the midst of the fury for the Constitution, the Union, and the flag, yet the natural and inexorable logic of revolutions would, sooner or later, drive them into that policy, and with it to its final but inevitable result, the change of our present democratical form of government into an imperial despotism. . . .

And now, sir, I recur to the state of the Union to-day. . . .

You have not conquered the South. You never will. It is not in the nature of things possible; much less under your auspices. But money you have expended without limit, and blood poured out like water. Defeat, debt, taxation, sepulchers, these are your trophies. In vain the people gave you treasure and the soldier yielded up his life. "Fight, tax, emancipate, let these," said the gentleman from Maine, (Mr. Pike,) at the last session, "be the trinity of our salvation." Sir, they have become the trinity of your deep damnation. The war for the Union is, in your hands, a most bloody and costly failure. The President confessed it on the 22d of September [1862], solemnly, officially, and under the broad seal of the United States. And he has now repeated the confession. The priests and rabbis of abolition taught him that God would not prosper such a cause. War for the Union was abandoned; war for the negro openly begun, and with stronger battalions than before. With what success? Let the dead at Fredericksburg and Vicksburg [sites of Civil War battles] answer. . . .

The Great Question

And now, sir, I come to the great and controlling question within which the whole issue of union or disunion is bound up: is there "an irrepressible conflict" between the slaveholding and non-slaveholding States? . . . If so, then there is an end of all union and

forever. You cannot abolish slavery by the sword; still less by proclamations, though the President were to "proclaim" every month. Of what possible avail was his proclamation of September? Did the South submit? Was she even alarmed? And yet he has now fulmined another "bull against the comet"—*brutum fulmen* [irrational threat]—and, threatening servile insurrection with all its horrors, has yet coolly appealed to the judgment of mankind, and invoked the blessing of the God of peace and love! But declaring it a military necessity, an essential measure of war to subdue the rebels, yet, with admirable wisdom, he expressly exempts from its operation the only States and parts of States in the South where he has the military power to execute it.

Neither, sir, can you abolish slavery by argument. As well attempt to abolish marriage or the relation of paternity. The South is resolved to maintain it at every hazard and by every sacrifice; and if "this Union cannot endure part slave and part free," then it is already and finally dissolved. . . .

But I deny the doctrine. It is full of disunion and civil war. It is disunion itself. Whoever first taught it ought to be dealt with as not only hostile to the Union, but an enemy of the human race. Sir, the fundamental idea of the Constitution is the perfect and eternal compatibility of a union of States "part slave and part free;" else the Constitution never would have been framed, nor the Union founded; and seventy years of successful experiment have approved the wisdom of the plan. In my deliberate judgment, a confederacy made up of slaveholding and non-slaveholding States is, in the nature of things, the strongest of all popular governments. African slavery has been, and is, eminently conservative. It makes the absolute political equality of the white race everywhere practicable. It dispenses with the English order of nobility, and leaves every white man, North and South, owning slaves or owning none, the equal of every other white man. It has reconciled universal suffrage throughout the free States with the stability of government. I speak not now of its material benefits to the North and West, which are many and more obvious. But the South, too, has profited many ways by a union with the non-slaveholding States. Enterprise, industry, self-reliance, perseverance, and the other hardy virtues of a people living in a higher latitude and without hereditary servants, she has learned or received from the North. Sir, it is easy, I know, to denounce all this, and to revile him who utters it. Be it so. The English is, of all languages, the most copious in words of bitterness and reproach. "Pour on: I will endure.". . .

Whoever hates negro slavery more than he loves the Union, must demand separation at last. I think that you can never abolish slavery by fighting. Certainly you never can till you have first destroyed the South

tainly you never can till you have first destroyed the South, and then . . . converted this Government into an imperial despotism. And, sir, whenever I am forced to a choice between the loss to my own country and race, of personal and political liberty with all its blessings, and the involuntary domestic servitude of the negro, I shall not hesitate one moment to choose the latter alternative. The sole question today is between the Union with slavery, or final disunion, and, I think, anarchy and despotism. I am for the Union. It was good enough for my fathers. It is good enough for us and our children after us.

II

The public journals of the North have been received, containing a proclamation, dated on the 1st day of the present month [January 1863], signed by the President of the United States, in which he orders and declares all slaves within ten of the States of the Confederacy to be free, except such as are found within certain districts now occupied in part by the armed forces of the enemy. We may well leave it to the instincts of that common humanity which a beneficent Creator has implanted in the breasts of our fellowmen of all countries to pass judgment on a measure by which several millions of human beings of an inferior race, peaceful and contented laborers in their sphere, are doomed to extermination, while at the same time they are encouraged to a general assassination of their masters by the insidious recommendation "to abstain from violence unless in necessary self-defense." Our own detestation of those who have attempted the most execrable measure recorded in the history of guilty man is tempered by profound contempt for the impotent rage which it discloses. So far as regards the action of this Government on such criminals as may attempt its execution, I confine myself to informing you that I shall, unless in your wisdom you deem some other course more expedient, deliver to the several State authorities all commissioned officers of the United States that may hereafter be captured by our forces in any of the States embraced in the proclamation, that they may be dealt with in accordance with the laws of those States providing for the punishment of criminals engaged in exciting servile insurrection. The enlisted soldiers I shall continue to treat as unwilling instruments in the commission of these crimes, and shall direct their discharge and return to their homes on the proper and usual parole.

The Designs of Lincoln

In its political aspect this measure possesses great significance, and to it in this light I invite your attention. It affords to our whole people the complete and crowning proof of the true nature of the designs of the party which elevated to power the present occupant of the Presidential chair at Washington and which sought to conceal its purpose by every variety of artful device and by the perfidious use of the most solemn and repeated pledges on every possible occasion. . . .

The people of this Confederacy, then, cannot fail to receive this proclamation as the fullest vindication of their own sagacity in foreseeing the uses to which the dominant party in the United States intended from the beginning to apply their power, nor can they cease to remember with devout thankfulness that it is to their own vigilance in resisting the first stealthy progress of approaching despotism that they owe their escape from consequences now apparent to the most skeptical. This proclamation will have another salutary effect in calming the fears of those who have constantly evinced the apprehension that this war might end by some reconstruction of the old Union or some renewal of close political relations with the United States. These fears have never been shared by me, nor have I ever been able to perceive on what basis they could rest. But the proclamation affords the fullest guarantee of the impossibility of such a result; it has established a state of things which can lead to but one of three possible consequences—the extermination of the slaves, the exile of the whole white population from the Confederacy, or absolute and total separation of these States from the United States.

———— • ————

"You cannot abolish slavery by the sword; still less by proclamations."

———— • ————

This proclamation is also an authentic statement by the Government of the United States of its inability to subjugate the South by force of arms, and as such must be accepted by neutral nations, which can no longer find any justification in withholding our just claims to formal recognition. It is also in effect an intimation to the people of the North that they must prepare to submit to a separation, now become inevitable, for that people are too acute not to understand a restoration of the Union has been rendered forever impossible by the adoption of a measure which from its very nature neither admits of retraction nor can coexist with union.

For Further Reading

Ira Berlin et al., eds., *Free at Last: A Documentary History of Slavery, Freedom, and the Civil War.* New York: New Press, 1992.

David W. Blight, *Frederick Douglass' Civil War: Keeping Faith in Jubilee.* Baton Rouge: Louisiana State University Press, 1989.

Robert F. Durden, *The Gray and the Black: The Confederate Debate on Emancipation*. Baton Rouge: Louisiana State University Press, 1972.

Clement Eaton, *Jefferson Davis*. New York: Free Press, 1977.

John Hope Franklin, *The Emancipation Proclamation*. Doubleday: Garden City, NY: 1963.

Forrest Wood, *Black Scare: The Racist Response to Emancipation and Reconstruction*. Berkeley: University of California Press, 1968.

VIEWPOINT 37A

War Justifies the Restriction of Civil Liberties (1863)

Abraham Lincoln (1809–1865)

The question of whether and how to maintain civil liberties while conducting a war confronted leaders on both sides of the Civil War. Abraham Lincoln, the sixteenth president of the United States, and Jefferson Davis, the first and only president of the Confederacy, took contrasting approaches. Davis maintained civil liberties for most Southerners except slaves. Abraham Lincoln, however, issued on several occasions proclamations suspending the writ of *habeas corpus*, a constitutional provision forbidding unlawful detention. Union military forces arrested and detained thousands of suspected Confederate sympathizers.

In 1863 a group of Democrats from Albany, New York, wrote to Lincoln, offering general support of the war but decrying what they saw as serious violations of the Constitution and the Bill of Rights. High among their concerns was the fate of Clement L. Vallandigham, a Democratic congressman who had actively opposed conscription and denounced Lincoln and other Union leaders. (See viewpoint 36B, Part I.) In May 1863 he was arrested in Ohio and tried by the army for treason. After being found guilty of "weakening the power of the Government" in putting down "an unlawful rebellion," he was sentenced to imprisonment—a sentence commuted by Lincoln to banishment to the Confederacy.

Lincoln replied to the Albany Democrats' pleas on June 12, 1863, in a letter that was widely reprinted in pamphlet form and is excerpted here. Defending his war policies, he argues that the "inherent power" of the executive justifies using whatever measures are necessary to protect the "public safety" during a rebellion or invasion, and cites the dangers of spies and traitors to the Union cause.

Why are civil liberties not accorded as much pro-

Reprinted from the *Complete Works of Lincoln*, edited by J. Nicolay and J. Hay (New York: F.D. Tandy, 1905).

tection during a rebellion as during peaceful times, according to Lincoln? How does he justify the detention of Clement L. Vallandigham?

Gentlemen:
Your letter of May 19, inclosing the resolutions of a public meeting held at Albany, New York, on the 16th of the same month, was received several days ago. . . .

Critical Resolutions

The resolutions promise to support me in every constitutional and lawful measure to suppress the rebellion; and I have not knowingly employed, nor shall knowingly employ, any other. But the meeting, by their resolutions, assert and argue that certain military arrests and proceedings following them, for which I am ultimately responsible, are unconstitutional. I think they are not. The resolutions quote from the Constitution the definition of treason, and also the limiting safeguards and guarantees therein provided for the citizen on trials for treason, and on his being held to answer for capital or otherwise infamous crimes, and in criminal prosecutions his right to a speedy and public trial by an impartial jury. They proceed to resolve "that these safeguards of the rights of the citizen against the pretensions of arbitrary power were intended more especially for his protection in times of civil commotion." And, apparently to demonstrate the proposition, the resolutions proceed: "They were secured substantially to the English people after years of protracted civil war, and were adopted into our Constitution at the close of the revolution." Would not the demonstration have been better if it could have been truly said that these safeguards had been adopted and applied during the civil wars and during our revolution, instead of after the one and at the close of the other? I, too, am devotedly for them after civil war and before civil war, and at all times, "except when, in cases of rebellion or invasion, the public safety may require" their suspension. . . . But these provisions of the Constitution have no application to the case we have in hand, because the arrests complained of were not made for treason—that is, not for the treason defined in the Constitution, and upon the conviction of which the punishment is death—nor yet were they made to hold persons to answer for any capital or otherwise infamous crimes; nor were the proceedings following, in any constitutional or legal sense, "criminal prosecutions." The arrests were made on totally different grounds, and the proceedings following accorded with the grounds of the arrests. . . . [The rebel] sympathizers pervaded all departments of the government and nearly all communities of the people. From this material, under cover of "liberty of speech," "liberty of the press," and "*habeas corpus*," they hoped to keep on foot amongst us a most efficient corps of spies, informers, suppliers and aiders and abettors of their cause in a thousand ways. They knew that in times such as they were inaugurating, by the Constitution itself the "*habeas corpus*" might be suspended; but they also knew they had friends who would make a question as to who was to suspend it; meanwhile their spies and others might remain at large to help on their cause. Or if, as has happened, the Executive should suspend the writ without ruinous waste of time, instances of arresting innocent persons might occur, as are always likely to occur in such cases; and then a clamor could be raised in regard to this. . . . Yet . . . I was slow to adopt the strong measures which [are] . . . indispensable to the public safety. Nothing is better known to history than that courts of justice are utterly incompetent to such cases. Civil courts are organized chiefly for trials of individuals, or, at most, a few individuals acting in concert—and this in quiet times, and on charges of crimes well defined in the law. Even in times of peace bands of horse-thieves and robbers frequently grow too numerous and powerful for the ordinary courts of justice. But what comparison, in numbers, have such bands ever borne to the insurgent sympathizers even in many of the loyal States? Again, a jury too frequently has at least one member more ready to hang the panel than to hang the traitor. And yet again, he who dissuades one man from volunteering, or induces one soldier to desert, weakens the Union cause as much as he who kills a Union soldier in battle. Yet this dissuasion or inducement may be so conducted as to be no defined crime of which any civil court would take cognizance.

A Case of Rebellion

Ours is a case of rebellion. . . . [The Suspension Clause from Section 9 of Article I of the Constitution] plainly attests the understanding of those who made the Constitution that ordinary courts of justice are inadequate to "cases of rebellion"—attests their purpose that, in such cases, men may be held in custody whom the courts, acting on ordinary rules, would discharge. *Habeas corpus* does not discharge men who are proved to be guilty of defined crime; and its suspension is allowed by the Constitution on purpose that men may be arrested and held who cannot be proved to be guilty of defined crime, "when, in cases of rebellion or invasion, the public safety may require it."

This is precisely our present case—a case of rebellion wherein the public safety does require the suspension. . . . Arrests in cases of rebellion do not proceed altogether upon the same basis. In the latter case arrests are made not so much for what has been done, as for what probably would be done. The latter is more for the preventive and less for the vindictive than the former. In such cases the purposes of men are much more easily understood than in cases of ordinary crime. The man who stands by and says nothing when the peril of his government is discussed, cannot be misunderstood. If not hindered, he is sure to help the enemy; much more if he talks ambiguously—talks for his country with "buts," and "ifs" and "ands." [Several Confederate leaders] were all within the power of the government since the rebellion began, and were nearly as well known to be traitors then as now. Unquestionably if we had seized and held them, the insurgent cause would be much weaker. But no one of them had then committed any crime defined in the law. Every one of them, if arrested, would have been discharged on *habeas corpus* were the writ allowed to operate. In view of these and similar cases, I think the time not unlikely to come when I shall be blamed for having made too few arrests rather than too many.

———— • ————

"The Constitution is not in its application in all respects the same in cases of rebellion or invasion involving the public safety, as it is in times of . . . peace."

———— • ————

By the third resolution the meeting indicate their opinion that military arrests may be constitutional in localities where rebellion actually exists, but that such arrests are unconstitutional in localities where rebellion or insurrection does not actually exist. They insist that such arrests shall not be made "outside of the lines of necessary military occupation and the scenes of insurrection." Inasmuch, however, as the Constitution itself makes no such distinction, I am unable to believe that there is any such constitutional distinction. I concede that the class of arrests complained of can be constitutional only when, in cases of rebellion or invasion, the public safety may require them; and I insist that in such cases they are constitutional wherever the public safety does require them, as well in places to which they may prevent the rebellion extending, as in those where it may be already prevailing; as well where they may restrain mischievous interference with the raising and supplying of armies to suppress the rebellion, as where the rebellion may actually be; as well where they may restrain the enticing men out of the army, as where they would prevent mutiny in the army; equally constitutional at all places where they will conduce to the public safety, as against the dangers of rebellion or invasion.

Clement L. Vallandigham

Take the particular case mentioned by the meeting. It is asserted in substance, that Mr. Vallandigham was, by a military commander, seized and tried "for no other reason than words addressed to a public meeting in criticism of the course of the administration, and in condemnation of the military orders of the general." Now, if there be no mistake about this, if this assertion is the truth and the whole truth, if there was no other reason for the arrest, then I concede that the arrest was wrong. But the arrest, as I understand, was made for a very different reason. Mr. Vallandigham avows his hostility to the war on the part of the Union; and his arrest was made because he was laboring, with some effect, to prevent the raising of troops, to encourage desertions from the army, and to leave the rebellion without an adequate military force to suppress it. He was not arrested because he was damaging the political prospects of the administration or the personal interests of the commanding general but because he was damaging the army, upon the existence and vigor of which the life of the nation depends. He was warring upon the military, and this gave the military constitutional jurisdiction to lay hands upon him. . . . Long experience has shown that armies cannot be maintained unless desertion shall be punished by the severe penalty of death. . . . Must I shoot a simpleminded soldier boy who deserts, while I must not touch a hair of a wily agitator who induces him to desert? This is none the less injurious when effected by getting a father, or brother, or friend into a public meeting, and there working upon his feelings till he is persuaded to write the soldier boy that he is fighting in a bad cause, for a wicked administration of a contemptible government, too weak to arrest and punish him if he shall desert. I think that, in such a case, to silence the agitator and save the boy is not only constitutional, but withal a great mercy.

If I be wrong . . . my error lies in believing . . . that the Constitution is not in its application in all respects the same in cases of rebellion or invasion involving the public safety, as it is in times of profound peace and public security. The Constitution itself makes the distinction, and I can no more be persuaded that the government can constitutionally take no strong measures in times of rebellion, because it can be shown that the same could not be lawfully taken in time of peace, than I can be persuaded that a particular drug is not good medicine for a sick man because it can be shown to not be good food for a well one. Nor am I able to appreciate the danger apprehended by the meeting, that the American people will by means of military arrests during the rebellion lose the right of public discussion, the liberty of speech and the press, the law of evidence, trial by jury, and *habeas corpus* throughout the indefinite peaceful future which I trust lies before them, any more than I am able to believe that a man could contract so strong an appetite for emetics during temporary illness as to persist in feeding upon them during the remainder of his healthful life. . . .

I am specifically called on to discharge Mr. Vallandigham. . . . In response to such appeal I have to say . . . it will afford me great pleasure to discharge him so soon as I can by any means believe the public safety will not suffer by it.

VIEWPOINT 37B

War Does Not Justify the Violation of Civil Liberties (1863)

Ohio Democratic Convention

Throughout the Civil War President Abraham Lincoln came under criticism from many people for actions that they believed violated the U.S. Constitution. One such action was the arrest of Clement L. Vallandigham, a Democratic representative from Ohio who was perhaps the most prominent of Northern political dissenters (known as "Copperheads") during the Civil War. Vallandigham was the most famous of the thousands of people in the North arrested for hindering the Union war effort during the Civil War; his case provoked much public controversy and at least two petitions to the president. The first petition, sent by a group of Democrats from Albany, New York, on May 19, 1863, was answered by a letter from Lincoln in which he argued his actions were justified, given the national crisis the United States was facing.

Many people remained unconvinced—including the group of Ohio Democrats who, on June 26, 1863, sent Lincoln the letter and set of resolutions excerpted in this viewpoint. Responding in part to statements Lincoln had made in his June 12 letter (see viewpoint 37A), the Ohio politicians argue that the arrest of Vallandigham, whom they had just nominated for governor, is unjustifiable. They contend that freedom of speech and of the press are indispensable in wartime as in peace. The petitioners also criticize Lincoln for his suspension of the writ of *habeas corpus* (which prevents government from

Reprinted from *A Life of Clement L. Vallandigham* by James L. Vallandigham (Baltimore: Turnbull Bros., 1872).

arbitrarily arresting individuals without showing just cause to the courts), arguing that under the Constitution only Congress, not the president, has the power to make such a decision.

What constitutional liberties are being threatened by Lincoln's actions, according to the Ohio petitioners? How do they characterize Vallandigham?

---

*T*o His Excellency, the President of the United States:

The undersigned having been appointed a committee, under the authority of the resolutions of the State Convention held at the City of Columbus, Ohio, on the 11th inst., to communicate with you on the subject of the arrest and banishment of Clement L. Vallandigham, most respectfully submit the following as the resolutions of that Convention bearing upon the subject of this communication, and ask of your Excellency their earnest consideration. And they deem it proper to state that the Convention was one in which all parts of the State were represented, and one of the most respectable as to numbers and character, one of the most earnest and sincere in the support of the Constitution and the Union, ever held in that State.

[The resolutions—some of which appear below— were inserted into the letter here.]

The Resolutions

That the arrest, imprisonment, and pretended trial and actual banishment of C.L. Vallandigham, a citizen of the State of Ohio, not belonging to the land or naval forces of the United States, nor to the militia in actual service, by alleged military authority, for no other pretended crime than that of uttering words of legitimate criticism upon the conduct of the Administration in power, and of appealing to the ballot-box for a change of policy—said arrest and military trial taking place where the courts of law are open and unobstructed, and for no act done within the sphere of active military operations in carrying on the war—we regard as a palpable violation of the provisions of the Constitution of the United States.

That Clement L. Vallandigham was, at the time of his arrest, a prominent candidate for nomination by the Democratic party for the office of Governor of the State; that the Democratic party was fully competent to decide whether he was a fit man for that nomination, and that the attempt to deprive them of that right by his arrest and banishment was an unmerited imputation upon their intelligence and loyalty, as well as a violation of the Constitution.

That we respectfully, but most earnestly, call upon the President of the United States to restore Clement L. Vallandigham to his home in Ohio, and that a committee of one from each congressional district of the State, to be selected by the presiding officer of this convention, is hereby appointed to present this application to the President.

The undersigned, in the discharge of the duty assigned them, do not think it necessary to reiterate the facts connected with the arrest, trial, and banishment of Mr. Vallandigham—they are well known to the President, and are of public history—nor to enlarge upon the positions taken by the Convention, nor to recapitulate the CONSTITUTIONAL PROVISIONS which it is believed have been violated: they have been stated at length, and with clearness, in the resolutions which have been recited. The undersigned content themselves with a brief reference to other suggestions pertinent to the subject.

They do not call upon your Excellency as suppliants, praying the revocation of the order banishing Mr. Vallandigham as a favor; but by the authority of a Convention representing a majority of the citizens of the State of Ohio, they respectfully ask it as a right due to an American citizen in whose personal injury the sovereignty and dignity of the people of Ohio as a free State have been offended. And this duty they perform the more cordially from the consideration that, at a time of great national emergency, pregnant with danger to our Federal Union, it is all-important that the true friends of the Constitution and the Union, however they may differ as to *the mode* of administering the Government, and the measures most likely to be successful in the maintenance of the Constitution and the restoration of the Union, should not be thrown into conflict with each other.

Unjust Arrest and Banishment

The arrest, unusual trial, and banishment of Mr. Vallandigham, have created wide-spread and alarming disaffection among the people of the State, not only endangering the harmony of the friends of the Constitution and the Union, and tending to disturb the peace and tranquillity of the State, but also impairing that confidence in the fidelity of your Administration to the great landmarks of free government essential to a peaceful and successful enforcement of the laws of Ohio.

You are reported to have used, in a public communication on this subject, the following language:

> It gave me pain when I learned that Mr. Vallandigham had been arrested—that is, I was pained that there should have seemed to be a necessity for arresting him; and that it will afford me great pleasure to discharge him so soon as I can by any means believe the public safety will not suffer by it.

The undersigned assure your Excellency, from our personal knowledge of the feelings of the people of Ohio, that the public safety will be far more endangered by continuing Mr. Vallandigham in exile than by releasing him. It may be true that persons differing from him in political views may be found in Ohio, and elsewhere, who will express a different opinion; but they are certainly mistaken.

Mr. Vallandigham may differ with the President, and even with some of his own political party, as to the true and most effectual means of maintaining the Constitution and restoring the Union; but this difference of opinion does not prove him to be unfaithful to his duties as an American citizen. If a man, devotedly attached to the Constitution and the Union, conscientiously believes that, from the inherent nature of the Federal compact, the war, in the present condition of things in this country, can not be used as a means of restoring the Union; or that a war to subjugate a part of the States, or a war to revolutionise the social system in a part of the States, could not restore, but would inevitably result in the final destruction of both the Constitution and the Union—is he not to be allowed the right of an American citizen to appeal to the judgment of the people for a change of policy by the constitutional remedy of the ballot-box?

———— • ————

"The undersigned are unable to agree . . . that the Constitution is different in time of insurrection or invasion from what it is in time of peace and public security."

———— • ————

During the war with Mexico many of the political opponents of the Administration then in power thought it their duty to oppose and denounce the war, and to urge before the people of the country that it was unjust and prosecuted for unholy purposes. With equal reason it might have been said of them that their discussions before the people were calculated to "discourage enlistments," "to prevent the raising of troops," and to "induce desertions from the army," and "leave the Government without an adequate military force to carry on the war."

Freedom of Speech Indispensable

If the freedom of speech and of the press are to be suspended in time of war, then the essential element of popular government to effect a change of policy in the constitutional mode is at an end. The freedom of speech and of the press is indispensable, and necessarily incident to the nature of popular government itself. If any inconvenience or evils arise from its exercise, they are unavoidable.

On this subject you are reported to have said, further:

It is asserted, in substance, that Mr. Vallandigham

was by a military commander seized and tried for no other reason than words addressed to a public meeting in criticism of the course of the Administration, and in condemnation of the military order of the General. Now, if there be no mistake about this—if there was no other reason for the arrest—then I concede that the arrest was wrong. But the arrest, I understand, was made for a very different reason. Mr. Vallandigham avows his hostility to the war on the part of the Union; and his arrest was made because he was laboring with some effect to prevent the raising of troops, to encourage desertions in the army, and to leave the rebellion without an adequate military force to suppress it. He was not arrested because he was damaging the political prospects of the Administration, or the personal interest of the Commanding General, but because he was damaging the army, upon the existence and vigor of which the life of the nation depends. He was warring upon the military, and this gave the military constitutional jurisdiction to lay hands upon him. If Mr. Vallandigham was not damaging the military power of the country, then his arrest was made on a mistake of facts, which I would be glad to correct on reasonable satisfactory evidence.

In answer to this, permit us to say, first, that neither the charge, nor the specifications in support of the charge on which Mr. Vallandigham was tried, impute to him the act of either laboring to prevent the raising of troops, or to encourage desertions from the army. Secondly, no evidence on the trial was offered with a view to support, or even tended to support, any such charge. In what instance and by what act did he either discourage enlistments or encourage desertions from the army? Who is the man who was discouraged from enlisting, and who was encouraged to desert, by any act of Mr. Vallandigham? If it be assumed that perchance some person might have been discouraged from enlisting, or that some person might have been encouraged to desert on account of hearing Mr. Vallandigham's views as to the policy of the war as a means of restoring the Union, would that have laid the foundation for his conviction and banishment? If so, upon the same grounds every political opponent of the Mexican War might have been convicted and banished from the country.

When gentlemen of high standing and extensive influence, including your Excellency, opposed in the discussions before the people the policy of the Mexican War, were they "warring upon the military," and did this "give the military constitutional jurisdiction to lay hands upon" them? And finally, the charge in the specifications upon which Mr. Vallandigham was tried, entitled him to a trial before the civil tribunals, according to the express provisions of the late Acts of Congress, approved by yourself, of July 17, 1862, and March 3, 1863, which were manifestly designed to supersede all necessity or pretext for arbitrary military arrests.

Examining the Constitution

The undersigned are unable to agree with you in the opinion you have expressed, that the Constitution is different in time of insurrection or invasion from what it is in time of peace and public security. The Constitution provides for no limitation upon, or exceptions to, the guarantees of personal liberty, except as to the writ of *habeas corpus.* Has the President, at the time of invasion or insurrection, the right to engraft limitations or exceptions upon these constitutional guarantees whenever, in his judgement, the public safety requires it?

True it is, the article of the Constitution which defines the various powers delegated to Congress, declares that the "privilege of the writ of *habeas corpus* shall not be suspended unless where, in case of rebellion or invasion, the public safety may require it." But this qualification or limitation upon this restriction upon the powers of Congress has no reference to, or connection with, the other constitutional guarantees of personal liberty. Expunge from the Constitution this limitation upon the power of Congress to suspend the writ of *habeas corpus*, and yet the other guarantees of personal liberty would remain unchanged.

Although a man might not have a constitutional right to have an immediate investigation made as to the legality of his arrest upon *habeas corpus*, yet his "right to a speedy and public trial by an impartial jury of the State and District wherein the crime shall have been committed," will not be altered; neither will his right to the exemption from "cruel and unusual punishments;" nor his right to be secure in his person, houses, papers and effects against any unreasonable seizures and searches; nor his right [not] to be deprived of life, liberty or property, without due process of law; nor his right not to be held to answer for a capital or otherwise infamous offence unless on presentment or indictment of a grand jury, be in anywise changed.

And certainly the restriction upon the power of Congress to suspend the writ of *habeas corpus* in time of insurrection or invasion, could not affect the guarantee that the freedom of speech and of the press shall not be abridged. It is sometimes urged that the proceedings in the civil tribunals are too tardy and ineffective for cases arising in times of insurrection or invasion. It is a full reply to this to say, that arrests by civil process may be equally as expeditious and effective as arrests by military orders.

True, a summary trial and punishment are not allowed in the civil courts. But if the offender be under arrest and imprisoned, and not entitled to a discharge under a writ of *habeas corpus*, before trial, what more can be required for the purposes of the Government? The idea that all the constitutional guarantees of personal liberty are suspended throughout the country at a time of insurrection or invasion in any part of it, places us upon a sea of uncertainty, and subjects the life, liberty and property of every citizen to the mere will of a military commander, or what he may say he considers the public safety requires. Does your Excellency wish to have it understood that you hold that the rights of every man throughout this vast country are subject to be annulled whenever you may say that you consider the public safety requires it, in time of invasion or insurrection? You are further reported as having said that the constitutional guarantees of personal liberty have "no application to the present case we have in hand, because the arrests complained of were not made for treason—that is, not for the treason defined in the Constitution, and upon the conviction of which the punishment is death—nor yet were they made to hold persons to answer for capital or otherwise infamous crime; nor were the proceedings following in any constitutional or criminal sense legal prosecutions. The arrests were made on totally different grounds, and the proceedings following accorded with the grounds of the arrests," &c. The conclusion to be drawn from this position of your Excellency is, that where a man is liable to a "criminal prosecution," or is charged with a crime known to the laws of the land, he is clothed with all the constitutional guarantees for his safety and security from wrong and injustice; but where he is not liable to a "criminal prosecution," or charged with any crime known to the laws, if the President or any military commander shall say that he considers that the public safety requires it, this man may be put outside of the pale of the constitutional guarantees, and arrested without charge of crime, imprisoned without knowledge what for, and any length of time, or be tried before a court-martial and sentenced to any kind of punishment unknown to the laws of the land which the President or the military commander may see proper to impose.

Important Questions

Did the Constitution intend to throw the shield of its securities around the man liable to be charged with treason as defined by it, and yet leave the man not liable to any such charge unprotected by the safeguard of personal liberty and personal security? Can a man not in the military or naval service, nor within the field of the operations of the army, be arrested and imprisoned without any law of the land to authorise it? Can a man thus in civil life be punished without any law defining the offence and prescribing the punishment? If the President or a court-martial may prescribe one kind of punishment unauthorised by law, why not any other kind? Banishment is an unusual punishment, and unknown to our laws. If the President has the right to prescribe the punishment of banishment, why not that of death and confiscation of property? If the President has the right to change the punishment prescribed by the court-martial from imprisonment to banishment, why not from imprisonment to torture upon the rack, or execution upon the gibbet?

Redefining Treason

If an indefinable kind of constructive treason is to be introduced and engrafted upon the Constitution, unknown to the laws of the land, and subject to the will of the President whenever an insurrection or invasion shall occur in any part of this vast country, what safety or security will be left for the liberties of the people?

The "constructive treason" that gave the friends of freedom so many years of toil and trouble in England, was inconsiderable compared to this. The precedents which you make will become a part of the Constitution for your successors, if sanctioned and acquiesced in by the people now.

The people of Ohio are willing to co-operate zealously with you in every effort warranted by the Constitution to restore the Union of the States, but they cannot consent to abandon those fundamental principles of civil liberty which are essential to their existence as a free people.

In their name we ask that, by a revocation of the order of his banishment, Mr. Vallandigham may be restored to the enjoyment of those rights of which they believe he has been unconstitutionally deprived.

For Further Reading

Frank L. Klement, *Dark Lanterns: Secret Political Societies, Conspiracies, and Treason Trials in the Civil War.* Baton Rouge: Louisiana State University Press, 1984.

Michael Linfield, *Freedom Under Fire: U.S. Civil Liberties in Times of War.* Boston: South End Press, 1990.

Mark E. Neely, *The Fate of Liberty.* New York: Oxford University Press, 1991.

VIEWPOINT 38A

Sherman's War Tactics Are Inhumane (1864)

James M. Calhoun (1811–1875), E.E. Rawson (1818–1893), and S.C. Wells (dates unknown)

The Civil War was unprecedented in American history in the amount of destruction and carnage it

caused. A small glimpse of its effects can be seen in the following exchange between the leaders of the Southern city of Atlanta, Georgia and William T. Sherman, the commanding general of the Union forces that captured Atlanta on September 2, 1864. Over the course of the Civil War Sherman had determined that the war and its effects needed to be fully brought to bear on the Southern people. Following Atlanta's surrender, Sherman decided not to remain and occupy the city, but to burn all of military value in it and take his troops on a march through Georgia. He ordered all civilians to evacuate the city. On September 11, James M. Calhoun, the mayor of Atlanta, and two members of the City Council wrote Sherman a letter, reprinted here, telling him of the hardships his order caused, and asking him to reconsider.

What hardships do Calhoun and the others describe? On what grounds do they appeal to Sherman?

---

*M*ajor-General W.T. Sherman.

Sir: We the undersigned, Mayor and two of the Council for the city of Atlanta, for the time being the only legal organ of the people of the said city, to express their wants and wishes, ask leave most earnestly but respectfully to petition you to reconsider the order requiring them to leave Atlanta.

Appalling Hardships

At first view, it struck us that the measure would involve extraordinary hardship and loss, but since we have seen the practical execution of it so far as it has progressed, and the individual condition of the people, and heard their statements as to the inconveniences, loss, and suffering attending it, we are satisfied that the amount of it will involve in the aggregate consequences appalling and heart-rending.

Many poor women are in advanced state of pregnancy, others now having young children, and whose husbands for the greater part are either in the army, prisoners, or dead. Some say: "I have such a one sick at my house; who will wait on them when I am gone?" Others say: "What are we to do? We have no house to go to, and no means to buy, build, or rent any; no parents, relatives, or friends, to go to." Another says: "I will try and take this or that article of property, but such and such things I must leave behind, though I need them much."....

We only refer to a few facts, to try to illustrate in part how this measure will operate in practice. As you advanced, the people north of this fell back; and

Reprinted from *Memoirs of Gen. W.T. Sherman* by William T. Sherman, 1875.

before your arrival here, a large portion of the people had retired south, so that the country south of this is already crowded, and without houses enough to accommodate the people, and we are informed that many are now staying in churches and other outbuildings.

This being so, how is it possible for the people still here (mostly women and children) to find any shelter? And how can they live through the winter in the woods—no shelter or subsistence, in the midst of strangers who know them not, and without the power to assist them much, if they were willing to do so?

---•---

"You know the woe, the horrors, and the suffering, cannot be described by words; . . . we ask you to take these things into consideration."

---•---

This is but a feeble picture of the consequences of this measure. You know the woe, the horrors, and the suffering, cannot be described by words; imagination can only conceive of it, and we ask you to take these things into consideration.

A Plea to Reconsider

We know your mind and time are constantly occupied with the duties of your command, which almost deters us from asking your attention to this matter, but thought it might be that you had not considered this subject in all of its awful consequences, and that on more reflection you, we hope, would not make this people an exception to all mankind, for we know of no such instance ever having occurred—surely never in the United States—and what has this *helpless* people done, that they should be driven from their homes, to wander strangers and outcasts, and exiles, and to subsist on charity?

We do not know as yet the number of people still here; of those who are here, we are satisfied a respectable number, if allowed to remain at home, could subsist for several months without assistance, and a respectable number for a much longer time, and who might not need assistance at any time.

In conclusion, we most earnestly and solemnly petition you to reconsider this order, or modify it, and suffer this unfortunate people to remain at home, and enjoy what little means they have.

Respectfully submitted:

James M. Calhoun, *Mayor.*
E.E. Rawson, *Councilman.*
S.C. Wells, *Councilman.*

VIEWPOINT 38B

War Is Necessarily Inhumane (1864)

William T. Sherman (1820–1891)

William T. Sherman was, after Ulysses S. Grant, the second most important Union general of the Civil War. Rising from colonel at the First Battle of Bull Run (Manassas) in 1861 to commanding general of Union forces in the West in 1864, he won his most important victory in September of that year when his army captured Atlanta, Georgia. Wanting to move his troops on, and not wishing to see Atlanta and its factories fall back into the hands of the Confederacy, he determined to burn the city, and ordered its inhabitants evacuated.

Sherman received several letters of protest over his decision to evacuate Atlanta, including one dated September 11, 1864, from the mayor and two members of the City Council, who asked Sherman to take into account the hardships he was causing. Sherman replied the next day in the letter that is reprinted here.

What beliefs does Sherman express about the nature of war? What is the only way for Southerners to end their suffering, according to Sherman?

James M. Calhoun, Mayor, E.E. Rawson and S.C. Wells, representing City Council of Atlanta.

Gentlemen: I have your letter of the 11th, in the nature of a petition to revoke my orders removing all the inhabitants from Atlanta. I have read it carefully, and give full credit to your statements of the distress that will be occasioned, and yet shall not revoke my orders, because they were not designed to meet the humanities of the case, but to prepare for the future struggles in which millions of good people outside of Atlanta have a deep interest. We must have peace, not only at Atlanta, but in all America. To secure this, we must stop the war that now desolates our once happy and favored country. To stop war, we must defeat the rebel armies which are arrayed against the laws and Constitution that all must respect and obey. To defeat those armies, we must prepare the way to reach them in their recesses, provided with the arms and instruments which enable us to accomplish our purpose. Now, I know the vindictive nature of our enemy, that we may have many years of military operations from this quarter; and, therefore, deem it wise and prudent to prepare in time. The use of Atlanta for warlike purposes is

Reprinted from *Memoirs of Gen. W.T. Sherman* by William T. Sherman, 1875.

inconsistent with its character as a home for families. There will be no manufactures, commerce, or agriculture here, for the maintenance of families, and sooner or later want will compel the inhabitants to go. Why not go now, when all the arrangements are completed for the transfer, instead of waiting till the plunging shot of contending armies will renew the scenes of the past month? Of course, I do not apprehend any such thing at this moment, but you do not suppose this army will be here until the war is over. I cannot discuss this subject with you fairly, because I cannot impart to you what we propose to do, but I assert that our military plans make it necessary for the inhabitants to go away, and I can only renew my offer of services to make their exodus in any direction as easy and comfortable as possible.

War Is Cruel

You cannot qualify war in harsher terms than I will. War is cruelty, and you cannot refine it; and those who brought war into our country deserve all the curses and maledictions a people can pour out. I know I had no hand in making this war, and I know I will make more sacrifices to-day than any of you to secure peace. But you cannot have peace and a division of our country. If the United States submits to a division now, it will not stop, but will go on until we reap the fate of Mexico, which is eternal war. The United States does and must assert its authority, wherever it once had power; for, if it relaxes one bit to pressure, it is gone, and I believe that such is the national feeling. This feeling assumes various shapes, but always comes back to that of Union. Once admit the Union, once more acknowledge the authority of the national Government, and, instead of devoting your houses and streets and roads to the dread uses of war, I and this army become at once your protectors and supporters, shielding you from danger, let it come from what quarter it may. I know that a few individuals cannot resist a torrent of error and passion, such as swept the South into rebellion, but you can point out, so that we may know those who desire a government, and those who insist on war and its desolation.

———— • ————

"You might as well appeal against the thunder-storm as against these terrible hardships of war."

———— • ————

You might as well appeal against the thunder-storm as against these terrible hardships of war. They are inevitable, and the only way the people of Atlanta can hope once more to live in peace and quiet at home, is to stop the war, which can only be done by admitting that it began in error and is perpetuated in pride.

We don't want your negroes, or your horses, or your houses, or your lands, or any thing you have, but we do want and will have a just obedience to the laws of the United States. That we will have, and, if it involves the destruction of your improvements, we cannot help it.

You have heretofore read public sentiment in your newspapers, that live by falsehood and excitement; and the quicker you seek for truth in other quarters, the better. I repeat then that, by the original compact of Government, the United States had certain rights in Georgia, which have never been relinquished and never will be; that the South began war by seizing forts, arsenals, mints, customhouses, etc., etc., long before Mr. Lincoln was installed, and before the South had one jot or tittle of provocation. I myself have seen in Missouri, Kentucky, Tennessee, and Mississippi, hundreds and thousands of women and children fleeing from your armies and desperadoes, hungry and with bleeding feet. In Memphis, Vicksburg, and Mississippi, we fed thousands upon thousands of the families of rebel soldiers left on our hands, and whom we could not see starve. Now that war comes home to you, you feel very different. You deprecate its horrors, but did not feel them when you sent car-loads of soldiers and ammunition, and moulded shells and shot, to carry war into Kentucky and Tennessee, to desolate the homes of hundreds and thousands of good people who only asked to live in peace at their old homes, and under the Government of their inheritance. But these comparisons are idle. I want peace, and believe it can only be reached through union and war, and I will ever conduct war with a view to perfect and early success.

When Peace Comes

But, my dear sirs, when peace does come, you may call on me for any thing. Then will I share with you the last cracker, and watch with you to shield your homes and families against danger from every quarter.

Now you must go, and take with you the old and feeble, feed and nurse them, and build for them, in more quiet places, proper habitations to shield them against the weather until the mad passions of men cool down, and allow the Union and peace once more to settle over your old homes at Atlanta. Yours in haste,

W.T. Sherman, *Major-General commanding.*

For Further Reading
James L. McDonough and James P. Jones, *"War So Terrible": Sherman and Atlanta.* New York: Norton, 1987.
James M. McPherson, *Battle Cry of Freedom: The Civil War Era.* New York: Oxford University Press, 1988.

Charles Royster, *The Destructive War: William Tecumseh Sherman, Stonewall Jackson, and the Americans.* New York: Knopf, 1991.

William T. Sherman, *Memoirs of General W.T. Sherman.* New York: Library of America, 1990.

Reconstruction

VIEWPOINT 39A

The South Is a Separate, Conquered Nation (1866)

The Joint Committee on Reconstruction

Following the Civil War the nation faced the dilemma of how to reintegrate the Southern states that had rebelled. The years 1865–1868 were marked by an intense struggle between Radical Republicans in Congress and President Andrew Johnson over the proper way to do this. In the summer of 1865 former vice president Johnson, a Tennessean and erstwhile Democrat who became president following Abraham Lincoln's assassination, officially pardoned many Confederates and instituted a moderate reconstruction program that aimed to quickly reinstate the former Confederate states and restore the Union with a minimum of federal involvement. These goals were in large part a continuation of the reconstruction policies and initiatives of Lincoln. The new state governments organized under Johnson's reconstruction program were criticized by some, however, for electing former rebels to positions of leadership (including Congress) and for passing laws designed to restrict the political and economic activities of blacks.

Johnson's policies were harshly criticized by some Republicans in Congress. Dubbed Radical Republicans, they advocated a thorough restructuring of Southern society, including the providing of civil rights protection and educational opportunity for the former slaves. An able summary of Radical Republican views is found in the following viewpoint, taken from the June 20, 1866, report to Congress of the Joint Committee on Reconstruction. Congress had established the committee in December 1865, instructing its fifteen members to investigate the condition of the South and to make recommendations for all bills concerning reconstruction. Thaddeus Stevens, a Radical Republican congressman, set the agenda for the committee, which consisted primarily of Republicans; only three members were Democrats. In these excerpts from the committee's

From Part 3 of the *Report of the Joint Committee on Reconstruction*, 39th Cong., 1st sess., 1866.

report, the majority members argue that the states of the former Confederacy have forfeited all rights previously held as states of the Union. The report contends that the South is in effect a conquered nation, separate from the Union, and therefore could not claim any constitutional guarantees or congressional representation. The implications of this argument were important: Without rights as states, the South could be remolded as the Radical Republicans saw fit; without representation, the Southern Democrats would be barred from the U.S. Congress.

What has been the reaction of the former Confederates toward their defeat in the Civil War, according to the committee? Why, in their view, is it important that Confederate states not be immediately brought back into the Union? What does the committee argue about the authority of Congress in making reconstruction policy?

A claim for the immediate admission of Senators and Representatives from the so-called Confederate States has been urged, which seems to your committee not to be founded either in reason or in law, and which cannot be passed without comment. Stated in a few words, it amounts to this: That inasmuch as the lately insurgent States had no legal right to separate themselves from the Union, they still retain their positions as States, and consequently the people thereof have a right to immediate representation in Congress without the imposition of any conditions whatever; and further, that until such admission Congress has no right to tax them for the support of the Government. It has even been contended that until such admission all legislation affecting their interests is, if not unconstitutional, at least unjustifiable and oppressive.

It is believed by your committee that all these propositions are not only wholly untenable, but, if admitted, would tend to the destruction of the Government.

It must not be forgotten that the people of these States, without justification or excuse, rose in insurrection against the United States. They deliberately abolished their State governments so far as the same connected them politically with the Union as members thereof under the Constitution. They deliberately renounced their allegiance to the Federal Government, and proceeded to establish an independent government for themselves. In the prosecution of this enterprise they seized the national forts, arsenals, dockyards, and other public property within their borders, drove out from among them those who remained true to the Union, and heaped every imaginable insult and injury upon the United States and its citizens. Finally they opened hostilities, and levied war against the Government.

They continued this war for four years with the most determined and malignant spirit, killing in battle and otherwise large numbers of loyal people, destroying the property of loyal citizens on the sea and on the land, and entailing on the Government an enormous debt, incurred to sustain its rightful authority. Whether legally and constitutionally or not, they did, in fact, withdraw from the Union and made themselves subjects of another government of their own creation. And they only yielded when, after a long, bloody, and wasting war, they were compelled by utter exhaustion to lay down their arms; and this they did not willingly, but declaring that they yielded because they could no longer resist, affording no evidence whatever of repentance for their crime, and expressing no regret, except that they had no longer the power to continue the desperate struggle.

•

"They did, in fact, withdraw from the Union and made themselves subjects of another government of their own creation."

•

It cannot, we think, be denied by any one, having a tolerable acquaintance with public law, that the war thus waged was a civil war of the greatest magnitude. The people waging it were necessarily subject to all the rules which, by the law of nations, control a contest of that character, and to all the legitimate consequences following it. One of those consequences was that, within the limits prescribed by humanity, the conquered rebels were at the mercy of the conquerors. That a government thus outraged had a most perfect right to exact indemnity for the injuries done and security against the recurrence of such outrages in the future would seem too clear for dispute. What the nature of that security should be, what proof should be required of a return to allegiance, what time should elapse before a people thus demoralized should be restored in full to the enjoyment of political rights and privileges, are questions for the law-making power to decide, and that decision must depend on grave considerations of the public safety and the general welfare.

It is moreover contended, and with apparent gravity, that, from the peculiar nature and character of our Government, no such right on the part of the conqueror can exist; that from the moment when rebellion lays down its arms and actual hostilities cease, all political rights of rebellious communities are at once restored; that, because the people of a State of the Union were once an organized commu-

nity within the Union, they necessarily so remain, and their right to be represented in Congress at any and all times, and to participate in the government of the country under all circumstances, admits of neither question or dispute. If this is indeed true, then is the Government of the United States powerless for its own protection, and flagrant rebellion, carried to the extreme of civil war, is a pastime which any State may play at, not only certain that it can lose nothing in any event, but may even be the gainer by defeat. If rebellion succeeds, it accomplishes its purpose and destroys the government. If it fails, the war has been barren of results, and the battle may be still fought out in the legislative halls of the country. Treason, defeated in the field, has only to take possession of Congress and the cabinet.

Your committee does not deem it either necessary or proper to discuss the question whether the late Confederate States are still States of this Union, or can even be otherwise. Granting this profitless abstraction, about which so many words have been wasted, it by no means follows that the people of those States may not place themselves in a condition to abrogate the powers and privileges incident to a State of the Union, and deprive themselves of all pretence of right to exercise those powers and enjoy those privileges. A State within the Union has obligations to discharge as a member of the Union. It must submit to federal laws and uphold federal authority. It must have a government republican in form, under and by which it is connected with the General Government, and through which it can discharge its obligations. It is more than idle, it is a mockery, to contend that a people who have thrown off their allegiance, destroyed the local government which bound their States to the Union as members thereof, defied its authority, refused to execute its laws, and abrogated every provision which gave them political rights within the Union, still retain, through all, the perfect and entire right to resume, at their own will and pleasure, all their privileges within the Union, and especially to participate in its government, and to control the conduct of its affairs. To admit such a principle for one moment would be to declare that treason is always master and loyalty a blunder. Such a principle is void by its very nature and essence, because inconsistent with the theory of government, and fatal to its very existence. . . .

The Attitude of Former Rebels

Hardly is the war closed before the people of these insurrectionary States come forward and haughtily claim, as a right, the privilege of participating at once in that Government which they had for four years been fighting to overthrow. Allowed and encouraged by the Executive to organize State governments, they at once placed in power leading rebels, unrepentant and unpardoned, excluding with contempt those who had manifested an attachment to the Union and preferring, in many instances, those who had rendered themselves the most obnoxious. In the face of the law requiring an oath which would necessarily exclude all such men from federal offices, they elect, with very few exceptions, as Senators and Representatives in Congress men who had actively participated in the rebellion, insultingly denouncing the law as unconstitutional. It is only necessary to instance the election to the Senate of the late vice president of the Confederacy [Alexander H. Stephens of Georgia], a man who, against his own declared convictions, had lent all the weight of his acknowledged ability and of his influence as a most prominent public man to the cause of the rebellion, and who, unpardoned rebel as he is, with that oath staring him in the face, had the assurance to lay his credentials on the table of the Senate. Other rebels of scarcely less note or notoriety were selected from other quarters. Professing no repentance, glorying apparently in the crime they had committed, avowing still, as the uncontradicted testimony of Mr. Stephens and many others proves, an adherence to the pernicious doctrine of secession, and declaring that they yielded only to necessity, they insist, with unanimous voice, upon their rights as States, and proclaim that they will submit to no conditions whatever as preliminary to their resumption of power under that Constitution which they still claim the right to repudiate. . . .

The testimony is conclusive that after the collapse of the Confederacy the feeling of the people of the rebellious States was that of abject submission. Having appealed to the tribunal of arms, they had no hope except that by the magnanimity of their conquerors their lives, and possibly their property, might be preserved. Unfortunately, the general issue of pardons to persons who had been prominent in the rebellion, and the feeling of kindness and conciliation manifested by the Executive, and very generally indicated through the northern press, had the effect to render whole communities forgetful of the crime they had committed, defiant towards the Federal Government, and regardless of their duties as citizens. The conciliatory measures of the Government do not seem to have been met even half way. The bitterness and defiance exhibited toward the United States under such circumstances is without a parallel in the history of the world. In return for our leniency we receive only an insulting denial of our authority. In return for our kind desire for the resumption of fraternal relations we receive only an insolent assumption of rights and privileges long since forfeited. The crime we have punished is paraded as a virtue, and the principles of republican government which we have vindicated at so terrible cost are denounced as unjust and oppressive. . . .

A Hostile Act

We now purpose to re-state, as briefly as possible, the general facts and principles applicable to all the States recently in rebellion.

First. The seats of the senators and representatives from the so-called Confederate States became vacant in the year 1861, during the second session of the Thirty-sixth Congress, by the voluntary withdrawal of their incumbents, with the sanction and by direction of the legislatures or conventions of their respective States. This was done as a hostile act against the Constitution and Government of the United States, with a declared intent to overthrow the same by forming a southern confederation. This act of declared hostility was speedily followed by an organization of the same States into a confederacy, which levied and waged war, by sea and land, against the United States. This war continued more than four years, within which period the rebel armies besieged the national capital, invaded the loyal States, burned their towns and cities, robbed their citizens, destroyed more than 250,000 loyal soldiers, and imposed an increased national burden of not less than $3,500,000,000, of which seven or eight hundred millions have already been met and paid. From the time these confederated States thus withdrew their representation in Congress and levied war against the United States, the great mass of their people became and were insurgents, rebels, traitors, and all of them assumed and occupied the political, legal, and practical relation of enemies of the United States. This position is established by acts of Congress and judicial decisions, and is recognized repeatedly by the President in public proclamations, documents, and speeches.

Second. The States thus confederated prosecuted their war against the United States to final arbitrament, and did not cease until all their armies were captured, their military powers destroyed, their civil officers, State and confederate, taken prisoners or put to flight, every vestige of State and confederate government obliterated, their territory overrun and occupied by the federal armies, and their people reduced to the condition of enemies conquered in war, entitled only by public law to such rights, privileges, and conditions as might be vouchsafed by the conqueror. This position is also established by judicial decisions, and is recognized by the President in public proclamations, documents, and speeches.

Third. Having voluntarily deprived themselves of representation in Congress, for the criminal purpose of destroying the Federal Union, and having reduced themselves, by the act of levying war, to the condition of public enemies, they have no right to complain of temporary exclusion from Congress; but on the contrary, having voluntarily renounced the right to representation, and disqualified themselves by crime from participating in the Government, the burden now rests upon them, before claiming to be reinstated in their former condition, to show that they are qualified to resume federal relations. In order to do this, they must prove that they have established, with the consent of the people, republican forms of government in harmony with the Constitution and laws of the United States, that all hostile purposes have ceased, and should give adequate guarantees against future treason and rebellion—guarantees which shall prove satisfactory to the Government against which they rebelled, and by whose arms they were subdued.

Fourth. Having, by this treasonable withdrawal from Congress, and by flagrant rebellion and war, forfeited all civil and political rights and privileges under the Constitution, they can only be restored thereto by the permission and authority of that constitutional power against which they rebelled and by which they were subdued.

Fifth. These rebellious enemies were conquered by the people of the United States, acting through all the co-ordinate branches of the Government, and not by the executive department alone. The powers of conqueror are not so vested in the President that he can fix and regulate the terms of settlement and confer congressional representation on conquered rebels and traitors. Nor can he, in any way, qualify enemies of the Government to exercise its lawmaking power. The authority to restore rebels to political power in the Federal Government can be exercised only with the concurrence of all the departments in which political power is vested; and hence the several proclamations of the President to the people of the Confederate States cannot be considered as extending beyond the purposes declared, and can only be regarded as provisional permission by the commander-in-chief of the army to do certain acts, the effect and validity whereof is to be determined by the constitutional government, and not solely by the executive power.

The Rights of Conquered Enemies

Sixth. The question before Congress is, then, whether conquered enemies have the right, and shall be permitted at their own pleasure and on their own terms, to participate in making laws for their conquerors; whether conquered rebels may change their theater of operations from the battle-field, where they were defeated and overthrown, to the halls of Congress, and, through their representatives, seize upon the Government which they fought to destroy; whether the national treasury, the army of the nation, its navy, its forts and arsenals, its whole civil administration, its credit, its pensioners, the widows and orphans of those who perished in the war, the public honor, peace and safety, shall all be turned over to the keeping of its recent enemies without delay, and without imposing such conditions as, in the opinion of Congress, the security of the country and its institutions may demand.

Seventh. The history of mankind exhibits no example of such madness and folly. The instinct of self-preservation protests against it. . . .

Tenth. The conclusion of your committee therefore is, that the so-called Confederate States are not at present entitled to representation in the Congress of the United States; that, before allowing such representation, adequate security for future peace and safety should be required; that this can only be found in such changes of the organic law as shall determine the civil rights and privileges of all citizens in all parts of the Republic, shall place representation on an equitable basis, shall fix a stigma upon treason, and protect the loyal people against future claims for the expenses incurred in support of rebellion and for manumitted slaves, together with an express grant of power in Congress to enforce those provisions.

VIEWPOINT 39B

The South Is Not a Separate, Conquered Nation (1867)

Andrew Johnson (1808–1875)

Andrew Johnson was the only Southern senator to support the Union during the war, keeping his seat in the Senate after his fellow Southerners withdrew. Selected to be Abraham Lincoln's running mate for the 1864 presidential election, Johnson was propelled into the presidency by the assassination of Lincoln in April 1865. As president he attempted to administer a reconstruction program that emphasized the rapid readmission of former Confederate states into the Union, while he opposed such measures as federal enforcement of black suffrage and civil rights. Over the next few years he was enmeshed in a power struggle with Congress over reconstruction, Congress being controlled by Radical Republicans, passing numerous reconstruction laws over his veto.

One of the hotly debated points between the president and Republican members of Congress was the status of the former Confederate states. Among the congressional actions taken over Johnson's veto were the dismantling of the provisional state governments

From Andrew Johnson's third Annual Message, December 3, 1867.

Johnson had established and the division of the South into military districts under Union army rule. In his State of the Union address of December 3, 1867, excerpted here, Johnson asserts that the Southern states have never been separated from the Union. Supporting his argument with a strict interpretation of the Constitution, Johnson declares that the Union is indivisible, and that the Southern states, having never been separated from the Union, cannot be denied their basic constitutional rights and representation. Johnson's clashes with Congress over reconstruction policy would eventually lead to an (unsuccessful) attempt to impeach him in 1868.

What does Johnson mean when he says that "there is no Union as our fathers understood the term"? What threats to the Constitution does Johnson perceive in the Radical Republicans' programs?

When a civil war has been brought to a close, it is manifestly the first interest and duty of the state to repair the injuries which the war has inflicted, and to secure the benefit of the lessons it teaches as fully and as speedily as possible. This duty was, upon the termination of the rebellion, promptly accepted, not only by the executive department, but by the insurrectionary States themselves, and restoration in the first moment of peace was believed to be as easy and certain as it was indispensable. The expectations, however, then so reasonably and confidently entertained were disappointed by legislation from which I felt constrained by my obligations to the Constitution to withhold my assent.

There Is No Union

It is therefore a source of profound regret that in complying with the obligation imposed upon the President by the Constitution to give to Congress from time to time information of the state of the Union I am unable to communicate any definitive adjustment, satisfactory to the American people, of the questions which since the close of the rebellion have agitated the public mind. On the contrary, candor compels me to declare that at this time there is no Union as our fathers understood the term, and as they meant it to be understood by us. The Union which they established can exist only where all the States are represented in both Houses of Congress; where one State is as free as another to regulate its internal concerns according to its own will, and where the laws of the central Government, strictly confined to matters of national jurisdiction, apply with equal force to all the people of every section. That such is not the present "state of the Union" is a melancholy fact, and we must all acknowledge that the restoration of the States to their proper legal

relations with the Federal Government and with one another, according to the terms of the original compact, would be the greatest temporal blessing which God, in His kindest providence, could bestow upon this nation. It becomes our imperative duty to consider whether or not it is impossible to effect this most desirable consummation.

The Union and the Constitution are inseparable. As long as one is obeyed by all parties, the other will be preserved; and if one is destroyed, both must perish together. The destruction of the Constitution will be followed by other and still greater calamities. It was ordained not only to form a more perfect union between the States, but to "establish justice, insure domestic tranquility, provide for the common defense, promote the general welfare, and secure the blessings of liberty to ourselves and our posterity." Nothing but implicit obedience to its requirements in all parts of the country will accomplish these great ends. Without that obedience we can look forward only to continual outrages upon individual rights, incessant breaches of the public peace, national weakness, financial dishonor, the total loss of our prosperity, the general corruption of morals, and the final extinction of popular freedom. To save our country from evils so appalling as these, we should renew our efforts again and again.

To me the process of restoration seems perfectly plain and simple. It consists merely in a faithful application of the Constitution and laws. The execution of the laws is not now obstructed or opposed by physical force. There is no military or other necessity, real or pretended, which can prevent obedience to the Constitution, either North or South. All the rights and all the obligations of States and individuals can be protected and enforced by means perfectly consistent with the fundamental law. The courts may be everywhere open, and if open their process would be unimpeded. Crimes against the United States can be prevented or punished by the proper judicial authorities in a manner entirely practicable and legal. There is therefore no reason why the Constitution should not be obeyed, unless those who exercise its powers have determined that it shall be disregarded and violated. The mere naked will of this Government, or of some one or more of its branches, is the only obstacle that can exist to a perfect union of all the States. . . .

It is clear to my apprehension that the States lately in rebellion are still members of the National Union. When did they cease to be so? The "ordinances of secession" adopted by a portion (in most of them a very small portion) of their citizens were mere nullities. If we admit now that they were valid and effectual for the purpose intended by their authors, we sweep from under our feet the whole ground upon which we justified the war. Were those

States afterwards expelled from the Union by the war? The direct contrary was averred by this Government to be its purpose, and was so understood by all those who gave their blood and treasure to aid in its prosecution. It can not be that a successful war, waged for the preservation of the Union, had the legal effect of dissolving it. The victory of the nation's arms was not the disgrace of her policy; the defeat of secession on the battlefield was not the triumph of its lawless principle. Nor could Congress, with or without the consent of the Executive, do anything which would have the effect, directly or indirectly, of separating the States from each other. To dissolve the Union is to repeal the Constitution which holds it together, and that is a power which does not belong to any department of this Government, or to all of them united.

"It can not be that a successful war, waged for the preservation of the Union, had the legal effect of dissolving it."

This is so plain that it has been acknowledged by all branches of the Federal Government. The Executive (my predecessor as well as myself) and the heads of all the Departments have uniformly acted upon the principle that the Union is not only undissolved, but indissoluble. Congress submitted an amendment of the Constitution to be ratified by the Southern States, and accepted their acts of ratification as a necessary and lawful exercise of their highest function. If they were not States, or were States out of the Union, their consent to a change in the fundamental law of the Union would have been nugatory, and Congress in asking it committed a political absurdity. The judiciary has also given the solemn sanction of its authority to the same view of the case. The judges of the Supreme Court have included the Southern States in their circuits, and they are constantly, *in banc* [on the bench] and elsewhere, exercising jurisdiction which does not belong to them unless those States are States of the Union.

If the Southern States are component parts of the Union, the Constitution is the supreme law for them, as it is for all the other States. They are bound to obey it, and so are we. The right of the Federal Government, which is clear and unquestionable, to enforce the Constitution upon them implies the correlative obligation on our part to observe its limitations and execute its guaranties. Without the Constitution we are nothing; by, through, and under the Constitution we are what it makes us. We may doubt the wisdom of the law, we may not approve of its provisions, but we can not violate it merely because it seems to confine our powers within limits narrower than we could wish. It is not a question of individual or class or sectional interest, much less of party predominance, but of duty—of high and sacred duty—which we are all sworn to perform. If we can not support the Constitution with the cheerful alacrity of those who love and believe in it, we must give to it as least the fidelity of public servants who act under solemn obligations and commands which they dare not disregard.

The constitutional duty is not the only one which requires the States to be restored. There is another consideration which, though of minor importance, is yet of great weight. On the 22d day of July, 1861, Congress declared by an almost unanimous vote of both Houses that the war should be conducted solely for the purpose of preserving the Union and maintaining the supremacy of the Federal Constitution and laws, without impairing the dignity, equality, and rights of the States or of individuals, and that when this was done the war should cease. I do not say that this declaration is personally binding on those who joined in making it, any more than individual members of Congress are personally bound to pay a public debt created under a law for which they voted. But it was a solemn, public, official pledge of the national honor, and I can not imagine upon what grounds the repudiation of it is to be justified. If it be said that we are not bound to keep faith with rebels, let it be remembered that this promise was not made to rebels only. Thousands of true men in the South were drawn to our standard by it, and hundreds of thousands in the North gave their lives in the belief that it would be carried out. It was made on the day after the first great battle of the war had been fought and lost. All patriotic and intelligent men then saw the necessity of giving such an assurance, and believed that without it the war would end in disaster to our cause. Having given that assurance in the extremity of our peril, the violation of it now, in the day of our power, would be a rude rending of that good faith which holds the moral world together; our country would cease to have any claim upon the confidence of men; it would make the war not only a failure, but a fraud. . . .

Unjust Punishment

I have no desire to save from the proper and just consequences of their great crime those who engaged in rebellion against the Government, but as a mode of punishment the measures under consideration are the most unreasonable that could be invented. Many of those people are perfectly innocent; many kept their fidelity to the Union untainted to the last; many were incapable of any legal offense; a large proportion even of the persons able to bear arms were forced into rebellion against their will, and of those who are guilty with their own consent the degrees of guilt are as various as the shades of their character and temper. But these acts of Congress confound them all together in one common doom. Indiscriminate vengeance upon classes, sects, and parties, or upon whole communities, for offenses committed by a portion of them against the governments to which they owed obedience was common in the barbarous ages of the world; but Christianity and civilization have made such progress that recourse to a punishment so cruel and unjust would meet with the condemnation of all unprejudiced and right-minded men. The punitive justice of this age, and especially of this country, does not consist in stripping whole States of their liberties and reducing all their people, without distinction, to the condition of slavery. It deals separately with each individual, confines itself to the forms of law, and vindicates its own purity by an impartial examination of every case before a competent judicial tribunal. If this does not satisfy all our desires with regard to Southern rebels, let us console ourselves by reflecting that a free Constitution, triumphant in war and unbroken in peace, is worth far more to us and our children than the gratification of any present feeling.

I am aware it is assumed that this system of government for the Southern States is not to be perpetual. It is true this military government is to be only provisional, but it is through this temporary evil that a greater evil is to be made perpetual. If the guaranties of the Constitution can be broken provisionally to serve a temporary purpose, and in a part only of the country, we can destroy them everywhere and for all time. Arbitrary measures often change, but they generally change for the worse. It is the curse of despotism that is has no halting place. The intermitted exercise of its power brings no sense of security to its subjects, for they can never know what more they will be called to endure when its red right hand is armed to plague them again. Nor is it possible to conjecture how or where power, unrestrained by law, may seek its next victims. The States that are still free may be enslaved at any moment; for if the Constitution does not protect all, it protects none.

For Further Reading

Harold M. Hyman, ed., *The Radical Republicans and Reconstruction, 1861–1870.* Indianapolis: Bobbs-Merrill, 1967.

Eric McKitrick, *Andrew Johnson and Reconstruction.* Chicago: University of Chicago Press, 1960.

Hans L. Trefousse, *The Radical Republicans: Lincoln's Vanguard for Racial Justice.* New York: Knopf, 1969.

VIEWPOINT 40A

Blacks Should Have the Right to Vote (1865)

Frederick Douglass (1817–1895)

Born in Maryland to a white father and a slave mother, Frederick Douglass escaped from slavery in 1838 and soon became a prominent abolitionist, lecturing throughout the North and in England. Unlike some abolitionists, Douglass was not content with mere emancipation; he insisted that their work would not be done until the right of blacks to all civil liberties, including the vote, was firmly secured.

On January 26, 1865, with the end of the Civil War a few months away, Douglass delivered a speech entitled "What the Black Man Wants" to the members of the Massachusetts Anti-Slavery Society. The following viewpoint is excerpted from that speech. Taking issue with those abolitionists who felt black enfranchisement should be gradual, Douglass calls for immediate suffrage for black men. Not only are blacks prepared for the responsibility of suffrage, Douglass insists, but once armed with the vote, they will be able to stand on their own, without any differential treatment.

What practical and moral reasons does Douglass give for black suffrage? How does he respond to charges of black inferiority?

I have had but one idea for the last three years to present to the American people, and the phraseology in which I clothe it is the old abolition phraseology. I am for the "immediate, unconditional and universal" enfranchisement of the black man, in every State of the Union. (Loud applause.) Without this, his liberty is a mockery; without this, you might as well almost retain the old name of slavery for his condition; for, in fact, if he is not the slave of the individual master, he is the slave of society, and holds his liberty as a privilege, not as a right. He is at the mercy of the mob, and has no means of protecting himself.

The Time Is Ripe

It may be objected, however, that this pressing of the negroes' right to suffrage is premature. Let us have slavery abolished, it may be said, let us have labor organized, and then, in the natural course of events, the right of suffrage will be extended to the negro. I do not agree with this. The constitution of the human mind is such, that if it once disregards the

From "What the Black Man Wants" by Frederick Douglass, *Liberator,* February 1865.

conviction forced upon it by a revelation of truth, it requires the exercise of a higher power to produce the same conviction afterwards. The American people are now in tears. The Shenandoah has run blood—the best blood of the North. All around Richmond the blood of New England and of the North has been shed—of your sons, your brothers, and your fathers. We all feel, in the existence of this rebellion, that judgments terrible, widespread, far-reaching, overwhelming, are abroad in the land; and we feel, in view of these judgments, just now, a disposition to learn righteousness. This is the hour. Our streets are in mourning, tears are falling at every fireside, and under the chastisement of this rebellion, we have almost come up to the point of conceding this great, this all-important right of suffrage. I fear that if we fail to do it now, if Abolitionists fail to press it now, we may not see, for centuries to come, the same disposition that exists at this moment. (Applause.) Hence, I say, now is the time to press this right.

———— • ————

"Here, where universal suffrage is the rule, where that is the fundamental idea of the government, to rule us out is to make us an exception, to brand us with the stigma of inferiority."

———— • ————

It may be asked, "Why do you want it? Some men have got along very well without it. Women have not this right." Shall we justify one wrong by another? That is a sufficient answer. Shall we at this moment justify the deprivation of the negro of the right to vote because some one else is deprived of that privilege? I hold that women as well as men have the right to vote (applause), and my heart and my voice go with the movement to extend suffrage to woman. But that question rests upon another basis than that on which our right rests. We may be asked, I say, why we want it. I will tell you why we want it. We want it because it is our right, first of all. (Applause.) No class of men can, without insulting their own nature, be content with any deprivation of their rights. We want it, again, as a means for educating our race. Men are so constituted that they derive their conviction of their own possibilities largely from the estimate formed of them by others. If nothing is expected of a people, that people will find it difficult to contradict that expectation. By depriving us of suffrage, you affirm our incapacity to form an intelligent judgment respecting public men and public measures; you declare before the world that we are unfit to exercise the elective franchise, and by this means

lead us to undervalue ourselves, to put a low estimate upon ourselves, and to feel that we have no possibilities like other men. Again, I want the elective franchise, for one, as a colored man, because ours is a peculiar government, based upon a peculiar idea, and that idea is universal suffrage. If I were in a monarchical government, or an autocratic or aristocratic Government, where the few bore rule and the many were subject, there would be no special stigma resting upon me because I did not exercise the elective franchise. It would do me no great violence. Mingling with the mass, I should partake of the strength of the mass; I should be supported by the mass, and I should have the same incentives to endeavor with the mass of my fellow-men; it would be no particular burden, no particular deprivation. But here, where universal suffrage is the rule, where that is the fundamental idea of the government, to rule us out is to make us an exception, to brand us with the stigma of inferiority, and to invite to our heads the missiles of those about us. Therefore I want the franchise for the black man.

Preventing Future Rebellion

There are, however, other reasons, not derived from any consideration merely of our rights, but arising out of the condition of the South and of the country . . . considerations which must arrest the attention of statesmen. I believe that when the tall heads of this rebellion shall have been swept down, as they will be swept down, when the [Jefferson] Davises and [Robert A.] Toombses and [Alexander H.] Stephenses and others who are leading in this rebellion shall have been blotted out, there will be this rank undergrowth of treason, to which reference has been made, growing up there, and interfering with and thwarting the quiet operation of the Federal Government in those States. You will see those traitors handing down from sire to son the same malignant spirit which they have manifested and which they are now exhibiting, with malicious hearts, broad blades and bloody hands in the field, against our sons and brothers. That spirit will still remain; and whoever sees the Federal Government extended over those Southern States will see that government in a strange land and not only in a strange land but in an enemy's land. A postmaster of the United States in the South will find himself surrounded by a hostile spirit; a collector in a Southern port will find himself surrounded by a hostile spirit; a United States marshal or United States judge will be surrounded there by a hostile element. That enmity will not die out in a year, will not die out in an age. . . . They will endeavor to circumvent, they will endeavor to destroy the peaceful operation of this government. Now, where will you find the strength to counterbalance this spirit, if you do not find it in the negroes of the South! They are your friends, and have always been your friends. They were your friends even when the Government did not regard them as such. They comprehended the genius of this war before you did. It is a significant fact, it is a marvellous fact, it seems almost to imply a direct interposition of Providence, that this war, which began in the interest of slavery on both sides, bids fair to end in the interests of liberty on both sides. (Applause.) It was begun, I say, in the interest of slavery, on both sides. The South was fighting to take slavery out of the Union and the North fighting to keep it in the Union; the South fighting to get it beyond the limits of the United States Constitution, and the North fighting to retain it within those limits, the South fighting for new guarantees and the North fighting for the old guarantees;—both despising the negro, both insulting the negro. Yet the negro, apparently endowed with wisdom from on high, saw more clearly the end from the beginning than we did. When [William H.] Seward said the status of no man in the country would be changed by the war, the negro did not believe him. (Applause.) When our generals sent their underlings in shoulder straps to hunt the flying negro back from our lines into the jaws of slavery from which he had escaped, the negroes thought that a mistake had been made, and that the intentions of the Government had not been rightly understood by our officers in shoulder straps, and they continued to come into our lines, threading their way through bogs and fens, over briars and thorns, fording streams, swimming rivers, bringing us tidings as to the safe path to march, and pointing out the dangers that threatened us. They are our only friends in the South, and we should be true to them in this their trial hour, and see to it that they have the elective franchise.

The Fallacy of Inferiority

I know that we are inferior to you in some things— virtually inferior. We walk about among you like dwarfs among giants. Our heads are scarcely seen above the great sea of humanity. The Germans are superior to us; the Irish are superior to us; the Yankees are superior to us (laughter); they can do what we cannot, that is, what we have not hitherto been allowed to do. But, while I make this admission, I utterly deny that we are originally, or naturally, or practically, or in any way, or in any important sense, inferior to anybody on this globe. . . .

It is said that we are ignorant; I admit it. But if we know enough to be hung, we know enough to vote. If the negro knows enough to pay taxes to support the Government, he knows enough to vote—taxation and representation should go together. If he knows

enough to shoulder a musket and fight for the flag, fight for the Government, he knows enough to vote. If he knows as much when he is sober as an Irishman knows when drunk, he knows enough to vote, on good American principles. (Laughter and applause.)

But I was saying that you needed a counterpoise in the persons of the slaves to the enmity that would exist at the South after the rebellion is put down. I hold that the American people are bound, not only in self-defence, to extend this right to the freedmen of the South, but they are bound by their love of country and by all their regard for the future safety of those Southern States to do this—to do it as a measure essential to the preservation of peace there. But I will not dwell upon this. I put it to the American sense of honor. The honor of a nation is an important thing. It is said in the Scriptures, "What doth it profit a man if he gain the whole world, and lose his own soul!" It may be said also, what doth it profit a nation if it gain the whole world, but lose its honor? I hold that the American Government has taken upon itself a solemn obligation of honor to see that this war, let it be long or let it be short, let it cost much, or let it cost little,—that this war shall not cease until every freedman at the South has the right to vote. (Applause.) It has bound itself to do it. What have you asked the black men of the South, the black men of the whole country to do? Why, you have asked them to incur the deadly enmity of their masters, in order to befriend you and to befriend this government. You have asked us to call down, not only upon ourselves, but upon our children's children, the deadly hate of the entire Southern people. You have called upon us to turn our backs upon our masters, to abandon their cause and espouse yours; to turn against the South and in favor of the North; to shoot down the Confederacy and uphold the flag—the American flag. You have called upon us to expose ourselves to all the subtle machinations of their malignity for all time. And now, what do you propose to do when you come to make peace? To reward your enemies, and trample in the dust your friends? Do you intend to sacrifice the very men who have come to the rescue of your banner in the South and incurred the lasting displeasure of their masters thereby? Do you intend to sacrifice them, and reward your enemies? Do you mean to give your enemies the right to vote, and take it away from your friends? Is that wise policy? Is that honorable? Could American honor withstand such a blow? I do not believe you will do it. I think you will see to it that we have the right to vote. There is something too mean in looking upon the negro when you are in trouble as a citizen, and when you are free from trouble as an alien. When this nation was in trouble, in its early struggles, it looked upon the negro as a citizen. In

1776, he was a citizen. At the time of the formation of the Constitution, the negro had the right to vote in eleven States out of the old thirteen. In your trouble you have made us citizens. In 1812, Gen. [Andrew] Jackson addressed us as citizens, "fellow citizens." He wanted us to fight. We were citizens then! And now, when you come to frame a conscription bill, the negro is a citizen again. He has been a citizen just three times in the history of this government, and it has always been in time of trouble. In time of trouble we are citizens. Shall we be citizens in war, and aliens in peace? Would that be just?

Less Sympathy, More Rights

I ask my friends who are apologizing for not insisting upon this right, where can the black man look in this country for the assertion of this right if he may not look to the Massachusetts Anti-Slavery Society? Where under the whole heavens can he look for sympathy in asserting this right if he may not look to this platform? Have you lifted us up to a certain height to see that we are men, and then are any disposed to leave us there, without seeing that we are put in possession of all our rights? We look naturally to this platform for the assertion of all our rights, and for this one especially. I understand the anti-slavery societies of this country to be based on two principles—first, the freedom of the blacks of this country; and, second, the elevation of them. Let me not be misunderstood here. I am not asking for sympathy at the hands of Abolitionists, sympathy at the hands of any. I think the American people are disposed often to be generous rather than just. . . . What I ask for the negro is not benevolence, not pity, not sympathy, but simply *justice*. (Applause.) The American people have always been anxious to know what they shall do with us. . . . Everybody has asked the question, and they learned to ask it early of the abolitionists: "What shall we do with the negro?" I have had but one answer from the beginning. Do nothing with us! Your doing with us has already played the mischief with us. Do nothing with us! If the apples will not remain on the tree of their own strength, if they are worm-eaten at the core, if they are early ripe and disposed to fall, let them fall! I am not for tying or fastening them on the tree in any way, except by nature's plan, and if they will not stay there let them fall. And if the negro cannot stand on his own legs, let him fall also. All I ask is, give him a chance to stand on his own legs! Let him alone! If you see him on his way to school, let him alone,—don't disturb him! If you see him going to the dinner table at a hotel, let him go! If you see him going to the ballot box, let him alone!—don't disturb him! (Applause.) If you see him going into a workshop, just let him alone,—your interference is doing him positive

injury. . . . Let him live or die by that. If you will only untie his hands, and give him a chance, I think he will live.

VIEWPOINT 40B

Blacks Should Not Have the Right to Vote (1866)

Benjamin M. Boyer (1823–1887)

The freeing of four million slaves by the passage of the Thirteenth Amendment to the Constitution in 1865 brought the issue of black suffrage to the fore. Many former Confederate states quickly passed laws banning the newly freed black slaves from voting—following the example set by the majority of the Northern states. Although the Northern states had abolished slavery long before the Civil War, in 1866 only five allowed blacks to vote on equal terms with whites. Hoping to set an example, Radical Republicans in Congress led by Thaddeus Stevens of Pennsylvania proposed a bill to enfranchise blacks in the District of Columbia.

On January 10, 1866, Pennsylvania democrat Benjamin M. Boyer spoke on the House floor, explaining his opposition to the measure. In his remarks, excerpted here, Boyer attacks the Radical Republican interpretation of the axiom "all men are created equal," arguing that the Founding Fathers never intended for suffrage to be extended to blacks. Boyer argues that biological and cultural differences create inequalities that cannot be ignored, and suggests, moreover, that enforcing black enfranchisement in regions where white public opinion is strongly against it would endanger, not protect, blacks.

The District of Columbia suffrage bill passed the House of Representatives, but it met with disapproval from moderate Republicans and was allowed to die in a Senate committee without coming to a vote. Proponents of black suffrage were eventually successful in passing the Fifteenth Amendment to the Constitution in 1870.

Why are blacks not qualified to vote, according to Boyer? How do his views on education and on racial differences differ from those of Frederick Douglass, author of the opposing viewpoint?

———

M r. Speaker [of the House, Schuler Colfax], however atrocious some gentlemen in this House may pronounce the sentiment that this is a white man's Government, and although I have lately heard in this Hall even the spirit of the

From *Congressional Globe*, 39th Cong., 1st sess., January 10, 1866.

illustrious dead condemned to everlasting fire for denying while upon earth the equality of the races, I am constrained notwithstanding to assume the responsibility of a respectful but firm and earnest opposition to this bill. I am opposed to it, sir, not only upon special and local grounds, but also upon the broad general principle that this is, and of right ought to be, a white man's Government.

Public Opinion Is Against Negro Suffrage

Sir, it is proposed by this bill to confer the elective franchise upon the colored population of the District of Columbia, and to elevate at once, without any qualification or preparation, a heterogeneous mass of about thirty thousand negroes and mulattoes to a complete political equality with the white inhabitants. It is proposed to do this, too, in opposition to the known wishes of a large majority of the citizens of the District, and in the face of an election held here only a few days ago in which the vote against negro suffrage was nearly unanimous. . . .

It would ill become us to fasten, by our votes, upon the people of this District, against their consent, a measure which the people of our own States have already pronounced a political degradation, and have provided against its infliction upon *them* by constitutional enactments. In eighteen out of twenty-five States now represented in this Congress negroes and mulattoes are not allowed to vote. In some of the others there are special restrictions imposed. In three of the States—Connecticut, Wisconsin, and Minnesota—elections were recently held, in which the people by heavy majorities decided against negro suffrage. Yet in each of the States the number of colored persons is comparatively small, while here it probably equals one third of the entire population.

In all the States the people have settled this question for themselves, and I claim the same privilege for the people of the District of Columbia. . . .

———— • ————

"The negroes are not the equals of white Americans, and are not entitled by any right, natural or acquired, to participate in the Government of this country."

———— • ————

But we were told the other day by my distinguished colleague, the chairman of the committee on reconstruction [Mr. Thaddeus Stevens], that "to say so is political blasphemy." And in support of his position he said further that "our fathers repudiated the whole doctrine of the legal superiority of races." But the truth is too plain for discussion, that our fathers recognized and practiced directly the opposite doctrine, and even fortified by the bulwarks of the Constitution itself the subjection of the inferior race. No man can read with open eyes and candid mind the Constitution of the United States, as made by our fathers, and fail to see that this Government was intended by its founders to be a white man's Government. It was on this very account that the early abolitionists denounced it as a covenant with hell, and the advocates of the higher law proposed to trample it under foot.

The Declaration of Independence

Arguments derived from the phraseology of the Declaration of American Independence would scarcely need a refutation, were it not for the pertinacity with which they are thrust upon us. If, however, by the expression therein contained, that "all men are created free and equal," we are to infer that the illustrious slaveholders who helped to frame that instrument intended to assert the political equality of the races, we must believe also the monstrous anomaly that they intended to proclaim their daily life a continuous lie and their supremacy over the negro a most atrocious and wicked usurpation. If so, what blasphemy would have been their appeal to the Supreme Judge of the world for the rectitude of their intentions, and what mockery to profess as they did a decent respect for the opinions of mankind. . . .

We find in the constitutions of many of the States the same words so much dwelt upon by the advocates of negro equality; and further on in the same constitutions we find words expressly excluding the negro from all participation in the government.

The constitution of Connecticut, adopted in 1818, says, "that all men, when they form a social compact, are equal in rights; and that no men or set of men are entitled to exclusive public emoluments or privileges in the community." But this declaration did not prevent the insertion of a clause in the same instrument confining the elective franchise to the *white* male citizens of the State.

Mr. Speaker, in the constitution of your own State of Indiana, adopted as late as 1851, I find these same talismanic words, "All men are created equal." But further on in the same constitution I find these other words, "No negro or mulatto shall have the right of suffrage." And in another place these additional words, "No negro or mulatto shall come into or settle in the State after the adoption of this constitution." And this last prohibition is enforced by heavy pains and penalties. Surely it will not be pretended that the intelligent people of Indiana intended to make a public proclamation of their injustice by asserting the equality of the negro, while by their organic law they denied to him all the rights of an equal, and even a home within the limits of their community.

In the constitution of the State of Oregon, adopted in 1857, there are these words: "We declare all men, when they form a social compact, are equal in rights." But in the same instrument we find also these other words, "No negro, Chinaman, or mulatto shall have the right of suffrage."

And Kansas, too, in her constitution, adopted in 1859, declares that "all men are possessed of equal and inalienable rights." But by the constitution of Kansas white male persons alone can vote.

In the constitution of the State of Iowa, adopted in 1857, are contained these words: "All men are by nature free and equal." But whether the right of suffrage should be confined to whites was submitted to a vote of the people of the State, and they decided that in that State white persons alone should vote. Yet the whole colored population of Iowa at that time did not exceed a thousand. . . .

Equality and the Laws of Providence

All men have indeed in some sense been created equal; but to apply this in its broadest signification, so as to ignore all national and ethnological inequalities among men, would involve the grossest absurdity. All men were endowed by their Creator with the equal right to receive, to do, and to enjoy according to their several capacities and in subservience to the common good. All men are equally entitled by nature to the enjoyment of "life, liberty, and the pursuit of happiness," but it does not follow from this that different races of men can all enjoy these blessings together in the same community and in the same form of government upon terms of complete equality. If it be true, as is affirmed by the greatest of the Apostles, that "God hath made of one blood all the nations of men," the same high authority informs us also that "he hath determined the bounds of their habitation." There is one extensive region of the earth where, all things considered, the negro is the superior of the white man, and where his race, defended by natural laws, has successfully defied the invading legions of conquering Rome and all the efforts of European enterprise. In Ethiopia the negro is and must ever continue to be the ruling race. But laws of Providence as imperative as those which have set apart Ethiopia for him will in the end preserve this Government for white men and their posterity, notwithstanding all the morbid excitements of this hour and all the temporary evils to which they are likely to lead. The ordinances of nature are not to be repealed by acts of Congress.

Of the same nature as the argument just answered is the one derived from that clause in the Constitution of the United States which guarantees to all the States a republican form of government. Strangely enough, it is insisted that to make a State republican in form its negro population must vote. But of this principle the founders of our Republic must surely have lived and died in blissful ignorance, for they certainly acted and talked as if they imagined they were living in republican communities, even when surrounded by negro slaves. If the negro has a natural right to vote because he is a human inhabitant of a community professing to be republican, then women should vote, for the same reason; and the New England States themselves are only *pretended* republics, because their women, who are in a considerable majority, are denied the right of suffrage.

Some of the reformers do say that after the negro will come the women. But I protest against this inverse order of merit; and if both are to vote I claim precedence for the ladies. There is one sense in which I will admit that negro votes will be needed at the South to make *Republican* States. And that is the sense in which the term "Republican" was used by my colleague [Mr. Thaddeus Stevens] in his speech already referred to, when, with even more than his characteristic candor, he assigned a reason for the coercion of southern communities into the adoption of negro suffrage. Said he:

> If they should grant the right of suffrage to persons of color, I think there would always be Union white men enough in the South aided by the blacks to divide the representation, and thus continue the Republican ascendency.

But I deny that to be the precise form of republican government guaranteed by the Constitution.

An Inferior Race

It is common for the advocates of negro suffrage to assume that the *color* of the negro is the main obstacle to his admission to political equality; and the gentleman from Iowa [Mr. James F. Wilson] dwelt long upon that argument. But it is not the complexion of the negro that degrades him, and I grant that it is but a shallow argument that goes no deeper than his skin. If he is to be excluded from equality in the Government it is not because he is black, nor because he has long heels and woolly hair, nor because the bones of his cranium are thick and inclose a brain averaging by measurement fewer cubic inches in volume than the skulls of white Americans, (although that fact is significant,) nor because of his odor, (although that is not always agreeable,) nor because his facial outline does not conform to our ideas of beautiful humanity. All these considerations I am willing to discard from the argument. But if the peculiarities I have mentioned are the outward badges of a race by nature inferior in mental caliber, and lacking that vim, pluck, and pose of character which give force and direction to human enterprise, and which are essential to the safety and progress of popular institutions, then the negroes are not the equals of white Americans, and are not entitled by any right, natural or acquired, to participate in the Government of this country. . . .

They are but superficial thinkers who imagine that the organic differences of races can be obliterated by the education of the schools. The qualities of races are perpetuated by descent, and are the result of historical influences reaching far back into the generations of the past. An educated negro is a negro still. The cunning chisel of a [Antonio] Canova could not make an enduring Corinthian column out of a block of anthracite; not because of its color, but on account of the structure of its substance. He might indeed with infinite pains give it the form, but he could not impart to it the strength and adhesion of particles required to enable it to brave the elements, and the temple it was made to support would soon crumble into ruin. . . .

It is argued that suffrage is necessary to the black man to enable him to protect himself against the oppression of the whites. But I do not think that this has been the experience of the country. In Pennsylvania we had, at the date of the last census, a colored population of 56,949, which since then has largely increased. They are there excluded from the polls; but in all my experience in the courts of my State, which has not been inconsiderable, I cannot recall to mind a single instance where justice was denied to a negro because of his complexion. I am satisfied that in those localities where such prejudice is allowed to corrupt the streams of justice you would only add force and acrimony to its operation by establishing a political rivalship between the races. The true friends of the negro race should save them from the fate which would be sure to follow. There is much to be done for the negro in which all parties can unite. In his emancipation the whole country has acquiesced, and a constitutional amendment enables Congress to secure to him the full measure of his liberty in all the States. It is our duty now to provide for his education, and to encourage and aid him in his efforts at improvement. Let the courts be opened to him; let his contracts be enforced, his labor protected, and his rights of property respected. Let public schools be provided for him; and after he shall have been first developed to the full measure of his intellectual and moral capacity there will be still time enough to decide the question whether he shall be a ruler in the land.

For Further Reading

William C. Gillette, *The Right to Vote: Politics and the Passage of the 15th Amendment.* Baltimore, MD: Johns Hopkins Press, 1965.

Harold M. Hyman, *A More Perfect Union: The Impact of the Civil War and Reconstruction on the Constitution.* New York: Knopf, 1973.

William S. McFeely, *Frederick Douglass.* New York: Norton, 1991.

James M. McPherson, *The Struggle for Equality.* Princeton, NJ: Princeton University Press, 1964.

VIEWPOINT 41A

Segregation Should Be Maintained (1872)

Henry Davis McHenry (1826–1890)

In 1866 Congress passed a national civil rights law, declaring blacks citizens of the United States and guaranteeing them equal protection under the laws. In 1870, Senator Charles Sumner introduced the second Civil Rights Bill, intended as a supplement to the 1866 law. Among the provisions of the proposed bill were measures strictly banning the segregation of blacks in public facilities and in transportation, and the exclusion of blacks from juries. The new bill, with its specific and far-reaching measures, found much greater opposition in Congress than the first Civil Rights Act had.

Among the proposed bill's opponents was Henry Davis McHenry, a Democratic representative from Kentucky, who on April 13, 1872, delivered the speech excerpted here. To allow blacks onto streetcars, in restaurants, and in public schools, McHenry argues, would force social associations with blacks onto unwilling whites. Listing the penalties for discrimination that would be authorized by the Civil Rights Bill, he insists that the bill actually gives special treatment to blacks while allowing discrimination against whites to go unpunished. Blacks have already obtained full political rights, McHenry contends; any rights of social equality must be granted by public opinion and sentiment, not mandated by law.

How are blacks specially favored by the proposed legislation, according to McHenry? What distinction does he make between "political" and "social" rights? Why is the proposed legislation an "outrage" against white people, in his view?

Whatsoever of personal privilege or individual right appertains to man, the local laws and courts as enforced in the States are far better adapted to enforce that privilege and maintain that right than any remedy we can devise and exe-

From *Congressional Globe*, 42nd Cong., 2nd sess., April 13, 1872.

cute through the instrumentality of the Federal Government.

Rights Are Already Secured

Everything that is really a right in this bill is already secured by State laws to the negro as well as the white man. He has the right to travel upon land and water; no one is forbidden to entertain him or to amuse him, and his right of education and burial are not denied him; but it is a far different thing when the law prescribes who shall do these things for him and the manner in which they are to be done. That is a matter of contract, in which the law has no right to interfere. Who shall restrict my right to keep a house of entertainment for such persons only as I see proper to entertain? Shall the law forbid the black man from opening a house of amusement for the black people alone; or the white man from establishing schools for the education of white children; or laying off cemeteries for the exclusive burial of their own race? This bill undertakes to compel every innkeeper to extend to the negro the full and equal enjoyment of every accommodation, advantage, facility, or privilege furnished by him to other guests. It gives the negro the right to demand the best bed, to occupy the best room, and to eat at the same table with the most favored guest, and to receive the same attention in every respect.

If a man sees proper to associate with negroes, to eat at the same table, ride on the same seat with them in cars, or sees proper to send his children to the same schools with them, and place himself upon the same level with them in any regard, I would not abridge his right to do so; but that is a very different thing from compulsory social equality and association with those whose company is distasteful to him. Under this law, if your wife should be traveling alone, any negro man who happened to be traveling in the same car has a right to seat himself by her side, and if the conductor or any one else should interfere for her protection they render themselves amendable to heavy penalties—penalties so heavy that no conductor would interfere to protect the most refined lady from such intrusion if there were a vacant seat by her side and the filthiest negro should see proper to occupy it. No man can afford to hold the place of a conductor and incur the heavy penalties of this bill by protecting a lady under the circumstances; and the result will be that she must submit to this degradation forced on her by the Congress of the United States.

If a man is in the habit of receiving travelers in his house, and furnishing them food and lodging for a compensation, he thereby becomes an innkeeper; a boarding-house keeper, who receives transient guests, is an innkeeper. It is not required that a sign shall be over the door or a license obtained to make an inn, and consequently not only the hotels in the cities, but the village inns and country taverns are included in this bill; and the negro can stop at the inn or tavern where the wife and daughters of the landlord wait on the table and demand entertainment, which must be given him, or severe penalties will fall upon the household, and there is no escape from them unless the man submits to the equality or quits his occupation. It will not do to take down his sign and surrender up his license. If he continues to receive and charge transient customers, he is an innkeeper under the law, and is embraced in this bill.

Legislating Private Business

Sir, hotels and inns are private property. The owners have no exclusive privilege or right to keep entertainment for the public. Any man can do it; and the State does nothing for him that it does not do for any other private citizen. He needs no special protection, nor is any special privilege given him. The entertainment he gives is a matter of contract between him and his guest, and the State has no interest in it, and no right to interfere between them, except to enforce the contract as it does in all other affairs. Then, upon what principle do we pretend to interfere and compel the innkeeper to receive guests distasteful to him? We levy specific taxes upon him, it is true; but I do not see that he has any exclusive right, privilege, or immunity granted him. He levies no toll upon the public, nor is he exempt from the duties and responsibilities which belong to other citizens. He simply gives a consideration for what he receives, as do men of all avocations of life, and he should be exempt from legislation which interferes with his individual rights. Hotels in this country have always discriminated as to the class of persons who they entertain. And they will continue to do it, even when this bill is passed.

Sir, let a poor, meanly-dressed white man, however worthy, if his appearance is such as to indicate that he moves in a sphere below that of the other guests, call at the Arlington or Metropolitan, and he would be refused entertainment, and would have no redress; but when the well-dressed negro with money in his pocket shall call and demand entertainment, notwithstanding his presence would be much more objectionable to those guests, the landlord cannot refuse him, because a special law has been passed for his benefit, and he is the representative of a race who are the wards and pets of the Federal Government.

The negro has the right to set up and keep an inn wherever and whenever he chooses, as they have the right to set themselves up in every other business; and they do have their boarding-houses, and in every city and town they will find those of their own race and color who are ready and willing to accommodate them with lodging and board; and the owners and proprietors of such houses do not want white guests, and would consider it a hardship if they were compelled to entertain them; and I would vote against a law compelling them to do so as a violation of their personal liberty. No doubt that in traveling they frequently suffer some inconvenience; but it is not for the law to furnish them conveniences at the expense of other people's rights; and if we are to consider the question of inconvenience, what shall be said of that of the white man whom we propose to compel to do subservience to the negro, and who is required to receive him in his parlor, entertain him at his table, and lodge him in his bed, or give up an occupation that he has followed all his life? Sir, it is a tyranny such as would not be imposed on its subjects by the most monarchical Government on the face of the earth.

"The right of a citizen to associate exclusively with those . . . whom he recognizes as his peers, is an individual liberty, and no Government can prostrate it to his inferiors."

The bill also undertakes to regulate the "benevolent institutions incorporated by national and State authority." Free Masons, Odd Fellows, Good Templars, and many other secret societies are benevolent institutions, and are in most instances incorporated by "national or State authority." Their rules, I believe, generally require a unanimous vote of all the members to admit new men to their fellowship. Suppose a negro puts in his petition to become a member of one of these societies where social equality and fraternity is the basis of their organization, would not some one vote against him? In my State not a white ball [favorable vote] would be found in the box. Then all the members are to be indicted, and if it shall be determined that the applicant was refused membership on account of his color or race, all are to suffer the severe penalties of this bill. The individual liberty of these men is violated, and their rights are taken from them by a despotism which is as unjust as it is iniquitous.

The asylums and alms-houses are "benevolent institutions, incorporated by national or State authority," and the poor unfortunate white men and women whom age and imbecility have rendered beneficiaries of such institutions, can only receive these charities by submitting to the social equality of the negro.

I would not prevent such charities from being extended to the negroes. I want provision made for them when they become old and helpless, but I would keep up a distinction between the races even in their misery and poverty.

Prejudice Is a Right

This is my feeling, and it is the feeling of those whom I represent. You may call it prejudice if you please, but it is a prejudice that will cling to the present generation, and will not be yielded up by the men now living; and all your laws, all your penalties, will not eradicate it. A prejudice is a right which belongs to a man as much as his love and partiality, and you cannot control it by law, and all your efforts in that direction only tend to increase it. The law can only prevent prejudice from interfering with the legal rights of others; but social prejudice is a social liberty that the law has no right to disturb. Whether it is a prejudice against the negro or a partiality for the whites, it is based upon a manifest and acknowledged superiority of class and race. I certainly have no sort of hostility to the negroes. I want them protected in all their just rights. But I do claim for my race a superiority over them in intelligence, morality, and in all the virtues of true manhood, and I can never consent to have it dragged down to their level; and it is in this view that I speak and protest against the great wrong and outrage this bill attempts against the white people.

The bill does not stop at the alms-house or the theater, but it goes to the school-house and the grave-yard, and forces this equality upon the little children at school and upon their parents under the sod. When a man's spirit shall have left this world his body becomes the dust of the earth, and there is no superiority. With him it is equality with all. But kind hearts and loving hands will mark his grave, not for any good to him, but to keep alive in the memories of those living his virtues, and his kindred and friends love to linger around his grave and feel that the spot is sacred, and reserve to themselves places by his side, when one day they must join him. But this reservation cannot be, for this law declares that the privilege of the negro to be buried there shall not be denied.

The rich man can educate his children in private schools, and this law will be no great hardship upon him; but the poor man's child must look to the common schools or go without education, and this bill forces that child to sit on the same seat with the negro, and to be raised up in fellowship with him. I believe, sir, that in my State the people will abandon the common-school system rather than submit to this unjust and unconstitutional regulation which is forced upon them by a fanaticism which heeds neither the liberty of the people nor the rights of the States.

This bill has not been debated. Gentlemen on the other side [Republicans] do not wish to discuss it. They well know that it cannot be defended under the Constitution, and hence for party purposes they silently cast their votes for it. All power belongs to the States, except such as has been delegated to the Federal Government, and there must be an authority found in the Constitution for all that we do here, and no advocate of this bill can point to a single clause in that instrument which can authorize or empower us to interfere with the schools in the States, which are supported not by any aid, nor maintained by any authority or permission, direct or indirect, derived from the Federal Government. We cannot force a State to establish a system of general education, and when she does establish it, it is an unwarranted interference if we assume to control or regulate it in any way.

It would not be right for a State to tax negroes to educate the whites unless they had the privilege of the schools, and in every State where they are so taxed they have that privilege. In my State we do not tax them for school purposes, nor have we undertaken to educate them, and we do not propose to be forced to do so by despotic laws. For many years we had no common-school system at all, and it is only of recent date that our system has become efficient, and after we have paid the enormous taxes imposed on us for the Federal Government, and the taxes to support our State government and educate the white children, it is unreasonable to ask us to tax ourselves further to educate the negroes who pay no tax, comparatively speaking.

Negroes Are the Favored Class

By this bill when a negro is excepted and excluded "from the full and equal enjoyment of any accommodation, advantage, facility, or privilege furnished by innkeepers, by common carriers, by owners of theaters," he has a remedy not given to the white man when the same "accommodation, advantage, facility, and privilege" are denied him. No remedy is by the bill given the white man for the denial of these rights; but when a negro is excepted or excluded from them he has a remedy in the Federal courts, and the amount of his damages is fixed by the law at $500, with full costs, and this remedy is not only against the innkeeper and owner of the steamboat, trustee, or commissioner, but is against any person aiding and inciting him to deny their rights; and not only this civil remedy is given to the negro, but the defendant is deemed to have committed a misdemeanor, and upon conviction thereof is to be fined from $500 to $1,000, or imprisonment not less than

thirty days nor more than one year.

Sir, any member of this House, if he happens to be one of the white members, can be kicked out of any hotel in this city or set ashore from any steamboat on the Potomac, or excluded from the theater, and no such remedy is given to him either by existing law or by this bill; and not only these remedies are given, but the same jurisdiction and powers are conferred, and the same duties enjoined, upon the courts and officers of the United States in the execution of this bill as are conferred in sections three, four, five, seven, and ten of the civil rights act [of 1866], and said sections are here again reënacted and made part of this bill.

By the provisions of those sections the district attorney, marshal, and commissioner appointed by Federal courts, the officers and agents of the Freedmen's Bureau, and every other officer who may be specially empowered by the President of the United States, are specially authorized and required at the expense of the United States to institute proceedings against all and every person who violates the provisions of this act, and if they shall fail to institute and prosecute such proceedings required by the bill, shall for every offense forfeit and pay the sum of $500 to the party aggrieved, and also be deemed guilty of a misdemeanor, and fined from $1,000 to $5,000.

The district courts are to have jurisdiction exclusive of the State courts for all offenses under this act. Penalties of $1,000 are imposed on marshals and deputy marshals for failure to execute the civil rights law. Extra commissioners are to be appointed, so as to afford a speedy and convenient means for the arrest and examination of persons charged with a violation of this act, and said commissioners are authorized and empowered to appoint one or more suitable persons in each county to execute any warrant or process, and they may call out the *posse comitatus* of the county or summon the Army and Navy of the United States or the militia to assist them in the performance of their duty.

It has never occurred that such extraordinary remedies have been given by Congress for the protection of any white man in his rights. To be a negro is to belong to the favored class.

All these remedies are given against trustees, commissioners, superintendents, teachers, and other officers of common schools and other public institutions of learning authorized by law, and against trustees and officers of cemetery associations and benevolent institutions. No such penalty is imposed against a trustee or commissioner for excluding a white child from the public schools, and the poor, decrepit old white man or woman would look in vain for such facilities to admit them to the alms-house. The object of this bill is to abolish distinctions on account of "race, color, or previous condition of servitude," but it in fact makes a discrimination against the white man on account of his color.

Negroes and Jury Duty

But, sir, the crowning infamy of this bill is to be found in the fourth section, which disregards the statutory regulations of the States and forces the negro in the jury-box, where, with his ignorance and prejudice, he is made the arbiter of the life, liberty, and property of the white man. Can any State right be more manifest than that of regulating her own courts and the forms of trial as between her own citizens? The Federal Government has no concern in it whatever; she cannot even prescribe to a State whether it will be governed by the common or civil law. She can only guaranty to them a republican form of government and provide that the Constitution of the United States, and laws made in pursuance thereof, shall be paramount and held sacred by the State courts, and this she only has the right to control through her judiciary department.

In my State the law requires the following qualifications for jurymen:

No person shall be a competent juryman for the trial of criminal, penal, or civil cases in the circuit court unless he be a free white citizen, at least twenty-one years of age, a house-keeper, likewise sober, temperate, discreet, and of good demeanor.

And the jury commissioners are sworn—

That they will not knowingly select any man as a juryman whom they believe to be unfit and not qualified.

Now, did my State have the right to make this qualification for her jurymen? If she had the right to say that they should be twenty-one years of age, and housekeepers, and that they should be sober and discreet, and of good demeanor, she had the right to say that they should be white. If it is a citizen's right to be a juryman, surely a man does not lose his right by not being a housekeeper or by being indiscreet, intemperate, and not of good demeanor. Then, if my State had the right to make these qualifications for her jurymen and compel her officers to swear to observe those qualifications in the selection of them, how can Congress repeal or modify or amend that law or in any way change the qualification as prescribed by the State? The Federal Government can prescribe the qualification of jurymen in her own courts, and whatever may be said of the policy of admitting negroes as jurors in those courts, the right and power of Congress to do it is not denied; but when we attempt to exercise that power in State courts we interfere where we have no authority.

The fifth section of this bill is short, but more comprehensive than all else that is in it, and is as follows:

That every discrimination against any citizen on account of color, by the use of the word "white" in any law, statute, ordinance, or regulation, is hereby repealed and annulled.

In this is asserted the power of Congress to repeal State laws, municipal ordinances, and corporate regulations, and takes from States the power to prescribe the qualifications of their own officers, and makes the negro eligible to all State offices, and I presume is intended, and will have the effect, to repeal the statutes in force in all the States preventing the intermarriage of whites and blacks. Except as to the penalties provided in the previous sections of the bill, this will cover all that is embraced in them. Its scope and intent is to establish perfect equality, legal and social. No distinction of race is to be tolerated. The African is not elevated, but the Anglo-Saxon is brought down to the same level with him. . . .

Equality and Liberty

The amendments to the Constitution have gone to the full extent of giving to the negro political rights. His freedom and citizenship, rights of property and protection, and right of franchise are recognized in all the States; and now it is intended to give him social rights enforced by law, and to secure this the liberty of the white man is made subservient to it. Sir, equality is one thing and liberty is another. The right of a citizen to associate exclusively with those who are congenial to him, and whom he recognizes as his peers, is an individual liberty, and no Government can prostrate it to his inferiors under the specious pretext of "equality before the law."

VIEWPOINT 41B

Segregation Should Be Abolished (1874)

James T. Rapier (1837–1883)

Born in Alabama, James T. Rapier was the son of a black mother and a white father. His father arranged for private tutors in Alabama and then sent Rapier to study law at universities in Canada and Scotland. After the Civil War, Rapier returned to Alabama and participated in state government. In 1872 he was elected to the U.S. House of Representatives. On June 9, 1874, Rapier delivered the following speech in support of the second Civil Rights Bill, which prohibited racial discrimination in public schools, theaters, hotels, jury selection, churches, cemeteries,

From *Congressional Record*, 43rd Cong., 1st sess., June 9, 1874.

and public transportation. Rapier cites his own experiences with racial discrimination and those of other prominent black politicians, such as Francis L. Cardozo. Racial segregation creates a caste system, Rapier contends, similar to those in Europe and India—a system that is unacceptable in a republic based on universal equality.

Minus the public school provisions, the Civil Rights Bill became law in 1875. It was rarely enforced, however, and was invalidated on constitutional grounds by the Supreme Court in 1883.

Why is the proposed civil rights bill necessary, according to Rapier? What experiences of discrimination does he describe in support of his position? How do his views on the relationship between laws and public opinion differ from those of Henry Davis McHenry, author of the opposing viewpoint?

———————

Mr. Speaker [of the House, James G. Blaine], I had hoped there would be no protracted discussion on the civil-rights bill. It has been debated all over the country for the last seven years; twice it has done duty in our national political campaigns; and in every minor election during that time it has been pressed into service for the purpose of intimidating the weak white men who are inclined to support the republican ticket. I was certain until now that most persons were acquainted with its provisions, that they understood its meaning; therefore it was no longer to them the monster it had been depicted, that was to break down all social barriers, and compel one man to recognize another socially, whether agreeable to him or not.

I must confess it is somewhat embarrassing for a colored man to urge the passage of this bill, because if he exhibit an earnestness in the matter and express a desire for its immediate passage, straight-way he is charged with a desire for social equality, as explained by the demagogue and understood by the ignorant white man. But then it is just as embarrassing for him not to do so, for, if he remain silent while the struggle is being carried on around, and for him, he is liable to be charged with a want of interest in a matter that concerns him more than any one else, which is enough to make his friends desert his cause. So in steering away from Scylla I may run upon Charybdis. But the anomalous, and I may add the supremely ridiculous, position of the negro at this time, in this country, compel me to say something. Here his condition is without a comparison, parallel alone to itself. Just think that the law recognizes my right upon this floor as a law-maker, but that there is no law to secure to me any accommodations whatever while traveling here to discharge my duties as a Representative of a large and wealthy constituency.

Here I am the peer of the proudest, but on a steamboat or car I am not equal to the most degraded. Is not this most anomalous and ridiculous? . . .

Half Slave, Half Free

I wish to say in justice to myself that no one regrets more than I do the necessity that compels one to the manner born to come in these Halls with hat in hand (so to speak) to ask at the hands of his political peers the same public rights they enjoy. And I shall feel ashamed for my country if there be any foreigners present, who have been lured to our shores by the popular but untruthful declaration that this land is the asylum of the oppressed, to hear a member of the highest legislative body in the world declare from his place, upon his responsibility as a Representative, that notwithstanding his political position he has no civil rights that another class is bound to respect. Here a foreigner can learn what he cannot learn in any other country, that it is possible for a man to be half free and half slave, or, in other words, he will see that it is possible for a man to enjoy political rights while he is denied civil ones; here he will see a man legislating for a free people, while his own chains of civil slavery hang about him, and are far more galling than any the foreigner left behind him; here he will see what is not to be seen elsewhere, that position is no mantle of protection in our "land of the free and home of the brave"; for I am subjected to far more outrages and indignities in coming to and going from this capital in discharge of my public duties than any criminal in the country providing he be white. Instead of my position shielding me from insult, it too often invites it.

Let me cite a case. Not many months ago Mr. [Francis L.] Cardozo, treasurer of the State of South Carolina, was on his way home from the West. His route lay through Atlanta. There he made request for a sleeping-berth. Not only was he refused this, but was denied a seat in a first-class carriage, and the parties went so far as to threaten to take his life because he insisted upon his rights as a traveler. He was compelled, a most elegant and accomplished gentleman, to take a seat in a dirty smoking-car, along with the traveling rabble, or else be left, to the detriment of his public duties.

I affirm, without the fear of contradiction, that any white ex-convict (I care not what may have been his crime, nor whether the hair on the shaven side of his head has had time to grow out or not) may start with me to-day to Montgomery [Alabama], that all the way down he will be treated as a gentleman, while I will be treated as the convict. He will be allowed a berth in a sleeping-car with all its comforts, while I will be forced into a dirty, rough box with the drunkards, apple-sellers, railroad hands, and next to any dead that may be in transit, regardless of how far decomposition may have progressed. Sentinels are placed at the doors of the better coaches, with positive instructions to keep persons of color out; and I must do them the justice to say that they guard these sacred portals with a vigilance that would have done credit to the flaming swords at the gates of Eden. Tender, pure, intelligent young ladies are forced to travel in this way if they are guilty of the crime of color, the only unpardonable sin known in our Christian and Bible lands, where sinning against the Holy Ghost (whatever that may be) sinks into insignificance when compared with the sin of color. If from any cause we are compelled to lay over, the best bed in the hotel is his if he can pay for it, while I am invariably turned away, hungry and cold, to stand around the railway station until the departure of the next train, it matters not how long, thereby endangering my health, while my life and property are at the mercy of any highwayman who may wish to murder and rob me.

Rights Under the Constitution

And I state without the fear of being gainsaid . . . that there is not an inn between Washington [D.C.] and Montgomery, a distance of more than a thousand miles, that will accommodate me to a bed or meal. Now, then, is there a man upon this floor who is so heartless, whose breast is so void of the better feelings, as to say that this brutal custom needs no regulation? I hold that it does and that Congress is the body to regulate it. Authority for its action is found not only in the fourteenth amendment to the Constitution, but by virtue of that amendment (which makes all persons born here citizens), authority is found in article 4, section 2 of the Federal Constitution, which declares in positive language "that the citizens of each State shall have the same rights as the citizens of the several States." Let me read Mr. [Frederick Charles] Brightly's comment upon this clause; he is considered good authority, I believe. In describing the several rights he says they may be all comprehended under the following general heads: "Protection by the Government; the enjoyment of life and liberty, with the right to acquire and possess property of every kind, and to pursue and obtain happiness and safety; the right of a citizen of one State to pass through or to reside in any other State for purposes of trade, agriculture, professional pursuits, or otherwise."

It is very clear that the right of locomotion without hindrance and everything pertaining thereto is embraced in this clause; and every lawyer knows if any white man in ante bellum times had been refused first-class passage in a steamboat or car, who was free from any contagious disease, and was com-

pelled to go on deck of a boat or into a baggage-car, and any accident had happened to him while he occupied that place, a lawsuit would have followed and damages would have been given by any jury to the plaintiff; and whether any accident had happened or not in the case I have referred to, a suit would have been brought for a denial of rights, and no one doubts what would have been the verdict. White men had rights then that common carriers were compelled to respect, and I demand the same for the colored men now.

A National Problem

Mr. Speaker, whether this deduction from the clause of the Constitution just read was applicable to the negro prior to the adoption of the several late amendments to our organic law is not now a question, but that it does apply to him in his new relations no intelligent man will dispute. Therefore I come to the national, instead of going to the local Legislatures for relief, as has been suggested, because the grievance is national and not local; because Congress is the law-making power of the General Government, whose duty it is to see that there be no unjust and odious discriminations made between its citizens. I look to the Government in the place of the several States, because it claims my first allegiance, exacts at my hands strict obedience to its laws, and because it promises in the implied contract between every citizen and the Government to protect my life and property. I have fulfilled my part of the contract to the extent I have been called upon, and I demand that the Government, through Congress do likewise. Every day my life and property are exposed, are left to the mercy of others, and will be so as long as every hotel-keeper, railroad conductor, and steamboat captain can refuse me with impunity the accommodations common to other travelers. I hold further, if the Government cannot secure to a citizen his guaranteed rights it ought not to call upon him to perform the same duties that are performed by another class of citizens who are in the free and full enjoyment of every civil and political right.

Sir, I submit that I am degraded as long as I am denied the public privileges common to other men, and that the members of this House are correspondingly degraded by recognizing my political equality while I occupy such a humiliating position. What a singular attitude for law-makers of this great nation to assume: rather come down to me than allow me to go up to them. Sir, did you ever reflect that this is the only Christian country where poor, finite man is held responsible for the crimes of the infinite God whom you profess to worship? But it is; I am held to answer for the crime of color, when I was not consulted in the matter. Had I been consulted, and my future fully described, I think I should have objected to being born in this gospel land. The excuse offered for all this inhuman treatment is that they consider the negro inferior to the white man, intellectually and morally. This reason might have been offered and probably accepted as truth some years ago, but no one now believes him incapable of a high order of culture, except someone who is himself below the average of mankind in natural endowments. This is not the reason, as I shall show before I have done.

Sir, there is a cowardly propensity in the human heart that delights in oppressing somebody else, and in the gratification of this base desire we always select a victim that can be outraged with safety. As a general thing the Jew has been the subject in most parts of the world; but here the negro is the most available for this purpose; for this reason in part he was seized upon, and not because he is naturally inferior to anyone else. Instead of his enemies believing him to be incapable of a high order of mental culture, they have shown that they believe the reverse to be true, by taking the most elaborate pains to prevent his development. And the smaller the caliber of the white man the more frantically has he fought to prevent the intellectual and moral progress of the negro, for the simple but good reason that he has most to fear from such a result. He does not wish to see the negro approach the high moral standard of a man and gentleman. . . .

A Question of Manhood

Mr. Speaker, nothing short of a complete acknowledgment of my manhood will satisfy me. I have no compromises to make, and shall unwillingly accept any. If I were to say that I would be content with less than any other member upon this floor I would forfeit whatever respect anyone here might entertain for me, and would thereby furnish the best possible evidence that I do not and cannot appreciate the rights of a freeman. Just what I am charged with by my political enemies. I cannot willingly accept anything less than my full measure of rights as a man, because I am unwilling to present myself as a candidate for the brand of inferiority, which will be as plain and lasting as the mark of Cain. If I am to be thus branded, the country must do it against my solemn protest. . . .

After all, this question resolves itself to this: either I am a man or I am not a man. If one, I am entitled to all the rights, privileges, and immunities common to any other class in this country; if not a man, I have no right to vote, no right to a seat here; if no right to vote, then 20 percent of the members on this floor have no right here, but, on the contrary, hold their seats in violation of law. If the negro has no right to vote, then one-eighth of your Senate consists of

members who have no shadow of a claim to the places they occupy; and if no right to a vote, a half-dozen governors in the South figure as usurpers.

———— • ————

"The solution . . . is to enact such laws and prescribe such penalties for their violation as will prevent any person from discriminating against another in public places on account of color."

———— • ————

This is the legitimate conclusion of the argument, that the negro is not a man and is not entitled to all the public rights common to other men, and you cannot escape it. But when I press my claims I am asked, "Is it good policy?" My answer is, "Policy is out of the question; it has nothing to do with it; that you can have no policy in dealing with your citizens; that there must be one law for all; that in this case justice is the only standard to be used, and you can no more divide justice than you can divide Deity." On the other hand, I am told that I must respect the prejudices of others. Now, sir, no one respects reasonable and intelligent prejudices more than I. I respect religious prejudices, for example; these I can comprehend. But how can I have respect for the prejudices that prompt a man to turn up his nose at the males of a certain race, while at the same time he has a fondness for the females of the same race to the extent of cohabitation? Out of four poor unfortunate colored women who from poverty were forced to go to the lying-in branch of the Freedmen's Hospital here in the District last year three gave birth to children whose fathers were white men, and I venture to say that if they were members of this body, would vote against the civil-rights bill. Do you, can you wonder at my want of respect for this kind of prejudice? To make me feel uncomfortable appears to be the highest ambition of many white men. It is to them a positive luxury, which they seek to indulge at every opportunity.

I have never sought to compel anyone, white or black, to associate with me, and never shall; nor do I wish to be compelled to associate with anyone. If a man does not wish to ride with me in the street-car I shall not object to his hiring a private conveyance; if he does not wish to ride with me from here to Baltimore, who shall complain if he charters a special train? For a man to carry out his prejudices in this way would be manly, and would leave no cause for complaint, but to crowd me out of the usual conveyance into an uncomfortable place with persons for whose manners I have a dislike, whose language is not fit for ears polite, is decidedly unmanly and cannot be submitted to tamely by any one who has a particle of self-respect.

Sir, this whole thing grows out of a desire to establish a system of "caste," an anti-republican principle, in our free country. In Europe they have princes, dukes, lords, etc., in contradistinction to the middle classes and peasants. Further East they have the brahmans or priests, who rank above the sudras or laborers. In those countries distinctions are based upon blood and position. Every one there understands the custom and no one complains. They, poor innocent creatures, pity our condition, look down upon us with a kind of royal compassion, because they think we have no tangible lines of distinction, and therefore speak of our society as being vulgar. But let not our friends beyond the seas lay the flattering unction to their souls that we are without distinctive lines; that we have no nobility; for we are blessed with both. Our distinction is color (which would necessarily exclude the brahmans), and our lines are much broader than anything they know of. Here a drunken white man is not only equal to a drunken negro (as would be the case anywhere else), but superior to the most sober and orderly one; here an ignorant white man is not only the equal of an unlettered negro, but is superior to the most cultivated; here our nobility cohabit with our female peasants, and then throw up their hands in holy horror when a male of the same class enters a restaurant to get a meal, and if he insist upon being accommodated our scion of royalty will leave and go to the arms of his colored mistress and there pour out his soul's complaint, tell her of the impudence of the "damned nigger" incoming to a table where a white man was sitting. . . .

Public Opinion

Mr. Speaker, though there is not a line in this bill the democracy approve of, yet they made the most noise about the school clause. Dispatches are freely sent over the wires as to what will be done with the common-school system in the several Southern States in the event this bill becomes a law. I am not surprised at this, but, on the other hand, I looked for it. Now what is the force of that school clause? It simply provides that all the children in every State where there is a school system supported in whole or in part by general taxation shall have equal advantages of school privileges. So that if perfect and ample accommodations are not made convenient for all the children, then any child has the right to go to any school where they do exist. And that is all there is in this school clause. . . .

Mr. Speaker, to call this land the asylum of the oppressed is a misnomer, for upon all sides I am treated as a pariah. I hold that the solution of this whole matter is to enact such laws and prescribe such penalties for their violation as will prevent any person from discriminating against another in public places on account of color. No one asks, no one seeks the passage of a law that will interfere with anyone's private affairs. But I do ask the enactment of a law to secure me in the enjoyment of public privileges. But when I ask this I am told that I must wait for public opinion; that it is a matter that cannot be forced by law. While I admit that public opinion is a power, and in many cases is a law of itself, yet I cannot lose sight of the fact that both statute law and the law of necessity manufacture public opinion. I remember, it was unpopular to enlist negro soldiers in our late war, and after they enlisted it was equally unpopular to have them fight in the same battles; but when it became a necessity in both cases public opinion soon came around to that point. No white father objected to the negro's becoming food for powder if thereby his son would be saved. No white woman objected to the negro marching in the same ranks and fighting in the same battles if by that her husband could escape burial in our savannas and return to her and her little ones.

Suppose there had been no reconstruction acts nor amendments to the Constitution, when would public opinion in the South have suggested the propriety of giving me the ballot? Unaided by law when would public opinion have prompted the Administration to appoint members of my race to represent this Government at foreign courts? It is said by some well-meaning men that the colored man has now every right under the common law; in reply I wish to say that that kind of law commands very little respect when applied to the rights of colored men in my portion of the country; the only law that we have any regard for is uncommon law of the most positive character. And I repeat, if you will place upon your statute-books laws that will protect me in my rights, that public opinion will speedily follow.

For Further Reading

Richard Bailey, *Neither Carpetbaggers nor Scalawags: Black Officeholders During the Reconstruction of Alabama.* Montgomery, AL: R. Bailey Publishers, 1991.

Eric Foner, *Reconstruction: America's Unfinished Revolution, 1865–1877.* New York: Harper & Row, 1988.

Loren Schweninger, *James T. Rapier and Reconstruction.* Chicago: University of Chicago Press, 1978.

INDEX